FORT FISHER TO ELMIRA

The Fatal Journey of More than Five Hundred Confederate Soldiers

By

Richard H. Triebe

First published by Smokey River Publishing
All Rights Reserved.

ISBN-10: 0-9798965-5-X
ISBN-13: 978-0-9798965-5-2

Front and Back Cover Design by Richard H. Triebe.
Cover photograph: This picture of Fort Fisher was taken shortly after its capture by Timothy O'Sullivan, 1865.

All photographs in this book are from the author's collection unless otherwise noted.

Other books by this author:

Point Lookout Prison Camp and Hospital,
ISBN 978-1495310140
Confederate Fort Fisher
  ISBN 978-1484032497
Fort Fisher to Elmira paperback,
  ISBN 145368736X
On A Rising Tide, ISBN 1-4208-7849-2
Port Royal, ISBN 0-9798-9650-9

Printed in the United States of America

This book is printed on acid-free paper.

Contact Information:
Email: richtriebe@aol.com

Printed in the United States of America.

Smokey River Publishing

Table of Contents

Fort Fisher to Elmira

Cartography

Foreword

Researching and writing history are similar to putting together a giant jigsaw puzzle. Historians methodically and diligently explore repositories in their unending search for historical documents—letters, diaries, journals, reports, memoirs, recollections, and newspaper accounts—to help them reconstruct past events. At the same time, they fully understand that they will never find every piece of the puzzle, as many of them have been discarded and destroyed or too scattered across space and time to ever be retrieved. The best for which historians can hope in their quest to learn what really happened and why is to find enough pieces to create some semblance of the past event.

New technology has benefited researchers enormously by providing greater accessibility to the increasing number of digitized documents and official records put online through a myriad of internet sites. Historians of old could not have fathomed the great leap forward in methodology over the past ten years. Richard H. Triebe has taken advantage of the improved technology for his new book, *Fort Fisher to Elmira: The Fatal Journey of 518 Confederate Soldiers*. As a former Chicago policeman and U.S. Army provost marshal investigator, Triebe knows a thing or two about solving mysteries. Combine his sharply honed detective skills with his passion for the past, and you have one good historical researcher.

Fort Fisher to Elmira was a natural progression for Triebe. His first historical fiction publication—*On a Rising Tide: A Tale of Civil War Blockade Running*—concerned the war in southeastern North Carolina. Fort Fisher, the main protector of blockade running ships attempting to enter Wilmington, North Carolina, played a prominent role in the novel. In his first non-fiction work, *Fort Fisher to Elmira*, Triebe explores the real Fort Fisher story and the fate of its gallant gray-uniformed defenders.

Confederate engineers built Fort Fisher near New Inlet, the northernmost entranceway into the Cape Fear River and Wilmington's harbor, to protect the more than 100 sailing vessels and steamships that imported essential European supplies for the Confederacy. Union ships hovered just offshore to intercept and capture or destroy blockade-runners. Colonel William Lamb supervised the expansion of Fort Fisher from a patchwork of sand batteries into the mightiest fortress in America. Both Confederate and Union engineers considered Fort Fisher virtually impregnable and referred to it as the "Gibraltar of the South." Union attempts to capture the imposing stronghold at Christmas 1864, and again in mid-January 1865, comprised the two heaviest naval bombardments and largest combined operations of the war.

Fort Fisher and Wilmington's importance to the Confederate war effort were largely ignored by historians until the last twenty years. Since then it has been the subject of several important studies including Rod Gragg's *Confederate Goliath* (HarperCollins, 1991), Chris E. Fonvielle Jr.'s *The Wilmington Campaign: Last Rays of Departing Hope* (Savas Publishing, 1997), William M. Robinson III's *Hurricane of Fire* (Naval Institute Press, 1998), Richard B. McCaslin's *The Last Stronghold* (McWhiney Foundation Press, 2003), and James L. Walker Jr.'s *Rebel Gibraltar* (Dram Tree Press, 2005). Triebe's work, however, proves that there are still important questions to be asked about Fort Fisher and new ways to interpret its history.

Fort Fisher to Elmira provides a solid encapsulation of the history of Fort Fisher from construction to capture. Triebe challenges some old assumptions, including the strength of the Confederate garrison during the height of the second battle. Colonel Lamb claimed in his postwar memoir that only 350 South Carolina troops were sent into the fort on January 15, 1865, as reinforcements for the beleaguered garrison of North Carolinians. All of the survivors were overpowered by Union ground forces later that evening. In fact, Triebe discovered that the number totaled 482 Palmetto State musket-bearers, most of who were captured alongside their Tar Heel comrades and sent north to military prisons. While this nugget of information may seem relatively minor to some historians, it, in fact, contributes vital statistical information to the longstanding debate about the number of Fort Fisher's defenders during the final battle.

Triebe's most significant contribution to the historical record of Fort Fisher, however, concerns the fate of the captives themselves. More than 1,100 of them were held at the infamous Elmira prison in New York, and 518 were dead by war's end. The 46 percent death rate for Fort Fisher's captives at Elmira was two times higher than the worst military prisons in both the North and South for the duration of the war. Combined with the 500 Confederate soldiers killed and wounded in the second battle of Fort Fisher, and the garrison's casualty rate approached an astounding 50 percent. Triebe gleaned much of the information from online sources. Included in his work is an assessment of conditions at Elmira that contributed to the deaths, soldiers' accounts, statistical analysis, and service records for each of the Fort Fisher prisoners who survived or died at Elmira. Thanks to Richard H. Triebe, another key piece of the Fort Fisher puzzle has been put into place.

Chris E. Fonvielle Jr.
Dept. of History, UNC Wilmington
September 2010

<u>Dedication</u>

This book was written to honor all the soldiers who fought and died during the battles of Fort Fisher, North Carolina. It is hoped that in some small way this text will help to keep alive the memory of all the men who perished at Fort Fisher and later at Elmira prison camp.

<u>Acknowledgments</u>

There are so many people I wish to thank for helping me with the manuscript for this book. I thank all the people who helped me in my research at Fort Fisher State Historic Site. These include Richard Lawrence, Mark Wilde-Ramsing, Julep Gilman-Bryant and Amy Thorton. I thank Beverly Tetterton at the New Hanover County Public Library and all the kind and knowledgeable staff who assisted me in my research. Thank you Candace McGreevy, Shannon SanCartier and Colleen Griffith at the Lower Cape Fear Historical Society. A well deserved thank you goes to George Farr. George was my eyes and ears at Elmira. His took photographs at Woodlawn Cemetery and also provided the grave numbers for the roster section of this book.

I owe a deep debt of gratitude to Dr. Chris Fonvielle not only for his encouragement, but for writing an excellent foreword for my book. Thanks for everything, Chris!

I also would like to thank Rod Gragg for reviewing my manuscript. Rod, thank you so much for the wonderful quote for the back cover of my book.

I would like to thank Jean Nance, my editor, for keeping me straight grammatically and suggesting what I can and cannot do. I also need to thank Wanda Canada, Katie Freeman, Nan Graham, Greg Player and Ellen Rickert for their invaluable assistance in reviewing my manuscript.

A special thank you goes out to Christy Judah, my publisher at Coastal Books. Without her help none of this would be possible. I met Christy after I had already started this project. I was surprised to learn how much we have in common! Actually, to say that I was surprised is putting it mildly. I was astonished! I had been working on this book for a number of years and to find someone who had three relatives at the battle of Fort Fisher was simply astounding. Thomas G. Faircloth was killed in the second battle on January 15, 1865. Two other Faircloth relatives were sent to Elmira Prisoner of War Camp in New York State. Both of these men died of disease within two months of captivity.

Grave of T. H. Faircloth is on the far left. He died at Elmira of chronic diarrhea 3/14/1865 and is buried in Woodlawn Cemetery, Elmira, New York.

Grave of T. Faircloth died at Elmira of Rheumatism 3/17/1865 and is also buried at Woodlawn. *Photographs courtesy of George Farr.*

Introduction

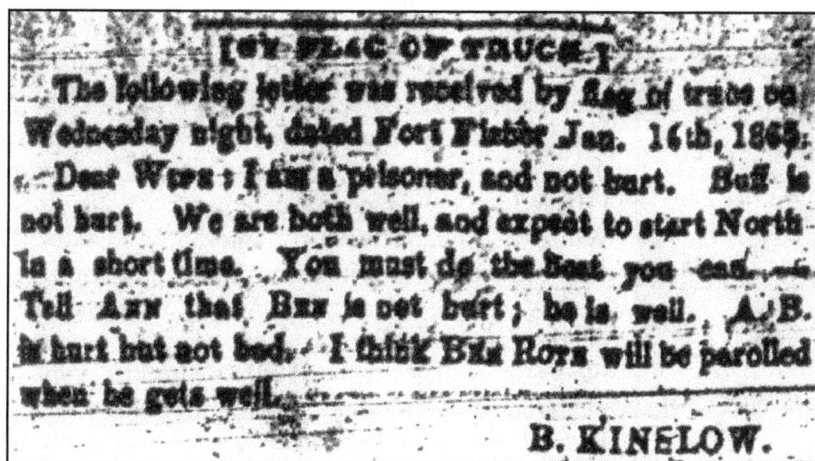

[BY FLAG OF TRUCE.]

The following letter was received by flag of truce on Wednesday night, dated Fort Fisher, Jan. 16th, 1865.

Dear Wife: I am a prisoner, and not hurt. Bud is not hurt. We are both well, and expect to start North in a short time. You must do the best you can. Tell Ann that Bax is not hurt; he is well. A. B. is hurt but not bad. I think Bud Boys will be paroled when he gets well.

B. KINELOW.

Corporal Benjamin Kinlaw's letter in the January 21, 1865, issue of the *Wilmington Daily Journal* which prompted the author's search.

The idea for this book came about in a most unusual way. A few years ago I was at the New Hanover Public Library in Wilmington, North Carolina, doing research for a book about the Civil War. I was searching the microfiche of the 1865 *Wilmington Daily Journal* for articles regarding the fall of Fort Fisher. Little did I know that I would uncover an article that would influence my life for the next six years. The newspaper had printed a letter that was passed through the lines from Fort Fisher under a flag of truce. This January 21, 1865 article caught my attention because it demonstrated how a husband and wife could be helplessly caught up in the throes of war. In it, Confederate soldier B. Kinelow assures his wife that he is well and will go north to prison in a short time. He tells her that she must do the best she can. After relating some news about friends who were also in the battle Benjamin ends this sad letter rather abruptly. This poignant letter kindled a fire in me. What became of this man and his friends after they went to prison? Did they ever return home to live a normal life? This 145-year-old newspaper article kept gnawing at me and would not let me rest until I knew the answers to these questions.

My writer's curiosity never let me forget that letter. I searched for B. Kinelow's records at the National Archives, but I was unable to locate him. However, I did find a Corporal Benjamin Kinlaw who was captured at Fort Fisher. I believe the *Wilmington Journal* editor misread this hastily scrawled note and incorrectly spelled Kinlaw's name. Upon further investigation I discovered Benjamin Kinlaw and his cousin Neil Kinlaw both died of disease at Elmira Prisoner of War camp. Ben died April 16, 1865 from chronic diarrhea and was buried in Woodlawn Cemetery at Elmira, New York. Neil died February 20, 1865 of the same disease. I was puzzled as to why two healthy, young men would die within three months of captivity.

I investigated other men who were captured at Fort Fisher and found an unusually large number of them also died of disease. What was going on here? I examined more records and several patterns began to emerge. The Confederate soldiers captured at Fort Fisher were transported by ship to five Union prisoner of war camps. 1,121 soldiers went to Elmira Prisoner of War Camp in Elmira, New York. The second largest group of soldiers, 639, went to Point Lookout Prison in Maryland. 97 soldiers went to Fort Columbus in New York Harbor, 61 men were sent to Fort Delaware, Delaware and finally 22 men were sent to Fort Monroe, VA.

Another more sinister pattern appeared when I began to look at these prisons individually. Of the 1,121 men sent to Elmira Prisoner of War Camp 46 percent of them died from disease within five months of captivity while at the same time Point Lookout Prison only had 9 percent die from disease.

Fort Delaware had 5 percent while Fort Columbus had less than 2 percent die from disease. Obviously something was horribly wrong at Elmira Prisoner of War Camp.

The typical Northern Prisoner of War Camp averaged an 11.7 percent death rate. Elmira had a 24.4 percent death toll making it by far the worst prison in the north. In comparison, the notorious Andersonville Prison in Georgia had a death rate of 28.7 percent. While Andersonville's mortality rate was unquestionably the highest during the war, it was closely rivaled by Elmira. Many of these Northern deaths can be attributed to an effective Union Naval blockade which reduced to a trickle vital food, medicine and clothing which might have aided the Federal prisoners. Sherman's march tore up Southern railroads and pursued a scorched earth policy that burned buildings and crops during the last six months of the war. It is difficult to understand why Elmira, a prison camp located in the heart of a lush Northern valley, had such a high mortality rate. What could have possibly made it so unhealthy that a quarter of its prisoners died from disease?

Corporal Benjamin Kinlaw's grave stone at Woodlawn Cemetery, Elmira, New York. *Photograph courtesy of George Farr.*

This book explores the causes that led to such a high death rate and uncovers the men responsible for creating such an unhealthy prison environment.

Part two of this book contains prisoner statements. It also has a section that has statistics for the Fort Fisher prisoners. The last part of this book has a roster containing the names of all Confederate soldiers who were captured at Fort Fisher and sent to Elmira Prisoner of War Camp. I have researched each soldier at the National Archives and have included all the information found. It is my wish people will have a better understanding of the prison system during the Civil War. I also wrote this book as a reference so the relatives of the men captured at Fort Fisher can trace their family history.

Chapter 1

Abraham Lincoln Takes Office and the South Secedes

Abraham Lincoln in 1860

When Abraham Lincoln ascended to the presidency on March 4, 1861, he was faced with the worst nightmare a president could have. South Carolina and six other states had announced their intention to secede and it appeared the nation was headed toward open rebellion and armed conflict. Lincoln, who wanted to preserve the Union at all costs, tried to calm the anxieties of the Southern states by assuring them their property and personal security would not be endangered because a Republican administration was taking office. In his inaugural address Lincoln vowed that he had no intention of interfering with the institution of slavery and he would enforce the Fugitive Slave Act. This controversial law declared that all runaway slaves be returned to their masters.

However, Lincoln also declared secession to be illegal and announced he would "hold, occupy and possess the property and places belonging to the government and collect the duties and imposts." South Carolina reacted to Lincoln's promises by bombarding Fort Sumter in Charleston Harbor on April 12, 1861. A discouraged but determined President Lincoln called for 75,000 volunteers to help put down the Southern insurrection.[1]

On April 19th President Abraham Lincoln declared a blockade of Confederate ports. Lincoln was aware the Confederacy did not have the weapons of war to sustain a rebellion past six months. He also knew that because the Southern states lacked the manufacturing necessary to produce these weapons, they would be forced to rely on trade with Europe. Therefore, the United States Navy must blockade the Confederacy. However, Lincoln's peacetime navy had only ninety warships to enforce a blockade of 3,549 miles of Southern coastline. Unfortunately, half of these vessels were obsolete sailing craft used mainly as training vessels.

When the Federal blockade began it was largely a blockade in name only because the United States lacked enough warships ships to enforce it.[2]

1861 Union recruitment poster

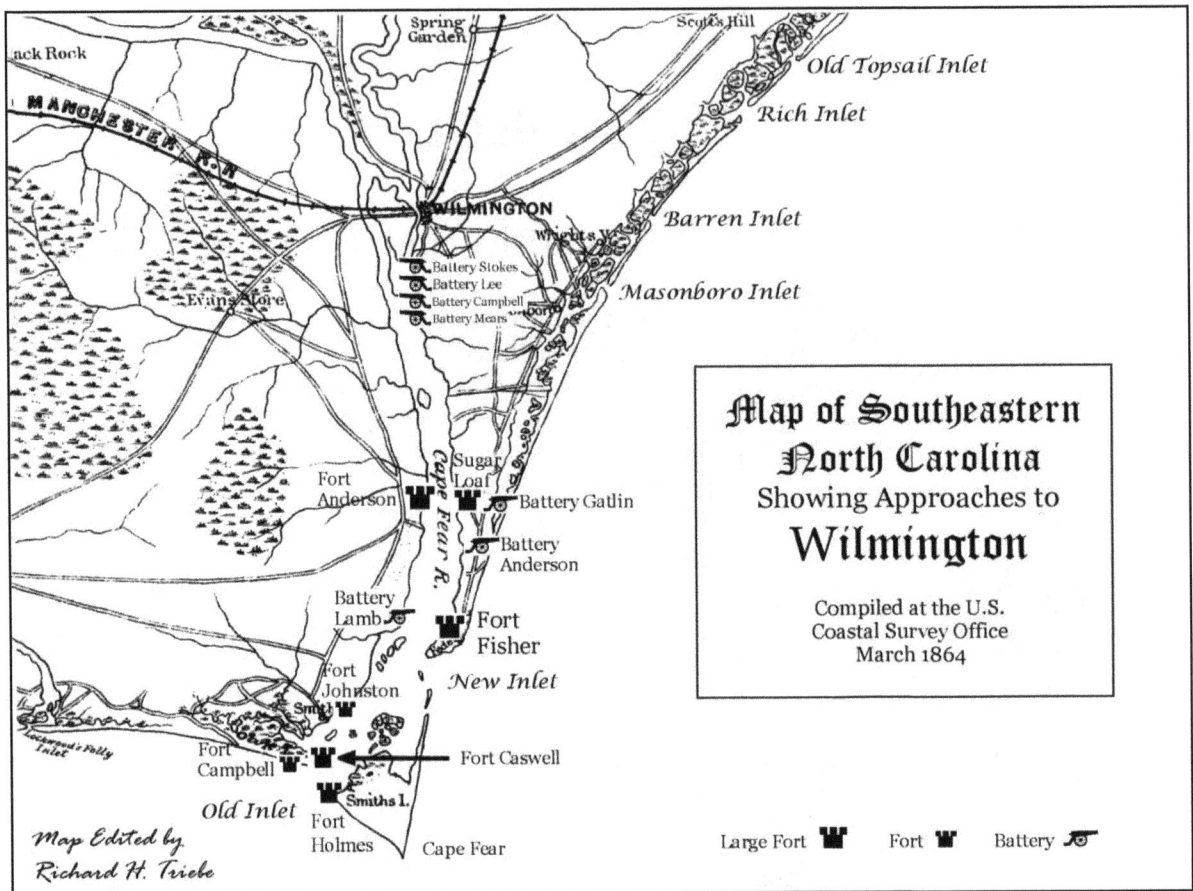

Map of the approaches to Wilmington, North Carolina, showing the Confederate forts and batteries guarding the Cape Fear River.

But as the war progressed, and more navy ships became available, the blockade became more effective. One by one the Confederate ports were closed by the Federal Navy until only the port of Wilmington, North Carolina, remained open. By the summer of 1864 Wilmington literally became the *Lifeline of the Confederacy* since it was the only seaport still able to supply the South with the materials it needed to survive. A large factor in making Wilmington ideal for blockade-runners and commerce raiders was its advantageous geography. The city lay twenty-eight miles up the Cape Fear River, well protected from the Federal fleet offshore. Blockade-runners could choose from two inlets to enter the Cape Fear River. Old Inlet and New Inlet were only six miles apart but due to the treacherous Frying Pan Shoals, this distance was extended to an arc of fifty miles. This meant the Federal Navy would have to blockade both entrances. Such an undertaking would require twice the men and ships. Perhaps the biggest factor in creating a superior blockade-running port was due to the presence of Fort Fisher. This mighty fort was the largest and most powerful earthwork fort in the Confederacy and guarded the entrances to the Cape Fear River and the crucial port of Wilmington.

Excellent transportation also made Wilmington a desirable destination for blockade-runners. Once the vessel's cargo was on the Wilmington docks it was relatively easy to ship these items to where they were needed. The city was served by three railroad lines that went to different parts of the South. The Wilmington & Weldon Railroad was the city's most important line because it became the main supply route for Robert E. Lee's Army of Northern Virginia. Another important line was the Wilmington & Manchester Railroad because it traveled into South Carolina and connected the port city with Charleston. Charleston was a major blockade-running port herself until the Federal Navy tightened its blockade and made it virtually impossible to run into or out of the city. A third line was the Wilmington, Charlotte & Rutherford Railroad which traversed the North Carolina Piedmont and was an important route into the interior. The Cape Fear River also served as a highway for the goods brought in through the blockade. This river flowed to the northwest and was navigable for 100 miles for small to medium-sized vessels.

Unlike most fortifications, Fort Fisher was only a two-sided structure. Since the fort was built near the end of Confederate Point peninsula, the mile-wide Cape Fear River acted as its third and final side. The fort resembled an enormous number seven with the long side facing the sea and the short, upper side crossing the peninsula. The woods had been cleared for a half-mile north of the land-face to provide a clear field of fire for the Confederate defenders. To discourage an infantry attack, an electrically detonated mine field and a nine-foot palisade fence of sharpened stakes was erected fifty feet in front of the fort. Its twenty-five foot high land-face stretched from the Cape Fear River on the west to the Atlantic Ocean on its right, a distance of one third mile.

Fort Fisher mounted a total of forty-four heavy cannon, not counting the field artillery and mortars. The land-face contained sixteen gun chambers, mounting twenty-three heavy seacoast artillery pieces, which were separated by fifteen-foot high mounds of sand called traverses. These traverses protected the gun chambers from enfilading fire and also gave Fort Fisher its characteristic bumpy appearance. Inside the hollowed-out traverse was a bombproof where the men could take refuge and an ordinance magazine. The land-face gun chambers were accessible from the rear by wooden stairs and a long interior passage connected all the bombproofs.

Colonel William Lamb, the commander of Fort Fisher.

The fort's gate, located in the western-most corner, was barricaded with sandbags and guarded by two field artillery pieces.

Halfway down the land-face was a tunnel through the earthen wall that ended in a raised gun platform for field artillery. In military jargon of the day this was known as a sally-port. Since these cannon were mobile, the gunners could push the artillery pieces inside the mound to seek shelter during a bombardment. Then, when the shelling ceased, the cannon could be run out to fire on an enemy approaching from the north. Since the sally-port extended outside the walls of the fort it was possible for the artillery pieces to have flanking fire on an enemy to the east or west of its position.[3]

Soldiers rest on a traverse beside Fort Fisher's 150-pounder Armstrong cannon. This huge artillery piece is on display at West Point. Image Timothy O'Sullivan, *Photograph courtesy of the National Archives.*

The earthwork continued at a right angle where the land-face meets the sea-face. Here a forty-three foot mound of sand known as the Northeast Bastion provided the commander, Colonel William Lamb, with a sweeping view of the Atlantic Ocean and the entire fort. Just to the south lay the Pulpit Battery, or Lamb's combat headquarters. Below the crescent-shaped Pulpit Battery lay the fort's field hospital. This structure extended twenty-eight feet into the mound of sand. The hospital's sides and roof were reinforced with huge oak timbers to hold the enormous weight of the Pulpit Battery. Surgeons Joseph C. Shepard and Spiers Singleton, along with a half-dozen assistant surgeons, would perform their operations by lantern light in the one-hundred foot long hospital. A semi-circular mound of sand lay nearly parallel to the hospital's entrance, protecting it from shell explosions in the fort's interior. As massive as the hospital was, it was still not roomy enough to house all the soldiers wounded during the second battle. Dozens of stretchers would be lined up outside the building while only the most seriously injured men were brought inside for surgery.[4]

Most of the sea-face was almost a duplicate of the land-face but it was only half as high and much longer in length. About midway down its rampart was the fort's heaviest gun, a monstrous 150-pounder Armstrong rifled cannon. The gun was a gift for the Confederacy from Sir W. G. Armstrong at Armstrong & Co. of London in 1864. This artillery piece was known for its accuracy and tremendous range. It came mounted on a beautiful mahogany and rosewood carriage fitted with brass hardware. It was said the gun crew took great pride in keeping the enormous cannon cleaned and polished.[5]

4

The sixty-foot Mound Battery anchored the south end of the fort and dominated the surrounding area armed with two heavy seacoast artillery pieces. The Mound kept Federal ships a respectable distance from the fort, and its gunners could direct a plunging fire onto the decks of enemy ships attempting to enter New Inlet. Since it was the tallest structure on Confederate Point, its summit was fitted with a beacon to signal blockade-runners. One of the most successful blockade-runner captains, John Wilkinson called the Mound Battery, "an excellent landmark. Joined by a long low isthmus of sand with the higher main land, its regular conical shape enabled the blockade-runner easily to identify it from the offing and in clear weather; it showed plain and distinct against the sky at night."[6]

On the tip of the peninsula, two-thirds of a mile southwest of the Mound Battery, Lamb constructed his final defensive work. Battery Buchanan was an elliptically-shaped earthwork designed to protect New Inlet and the fort's rear. Buchanan extended 320 feet and was enclosed with fifteen-foot sloping walls which mounted two 11-inch Brooke smoothbores and two 10-inch Columbiad cannons. Lamb later wrote, "Battery Buchanan was a citadel to which an overpowered garrison might retreat and with proper transportation be carried off at night, and to which reinforcements could be safely sent under the cover of darkness."[7]

Fortunately for the Confederacy, capturing the port of Wilmington remained low on the Federal list of priorities during the first years of the war. Northern generals focused their attention on the immediate threat posed by the Southern armies. The Federal armies of the Potomac and the James had been trying to defeat Robert E. Lee's Army of Northern Virginia and capture Richmond since the beginning of the war. Closing the port of Wilmington would have to wait until more men became available. The error with this thinking was that it gave the South a viable seaport that allowed supplies to flow uninterrupted to the Confederate Army. It also provided the Confederates with the opportunity to strengthen Fort Fisher and the other defenses around the mouth of the Cape Fear River.

The sixty-foot high Mound Battery served as a landmark for blockade-runners. Image Timothy O'Sullivan, *Photograph courtesy of the National Archives.*

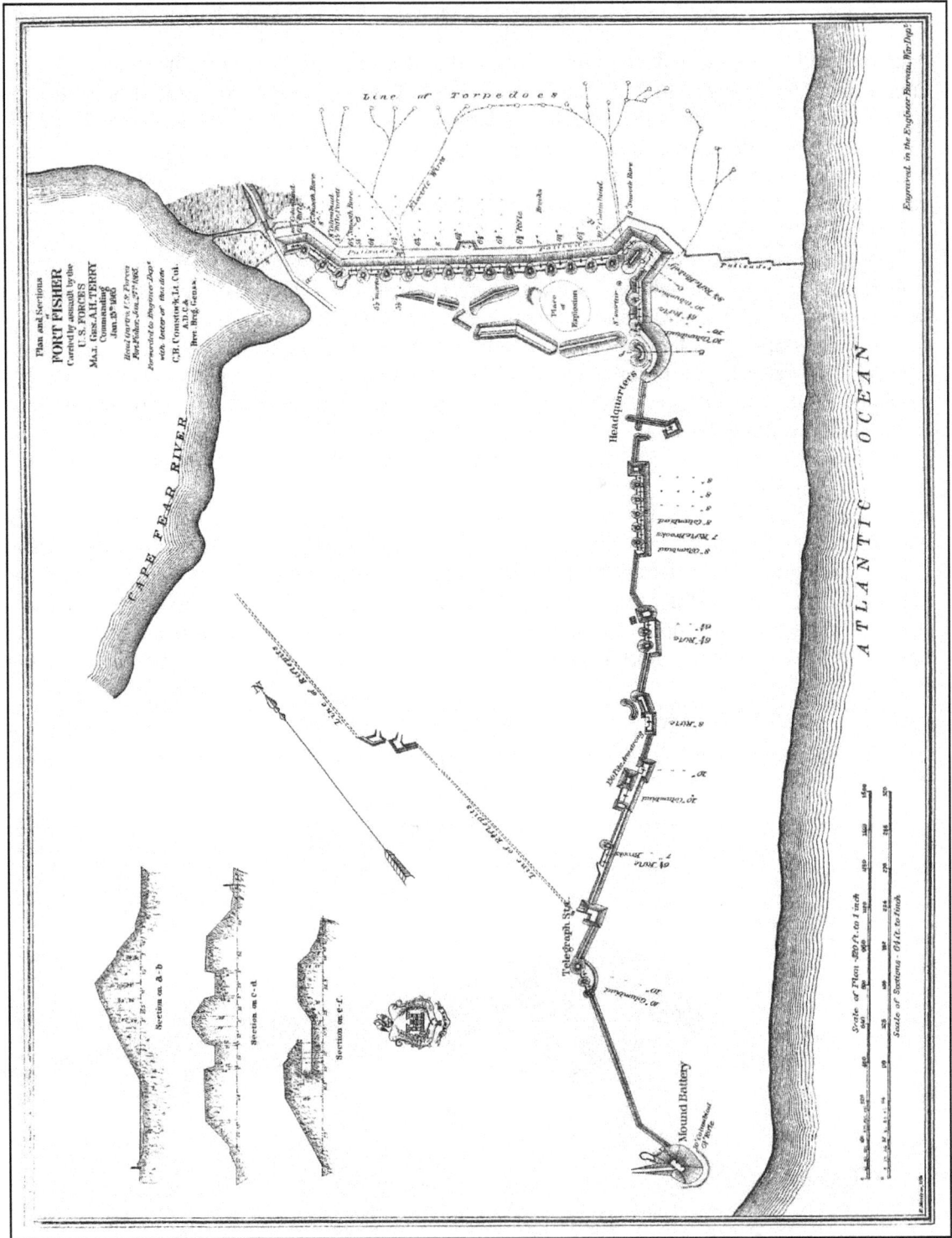

Map of Fort Fisher drawn by Lieutenant Colonel C. B. Comstock in 1865.

Firing at a blockade-runner off Wilmington, North Carolina, drawing from *Harper's Weekly*.

Chapter 2

Wilmington Takes On New Importance

"The importance of closing Wilmington and cutting off Rebel communication is paramount to all other questions—more important practically than the capture of Richmond." Gideon Wells, United States Secretary of the Navy, September 15, 1864

Capturing the port of Wilmington became more attractive to Lieutenant General Ulysses S. Grant in the fall of 1864. Union General William T. Sherman's army had nearly completed its March to the Sea and was nearing the Georgia coast. After capturing Savannah, Sherman then planned to drive north through the Carolinas, and he would need a seaport to resupply his army and reinforce it with more troops if necessary. Grant saw Wilmington as the perfect place to accomplish this. On September 12, 1864, he wrote to Sherman saying, "I want to send a force of from six to ten thousand men against Wilmington. This will give us the same control of the harbor of Wilmington that we now have of the harbor of Mobile."[1]

Federal War and Navy Departments organized a joint movement to insure the Fort Fisher expedition's success. Secretary of the Navy Gideon Welles chose Rear-Admiral David D. Porter to lead the naval assault against Fort Fisher, while General Grant selected Major General Godfrey Weitzel to command the army expedition. Weitzel's superior, Major General Benjamin F. Butler, felt that Weitzel was too young and inexperienced to handle such a complicated operation so he assumed command instead. In fact, Butler was looking for a way to redeem himself after his miserable failures at New Orleans and Bermuda Hundred.

Major General Benjamin Butler

Because of his infamous proclamation Butler's image decorates the bottom of thousands of chamber pots.

Bitterly resentful of the Union occupation of New Orleans, the ladies of that city took pleasure in heaping insults on the occupying soldiers. Whenever any of Butler's men were present they would contemptuously gather in their skirts, cross streets, flee rooms, cast hateful glances, or make disrespectful comments. Some sang spirited renditions of "The Bonnie Blue Flag" and other Confederate songs. Naval commander David G. Farragut became a target of the women's wrath when the contents of a chamber pot was emptied on his head by a Confederate

woman in an upstairs window as he walked down a street. Butler, infuriated by these insults, issued his notorious General Order Number 28 that declared any woman who was disrespectful to a Federal officer would be arrested as a prostitute plying her trade. Benjamin Butler's image decorated chamber pots throughout the South. President Jeff Davis also declared Butler a criminal to be hanged if captured. Butler's reputation took another serious hit in June of that year when he had a New Orleans man hanged for tearing down a United States flag.[2]

BUTLER'S PROCLAMATION

An outrageous insult to the Women of New Orleans!

Southern Men, avenge their wrongs!!!

Head-Quarters, Department of the Gulf,
New Orleans, May 15, 1862.

General Orders, No. 28.

As the Officers and Soldiers of the United States have been subject to repeated insults from the women calling themselves ladies of New Orleans, in return for the most scrupulous non-interference and courtesy on our part, it is ordered that hereafter when any Female shall, by word, gesture, or movement, insult or show contempt for any officer or soldier of the United States, she shall be regarded and held liable to be treated as a woman of the town plying her avocation.
By command of Maj.-Gen. BUTLER,
GEORGE C. STRONG,
A. A. G. Chief of Stables.

General Butler's Proclamation infuriated Southerners and prompted Confederate President Jefferson Davis to order Butler to be hanged if captured.

General Butler was known for his fanciful ideas regarding new weapons of warfare. He had once suggested that fire engines could be used to destroy Confederate earthworks by shooting jets of water at them, and for a while he had promoted a plan to tunnel under Richmond and launch a surprise attack from beneath the city. The latest brainstorm of the infamous general concerned a floating bomb. Butler was fascinated by this idea ever since a tremendous explosion of a munitions barge on the James River entirely destroyed a wharf, killing forty-three people and wounding one hundred twenty-six. It was later determined that Confederate agents had planted an explosive device on the barge.[3]

Butler concocted an ambitious scheme to blow down the walls of Fort Fisher and stun its garrison into submission with a giant floating bomb. Admiral Porter was skeptical of the plan at first, but after talking with Butler he reluctantly agreed to supply the sacrificial vessel that would be used. The *USS Louisiana* was a 295-ton, 143-foot long iron hulled steamer that only drew eight and a half feet of water when fully loaded. This shallow draft was important because the *Louisiana* would have to be towed into shore and run aground for the explosion to have the desired effect on the fort. She was stripped of her boiler and machinery and a fake smokestack was erected near the ship's single stack and the vessel painted a dull gray. On a dark night the ship could easily pass for a blockade-runner and get close to Fort Fisher without being fired upon. Once her disguise was complete, the *Louisiana* was towed a safe distance away from the federal fleet at Hampton Roads, Virginia, and loaded with 215 tons of gunpowder.

Admiral Porter gathered a variety of warships to pound Fort Fisher into submission. Sixty-four armed vessels with 635 guns took part in the bombardment in December 1864. This flotilla included four ironclad monitors propelled by either side-wheels or screw propellers, and wooden-hulled steam frigates. Porter's largest steam frigate was the *Colorado*, with fifty-two guns, followed by the

Minnesota and *Wabash*, with forty-six and forty-four respectively. The pride of Porter's fleet was the *New Ironsides*, whose hull was sheathed with four inches of iron. This warship carried fourteen 11-inch guns, two 150-pounders, and two 60-pounders. The monitor *Monadnock* boasted four 15-inch guns whose shells weighed three hundred pounds each.[4]

Admiral Porter's armada left Hampton Roads on December 13, 1864. Porter asked Butler to allow the navy at least twelve hours lead time because his heavily armed warships were weighty and slow, and the unseaworthy monitors and the *Louisiana* would have to be towed. He also needed to stop at Beaufort, North Carolina, to take on more fuel and ammunition for the monitors and more gunpowder for the *Louisiana*. Butler agreed with the admiral.

At Petersburg, Virginia, Confederate General Robert E. Lee received a report that the Federal armada had sailed from Hampton Roads. He knew the fleet could be bound for either Charleston, South Carolina, or Wilmington, North Carolina. As it happened, Lee was brooding over reports that his Army of Northern Virginia had less than a month's worth of rations. If Fort Fisher fell, Lee's most important artery of supply would be severed. Lee could not afford this, so he withdrew General Robert F. Hoke's Division of 6,150 men from the trenches around Petersburg, and ordered them to help defend Wilmington.[5]

When General Butler arrived twenty-five miles east of Cape Fear, North Carolina, on December 15th, he was surprised to find only a few naval vessels on station. He was told that Admiral Porter was in Beaufort with most of the fleet getting supplies. While Butler waited for Porter to arrive the weather was perfect with spring-like temperatures and calm seas. Unfortunately, the pleasant weather began to deteriorate after three days. Somehow the communication between General Butler and Admiral Porter was disrupted. Butler steamed north to Beaufort to seek shelter from the gale while Porter's fleet put out to sea and braced itself for the coming storm. Despite high seas and gale-force winds the naval fleet rode out the storm without loss of life or vessel. Unable to meet up with Butler or his army, Porter decided to explode the powder boat near Fort Fisher. When Butler's aide arrived on the morning of December 23rd, Porter informed him of his plans to tow the *Louisiana* toward shore that night and explode it. The aide returned to Beaufort to report Porter's intentions to General Butler.

The Federal armada sent to capture Fort Fisher contained powerful ships such as the forty-four gun frigate *USS Wabash*. Painting by artist Clary Ray. *Photograph courtesy of the Naval Historical Foundation.*

Butler was furious when he heard the news. He felt that Porter wanted to destroy Fort Fisher in the army's absence so he could claim all the credit for himself. "The Admiral supposed he would blow the fort all to pieces, and be able to land with his marines and take possession of it," Butler seethed. His officers agreed with their superior that Porter was seeking all the glory.[6]

Admiral Porter's fleet assembling at Hampton Roads, Virginia, for the Wilmington expedition. *Photograph courtesy of the Naval Historical Foundation.*

Chapter 3

The First Attack

"Suddenly a bright flash was observed and a stream of flames ascended to a great height."
Ensign John W. Gratten.

The steamer *USS Louisiana* was disguised to look like a blockade-runner, loaded with 215 tons of gunpowder and towed to Fort Fisher as a floating bomb. Drawing from *Harper's Weekly*.

Commander Alexander Rhind of the *USS Wilderness* put a crew aboard the *Louisiana* to detonate the ship when she grounded on the shallows near Fort Fisher. It was 10:30 PM when the *Wilderness* towed the floating bomb toward shore, cast it loose in the darkness and then picked up the crew after they had set the fuses.

Admiral Porter took the fleet to an anchorage twelve miles off shore and ordered all the ships to release the steam from their boilers so they would not rupture from the gigantic explosion that was sure to light up the night. Shortly after midnight sailors of the Federal fleet spotted several rockets in the western sky—Rhind's signal that the powder boat was set to detonate. For more than an hour they waited. At 1:40 AM the sailors saw a bright flame on the horizon. Commander Daniel Ammen on board the *Mohican* recalled the explosion resembled distant lightning. Seconds later a low rumble that sounded like an approaching thunderstorm raced across the water. As the rumble increased, the masts and spars on the vessels began to rattle, but the explosion failed to live up to expectations. Disappointed at the feeble explosion, Commander Rhind turned to the men on the *Wilderness*, shook his head and said, "There's a fizzle!" General Butler's idea of using a powder boat to destroy Fort Fisher had proved to be a loud and spectacular failure.[1]

Colonel William Lamb had already gone to bed when the *Louisiana* blew up. Fort Fisher was undamaged, but the fort's sentries immediately sounded the alarm, alerting Lamb and the garrison. When Lamb observed the burning wreckage of an unknown vessel, he wired General Whiting in Wilmington and informed him that, "a blockader got aground near the fort, set fire to herself and blew up."[2]

13

The first Confederate sentry to spot the Federal Fleet was Private Arthur Muldoon. He was detailed as a lookout upon of Fort Fisher's Pulpit Battery when the Federal warships materialize one by one out of the early morning mist. Muldoon sent for Colonel Lamb at once. Lamb wrote about what he observed in *Colonel Lamb's Story of Fort Fisher*:

> A grander sight than the approach of Porter's formidable armada toward the fort was never witnessed on our coast. On the vessels came, growing larger and more imposing as the distance lessened between them and the resolute men who had rallied to defend their homes. The *Minnesota, Colorado* and *Wabash* came grandly on, floating fortresses, each mounting more guns than all the batteries on land, and the first two combined carrying more shot and shell than all the magazines in the fort combined.[3]

Lamb watched the Federal fleet deploy with a mixture of awe and dread. Fort Fisher's garrison had always been undermanned even though General Whiting had pleaded with President Davis to send him more troops. Even after receiving reinforcements from the other Cape Fear defenses Colonel Lamb only commanded 1,371 soldiers, a third of whom were Junior Reservists, mere boys sixteen to eighteen years of age. Lamb was also worried there was too little ammunition for him to allow his gunners to fire at will. For all forty-four of the fort's cannon, Lamb had a total of 3,000 rounds—an average of 68 rounds per gun. Ammunition would have to be rationed and controlled. Lamb ordered that only long-range guns would fight the ships, and no piece would be permitted to fire more than once every half-hour. To spare the men from unnecessary exposure, the gun crews remained inside the bombproofs until the time came to fire their half-hourly shot. Lamb's largest artillery piece, the gigantic 150-pounder Armstrong cannon, had only thirteen rounds of ammunition and he ordered it to be fired only at his command.[4]

The forty-six gun frigate *USS Minnesota* was one of the ships which Colonel Lamb had seen on the morning of January 13, 1865. *Photograph courtesy of the Naval History & Heritage Command.*

Lamb was afraid Porter would use the same naval tactic that was employed by Admiral Farragut in Mobile Bay, Alabama. Farragut had run his fleet past three Confederate forts and captured all of them from behind. If Porter could cross the sandbar at the river's entrance and proceed up river, Fort Fisher could be taken from the rear because its defenses were directed seaward, away from the ships behind them. Lamb was determined that this would not happen here. He ordered his gunners to fire as rapidly as possible if any attempt was made to enter the Cape Fear River.

While still beyond the range of the fort, the wooden ships slowed and the ironclads steamed ahead. The *New Ironsides, Monadnock, Saugus, Canonicus* and *Mahopac* reached their anchorage about three-quarters of a mile off the beach. They came into line, dropped bow and stern anchors so their broadsides could bear on the fort. The gunboats deployed into three adjacent lines of battle forming an arc running north to south with lines of fire directed at specific gun chambers in Fort Fisher.

The honor of opening the battle went to the *USS New Ironsides*. A sudden flash of light and a great cloud of smoke billowed from one of her starboard cannon. An 11-inch shell screamed over the heads of the Confederate defenders and exploded harmlessly in the rear of the fort. The *New Ironsides* first shot started a chain of broadsides down the length of the lines. "It was a magnificent sight," Federal Naval officer B. F. Blair wrote to his mother, "and one never to be forgotten. [The ships'] sides seemed sheets of flame and the roar of their guns like a mighty thunderbolt. . . .Nothing could withstand such a storm of shot and shell as was now poured into this fort."[5]

The *USS New Ironsides* fired the first shot, an 11-inch shell, into Fort Fisher. Painting by artist Clary Ray. *Photograph courtesy of the Naval Historical Foundation.*

From his position atop the Pulpit Battery, Colonel Lamb could see the *New Ironside's* shell as it hurtled over the ocean. When it exploded, he ordered the fort's signal gun fired. The huge Columbiad cannon bellowed a deep roar and sent the fort's first round whizzing toward the fleet. The missile, a 10-inch solid shot cannonball, ricocheted off the sea, bounded over the rail of the *USS Susquehanna* and punched a gaping hole in the ship's smokestack. This was the signal the fort's gunners were waiting for. They sprang into action and the line of batteries on the fort's sea-face belched fire and sulfur-laden smoke. Several of Porter's ships were struck in this opening salvo. The *USS Minnesota* was struck four times, losing her anchor cable and sustaining damage to her rigging and masts.[6]

Anchored at their battle stations, the long line of Federal warships replied with a stunning barrage. A mile-wide storm of shot and shell screamed toward the fort, exploding overhead and sending hot iron fragments to plow up the fort's sandy interior. When the frigates *Minnesota, Colorado* and *Wabash* opened up, Captain Thomas Selfridge wrote:

> The enemy replied briskly, but when these frigates found the range and commenced firing rapidly, nothing could withstand their broadsides of twenty-five 9-inch guns. It was a magnificent sight to see these frigates fairly engaged, and one never to be forgotten. Their sides seemed a sheet of flame and the roar of their guns like a mighty thunderbolt.[7]

15

Aboard the large warships conditions were almost intolerable for the sailors working the guns. The constant roar, smoke and concussion of cannon fire in tight, confined spaces aboard ship prompted Acting Master's Mate Joseph Simms to comment, "The roar of the cannon was something terrible. Every particle of flesh upon one's bones seemed to be slipping off, eyes stinging, and we were almost blinded by the powder and smoke and refuse. The guns and our clothing were almost white from the saltpeter and several men at my gun bled at the nose."[8]

Colonel Lamb wrote about the federal bombardment in *Colonel Lamb's Story of Fort Fisher*:

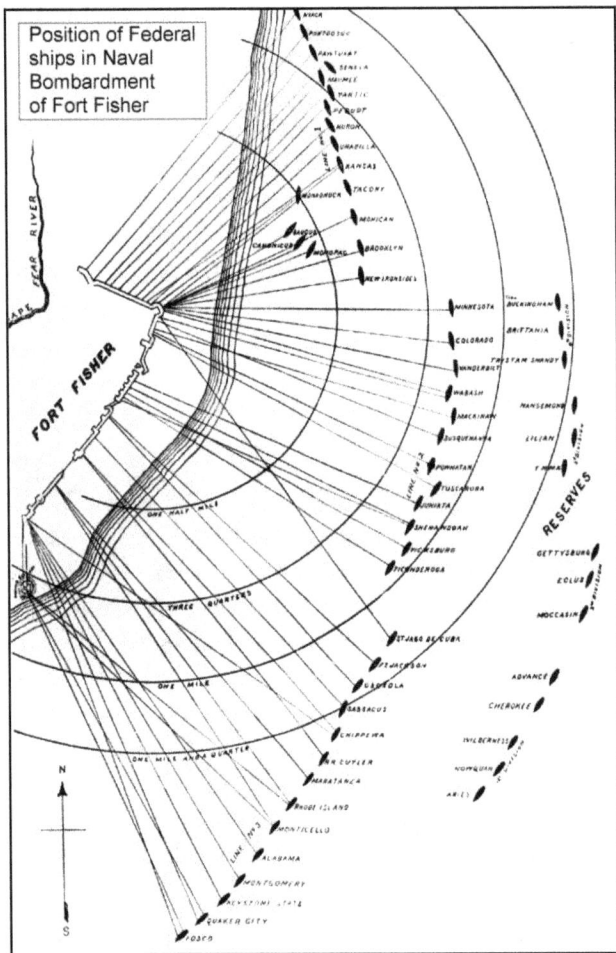

Walter A. Lane's drawing of the position of the Federal Fleet during the bombardment of Fort Fisher. Reprinted from *The Soldier In Our Civil War*.

This was the commencement of the most terrific bombardment from the fleet which war had ever witnessed. Ship after ship discharged its broadside, every description of deadly missile, from a 3-inch rifle bolt to a 15-inch shell flying wildly over the fort. In the rear of the flagstaff the wooden quarters of the garrison were situated, and these were soon set on fire by the bursting shells and more than one half of them were consumed. The day being balmy most of the men had left their overcoats and blankets in their bunks and these were consumed.

This lack of overcoats and blankets would play an important role later in promoting disease among the Confederate prisoners in Northern prisoner of war camps during one of the harshest winters in years.[9]

About 4:30 PM that afternoon General William Whiting and his staff arrived at Battery Buchanan to assist in the defense of Fort Fisher. Ordinarily the general and his staff would be met by saddle horses so they could ride to the fort. But the stable was destroyed during the bombardment and the horses were either killed or scattered throughout the fort. Braving the naval bombardment the men hurried across the mile and a half of deep sand to Colonel Lamb's combat headquarters in the Pulpit Battery. Lamb was surprised to see General Whiting and his staff climbing the path to the Pulpit. He offered to relinquish command to Whiting, but the general told Lamb that he had come merely to assist and observe. Whiting also brought with him some badly needed reinforcements and the welcome news that advance elements of General Robert F. Hoke's Division had arrived at Sugar Loaf, a fortified natural earthwork, six miles north of the fort.

Colonel Lamb made an important discovery after the fort's garrison flag was shot away. When Private Christopher C. Bland climbed the shattered staff to reattach the flag, the Federal fleet concentrated a heavy fire on it. Taking a cue from this, Lamb decided to plant a flag where the fleet's cannon fire would do the least damage. He personally planted a company flag on Sheperd's Battery, the westernmost mound in the fort. Here, Lamb figured, at least half of the shells aimed at the flag would overshoot their target and fall harmlessly into the Cape Fear River.

However, some shots from the Federal fleet found their mark. A Confederate courier dashed across the open plain to deliver a message to the Brooke Battery. Before he could reach his destination a 15-inch shell scored an almost direct hit on him, exploding and blowing him into so many pieces that the soldiers could hardly find enough to bury in the shallow grave they scraped out of the sand. The Brooke Battery itself took a hit some moments later, and a shell fragment tore off the leg of one of the Confederate gunners.[10]

The Federal fleet did not escape unscathed, either. Confederate gunners made their shots count even though they were only allowed to fire their cannon once every half-hour. A shell struck the gunboat *Mackinaw* at the waterline, tearing through a coal bunker and smashing into the port boiler. The engine room was flooded and filled with steam, nearly extinguishing the fires in the furnace and scalding ten men. A similar fate occurred to the *Osceola*. A 10-inch solid shot penetrated the hull below the waterline and pierced a boiler. Six men were scalded and the engine room began to take on so much water that the captain pulled his vessel out of line and signaled that his ship was sinking. The former blockade-runner *A. D. Vance* came to the *Osceola*'s aid and towed the stricken ship to a safe anchorage where emergency repairs could be made. On board the frigate *Wabash* five sailors were injured by shrapnel. The fleet's largest frigate, the *Colorado*, received at least four rebel cannonballs. One shot hit the cut-water, the bow was struck by another, the starboard gangway was hit twice, shattering some deck planks, the main topmast and head of the topgallant mast also received damage. Luckily, only one man was injured on the *Colorado*.[11]

Drawing of exploding Parrott Rifle from *Harpers Weekly*.

Ironically, most of the damage and casualties suffered by the Federal fleet occurred when five of the Navy's 100-pounder Parrott rifles burst upon firing. Two sailors were mortally wounded when the *Yantic*'s Parrott rifle exploded, damaging the vessel so severely that her commander pulled her out of the battle. The *Ticonderoga* suffered the most from the malfunctioning Parrotts. A cannon exploded killing eight sailors and wounded twelve others. The ship was such a bloody mess that the decks had to be covered with sand to absorb the blood. Seeing the demoralizing effect the mangled bodies were having on his men, Coxswain William Shipman shouted encouragement to his shipmates, "Go ahead, boys, this is only the fortune of war." Under Shipman's guidance his fellow sailors returned to their posts and continued loading and firing. Coxswain Shipman would later receive the Medal of Honor for his coolness under fire.[12]

Another Parrott rifle exploded on the screw sloop *Juanita*, turning her deck into a slaughter house. The blast sprayed pieces of the gun in all directions, killing five and wounding eight. With forty-five casualties on five ships from exploding Parrott rifles, Porter ordered all the 100-pounders retired from the battle.[13]

At 5:50 PM the fire from the Federal fleet sputtered to a stop and the vessels withdrew to their anchorage five miles offshore. Describing the first day's battle Lamb wrote:

> Never since the invention of gun powder was there so much harmlessly expended as in the first day's attack on Fort Fisher. I had about one-half of the quarters burned, three gun carriages disabled, a light artillery caisson exploded, large quantities of the earth work torn and plowed up, with some revetments broken and splintered, but not a single bombproof or magazine injured. Only twenty-three men wounded, one mortally, three seriously and nineteen slightly.

Lamb also noted that the fort had only fired 672 projectiles while the navy expended at least 10,000. At the height of the bombardment on the 24th Admiral Porter estimated the rate of fire at Fort Fisher as 115 shells per minute.[14]

The limited return fire from Fort Fisher was proof enough to Admiral Porter that most of the fort's guns had been rendered useless. This prompted him to send a telegram to Secretary of the Navy Gideon Welles boasting:

> Sir: I have the honor to inform you that I attacked the forts at the mouth of Cape Fear River this morning at 12:30, and after getting the ships in position silenced them in about an hour and a half. There being no troops here to take possession, I am merely firing at it now to keep up practice. The forts are nearly demolished, and as soon as troops come we can take possession. We have set them on fire, blown some of them up, and all that is wanted now is the troops to land to go into them.[15]

General Butler did not arrive with the army transports until the evening of December 24th, just as the Navy was finishing its bombardment of Fort Fisher. Butler learned of the utter destruction of the fort from the boastful Admiral Porter. Although Butler was angry that he had missed the powder boat explosion, he was hopeful that when his troops landed they would capture the fort with ease.

Rear Admiral David Dixon Porter

Shortly after sunrise on the 24th, Confederate General William W. Kirkland had left Wilmington with his brigade and followed Confederate Point Road south toward Fort Fisher. Kirkland's Brigade, which was the vanguard of General Robert F. Hoke's Division, consisted of 1,300 troops from the 17th, 42nd and a portion of the 66th North Carolina Infantry regiments. The general rode ahead of

18

his troops and reached Sugar Loaf about 1:00 PM. In the distance he could hear the Federal fleet pounding Fort Fisher. There he was met by a ragtag Confederate force of 1,200 Junior and Senior Reserves. These old men and boys were drafted into service to fill the depleted ranks. On April 16, 1862, the Confederacy began conscription for three years' service of all white males between 18 and 35 who were not legally exempt. The age was raised several times until the Confederacy conscripted nearly everyone from seventeen to fifty who could shoulder a rifle.[16]

Kirkland placed his brigade on a line of defensive works across the peninsula from the Cape Fear River, near Sugar Loaf, to Battery Gatlin on the beach. He also sent a small force of eighty men two miles down the beach to a one-gun earthwork called Battery Anderson.

At 10:30 AM Christmas morning the Federal fleet resumed its bombardment of Fort Fisher. Federal Chaplain Henry Turner described the scene in his diary: "Broadside after broadside was fired, until the reports became so continuous that, in many instances it was one unbroken roar, which seemed to be awful enough to shake the world."[17]

Federal Sergeant Edward K. Wightman observed the bombardment with awe. Only one day later, while the events were fresh in his mind, Wightman wrote a vivid account of the shelling to his brother:

Confederate General William Kirkland's Brigade was the first unit from Hoke's Division to arrive at Wilmington.

> I can imagine nothing like the bellowing of our fifteen-inch guns. The belching of a volcano with accompanying explosions may suggest a corresponding idea. The din was deafening. Above the fort the countless flashes and puffs of smoke from bursting shells spoke for the accuracy of our guns while columns of sand heaved high in the air suggested that possibly the [fort's] casements were not so safe and cozy after all.[18]

On Christmas morning nineteen Federal warships moved into position between Battery Gatlin and Battery Anderson, three miles north of Fort Fisher. These gunboats were ordered to shell the batteries and the woods in preparation for the Federal landing. Admiral Porter, observing the action from the deck of his flagship *Malvern*, thought the gunboats were positioned too far from shore for their gunfire to be effective. Porter signaled the *Brooklyn* to show the others how a beach should be shelled. The *Brooklyn*, the fourth-largest ship-of-the-line in the armada, was a powerful screw sloop with twenty-six big guns. Porter respected the ability of its commander, Captain James Alden. The *Brooklyn* had helped Admiral Farragut capture New Orleans and Alden knew how to bombard a shore installation.

The intense shelling by the Federal gunboats killed and wounded twenty soldiers of Kirkland's Brigade and an undetermined number of reserves. As Kirkland's brigade advanced in line-of-battle through the woods they encountered several dead from the Senior Reserves. Confederate Captain Charles G. Elliott wrote, "It was pitiful to see some gray-haired patriots dead in the woods, killed by shells from the fleet. I saw the ships extending as far as I could see down the beach and rode down through the woods and found a large [Federal] force on the beach and more coming while the woods around us were filled with shrieking shells."[19]

Because of his skill in the capture of New Orleans, Captain James Alden of the *USS Brooklyn* led the bombardment three miles north of Fort Fisher prior to the army coming ashore. *Photograph courtesy of the Naval Historical Foundation.*

Around 2:00 PM General Butler's landing force shoved off from the fleet for the shore. The long, blue column snaked through the rolling swells and then fanned out as they came ashore. Before they reached the beach, the men were over the sides of the boats, waist deep in water, and were deploying as skirmishers. To his surprise, General N. Martin Curtis' came ashore unopposed and secured the landing site with a strong skirmish line. Curtis, and a reconnoitering party of five hundred men from the 142nd and the 112th New York, was to push as close as possible to Fort Fisher, ascertain its condition, and report whether the rest of the troops should be landed and an assault made.[20]

Noticing Confederate Battery Anderson was three-quarter of a mile due south, and between him and Fort Fisher, Curtis promptly led a force down the beach to assault the battery. In the distance he saw a white flag appear above the battery. General Butler, noticing the landing was unopposed and allowed the rest of Curtis' brigade to go ashore also.

There has always been a fierce competition between the army and the navy and so it was at Fort Fisher. When Lieutenant Samuel Huse of the *Britannia* saw the white flag and Curtis' Brigade

Federal landing site three miles north of Fort Fisher, *Harper's Weekly*.

approaching the battery, he ordered Ensign W. H. Bryant to take a boat ashore and receive the surrender before the army got there. Boats were also sent out from the *Tristram Shandy, Howquah* and the *Santiago de Cuba*, each eager to receive the battery's surrender. When the army troops noticed the boats racing ashore, they ran as quickly as they could, trying to get there before the navy.

Confederate Major General Robert F. Hoke's Division was taken from the Petersburg, Virginia, defenses and sent to Wilmington, North Carolina.

The *Britannia*'s crew arrived there ahead of the army and Ensign Bryant planted a United States flag atop the battery. He was met by the demoralized battery commander, Captain Koonts, holding out his sword in surrender. He and eighty men from the 42nd North Carolina had been badly battered by the navy's intense shelling. When his only cannon exploded and he saw his soldiers were outnumbered six-to-one, he decided to give up.[21]

General Kirkland and his staff had just left Battery Gatlin and were riding south to Battery Anderson when he heard a deafening cheer from the fleet. A courier dashed up to the general and reported the surrender of Battery Anderson. Kirkland's regiment was stretched thin, but he thought if he attacked the Federal-occupied battery it might be possible to release the prisoners. Kirkland needed to know more about the Federal advance so he conducted a closer reconnaissance of the beach. He saw his men were facing at least three Federal brigades with more men coming ashore. The enemy was overlapping his flanks so Kirkland deployed his whole regiment as skirmishers. As soon as Lieutenant Colonel Sharp's 17th North Carolina regiment was deployed, they advanced on Battery Anderson.

In a short while they encountered the enemy and pushed their skirmish line back upon the main body. Once the Confederates left the woods and came out on the beach they found they were covered by the guns of nineteen warships. "It would have been madness to have advanced farther," Kirkland said, "besides I was fearful the enemy would land a force at Gatlin and push up the Wilmington Road which was covered by one regiment."[22]

General Whiting sent numerous telegrams to Confederate Headquarters in Wilmington pleading for help. "A large force of the enemy has landed near the fort, deploying as skirmishers. May be able to carry me by storm." In another telegram Whiting told Bragg, "Our case is critical. The enemy have landed and are now skirmishing with our troops on the parapet. If you send reinforcements for Kirkland to attack in the rear we can hold out." Major General Bragg sent no help to Whiting, in fact, "in an alarming display of pessimism he made arrangements for his wife, Elisa, to flee the city." This single move by the commanding general caused widespread panic in Wilmington.[23]

While the Federal infantry was skirmishing and moving down Confederate Point, Admiral Porter was contemplating an attack on the south end of Fort Fisher. Porter figured if several warships could enter New Inlet, and steam up the Cape Fear River, they could bombard the fort from the rear and perhaps force it to surrender. However, the inlet was hazardous due to the wrecks of blockade-runners and shifting sandbars. Porter needed accurate soundings and the channel marked with buoys before he would commit his ships to such a daring plan. The inlet was well guarded by the Mound Battery and Battery Buchanan which bristled with Confederate cannon. A mission like this was practically suicide and would require a man who was fearless in battle. Admiral Porter knew Lieutenant Commander William B. Cushing was such a man.

Cushing formed his reputation for reckless bravery by leading a small party of volunteers in a commando style raid against the powerful ironclad *CSS Albemarle* in the Roanoke River. Brandishing only a fourteen-foot long spar torpedo and the audacity to try something that everyone else thought was impossible, Cushing set out in a thirty-foot steam launch and destroyed the rebel ship.

Cushing became a national figure in the North for sinking the *CSS Albemarle* and this exploit earned him an audience with President Abraham Lincoln. When the media learned of the story they dubbed him "Lincoln's Commando". Cushing also conducted several small raids into the Cape Fear River the previous year, capturing a number of prisoners and embarrassing the Confederate military.[24]

Lieutenant Commander William B. Cushing became known as "Lincoln's Commando" after leading several daring missions. *Photograph courtesy of the Naval Historical Foundation.*

At Fort Fisher Commander Cushing led a force of ten launches into New Inlet while Commander John Guest of the *USS Iosco* and eight other warships unleashed a heavy, suppressing fire against the Mound Battery and nearby Battery Buchanan. Even though the increased Federal cannon fire made it hazardous for the Confederates to man their guns, they still gave a good account of themselves. Before the battle began Colonel Lamb had specifically ordered the gunners to fire as rapidly as possible if anyone tried to enter New Inlet because the enemy might try to take the fort from the rear. Although countless Rebel shells fell all around the boats, the sailors coolly took soundings and marked the shipping channel. So many shell fragments peppered the water's surface that the sailors had to stop what they were doing and bail out the launches several times.

Ironically, the first casualties from this action occurred when one of the Confederate Brooke rifles exploded. The barrel split, spraying red-hot iron in all directions. Seven gunners were wounded but no one was killed.[25]

One of the Confederate cannon found the range of a Federal launch from the *USS Tacony* and shot the flagstaff from its stern. A sailor picked up the pennant and was busy tying it to the broken staff when another shell smashed into the boat, cutting it in two. One man received several splinters in his backside while seaman Henry Sand's legs were severed at the knees, mortally wounding him. The other boats rescued the men in the water and Cushing ordered a hasty withdrawal. This was the last attempt by the Federals to enter the river.[26]

The *USS Powhatan* was hit by four cannonballs. One shell caused the ship to leak badly. *Photograph courtesy of the Naval History & Heritage Command.*

The Federal fleet also suffered under the Confederate fire. At 3:30 PM the fort's gunners found the range of the *USS Powhatan* and hit the ship with four cannonballs in quick secession. One ball struck below the waterline where it destroyed some copper sheathing and caused the ship to leak badly.[27]

At 4 PM Admiral Porter's flagship signaled the fleet to cease fire and retire to avoid hitting the Federal Army as it approached the fort. For some reason the *USS Colorado* and the *USS Minnesota* ceased fire but remained at anchor. Since the other Federal ships were steaming out of range, the Confederate gunners concentrated their fire on the two largest ships in the Federal fleet. At 4:30 PM a ten-inch solid shot struck the *Colorado* over the No. 4 gun on the starboard side damaging two guns and killing one man and wounding five more. Commodore Thatcher of the *Colorado* wrote:

> Near the close of the second day's action, we perceived the approach of the advanced skirmishers of our army force when our fire ceased for nearly thirty minutes, and was resumed after we had been hulled several times by a vicious gun which appeared to be fired from the N. E. angle of Fort Fisher. We then reopened heavily, but more to the left than we had preciously fired, to avoid annoying our own troops who were seen approaching the fort.[28]

At 4:40 P.M. the *Colorado* signaled to the *Minnesota*, Enemy are hulling us; fire for your own protection.

But the *USS Minnesota* was struck below the starboard waterline, and another shell struck amidships and lodged in the stern of one of the cutters. Shortly after, a rebel shell exploded on the chain armor, scattering shrapnel on both sides of the ship.[29]

Leading 250 soldiers of the 142nd New York, General Weitzel and Colonel Curtis advanced within 800 yards of the fort's land-face. From there, the officers studied the sprawling fort through binoculars. General Weitzel wrote, "I counted seventeen guns in position, bearing up the beach, and between each pair of guns there was a traverse so thick and so high above the parapet that I have

Major General Godfrey Weitzel advised Butler against attacking Fort Fisher. *Photograph courtesy of Library of Congress.*

no doubt they were all bombproofs. I saw plainly that the work had not been materially injured by the heavy and very accurate shell fire of the navy." Weitzel recalled the Federal slaughter that had occurred in repeated attacks against Battery Wagner near Charleston. Their present situation was virtually the same except the Rebel fort was at least ten times as strong. General Weitzel did not want to make that same mistake here. He returned to the fleet and told General Butler about his findings. He strongly advised against an attack, saying, "it would be butchery to order an assault."[30]

Before General Weitzel left, Colonel Curtis asked for permission to conduct a reconnaissance of the area. Weitzel reluctantly agreed, but insisted Curtis not bring on a general engagement with the enemy. Curtis said he wouldn't, then led a reconnaissance force toward the western part of the fort. Skirmishers located a telegraph pole which linked the fort to Sugar Loaf and Confederate headquarters in Wilmington. Lieutenant George Simpson shinnied up the pole and chopped the wires with a hatchet.

Curtis' men advanced within 500 yards of the fort and halted at an abandoned Confederate battery. The colonel used this slightly higher ground to get a better view of the fort. Although he saw many serviceable cannon on the fort's wall the guns appeared unmanned. Encouraged by this, Curtis and 40 soldiers from the 142nd New York advanced to within 75 yards of the fort. Some of the more daring men slipped through a jagged hole blown in the palisade fence.

A huge naval shell exploded on the fort's ramparts, throwing a plume of sand into the air and knocking down the Confederate flag staff so it extended past the parapet walls. Captured enemy flags were highly prized and seizing one made a soldier an instant legend. Witnessing what had happened, Lieutenant William Walling scaled the exterior slope of the fort and grabbed the flag along with a twelve-foot section of the pole and brought it back as a trophy. Walling describes the incident in the book *Deeds of Valor*:

Lieutenant William Walling captures a fallen Confederate flag from Fort Fisher's land-face. Picture Reprinted from *Deeds of Valor*.

> [A] shot from the fleet cut down the Confederate flag on the fort. . . .I said to my men: 'I'll go and get the flag; you keep a sharp lookout for the riflemen on the works. Let every man have his gun in position to fire.' 'We will, Lieutenant; we will!' came the response from my men as with one voice. I started off. I had gone but a few steps when one of the great monitor shells passed in front of me and exploded before reaching the river. I confess I was frightened, and for an instant halted involuntarily, stunned by the fearful crash. But, quickly recovering my wits, I proceeded and came to a place where a shell had cut a hole in the palisade a little to the left of the flag. Through this opening I entered, passed along toward the river, gained the parapet, secured the flag and returned, uninjured as I had gone.

This daring deed earned Lieutenant Walling the Medal of Honor.[31]

Several minutes later a Confederate courier on horseback emerged from the fort's gate and clattered over the wooden bridge that crossed the marsh. Nineteen-year-old Private Amos H. Jones carried a dispatch from Major William Saunders to General Hebert's chief of artillery, requesting a battery of light artillery be placed in the fort. As Jones galloped down

River Road toward Sugar Loaf, a Federal soldier rose up from his hiding place beneath the bridge and shot him from the saddle, killing him.[32]

Colonel N. Martin Curtis was wounded four times in the second battle of Fort Fisher, winning him the Medal of Honor. His last wound was from a shell fragment which carried away his left eye and orbital bone. *Photograph courtesy of Library of Congress.*

The lack of Confederate soldiers on the fort's walls convinced Colonel Curtis that Fort Fisher could easily be taken by assault. He sent a dispatch back to the rear guard and ordered Lieutenant Colonel Barney to bring forward the rest of the First Brigade. Curtis took the captured flag to the beach and began waving it to signal the fleet that the army's assault was about to begin and for them to shift their fire away from his advancing soldiers. The sailors on the ships did not understand Curtis' signal and cheered the plucky Federal officer waving the Confederate flag from the beach.

It had been twenty minutes since Curtis called for reinforcements. Curious why it was taking so long, he looked down the beach and his soldiers appeared to be milling around the landing site instead of moving forward as ordered. Curtis stormed down the beach.

Lieutenant Colonel Barney informed Curtis that he had received orders from General Butler to withdraw and re-embark the troops. Curtis was bewildered by the orders. Clearly Butler did not understand the situation. He scribbled a message, appraising his commanding officer of the conditions at Fort Fisher. "Your order is held in abeyance that you may know the true condition of the fort; the garrison has offered no resistance; the flagstaff of the fort was cut by a naval shot and one of my officers brought from the rampart the garrison flag; another cut the telegraph wire connecting the fort with Wilmington; my skirmishers are now at the parapet."[33]

About 8:00 PM Colonel Curtis received another dispatch from General Butler calling off the attack and ordering him to return to the landing site and load his men on the ships. Captain Birney B. Keeler brought the message to his friend and told Curtis, "All the troops which have landed, including the larger part of your brigade, Pennypacker's brigade, and Bell's brigade, have been taken on board the ships, and there is no one on land but your force and the flankers and pickets you have left out, and it will be entirely useless for you to expect any assistance." Saddened, Curtis had no choice but to return to the landing site.

Curtis reached the beach sometime after 9 PM and saw the reembarkation process was well underway. The wind had been increasing all evening and the seas were running so high that boats approaching the beach faced the dangerous prospect of being swamped or overturned. The Federal boats bravely continued coming ashore, tossed about by the wind-driven waves. After they were loaded, the boats ferried the men to the ships while the gale increased in intensity. Six boats were destroyed and one man drown in the rough surf before General Adelbert Ames called a halt to the reembarkation, leaving 600 of Curtis' men and 200 prisoners stranded on the beach.

Regimental Surgeon James A. Mowris of the 117th New York, recalled being left behind:

> The 3rd brigade had already departed, and the 2nd [brigade], despite the increasing sea, had nearly all recovered their places on the transports. Soon after they had all done so, the 1st brigade attempted it, but the violence of the surf promptly arrested the work and emphatically, forbade its renewal. Then followed a gloomy night for the 1st brigade. Darkness was about us—we were destitute of materials for shelter, or tools for entrenching—a heavy and cold rain was upon us—the forbidding sea roared on one side and Hoke's division threatened on the other.[34]

Confederate First Lieutenant William Drew was wounded and captured at Fort Fisher. Photograph reprinted *from State Troops and Volunteers.*

General Butler retired to his cabin aboard the *USS Ben De Ford.* Nothing seemed to be going right for him. Butler's troubles began with the ill-fated powder boat explosion. He was convinced if he had been here to supervise things would have gone as planned and Fort Fisher would have been captured by now.

Now, Butler was faced with another set of problems. Colonel Curtis had captured some prisoners from Confederate General Hoke's army. These prisoners reported that General Lee had ordered their division from the Petersburg trenches to help defend Wilmington and Fort Fisher. Butler had seen evidence of this himself because his troops were already skirmishing with Confederate soldiers moving south from Wilmington and into the Federal rear. This certainly added to Butler's worries, but the bad news didn't stop there. The weather was deteriorating quickly and night was coming on. If Butler left his troops ashore these men would be extremely vulnerable to an assault. To the north was General Hoke's 6,000 man division and to the south was Fort Fisher's garrison. These Confederate forces were numerically superior to the Federal troops ashore. If they coordinated their attacks, his invasion force could very well be captured. With night falling, and the weather blowing a gale, even the navy with its 640 guns would be useless to help the troops ashore.

Butler had also received a report from General Weitzel that Fort Fisher appeared uninjured from the naval bombardment and, in his opinion, it would be butchery to assault the fort now. General Ames agreed with Weitzel that any Federal land assault now would end in failure. Butler trusted Weitzel's assessment of the situation, but he needed to see for himself before he called off the assault.[35]

Butler transferred from his flagship to the *Chamberlain,* a shallow draft vessel, so he could get in close to study the fort. As the *Chamberlain* steamed by the Northeast Bastion, Butler saw that Fort Fisher appeared as formidable as ever after the naval attack. While he scanned the fort with his binoculars, the naval bombardment ceased and the fort's parapets were soon fully manned with Confederate defenders. Apparently General Weitzel had been right about the soldiers seeking shelter in bombproofs, waiting for the naval fire to end. Butler could plainly see his army would be slaughtered in a futile attempt to capture Fort Fisher.

Due to the severe weather even the evacuation did not go right for General Butler. Colonel Curtis' 600 man brigade was stranded ashore for an indefinite period until the storm abated. It didn't seem to matter what course of action Butler took, the situation kept getting worse. Now Curtis' men were surrounded by a vastly superior enemy who outnumbered his men twelve to one. Apparently this news was too much for Butler to handle for he sailed north to Hampton Roads, leaving Colonel Curtis' Brigade to its fate.

The survival of Fort Fisher depended upon a vigorous Confederate defense led by a bold commander. Unfortunately General Braxton Bragg would let the soldiers down. *Photograph courtesy of Library of Congress.*

As history would eventually show, Major General Butler worried needlessly about the Federal brigade stranded on the beach for a day and a half. Confederate Major General Braxton Bragg appeared paralyzed by fear and indecision and thus made no move to capture the enemy. A cold, driving rain fell that evening while the wet and hungry Federal soldiers hunkered down behind their sand breastworks, and waited for an attack that never came. Finally, the weather moderated on the morning of the 27th of December, allowing the fleet to send boats ashore to rescue the men. The choppy water was so turbulent that many of the naval launches had to be hooked to hawsers running from the beach back to the ship. True to his nature, the gallant Colonel Curtis was the last man to leave the beach at two that afternoon.

When Curtis came aboard the *Nereus* both he and his staff complained bitterly about the handling of the invasion force. "Fort Fisher would have been captured if General Butler had properly supported my men," Curtis contended. Lieutenant George Simpson of the 142nd New York seemed to sum up the Wilmington Campaign succinctly by saying, "One of the grandest and most expensive expeditions ever organized in our country has been terminated in a complete farce."[36]

Confederate Major General Bragg's inaction dumbfounded Whiting. "It was a matter of grave charge against [Bragg] that the whole [Federal] force was not captured," Whiting wrote in a letter to General Benjamin Butler while he was a prisoner on Governor's Island, New York. "I agree with General Whiting," wrote Colonel Lamb, "that but for the supineness of General Bragg the 3,500 men who landed would have been captured on Christmas night, and it is incomprehensible why he should have allowed the 700 demoralized troops who were forced to remain on the beach on the night of the 26th of December escape unmolested."[37]

Admiral David D. Porter was aghast at Butler's withdrawal. He sent a telegram to Secretary of the Navy Gideon Wells:

I can't conceive what the army expected when they came here. [Fort Fisher] was so blown up, burst up, and torn up that the people inside had no intention of fighting any longer. Had the army made a show of surrounding it, it would have been ours, but nothing of the kind was done. I feel ashamed that men calling themselves soldiers should have left this place so ingloriously.

Porter confided privately to Welles, "It was however nothing more than I expected when General Butler got himself mixed up in this expedition."[38]

The unpleasant duty of informing President Lincoln about the failure at Wilmington fell upon General Ulysses S. Grant. *Photograph courtesy of Library of Congress.*

On December 28, 1864, Lieutenant General Ulysses S. Grant undertook the unpleasant task of informing President Lincoln about the expedition's lack of success. "The Wilmington expedition has proven a gross and culpable failure. Many troops are now back here. Delays and free talk of the object of the expedition enabled the enemy to move troops to Wilmington to defeat it."[39]

General Grant decided the best way to capture Fort Fisher was to immediately select a new commander and renew the attack before the Confederates had a chance to repair the damage from the first assault. Grant was aware that General Butler could use his considerable political influence to absolve himself of any blame in the Wilmington affair. If he did so, Grant wondered if the president would approve of his decision to replace Butler. To his relief Lincoln agreed, but he cautioned Grant that this time he must select a commander who was both aggressive and dependable.

Grant already had a new commander in mind when he spoke to the president. Unlike the quarrelsome Butler, Major General Alfred H. Terry was a mild-mannered officer who got along easily with his superiors. He was a seasoned combat veteran and his proven ability instilled confidence in the men around him. "Although the General was a brave soldier," observed one of Terry's staff officers, "pomposity, arrogance, cowardice and self-conceit seemed to be elements foreign to his character."[40]

As the Federal ships faded into the horizon, General Whiting and Colonel Lamb realized that Fort Fisher was safe for the moment. The Confederates had won a major victory and the casualties were light: The total for the two days inside the fort was three killed, sixty-one wounded, two mortally. General Hoke's forces had five killed, sixteen wounded and 307 missing. The damage to the fort was relatively light and could easily be fixed. Only two guns were dismounted by enemy fire, another two were dismounted by recoil, three Brooke guns had burst and the headquarters and barracks buildings were destroyed.[41]

On January 4th, 1865, the Ladies Soldier's Aid Society travelled to Fort Fisher to show their appreciation to the soldiers by serving them a warm meal. A reporter from the *Wilmington Daily Journal* accompanied the women and wrote about the damage to the fort. "Deep holes are dug in the parapets and many of the traverses are marked and scarred. The outside and top of the ramparts looked as though rooted by gigantic hogs; none of this rooting, however, seemed to do more than roughen the surface."[42]

Confederate Major General Braxton Bragg continued to be Fort Fisher's worst enemy. He erroneously believed the fort and Wilmington were no longer in any danger. General Robert E. Lee even offered to send more ammunition to Fort Fisher but Bragg refused the supplies. In fact, Bragg sent Hoke's troops to Wilmington for a victory parade and then made plans for them to return to Richmond.[43]

The Federal Army suffered one man killed, eleven men wounded and one captured from the 142nd New York, while the navy had twenty killed and sixty-three wounded. The navy's sixty-four warships expended 20,271 projectiles against Fort Fisher, or fifteen shells for every defender.[44]

A drawing of Fort Fisher's interior showing Sheperd's Battery and the main gate. Horrific fighting for possession of the fort would take place in this area. Picture is from *The Seventh Regiment New Hampshire Volunteers in the War of the Rebellion. 1861-1865.*

Chapter 4

The Second Attack

"The country will not forgive us for another failure at Wilmington." Gustavas V. Fox, Assistant Secretary of the United States Navy[1]

In January, 1865, Lieutenant General Ulysses S. Grant had Confederate General Robert E. Lee right where he wanted him. Lee was a brilliant commanding general who had out-fought and embarrassed a much larger, better equipped Federal army. The daring Lee was not opposed to splitting his smaller force in the face of the enemy and boldly marching a portion of his army around an opponent to deliver a devastating blow where it was least expected. Unfortunately, Grant denied Lee the ability to maneuver by pinning him down in the trenches around Richmond and Petersburg. Lee was woefully aware that his smaller, poorly supplied army could not win a battle of attrition. Before his army was in the Petersburg trenches, Lee stated to the Reverend J. William Jones, a former Chaplain in the Army of Northern Virginia, "We must destroy this army of Grant's before he gets to the James River. If he gets there, it will become a siege, and then it will be a mere question of time."[2]

One of Lee's constant worries was feeding his 52,000-man army. Much of the rich farm land of the Southern states was devastated by General William T. Sherman during his march through Georgia and the Carolinas. General Philip Sheridan's cavalry conducted a similar scorched earth policy in the Shenandoah Valley, commonly referred to as "the breadbasket of the Confederacy." These men systematically tore up the

General Robert E. Lee knew the assault on Wilmington would be renewed. *Photograph courtesy of Library of Congress.*

Southern railroad, destroyed crops, burned government buildings and homes of suspected Southern sympathizers.

Blockade-runners provided much of the food for Lee's starving army. By mid-1864 Wilmington, North Carolina, was the only viable blockade-running seaport left in the South. As early as January 1863, Lee told Major General Gustavus Smith the city must be "defended at all hazards." Lee also sent word to Colonel Lamb warning, "if the fort fell he could not maintain his army." This statement had severe implications regarding the Confederacy; Lee was saying he could no longer defend Richmond and would have to evacuate the city if Fisher fell. As outnumbered as he was, Lee could not afford to send any troops to Wilmington. And yet, he realized if he did not defend Wilmington vigorously, the Confederacy's last line of supply might be severed. Lee could not afford to lose Wilmington and so he sent one of his best generals and 6,000 men to the port city.[3]

General Lee at first had been greatly relieved when he heard that the December attack against Fort Fisher had been repulsed. But now he had received alarming information which pointed to a renewal of the attack on Wilmington. Lee sent a telegram to Secretary of War Sedden, warning him

Confederate Robert Church, Company F, 10th North Carolina, killed at Fort Fisher. Photograph reprinted from *State Troops and Volunteers, Vol I*

about the new campaign and telling him the commander was General Alfred H. Terry. Lee also told Sedden that General Bragg had been notified and had reported "nothing has yet appeared off here."[4]

Colonel Lamb was aware that the Federal fleet had gone to Beaufort, North Carolina, to resupply but he could only guess when Admiral Porter might resume his attack of Fort Fisher. At 10 PM on January 12th, Colonel Thomas J. Lipscomb of the 2nd South Carolina Cavalry reported to headquarters that the enemy fleet of at least thirty vessels was off of Masonboro and steaming south. Later that night, Colonel Lamb was summoned to the Pulpit Battery. He later wrote, "I saw from the ramparts of the fort the lights of the great armada, as one after another appeared above the horizon." Lamb immediately prepared the fort for action. Only 800 soldiers from the 36th North Carolina were inside the fort. This prompted Lamb to telegraph an urgent plea to Wilmington Headquarters for reinforcements and call for the return of General Hoke's division. By January 15th, 700 men arrived from the other forts in the area and a detachment of 50 sailors and marines of the Confederate Navy.[5]

Major General Whiting and his staff traveled to Battery Buchanan on Friday the 13th of January, and walked across the deep sand to the Pulpit Battery at Fort Fisher. Lamb greeted Whiting and offered to turn over command of Fort Fisher's defense. Whiting declined, saying that he had come only as an advisor. Then he said, "Lamb, my boy, I have come to share your fate. You and your garrison are to be sacrificed." Colonel Lamb was shocked that his friend and mentor was so pessimistic after their glorious victory less than a month before. "Don't say so, General! We shall certainly whip the enemy again." Whiting then told him that when he left Wilmington General Bragg was removing his stores and ammunition and was looking for a place to fall back upon.[6]

32

When Lamb told General Whiting of the Federal landing, he wasn't surprised. Whiting had predicted this was going to happen for some time. Months earlier he had told President Davis and General Lee that this was the location where a Federal landing would take place. Whiting also told them he needed reinforcements so he might station a brigade there to oppose such a landing. It appeared he had been branded an alarmist because no would listen to him. Whiting would never let Fort Fisher slip away without a fight. He immediately sent several urgent messages to General Bragg advising him of the situation. "The enemy have landed in large force. Garrison too weak to resist assault and prevent their advance. You must attack them at once."

Whiting expected Bragg to wire him back with some sort of plan but as the minutes turned to hours and there was still no reply he began to wonder if his message had gotten through. Whiting sent another telegraph message, "Enemy have landed a large force. They will assault me tonight, or try to do it. You must attack." Still Bragg was curiously silent, so General Whiting sent a third message at 1:30 PM:

Confederate Major General William Whiting was appalled by Braggs inaction against the 700 Federals left on the beach during the December attack.

The game of the enemy is very plain to me. They are now furiously bombarding my land front; they will continue to do that, in order, if possible, to silence my guns until they are satisfied that their land force has securely established itself across the neck and rests on the river; then Porter will attempt to force a passage to co-operate with the force that takes the river-bank. I have received dispatches from you stating that the enemy had extended to the river. This they never should have been allowed to do; and if they are permitted to remain there the reduction of Fort Fisher is but a question of time. I will hold this place till the last extremities; but unless you drive that land force from its position I cannot answer for the security of this harbor. The fire has been and continues to be exceedingly heavy, surpassing not so much in its volume as in its extraordinary condition even the fire of Christmas.[7]

For some reason Bragg would not telegraph Whiting directly. If he needed to communicate with Whiting, he would send a message to him through Lieutenant Colonel Archer Anderson. Anderson sent Whiting a message at 2 PM saying General Bragg would send a brigade of 1,000 men to Fort Fisher that evening. Still not pacified by this report that promised re-enforcements, Whiting sent Bragg another telegraph at 8 PM. "Enemy are on the beach, where they have been all day. Why are they not attacked?" As he had done all day, Bragg virtually ignored Whiting, and reported to General Lee on the afternoon of the 15th that, "It is believed by the commander of your troops that the (Federal) effort will fail if made, and at a heavy sacrifice. If defended, as I believe it will be, by your veterans and the former garrison, it cannot be taken."[8]

Admiral Porter's plan of battle was similar to that of the first bombardment. Three lines of warships would anchor off the fort while the five ironclads would be positioned in front of the first line. Porter had instructed the captains in the fleet that for the first few hours they were to fire into the woods north of the fort in the vicinity of Battery Anderson and Battery Gatlin. This would destroy any Confederate resistance to General Terry's landing. After this, the ships were to concentrate their fire on the fort's artillery. Special attention was to be paid to the gun chambers on the land-face because this is where the Federal assault was to be made.

Sailors on board the *USS Unadilla. Photograph courtesy of the Naval Historical Foundation.*

At 8:30 AM the *USS New Ironsides* dropped anchor and waited for Fort Fisher to begin the battle. The Federals did not have to wait long. The Columbiad cannon in the Pulpit Battery roared to life, signaling the rest of the fort's gunners to open fire. Waiting for the fort to fire first was not as chivalrous as it sounds. Commodore William Radford wanted to count the fort's guns and see where they were located so very little ammunition would be wasted. One by one the ironclad's guns fired methodically to get the range of their targets. Gunners were instructed to note the elevation required for their cannon because when the bombardment began in earnest, the gun smoke would be so thick it would be impossible to tell where the shots were falling.

Fort Fisher's gun crews took advantage of the Federal's sporadic firing. Apparently the artillerists had honed their marksmanship during the first battle because the *New Ironsides* was struck by a series of shells. A ten-inch shot smashed through a starboard porthole into the ship's sick bay. The ship's iron hull was badly battered, her stern pennant and lightning rod were shot away, and a wooden launch was damaged severely along with sections of her railing.[9]

Federal soldier Augustus Buell wrote about the monitors in action at Fort Fisher in a book called *The Cannoneer:*

> The day was bright and clear, but cold and crisp, which made the smoke light, and the wind from the northwest lifted it quickly seaward, so that the flash of every gun could be seen. I wouldn't have missed seeing that bombardment of Fort Fisher for 10 years of my life. It beat anything in history for weight of ordinance used, even greater than the bombardment of the Sebastopol forts by the English and French fleets, because the guns we used were so much heavier. I cannot describe the discharges of those 13 and 15-inch Rodman guns of the monitors, or the explosion of their great shells in the air over the fort or among its traverses. To me it seemed like firing meteors out of volcanoes. I would watch the turrets of

the monitors through my glass. They would turn their iron backs on the enemy to load, and I could distinctly see the big rammer staves come out of the ports. Then they would wheel round on a line with the fort, there would be two puffs of blue smoke about the size of a thunder cloud in June, and then I could see the big shell make a black streak through the air with a tail of white smoke behind it and then it would come over the water, not the quick bark of a field gun, but a slow, quivering, over powering roar like an earthquake, and then, away among the Rebel traverses, there would be another huge ball of mingled smoke and flame as big as a meeting house."[10]

Quartermaster Daniel D. Stevens replaced the flag on the *USS Canonicus* two times after it was shot down by Confederate fire. Drawing from *Deeds of Honor, Volume 2, Photograph courtesy of the Naval Historical Foundation.*

For the first several hours the fort's gunners concentrated on the ironclads because the wooden warships were two miles north, shelling the beach for General Terry's landing. During this time the *Canonicus* was struck thirty-six times, the *New Ironsides* took twenty-five hits and the *Saugus* suffered eleven direct shots. Although the Confederate gunners' aim was excellent the cannonballs merely dented the iron sides of the ships and bounced harmlessly off.

Quartermaster Daniel D. Stevens had one of the most hazardous duties in the Federal fleet. His job was to stand outside on the deck of the *Canonicus* and act as an artillery spotter, watching for the effects of her shots on the fort. He was also required to take soundings so the ironclad would not run aground. The heavy Confederate fire twice shot away the *Canonicus* flag. Stevens, at great risk to his safety, replaced the flag both times, winning the Medal of Honor for his bravery.[11]

At 8:45 AM twenty-two troop transports anchored four miles north of Fort Fisher and began lowering boats of every type. Captain Adrian Terry (General Alfred Terry's brother) described the landing to his wife in a letter dated January 24, 1865:

The transports had hardly anchored when the water was covered with the small boats of the navy, varying in size from the small cutter to the huge launch, the former pulling six oars and the latter between twenty and thirty, which pulled rapidly up to the transports and were quickly filled with the soldiers who evinced the utmost eagerness to reach shore as soon as possible, more I fear in order to get on solid land once more than from their desire to meet the enemy.[12]

Terry's force of 9,600 men had three day's rations and forty rounds of ammunition in their cartridge boxes. The sea was rough due to a recent gale and the soldiers rarely came ashore dry. Eager to be on land once more, many men jumped over the side as the launches came into shallow water. "Loaded down as they were with ammunition, provisions, blankets, etc," one Union soldier observed, "there was some tall scrambling done on all-fours before they extricated themselves from their involuntary saltwater bath."[13]

Lieutenant Henry F. Little of the 7th New Hampshire recorded in his diary the rough sea conditions during the landing:

> As the boats were rowed up to the beach, the heavy waves would recede, and for an instant the bow of the boat would rest upon the sand, when the order would be given to jump, which order was supposed to be executed on the instant. . . .[to] clear the next wave. The men being in heavy marching order, and judging from the size of their knapsacks, perhaps a little top-heavy, could not all execute the movement promptly at the right moment, and those who were late in the execution of the command would invariably be caught by the next big roll, when they would find themselves in water perhaps ten feet deep. Many came near being drowned, and were very fortunate in getting off with only a thorough drenching.[14]

Pictured is the back of the Medal of Honor awarded to Ordinary Seaman Thomas Harcourt by the Navy for his bravery during the Naval Brigade's charge at Fort Fisher. The medal's red, white and blue ribbon is missing. *Photograph courtesy of the Naval Historical Foundation.*

The soldiers were not the only thing to get soaking wet that day. Provisions and ammunition got drenched as well. General Terry ordered 300,000 cartridges and six days' rations to replace the ruined supplies.[15]

Lieutenant Samuel Little also recalled several humorous incidents that occurred during the landing:

A very broad smile was caused by those who witnessed the misfortune which befell an officer, in a brand new uniform, whose foot slipped just as he was ready to jump, sending him headlong into the water. The sailors pulled him out by the collar, and seemed much pleased at the opportunity to lend a hand at his rescue. Again, two company cooks, who had been closely watching this operation of jumping, were anxiously waiting their chance to land. They were in charge of quite an accumulation of sugar and coffee belonging to their company, and resolved to keep it dry if possible; in order to do so, one fastened the bag of sugar around his neck, and the other secured the bag containing coffee in a like manner around his own. They jumped just quick enough to get caught in one of the largest of the incoming waves. The one having charge of the sugar was fished out just in time to save his life, while the one having the coffee came near being drowned, but was finally rescued in an exhausted condition by one of the sailors belonging to the boat, but the sugar and coffee were spoiled.[16]

Once General Terry's army was on shore, his greatest fear was that Confederate General Robert Hoke would assault him before he was ready. He wanted to construct a defensive line across Federal Point to protect the rear of the force that would advance on the fort. This would isolate Fort Fisher and make it more vulnerable to attack. Taking the bulk of his army on the evening of January 14th, General Terry marched south in the darkness through the pines and scrub oaks toward Fort Fisher. Terry found most of the ground was low and swampy with thick underbrush unsuitable for defense. By 2 AM the soldiers reached a point of fairly high ground, two miles north of the fort where Terry ordered his troops to establish a line of entrenchments from the river to the beach.

"All night long the troops labored most vigorously, the tools passing from hand to hand," reported an officer, "until by sunrise we had a line of breastworks across from the river to the sea, behind which our men could easily repel the attack of double their force." The 142nd New York, under Colonel Joseph McDonald, was ordered to establish a skirmish line as close to the fort as possible. The New York regiment pressed on through the dense underbrush in the darkness until they came to a large clearing. Across the moonlit silvery-white sand was an impressive sight. Fort Fisher's immense twenty-five foot wall, dotted by fifteen-foot high traverses, stretched as far as the eye could see. In anticipation of a land assault, Colonel Lamb had ordered the trees and underbrush removed for half a mile north of the fort to provide a clear field of fire for the fort's gunners. Colonel McDonald, knowing he could go no farther without being observed by the enemy, ordered the 142nd New York to deploy their skirmish line here.[17]

Colonel N. Martin Curtis was not satisfied with halting his men at the tree line. He had been on this same ground during the last expedition and his brigade was allowed to approach the fort without a shot being fired. Curtis felt that Fort Fisher's garrison lacked vigilance and that his brigade could

100-pounder rifled Parrott aboard the *USS Wabash*. Although this cannon did not explode during the battle five other similar guns blewup on Federal ships causing forty-five casualties.

have easily captured the fort if only General Butler had given him the opportunity. This time Butler wasn't here to hold Curtis back and the expedition had a bold new commander in General Terry. Because Curtis had knowledge of the enemy and terrain, Terry trusted his opinion on matters concerning the assault. This knowledge gave Curtis the confidence to move his brigade out of the tree line to within 900 yards of Fort Fisher for the assault the next day. Curtis also sent skirmishers even closer to the fort and had men dig a series of rifle pits for sharpshooters so they could clear the fort's parapet of enemy marksmen.[18]

While the Federal army was landing 9,000 troops, General Hoke's division was marching from Wilmington to Sugar Loaf. Kirkland's Brigade, which had been transported downriver on steamers, arrived in time to watch the Federal landing. Hoke's soldiers were confident they could push the Federals back into the sea if only their commander would order an attack. "We did nothing," complained a disgusted Asa King of the 66th North Carolina infantry, "just lay quiet . . . and let the enemy land. We could have repulsed them if we had fired on them as they landed, which we were anxious to do. We received no orders from our officers, just let the Federals assemble a force together, then they commenced firing on us."[19]

Meanwhile, at Fort Fisher, Colonel Lamb was observing the Federal landing with growing alarm. He telegraphed Wilmington headquarters asking, "Where is Hoke? The Yankees are landing a heavy force. I should have a regiment of veterans before sundown. I have plenty of shelter, and the firing is slow. They can come in. I have fewer men than on the 24th (of December)."[20]

Chapter 5

The Final Day of Battle

"Our fleet and the ironclads were doing some beautiful marksmanship, landing their shells between and in the enemy's traverses, throwing up clouds of sand and driving the rebels from their guns."
Federal Captain Benjamin Sand

Fort Fisher's land-face takes a pounding prior to the Federal ground assault. Drawing from *Battles and Leaders of the Civil War*.

Colonel Lamb wrote about the severity of January 15th's Federal bombardment:

On the morning of the 15th, the fleet, which had not ceased firing during the night, redoubled its fire on the land-face. The sea was smooth, and the navy having become accurate from practice, by noon had destroyed every gun on that face except one Columbiad, which was somewhat protected by the angle formed by the northeast salient. The palisade had been practically destroyed as a defensive line and was so torn up that it actually afforded cover for the assailants. The harvest of wounded and dead was hourly increasing and at that time I had not 1,200 effective men to defend the long line of works.[1]

Sea-face cannon muzzle broken off from direct hit. Timothy O'Sullivan image, 1865, *Photograph courtesy of the Library of Congress.*

The successful landing by General Terry's troops allowed the wooden warships to join the fight at Fort Fisher by late afternoon. From this point on, Fort Fisher began to take a terrible beating from the increased firepower. The Federal Navy, which had been criticized for their failure to destroy Fort Fisher's defenses in the previous assault, wanted desperately to have another chance to show the navy's destructive power. This time they resolved that nothing was going to prevent them from reducing the fort to a pile of useless rubble. The naval fire was far more accurate and destructive than it had been in the previous battle. The Federal gunners had been instructed to concentrate their fire on the gun

Fort Fisher gunners return the fire of the Federal fleet during the second bombardment. Drawing from the March 15, 1865 issue of the *Illustrated London News.*

40

Confederate Sergeant Murdock Smith, 36th North Carolina, captured at Fort Fisher.

chambers of the land-face and not waste any ammunition by shooting at the Confederate flags. Furthermore, each warship had been assigned certain gun chambers to destroy, to avoid repetition. All day and night on the 13th and 14th of January the fleet kept up its relentless bombardment. After the wooden warships withdrew for the evening the ironclads would remain at anchor and continue shelling the fort with their huge 11-inch and 15-inch cannonballs to prevent the Confederate soldiers from retrieving their wounded and making any repairs to the gun chambers. Sergeant Thomas A. McNeill of Company D, First Battalion, North Carolina Artillery, wrote of the intense bombardment:

The 15-inch shells landed often on the guns, knocking off trunnions, breaking off great pieces of the Columbiad muzzles, wrecking gun carriages, and often bespattering the walls of the gun chambers with blood and brains of the men of the detachments, yet the gunners coolly adjusted the degrees. The men obeyed every order. . . .often mounting the parapet amid a storm of exploding shells when necessary to sponge a gun, the flannel bursting into flame as soon as out of the muzzle.[2]

Colonel Lamb had given orders to the Confederate gun crews they could only fire their artillery pieces once every thirty-minutes, but even then the increased naval fire did not allow his gunners much opportunity to man their cannon. The tremendous hail of iron kept the men in their bombproofs for long periods of time, interrupting the fort's return fire. Nearly all of the fort's artillery pieces would suffer a direct hit that would either destroy or dismount the gun. As the damage to the fort increased, so did the number of casualties. In the first two days of the fight, over two hundred Confederate soldiers had been killed or wounded.[3]

Federal Captain Benjamin Sand of the *Fort Jackson* later wrote about the severity of the bombardment:

Our fleet and the ironclads were doing some beautiful marksmanship, landing their shells between and in the enemy's traverses, throwing up clouds of sand and driving the rebels from their guns. I saw several alight near a gun, between a couple of traverses, and the men kept loading their gun and were training it on the fleet, when another shell exploded right over them and cleaned them away entirely, that gun not being fired afterwards.[4]

Private James Montgomery of company B, 36th North Carolina, noted, "Shot and shell rained on us. We could not repair our displaced guns, cook or eat or bury our dead lying around us. We were

41

helpless . . . our guns were disabled and our front shot to pieces." Confederate seaman Robert Watson, who was manning the Brooke Battery on the sea-face, wrote in his diary, "Several of us were knocked down with sand bags. We were all nearly buried in sand several times. This was caused by shells bursting in the sand. Whenever one would strike near us, it would throw the sand over us by the cartload." A group of army signal corpsmen assigned to Battery Buchanan had a spectacular view of the bombardment. "[The shells were] exploding so fast that it would seem to be one roaring sound. . . .and the sand and water rising in great clouds—so that you could not see ten feet in any direction and the atmosphere was filled, it seemed, by sulfur," explained one soldier.[5]

Confederate Private Thomas Yarborough and wife Martha. Yarborough, a private in the 21st South Carolina, was captured but later died of pneumonia at Elmira Prisoner of War Camp.

Despite the fierce Federal bombardment, some Confederate artillery on the fort's sea-face did survive and saw good service. Seaman Robert Watson served as a gunner for a Brooke rifle and saw the effect his shots had on the fleet. Fortunately for us, Watson was one of the few Confederate seamen who kept a journal and wrote of his experiences at Fort Fisher. "Our shot and shell would strike the monitors iron sides and break in pieces and of course did them no injury, but the wooden vessels did not fare so well for several of them had to haul off." Indeed, the *Huron* and the *Unadilla* were forced to retire when they were struck repeatedly by Fort Fisher's cannon. The *Huron* was struck four times and had her mainmast shot away and main shroud cut. The *Unadilla* was hit several times and sailed out of range, leaking badly.[6]

Federal Captain Adrian Terry was so impressed by the bombardment of Fort Fisher's land-face that he described it in a letter to his wife:

The fleet was throwing into the fort tremendous broadsides of shells and solid shot of all sizes from the 30-pounder Parrott to the huge 15-inch shells, the explosions seeming. . . .to shake the solid earth and throwing huge clouds of sand high in [the] air from every part of the fort.[7]

Confederate Sergeant Thomas A. McNeill of the 1st Battalion, North Carolina Artillery, was on the receiving end of this bombardment and observed, "All the land-face looked as if wrapped in flame and smoke. The screaming, exploding shells [were] tearing the earthwork, making holes in the traverses, and in all the history of war it is doubtful if a more infernal fire ever fell upon a fort."[8]

Bragg ordered 1,100 men of the 11th, 21st and 25th South Carolina infantry to proceed by three steamers to Battery Buchanan and reinforce Fort Fisher, but it was another example of too little too late. The soldiers on the transport *Sampson* did not arrive at Battery Buchanan until the early morning hours of the 15th, the third day of the Federal assault. Unfortunately the two other steamers, *Petteway* and *Harlee*, ran aground on a shoal near the docks at Gander Hall. After unloading her soldiers at Battery Buchanan the *Sampson* returned to the stranded steamers and began the tedious task of transferring the rest of the troops in small boats. By the time the *Sampson* had taken on a load of men and returned to Battery Buchanan, the Federal warships had resumed their bombardment of the fort. Only 482 men from the South Carolina regiments had been put ashore when the severe fire of the fleet forced the *Sampson* to retreat to safer waters.

The South Carolinians had never experienced such a terrific bombardment as the one they were witnessing at Fort Fisher. After a short rest, they had to double-quick a mile and a half to the main fort. Unfortunately, these troops were so traumatized by the shells exploding all around them they were practically useless for the rest of the battle. Lamb wrote, "They were out of breath, disorganized and more or less demoralized. They reached our front about thirty minutes before the attacking columns came like avalanches on our right and left. I sent them to an old commissary bombproof to recover their breath."[9]

Confederate Captain John Anderson Richardson, 19th Georgia, Hoke's Division.

General Terry's battle plan called for General Adelbert Ames' division to attack in echelon, with Colonel Curtis' First Brigade; the 112th, 117th and 142nd New York infantry regiments, leading the charge and angling toward the area between the second traverse and the main gate. The second brigade, led by Colonel Galusha Pennypacker, would then advance to the line vacated by Curtis' brigade. Colonel Bell's third brigade would move forward and occupy the line vacated by Pennypacker's brigade. The second and third brigades would halt their advance and wait for further orders from General Ames. If the assault stalled, Ames could send in a fresh brigade to keep the advance moving forward. Colonel Abbott's 1,400-man brigade would stand by in reserve. The 3,600 black soldiers of Paine's division would hold the Federal rear line against Hoke's Confederates and would not be put into action unless it was absolutely necessary.[10]

Federal Private Simeon Chase, 97th Pennsylvania, died of wounds suffered at Fort Fisher.

By 2 PM, on January 15th, 3,700 Federal soldiers were in position for their assault against Fort Fisher's western land-face. The troops waited inside the tree line, half-a-mile north of the fort, for the signal from General Adelbert Ames to advance. Unlike the largely untried Fort Fisher garrison, these men were veterans of the Army of the James. They had survived difficult combat at places like Malvern Hill, Antietam, Fredericksburg, Chancellorsville, Gettysburg, Cold Harbor and the trenches around Petersburg.[11]

Regimental Surgeon James A. Mowris of the 117th New York was busy setting up the field hospital for the coming battle. There were operating tables to construct, medicine and instruments needed to be unpack and stretcher bearers to assign. As Mowris worked, he was struck by the men's somber behavior before they would charge the fort and described it in his book, *History of the 117th Regiment, New York Volunteers*:

> We again reached a time that "tries men's souls." It was traceable in the faces of those about us. One could read there the silent language of stern determination and high resolve. Men were cheerful, but not mirthful; serious but not solemn. In every eye might be read, not fear, but volumes of thought, too deep for utterance. . . .Not far in advance towered the frowning Fortress. . . .and, though none saw, all knew, that above, in imperial majesty, sat the Angel of Death. It was an awful moment, and, with compressed lips, our troops were breathing a silent petition for home and country.[12]

Interior of Fort Fisher's Hospital. *Frank Leslie's Illustrated Newspaper* February 18, 1865.

Admiral Porter was not satisfied with the navy's limited role in this campaign. According to General Grant's plan the navy was to soften the fort's defenses so Terry's army could march in and accept the Confederate surrender. This subservient role to the army was unacceptable to Porter. He wanted the navy to take a more active part in Fort Fisher's capture. Porter realized with his vast armada that he could easily find 2,000 volunteers to storm the fort and share in the glorious victory. It was possible, he reasoned, that the navy might even show the army a thing or two about storming a fort and forcing it to surrender. His supreme confidence in the navy's fighting ability prompted

44

Admiral Porter to issue General Order 81 to the commanders of the fleet. Upon reading the admiral's order, the sailors volunteered in droves. They thought this would be a grand adventure and likened the assault to the spirited race they had against the army to capture the Confederate batteries on the beach north of Fort Fisher.

General Order 81 stated that each vessel was to provide as many men that could be spared for a landing party. "The sailors will be armed with cutlasses, well sharpened, and with revolvers. When the signal is made to assault. . .[the sailors will] board the fort on the run in a seaman-like way." The admiral had high hopes for the success of the campaign and bragged to Secretary Wells that if the army failed again, the navy would "show the soldiers how to do it. I can do anything with . . . my own good officers and men and you need not be surprised to hear that the webfooters have gone into the forts."[13]

The night before the Federal ground assault, General Terry met with Admiral Porter on the *Malvern* so they could coordinate their attacks for the following day. Terry agreed to signal the flagship right before the army's assault was to begin using a system of semaphore flags, so the fleet could shift its fire away from the land-face to avoid hitting the attacking force. The admiral's flagship would then hoist a signal flag and announce the charge with two long blasts from her steam whistle. This shrill blast was then to be repeated by the rest of the fleet.

Although the land assault was scheduled to begin at 3 PM, it appears there was some confusion over the time. In a letter to Gideon Wells, the Secretary of the Navy, Porter states he was under the impression the assault was to begin at 2 PM. "It was arranged between the General and myself that the ships should all go in early and fire rapidly through the day until the time for the assault came off. The hour named was 2 PM." Porter goes on to say, "At 2 o'clock I expected the signal for the vessels to change the direction of their fire, so that the troops might assault. The sailors and marines had worked, by digging ditches or rifle pits, to within 200 yards of the fort, and were all ready. The troops, however, did not get into position until later, and at 3 o'clock the signal came."[14]

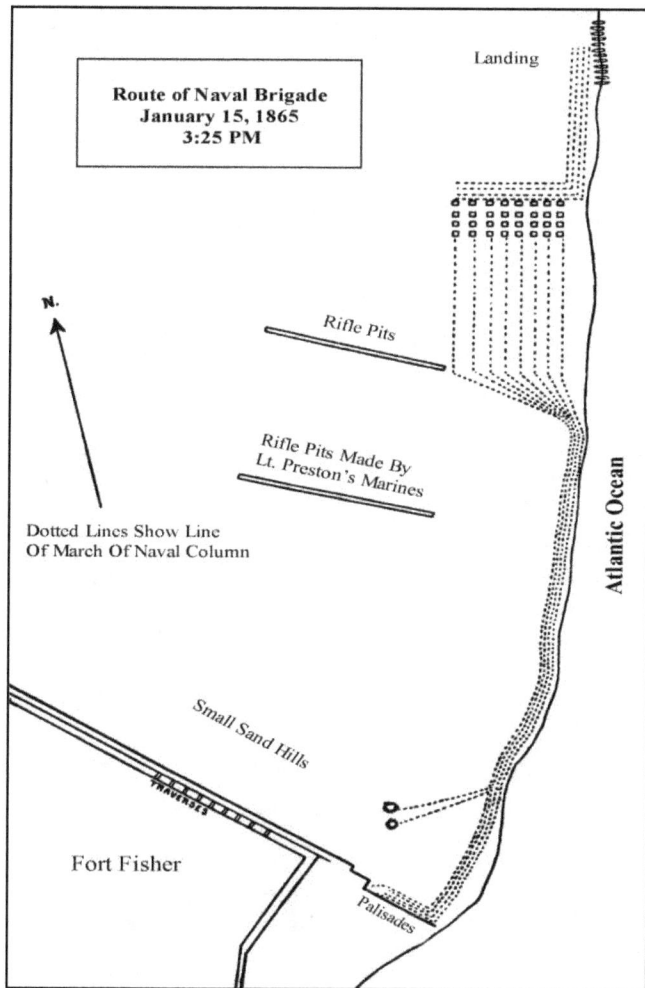

The Naval Brigade's assault targeted Fort Fisher's Northeast Bastion. Drawing from: *The Official Records of the Union and Confederate Navies in the War of the Rebellion*, Series I, Vol. XI.

Had Porter given his officers the wrong time for the army's assault to begin? If he did, this could help explain why the naval brigade was in position so early and why Lieutenant Commander Breese, after waiting nearly an hour and a half for the army to begin their attack, went ahead with their assault.

Lieutenant Commander K. Randolph Breese would lead the Navy's ground assault.

Admiral Porter's plan called for three columns of sailors to get into position for the assault a half-mile north of the fort. The sailors were ordered not to charge until they saw the army going over the northwest parapet of the fort. The marines were to act as sharpshooters and keep the fort's wall clear of Confederate defenders while the naval brigade charged. The route of the attack would take the sailors down the beach where they would skirt the end of the palisade fence and continue on to the fort. They were to scale its mounds and kill or capture the Confederate garrison.[15]

The landing party of 1,600 sailors and 400 marines came ashore at 11 AM and was put in charge of Lieutenant Commander K. Randolph Breese. Breese instructed the officers of the naval brigade that it was imperative to coordinate their attack with the army, a half mile to the west. Doing so would divide the fort's defenders and make the fort more vulnerable to the Federal ground assault. The sailors were divided into three divisions or columns.

Lieutenant Commander Charles H. Cushman was assigned command of the first column, the second, Lieutenant Commander James Parker, and Lieutenant Commander Thomas O. Selfridge had the third column. The marines were led by Captain Lucien L. Dawson.

Sailors armed with spades had orders to construct a series of entrenchments for the marine sharpshooters as close to the fort as possible. A marine detachment under Lt. Louis Fagan was to provide covering fire for the sailors while they dug. Despite this protection the naval brigade was peppered with grape and canister from Fort Fisher's remaining eight-inch Columbiad on the land-face and from two 12-pounder Napoleon cannons at the main sally-port. The sailors persevered and managed to construct breastworks 600 yards in front of the fort and then gradually advanced them within 200 yards of the fort's northern wall.[16]

Lieutenant Commander James Parker led the second column in the attack.

Breese marched the naval brigade from their landing site to a half mile north of the fort's land-face. This distance was adequate if the men were to begin the assault within the next few minutes. However, this was far too close if they were to remain there long. The problem was Breese was under the mistaken impression the assault was scheduled for 2 PM instead of 3 PM. This exposed his large column of blue-jackets to Confederate sharpshooters for over an hour while the army moved into position. The sailors, armed only with Remington and Whitney revolvers, were too far away from the fort to return fire. Several men were killed and wounded because of this failure to coordinate the time for the assault. Breese ordered his brigade to move closer to the water, so the sloping beach might provide some cover, and instructed them to lie flat on the sand.

Two o'clock passed without any significant movement by the army toward the fort. Two thirty came and went and there was still no signal from the army. The fire from the fort was growing heavier. Besides receiving fire from the Confederate cannon, a few of the artillery rounds from the Federal fleet fell short of the fort and sprayed the naval brigade with red-hot shrapnel. "We were under a galling fire from a hateful gun mounted upon a field carriage at the fort's sally port, as well as musketry along the land face," Acting Master's Mate Joseph Simms recalled. "Together with musketry, canister, and grape fired by the enemy in front of us, fragments of bursting shell fired by our ships at the rear and left of us, entrenching (sic) near the face of Fort Fisher was not a pleasant job." Ensign Ira Harris of the *Powhaten* noted the stray shells of the Federal fleet in a letter, "The shells from fifty-eight men-of-war made a horrible screeching and one eleven-inch gun [said to be the after pivot-gun of the *Vanderbilt*] fired several shells into our column. The wounded had to be carried through our ranks, and it seemed to discourage the men somewhat."[17]

When 3:15 PM came the army was still getting into position. Breese was irritated because his men were being needlessly exposed to hostile fire for over sixty minutes. Gazing anxiously to the west one more time, Breese saw some troop movements and determined the army was preparing to attack. At this point one has to question the

Lieutenant Roswell Lamson, commander of the *USS Gettysburg*, would be wounded in the shoulder.

movements that Breese saw. Were they meaningful troop movements signaling the army was beginning their assault, or were they merely wishful thinking on Breese's part? It is important to know the answer to this question because the navy suffered terribly during the ground assault. Was this a direct result of Breese launching his assault too early? It would appear some thought it was. This is part of the report Marine Captain Lucien L. Dawson made on January 27, 1865 to Colonel Jacob Zeilin, United States Marine Commandant, in Washington, D.C. Dawson is addressing the criticisms made by Rear-Admiral Porter in which he blames the Marine Corps for failing to support the naval ground assault at Fort Fisher and thus contributing to the severe casualties suffered by the Navy:

> The naval party assaulted before the army instead of after, thereby not only drawing nearly the whole fire of the rebels upon themselves, but acting in direct violation of the admiral's express written order, which was that the naval party should not move to the assault until the army was seen going in over the northwest parapet of the fort.[18]

47

Ensign Robley Evans also wrote of the naval brigade assaulting before the army in his book, *A Sailor's Log*, saying, "At three o'clock the order to charge was given, and we started for our long run of twelve hundred yards over the loose sand. . . .The army had not yet assaulted, so the whole garrison concentrated its fire on us."[19]

The fateful 3 PM deadline for the ground assault had long since passed. Tired of waiting for the army, Lieutenant Commander Breese drew his sword and turned to look at the men gathered around him. Dozens of brightly colored United States flags fluttered in the breeze. Beneath these flags, hundreds of men with determination deeply etched on their faces were watching him. Brimming with confidence, he thrust his sword toward the fort, and bellowed, "Charge! Charge!"[20]

Medal of Honor winner Marine Sergeant Richard Binder advances on Fort Fisher during the naval ground assault. Drawing from *Deeds of Valor*, Vol. 2.

Armed with cutlasses and revolvers, the sailors raced down the beach toward the Northeast Bastion, cheering wildly. The marines, who were instructed to stay in their entrenchments and provide covering fire for the navy, became caught up in the excitement of the charge and joined the sailors. This proved to be a fatal mistake because the lack of the marine support allowed the Confederate defenders to fire at will from the fort's parapet. In Breese's official report of the incident he wrote, "(The naval brigade) assaulted to within 50 yards of the parapet, which was lined with one dense mass of musketeers, who played sad havoc with our men. The marines having failed to occupy their position, gave the enemy an almost unmolested fire upon us."[21]

When the Federal fleet saw the naval brigade running down the beach, they sounded the charge with dozens of steam whistles. Admiral Porter beamed with fatherly pride as he stood on the deck of the *Malvern* and closely followed the progress of his men. He had every reason to be proud. Not only was this charge his idea, but his own seventeen-year-old son, Carlisle P. Porter, was participating in the assault. Porter could understand his son's eagerness to join the attack on the fort. The war was quickly drawing to a close and Carlisle was afraid he would miss the last great battle. Admiral Porter mentioned this to Lieutenant Commander Breese, who had the responsibly of organizing the Navy's ground assault, and now was ordered to keep an eye on the admiral's son. Breese decided the best way to get young Porter involved was to put him to work as a courier delivering dispatches, thus keeping him away from the hazardous assault.

Aboard other ships, crewmen scaled the rigging and crowded the rails to watch their shipmates charging down the beach toward the rebel fort. "We almost held our breath as they charged," reported Seaman John Grattan. "The noise of the guns, whistles, cheers and yells of the sailors and marines was terrific and made the most exciting and indescribable event."[22]

Upon hearing the fleet's steam whistles and the wild cheering from thousands of sailors and marines, the Confederate defenders were aware that the long awaited ground assault had finally begun. When the naval bombardment shifted to another area of the fort, they stormed out of their bombproof and raced to the top of the northeast bastion. Suddenly the fort came to life, bristling with guns. Men clad in a mix of butternut-brown and dirty gray uniforms lined the walls. Colonel Lamb climbed to the crest of the parapet and scanned the beach with his binoculars. Half a mile to the north he detected an undulating blue mass, topped by curious flashes of light. As they drew closer, Lamb discovered the men of the naval brigade were running down the beach and waving their cutlasses. The steel from these cutlasses caught the sunlight and reflect it toward the fort creating the flashes of light Lamb saw.

The Naval Brigade was ordered to charge through the palisade fence and scale the formidable 43-foot-high Northeast Bastion. Image Timothy O'Sullivan, *Photograph courtesy of Library of Congress.*

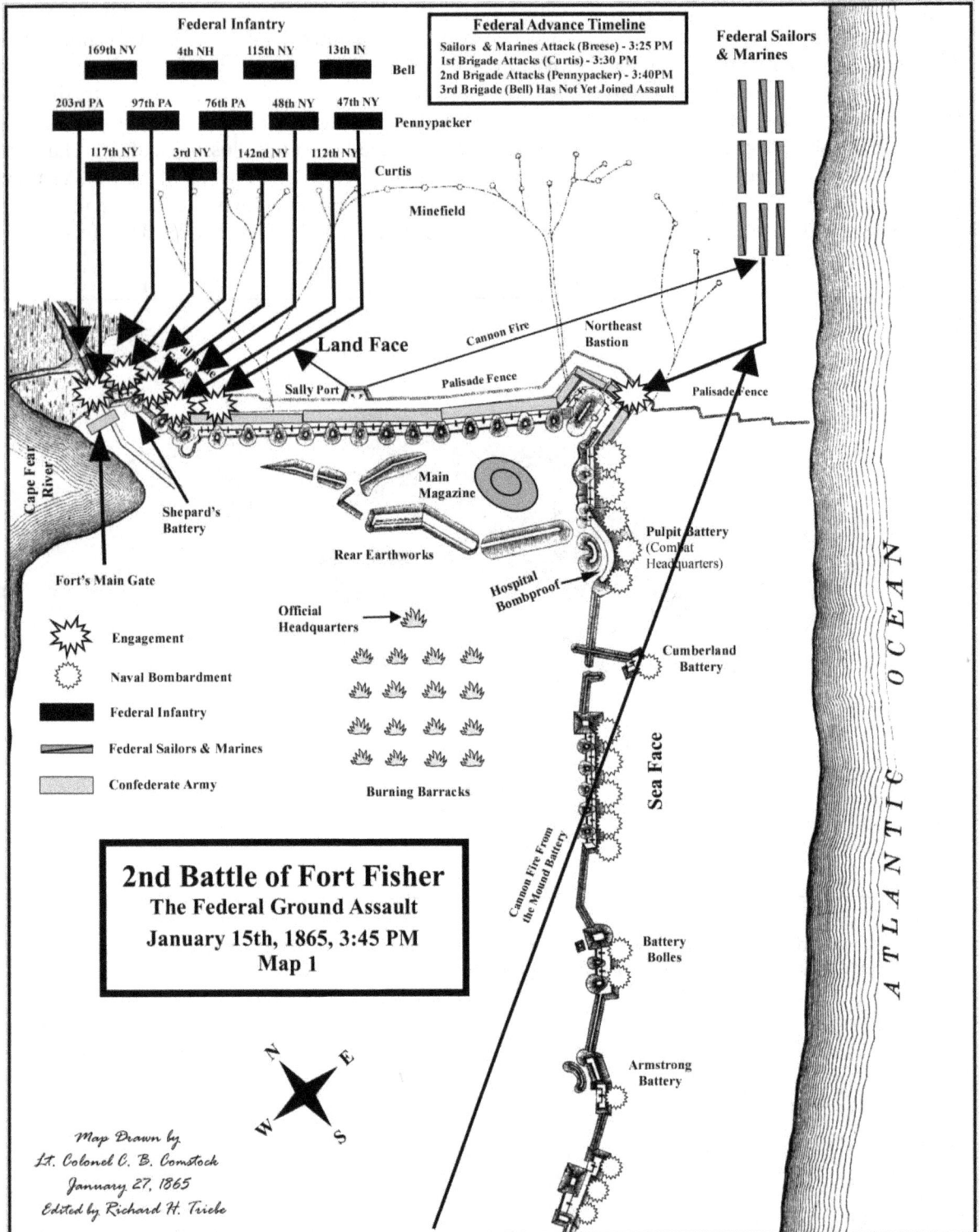

Federal Infantry

169th NY	4th NH	115th NY	13th IN

Bell

203rd PA	97th PA	76th PA	48th NY	47th NY

Pennypacker

117th NY	3rd NY	142nd NY	112th NY

Curtis

Federal Advance Timeline

Sailors & Marines Attack (Breese) - 3:25 PM
1st Brigade Attacks (Curtis) - 3:30 PM
2nd Brigade Attacks (Pennypacker) - 3:40PM
3rd Brigade (Bell) Has Not Yet Joined Assault

Federal Sailors & Marines

Minefield

Land Face

Cannon Fire

Northeast Bastion

Sally Port

Palisade Fence

Palisade Fence

Cape Fear River

Shepard's Battery

Fort's Main Gate

Main Magazine

Rear Earthworks

Hospital Bombproof

Pulpit Battery (Combat Headquarters)

Official Headquarters

Cumberland Battery

Engagement

Naval Bombardment

Federal Infantry

Federal Sailors & Marines

Confederate Army

Burning Barracks

Sea Face

Cannon Fire From the Mound Battery

Battery Bolles

2nd Battle of Fort Fisher
The Federal Ground Assault
January 15th, 1865, 3:45 PM
Map 1

Armstrong Battery

N E
W S

Map Drawn by
Lt. Colonel C. B. Comstock
January 27, 1865
Edited by Richard H. Triebe

ATLANTIC OCEAN

Colonel Lamb planned to withhold the Confederate fire until the naval brigade had come within 150 yards of the fort, then give the order to detonate the underground torpedoes, trapping half of the enemy between the explosion and the fort. Volleys of Confederate gunfire would decimate the soldiers left standing and any remaining sailors would be so thoroughly demoralized that they would retreat in confusion.

Ensign Robley Evans was severely wounded in the assault on Fort Fisher.

To his dismay, Lamb noticed the attacking column was keeping close to the water's edge and would miss the line of buried torpedoes. It became clear that Fort Fisher's fate rested solely on the soldier's ability to throw back the assaulting column. Once his troops were in position behind the sandbagged parapet, Lamb instructed his men "to pick off the officers in the assaulting columns" but not to fire yet. The sharpshooters and the few remaining artillery crews would continue to fire at targets of opportunity, but Lamb wanted his main troops held in reserve. He needed to draw the enemy closer to the fort before unleashing the first devastating Confederate volley. A sudden blast of gunfire delivered at close range could shatter the enemy's resolve and force them to withdraw.[23]

The Confederate defenders, their rifles at the ready, tensed as they watched the mass of enemy troops surging toward them, unchecked. The two sally-port field pieces, the lone land-face Columbiad and the two cannons at the mound battery fired, reloaded and fired again, but this wasn't enough. Still the blue clad horde ran on, cheering and waving their cutlasses and revolvers. Nothing was going to stop them from reaching the fort. As the naval brigade neared the palisade fence they angled toward the opening where the fence meets the sea. A bottleneck occurred in this small area, cramming the sailors and marines together.

This was the moment Lamb had been waiting for; the enemy was within easy range and densely packed so that his men could not miss. Colonel Lamb commanded his soldiers, "Men of the thirty-sixth North Carolina, prepare to fire!" All along the line hammers clicked as men cocked their guns. He thrust his sword at the Yankees and shouted, "Fire!" The parapet of the Northeast Bastion exploded into a forbidding wall of flame and gun smoke.

Lieutenant Commander Breese led the naval brigade's charge down the beach when suddenly white gun smoke exploded on the fort's parapet along with the roar from hundreds of Confederate rifles. All of the men fell to the sand, either struck by bullets or desperately seeking any sort of shelter they could find. Ensign Robley Evans recalled the incident in his book *A Sailor's Log*, "About five hundred yards from the fort the head of the column suddenly stopped, and, as if by magic, the whole mass of men went down like a row of falling bricks; in a second every man was flat on his stomach," Ensign Robley Evans recalled.[24]

One of the first seamen to be shot was James Flannigan. The night before the assault, Flannigan shared a premonition of his death with fellow *Powhatan* shipmate Ensign Evans. The sailor came to Evan's room with a small box and said, "Mr. Evans, will you be kind enough to take charge of this box for me—it has some little trinkets in it—and give it to my sister in Philadelphia?" Evans asked why he did not deliver it himself. Flannigan replied, "I am going ashore with you tomorrow and will be killed." Evans wrote of the incident later:

> He showed no nervousness over it, but seemed to regard it as a matter of course. I took the box and, after making a proper memorandum, put it away among my things. On the afternoon of the next day, when we were charging the fort and just as we came under fire, at eight hundred yards, I saw Flannigan reel out to one side and drop, the first man hit, with a bullet through his heart. I stepped up quickly to his side and asked if he were badly hurt; the only reply was a smile as he looked up into my face and rolled over dead.[25]

Picture by Frank Vizetelly artist for the *London Illustrated News*.

Several Federal officers got to their feet, urging the men to get up and resume the charge, which they did. The naval brigade raced forward another 50 yards when they encountered a second murderous Confederate volley. The men instantly dropped to the sand and tried to present as small a target as possible. Because the beach was relatively flat with no cover, men began scooping sand in front of them with their bare hands. In a letter to his sisters Lieutenant John Bartlett wrote about his experience:

> I began to dig a hole with my hands. You would have laughed to have seen me. It did not take me long to get a pile of sand in front of me high enough to screen me from fire. This was at about half past 3. I kept on digging until I had a hole that I could stand up in. The sand was very soft and dry, so that it was easily thrown up. Every time I threw up a handful of sand on the edge of my pit, a dozen bullets would skip over my head. It was rather unpleasant, as it knocked the sand all down on me.[26]

52

Ensign Benjamin Porter was killed in the Naval Brigade's charge while carrying the Admiral's flag.

Once more Lieutenant Commanders Breese, James Parker and Captain Thomas Selfridge encouraged the naval brigade to get to their feet and continue the charge. When the head of the column reached the palisade fence, they were stopped in their tracks by a devastating volley of rifle fire delivered at close range. Commodore Joseph Lanman noted the assault in his report:

The enemy opened a heavy fire upon us of musketry and grape, which soon became very hot. A few of the officers and men pressed beyond the palisades, but the advance along the beach was there checked, and turned along the palisades toward the fort. In the hurry of the advance, the different divisions had somewhat intermingled, and almost every shot from the enemy carried its message of wound or death to some one of our number.[27]

Flag Lieutenant Samuel W. Preston and Ensign Benjamin Porter were killed moments apart. They were the best of friends and shared everything together, even death on the sands of Fort Fisher.

At the head of the column Lieutenant Benjamin Porter was proudly carrying the Admiral's flag. Porter, who was no relation to Admiral David D. Porter, was the 19-year-old commander of the Admiral's flagship, the *Malvern*. Lieutenant Porter had boasted that the admiral's flag would be the first on the fort. Accompanying him was his longtime friend, Flag Lieutenant Samuel W. Preston. The blue banner with two white stars which Porter held aloft made him an irresistible target for the fort's marksmen. It's amazing Porter was able to get as far as he did. When he was only fifty feet from the palisade fence a Confederate bullet struck him square in the chest, killing him instantly. Lieutenant Preston, unaware that Porter had been shot, raced on and moments later he too was fatally shot.

Lieutenant Roswell H. Lamson wrote of this incident in his official report:

The men pressed forward, and when near the palisades Mr. Preston was struck in the left thigh or groin, the femoral artery being severed. He fell forward, and one of the men stooped to assist him and was shot, falling on Mr. Preston. Someone pulled him off, and Mr. Preston turned over on his back and soon expired. . . . I had got forward some twenty paces more, when I was knocked down by a

53

shot through the left arm and shoulder. I arose again and got up nearer the parapet, when I fell from loss of blood and exhaustion.[28]

True to his calling, assistant Surgeon William Longshaw Jr. selflessly moved from one wounded man to another, carrying medical instruments, tourniquets and canteens of water. Ensign Robley D. Evans was wounded in both legs and remembers Surgeon Longshaw treating him and giving him a sip of water. "We will have you all off the beach tonight," the doctor said, and continued on to the next man. Longshaw's lifeless body was found on the beach the following morning. He had been binding up the wounds of a mortally wounded marine when his skull was shattered by a Confederate bullet.[29]

Terrified by the hail of lead and iron whizzing by them, most men refused to go any farther. Some sought out bomb craters for protection while others hid behind the dead bodies of fallen comrades. The palisade fence, intended as a defensive structure for the Confederates, was now being sought out by the enemy for shelter. After catching their breath, a few of the men ran through

The Capture of Fort Fisher, painting by J. O. Davidson, 1887, print by L. Prang & Co. This picture portrays the climactic moment when the Naval Brigade broke through the palisade fence and stormed Fort Fisher's Northeast Bastion.

splintered gaps in the fence and continued on to the fort. Most of the men who ventured beyond the palisade fence were shot down before they reached the fort, but a few managed to elude the storm of minie balls. One man, quarter gunner James Tallentine from *USS Tacony*, scaled the fort's steep slope alone. Apparently he did not realize the other men had been killed or wounded. Up he went, toward the horde of Confederate soldiers trying to shoot him. Bullets plucked at his coat and kicked up the sand around him, but none found their mark. One has to wonder why he got as far as he did. Was he just lucky, or did the Confederate soldiers reward his determination and bravery by allowing him to finish his climb? We will never know. What we do know is that James Tallentine reached the crest of the parapet, and was shot by a Confederate soldier, causing him to fall into the ranks of the fort's defenders.[30]

Lamb wrote of this brave charge in his book, *Colonel Lamb's Story of Fort Fisher*:
The sailors and marines reached the berme (sic) and sprang up the slope, but a murderous fire greeted them and swept them down. Volley after volley was poured into their faltering ranks by cool, determined men, and in half an hour several hundred dead and wounded lay at the foot of the bastion.[31]

There were no more Confederate volleys. Now each man fired his rifle-musket as rapidly as possible. Colonel Lamb wisely placed the best marksmen that Fort Fisher had to offer along the fort's walls. After these men had fired their rifles, they would pass their weapons back to the soldiers behind them to be reloaded. In turn, these expert sharpshooters would be handed a loaded rifle so they could keep up a steady, accurate fire. Through the thick smoke General Whiting could be seen scaling the parapet. He boldly stood on the wall with his sword raised, pointing at the Yankees and urging his men to fire. Ramrods rattled and scraped in hot rifle barrels as soldiers reloaded, then fired again. Federal ensign Ira Harris recalled the intense Confederate fire:
From where I lay on the glacis, we could see four rows of [Confederate] soldiers in the fort, two ranks firing, and two loading, and hear their taunts to "come on". . .

Seaman William Cobb survived the charge of the Naval Brigade and wrote about the death that surrounded him.

. .At this time there was no distinct sound of bullets, but only a steady rush, and the water close to the beach was lashed to foam. I would not have supposed men could fire so fast.[32]

The area in front of the Northeast Bastion became a killing zone. The smoke-filled beach was strewn with dead and wounded seamen, struggling to get out of the line of fire. The moans and cries of the injured along with the rattle of gunfire and the bursting of shells combined to create a cacophony of sounds which seemed to emanate from the bowels of hell.

"I have been in a great number of battles," reported Seaman William Cobb, "but I never saw men fall so fast in my life. There was a shower of canister (that came) through the ranks where I was running up the beach and out of about twenty that stood within eight paces of me, there was but four of us that came out." It was clear to the sailors and marines that they could not advance without being slaughtered, but it was equally clear they could not remain where they were because their only shelter was the shattered remnant of the palisade fence. As things stood right now it was only a matter of time before the rest of the sailors were picked off by Confederate sharpshooters.[33]

As before, Lieutenant Commander Breese was on his feet, waving his sword and his arms, trying to encourage the men to renew the attack. No matter how hard he tried, nobody would budge. The only thing he succeeded in doing was attracting more Confederate gunfire in his direction. Frustrated, Breese turned to the rear thinking maybe he could rally the men back there. What he saw made him sick to his stomach. Dozens of men in the rear of the formation were drifting back up the beach toward the Federal lines. Breese chased after them, shouting, "No, men, charge! Charge the fort! Don't be cowards! Don't retreat!"[34]

Pinned down by an avalanche of Confederate fire, the sailors began to grumble amongst themselves about the hopelessness of their situation. Those men who had heard Breese shouting at the retreating sailors misinterpreted what he was saying. They heard the word retreat, and they repeated it. "Retreat! Retreat!" That was all it took. What began as a few stragglers going to the rear soon escalated into a panicked mob, shoving at each other in a mad dash to get away from the fort. "Flesh and blood could not long endure being killed in this slaughter-pen, and the rear of the sailors broke, followed by the whole body, in spite of all efforts to rally them," Lieutenant Commander Selfridge recalled with bitterness. His sentiments were echoed by Lieutenant John Bartlett, "I shouted and waved my sword for the sailors to come back, but no, off they went down the beach. . . .I could have cried when the blue jackets retreated."[35]

Drawing of the Naval Brigade assault by Ensign John W. Grattan. Notice the cluster of men around the palisade fence and in the shallow water. Photograph reprinted from *Under the Blue Pennant.*

As Lieutenant Commander Breese chased the deserting sailors down the beach, it soon became obvious that the men were ignoring his curses and threats; if anything, his pursuit was making them run even faster. Disheartened, Breese slowed to a stop and returned to the front amid a shower of enemy bullets. "How [Breese] escaped death is a marvel to me," Lieutenant Commander Parker said.[36]

Only sixty sailors remained near the foot of the fort, hiding behind the remains of the palisade fence. A wave of relief and jubilation overcame the Confederate soldiers, and they began tossing their hats into the air and cheering the retreating mob of sailors. Even the normally reserved General

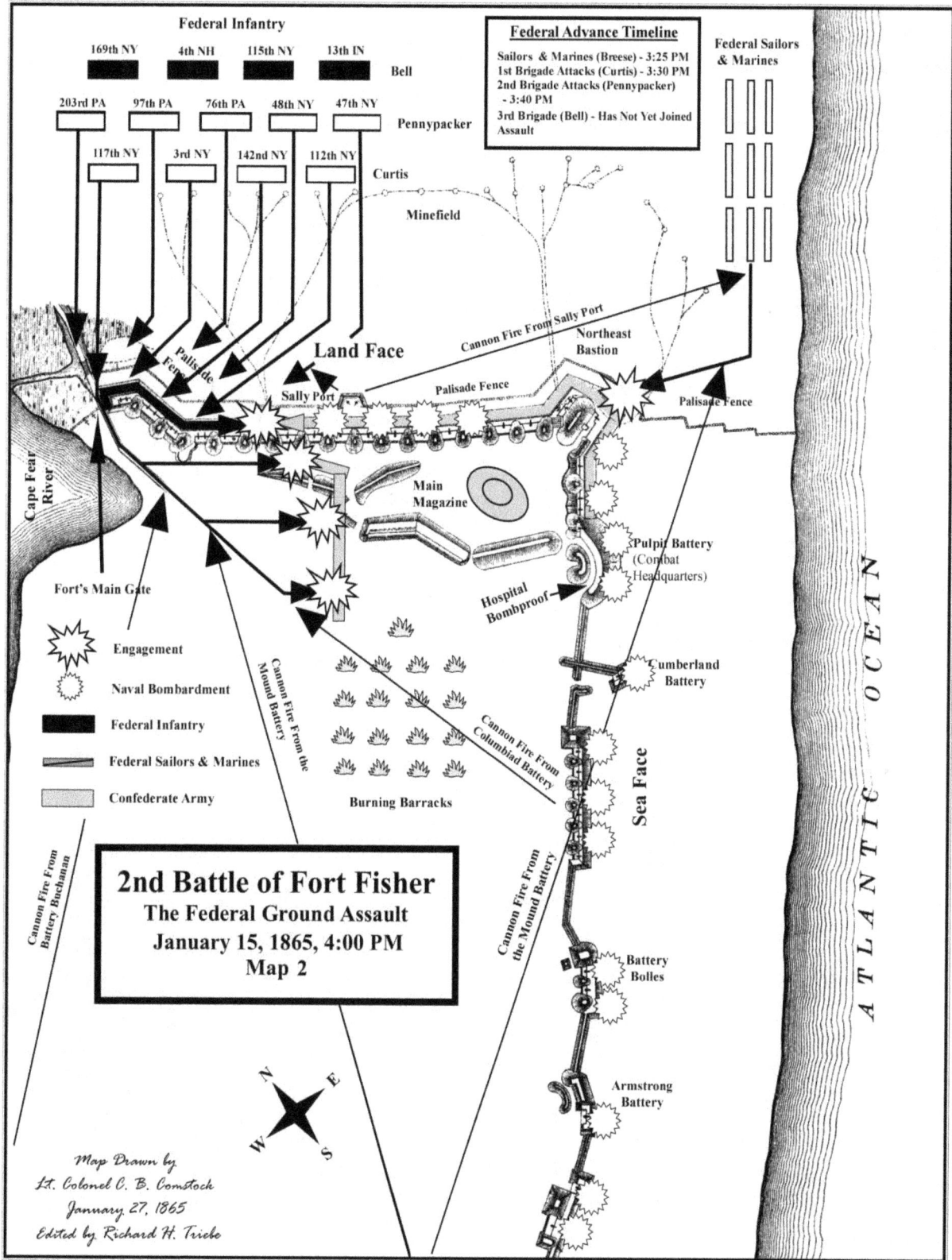

Federal Infantry

169th NY 4th NH 115th NY 13th IN Bell

203rd PA 97th PA 76th PA 48th NY 47th NY Pennypacker

117th NY 3rd NY 142nd NY 112th NY Curtis

Minefield

Federal Advance Timeline

Sailors & Marines (Breese) - 3:25 PM
1st Brigade Attacks (Curtis) - 3:30 PM
2nd Brigade Attacks (Pennypacker) - 3:40 PM
3rd Brigade (Bell) - Has Not Yet Joined Assault

Federal Sailors & Marines

Cannon Fire From Sally Port Northeast Bastion

Land Face

Sally Port Palisade Fence Palisade Fence

Palisade Fence

Cape Fear River

Main Magazine

Pulpit Battery (Combat Headquarters)

Fort's Main Gate

Hospital Bombproof

Cumberland Battery

Engagement

Naval Bombardment

Federal Infantry

Federal Sailors & Marines

Confederate Army

Cannon Fire From the Mound Battery

Cannon Fire From Columbiad Battery

Sea Face

Burning Barracks

Cannon Fire From Battery Buchanan

2nd Battle of Fort Fisher
The Federal Ground Assault
January 15, 1865, 4:00 PM
Map 2

Cannon Fire From the Mound Battery

Battery Bolles

Armstrong Battery

N E S W

Map Drawn by
Lt. Colonel C. B. Comstock
January 27, 1865
Edited by Richard H. Triebe

ATLANTIC OCEAN

57

Whiting and Colonel Lamb were dancing about and shouting with glee. But the festive mood soon faded when they realized that not all of the sailors had withdrawn. The Confederate defenders began to concentrate their fire on the small band of men who had not fled. In a matter of moments, four Federal officers fell wounded. Seeing the futility of continuing the advance, Lieutenant Commander Parker ordered everyone to stay put until they were able to withdraw under the cover of darkness.[37]

Some of the wounded sailors and marines were unable to move and drowned when the tide came in.

Death for the sailors and marines did not end there, however. Another tragedy occurred when the tide came in. The assault had been at low tide to allow the naval brigade as much room as possible to slip between the end of the palisade fence and the ocean. Some of the wounded men, either too weak from loss of blood or severely injured, were unable to escape the rushing sea and drowned. Landsman Edward Lindsay was wounded in his right hip and his left leg was broken by grapeshot. Unable to stand, Lindsay was swept out to sea where he disappeared beneath the waves. Lieutenant John Bartlett wrote of his frustration over not being able to help these injured men. "It was low tide when we made the charge and a few fell close to the water. Before dark the tide rose and the waves washed up on the poor fellows, some only wounded. It was hard to look on and not be able to give them any help."[38]

The charge of the naval brigade was considered a failure because it did not achieve its objective and left over three hundred sailors and marines killed or wounded in the twenty-five minute assault. This amounts to twelve men being shot every sixty seconds. One thing the naval ground assault did accomplish, however, was a diversion for the army's attack a half mile to the west. It is questionable if the army would have been successful in their assault had it not been for the navy's sacrificial charge that divided the enemy's attention at such a crucial time. When considered in this light, it would appear that the naval assault was a success of sorts because it did contribute to the expedition's ultimate goal, the capture of Fort Fisher.[39]

Colonel William Lamb and his Confederates leaped upon the parapets, whooping for joy at the retreating naval brigade which was flying down the beach. Men dressed in butternut brown and gray were laughing, dancing and waving their battered hats, shouting, "Come aboard, Billy Yank! Don't run away! Come aboard an' we'll show you some real Southern hospitality!" The cheering Confederates believed they had thrown back the main assault. "The heroic bravery of [the Federal] officers, twenty-one of whom were killed and wounded, could not restrain the men from panic and retreat, and with small loss to ourselves, we witnessed what had never been seen before, a disorderly rout of American

General Adelbert Ames, Commander of the Second Division, had the honor of leading the Federal assault.

58

sailors and marines," Lamb wrote.[40]

As the cheering began to subside, Lamb's attention was drawn to his left by an ominous swell of gunfire. He stared in stunned disbelief at several Federal battle flags amid a smoky swirl of activity upon the fort's westernmost ramparts. Blue-clad soldiers were clamoring over the parapet and fighting with the gray defenders for possession of the gun chambers. Incensed, General Whiting called for volunteers to "Haul down those flags and drive the enemy from the works!" Flushed with the taste of victory, hundreds of Confederate soldiers rushed to obey. They swarmed down the Northeast Bastion and swept along the fort's land-face until they met the Yankees in mortal combat at the third gun chamber.[41]

Federal General Adelbert Ames' brigade had been given a daunting task. They were to charge across a half mile of barren, sandy plain while their every movement was being observed by an enemy in an elevated, fortified position. Confederate defenders would be firing a storm of iron and lead projectiles at these soldiers from four sally-port cannons. One of the 8-inch Columbiad artillery pieces next to the Northeast Bastion had miraculously survived the bombardment and would join the assault on the Federal troops. Also firing with these cannons would be hundreds of rifle muskets. Even if the Federals were able to penetrate this barrage, a muddy ditch blocked their approach to the fort's main gate. Although a wooden bridge that spanned the River Road marsh was left in place, the Confederates had removed the planks and left only several grease-coated stringers for the Federals to navigate. [42]

Major General Alfred H. Terry, Commander of the Wilmington expedition.

General Alfred Terry was aware these men's lives depended on his decisions. This was a grave responsibly and it weighed heavily on his mind all morning. Terry needed to give this assault every opportunity to succeed. After much consideration, he sent 100 sharpshooters forward to entrench within 175 yards of the fort. These men would cover the area with a suppressing fire while the other troops advanced. The sharpshooters were armed with the latest weapon, a lever-action Spencer repeating rifle with a seven-shot magazine, and were instructed to pick off any Confederate riflemen that appeared on the fort's walls. Because the palisade fence on the western side of the fort survived the bombardment largely intact, some of these men also carried axes so they could chop openings for the charging infantry.[43]

General Terry also had Curtis' brigade move out of the woods in a line of battle and rush to within 200 yards of the fort. They dropped to the sand and quickly began to construct crude breastworks with anything they had, scooping up the loose sand with bayonets, swords, tin plates, cups and bare hands. Curtis waited until the naval bombardment drove the Confederates back to their bombproofs, then sent his brigade forward, one regiment at a time.[44]

Satisfied with the disposition of his army, General Terry issued orders for the fleet to shift their bombardment away from the land-face because the land assault was about to begin. Immediately a huge signal flag was waving back-and-forth above the command-post earthwork, alerting Admiral Porter on the *Malvern*. Lieutenant F.E. Beardsley, the signal officer who was waving this large flag, became a prime target for Confederate sharpshooters. These rebel marksmen were instructed to pick off the officers, but they were also told to disrupt Federal communications by shooting at the signalmen.[45]

General Terry turned to his division commander, and said, "Colonel Ames, the signal agreed upon for the assault has been given. Your division is ready to advance."[46]

As the naval column was being slaughtered a half-mile to his left, Colonel Curtis rose in the center of his line, waved his hat and called out to his men, "Forward!" Each man sprang to his feet, charging the fort without saying a word. Curtis had forbidden cheering because every man would need his breath to charge up the fort's steep parapet.[47]

"The enemy quickly showed themselves upon the ramparts and was pouring into [us] a tremendous fire of musketry while four or five cannon threw showers of grape and canister into [our ranks]," Captain Adrian Terry recalled in a letter. The Federal troops were just beginning their charge, and not yet fully upright, causing the first volley to pass overhead. The second did not miss, however. All along the line men began to fall. Colonel John F. Smith, the commanding officer of the 112th New York, was struck in the bowels shortly after he rose. Bullets furiously kicked up the sand around his body as he lay wounded. Several men saw their colonel in the line of fire and dropped their weapons to help him. Under a hail of lead, they carried the severely wounded Smith to a depression in the sand, so he would be safe until a surgeon could tend to him. Despite the surgeon's best efforts, Smith would die of his wounds three days later. On the day of his death, the colonel revived for a short time and asked, "Do we still hold the fort?" He was assured they did. Colonel Smith smiled briefly, closed his eyes and passed away.[48]

The same Confederate volley also felled Lieutenants Frank Lay and Paul Horvath. Lay would later rejoin the battle, but Horvath was killed instantly. Federal soldier Leonard Thomas was so impressed by the deadly accurate fire that he wrote:

> It was not a blinding fire whistling and humming overhead. The number of stricken men, increasing from moment to moment, showed how well the veterans on the ramparts could aim. Caps and clothing were pierced, swords and scabbards were hit, belts and canteen straps were cut."[49]

Captain Albert G. Lawrence, Ames' aide-de-camp, was the first man through the palisade fence. He stepped through the jagged opening and turned around to help a color bearer behind him. He grabbed the man's guidon, and was turning to resume the charge when a Confederate shell exploded beside him, tearing off his left arm and fatally wounding him.[50]

Confederate rifle fire along with blasts of grape and canister from the middle sally-port artillery began to take a fearful toll on the left of Curtis' line. Federal Captain George F. Towle recalled the terrible slaughter, "For the first few minutes out of every five [men] who gained the slope of the parapet, three went down dead or wounded."

Captain Albert Lawrence was killed by an artillery fragment moments after he stepped through the palisade fence.

The 112th New York had twice as far to charge as the other regiments because it needed to right oblique from its position on the left and advance toward the far side of the fort. Thus these soldiers were exposed to the withering Confederate fire for a longer period of time.

Federal soldier N. M. Robinson described the hazards of charging Fort Fisher in a letter dated February 27, 1865:

> We had to run about 50 rods right under the fire of the rebs sharpshooters & there (sic) grape and canister & I tell you it thinned out our men very bad, going to the fort I could see them fall on every side of me. . . .I considered it more dangerous going up to the fort than it was after we got into it.[51]

The most destructive fire came from the two cannons at the fort's sandbagged River Road entrance. A 12-pounder Napoleon and a 3.2-inch Parrott rifle were pointed menacingly up River Road, blocking the entrance to the main gate. These cannons were manned by gunners from Captain Kinchen Braddy's men of Company C, 36th North Carolina and men from Captain James McCormic's First Battalion North Carolina Artillery. Lead case-shot spewed from these guns and tore gaping holes in Curtis' charging Federals. Judge Zachary F. Fulmore, who was a Confederate private during the assault at Fort Fisher, wrote Colonel Lamb a letter regarding the battle at the River Road sally-port in 1883:

Confederate Captain Kinchen Braddy, 36th North Carolina, commanded the River Road battery during the Federal assault.

"Company D was [to] the extreme left of the fort, occupying the space on both sides of the Napoleon, and although protected only by a shallow ditch and the remnants of the palisade, successfully repulsed every charge made by Curtis' brigade in front, and compelled the charging columns to abandon this. . . .entrance to the fort and go off to the right, to climb the high parapets in order to get into the fort. . . .There was another piece, however, a Parrott gun. . . .which we used once or twice very effectively in blowing to atoms a bridge on the main road into the fort. At the [Federals] first charge the boys at the Napoleon made a shot which cleared that road and caused many to take refuge under that bridge."[52]

The Federals, who witnessed dozens of their fellow soldiers being blown away by the Confederate artillery, chose wading through the cold, murky water rather than certain death on the bridge. Unfortunately, this route did not provide the shelter the men sought. Chaplain William L. Hyde, a veteran of the 112th New York wrote:

61

(The men of our regiment) moved forward in the charge, were greeted by a murderous fire from the fort! Many a brave fellow fell. Soon they reached the marsh in front, which some attempting to cross, were mired, and became the easy

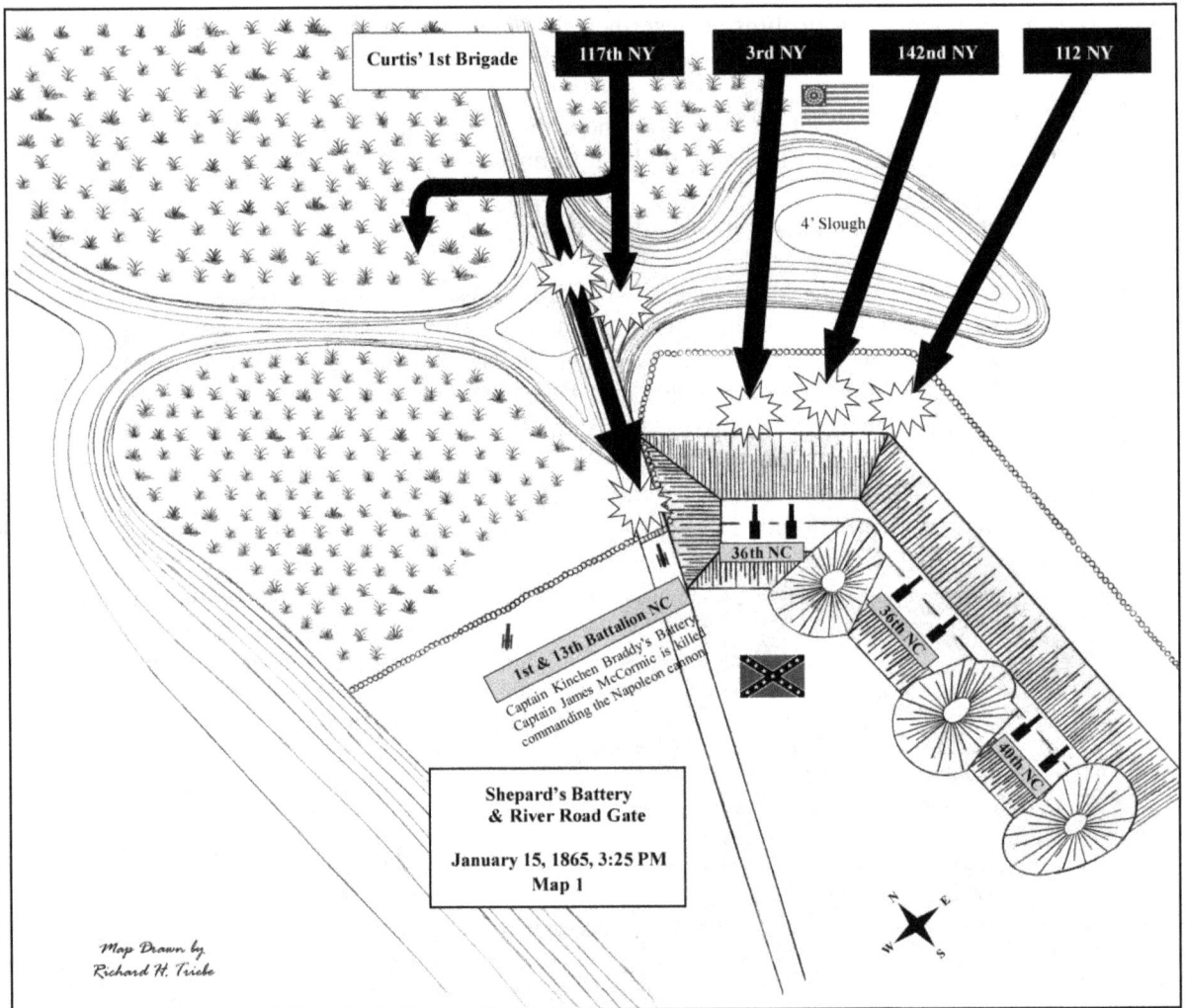

Curtis' 1st Brigade
117th NY
3rd NY
142nd NY
112 NY

4' Slough

36th NC

1st & 13th Battalion NC
Captain Kinchen Braddy's Battery
Captain James McCormic is killed commanding the Napoleon cannon

36th NC

40th NC

Shepard's Battery
& River Road Gate

January 15, 1865, 3:25 PM
Map 1

Map Drawn by
Richard H. Triebe

mark for riflemen in the fort.[53]

Colonel Curtis' Brigade charged Fort Fisher and met a storm of cannon and rifle fire. Many soldiers decided it was safer to wade through the marsh because of the barrage of Confederate fire on the bridge.

Confederate Captain Kinchen Braddy's small detachment of thirty-five soldiers was in extreme peril at the River Road gate. His men bravely stood their ground against hundreds of charging Federal troops, loading and firing the battery's two cannons. There were not enough men to stem the tide and the battery was in danger of being overrun. Hordes of screaming Federals stormed the sandbagged sally-port gate, trying to force their way through. These men were met by equally determined Rebel defenders, who fired their muskets point-blank into the charging Federals. It

62

seemed like the harder these men fought, the more determined their attackers became. One after another, the Confederates soldiers fell dead and wounded. When it appeared the Northern troops would burst through the entrance, the defenders were reinforced by soldiers from the First North Carolina Heavy Artillery. These men had seen the desperate fight from the gun chamber above and rushed over to keep the Yankees out of the fort.

Confederate Sergeant Thomas A. McNeill recalled the deadly combat at the River Road gate:

> The men of [Company D] rushed to the . . . sally-port [and] at once opened fire on the enemy, and a destructive fire was kept up. . . .After a few rounds from the battery, the detachments, two or three in succession, were all shot down at their guns, and the pieces were not after this served . . . The [Yankee] column advanced to the right of this company's position, under a heavy fire poured on it from the palisades between the sally-port and the river's edge, moving as if to effect a lodgment on the fort. . . .In the midst of this fire, it was found that the enemy were [sic] inside the palisades, to the right of Company D, and then a desperate struggle succeeded almost hand-to-hand, some of [our men] clubbing their muskets and fighting the width of the palisade between them and the enemy.[54]

Confederate Private Zachary Fulmore recalled the terrible bloodbath in a letter to Colonel Lamb, "On the afternoon of the fight my recollection is that there were eleven men killed and seventeen wounded in Company B, during the three charges. . . .[made by] Curtis' Brigade."[55]

As brutal as the fighting was for the Confederates, it was just as hard for the Federal soldiers. It's true that the Northern troops greatly outnumbered the Confederates inside the fort, but the men on the firing line knew no such advantage. To them it was kill or be killed. Shoot the man in the gray uniform aiming his rifle before he gets the chance to shoot you. This was the most brutal combat imaginable. The men were so close, many times only a few feet separated them, that the struggle became personal. Not only could you look your opponent in the eye, but you could hear him scream in pain as you shot him or clubbed him with your musket. The fighting at the gate became so bitter that many veterans of the battle would later refer to this entrance as the "bloody gate". For one Federal veteran this was an unusually apt name. "The fighting at the sally-port was terrific and the carnage the most terrible that I had ever witnessed," recalled Federal 2nd Lieutenant George Simpson of the 142nd New York. "Rivulets of blood ran from the gateway."[56]

Colonel Curtis saw the desperate fight for the River Road gate and realized his frontal assault was not working. He was losing too many men and no ground was being gained. Curtis figured the best way to capture the gate was to flank it by taking

Federal Lieutenant George Simpson of the 142nd New York, recalled, "[The fighting] was terrific and the carnage the most terrible that I had ever witnessed . . . rivulets of blood ran from the gateway."

the elevated gun chamber next to it. Once this had been captured, his men could either fire down on the stubborn Confederate defenders at the gate or move around behind them and attack from the rear.

While Curtis was contemplating the best way to capture the Confederate battery, his men veered to their left to get away from the murderous cannons at the fort's gate. Dozens of Federal soldiers gathered at the base of the fort's sloping walls. Here they found temporary shelter from the Confederate guns. A serious mistake was made by Major Riley's Confederate defenders in the gun chambers. Unlike Colonel Lamb's soldiers at the Northeast Bastion, who stood on top of the fort's parapets, shooting down at the charging Federals, these Confederate defenders remained inside their gun chamber waiting for the Union soldiers thus limiting their field of fire. This inadvertently created a blind spot for the defenders and allowed the enemy a brief respite to catch their breath and regroup before continuing their charge up the steep slope. This error in judgment exacerbated the already small number of Confederate troops available. As a result, the soldiers were unable to see the advancing Federals until they were practically on top of them. By then it would be too late. Large numbers of Federal troops would swarm over the fort's walls and overwhelm the Confederate defenders.[57]

Federal Captain Joseph S. Mathews' regiment, the 112th New York, was severely raked by cannon fire from the main sally-port.

Colonel Lamb mentioned this grave error in 1893 while addressing the Cape Fear Camp of the United Confederate Veterans in Wilmington, North Carolina:

> I knew my only hope of repelling greatly superior numbers was to man the top of the parapet and fire down upon the assaulting columns. . . .The guns immediately to the right of Sheperd's Battery were manned by some of the bravest officers and men, but the fatal mistake of the commander was fighting from behind the revetment instead of from the top of the parapet, as ordered. Only two of the men mounted the parapet, and they were instantly shot down. One was Bob Harvey, a recklessly brave boy, the last male member of an old family of Bladen County. I have been unable to learn the name of his heroic companion. Had [the soldiers] been on top of the parapet they could have used their bayonets or clubbed their guns, and thus delayed a lodgment until reinforcements came.[58]

The Confederate defenders in Sheperd's Battery watched the area over the sandbagged parapet, anxiously waiting for the Yankees to appear. First the brass eagle of the national flag came into view, then the silver spear point at the top of the blue and gold banner of the 117th New York. The flags were rising higher, billowing gracefully in the smoky, sulfur laden breeze. Below these flags appeared scores of bearded veterans of the Federal Army of the James, determined to be the first to plant their flags on Fort Fisher's parapet.

A sudden explosion of Confederate gunfire shattered the Federal ranks, hurling back the dazed survivors. The color bearer for the 3rd New York was shot and fell down the steep slope. Sergeant Frederick Boden, who was carrying the 117th New York's flag up the sandy hill, had to quickly step out of the way so he would not be bowled over by the dead and wounded soldiers as they tumbled past him. Grim men in brown and gray rushed forward to meet the Yankee charge. These soldiers became locked in mortal combat, shooting their rifles at point-blank range, swinging muskets, slashing with swords and bowie knives, and stabbing with bayonets. Confederate defenders bit open cartridges, loaded their weapons and rammed the charges down smoking gun barrels. If these men were lucky, and somehow avoided being shot, they raised their rifles and blasted away at the surging blue mob before them. Corporal Henry Clay McQueen of the First North Carolina Artillery Battalion remembered his company lost twelve men in the bloody struggle for the gun chamber. "A comrade next to me on the traverse was shot in his brains and killed," McQueen recalled. "His brains splattered in my face." Another bullet knocked off McQueen's hat, and then he fell wounded in the left thigh.[59]

Harper's Weekly drawing of Federal Infantry assaulting Sheperd's Battery and the River Road gate.

James A. Mowris, Regimental Surgeon for the 117th New York, recalled the desperate fight:

(Though) the roar of artillery abated, it was more than supplied by the yelling and the din of deadly musketry. All along on the crest of the parapet, as far to the left as our line extended, might be seen the desperate contest. The national colors and the insurgent rag were seen simultaneously and then alternately, on the same traverse. Hand to hand, foot to foot, the combatants fought.[60]

Colonel Curtis, a guidon from the 117th New York in one hand and a sword in the other, appeared in the midst of this free-for-all. Several men from a Confederate gun crew were desperately trying to fire a huge Columbiad artillery piece into the mass of Yankees swarming over the parapet. A shot had been jammed into the cannon's muzzle, but the crew was overpowered as they were ramming the charge home. The Confederate gunner was still trying to get a shot off even though the rammer's shaft was protruding from the barrel. Curtis called for the man's surrender. Ignoring him, the Confederate gunner inserted a friction primer into the cannon's vent hole. Curtis angrily leaped into the gun chamber and struck the gunners outstretched hand with his sword, forcing him to surrender.[61]

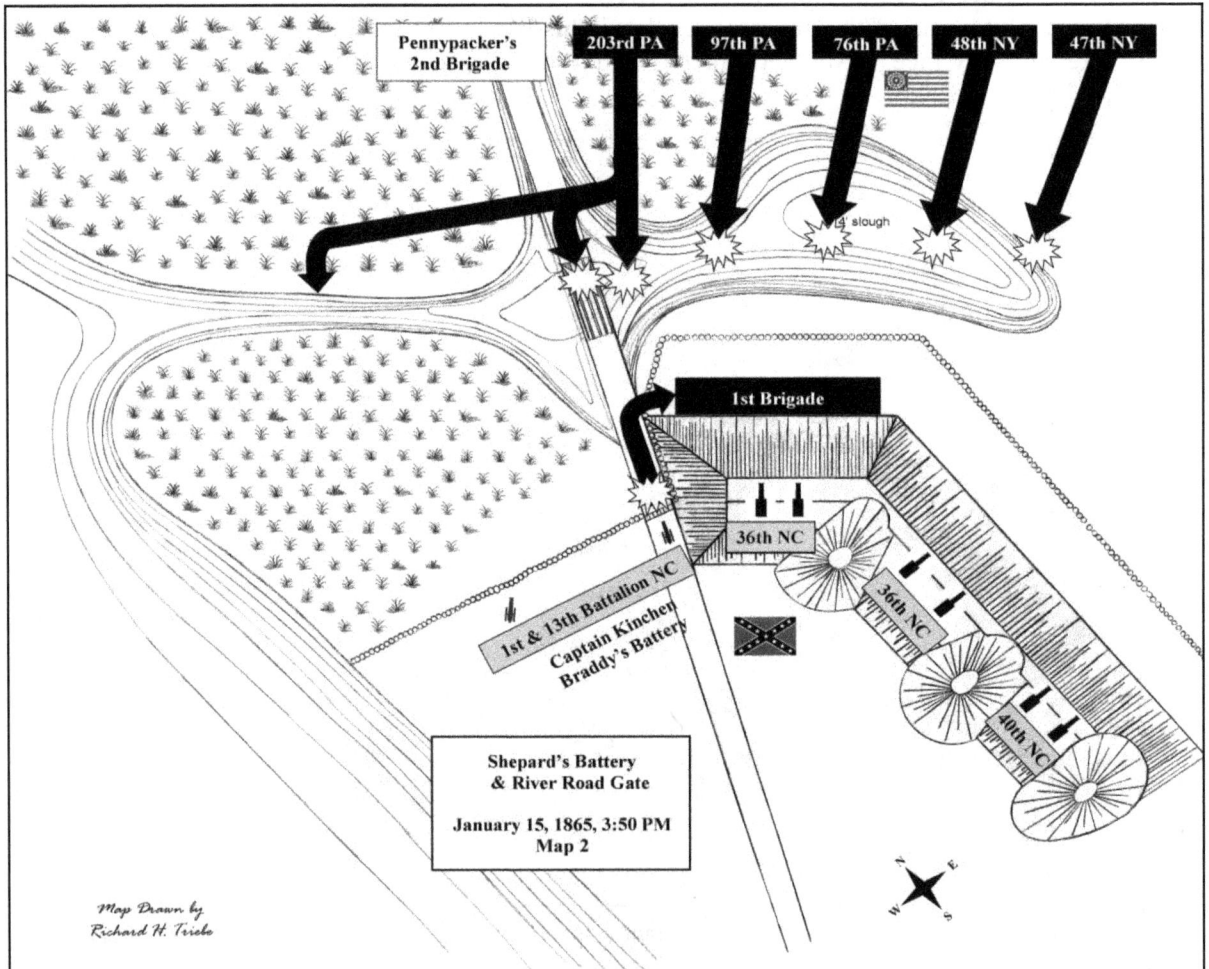

The 3rd Brigade joins the Federal assault. The 1st and 2nd Brigades charge up the earthworks and fight a bloody hand-to-hand struggle with the 10th North Carolina Heavy Artillery.

Federal soldiers swarmed over the parapet in such large numbers that halting their advance was near impossible. Hopelessly outnumbered, the Rebels were unable to contain this serious breach of the fort's walls. One-by-one the ranks of the Confederates were being thinned as more men were

66

shot down. With so few men available, there was no one to replace those who had fallen. Such was not the case for the Union army. For every Northern soldier killed, it seemed two appeared to take his place.

However, everything was not fine with the Federal advance. No one knew this better than Colonel Curtis. Curtis was aware they needed to exploit this breach in the Rebel defenses, but how could he possibly do this when his men barely had the strength to hold on. His brigade had done their job well, spearheading the Federal attack, but the soldiers were quickly running out of steam. The unexpected Confederate resistance had fought his men to a standstill. What Curtis needed more than anything was for General Ames to send in the second brigade so he could fill this gap in the Confederate defense with more men.   A sudden swell of gunfire and men cheering outside of the fort was a glorious sound to Curtis. Ames had answered his prayers by sending in a fresh brigade!

Federal Sergeant Henry Odiorne, 97th Pennsylvania, died of wounds suffered at Fort Fisher.

General Adelbert Ames saw that Colonel Curtis' brigade had stalled and decided to send in Colonel Galusha Pennypacker's brigade to get them moving forward again.   Ames planned on accompanying this new attack and commanded his staff, "Gentlemen, we will now go forward." Leaving the relative safety of their earthwork, the large group of officers made an irresistible target for Confederate sharpshooters. Noticing the bullets whizzing around them, Ames warned his staff, "We had better separate somewhat from each other." He had no sooner spoken these words when two of his aides, Captain Richard W. Dawson and Captain Birney Keeler, were both struck by enemy fire. Dawson was severely wounded in the left elbow and would later die from his injuries.[62]

The 2nd brigade began to take casualties even before they began their advance on Fort Fisher. Lieutenant Colonel William B. Coan was severely wounded while forming the 48th New York battle line and carried from the field. Moments later Captain James W. Dunn and Private Ferdinand Walser were shot down. Dunn was killed instantly while Walser was wounded so severely that his right arm had to be amputated to save his life. As the brigade rose to their feet to charge, they were met by a murderous fire.

The 47th New York, commanded by Colonel Joseph M. McDonald, held the left of the brigade line, north of the center sally-port. The assault route took the regiment close to the Confederate battery commanded by Captain Zachariah Adams. As the 47th New York moved forward, the entire color guard was swept away by a vicious blast from a Napoleon cannon at the sally-port. Although these men had been horribly killed, this didn't halt the Federal advance. Other soldiers quickly snatched up the battered flags and continued the charge. These silk banners were a source of regimental pride, and it was a considered a terrible disgrace to let them fall in battle. These men would rather die than let that happen.[63]

All of the Federal regiments suffered during the battle of Fort Fisher, but none had it worse than the 203rd Pennsylvania. The regiment was on the extreme right of the Federal line, alongside the river. This area was covered by Confederate Captain Kinchen Braddy's battery which guarded the fort's "bloody gate". The 203rd bravely charged the western side of the fort and were slaughtered wholesale. This single regiment would earn the dubious distinction of having the most men killed and wounded at Fort Fisher. This figure was high enough to earn it a place on the list of the most casualties suffered by a single regiment during a Civil War battle. By battle's end the 203rd

Pennsylvania would suffer 191 casualties. Colonel Pennypacker's 2nd brigade, to which the 203rd belonged, also suffered 280 casualties in the same charge. One Union officer recalled, "(The 203rd Pennsylvania) was being mowed down in windrows," by the Confederate gunners at the gate. Another soldier from the 203rd Regiment commented, "(It was) Sure death to stop-almost certain destruction to go on."[64]

Color Sergeant William McCarthy, 97th PA, with the regiment's flag he carried at Fort Fisher. McCarthy was wounded in the knee and the flag was snatched up by Colonel Pennypacker. Pennypacker was severely wounded moments later and carried to the rear. Photograph reprinted from *Advance the Colors!* Vol. 2.

Pennypacker's brigade came on like a surging blue wave, rushing up the fort's sloping walls and joining the rear of Curtis' soldiers. The regimental flags of the 97th and 203rd Pennsylvania now joined the banner of the 117th New York on the crest of the parapet. Holding the 97th flag aloft, colorbearer William McCarty was leading the way for his regiment when he fell, shot through the knee. Colonel Pennypacker grabbed the fallen banner, inspiring his men to greater efforts by his bravery. A short distance away, Colonel John W. Moore of the 203rd Pennsylvania was climbing the fort's sandy slope and saw color bearer George Deitrich get shot down. Moore picked up the fallen flag. Seeing him, Pennypacker called to him. "Moore," he shouted, holding up the banner, "I want you to take notice that this is the flag of my old regiment." Moore, who had been "waving his colors and commanding his men to follow," glanced up at Pennypacker and then toppled over, taking a bullet through the heart. "The flag of the 97th Pennsylvania was pierced by one hundred and seven bullets and canister shot and its staff cut in two in the action," recalled Major Isaiah Price.[65]

Reinforced with a fresh brigade, Curtis boldly pushed more men into the gap in the Confederate defensive line. The bitter hand-to-hand struggle was reaching a crescendo as more men fought for control of the gun chamber. The Confederate soldiers were fighting with everything they had, but it still wasn't enough. They could not halt the aggressive Federal attack and were being driven back. The defenders were paying dearly for their stubborn resistance by leaving behind a bloody trail of dead and wounded men as they doggedly backed away, firing as they went. It was clear the Southerners were running out of room and needed to take immediate action. They could leave the gun chamber or be killed in a valiant attempt to save that which was probably already lost. At this point there was no officer left alive to order the men to retreat, yet the men instinctively withdrew over and around the traverse to the next gun chamber. Those men, who were not carrying an ounce of lead in their body, fell back and left Sheperd's Battery to the Yankees.

Colonel Curtis now turned his attention to the stubborn Confederates at the River Road gate to his right. Attacking them and holding on to the gun chamber was more difficult than Curtis had imagined. The Federal soldiers now had to fight on three fronts. A few of the Confederates they had been fighting had escaped by retreating over the traverse to the next gun chamber. Curtis urged his soldiers to keep up the pressure on these men by scaling the traverse and firing into the enemy, but he also needed to divert some men to the other side to attack the Rebel right flank at the River Road gate. To make the situation worse, he was receiving hostile fire from the parade ground in back of the gun chamber. Captain George F. Towle recalled, "A foothold was barely obtained, and the brigade here came to a stand [still], holding on by the eyelids, as it were, while men fell fast on every side."

Curtis had learned from his battlefield experience that the longer his men remained in one place the more difficult it was to get them moving again. He knew his best strategy was to stay on the offensive because this would keep the enemy off balance and prevent him from mounting an effective counterattack. Curtis needed to organize a thrust where the Confederates least expected it. He turned his attention to the stubborn enemy battery that was preventing his men from entering the fort through the River Road gate. Curtis knew what he had to do. He would lead a charge down the traverse to smash into the Confederate right flank.

The national flag of the 203rd Pennsylvania displays the battle scars from Fort Fisher. Photograph from *Advance the Colors!*, Vol. 2.

The toll on Confederate officers leading the courageous band of soldiers at the River Road gate was heavy. In a matter of minutes Lieutenant Thomas M. Argo fell wounded and Captain James McCormic was killed. Without these two officers there was no one in authority left to lead the men. The only other officer, Captain Kinchen Braddy, had departed moments before in search of men to reinforce his besieged battery. The South Carolinians that General Hoke had sent to the fort had been ordered to reinforce the riverside battery, but they stayed in their bombproof and refused to come out. A few of the soldiers that did venture forth thought Braddy was the enemy and fired at him, killing men on either side of the captain.

The bravery of the Confederates at the River Road gate was no match for the overwhelming numbers of Union soldiers. The massive Federal juggernaut seemed invincible. Blue-coated soldiers appeared everywhere. Some of the determined Union troops were even wading through the supposedly impassable swamp to the left. Others were putting incredible pressure on the gun chamber to the right. Private Zachary Fulmore described this desperate action in a letter to Colonel Lamb, dated May of 1897:

Our captain was killed . . . one lieutenant had been shot down, so that we . . . were in charge of a non-commissioned officer. As Adams men were being shot down one by one, our boys took the places of the dead or disabled. Our non-commissioned officer was killed, and four of our force on the left of the gate, within a very few minutes. . . .One of our boys was killed by a shot coming from our rear. I looked around and saw the stars and stripes floating from the top of the parapet, with what seemed to me to be a thousand bluecoats around it—some shooting at us. As soon as I saw this, I jumped to the Napoleon to see if I could spike it when they dashed down on us [from the traverse] and demanded our surrender. . . .I saw they had us

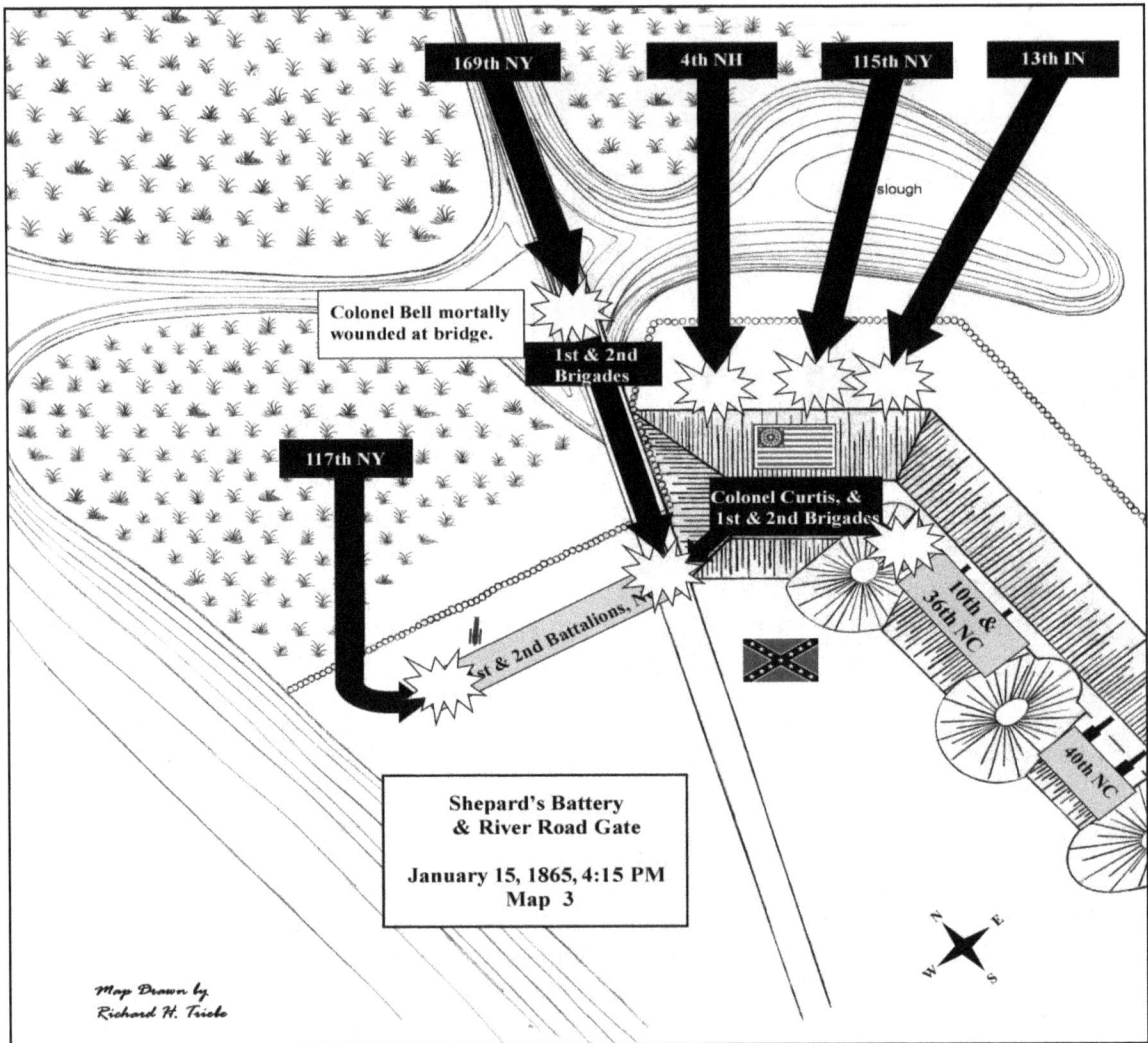

Colonel Curtis captures Sheperd's Battery and launches an attack against the right flank of the men at the River Road Gate Battery. The 117th New York attacks the Confederate left simultaneously.

completely surrounded—knew we would have to give up the gun, and in that event they would turn it on our men in the fort, hence my determination to spike it if possible. [66]

Seeing that further resistance would cause useless bloodshed, the Confederate defenders at the Bloody Gate dropped their weapons and surrendered.

Cannon fire from Battery Buchanan was targeting the Federal attack at the River Road gate. Unfortunately, the shells were killing friend and foe alike. Federal soldier George G. Spencer of the 117th New York was celebrating his 19th birthday in a very unusual way. He had mentioned to a friend that he thought the battle would be a "great birthday excursion". Spencer had managed to survive the horrific fighting at the fort's entrance only to be killed by a shell that fragment shattered his skull. On the other side, Confederate Privates John Cooper and Angus Blue were struck by shell fragments from their own men. Cooper, who was one of Braddy's best men, was killed instantly while Blue was wounded from behind by a shell that put him out of the fight. [67]

Colonel Galusha Pennypacker had taken the 97th Pennsylvania's flag after colorbearer William McCarty was wounded in the knee. As he led his men up to the third traverse, a dozen Rebels rose up and fired a volley. Pennypacker was struck in the hip, the bullet passing close to his spine, doing tremendous damage. He would spend eleven months in the hospital. Forty-six years later, Pennypacker was asked by journalist Philip R. Dillon if he had seen the man who shot him. The Colonel said, "I did see him—a big North Carolinian. I took my flag and planted it on the parapet, which was 20 feet high. There were eight or ten men with me going over. When we got over the top there was the traverse, 10 feet above us, and a whole platoon, 20 men . . . rose up from behind the traverse and fired. I saw the man who shot me. I saw him aim his gun, and I felt his bullet."

Seeing they were outnumbered, the Confederates surrendered. While they were being led away, Pennypacker's orderly saw a Confederate soldier with a blanket wrapped around him, trying to stay warm. "Take off that blanket and give it to us to carry away this wounded officer!" he demanded.

The soldier refused to give up his blanket, saying, "I'm a prisoner and I'm entitled to my blanket!"

Colonel Galusha Pennypacker, commander of the 2nd Brigade, was severely wounded in the hip at Fort Fisher. What his soldiers did next would stay with him forever.

Confederate Major James Stevenson lived through the battle only to die of pneumonia at Fort Columbus Prison in New York Harbor.

Pennypacker remembered what happened immediately after. "The next instant my men, with clubbed muskets, dashed out his brains; he died instantly. For the blood of my men was up, and they were as savage as the Carolinian. I closed my eyes and they carried me away in that blanket, but the horror of it has never gone out of my mind to this day!"[68]

General Whiting led 500 Confederate soldiers in a wild counterattack that slammed into the Yankees at the fourth gun chamber. "The Rebels attacked our men like savage dogs," exclaimed E. D. Williams of the 117th New York. "Give and take was the watchword on both sides, face to face and gun to gun." The Confederates would, "jump up on the top of a traverse and shoot down upon our men, and if that failed, they would attempt their slaughter with clubbed muskets," wrote a Federal soldier. "A few instances were found in which our men and theirs had pinned each other with their bayonets, and died together." There was little room for the opponents to maneuver. Men fired their muskets point-blank into the enemy, then plunged into brutal hand-to-hand combat—grappling with each other and killing their attacker any way they could.

"It was a soldier's fight now," recalled Confederate Private James A. Montgomery, Company B, 36th North Carolina. "As a man would fall, another sprang up to take his place, our officers loading and firing with us." The combatants trampled on the dead and wounded, stumbling over bodies, all the while keeping their eyes focused on the enemy. "Our killed and wounded on the parapet impeded our advance to the fourth traverse so that we were scarcely able to go forward without treading upon them," explained Colonel Curtis. "The struggle was the hottest and most prolonged single contest of the day. The loss of life was great on both sides."

Colonel Zent, of the 13th Indiana, had a close call during the fight for the fourth traverse. Zent climbed to the top of the mound of sand and peered over the crest. "All I remember seeing was a flash and feeling a sensation similar to an electric shock," the officer recalled. "The fellow had pulled the trigger a little too soon and the ball passed through my hat just grazing the top of my head."[69]

A big man with a drooping mustache and wild, brown hair spilling out from beneath his cap, moved in front of the Third Brigade and observed the battle, intently. Colonel Louis Bell had picked up a soldier's discarded rifle ramrod to use as a walking stick. Right now the long metal rod was being bent by powerful hands, revealing his frustration at being left behind while his army was fighting for its life. Bell was a man of action. He could not sit idly by and watch his army being destroyed without doing everything in his power to help. Each time the United States flag fell to the ground he took it as a personal insult and wanted to rush over and raise it up again. When the banner went down for the fifth time, Bell anxiously turned his gaze to the abandoned Confederate earthwork where General Terry had his combat headquarters. He was hoping to see a runner coming toward him with an order from the general to advance.[70]

72

Colonel Louis Bell suffered a fatal wound crossing the River Road bridge.

At that moment, General Terry had received an urgent dispatch from General Ames inside the fort reporting that the Federal assault was stalled. His troops were holding their own, but they needed help. Send in the Third Brigade and he could take the fort. Terry quickly wrote the order for the 3rd Brigade to join the assault in his notebook, tore off the sheet and gave it to Captain George F. Towle to deliver.[71]

Captain Towle, General Terry's aide, hand carried the order to Colonel Bell. Bell jammed his ramrod into the sand and read the order. He gave Towle a brief smile, then went to the front of his brigade. Bell nodded to Colonel Alonzo Alden to proceed with the advance. Alden shouted the preparatory command, "Third Brigade!"

The regimental commanders from the four regiments that made up the Third Brigade drew their swords and echoed the command to their men. Colonel Alden then gave the command of execution, "Forward! Double-quick!"

The men shifted their rifles to a loose form of port-arms and began to trot toward the fort. Bell raced out ahead, leading his troops into battle. The same devastating Confederate fire which greeted the two previous brigades now fell upon Bell's men.

Some of Pennypacker's soldiers had replaced several of the planks on the bridge and the Third Brigade angled to the right so they could cross it.

"How well the brigade is coming on under so severe a fire," Bell told one of his staff officers as they raced to the fort.[72]

The men began to bunch up on the north side of the bridge as they funneled over it. A Confederate marksman singled out Bell because a high ranking officer was leading the brigade. A bullet slammed into Bell's chest, exiting his lower back and knocking him to the ground. At first Bell did not realize how seriously he was wounded. He said to Lieutenant Hugh Sanford, his aide, "My arm is broken."

The aide knew better. He had heard the sickening thud of a body wound and saw the growing stain of blood on his colonel's left chest. A crowd had gathered around the prostrate officer, picked up their wounded colonel and carried him to the rear.

Surgeon David Dearborn hurried to Bell's side and began cutting off the colonel's bloody clothing so he could examine the wound. "Is the wound mortal?" Bell asked. "I am fearful it is, Colonel," Dearborn replied. "Well," Bell said in a calm, matter of fact voice, "I thought as much myself."

Someone told Bell his men had planted their flags on the enemy ramparts. Bell struggled to raise himself a little, saying, "I want to see my colors on the parapet." He spied a distant flag and smiled because his dying wish had been satisfied.[73]

Whiting and his Confederates drove the Federals from the fourth gun chamber, then climbed up the traverse to continue the fight. "Much hand-to-hand fighting of a desperate character ensued upon these huge traverses," recalled Captain Edson J. Harkness. "Our men would make a charge to the summit of a traverse, to be met by Confederates coming from the other side, where these hand-to-hand struggles occurred. One or two of these traverses were retaken, and held for a short time by the Confederates, but they were soon driven out for the last time."

Atop the traverse General Whiting grabbed a Federal flagstaff. He was instantly surrounded by Northern troops, demanding his surrender. "Go to hell, you Yankee bastards!" he shouted. They fired and Whiting fell with two wounds in his right thigh. Some of his men saw him go down, rushed to his side and carried him to the fort's hospital.[74]

Colonel Alonzo Alden 169th New York. Alden took command of the Third Brigade after Bell was wounded.

The fire of the Federal fleet was largely responsible for halting the Confederate counterattack on the fort's parapets. Colonel Curtis had communicated with Terry, who in turn signaled the fleet to shift their fire back to the land-face and stay ahead of the attacking Federal army. This is the earliest incident the author is aware of in which artillery fire was adjusted by the attacking commander to provide close-ground-support for his troops.

Colonel Lamb credited the Federal fleet's accurate artillery fire for stopping the Confederate attack:

We had retaken one of these [gun chambers] in the charge led by Whiting, and since we had opened on their flank we had shot down their standard bearers and the Federal battle flags had disappeared from our ramparts; we had become assailants and the enemy were on the defensive, and I felt confident that we would soon drive them out of the fort. Just as the tide of battle seemed to have turned in our favor, the remorseless fleet came to the rescue of the faltering Federals. Suddenly the bombardment which had been consigned to the sea-face during the assaults turned again on our land front and with deadly precision. They swept the recaptured gun chamber of its defenders, and their 11 and 15 inch shells rolled down into the interior of the work, carrying death and destruction in their pathways. They drove from the parapets in front of the enemy all of my men except those so near that to have fired on them would have been slaughter to their own troops.[75]

Back at Sugar Loaf, Confederate General Braxton Bragg ordered Hoke to probe the Federal's northern defensive line. At 4:00 PM Hoke sent the brigades of Kirkland and Clingman forward to make a reconnaissance of the enemy position. According to Captain Elliott of Kirkland's Brigade, "We easily drove in the enemy's skirmish line, occupied their rifle pits, and our skirmishers were making their main line keep their heads down behind their entrenchments."

Hoke rode down from his headquarters at Sugar Loaf to observe the action. He later reported to General Bragg that his men were involved in a sharp firefight in which he had gotten, "two balls in his clothes, between the left arm and breast." Should he proceed with the attack? Hoke asked Bragg.

74

Captain John T. Thomas, Company F, 117th New York. Thomas would be killed trying to take the 3rd traverse. *Photograph courtesy of Chris Fonvielle Jr.*

Captain Elliott later recalled the anticipation of many of the soldiers: "We confidently expected to run over the troops in our front and drive them in confusion upon Terry's attacking column." But Bragg was not of that opinion. He considered the Federal entrenchments too formidable for Hoke. "Their line was impracticable for his small command," Bragg said, "and I did not hesitate to recall him. [Hoke] could not have succeeded." Captain Elliott was dismayed. "When we all expected an order to charge a courier came to Hoke from Bragg advising him to withdraw to Sugar Loaf." Bragg had made the grim decision that Fort Fisher would stand or fall on its own.[76*]

Federal Colonel John W. Ames of the 6th U.S. Colored Troops commented on Hoke's so-called attack, saying, "It was little more than a weak attempt to carry the picket line. It's feebleness was so striking that it did us good service in showing how little we had to fear from that quarter." Federal General Charles J. Paine agreed with Colonel Ames and confessed, "If [Hoke] had made an attack, and if he had carried my line and they held out in the fort, we should have been in a tight place."

Years later, Captain Edson J. Harkness wrote:

> It is difficult to understand why General Hoke, with his splendid record as a fighting Confederate, and with the magnificent troops which he brought with him from Richmond, should have allowed himself to remain at Sugarloaf, seven miles above Fort Fisher, without making any attempt to relieve Whiting or to attack Paine's defensive line. There has never been any question in my mind, either from the reports made of these operations, or from my own observation, that the landing of our forces at Masonborough Sound, or, at any rate, the establishment of a line across the peninsula from the ocean to the river, could have been prevented by a resolute and determined enemy. Neither has there been any doubt that after the line was established, an attack by Hoke upon the north line would have been so serious a diversion as to have withdrawn a large portion of the assaulting force from Fort Fisher, and rendered that assault impracticable.[77]

Unlike General Braxton Bragg, Colonel Lamb was the correct officer to defend Fort Fisher. Lamb was both resourceful, could think clearly in time of great stress. Like any good field commander, Colonel Lamb was flexible. He could appraise the combat situation

75

immediately and adapt to the ever changing tide of battle. This ability led Lamb to do the unthinkable in his search for information on how to defeat his enemy. Lamb describes this in Walter Clark's book the *Histories of North Carolina Regiments and Battalions*:

> I doubt if ever before the commander of a work went outside the fort and looked upon the conflict for its possession, but from the construction of the fort it was absolutely necessary for me to do so in order to quickly comprehend the position of affairs. . . . I rushed through the sally-port, and outside the work and witnessed a fierce hand-to-hand conflict for the possession of the fourth gun chamber. The men led by the fearless Whiting had driven the standard bearer from the top of the traverse and the enemy from the parapet in front. They had recovered one gun chamber with great slaughter, and on the parapet and on the long traverse of the next gun chamber the contestants were savagely firing into each other's faces, and in some cases clubbing their guns.[78]

Seeing his men savagely fighting the enemy convinced Colonel Lamb a determined assault would drive the enemy from the fort. Lamb rushed to the various gun chambers and bombproofs to appeal to his men to come with him and defeat the Yankees. He was saddened to see the magnificent fort which he had helped build reduced to smoldering wreckage. He describes the grisly death and destruction in an address to the Cape Fear Camp, United Confederate Veterans of Wilmington. "As I passed through portions of the work, the scene was indescribably horrible. Great cannon broken in two, their carriages wrecked and among their ruins the mutilated bodies of my dead and dying comrades."[79]

Lamb returned around 4:30 PM with several hundred soldiers and placed them behind a breastwork on the parade ground. The Confederates were within one-hundred feet of the enemy, close enough to see their faces distinctly. Lamb asked the officers and men if they would follow him in a charge against the Yankees, and they all agreed. Encouraged by the overwhelming support of his men, Lamb jumped upon the breastwork, waving his sword. "Charge, bayonets! Forward, double quick, march!"

The moment Lamb uttered the command, a rifle bullet slammed into his hip, knocking him off the breastwork. The same volley that wounded Lamb also fatally wounded Lieutenant Daniel R. Perry. The Confederate soldiers were starting over the breastworks when they met a storm of Federal gunfire. The men went back behind their mounds of sand and returned fire.

Lamb turned over defense of the breastwork to Captain Daniel Munn, telling him he would return after he had his wound bandaged. Before reaching the hospital Lamb became so weak from loss of blood that he knew he could not return to the battle. Surgeon Joseph Shepard had Lamb's litter set down next to General Whiting. Whiting told Lamb that General Bragg had ignored his messages and they could expect no help from him.

Confederate Surgeon Joseph Shepard treated both General Whiting and Colonel Lamb.

Lamb ordered his adjutant, Lieutenant John Kelly, to find Major Reilly because he was the next senior officer in line to take command of Fort Fisher. When

Major Reilly arrived at the hospital, he was given command of the fort from Lamb and Whiting, and promised he would keep fighting, "as long as a man or a shot was left."[80]

General Whiting sent a message to General Bragg at 6:30 PM, downplaying his severe wounds and appealing for help. "The enemy are assaulting us by land and sea," he reported. "Their infantry outnumber us. Can't you help us? I am slightly wounded." Whiting never received a direct response to his dispatch from General Bragg. Instead, Colonel Archer Anderson, Bragg's assistant adjutant, sent a dispatch about 7:40 PM, telling Whiting General Colquitt was coming to the fort to relieve him and take immediate command. Whiting was also ordered to report to General Bragg at his headquarters.[81]

Confederate Major James Reilly assembled some of the men from the earlier charge Colonel Lamb had led. Reilly managed to deploy a force of 150 men behind the huge main magazine. With a color bearer from Captain Izlar's South Carolinians, the small band of Confederate soldiers advanced to do battle with the Federal troops massed behind Sheperd's Battery.

Sheperd's Battery with the Bloody Gate to the left. Timothy O'Sullivan image, 1865. *Photograph courtesy of the Library of Congress.*

77

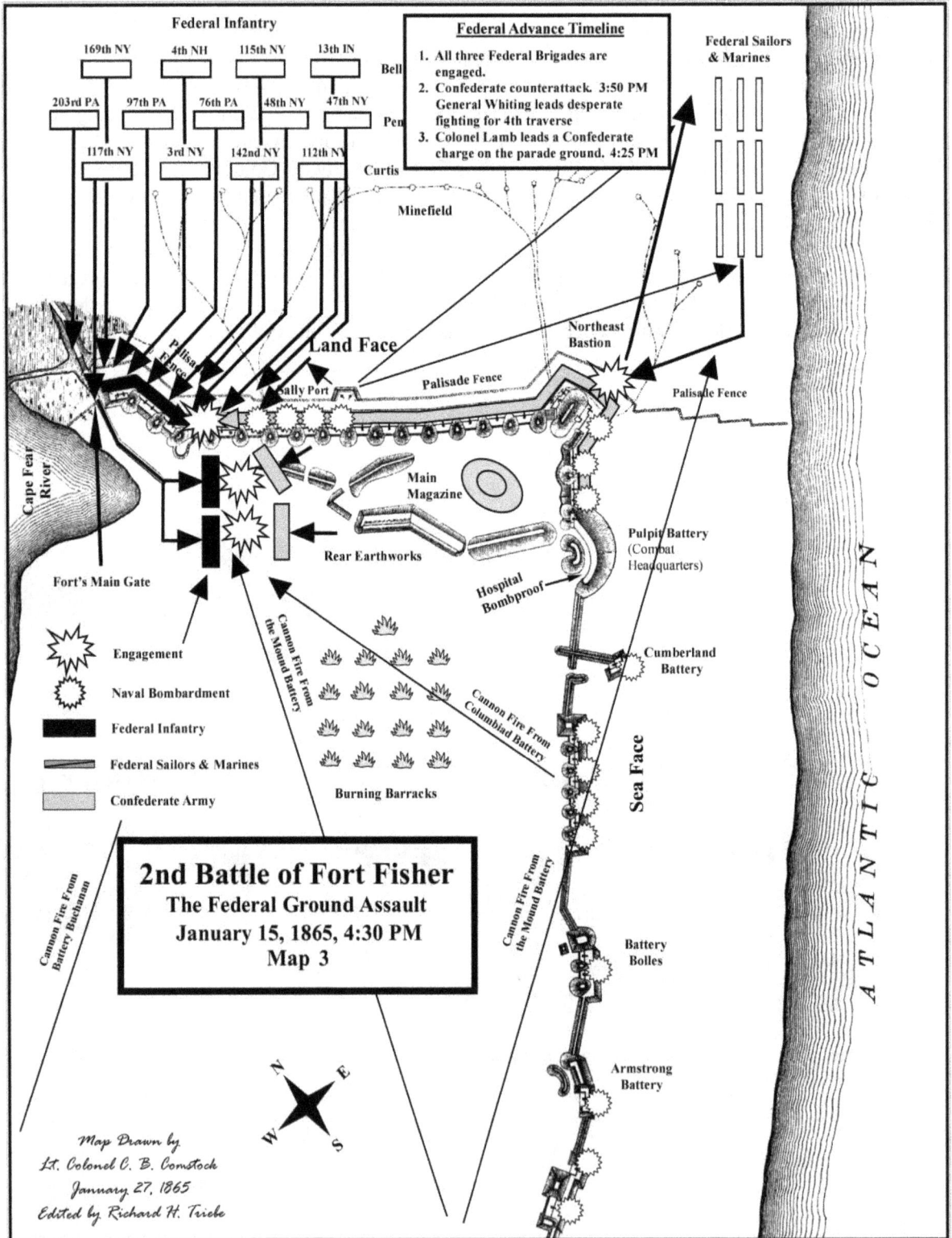

Federal Infantry

169th NY	4th NH	115th NY	13th IN
203rd PA	97th PA	76th PA	48th NY	47th NY
117th NY	3rd NY	142nd NY	112th NY

Bell

Pen

Curtis

Minefield

Federal Advance Timeline

1. **All three Federal Brigades are engaged.**
2. **Confederate counterattack.** 3:50 PM General Whiting leads desperate fighting for 4th traverse
3. **Colonel Lamb leads a Confederate charge on the parade ground.** 4:25 PM

Federal Sailors & Marines

Land Face

Northeast Bastion

Palisade Fence

Sally Port

Palisade Fence

Palisade Fence

Cape Fear River

Main Magazine

Rear Earthworks

Pulpit Battery (Combat Headquarters)

Hospital Bombproof

Fort's Main Gate

Cannon Fire From the Mound Battery

Cumberland Battery

Sea Face

Cannon Fire From Columbiad Battery

Engagement

Naval Bombardment

Federal Infantry

Federal Sailors & Marines

Confederate Army

Burning Barracks

Cannon Fire From the Mound Battery

Battery Bolles

2nd Battle of Fort Fisher
The Federal Ground Assault
January 15, 1865, 4:30 PM
Map 3

Cannon Fire From Battery Buchanan

Armstrong Battery

N E W S

Map Drawn by Lt. Colonel C. B. Comstock January 27, 1865 Edited by Richard H. Triebe

ATLANTIC OCEAN

78

"As soon as the enemy observed our object, they opened a very destructive fire on our advancing column," Reilly later reported. "Under such a fire our men began to waver and fall back." The color bearer was shot dead and Reilly's troops dispersed in confusion. "By the time I reached near the [Northeast Bastion] I had not sixty men with me." The major withdrew to his position near the main magazine and "kept up as heavy and destructive a fire as [his] small command would allow." Nearly two-thirds of his men had become casualties.[82]

Confederate Lieutenant William C. Daniel, 36th North Carolina, captured at Fort Fisher.

While Curtis' men were capturing the traverses, other Federal soldiers were keeping pace with the advance on the floor of the fort. The going was difficult because these troops were battling Confederates hiding behind debris from the burned-out buildings, shell craters and any other obstruction that afforded any sort of cover. It was during this action that Lieutenant Colonel Jonas W. Lyman of the 203rd Pennsylvania was killed while urging his troops forward. Captain Heber B. Essington described what happened after his regiment entered the fort:

After having assisted in capturing the first two mounds, a portion of the regiment went with the first Brigade over the traverses, and the remainder went to the right and stationed themselves behind a bank [of sand] in the open field south of the fort. The latter portion then charged across the plain, until opposite the seventh or eighth traverse, where they threw up an embankment with their tin plates and shovels, keeping up a steady fire upon the enemy.[83]

The Federal fleet kept up its accurate bombardment of the fort firing three shots per second amid the Confederates on the parapet. Colonel Curtis describes the action when one of these shells went astray:

At the fifth traverse a shot went wide of its mark and killed or disabled all but four men in our front line. Fearing that a slackening of our fire would invite a countercharge, I myself discharged the guns of the killed and disabled men until reinforcements were brought forward. A sudden emergency compelled this action. It was not done to encourage the soldiers—no such efforts were needed to quicken their zeal. Men unable to stand and fire their pieces handed up the guns of their dead and helpless comrades, and when given back reloaded them again and again, exhibiting an unselfish devotion that seemingly nothing but death could chill. Within twenty minutes I found wounded men dead who had handed me their guns.[84]

Captain Albert M. Barney's regiment, the 142nd New York, was in the first Federal wave to assault the fort.

From the seventh traverse, Colonel Curtis noticed that a

79

troublesome Columbiad Battery on the sea-face could be silenced by some expert marksmen. He sent Corporal John Jones, of the 117th New York, to the west end of the fort to bring back some Union sharpshooters. When Jones returned, he told Curtis that General Ames refused to send these men forward. Ames also told him he would issue spades so the soldiers could entrench for the night. Curtis then sent his orderly, Captain Arthur O. Knight to explain to General Ames why these men were needed.

Confederate Captain Daniel Munn, 36th North Carolina, captured at Fisher.

Knight returned shortly and told Colonel Curtis that Ames said the men were exhausted and no further advance would be attempted until morning. He also ordered Knight to tell Curtis to hold onto the ground now occupied and he would send forward entrenching tools. Curtis ordered Knight to go back and request officers under his rank to come to the front, so that an attack could be made before dark. If Ames would not provide him with soldiers, Curtis would attack with his own men.

Knight came back with an armful of spades from General Ames. Curtis, a huge man six-feet-six inches in height, grabbed the spades and threw them over the traverse to the Confederates. Curtis went over General Ames head by sending Seaman Silas W. Kempton to Major General Terry, urging Terry to have the troops then engaged in digging entrenchments join in an advance and take possession of the fort before reinforcements could be sent by the Confederate army.[85]

Curtis ordered Captain David B. Magill of the 117th New York to keep pressing the next traverse while he went to the west end of the fort to obtain some men. While Curtis was assembling some soldiers, he was met by General Ames, who said, "I have two or three times sent you word to fortify your position and hold it until reinforcements can be sent to aid us, the men are exhausted, and I will not order them to go forward."

Curtis reminded Ames that the Confederates had two steamboats in the river loaded with troops waiting for darkness so they could put them ashore. "Should they succeed in landing, they may be able to drive us out," he said. "Therefore, the fort should be captured before fresh troops come to the enemy." Curtis had no sooner said this when he was struck in the face by two shell fragments. One destroyed his left eye while the other carried away portions of the front orbital bone. Unconscious and believed by his men to be fatally wounded, Colonel Curtis was carried from the battlefield. This was Curtis' fifth wound of the day. Ames promptly informed General Terry that Curtis was mortally wounded.[86]

General Terry was concerned. He had over four thousand troops engaged at Fort Fisher and still the fort had not fallen. Casualties were heavy, especially among the senior officers. Colonels Lyman, and Moore had been killed. Colonels Bell, Coan, Curtis, Littell, Pennypacker and Smith were severely wounded, perhaps mortally. The troops were tired and disorganized. Darkness was coming and the Confederates would probably reinforce the fort. Terry asked his aide, Lieutenant Colonel Cyrus B. Comstock for advice. Comstock had a definite opinion: Bring up Abbott's Brigade and throw it into the fort against the Rebels. Bring up Pain's troops too. Leave just a skeletal force behind to guard the entrenchments against Confederate General Hoke. Overwhelm the Rebels with fresh troops and finish the job.[87]

Terry agreed with Comstock and sent orders to General Abbott to enter the fort with his brigade as soon as possible. Abbott was told to report to General Ames and ask where he should deploy his troops. General Paine was ordered to send his best regiment into the fort and then report to Ames for further orders.

General Abbott withdrew his soldiers from the entrenchments on the northern defensive line and replaced them with sailors and marines who had participated in the

Lieutenant Colonel Cyrus B. Comstock advised General Terry to throw in Abbott's Brigade and overwhelm the Rebels with fresh troops.

assault of the naval brigade. It was about dusk when Abbott's brigade filed through the River Road gate. Abbott located the division command post and reported to General Ames. He was told to replace Ames' tired troops with fresh soldiers.

General Abbott's troops would be the fourth Federal brigade to fight at Fort Fisher.

General Terry had found that the sound of gunfire was a reliable indicator of how the battle was going. When the first three brigades had stalled in their advance, the rifle fire had slackened. It was over an hour since Terry had sent in Abbott's brigade, but the firing had not increased as expected. Curious, General Terry went inside the fort to investigate. What he found alarmed him greatly. Troops were milling around, brigades and regiments intermingled, showing no form of cohesion or purpose. Instead of rushing Abbott's Brigade to the front, Ames put some of the men to work digging entrenchments and placed one regiment, the 7th Connecticut, on picket duty in his rear. A single regiment, the 3rd New Hampshire, had been sent to the front, but instead of renewing the Federal assault, they were ordered to relieve the weary troops already there.[88]

81

Ames explained to General Terry he was fortifying his position for the night and would resume the assault in the morning, after his men were rested. Ames then went on to tell Terry his troop losses had been especially heavy. "Ten of my officers had been killed, forty-seven wounded, and about 500 men were killed and wounded." Terry agreed that many a good man had been lost that day. He also agreed the soldiers were tired, but so were the Rebels. Terry pointed out that the Confederate troops had barely survived the nonstop, three-day bombardment and then fought a bloody hand-to-hand struggle all afternoon. One final push was all that was needed to convince them to surrender. Besides, General Terry had noticed the Confederate troop transports in the Cape Fear River, waiting for dark so they could unload thousands of fresh troops. No! General Terry told Ames. The Federal advance would go forward tonight as planned.[89]

Captain William H. Trickey led the Federal assault on the last land-face traverses.

The Federal troops had captured two-thirds of the land-face, but the Confederates held the rest. General Abbott ordered his brigade forward around 9:00 PM. Captain Trickey's regiment, the 3rd New Hampshire, captured all the remaining land-face traverses but one. Abbott surrounded the gun chamber with the 7th New Hampshire and the 6th Connecticut. The Federal soldiers charged up the slope and met a sharp fire from the Confederates waiting for them behind the parapet. The scene had a terrifying, surreal quality. Darkness had fallen and the slopes and traverses were eerily illuminated by the brilliant flashes of gunfire. Abbott's troops, who were armed with Spencer repeating rifles, made short work of the few remaining defenders who were hiding in the gun chamber. Those who were not killed, wounded or captured escaped southward along the sea-face.[90]

Confederate Major James Reilly led the retreat to Battery Buchanan.

Inside the Confederate hospital, Colonel Lamb could hear the sounds of battle drawing closer. Things had gone terribly wrong. Apparently Fort Fisher had been deserted by General Bragg, the minefield had failed to explode because of damage to the wires by the intense naval bombardment. Now Lamb heard more bad news from several of his officers. Major Reilly reported that one of the fort's officers had raised a white flag, let the Yankees into the main sally-port and surrendered a large part of the garrison. That wasn't all. Around 8:00 PM Lamb's aide returned to the hospital and reported that the troops were almost out of ammunition. Chaplain McKinnon had gathered all he could from the dead and wounded in a blanket and distributed it among the troops. The situation appeared hopeless, the aide lamented. He told Lamb that the Yankees nearly had all the land-face and appeared to be regrouping for another attack. Since it was nearly impossible to hold out much longer, he asked, wouldn't it be wise to surrender to prevent further bloodshed?[91]

"I replied that while I lived I would not surrender as Bragg would surely come to our rescue in time to save us," Colonel Lamb later wrote. "General Whiting declared if I died he would assume command and would not surrender." Lamb also had promised the women of Wilmington who had visited the fort after the first battle that their homes would be protected by his garrison. Lamb had an

Confederate Captain Edward B. Dudley, 36th North Carolina, made sure no Yankee would ever take Colonel Lamb's sword.

even more substantial reason for refusing to surrender. General Lee had sent word that if Fort Fisher fell, he could not maintain his army. This meant the South would lose the war. All the sacrifices they had made for four long years would have gone for nothing. Lamb refused to be the man who had lost the war for the South. "Is it to be wondered that I felt it my sacred duty, even after I was shot down," Lamb asked, "to appeal to officers and men to fight in defense of the last gateway to the South?"[92]

After the land-face had fallen, the fighting for the sea-face intensified. The gunfire moved steadily closer to the hospital and prompted an evacuation of the structure. General Whiting and Colonel Lamb were hurriedly removed on stretchers to Battery Buchanan, while Major Reilly's troops covered their retreat. "When we left the hospital the men were fighting over the adjoining traverse, and the spent balls fell like hailstones around us," Lamb recalled. "The remnant of the garrison then fell back in an orderly retreat along the sea-face, the rear guard keeping the enemy engaged as they advanced slowly and cautiously in the darkness as far as the Mound Battery."

As Lamb was being carried away, Captain Edward B. Dudley, 36th North Carolina, took the colonel's saber and sword belt. "No damned Yankee shall ever have the sword!" he exclaimed as he tossed it into the Atlantic Ocean.[93]

Colonel Lamb had designed Battery Buchanan as a citadel where the Fort Fisher garrison could retreat if they were under great pressure from a Federal assault. The earthwork had four large artillery pieces and was served by a dock on the Cape Fear River. Here the garrison could join forces with Lieutenant Robert T. Chapman's Naval detachment and continue their defense of Confederate Point. Should it become necessary, the embattled troops could either be reinforced by soldiers from the mainland or evacuated under the cover of darkness.[94]

Major Reilly planned on reforming his scattered command once they reached Battery Buchanan. If the Confederates could put up a stubborn defense for only two hours it was believed substantial numbers of troops could be ferried across the river before the Federals captured them.[95]

When Reilly's column of refugees arrived at Battery Buchanan, he and his men were shocked. The sailors and marines had fled. They had spiked the guns, and worst of all, they had taken the boats that the garrison was relying on to take them to safety. About 600 soldiers had fallen back from Fort Fisher and were milling about the battery, at least three-fourths were without weapons and could offer no defense against the pursuing Federal troops.[96]

Confederate Naval Lieutenant Robert T. Chapman evacuated Battery Buchanan against Major Reilly's orders and left the garrison to be captured.

Colonel Lamb and General Whiting would have passed these sea-face gun chambers when the hospital was evacuated. Note that two of the cannon have been turned around to fire at the Federal troops near Sheperd's Battery. Timothy O'Sullivan image, 1865. *Photograph courtesy of the Library of Congress.*

Reilly was furious. First Fort Fisher had been deserted by General Bragg; but the final, devastating blow was delivered by Lieutenant Chapman when he fled Battery Buchanan and left the garrison to be captured by the Yankees.

Reilly later recalled that he had sent Captain Zachariah Adams to Battery Buchanan around 4 PM with orders for the naval commander to hold the battery and be ready to fight the enemy. Reilly further stated, "not to abandon the Battery for when I was forced out of Fort Fisher I would fall back on Buchanan and fight the enemy there." Captain Adams reported back with Chapman's cryptic reply. "Very well." Major Reilly "was confident Chapman was still in the battery for I thought him too good a soldier to abandon us." Major Reilly was gravely mistaken about Chapman.

"We had a splendid opportunity to retrieve our defeat and get away," Reilly recalled about the Confederates ability to defend Battery Buchanan. "If the armament of the battery was serviceable. . . .Our men were free from the destructive and demoralizing effect of the fire from the fleet. . . .The whole mode of fighting was changed. We would have regained courage and the enemy would not have captured us."[97]

Seaman Robert Watson kept a diary of the events of the battle including Lieutenant Chapman's decision to abandon his post at Battery Buchanan:

> As soon as we saw that the enemy had gained a footing and planted their hateful flag on the left of the works we knew that the fort was lost and Captain [Robert T.] Chapman had all hands mustered, the roll called, and he then informed us that the fort was lost and that it was useless for him to keep us here to be taken prisoners or slaughtered, that we could fight the battery for some time and probably do the enemy some damage but that we could not hold it for any length of time. He then ordered us in the boats.[98]

84

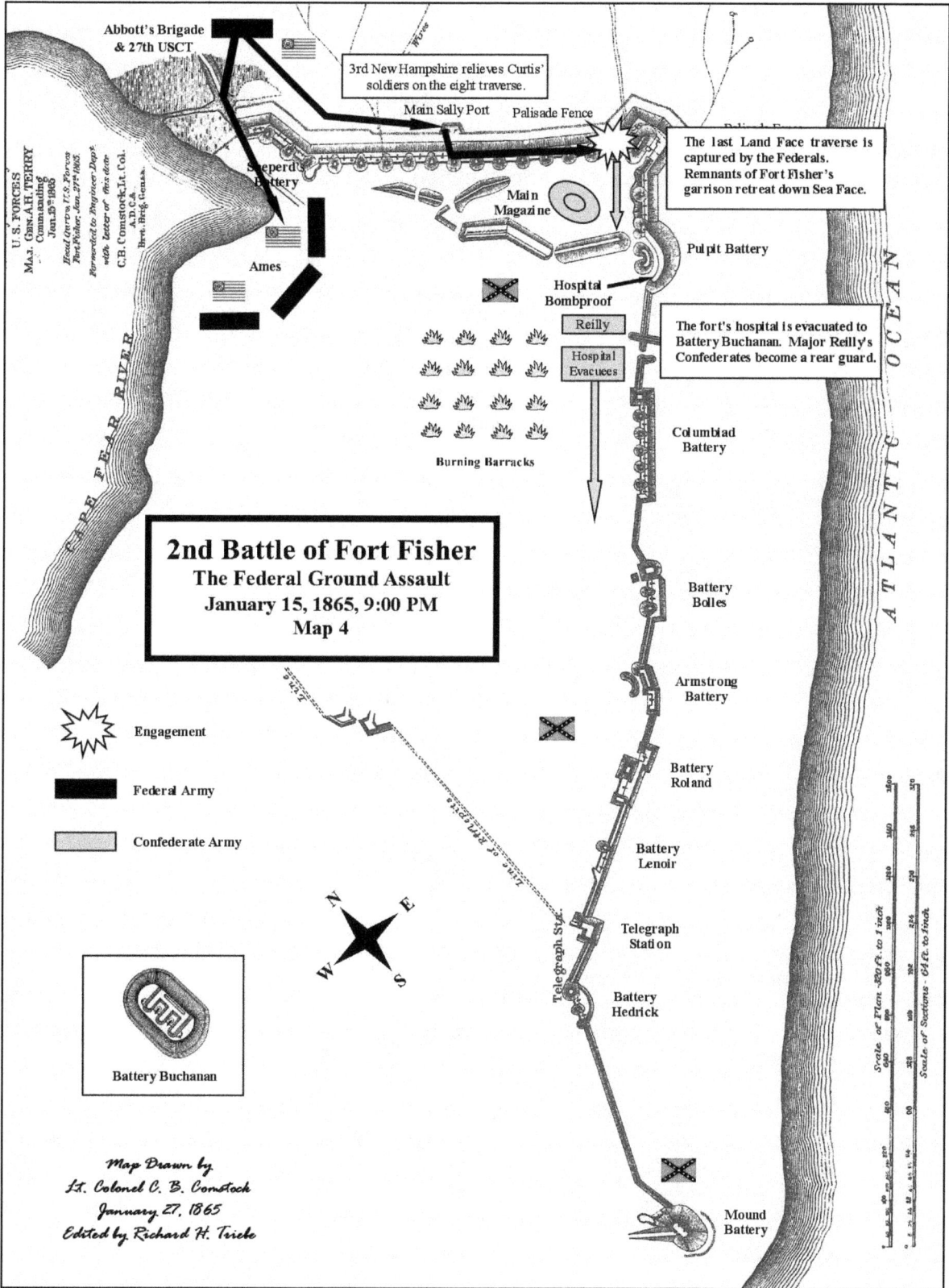

Abbott's Brigade
& 27th USCT

3rd New Hampshire relieves Curtis'
soldiers on the eight traverse.

Main Sally Port   Palisade Fence

Palisade Fence

The last Land Face traverse is
captured by the Federals.
Remnants of Fort Fisher's
garrison retreat down Sea Face.

Sheperd's
Battery

Main
Magazine

Pulpit Battery

Ames

Hospital
Bombproof

Reilly

The fort's hospital is evacuated to
Battery Buchanan. Major Reilly's
Confederates become a rear guard.

Hospital
Evacuees

Columbiad
Battery

Burning Barracks

Battery
Bolles

2nd Battle of Fort Fisher
The Federal Ground Assault
January 15, 1865, 9:00 PM
Map 4

Armstrong
Battery

Engagement

Battery
Roland

Federal Army

Battery
Lenoir

Confederate Army

Telegraph
Station

N
E
W
S

Battery
Hedrick

Battery Buchanan

Map Drawn by
Lt. Colonel C. B. Comstock
January 27, 1865
Edited by Richard H. Triebe

Mound
Battery

CAPE FEAR RIVER

ATLANTIC OCEAN

U.S. FORCES
Maj. Gen. A.H. TERRY
Commanding
Jan 15th 1865

Head Qtrs. U.S. Forces
Fort Fisher, Jan. 27th 1865.
Forwarded to Engineer Dept.
with letter of this date
C.B. Comstock, Lt. Col.
A.D.C.A.
Bvt. Brig. Genaa.

Scale of Plan - 320 ft. to 1 inch

Scale of Sections - 64 ft. to 1 inch

It appeared to Major Reilly no one was in command of the Confederate soldiers that crowded Battery Buchanan because all discipline had vanished. Men wandered about aimlessly or huddled into despondent groups to await the Yankees. Reilly was worried the Federal troops would assault the battery before they had a chance to surrender. If that happened, the unarmed men inside wouldn't stand a chance.

Captain Edgerly hauled down the Confederate flag atop the Mound Battery. Picture reprinted from *The Third New Hampshire and All About It, 1861-1865.*

The only safe thing to do was to go out and meet the Yankees and surrender before they reached the battery. Major Reilly, accompanied by Major James H. Hill, General Whiting's chief-of-staff, and Captain Alfred C. VanBenthuyson of the Confederate States Marine Corps, went toward Fort Fisher to meet the enemy commander. After they had gone 300 hundred yards from Battery Buchanan, Reilly halted and tied a white handkerchief to his sword. "It was a distressing time to me and the brave officers and men under my command," Reilly admitted.[99]

By 9:00 PM Federal troops had occupied so much of Fort Fisher that further bombardment was dangerous. General Terry signaled the fleet to cease-fire so his soldiers would have a clear path to Battery Buchanan. Regiments of General Abbott's brigade cautiously advanced in skirmish formation, securing the deserted Confederate batteries. Abbott's troops were joined by Colonel Albert M. Blackman's 27th Colored Troops in the mopping-up operation. The gunfire ceased and for the first time in many hours the soldiers could hear the crash of the surf on the beach nearby over the low moans of the wounded.

When Abbott's troops closed in on the Mound Battery, Captain J. Homer Edgerly of the 3rd New Hampshire, spied the Confederate flag flying on the crest of the battery. He raced up the huge sand hill, cut down the banner and rejoined his regiment. This was the same flag that Confederate Private Christopher Bland had replaced twice when it was shot down by the Federal Fleet.

The 7th Connecticut, commanded by Captain E. Lewis Moore, continued their cautious advance. As the line of skirmishers approached Battery Buchanan, Moore noticed a small group of Confederate officers holding a white flag. He halted his soldiers, selected a few men to accompany him, and went out to meet the Confederates.

Asked about the incident years later, Major Reilly recalled what he had said to Captain Moore. "I told that officer we surrendered and requested him to halt and retire his line and not let them fire on our defenseless troops. Capt. [Moore] with the instinct of a true soldier . . . complied with my request and reported, I think, to Genl. Abbott."[100]

The Confederate soldiers retreated from Fort Fisher to Battery Buchanan where they planned to renew their defensive struggle. Image Timothy O'Sullivan. *Photograph courtesy of the National Archives.*

Shortly before James Reilly's surrender, Confederate General Alfred H. Colquitt took a row boat downriver from Sugar Loaf to Battery Buchanan. Colquitt was ordered to take command of Fort Fisher and replace General Whiting. He was appalled by what he found at the battery. "[The] men were without guns, without accoutrements, some of them without hats, and all in a very bad state of demoralization," he reported to General Bragg.

Colquitt found General Whiting and Colonel Lamb on stretchers and told them Bragg had given him command of Fort Fisher. Lamb said that a fresh brigade of Confederate troops might retake Fort Fisher from the battle-weary Federals. Colquitt told Lamb that he could not help because he brought no troops. Lamb asked if he would take the seriously wounded General Whiting with him. "It was suggested that the general should take me with him as I was probably fatally wounded," Lamb recalled, "but I refused to leave, wishing to share the fate of the garrison, and desiring that my precious wife anxiously awaiting tidings across the river, where she watched the battle, should not be alarmed, spoke lightly of my wound." Suddenly, one of Colquitt's staff officers appeared, urging him to leave at once because it was reported that the Yankees were advancing on the battery. General Colquitt left abruptly, leaving Lamb and Whiting behind.[101]

General Terry was summoned to Battery Buchanan to receive the formal surrender of Fort Fisher from its commanding officer. Captain Adrian Terry, the general's brother, recalled what happened as they approached Battery Buchanan. "We saw a thin line of men standing by the shore several hundred in number . . . utterly cast down and helpless. Lying upon a stretcher . . . was Major General Whiting and near him was Colonel Lamb."

87

Confederate General Alfred H. Colquitt was sent to Battery Buchanan to relieve General Whiting of command. *Photograph courtesy of GeorgiaInfo.com.*

Seeing several blue-coated officers around him, General Whiting asked for the commanding officer. Major General Alfred H. Terry stepped forward and identified himself. "Alfred walked up to him and stated his name and rank," Captain Terry recalled. "Gen. Whiting said, 'I surrender, sir, to you the forces under my command. I care not what becomes of myself.'" General Terry promised Whiting that he and his solders would receive kind treatment.[102]

During the early morning hours of January 16th, the Confederates were taken under guard to the beach two miles north of the fort. Federal Colonel Alfred P. Rockwell wrote in his report:

The prisoners . . . were marched out of the work. My regiment [sixth Connecticut], with the Seventh New Hampshire, formed the guard to these prisoners, and marched them back through Fort Fisher, collecting others on the way, to the beach about two miles north of the fort, where they bivouacked. . . .My regiment was detailed to guard the camp of prisoners (about 1,800 in number) until about noon, when I was relieved.[103]

General Terry was presented with the Confederate flag that Captain Jonathan H. Edgerly had cut down from the Mound Battery. Eager to inform General Grant of the victory at Fort Fisher, Terry commandeered a horse from the battery. In a highly controversial act, General Terry then wrapped himself in the captured Confederate banner and rode to his headquarters. Captain Elridge remembered Terry's triumphant appearance. "Gen. Terry rode into the fort with the flag of [the Mound Battery] wound around his body. We gave him three cheers, when he made this remark: 'Boys, rather than that you should cheer for me, I ought to cheer for you.'"[104]

About 10:00 PM a rocket was fired from atop Fort Fisher's Northeast Bastion. This was the prearranged signal announcing the army's capture of the fort. Admiral Porter ordered three cheers to celebrate the fall of Fort Fisher. Ensign John Gratten wrote about this memorable night in his book, *Under the Blue Pennant*:

The Admiral never before gave an order which was so heartily obeyed. Everyone appeared to be wild with joy. . . .The flag ship signaled the fleet and repeated the Admiral's order, and in a few seconds thousand of voices were united in tremendous cheering. All the vessels were quickly illuminated, rockets and signal lights were flashing in the air, bells were rung and steam whistles were screaming forth the glad tidings.[105]

88

"My very heart went up in thanksgiving," reported Lieutenant Frank Lay of the 117th New York, who realized he was the only officer in his regiment not dead or wounded. "Never did I feel as I felt then," he wrote his wife. "Men grasped each other's hands and wept as brave men can in the hour of victory."[106]

While searching Battery Buchanan for important papers, Colonel Albert M. Blackman's officers discovered many letters written by the Confederate soldiers. Two of these letters were written by the same man and appeared in the *New York Herald-Tribune*, January 26, 1865:

Fort Fisher, Jan. 15th,

Dear Father: I am safe thus far but have suffered one of the most terrific bombardments that the world has ever known. No material damage is done the fort. The Confederate flag still floats triumphantly over old Fort Fisher. There is nothing left but her works; all the barracks are demolished. We are attacked by four monitors, eleven iron sides and fifty-six other vessels. The enemy has landed a very heavy force, and we are looking for an assault every moment from that direction. May God bless our arms with victory. I volunteered as courier and have been exposed in the hottest of the shelling most of the time. It is now 11 o'clock. I have been to the land front. Our pickets are firing into each other. Gen. Whiting and staff are down, all the boys are in fine spirits, and as long as we can fire a gun this fort will never show the white flag. May God bless you all and give us victory.
Yours, & c., (company) S. B. H.

Please send this note to Miss Sue M_____ and write soon.
J. B. H.

Fort Fisher, Jan. 15th, 1865,

My Dearest Sue: Night is about to close one of the most terrific bombardments that have ever happened on the continent. For 48 hours the enemy have shelled us most furiously, commencing Friday morning at 8:15. They have landed many troops, and we are looking for an assault any moment by land. Dear one, I can alone attribute my safety to a merciful Providence. I volunteered as courier on the morning of the engagement, and have been exposed to the hottest of the shelling. Several times I have escaped most miraculously; and if it is the Lord's will, I hope to endure all and come home safe. I have no time to write anymore. May God bless you; and if I never see you again, believe that I loved you, and have died fighting for my country and my all. Good bye my dear Sue. Yours forever.

J. B. H. [107]

Civil War soldiers had a habit of writing their initials instead of their names. This can be frustrating for a researcher especially when he is trying to identify a particular soldier. There was only one Confederate soldier in Fort Fisher with the initials J. B. H.. James B. Hunter of company F, 36th North Carolina Artillery, was killed in the battle. His letters were brought to Battery Buchanan to be put aboard the next steamer. The Confederate troopship *Sampson* was driven away from Battery Buchanan by the Federal bombardment before she could pick up the mail. This would explain why Hunter's letters were never delivered.[108]

Sheperd's Battery showing dismounted cannon and holes in palisade fence. *Photograph courtesy of Library of Congress.*

Chapter 6

The Aftermath

A Union soldier stands before a sea-face gun chamber. Note the blood on the dismounted cannon barrel to the left. Image Timothy O'Sullivan, *Photograph courtesy National Archives.*

Exhausted by the fierce combat the day before, many of the soldiers of both armies literally dropped where they were and slept. A few men were surprised when they awoke and found themselves sleeping next to the enemy or possibly a corpse. As the men slowly came awake the first thing they noticed was the smell. The pervasive odors of burnt sulfur, charred wood and the horrible stench of death were in the air. While some of the soldiers were visiting the latrine others were building campfires to cook their breakfast. Some men were early risers and as soon as it was light enough to see, they explored the fort. One *New York Tribune* correspondent aptly wrote these men were "breakfasting on horrors." The gruesome sights were everywhere:

Within the fallen fort were sights sickening and dreadful. Guns dismounted, guns split, guns broken; caps, clothes, bayonets, swords, muskets, rifles, scattered, battered, blood-stained; knapsacks, powder in bags, cartridges, dead horses, broken bottles, shells exploded, bullets, scabbards, bedding. And then the dead! Men in all postures, mangled in the head and body, with brains out, but with perfect features, covered with sand and grimed with powder. Arms, legs, hands, faces distorted, swollen, in all the traverses, in the trenches, in green water pools, in the bombproofs, upon the parapet, down in the embankments, here, there, everywhere. . . .The carrying past of the wounded, the groans of the dying, and the smell of blood and powder.[1]

Sailor James Cleer of the *Maratanza* was so frightened by the horrible things he saw inside Fort Fisher that he took a few swallows of whiskey to calm his nerves. "I never saw such a sight in all my life," he wrote his parents. "There was soldiers and sailors laying around me dead, some with arms and legs and heads off. I [found] a demijohn of whiskey. I filled a quart bottle with the whiskey, took a drink of it and I tell you it did not come amiss. I never wanted it more in my life than I did then."[2]

This picture from *Frank Leslie's Illustrated* shows the Federal troops preparing to bury the dead from the battle. One soldier is carrying a bundle of wooden stakes to use as grave markers while another stirs a can of paint to write the men's names.

SCENE AFTER THE BOMBARDMENT OF FORT FISHER—LAYING OUT DEAD U. S. SOLDIERS FOR BURIAL.

Another soldier wrote a letter to his brother describing the carnage inside the fort:

The scenes. . .were indescribably horrible. Great cannon lay in ruins, surrounded by the bodies of the defenders; men were found partly buried in graves dug by the shells which had slain them. . . .Some lay face downward in the sand, and others who had been close together when struck by an exploding shell had fallen in a confused mass, forming a mingled heap of broken limbs and mangled bodies.[3]

SUMMIT OF MOUND BATTERY, NEAR FORT FISHER.

Federal soldiers examine the Mound Battery's cannon. Notice the two lanterns used to signal blockade-runners. Picture is from *Frank Leslie's Illustrated Newspaper*, March 4, 1865.

After breakfast some of the more hearty men climbed the sixty-foot Mound Battery to get a view of the fort and to see the battery that had given them so much trouble during the battle. Federal Ensign John W. Grattan wrote of these experiences in his book *Under the Blue Pennant*:

[The Mound Battery] mounted two heavy guns which were in good order, the enemy having neglected to spike them before the surrender. The ground was thickly covered with the iron fragments of our shells, and one of the guns was splattered with the blood and brains of a rebel gunner who must have been engaged in training the gun—which was loaded—on our soldiers . . . when a fragment of a shell from the [fleet] struck him down."[4]

Paymaster Henry M. Rogers of the *Gettysburg* recalled the sights in Fort Fisher would "horrify even the stoutest heart. Devastation, ruin, [and] death in every attitude and every form, these are the things we lose sight of when the pride, pomp and circumstance of 'Glorious War' are mentioned."[5]

Visiting a wounded friend in a field hospital could also be a traumatic experience. The three Union hospitals were filled with so many patients that there was a shortage of surgeons to tend them. Regimental Chaplain T. D. Jones wrote:

The wounds are terrible on both sides and in the hospitals a heart of stone would have bled to see such sights. It was very cold by this time and many had to lie on the ground without covering while others lay in their blood for hours outside the fort where they had fallen. We were short of doctors and there was only one chaplain in Ames' command to help them. Everyone did their best. We were on our feet for three days and nights with little food or sleep, cleaning and binding up wounds.[6]

Chaplain Henry M. Turner also spent much of his time in the hospitals comforting the dying and the wounded:

It would be impossible to describe what I witnessed among the wounded. But one thing I must mention as a fact. I found twice the number of rebels calling upon God for mercy to what I found among our own wounded soldiers. One rebel particularly, whom I passed, was saying in a most pathetic tone, "O, Lord God, have mercy on me! Please have tender compassion on one who is a sinner, and comfort me in this hour of trial! O Lord, have mercy on me this one time more." When I commenced talking with him, and he discovered I was a chaplain, his countenance seemed to be illuminated with joy. But the prayer that went up from the rebel wounded bought off my prejudice, and I rendered them every comfort in my power.[7]

Shortly after the surrender of Fort Fisher General Ames ordered Lt. Colonel Zent to place guards on thirty-one bombproofs and magazines. Weary from the long night of battle, Zent made a deadly mistake by not any posting sentries on the main magazine. Apparently he was unaware the large mound of sand in the northeast corner of the fort was a powder magazine. It didn't seem to matter if he had posted guards or not because troops were allowed inside despite orders. Many Union soldiers, sailors and marines went from bombproof to bombproof searching for liquor, souvenirs and the spoils of war. "The soldiers were ransacking every nook and corner," Chaplain Henry M. Turner claimed, "in search of trophies and other memorials, such as tobacco, segars, clothes, pistols, etc." Some of the soldiers found a large quantity of liquor used for medicinal purposes and became intoxicated.[8]

The explosion of the main powder magazine occurred on the morning after the fort's surrender. *Harpers Weekly.*

In the early morning hours of January 16th a tremendous explosion rocked the fort. The fort's large reserve magazine, which contained 13,000 pounds of gunpowder, blew up. Unfortunately, the top of this magazine was an inviting area for weary soldiers to bed down for the night. The 4th New Hampshire, 115th and 169th New York regiments were among those who chose this grassy mound for their camp. A *New York Tribune* correspondent wrote:

This morning about 8 o'clock, as I had just entered and was walking leisurely through Fort Fisher, studying the record of horror before me, torn traverse by traverse, dismounted gun by gun, ghastly corpse by corpse, death and destruction all around that I might know of what I speak, I was suddenly startled by a terrific explosion and the sight of an immense column going high into the air. Following the instincts of nature and the example of those around me . . . I put myself under the best cover within reach.[9]

Surgeon James A. Mowris was searching for the dead of his regiment near the crest of a gun chamber when he heard a deep explosive sound. The violent explosion hurled him to the ground and buried him with falling sand and debris. Mowris wrote about his near death experience:

> I beheld an immense shaft of earth and rubbish . . . rising to the very clouds. . . . I found myself the victim of the most intense violence . . . Then came a distressing sense of suffocation with a clear conviction that my immediate death was inevitable. I felt the grave rudely closing around me, and realized the horrors of being buried alive. Then a temporary lull in the descent of the debris. Instinctively I thrust out a hand . . . [and] gained the air. Again was I . . . overwhelmed by a fresh fall of sand and rubbish . . . another struggle for life and I gained the atmosphere. The danger had passed, and I was still alive.[10]

Men from all over the fort rushed to the scene of the explosion to help rescue the victims. The huge magazine had disappeared leaving only a large crater. The victims of the disaster were seen here and there amid shattered pieces of timber. "On my right, lay a quivering face, all that was visible of a victim," Mowris recalled. "All the bodies [from the battle] that lay along the [slope], before the explosion had been suddenly buried in many nameless unmarked graves, while the surface of that general grave-yard was already dotted with the mutilated members of scores of new victims."[11]

The temporary graveyard for the Federal dead was about 250 feet north of the center of the landface. This photograph also shows the main sally-port and tunnel through the landface. *Photograph courtesy of the National Archives.*

There would never be an exact count of the casualties from the magazine explosion. Estimates of the dead and wounded ranged from 130 to 265 with most historians agreeing there were at least 200. However, the 3rd brigade reported that the 115th New York had 110 casualties; the 169th New York had 105 casualties; and the 4th New Hampshire had 50 casualties. This would place the army's casualties at 265. To complicate matters further, both the Federal Navy and Colonel Lamb also claimed to have lost men in the explosion.[12]

Confederate Private James Wright Farmer of the 3rd Battalion, North Carolina Light Artillery was captured and sent to Point Lookout Prison, Maryland. *Photograph courtesy of Pat Hoggard.*

Many of the Federal soldiers blamed the magazine explosion on rebel saboteurs. They knew about the Confederate minefield in front of the fort, so it was not beyond comprehension that the rebels would rig the powder magazine also. Lt. Colonel Nathan J. Johnson found some suspicious copper wires among the debris of the magazine. These wires were concealed underground and led to the Cape Fear River. Some Northern soldiers believed the copper wire was proof positive that this tragedy was no accident.

"I heard that the Yankees thought we blew the magazine up," Confederate Private John M. Johnston said, "and they were going to kill as many Confederates as the explosion had killed in Yankees. I felt sure if the report was true, I would be among the number killed."[13]

"This circumstance cast a serious gloom over our army than all the casualties which had happened on the previous day and caused more oaths to be uttered than I ever heard before," said Chaplain Henry M. Turner. "Many were for killing all the rebel prisoners, while others were for blowing them up too."[14]

On January 20th the Union Army held a "court of inquiry" to determine the cause of the magazine explosion. Following the testimony of many witnesses it was concluded "that the explosion was the result of carelessness" on the part of Federal soldiers, sailors and marines who were running about with burning torches in the fort and entering bombproofs while intoxicated.[15]

Lieutenant George Quimby of the 4th New Hampshire testified that as he was walking past the main magazine he saw several soldiers standing around the entrance, examining something that had been carried out:

One man said, 'Have you got all out?' The other replied, 'I have—perhaps not; they've got a light in there now,' (meaning the magazine). I then stepped to the entrance and inquired what it contained. Someone inside said, 'Boxes of powder.' I then ordered if they had a light to put it out, and cautioned them not to have any more, as it was very careless and dangerous. I then left the fort, and ten or fifteen minutes afterward the explosion took place.[16]

96

The number of casualties from the second battle of Fort Fisher is difficult to determine. The Union army records showed 184 killed and 749 wounded with 22 missing. This figure, however, does not include the casualties suffered by the navy. The Federal navy had 82 men killed, 269 wounded and 35 missing. This makes the combined total casualties for the Federal armed forces in the second battle of Fort Fisher, 266 men killed and 1,018 wounded and 57 missing.[17]

The Confederate casualties are difficult to determine since we have no official figures. Typically after a battle both the Union and Confederate officers would submit a written report to their superiors explaining their regiment's activities and casualties. Because the Confederate officers at Fort Fisher were sent to prison no report was ever submitted. Any Confederate histories written about the battle of Fort Fisher were done years later and usually appear in regimental histories and contain no useful information as to numbers. This being the case, we can only piece together the facts that we have. We know from General Terry's report that 1,546 Confederate soldiers were captured at Fort Fisher. Of these 286 were wounded. We could perhaps determine the Confederate dead by subtracting 1,546 men from the size of the garrison. Colonel Lamb had reported this to be about 1,900. But was this the true size of the garrison on January 15th?

When Colonel Lamb was asked how many South Carolina soldiers were inside Fort Fisher on the 15th of January, his response was there were 350 men from the 11th, 21st and 25th South Carolina. It is difficult to tell how many men landed since only part of Hagood's 1,100 man brigade had been allowed to come ashore before the Federal bombardment drove the Confederate troopship away from Battery Buchanan. The only sure way to achieve an accurate account would be to examine each soldier's record at the National Archives to see if he had been killed or captured at Fort Fisher on January 15, 1865. This was no small task since Hagood's entire Brigade numbered several thousand. However, every man in this brigade was checked to see if he had been at Fort Fisher. Of this group 482 South Carolina troops were reported inside the walls of the Fort. This new information would add 132 more soldiers to the fort's garrison than previously thought. Lamb's force would now total 2,032. If we subtract the 1,546 men General Terry reported as captured, we arrive at a total of 486 Confederate dead. This figure is close to the original estimate of 500 dead.[18]

Colonel Alfred P. Rockwell's 6th Connecticut was assigned to guard the Confederate prisoners.

The Federal dead were buried in two temporary cemeteries in front of the land-face. One graveyard for Federal officers was located 250 feet north of the center of the main sally-port. The other much larger cemetery for the enlisted men was in front of Sheperd's Battery at the western end of the land-face. The Confederate dead were buried in the post cemetery. These men were later reinterred at Wilmington's Oakdale Cemetery and Wilmington National Cemetery.[19]

Federal Colonel Alfred P. Rockwell and the 6th Connecticut were assigned to guard the Fort Fisher prisoners two miles north of the fort. The Confederate soldiers were separated into manageable 150 man groups and spent a miserable night on the exposed seashore. "We slept on the cold beach," Private William Haigh remembered, "the screaming winter blast blowing unobstructed fresh from the ocean, and the damp ground, (always colder and damper near salt water) chilling us through our blankets."[20]

The morning of the 16th brought many changes for the prisoners. As the Confederates awoke they were reminded that life would never be the same. Above the fort a large Federal flag had replaced the Confederate banner on the post's flagpole. Evidence of the terrible struggle was everywhere. The dead were strewn along the Federal navy's route where they had charged the Northeast Bastion. The Confederates comfortable barracks had been destroyed and replaced by the bitterly cold, windswept beach. "The morning found us strongly guarded," William Haigh remembered. "A line of sentinels surrounded us, and gunboats & frigates lay off [the fort]." The Confederate prisoners were saddened by the loss of so many of their friends, but they were also relieved that the bloody fighting was finally over. As the haggard men looked around and saw the strong Union guard watching them, the reality of their uncertain future seeped in. If they were sent to prison, who would care for their families? The men's anxiety was heightened when the fort's powder magazine exploded, causing the guards to cast vengeful glances at the prisoners.[21]

Sergeant Alfred B. Beers, 6th Connecticut.

Fortunately, not all the guards saw their captives as the despicable enemy, but fighting men just like themselves. These rugged men were basically of the same mold. The Confederates had the same complaints that soldiers have griped about for ages; the quality of their rations, the officers, and the foolish orders they were forced to obey. Like any devoted husband or father they also talked lovingly of their families. Although it remained unspoken, the Federal soldiers knew if things had gone badly for them during the battle they could be the ones being guarded instead of the Confederates. It wasn't long before the Federal and Confederate soldiers began freely talking to one another. One thing led to another, and a few of the guards began to share what food they had in their haversacks.

"They appreciated those Union rations," remembered Captain Leonard R. Thomas, "for those of the Confederacy in January 1865 were poor in quality and meager in quantity . . . composed mostly of coarse corn and not an ounce of sugar or coffee. It was almost pathetic to see how those iron-sided veterans took to the Union coffee. As they drank it, they were heard to say, 'This is the first we've tasted since early in 1862.' Those men had marched, toiled and fought during the last year of the war on rations which might have caused a mutiny had they been served to the Union army. . . There was not a man among the victors who did not thereby get an access (sic) of admiration for the gallant men whom the fortunes of war had made our prisoners."[22]

"Glad enough were we to get anything to eat, and thanks to the Masonic Order, I found friends among my enemies," said William H. Haigh. "I shall ever remember with grateful heart Captain Wm. S. Marble, 7th Conn. Vols, and Rev. Mr. Eaton, Chaplain of the same Regt. who not only ministered to my then present necessities, but gave me money to aid me as a prisoner."[23]

98

On Wednesday morning the Confederate prisoners were marched back through the fort to the wharf near Battery Buchanan. Here they were loaded onto the transports *California, DeMolay, General Lyon* and *North Point* to begin the arduous five-day voyage north to their respective prisons.

Private Haigh describes his journey aboard the *North Point* in a letter to his wife Kate:

You know that the prisoners from Fort Fisher arrived here [Point Lookout, MD] on Sunday the 22nd of January, 1865, but you do not know, for no pen could describe, or tongue tell the awful horrors of that terrible sea voyage from Fort Fisher to this place. . . .From Wednesday the 18th until Sunday the 22nd, late in the evening, six hundred of us were in the hold of the ship *North Point*. I will not attempt to describe the scene. Memory sometimes sickens me with a retrospective view of that motley medley of men, almost stifled and crushed to death. There poor McNeill fell a victim to "Black Hole in Calcutta" cruelty [prisoners dying from suffocation and crushing]; and others had sown the fatal seed of these terrible maladies that made them inmates of Point Lookout Grave Yard. Cooped up in that 'cattle transport' (for such it literally was) midst the darkness of night, the hatches down, men writhing in agony, many blaspheming, cursing and quarrelling, it made one feel that he was next door neighbor to the damned spirits of the infernal regions.

Morning after morning came, but still the endless waste of waters, tossed and heaving with a winter's storm. I was one of those whose duty it was to give out the rations—and this enabled me to move about a little on deck, and thus get a little fresh air, though bitter cold with drifting snow.[24]

Private John M. Johnston also wrote of his experience:

After remaining [on the beach at Fort Fisher] for about two days, [we] were marched back to the fort . . . and put into small boats and carried to a large steamer. After being put on the steamer, we were put in charge of a Negro guard. We had been guarded by white men up to this time. I had never seen a Negro soldier before so you can imagine how we Confederate prisoners felt. We didn't know what they were going to [do] with us or where they were going to cary (sic) us. And right then, I felt like I didn't care where they carried us or what became of us. I was reckless, felt like I had rather be dead than alive. Anyway the vessel with about 800 prisoners put out to sea, I stood on its stern and looked and watched as long as I could see a sight of land. When I could no longer see land I felt that all hope was lost. [Where] I was going I knew not . . . but found out after a while that we were bound for Point Lookout, a Yankee prison situated on the Chesapeak (sic) Bay.

After being on the ocean for about five days about 10 o'clock on 22 of January. We anchored in sight of the prison. It was my first and last sea voyage and rough one it was. The vessel came very near being broken to pieces by striking a rock as we

Chaplain Jacob Eaton was kind to the prisoners. Eaton died of disease a few months later in Wilmington.

99

passed Cape Lookout. One of the prisoners died on the way and was buried after we arrived at prison.[25]

The fall of Fort Fisher sent shock waves racing throughout the world. Like all disasters it was felt hardest in the area closest to the epicenter. The Confederacy was already reeling from one calamity after another and now this terrible news seemed to seal her fate as surely as the port of Wilmington had been sealed from the outside world. Not only had the Confederacy lost their last major seaport, but it also lost its ability to supply General Lee's army with food and equipment. By late February Lee was already feeling the pinch of not enough provisions and reported that his men were deserting by the hundreds every night.

Confederate President Jefferson Davis sent Congressman Duncan F. Kenner to Europe a week after the fall of Fort Fisher. Kenner was to advise the governments of Great Britain and France of the Confederacy's willingness to emancipate its slaves if either nation would recognize the sovereignty of the Confederate States. Both governments declined to do so, seeing the fall of Fort Fisher as the death knell of the Confederacy.

President Davis realized the Confederacy was sinking and tried to salvage what he could. He appointed a three-man team to travel to Hampton Roads, Virginia, to discuss a peace settlement with United States officials. These men met with President Abraham Lincoln and Secretary of State William Seward aboard the ship *River Queen* on February 3, 1865. Historian Rod Gragg wrote: "The meeting failed to produce a settlement. Lincoln offered amnesty to Confederate leaders and indicated slave owners might receive some Federal compensation for their freed slaves, but rejected the suggestion of an armistice. Instead, he insisted the Southern states surrender, return to the Union and comply with some form of compensated emancipation. Lincoln was unyielding on the question of an armistice— the South *had* to surrender and rejoin the Union. The peace conference was a failure. Lincoln was no longer interested in negotiating a peace settlement, Davis said, and instead now insisted on a 'humiliating surrender.' The Confederate President attributed Lincoln's change in attitude to the fall of Fort Fisher: the loss of the Confederacy's last major port and the resulting isolation of the South had convinced Lincoln that the death of the Confederacy was only a matter of time."[26]

Confederate President Jefferson Davis tried to negotiate a peace settlement with the Federal government.

No one seemed more shocked about the fall of Fort Fisher than General Bragg. After learning of the fort's surrender from General Colquitt, Bragg telegraphed General Lee at 1 AM on January 16, 1865:

"I am mortified at having to report the unexpected capture of Fort Fisher, with most of its garrison, at about 10 o'clock to-night. Particulars not known."[27]

Bragg's reputation was on shaky ground after his defeats at Murfreesboro, Missionary Ridge, and at Chattanooga, Tennessee. Bragg, knowing his critics would relish the opportunity to blame him for the loss of Fort Fisher, began a search for a scapegoat to divert attention from himself. The most logical choice would be to find fault with General Whiting's or Colonel Lamb's leadership. Bragg was unable do this since both men had been severely wounded during the battle and were considered heroes. The citizens would never allow these patriotic men to be attacked. However, the fort's garrison was another story.

In his official report Bragg wrote: "The (Federal) army column, preceded by a single regiment, approached along the river and entered the work on that flank almost unopposed."[28] This must have been news to the men who fought a life and death struggle at the River Road gate. Private Zachery T. Fulmore, who was captured at the gate, would have to live with the shame of General Bragg's lies the rest of his life. In 1883 he wrote to Colonel Lamb about an experience he had returning home:

Confederate General Braxton Bragg tried to save his reputation by shifting the blame for Fort Fisher's surrender to someone else.

On my way home from prison in the later part of May, 1865, I was put off the boat up at Meares' Bluff and walked the ties up to Lumberton. At the end of the first day's journey we stopped at the farm house of Colonel Joe Green, a prominent citizen of Bladen County, to get something to eat. We received excellent treatment, as he knew some of my family connection, but he said he was very much mortified to know that we had acted so cowardly as to let the enemy come in at that gate unopposed. I protested that we had done all that we could; told how many men we had killed and wounded right there, etc, etc. He said General Bragg was an experienced fighter—saw the whole affair, and his statement would outweigh the statement of anybody else, but seeing our ragged and starved condition and knowing of our sufferings subsequently, he expressed a kindly sympathy, and gave us food. I assured him he would learn the truth someday, and hoped it would be soon. I have never seen him since, but presume he died under the impression that General Bragg had given us our just deserts. Many years afterwards, however, I left the State of Virginia on a big disgust over the war reminiscences . . . I despaired of ever overcoming the impression created by General Bragg and dropped the whole subject.[29]

General Whiting was extremely vocal in their criticism of Bragg. Whiting wrote to General Lee from his death bed at Governors Island in New York Harbor:

I think that the result might have been avoided, and Fort Fisher held, if the commanding general had done his duty. I charge him with this loss; with neglect of

101

duty in this, that he either refused or neglected to carry out every suggestion made to him in official communications by me for the disposition of the troops. . . . I charge him further with making no effort whatever to create a diversion in favor of the beleaguered garrison during the three days' battle, by attacking the enemy. . . . I desire that a full investigation be had of this matter and these charges which I make; they will be fully borne out by the official records. . . . I demand in justice to the country, to the army, and to myself, that the course of this officer be investigated.[30]

No investigation of Bragg's conduct was ever done. Some say it was too late in the war to do anything. Others said it was because General Bragg and President Jefferson Davis were friends.

General Whiting was healing from his wounds and appeared to be doing better, but died unexpectedly of chronic diarrhea on March 10, 1865. Known as the soldier's disease, this illness claimed more lives than any other disease in the Civil War.

Fort Fisher's importance to the Confederate war effort was largely ignored by historians until fairly recently. Even Ken Burns' lengthy Civil War documentary failed to mention Fort Fisher. Perhaps the battle's significance was overshadowed by President Lincoln's assassination and then by the end of the war itself. In either case, Fort Fisher was mostly forgotten by everyone except the people in southeastern North Carolina.

Colonel Lamb could not forget the sacrifice made by those brave men who defended the fort against all comers. At a reunion in 1875, Lamb addressed the gallant veterans of Fort Fisher and paid them the ultimate compliment:

I stand here a witness to the heroic bravery of that small body of North Carolina troops, assisted by a mere handful of Confederate sailors and marines, who after the fort was entered and its citadel captured, and they might have surrendered with honors, refused to submit, but withstood for hours the fierce assaults of three splendid brigades of Federal soldiers led by gallant officers. They disputed hand-to-hand every inch of ground until pushed by the force of irresistible numbers to the very brink of the sea, and then surrendered only when their ammunition was expended and all hope lost.

North Carolina need cross no ocean to search amid Roman and Grecian stories for examples of self-sacrifice in defense of home and country, for here among her own sons, upon her own soil, the valor of Pharsalia and of Thermopylae were reproduced, and no correct history of this grand old State can be written unless the defense of Fort Fisher by North Carolinians in January, 1865, be placed among the most heroic deeds in the drama of our Civil War.[31]

Chapter 7

ELMIRA PRISONER OF WAR CAMP

The Fatal Journey of 518 Confederate Soldiers

"If there ever was a hell on Earth, Elmira Prison was that hell, but it was not a hot one, for the thermometer was often 40 degrees below zero," Former Confederate prisoner F.S. Wade, 1865. [1]

An artist's sketch of Elmira Prisoner of War Camp appeared in the April, 1865, issue of *Harper's Weekly*.

The American Civil War has often been thought of as the first modern war. Certainly, it saw many warfare firsts: the first use of extensive trench warfare; the first use of rifled weapons; the first bombardment of civilian areas like Atlanta, Charleston and Vicksburg. It was also the first time mines and hand grenades were used. Unfortunately these destructive ideas extended to the prison system as well.

As the war dragged on and feelings became more bitter, the prisons became less of a temporary detention center and more like long-term concentration camps. During the last year of the war, prison camps ultimately evolved into retaliatory prisons or death camps.

The Confederate soldiers captured at Fort Fisher saw the worst that the Northern prisons had to offer. Unfortunately these men became prisoners during a critical time in Elmira Prison camps development. These prisoner of war camps had four long years to fester, and they were ready to spew their poison onto anyone who entered their gates. Most of the soldiers captured at Fort Fisher lost their winter clothing when their barracks caught fire and burned to the ground from the Federal bombardment. When these men were sent north in January all they had was the clothing they wore during the battle. This was woefully insufficient for the frigid temperatures and snowy conditions of upstate New York where Elmira Prisoner of War Camp is located. Fort Fisher prisoner Thaddeus C. Davis recalled, "We arrived (at Elmira) about eight o'clock in the evening, in four feet of snow, and many prisoners had neither blankets nor coats. We were kept standing in ranks in the street for half an hour before starting for the prison."[2]

The retaliatory phase of the Northern prison system was at its height just as the Fort Fisher prisoners arrived at Elmira. This unwritten policy prescribed that high ranking Union officials were to give the Confederate prisoners the same sort of treatment that the Union prisoners were receiving in the South. All of these things along with an unhealthy environment, an inadequate diet, and lack of proper clothing, shelter and medical attention contributed to Elmira's staggering 46 percent death toll in just a few months.

The soldiers from Fort Fisher had to endure many hardships in the perilous months ahead. To understand why these men were so susceptible to disease we must appreciate their desperate situation. These men were physically and mentally exhausted. Not only had they been captured after a furious battle but they were being taken North to prison and an uncertain future. They did not know what would become of them or their families. The overwhelming worry, the drastic change in climate and diet and overcrowded conditions all added up to make these men prime candidates for death and disease. Is it any wonder that in February of 1865 inspecting officer Lieutenant James R. Reid, wrote, "The Fort Fisher prisoners arrived in cold weather very much depressed, poorly clad, and great numbers were soon taken sick with pneumonia and diarrhea, rapidly assuming a typhoid character." Prisoner James Huffman also remembered the influx of soldiers from Fort Fisher. "A large number of North and South Carolinians had been captured at a fort on the North Carolina coast—hale, hearty looking fellows. These men crowded us very much at first, but in two or three weeks they were nearly all gone to the hospitals, and most of them died."[3]

To better understand what was happening in Northern prisons at the time Fort Fisher fell we must go back to the beginning of Elmira's existence and see how it evolved into the worst prison camp in the North.

Secretary of War Edwin McMasters Stanton

When the war began there was an orderly system of prisoner exchange that allowed the soldiers to go home after a brief period of captivity usually lasting 30 days or less. Many times commanding generals exchanged prisoners on the battlefield using only a gentleman's agreement. President Abraham Lincoln did not condone these exchanges because to do so he would have to recognize the Confederate government as a legitimate, sovereign power. Therefore, no general exchanges could be permitted. Secretary of War Edwin M. Stanton told Major General George B. McClellan, "*It is not deemed proper for officers bearing flags of truce in respect to the exchange of prisoners to hold any conference with the rebel officers upon the general subject of the existing contest or upon any other subject than what relates to the exchange of prisoners.*" The battlefield exchanges, which worked quite well, now ceased to exist.

Mounting pressure from politicians, newspapers, petitions, forced congress to act. On December 12, 1861, congress passed a joint-resolution that said, "*Resolved, by the Senate and House of Representatives of the United States of America in Congress assembled, that the President of the United States be requested to inaugurate systematic measures for the exchange of prisoners in the present rebellion.*" Now President Lincoln had no choice but to renew the prisoner exchange. After much debate the Dix-Hill Cartel was created and introduced July 22, 1862. Several important points of the new exchange policy were that prisoners should be exchanged within 10 days of capture and paroled prisoners could not rejoin the military until their enemy counterpart had reached his own lines.

The prisoner exchange cartel was extremely fragile because of distrust and hostility on both sides. Finally the cartel broke down because Confederate President Jefferson Davis suspended the parole of Union officers following the execution of William Mumford, a New Orleans citizen, by Union General Benjamin F. Butler earlier that year. In reaction, Union Secretary of War Edwin M. Stanton ordered a halt to all exchanges of commissioned officers.

This photograph shows a prisoner exchange at Camp Fisk near Vicksburg, Mississippi. Early in the war prisoners were exchanged on the battlefield using only a gentleman's agreement.

In early 1863 Secretary of War Edwin M. Stanton directed General Henry Halleck to drastically reduce the number of exchanges. On May 20th Stanton ordered Colonel Hoffman to halt the prisoner exchanges, giving no reason for the abrupt stop. Historians differ on the motivation behind Stanton's order. The most popular theory suggests the Federal government halted the prisoner exchanges because the Confederate authorities refused to exchange black soldiers. It is true the South would not exchange the black troops who had been captured. The Confederates maintained that these Negro soldiers were escaped slaves and were therefore recaptured property. Judge Robert Ould, the Confederate Commissioner of Exchange, said these soldiers would be returned to where they had been captured so they could be dealt with according to the laws of that state. He also added the South was willing to make an exception and exchange free blacks. However, the Confederates

105

refused to exchange white officers who had been captured in command of black troops. The South claimed these men were guilty of inciting servile insurrection and would either be put to death or otherwise punished at the discretion of the courts. Despite all the threats no white officer was ever executed for commanding a Negro regiment.[4]

The reason Secretary of War Edwin M. Stanton and General Ulysses S. Grant did not want to exchange Union prisoners is because it was felt these men would take resources away from the Confederacy and drain its strength further by having to care for thousands of Union prisoners. It was also felt the exchanged Confederate prisoners would be healthy enough to go right back into the Army while the North would only receive sick and broken men in return.

In mid-August of 1864 Lieutenant General Ulysses S. Grant helped to end the prisoner exchange cartel. Grant felt that the Confederate Government was violating the cartel's rules by allowing released prisoners to rejoin the military before they were paroled. Grant wrote General Benjamin Butler, the Union's commissioner of exchange, and said: "It is hard on our men held in Southern prisons not to exchange them, but it is humanity to those left in the ranks to fight our battles. Every man we hold, when released on parole or otherwise, becomes an active soldier against us at once either directly or indirectly. If we commence a system of exchange which liberates all prisoners taken, we will have to fight on until the whole South is exterminated." Then Grant wrote these hauntingly, prophetic words. "If we hold those caught they amount to no more than dead men."[5] Surely he did not mean that literally, but thousands of men in both armies would ultimately die because the prisoner exchange had ended. Because of this decision civil war prisons evolved from temporary detention facilities to long-term concentration camps and a few would become the closest thing to death camps the North had ever seen. Secretary of War Edwin McMasters Stanton agreed with General Grant that holding Confederate prisoners of war would weaken the Southern army and bring the war to an earlier conclusion.

The three-story Mears brothers' observatory can be seen to the right of this photograph. Northern entrepreneurs built these towers to profit from the prisoners' misery. *Photograph courtesy of the Chemung County Historical Society.*

While halting the prisoner exchange did not directly affect the prisoners from Fort Fisher, they were indirectly affected by the overcrowding in Northern prisons that led to disease raging out of control. During its twelve months of existence Elmira had a death rate of 24.4 percent, the highest for any Northern prison camp. My research has shown that Elmira was responsible for many more deaths than the history books tell us.

A new problem arose with the end of the prisoner exchange. If the North continued to capture prisoners and could not release any, where would the new prisoners be kept? A suitable camp was located just a few miles north of the Pennsylvania border in western New York State. In 1861 "Camp Chemung" was a new training facility built to answer President Lincoln's call for 75,000 volunteers to help put down the Southern insurrection. The camp now lay deserted only a mile west of Elmira, New York, then a city of 8,800 people. Elmira had many advantages for housing a prisoner of war camp. It had excellent railroad connections, a thriving lumber business to supply wood for barracks and fuel for the fires to fight the harsh northern winters, and abundant fresh water from the Chemung River. It was also located in a valley that produced ample fruits and vegetables. The addition of fruits and vegetables into a prisoner's diet was vital for the prevention of scurvy.

Camp Chemung officially became Elmira Prisoner of War Camp in June of 1864. The thirty-two acre site lay along the banks of the Chemung River. A one acre lagoon, called Foster's Pond, stood within the walls of the stockade. The pond was a backwash from the river that served as a latrine and garbage dump. Prison buildings were located on the high northern bank of the lagoon. The lower southern level, known to flood easily, later became a hospital area for thousands of smallpox and diarrhea victims. The entire prison was surrounded by a twelve-foot-high fence which contained a wooden walkway for the guards. This walkway was eight feet off the ground with forty-seven sentry boxes set at intervals in case of inclement weather.

Turning a dollar on someone else's misfortune seemed to be the motivation behind a man building an observation tower across the street from Elmira Prisoner of War Camp. Near the end of July Mr. Nichols purchased the northeast corner next to the prison and built a two-story observation platform. Then he erected a sign reading, "an observation tower from which to view the prisoners—admission 15¢, refreshments served below." The New York Evening Post of August 17, 1864, stated that "a man of genius" "who sought his opportunity and was equal to the occasion, suddenly appeared at the camp, and apparently determined that the rebels should make his fortune."[5]

el William Hoffman, the Commissary General of
ers, in front of his office. *Photograph courtesy of the*
ung County Historical Society.

The *Elmira Daily Advertiser* reported that it was "often crowded with sightseers and must prove a paying institution."[6] People flocked to the observatory to get a glimpse of the rebel prisoners. One business partner said the tower paid for itself in two weeks. *The Rochester Daily Union* reported that the proprietor of the observatory "intends to keep in this tower a powerful glass, by the aid of which visitors can see the vermin which are said to be so plenty upon the bodies of the prisoners."[7] Body lice called "graybacks" infested every part of Elmira. James Huffman remembered, "Some fellows did not wash their clothes nor themselves and you could see the graybacks crawling over their clothes on the outside."[6] This observatory was so successful that several weeks later another tower was built down the street from the original. W. and W. Mears made their observatory twenty feet higher and charged their customers five cents less. This new tower boasted three decks instead of two and promised "a fine view of the rebel prisoners." Wooden stands sprang up where hungry visitors could buy ginger cakes, crackers and peanuts or refresh themselves with a cool lemonade, beer or liquor. A writer would recall three decades later, "They took on the look of a long row of rude wooden booths like those at a fair, or more like those that spring up in a night along a street that is the route to the grounds where a circus tent is to be spread."[9]

One observer claimed the Confederates "have a rough appearance, wearing as they do, clothing of as many hues as the rainbow but none so brilliant. The men are generally of good size, and what would be called fair specimens of the race, if they were not Rebels."[10]

A Tennessee sergeant, G.W.D. Porter, recalled how "hundreds would crowd daily to get a view of the prisoners—many to gloat, perhaps, on their sufferings; some to gaze in wonder and awe upon the ragged, bob-tailed crew who had on many fields conquered their best armies; and some, no doubt, to sigh for an exchange of these men for fathers, sons, and brothers who were suffering kindred miseries at Libby, Salisbury and Andersonville."[11] James Huffman remembered there was "a constant stream of people winding their way to the top of these observatories to get a glimpse of the Rebs, as they supposed us to be like some kind of curious, monkey-shaped animals."[12]

The diary of Ausburn Towner was discovered thirty years lafter the war and described his visit to the observatories:

Colonel Benjamin Tracy became Elmira's post commander on September 20, 1864. Tracy would be in charge during the prison camp's most difficult months. *Photograph courtesy of the Chemung County Historical Society.*

"It was like looking down into an immense bee-hive. There was a constant motion on all sides, but without noise or confusion that could be heard. Groups were standing here and there, formed one minute, broken up the next; some men had built a fire underneath a tree and were baking corn-meal cakes; someone was coming or going every instant to or from every building whose entrance was in sight, and many were seated in the shadow of the trees whittling or fashioning some object, the character of which the distance forbade making out. In the space between the buildings and the fence nearest sat a small circle of men, with one on his feet who seemed to be speaking and making the most violent gestures. When he finished he seated himself in his place in the ring and another rose to go through similar exercises in his turn. A few feet from these men were five men playing cards. In the corner close at hand was a large tent that had a lonesome look. Into it, during the half hour of our visit, came two men five times, bearing each time on a stretcher the dead body of a man covered over with a piece of canvas." Towner did acknowledge that he and his friends all "speedily grew melancholy over the spectacle and cut our visit to the top of the tower very short."[13]

Both observatories and the refreshment stands did a thriving business through September. [14] The *Elmira Daily Gazette* proudly proclaimed: "Upper Observatory (the original observation tower) should be visited by all strangers and citizens. The pictures taken from there will always be remembered with delightful interest. Photograph views of the rebel camp, and surroundings . . . have been taken and can be obtained by the public in a few days."[15]

On September 19, the lucrative observatory business came to an end. The Elmira officials were concerned that the towers could be used for communication between rebel spies on the outside and the prisoners. It was also possible, they theorized, that the towers might be used to organize an escape. The commissary general of prisoners ordered Captain John Elwell, Elmira's assistant quartermaster, to seize the ground occupied by the two observatories. The Confederates were relieved that these observatories were no longer in use. "I am surprised that Barnum has not taken the prisoners off the hands of Abe, divided them into companies, and carried them in caravans through the country," wrote prisoner Anthony M. Keiley.[16]

About this time Federal Master Sergeant Washington S. Toland of the 83rd New York wrote a letter to the editor of the *New York Times*. He had been a prisoner in Confederate Belle Isle and Libby prisons in Richmond, Virginia. The newspaper printed his story in April, 1864, under the title of "Prison Life at Richmond—Its Cruelties." Toland described these cruelties as lack of adequate food, clothing and shelter. Lonnie Speer's book, *Portals Of Hell: Military Prisons of the Civil War,* lists Libby prison as having only twenty deaths at the end of the war and Belle Isle, 300 deaths. To put this into perspective, Belle Isle had as many prisoners as Elmira did but only 1/10 as many deaths.[17]

Secretary of War Edwin Stanton received a copy of Master Sergeant Toland's letter. About the same time Stanton also heard from the Commissary General of Prisoners, Colonel William Hoffman, who wrote, "I respectfully suggest, as a means of compelling the rebels to adopt a less barbarous policy toward the prisoners in their hands that the rebel officers at Johnson's Island be allowed only half rations; that their clothing be reduced to what is only sufficient to cover their nakedness, and that they be denied the privilege of purchasing the articles allowed to other prisoners."[18]

On May 3rd Colonel Hoffman filed a report of his observation of Union prisoners who had been returned from Richmond. The returning prisoners were so mentally and physically deteriorated that Hoffman became convinced that Union prisoners of war were being deliberately starved to death. Again Hoffman urged that retaliatory measures be put in place.

Secretary of War Stanton had always suspected that Union prisoners were receiving poor treatment from the Confederates. Now, with the aid of Colonel Hoffman and the *New York Times*, he urged a retaliation bill. On May 5th Stanton wrote President Lincoln, telling him of the abuses suffered by Union prisoners of war. The secretary of war then proposed that "precisely the same rations and treatment be henceforth practiced to the whole number of rebel officers remaining in our hands that are practiced against either soldiers or officers in our service held by the rebels."[19]

On May 4th Stanton wrote Senator Benjamin Wade, "The enormity of the crime committed by the rebels towards our prisoners for the last several months is not known or realized by our own people, and cannot but fill with horror the civilized world when the facts

Senator Benjamin F. Wade wrote Joint Resolution 97 and read it on the floor of the Senate. The resolution later became known as the Retaliation Bill.

are revealed. There appears to have been a deliberate system of savage and barbarous treatment and starvation."[20]

Senator Wade then wrote *Resolution 97* and read it on the floor of the Senate on January 26, 1865. This joint resolution would have the full effect of a law if passed by both houses of Congress and signed by the chief executive. Congress passed it, but to his credit President Lincoln did not sign it. The first part of the resolution is included here to show the mindset of the Northern politicians at the time. The men captured at Fort Fisher were going north to prison about this time and would feel the repercussions from this legislation.

Joint resolution 97 read:

S.R. 97
Mr. Wade submitted the following amendment.
JOINT RESOLUTION
Advising retaliation for the cruel treatment of prisoners by the insurgents.

"Whereas it has come to the knowledge of Congress that great numbers of our soldiers who have fallen as prisoners of war into the hands of the insurgents, have been subjected to treatment unexampled for cruelty in the history of civilized war, and finding its parallels only in the conduct of savage tribes; a treatment resulting in the death of multitudes by the slow but designed process of starvation and by mortal diseases occasioned by insufficient and unhealthy food, by wanton exposure of their persons to the inclemency of the weather and by deliberate assassination of innocent and unoffending men; and the murder in cold blood of prisoners after surrender; and whereas a continuance of these barbarities, in contempt of the laws of war and in disregard of the remonstrance's of the national authorities, has presented to us the alternative of suffering our brave soldiers thus to be destroyed, or to apply the principle of retaliation for their protection: Therefore, resolved by the Senate and House of Representatives of the United States of America in Congress assembled, That in the judgment of Congress, it has become justifiable and necessary that the President should, in order to prevent the continuance and recurrence of such barbarities, and to insure the observance by the insurgents of the laws of civilized war, resort at once to measures of retaliation."[21]

Clearly there was a recommended form of retaliation in place when the Fort Fisher prisoners arrived at their respective prison camps. Articles favoring retaliation frequently appeared in the Northern newspapers that autumn. The *New York Times* spoke of how the inhumane treatment of Union prisoners of war had "stained and sullied the vesture of Southern chivalry. No such disgrace, thank God, touches the North! Everything that our own soldiers are allowed by law is cheerfully given to our prisoners. Such clothing, such food as the poor Southron never enjoyed at home, is heaped before him when in our hands. . . . None suffer from want." The *Times* then proclaimed: "We believe that the most active measures should be undertaken to insure corresponding treatment of our own brave soldiers. We urge that rebel prisoners should no longer live in luxury while ours are dying of starvation and neglect."[22]

Ever the politician, President Abraham Lincoln did not want anything to reflect badly on his administration. In his book, *The Lincoln Nobody Knows*, Historian Richard N. Current wrote that the president had an arrangement with Secretary Stanton: "Such apparently was the division of labor between Lincoln and Stanton, between lenity and the law. If a life was spared, Lincoln could get the credit. If not, Stanton with would take the blame." Lincoln himself admitted, "I want to oblige everybody whenever I can and Stanton and I have an understanding that if I send an order to him which cannot be consistently granted, he is to refuse it." One thing was certain: Stanton was a major decision maker in Lincoln's scheme of things.[23]

dent Abraham Lincoln refused to sign Resolution 97.

Historian Michael Horrigan wrote, "The stark reality is this: Stanton and Hoffman wished to put forward a policy of retaliation; there is no documented objection to this idea from President Abraham Lincoln. Therefore, in the matter of retaliation, the virtually unbridled use of power on the part of the secretary of war would have no trouble quashing any opposition to his orders that demanded a reduction in rations."[24]

Colonel Hoffman, who was known for being tightfisted, found a way to save the United States government thousands of dollars. His plan not only saved money, but also supported his idea of retaliation. Hoffman theorized since the prisoners were sedentary and not actively fighting or marching in the field, they could get along with less food. The rations saved could then be sold back to the commissary. Secretary of War Edwin Stanton liked the idea and authorized Hoffman to implement the reduction of rations on April 20, 1862.[25]

Not satisfied with limiting the prisoner's food, Hoffman issued the following order on November 12, 1863:

> You will issue no clothing of any kind except in cases of utmost necessity. So long as a prisoner has clothing upon him, however much torn, you must issue nothing to him, nor must you allow him to receive clothing from any but members of his immediate family, and only when they are in absolute want.[26]

111

During the late summer days of 1864, 5,000 Confederate prisoners were housed in tents. Some men slept in tents through late December until the last of the winter barracks were completed. *Photograph courtesy of the Chemung County Historical Society.*

In November 1863 Union authorities placed further restraints on their POWs. "I do not think it well to permit them to receive boxes of eatables from friends," Colonel Hoffman advised his prison commandants in an official dispatch on November 9, "and I suggest you have them informed that such articles will not hereafter be delivered."[27]

Elmira prisoners line up for morning roll call. Men were required to stand in line for roll call regardless if the weather was bad or they were sick. *Photograph courtesy of the Chemung County Historical Society.*

The next year, Colonel Hoffman notified the secretary of war that rations for prisoners could once again be reduced without adversely affecting the men's health. Stanton ordered a 20 percent reduction in rations effective June 1, 1864. Savings on food purchases would be placed in a general prison fund. This fund would be used to purchase materials for the prison camps that were not provided by the War Department. Although Elmira existed only a year the prison camp fund amounted to $239,857. Fifty-eight thousand dollars remained unspent at the end of the war and was returned to the Federal Government. The prisoners of Elmira could have certainly used this money to stave off death by buying extra food and clothing.

"These orders put the prisoners on half rations," complained prisoner James F. Crocker. "The result of these orders was that the prisoners were kept in a state of hunger—I will say in a state of sharp hunger—all the time."[28]

"I know from personal observation that many of my comrades died from starvation," wrote John A. Wyeth. "Day after day it was easy to observe the progress of emaciation until they became so weak that when attacked with an illness which a well-nourished man would easily have resisted and recovered from, they rapidly succumbed."[29]

Under these new orders the Elmira prisoners were limited to two meals a day and ate in shifts that ran from 6 to 9 AM and from 3 to 6 PM. The mess hall had long chest-high tables with no seats. The prisoners filed into the building, stood at opposite sides of a table and had fifteen minutes to eat his meal. The ration was four ounces of bread and a thin piece of salt pork. Dinner had the same

113

amount of bread but the meat was replaced by a soup or broth so clear you could see the bottom of the cup.

On August 10th, 1864, Circular no. 4 was issued by the commissary general of prisoners forbidding the prisoners to purchase food, including fruits and vegetables, from the sutler's shop. The circular also advised that all articles of clothing and other items sent to prisoners from relatives or friends be restricted to those officially listed as sick. Elmira prisoner R. B. Ewan would note: "Many hundreds of boxes of provisions were brot (sic) in camp, but unless we were in the hospital, or could furnish a certificate of sickness, the ham, cheese, bread and pie were put back on the wagon and hauled to fill other stomachs."[30]

An outbreak of scurvy in August and September soon reached epidemic proportions and prompted Post Surgeon Eugene Sanger to ask Colonel Hoffman to increase the supply of vegetables. The vitamin deficiency caused assorted spots and irritations on the body, but John R. King remembered the way it "attacked the mouth and gums, becoming so spongy and sore that portions could be removed with the fingers." In addition to losing their teeth, victims frequently saw their hair fall out and felt their stomachs cramp, leaving some men too weak to walk.

Confederate prisoners sold rats for food at five cents apiece. This became a thriving business in the camp. *Photograph courtesy of the Chemung County Historical Society.*

If this were not bad enough, the beef rations were reduced on October 3rd by Special Order No. 336 issued by post commandant Colonel Benjamin Tracy: "Whereas the fresh beef now being furnished at this post is in the opinion of the Colonel commanding unfit for issue, and inferior in quality to that required by contract. Therefore: Colonel S. Moore and Major Henry V. Colt are hereby designated to hold a survey upon said beef and to reject such parts or the whole of the said beef as to them appears to be unfit for issue, or of a quality inferior to that contracted for."[31]

The daily meat inspection frequently resulted in large amounts of beef being rejected. The supposedly inferior beef was then sold to local meat markets while the prisoners simply had to do without meat. Many historians agree that Secretary Stanton's approval of this controversial order was intended to force a bread-and-water diet on the prisoners without actually going on record as ordering it.

The lack of food robbed the prisoners of more than their energy and will to live. It also made them very susceptible to more deadly diseases. The threat of scurvy became so acute that Colonel Hoffman eventually ordered that sutlers at all Northern prison camps be permitted to sell vegetables to the prisoners of war.

Former prisoner Barry Benson recalled, "Another item of fare which was not on the list furnished by the government was—rats! The prison swarmed with them—big rusty fellows which lived about the 'cook house' as the kitchen was always called, and also under the house used as quarters. The floors of these houses were close to the ground, and the sides came down all the way. The rats burrowed holes underneath to go in and out, sometimes as large as a man's leg."[32]

One evening a prisoner was arrested for prowling around the camp during the night. The next morning he was taken to headquarters and questioned by Major Colt. "What were you doing?" The prisoner answered, "Huntin', sir." Colt wondered what type of animal would be in his prison camp at night and asked, "What are you hunting?" The man replied, "Rats." The rodents were attracted to the cookhouse which had heaps of refuse from feeding ten thousand prisoners. Toward dusk, prisoners armed with rocks waited for the rats to gather. One prisoner remarked, "[when a rat was seen] such a hurrah and such a chase and such a volley of stones! You would have thought it was our Battalion of Sharpshooters in charge."[33]

Many of the prisoners at Elmira displayed their artistic talents by making drawings, fans, rings and watch chains. Here is a pencil sketch, entitled "Group of Rebel Prisoners," signed by W. Norman. *Photograph courtesy of the Chemung County Historical Society.*

After the rats were killed and cleaned they were either grilled or fried.[34] Marcus Toney remembered men catching and then eating the rats. "I am glad that I did not have to go on this diet; but I have tasted a piece of rat, and it is much like squirrel." Everything on a rat was used. After a prisoner got every bit of nourishment from the animal possible, he would sew several hides together to make gloves for the winter months.[35]

Walter D. Addison wrote, "Rats, dogs, cats nor any other animal would long exist amongst that hungry throng of prisoners. Catching rats and selling them for food became quite a business, and they pursued the avocation with quite a profit, the demand being steady."[36]

Killed and dressed rats were an important commodity in the prison camp and sold anywhere from four to twenty-five cents apiece. Former Elmira prisoner of war R.B. Ewan recalled, "Our mart of trade was about in the center of the ground, and at 10 o'clock every day dressed rats on boards and tin plates, and sick prisoners' rations were offered for five cents and sometimes more."[37]

Men gathered together at this market place, buying and selling various goods they had made. A fiddler entertained the men by playing an instrument he designed from a cracker box and string. Prisoners traded cups of coffee, slices of bread, and meat rations for tobacco. Many used old wooden crates as makeshift stands so they could display their wares.[38]

John R. King wrote, "The prisoners passed the time making trinkets. Capt. Munger and Capt. Peck, secured the material and after the articles were completed they sold them in the city for the best price possible, always remitting the money. In passing through the prison one would see a boisterous lot playing cards or some other game, numbers making rings out of Gutta-percha buttons and riveting sets on to them of real silver which the captains had purchased, others were making pretty trinkets out of bone, such as tooth picks and seals for watch chains, with birds, squirrels and other figures designed on them. Some made watch chains out of horsehair with single links, with two links interlocked and others with three links interlocked making a round chain. This was done with horsehairs and two common needles. Others in our pen made fans out of white pine wood, the board was cut in the shape of a paddle with a fancy handle, then the part which formed the paddle was notched and cut into thin slices with a very sharp knife. The wood was softened with warm water and then the slices bended like a fan. Different colored ribbons were worked through the notches and the ends tied in a bow around the handle. They were very pretty, but frail. One man made a small parasol on the same plan."[39]

Woodlawn Cemetery with the original wooden grave markers. These markers became weathered and cracked over the years and were replaced with head stones by the United States Government in 1907. Unfortunately, the numbers on these stones were changed so the records for the graves no longer match. *Photograph courtesy of the Chemung County Historical Society.*

Prisoners also had to abide by rules when writing letters. The letter could only be a single page and not mention anything critical of the camp or their treatment. The envelope remained unsealed so it could be examined by a censor. If a letter contained anything forbidden, it was not mailed.

Somehow Elmira prisoner John Brusnan got a letter past the military censors to his sister in Maryland. "I will give you some idea of my situation," Brusnan wrote. "I would have never written to you for money, but I am almost starved to death. I only get two meals a day, breakfast and supper. For breakfast I get one-third a pound of bread and a small piece of meat; for supper the same quantity of bread and not any meat, but a small plate of warm water called soup. When I came here this prison contained 10,000 prisoners, and they have all died except for about 5,000. They are now dying at the rate of twenty-five a day."[40] Apparently Brusnan's sister forwarded his letter to the War Department where it caused quite a stir.

Since money was not allowed at Elmira the prisoners needed to find another type of exchange. Tobacco proved to be an ideal substitute since it could easily be divided and was readily available. One pound of tobacco was worth about a dollar. The pound was usually divided into twenty squares or quids. These were often referred to as chews. The value of each quid was five cents. This system of trade made it possible to have a thriving marketplace.

Some of the 2,980 prisoner's graves with stone markers.

One of the leading causes of disease was the water supply. Foster's pond was a stagnant backwash of the Chemung River running through most of the camp. Prisoners were using this water for bathing and also as a latrine. On November 1, 1864, Surgeon Eugene Sanger wrote a lengthy report critical of Elmira's sanitary conditions to Surgeon General Joseph K. Barnes. Sanger wanted to absolve his department of any wrongdoing in regards to the overwhelming sickness and death among the prisoners. Sanger also noted there were serious delays in getting the medical supplies he needed and in building better hospital facilities. "Foster's Pond," he wrote, "remains green with putrescence, filling the air with its messengers of disease and death, the vaults give out their sickly odors, and the hospitals are crowded with victims for the grave." He estimated that "Seven thousand men will pass 2,600 gallons of urine daily. A portion of this is absorbed by the earth or runs into the pond to purify." Sanger concluded with, "Unless the laws of hygiene are carefully studied and observed in crowded camps, disease is the inevitable consequence."[41]

In August, Sanger requested that a drainage system be built to flush the pond and remedy the problem. Surgeon Sanger was not alone in sounding the alarm about the dangers of Foster's pond. At least four other officers, including Colonel Eastman, Colonel Tracy, Lt. Colonel Alexander and

Captain Munger, wrote more than a dozen letters to the Commissary General of Prisoners recommending a drainage system for Foster's Pond. These letters were largely ignored.

On October 23rd, 101 days after this unhealthy condition was brought to his attention, Colonel Hoffman finally gave his approval to build a drainage trench to the Chemung River, specifying that the money would come from the prison fund and the labor was to be performed by the prisoners. The trench was to be dug six feet deep and a two inch wooden pipe would carry water from the river. Earlier Colonel Tracy had estimated it would only take two weeks to complete the mile-long drainage project, but now there were delays because the ground was frozen. Twelve hundred sixty-three prisoners died of disease before work on the drainage system was completed in early January. Secretary Stanton and Colonel Hoffman had once again succeeded in bringing their policy of retaliation to fruition through the use of delaying tactics. Historian Michael Horigan wrote:

> The failure of the commissary general [Colonel Hoffman] to launch a work project
> in good weather of late summer is puzzling. It now appeared, in the eyes of some,
> that a tactic of deliberate delay was beginning to come into being. That tactic would
> become part of the Elmira Prison Camp's legacy.[42]

Every morning a wagon would make the rounds of the camp and pick up the dead bodies from the night before. *Photograph courtesy of the Chemung County Historical Society.*

Federal Lieutenant Frank Wilkeson wrote of guarding the Confederate prisoners as they dug the drainage trenches at Elmira: "They (the prisoners) were eager to work, to earn money to buy tobacco. On pleasant days a few hundred of them were employed outside the stockade in digging ditches and trenches. For this work they were paid about twenty-five cents per day, which sum they promptly invested in tobacco. And they worked faithfully and honestly, and earned their scanty pay. Thinly clad, with blankets wound around them instead of overcoats, poorly fed, hopeless, these unfortunate soldiers swung heavy picks, and bent low over their shovels, as the cold wind swept through their

118

emaciated frames as through a sieve. It was pitiful to see the poverty-stricken Confederates breaking the hard, frost-bound earth."[43]

Another factor affecting the water quality was the number of people in the camp. Camp Chemung was built to house 2,000 men. When it was converted into Elmira Prison Camp over a thousand tents were added, increasing the capacity of the camp to 4,000 men. Until the new barracks were completed the following January, 5,190 men camped outdoors in tents while 3,873 were housed in barracks. The camp designed to accommodate 4,000 men now had over 9,000 going into the harsh northern winter.

The severe winter weather of 1864-65 became a major story in Elmira's newspapers. The *Advertiser* noted January 16th "as being one of the wildest and most blustery days of the season. We were favored with blustery, blinding snow squalls which seem to have swept generally through this part of the state."[44] On February 11th the *Advertiser* reported that snow in the wooded areas near the town was two and a half feet in depth. Prisoner John N. Opie recalled in a memoir the cold winter mornings and said, "Imagine if you can, with the weather ten or fifteen degrees below zero, one hundred men trying to keep warm by one stove. Each morning the men crawled out of their bunks, shivering and half frozen, when a scuffle and frequently a fight, for a place by the fire occurred. God help the sick or the weak, as they were literally left out in the cold."[45] John R. King wrote, "The man who looked after the fires made only two fires in 24 hours. The first fire was made at 8:00 in the morning, the other at 8 p.m. Near noon and midnight we were comfortable, but during the twelve hours between fires when the temperature of the stoves lowered we often suffered with the cold."[46]

Prisoner James Huffman remembered the "weather being so extremely cold that some of the men froze their feet while standing on the snow and ice at (morning) roll call."[47] John R. King wrote, "While in the house I wrapped my feet in old rags which kept them warm, but in the late winter we were compelled to stand in

Chief Surgeon Eugene Sanger called attention to the hazards of Foster's Pond. *Photograph courtesy of the Chemung County Historical Society.*

the snow every morning for roll call, consequently my feet and shins were badly frozen. Many besides myself had frozen feet." Nine Fort Fisher prisoners died from disease that was attributed to gangrene. Gangrene is characterized by decay of body tissue where the flesh turns black and dies due to severe trauma or frostbite. These deaths occurred in February and March which suggests these men died as a result of frostbite. [48]

Captain Bennett F. Munger inspected Elmira on August 25, 1864, and reported that, "two hundred twenty-six prisoners were sick in hospital and a large number in quarters." He noted that a number of prisoners in their barracks were unable to attend sick call, and in some cases had not been visited by a surgeon in four days. "Some are destitute of blankets and proper underclothes, and all without hospital rations; clothing of prisoners deficient, especially in blankets and shirts. The stench arising from the stagnant water in the pond is still very offensive."[49]

In late September, Captain Munger conducted another inspection of Elmira and noted the weather was unseasonably cold. "There is still great destitution and those in tents especially suffer." The report told of a lack of stoves in the hospitals and barracks, and overcrowded hospital conditions that deprived about a hundred sick prisoners of war of a hospital bed. Captain Munger wrote, "During the past week there have been 112 deaths, reaching one day 29. There seems little doubt numbers have died both in quarters and hospital for want of proper food."[50]

John R. King wrote, "The poor fellows died rapidly, despondent, homesick, hungry and wretched, I have stood day after day watching the wagons carry the dead outside to be buried and each day for several weeks 16 men were taken through the gate."[51]

The Elmira prisoners also became sick due to the lack of adequate clothing. Between August 22nd and February 1st of the following year four attempts were made by different individuals to provide the prisoners with winter necessities. All four were thwarted by Secretary Stanton and General Henry W. Wessells. Wessells became the perfect ally of Stanton because he had been a prisoner of the Confederacy and readily accepted the idea of retaliation. Circular No. 4 dictated that clothing might be furnished to "destitute" prisoners of war by their relatives. "The outer garments must be gray, and only one suit and change of underwear would be allowed."[52]

Lt. Colonel Eastman sent a letter to the War Department asking what he should do with packages of clothing sent by prisoner's relatives. The government's lack of action appalled clothing giant Noah, Walker & Co. *Photograph courtesy of Minnesota Historical Society.*

Sergeant George W.D. Porter recalled, "A great number of the men were in rags, and but a small quantity of clothing was issued by the United States Government. Of that received from home and friends the amount was restricted, and only obtainable on a permit approved by headquarters. When the mercury got down to 35 degrees below zero in the winter of 1864-65, I saw numbers of my comrades with frost-bitten hands, feet, ears and faces."[53]

Noah Walker & Co., a Baltimore clothing retailer, notified Colonel Eastman that it had a number of clothing packages ordered by relatives of prisoners that were to be delivered to Elmira. The company explained the War Department restricted all deliveries of clothing to prison camps and asked Eastman if he would accept the packages for Elmira.

Colonel Eastman sent a letter to the War Department asking what he should do. No record was ever found regarding the War Department's reply. What they said can only be surmised by Eastman's refusal to allow the shipment of clothing from the Baltimore firm.

In another attempt to send clothing to Elmira, The Baltimore Relief Organization in early September sent John J. Van Allen to Elmira to see about providing a shipment of clothing for the prisoners. Colonel Eastman received Van Allen with courtesy and informed him that the prisoners of war at Elmira "were destitute of clothing and blankets; that one-half of them did not have a single blanket; that most of them had been captured during the hot summer months with nothing other than thin cotton clothes, which in most instances were in tatters."[54]

The War Department refused to allow Van Allen to enter the prison camp. He contacted the secretary of war in hopes of being allowed to help the prisoners. Stanton's response, Van Allen claimed, would only allow gray color clothing to be brought to the prison. Van-Allen was told he could not distribute the clothing or moneys himself, but would have to leave it with prison officials. Van-Allen was convinced that the Confederate prisoners would never see any of the clothing or money that he had brought. "I was actually forced to give the matter up in despair," a disappointed John Van Allen wrote, "The brutal Stanton was inexorable to all my entreaties, and turned a deaf ear to the tale of their sufferings."[55]

In April of 1876 *The Southern Historical Society Papers* reported that the Honorable A. J. Beresford Hope wrote Secretary Stanton for permission to raise money in England to alleviate the status of prisoners in Northern prisons. Stanton said, "Almighty God! No! The government of the United States is rich enough to provide for its prisoners and needs no foreign help."[56]

Judge Robert Ould, the Confederate agent for the exchange of prisoners.

Judge Robert Ould, the Confederate agent of prisoner exchange, wrote a letter in October to Major John E. Mulford, his Federal counterpart. Ould pointed out that thousands of prisoners of war would be held through the winter of 1864-65. Ould proposed a plan to ease the suffering of the Confederate prisoners. If the North would send a ship to Mobile, Alabama, 1,000 bales of cotton would be loaded aboard and sent to New York City. The cotton would be sold and the money collected would be used to purchase clothing, blankets, and other necessities for the Confederate soldiers being held in Northern prisons. General Grant was receptive to the idea.

Historian Michael Horigan wrote, "The simplicity of the plan raised hopes for success of the operation. However, a series of delays orchestrated by Secretary of War Stanton all but eliminated any possibility of the clothing and blankets arriving in Northern prison camps before the beginning of the winter season."[57]

In December the U.S. Transport *Atlanta*, under a flag of truce, sailed into the harbor at Mobile. The delays began when Secretary Stanton objected to the Confederate officer who was to sell the cotton in New York. Judge Ould wanted Major General Isaac R. Trimble to handle matters in New York. It took Stanton three weeks to find a suitable replacement in Confederate General William N. R. Beall. Beall had just been paroled from Fort Warren and was in the custody of Union General

Halbert E. Paine. Due to further delays in transferring the cotton the *Atlanta* did not dock in New York Harbor until January 24th. Unfortunately due to the rapidly declining cotton market the cargo yielded less than 50 percent of its value from November.

Colonel Tracy submitted Elmira's December clothing requisition for 1,000 jackets, 2,500 shirts, 3,000 pairs of trousers, 8,000 drawers, 7,000 pairs of socks and 1,500 caps. Tracy was informed by General Wessells that "a large amount of cotton has been shipped for New York . . . the proceeds to be applied for the purchase of clothing . . . for the comfort of rebel prisoners of war. In view of this fact it is desirable that no more clothing shall be provided by the Government than is absolutely demanded by the ordinary dictates of humanity." Wessells then closed his letter with the instruction, "You will please report your views on this subject."[58]

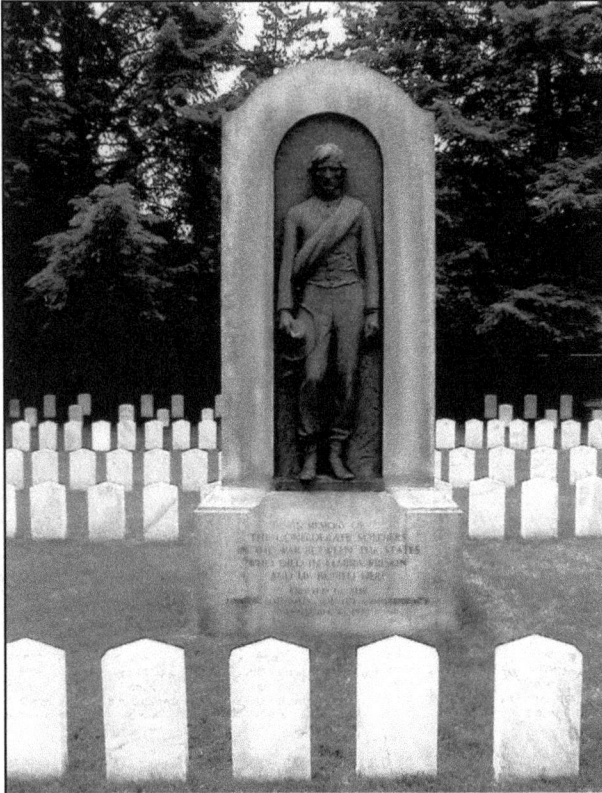

Daughters of the Confederacy monument honoring the Confederate soldiers who died at Elmira prison. *Photograph courtesy of Kathleen Walls.*

Colonel Tracy waited all month for the clothing he ordered in December but no shipment ever came. Finally Tracy wrote General Wessell's on January 5th and informed him he was still waiting for his December allotment of clothing to be delivered. Colonel Tracy asked, "that these amounts . . . be furnished immediately for issue to prisoners, unless the department is advised that supplies will be speedily forwarded by the rebel authorities."[59]

Wessell's responded to Colonel Tracy on January 19th and told him that his clothing requisitions for Elmira were not sent because Tracy had failed to report his views of the government's plan as ordered. This bureaucratic red tape was all part of Secretary Stanton's delaying tactics to exact punishment against the Rebels. If he could holdup the clothing shipment long enough, it would virtually have the same effect as refusing to fill it.

It was not until February 7th that three boxes of clothing finally arrived at Elmira for distribution among the prisoners. More boxes arrived in the weeks afterward. The question remains, how many prisoners died as a result of the lack of clothing and blankets during the harsh winter season?

In September 1864, with the end of the war in sight and apparently in favor of the North, the War Department reinstituted the prisoner exchange. Commissary General of Prisoners, William Hoffman, telegraphed Colonel Tracy, "By authority of the Secretary of War all invalid prisoners in your charge who will not be fit for service within sixty days will in a few days be sent South for exchange." This order refused to release men "who are too feeble to endure the journey." Those to be exchanged were to be accompanied by at least one medical officer and several able Confederates who had served in the camp hospital as attendants and nurses. Elmira's medical staff was to select only those prisoners who were healthy enough to survive the journey. Colonel Tracy hoped the prison hospital would be improved by eliminating over twelve hundred invalids.[60]

On the morning of October 11th, the 1,264 prisoners to be exchanged made the two-mile trip from the prison camp to the town's railroad depot. Nearly 300 men, who were unable to walk, rode in wagons to the depot and then were loaded onto boxcars. They were described by Anthony Keiley, an assistant nurse, as "hospital patients on crutches, borne in the arms of friends, creeping some of them, on hands and knees, pale, gaunt, emaciated; some with the seal of death stamped on their wasted cheeks and shriveled limbs. They were a ghastly tide, with skeleton bodies and lusterless eyes, and brains bereft of but one thought, and hearts purged of all feelings but one—the thought of freedom, the love of home."[61]

The prisoners were loaded onto three trains of boxcars for the 260-mile trip to Baltimore. During the forty hour trip death claimed five of the Confederates and another prisoner died shortly after he arrived at his destination. Medical officials in Baltimore were dismayed to learn no doctors had accompanied the men.

Surgeon Josiah Simpson, medical director of the Middle Department, VIII Army Corps, angrily reported to Colonel Hoffman that many of the prisoners arriving from Elmira were gravely ill. "I made a personal inspection of the men," Simpson stated, "and found a number unable to bear the journey. Many should never have been permitted to leave Elmira."[62]

Surgeon Artemus Chapel boarded the steamer at Baltimore to examine the Elmira prisoners going to Point Lookout. He reported to Surgeon Simpson that someone "is greatly censurable for sending such cases away from camp even for exchange."[63] Surgeon C.F. Campbell told Simpson that sixty of the men were suffering from extended illnesses and too debilitated to make the trip. "Such men," Campbell wrote, "should not have been sent from Elmira. If they were inspected before leaving the place in accordance with orders it was most carelessly done, reflecting severely

Surgeon Josiah Simpson told Colonel Hoffman that many prisoners were unable to bear the journey south.

on the medical officers engaged in that duty and is disgraceful to all concerned. The effect produced on the public by such marked displays of inefficiency or neglect of duty cannot fail to be most injurious to our cause both at home and abroad."[64]

Surgeon Simpson sent a letter to Colonel Hoffman regarding the Elmira exchange. An angry Simpson suggested there was "criminal neglect and inhumanity on the part of the medical officers in making the selection of men to be transferred."[65] Colonel Hoffman forwarded all the reports regarding the October prisoner exchange to Secretary of War Stanton. Stanton remained silent about the matter and never took any disciplinary action.

Richard H. Dibrell, a member of the "ambulance committee", was in Savannah, Georgia, to help receive the prisoners exchaned from Northern prison camps. Dibrell testified to the Committee to Investigate the Conditions and Treatment of Prisoners of War in March, 1865. "I have never seen a set of men in worse condition. They were so enfeebled and emaciated that we lifted them like little children. Many of them were like living skeletons. Indeed, there was one poor boy about 17 years old, who presented the most distressing and deplorable appearance I ever saw. He was nothing but skin and bone, besides this, he was literally eaten up by vermin. He died in the hospital in a few days. . . The mortality on the passage from Maryland was very great as well as that on the passage from the prisons to the port from which they started. I cannot state the exact number, but I think I heard that 3,500 were started, and we only received about 3,027"[66]

In the early spring of 1865 a similar incident occurred. On February 20th and again on March 3rd the Fort Fisher prisoners at Elmira participated in an exchange. The men were examined by a medical officer to insure they were invalids who were healthy enough to survive the trip. Of the 259 men exchanged 65 did not live long enough to return to their homes. There are several possible reasons why these gravely ill men were allowed to leave the prison camp. The first explanation suggests that the prisoners might have paid the medical officer to release them regardless of their

These soldier's records were found at the National Archives. All three men "died on the route" to be exchanged in February, 1865. The author had found sixty-five Confederate soldiers from Fort Fisher who were exchanged and then died of disease before they ever made it home. Were these soldiers released even though the Union medical officers knew the men were terminally ill?

condition. Since money was not allowed in prison, it would be difficult for a prisoner to have enough money to bribe anyone. If the man was fairly healthy and industrious, it was possible for him to earn some money by selling items that he had made. However, any sales inside the prison were paid for in chewing tobacco. If a man wanted hard cash, he needed to sell his trinkets outside the walls of the prison. Many of the Union soldiers were willing to sell the prisoner's wares for a percentage of the money made. In this way it would be possible for a prisoner to earn enough to bribe his way into an early exchange. However, there was still a catch he had to overcome. Any money an inmate earned while working at the prison would have been collected by the prison treasurer and entered into a ledger. Credit was then issued to the prisoner so he could purchase items from the sutler's store. It is unclear how inmates could obtain money to buy their freedom. Below are several examples of prisoners bribing officials.

W.W. Gramling wrote this in his diary entry for Feb 28, 1865. "Another load of 500 signed the paroles today. Don't know when they will get off. Have a load of sick made up also. Hope I will get out soon. Trust to Providence. Just whoever has money to buy his way out can go."[67]

On one occasion a examining surgeon approached a rebel prisoner who claimed to have a painful gunshot wound that would prevent him from carrying a musket for at least sixty days. This was the time allotted where an invalid prisoner could not return to the Confederate army. The man carefully rolled up his sleeve so only the doctor could see his arm. Instead of a wound the doctor found a five dollar bill. Apparently this was sufficient incentive for the medic to tell the parole clerk that the prisoner had a "gunshot wound in the left arm." [68]

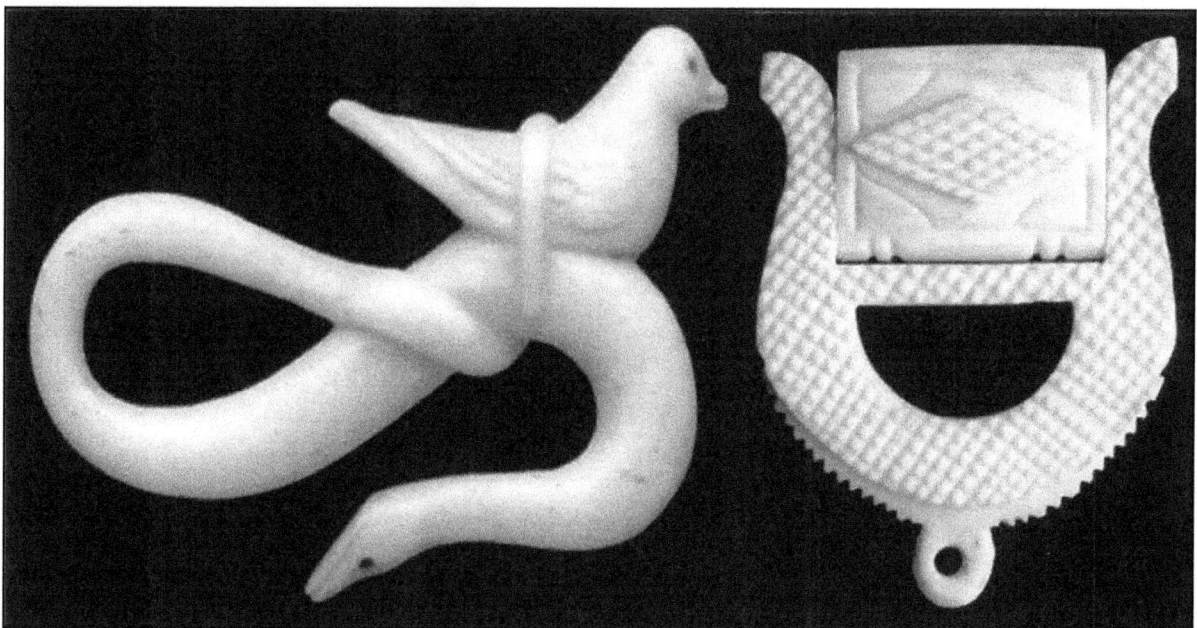

Two trinkets made by George W. Davis at Elmira Prison. Both the bird and snake and the watch fob were carved from beef bone. *Photograph courtesy of the North Carolina Museum of History.*

Another reason for exchanging gravely ill men seems more likely. The officers at Elmira were trying to prove to their superiors, and to the public, that conditions were healthful and not any worse than other Union Prisoner of War Camps. What better way to instantly improve the health of their camp than to get rid of hundreds of terminally-ill prisoners? Is it possible the officers at Elmira deliberately planned to exchange terminally ill prisoners before they died inside the camp? If they could to do so, those deaths would not go on Elmira's permanent record and the public would never know that they had occurred.

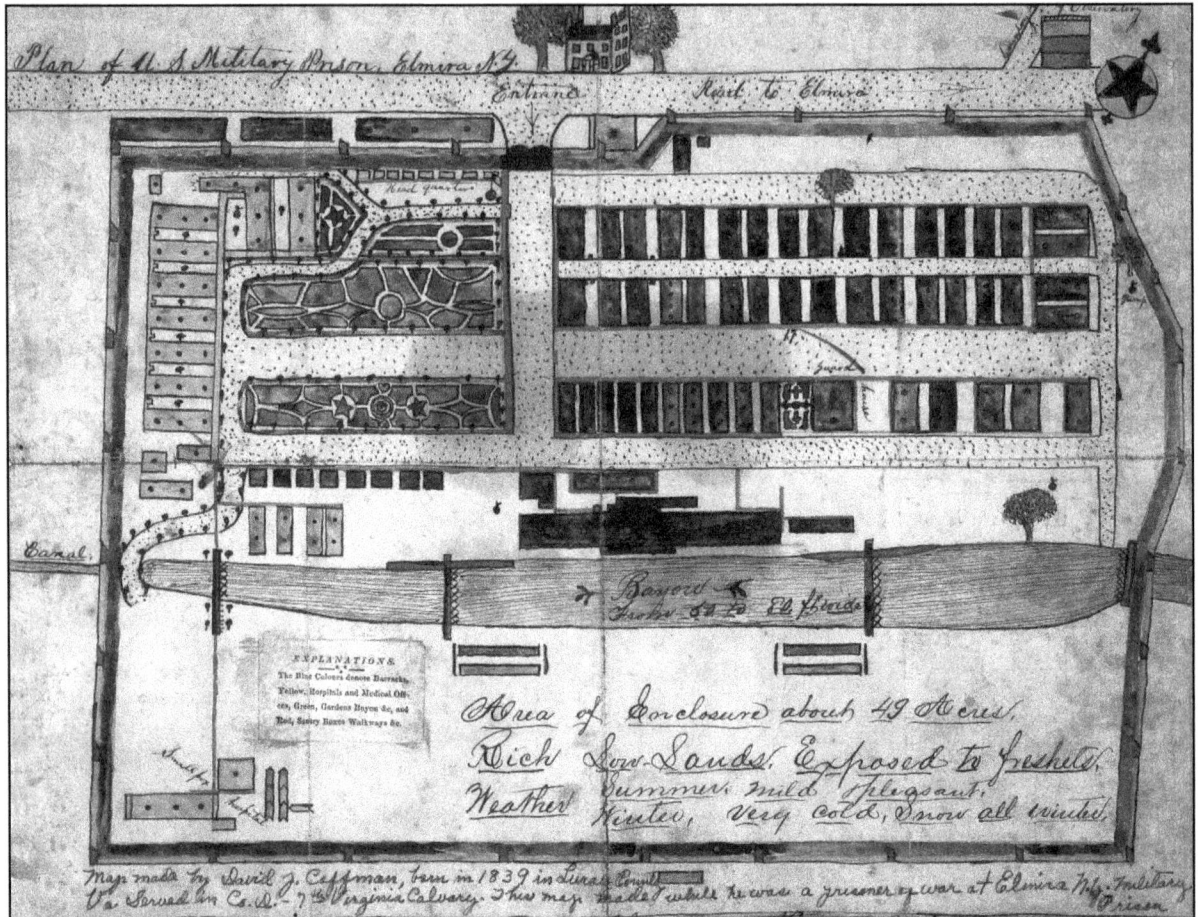

David Coffman drew this map of Elmira while he was a prisoner. The dark rectangles in the upper right are barracks. To the left of the barracks are gardens and the lighter rectangles on the left are prison hospitals. The body of water that runs through the prison compound is Foster's Pond. The large dark rectangle above the pond is the mess hall. The first observation tower can be seen in the upper right of the map. *Photograph courtesy of the Chemung County Historical Society.*

Anyone in a position of authority at a prisoner of war camp with a high death rate should not be surprised to find himself the target of intense scrutiny and criticism. The spotlight was especially harsh for Chief Surgeon Eugene Sanger because the prisoner's health was his responsibility. If prisoner reports are to be believed, the good doctor was not as benevolent as he appeared. Prisoner Anthony Keiley was one of the most severe critics of the medical department. Keiley was given the job of clerk in the prison's medical department because he had once been a newspaper editor in Petersburg, Virginia. One of his jobs was keeping a record of the deaths in the hospital wards each morning. After a particularly disturbing day he wrote about high number of prison deaths: "As I went over to the first hospital this morning early, there were eighteen dead bodies lying naked on the bare earth. Eleven more were added to the list by half-past eight o'clock!"[69] In October Keiley wrote, "The deaths yesterday were twenty-nine. Air pure, location healthy, no epidemic. The men are being deliberately murdered by the surgeon, especially by either the ignorance or malice of the

126

chief." Another prisoner, James Huffman, allegedly heard a doctor say, "He (Sanger) killed more Rebs than any soldier on the front."

In his book *In Vinculis* Anthony Keiley wrote, "Sanger is simply a brute, as we learned the whole truth about him from his own people. If he had not avoided court martial by resigning his position, it is likely that even a military commission would have found it impossible to screen his brutality to the sick."[70] Historian Clay Holmes wrote that many prominent citizens who personally knew the Chief Surgeon, believed "something was wrong with Dr. Sanger." Many believed that he "took a very considerable amount of the medicine which the Government furnished for the sick prisoners."[71] Further indictments came from within the hospital. Medical steward W.P. Whitesides commented that there were "plenty of stimulants, but a good deal of it drank by the doctor."[72]

In October, Major Sanger wrote to Brigadier General John L. Hodson, requesting a recruiting position in Augusta, MA. Sanger had never been happy at Elmira and claimed that his health suffered since he had been assigned to the prison. He also included in his letter this disturbing sentence: "I now have charge of 10,000 Rebels a very worthy occupation for a patriot, particularly adapted to elevate himself in his own estimation, but I think I have done my duty having relieved 386 of them of all earthly sorrow in one month." Was Sanger admitting that he murdered these prisoners?[73]

In Sanger's defense it must be noted that between August 13th and October 17th he wrote nine detailed reports that told of unhealthy conditions in the prison camp. Historian Michael Horigan wrote, "No other officer, in the duration of the camp, did so much in such a short period of time. Undoubtedly, the single greatest irony of the Elmira Prison Camp is this: the officer who most vociferously called attention to the unsanitary conditions and other major shortcomings of Barracks No. 3 (Elmira Prison Camp) became the nearest thing to a scapegoat in this very sad story."[74]

On December 23, 1864 Sanger got his wish and was replaced by Major Anthony E. Stocker as Chief Surgeon at Elmira Prison Camp. It should be noted that the two most deadly months, February and March, 1865, occurred at the prison after Sanger had left. However, it must also be remembered that this high death toll may have been a result of insufficient clothing during the unusually harsh winter.

Because of retaliatory articles in Northern newspapers a great number of people felt the South was guilty of brutal behavior in its treatment of Union prisoners of war. The South was hard-pressed to provide food and medicine for their own people, let alone prisoners of war. The devastating impact of three years of war had seriously depleted the region's agricultural production. General Sherman's March to the Sea and up through the Carolinas devastated cropland which until that time had produced substantial amounts of food. Sherman's powerful 62,000 man army carried out a scorched earth policy and destroyed all crops and centers of transportation. This seriously impaired any attempt to properly feed Union prisoners of war at places such as Andersonville.

Most people in the North were unaware that their own government was partly responsible for the mistreatment of Union prisoners. The Northern blockade of Southern ports slowed to a trickle the foods and medicine that might have helped Union prisoners. Every time the prisoner of war exchanges were halted it was done by the North. The Confederacy wanted to relieve itself of the burden of caring for thousands of Union prisoners and tried repeatedly to re-establish the exchange but all too often their appeals fell on deaf ears.

Several years after the war Federal Major-General Benjamin Butler wrote about the starving Confederate soldiers and reasoned they could only give a small amount of food and clothing to prisoners.

While I do not mean to apologize for the manner in which our prisoners were treated, I feel bound to say that from careful examinations of the subject I do not believe that either the people or the higher authorities of the Confederacy were in so great degree responsible as they have been accused. In the matter of starvation the fact is incontestable that a soldier of our army would have quite easily starved on the rations which in the latter days of the war were served out to the Confederate soldiers before Petersburg. I examined the haversacks of many Confederate soldiers captured on picket during the summer of 1864 and found therein, as their rations for three days, scarcely more than a pint of kernels of corn, none broken but only parched to blacken by the fire, a long piece of meat, most frequently bacon, some three inches long by an inch and a half wide and less than a half an inch thick. Now, no Northern soldier could have lived three days upon that, and the lank, emaciated condition of the (Confederate) prisoner fully testified to the meagerness of his means of sustenance.

With regard to clothing, it was simply impossible for the Confederates at that time to have any sufficient clothing upon the bodies of their soldiers, and many passed the winters barefoot. Necessity, therefore, would seem to have compelled the condition of food and clothing given by them to the Federal prisoners, for it was not possible for authorities to supply it without taking the clothing from their soldiers in the field. [75]

ANDERSONVILLE PRISON
AS SEEN BY
JOHN L. RANSOM,
Author and Publisher of "ANDERSONVILLE DIARY, ESCAPE AND LIST OF THE DEAD"

Elmira has become known as "The death camp of the North". Its similiarities to the infamous Andersonville cannot be avoided.

Elmira, with its 24.4 percent death rate, was without a doubt the worst camp in the North. Its comparison to Andersonville in southwestern Georgia cannot be avoided. During the war some 45,000 Union prisoners of war were incarcerated at Andersonville. Today there are 12,914 Federal graves in its National Cemetery, making Andersonville's death rate of 28.7 percent the highest of any Civil War prison.[76]

The unusually high death rates of Andersonville and Elmira are comparable, but this is where the similarity ends. Elmira had so much more than Andersonville. Elmira had excellent railroad connections which made it possible to ship in any supplies that the prison camp needed, plus an unlimited supply of fresh water from the Chemung River and plenty of timber for the construction of barracks. Elmira was also located in a valley that was known for growing an abundance of fruits and vegetables. Local newspapers in the summer of 1864 boasted of bumper crops of apples, pears, peaches and a variety of vegetables. There were also herds of cattle and sheep to supply healthful meat for the prisoners. It is difficult to understand why Elmira Prison Camp should be in need of anything in this land of plenty. Many of the deaths at Elmira could have been prevented by sufficient food, clean water, clothing and proper quarters, but officials in Washington chose to ignore the reports about the unsanitary conditions of the camp.

In a letter to President Lincoln, Secretary of War Stanton admits to retaliation and threatens strict measures if Union prisoners do not receive better treatment.

War Department, Washington City, December 5, 1863

Mr. President: The rebel prisoners of war in our possession have heretofore been treated with the utmost humanity and tenderness consistent with security. They have had good quarters, full rations, clothing when needed, and the same hospital treatment received by our own soldiers. Indulgence of friendly visits and supplies was formerly permitted, but they have been cut off since the barbarity practiced against our prisoners became known to the Government. If it should become necessary for the protection of our men, strict retaliation will be resorted to.

Respectfully submitted,
            Edwin M. Stanton
            Secretary of War [77]

Did Secretary of War Stanton ever implement the "strict retaliation" he refered to? The record seems to indicate he may have. Certainly the situation of the Northern prisoners did not improve. It probably got worse. The war had another year and a half to go and the South had yet to experience Sherman's devastating march to the sea and up through the Carolinas. This invasion burned buildings and crops, butchered livestock and tore up the rail road tracks. All of these things were needed to feed and clothe the Federal prisoners.

After reviewing all the evidence presented it is difficult not to arrive at the conclusion that there was some form of retaliation taking place. Admittedly, there is no hard proof such as documents that distinctly outline a plan of retaliation. However, we can put the pieces together to form a picture. The picture that takes shape is not very pretty because it clearly shows man's inhumanity toward man. Worse still, it reflects man's vindictiveness against helpless prisoners of war.

These examples suggest that during the last year of the Civil War certain officials of the United States War Department sought retaliation in the form of delaying or rejecting reasonable requests from prison personnel. These orders emanated from one man, Secretary of War Edwin M. Stanton, and were passed down to like minded officers, ie, General Henry W. Wessells, Colonel William Hoffman, General Ethan A. Hitchcock and others. Soldiers at Elmira enforced these mandates and turned Elmira into a death camp. In his own way, Stanton succeeded in creating his own Andersonville in the North.

PRISONER'S STATEMENTS

Recollections of a Confederate Soldier of the Prison-Pens of Point Lookout, Md., and Elmira, New York by Walter D. Addison

This article is from the Southern Historical Collection of the University of North Carolina Library, Chapel Hill.

So many exaggerated accounts of the treatment of Union soldiers in Southern prisons have been published from time to time creating as they have done such a wide spread prejudices throughout the country and which of course have been accepted all over the North as truth, the wonder is that such silence should be kept by Southerners as to the treatment of Confederate prisoners within Northern prison pens.

The writer having more than six months experience at Point Lookout, Maryland; and Elmira, New York, recalls that which he has witnessed himself, and desires to state truthfully herein, it being ever green in his memory.

I was a private in Company A, Breathed's battery of Stewart's Horse artillery commanded at the time by Captain Preston P. Johnson of Baltimore, Md., and now a resident of Kentucky. Major James Breathed of Hagerstown, Md., in command of the Battalion.

I was a captive in the summer of 1864 at the time of the Wilderness Campaign, and was sent to Point Lookout and there confined a few weeks, and when there was confined about sixteen thousand Southern prisoners many having been there as long as two years owing to the refusal on the part of the North, to exchange prisoners. During my entire confinement at Point Lookout we were under guard of Negro soldiers whose conduct and treatment of the prisoners was infamously cruel and in many instances they conducted themselves in a savage manner. I have witnessed them fire their muskets indiscriminately into crowded masses of prisoners, shooting two or three men at a single shot, and such outrages were tolerated by their white officers, and they never were punished nor their cases investigated. This repeatedly happened at Point Lookout, and I never heard that one was even reprimanded.

There was at one time an apprehended raid of Mosby's cavalry upon Point Lookout for the purpose of releasing the prisoners confined there. Stringent orders were given to the guard to fire upon any prisoners who were seen out of their quarters after eight o'clock at night. Many prisoners were unaware of the orders, and incautiously ventured out for the performance of nature calls, when they were ruthlessly shot down. Several cases of the kind occurred. All these outrages were perpetrated by Negroes as there were none others on guard.

Water for the use of the prison was collected in barrels distributed about the prison grounds, and the vessel for drinking purposes was conspicuously absent in many places, when the prisoners would drink from the barrel. The audacious Negro was always at hand, and seemed to delight in immersing the head of the drinker, and then gloat over the fun. All this was allowed, and there was no redress. Repeated remonstrances were made to the authorities, but were unnoticed, and such outrages continued to be of daily occurrence.

The Rev. Mr. Eddy, an English gentleman residing in Texas at the breaking of the war, and who espoused our cause, and gallantly fought in the ranks was a prisoner at Point Lookout, and attempted to expose to the outside world the outrageous shooting of our prisoners by the Negro guard was detected in his good work. He remained at Point Lookout after my transfer to Elmira. I next saw him in the guard house at Elmira, after suffering as he did cruelties which befitted a savage than the so called Samaritan of the Federal army. Mr. Eddy was for weeks confined at Elmira when all sorts of indignities were imposed upon him and when I was undergoing similar punishment for writing an article upon the treatment of the prisoners and which was intercepted in the Elmira PO. The Post Office was cautiously watched and it was almost impossible for a letter to pass such watching eyes as were employed, and the dread of having letters which could contain anything pertaining to the inside workings of the stockade. In any other prisoners served their sentence in the guard house for the same offense, and some marched at the command of the Negro guard with a barrel shirt.

From Point Lookout, and various other Northern prisons there were about Ten thousand prisoners transferred to Elmira, NEW YORK in the summer of 1864, the writer being amongst the number. The first installment from Point Lookout was dispatched by sea via New York City in the month of July upon a miserable old Government transport only fitted to carry cattle. About twelve hundred men were crowded upon this old tub between decks with only the hatches open, and there they remained crowded together like sheep for many days, only allowing one or two at a time on the main deck for a few minutes, when they were ordered into their horrible quarters below. The sight of these holds was sickening in the extreme, and the condition and sufferings of the prisoners therein confined was indeed horrible, and a large number of the men being already sick when placed on board their wretched condition upon the voyage can be imagined better than described. After reaching the harbor of New York we were released from the ship until the following day, and upon clearing the vessel the sight presented can never be forgotten. Think of their journey by sea, several hundred miles, crowded together as we were, with so many sick in the sweltering heat of July. It was on a par with the condition of the Yankee slave ships with a cargo of human souls purchased with a cargo of Boston rum. Our rations consisted of fat pork and a loaf of bread.

No beds nor straw to lie upon, only a blanket spread beneath us on the filth covered hard boards only comparable with hog or cattle pen. Never upon the whole voyage was there any attempt made to sweep or clean the floors. There was scarcely an inch of space where there could be a step between the crowded mass of human freight. The insufficient ventilation of the ships holds rendered the stench and the foul air unbearable, and many deaths were the result. The writer owes the preservation of his own life to the kindness of one of the prisoners (now residing in San Francisco) who was fortunate enough to enjoy a little more freedom than the rest, and who managed to smuggle me a small lump of ice, and a swallow of tea when I was lying jammed in amongst the rest of the hold and sick almost to death. Some were already dead when the ship reached New York, and I feel certain that many died afterward from the affects of that horrible voyage. The continuation of the trip afterward to Elmira was attended with less suffering.

When showing the prisoners on the ship at Point Lookout they were supplied with their rations for the voyage, consisting of a piece of very fat mess pork and a loaf of bread, and it can be imagined what was the condition of things between decks when rolling on the billows of the deep, and hardly one escaped the effects of his first experience at sea. It reminded me of only one other scene I witnessed when passengers upon a ship at sea, which was converging at market nearly two thousand huge densely crowded together upon deck, the animals having been fed upon raw potatoes just before starting. The sea affects them as it does a human being. Those swine were accommodated better than we, they being upon the upper decks in the fresh air, whilst we were between decks almost poisoned by the foul air, which was intensely polluted by human excrement.

The return trip to Richmond from Elmira was no more comfortable than the one described. We were marched from the prison to the depot in Elmira through about two feet of snow—the weather intensely cold—in February 1865. Upon reaching the depot wet and cold we were crowded into cattle cars wherein was a little dirty straw scattered over the floor, and not a particle of fire. Thus we were transferred to Baltimore in nearly forty-eight hours, including two whole nights. At Baltimore we were marched a long distance through a blinding sleet and snow storm to the steamboat upon the wharf from noon till night, when we were placed upon a dilapidated government cattle transport and landed at City Point below Richmond. A violent storm of wind, sleet, and snow raged the entire night of our passage down the bay, and unprotected as we were upon the hurricane deck with only a blanket the night was a hard one. Many of the sick of which there were a large numbers were placed below decks in the stalls formerly for cattle, and but slightly protected from the weather, and but little more comfortable than there on the hurricane deck. There can be no doubt that it was the grossest indifference on the part of the Government in thus permitting sick prisoners to be conveyed in such an inhuman and cruel manner. I do not believe that in any instance during the war when Northern prisoners suffered as much, if as, it was for lack of provisions and the refusal on the part of the North to exchange prisoners, it seeming their intention to let the latter die rather than refrain from their endeavor to eat out the substance of the South.

The conduct of many of the physicians in charge of the hospitals herein named deserves especial notice, and the strongest condemnation. If they had been dumb brutes, instead of human beings as they were supposed to be, they could not have exhibited greater brutality. I was ward master in one of the hospital barracks at Elmira which contained from eighty-five to ninety patients crowded, as they sometimes were to or three in a bunk. The physician, a doctor Van Ness made his visits once and sometimes twice every twenty-four hours. For the many different diseases incidental to such places, nearly every patient received opium pills. That being the favorite prescription no matter what the nature of the disease. On one occasion, three persons so being treated were visible shaking, the surgeon-in-chief, a Dr. Sanger, was called in. He directed Dr. Van Ness to write four or five drops of Fowler's solution of arsenic. He wrote forty-five and the patients in a very short time breathed their last breath. No investigation ensued. No reprimand. Dr. Van Ness continued in his position. Hundreds of our prisoners died. I can truthfully say not twenty percent of those in the hospital left it alive. This is no exaggeration of what I believe was a terrible crime growing out of, to put it mildly, the deplorable ignorance of the medical men in charge, if not willful murder.

They had our poor helpless soldiers at their mercy. Often have I heard them, when gathered together in the dispensary discussing their experiences of the day, exult over the numbers of the Rebs they had put through, i.e. killed' and expressing their desire to, in this way, get rid of the whole number of the Confederates there, thus avoiding an exchange. All in authority at Elmira seemed to

133

be of this opinion. Who that was confined at Andersonville can recall a single instance where there was a greater outrage than at Elmira, where thousands of prisoners were confined in small tents until early winter in such a dreadfully severe climate as that of northern New York where is situated Elmira. I have known persons to be frost bitten, and when some of them provided for themselves little mud chimneys to their tents,. gathering chips and other small fuel, the Yankee officers would send a guard to ruthlessly destroy them and Major Beall, who was then in command, would go to the rounds himself, in the middle of the night and deprive them of the extra blankets which were their own personal property, leaving the soldier to freeze to death. No coffee, no tea, no vegetables but a few beans to make tasteless watery soup consisting of the liquid in which the pork had been boiled. After many months the old soldier barracks—barns were used as hospitals. Hundreds were wedged in, and crowded together like packed sardines. Two and frequently three in a bunk. They had no opportunity to cleanse themselves of vermin there first found, therefore who can wonder at the fearful numbers of deaths, arising from ignorant medical supervision, and total lack of proper ventilation. Of the false statements of the humanity then boasted by the Yankee, the bored will get a truthful statement. Humanity equal to that shown at the time they burned, so termed witches. The Northern people, not descended from Yankees, will when the whole truth is known, believe the palm of humanity belonged to the South, and will see through the intentional falsehoods of a prejudiced press.

There is no doubt in my mind as to the intention of our enemies to rid themselves of as many of our prisoners as was possible, no matter what the means to which they resorted. Witness in various instances when contagious diseases were introduced into crowded prisons. I recollect, in one instance at Elmira hundreds of deaths were the result of small-pox introduced by patients from Blackwell's Island, New York. Up to that time not a case of the disease had been known there. In a few days it manifested itself in one of the new importations. Instead of being isolated, he was placed immediately adjoining one of the wards used as a hospital, and there remained for days. Other cases rapidly developed, and soon broke out in a virulent form. Tents were them placed inside the stockade where hundreds were confined, and immediately upon their convalescence were again distributed amongst the well prisoners, even occupying the same beds, thus spreading the disease to an appalling degree. No comfortable buildings were provided for the wretched victims, even when the temperature fell twenty degrees below zero. Very few small-pox patients survived. When discharging small-pox cases they were led to a pump, and there stripped and washed in the coldest weather, and then assigned new quarters for a brief time, when they were returned to the hospital to meet their deaths. Their sufferings were laughed at. Considering their ill usage, premeditated torture, insufficient food, and the prevailing lack of any show of humanity it seems a miracle that one again reached his home. I repeatedly heard it said by Federal officers that the mortality at Elmira far exceeded that at Andersonville. I will say in justice to two officers, Captains Whiton and Munger, that they did what they could to alleviate the sufferings of the prisoners, but were almost powerless to render the aid they deserved.

The outrageous manner in which men were vaccinated excelled anything I have ever witnessed even surpassing the acts of savages. The modus operandi was to assemble the man first in long lines with coats off and arms bared; then the butchering began by illiterate and irresponsible men. They would take hold of a thick piece of flesh, dip a lancet into the diluted virus, and then thrust it entirely through the pinched up flesh. The spurious virus soon produced such fearfully disastrous results that it became necessary to construct gangrene hospitals, from which arose a dreadful stench. Scores died

134

from the effects; others losing arms. I have there seen the sickening effects of their villainous vaccination. There are many who can verify the above.

A most horrible instrument of torture used at Elmira was called a sweat box. For trivial offenses our men were therein confined for hours, in the scorching suns of July and August, without food and water, and removed in many cases only when the victim was more dead than alive. I vividly recollect when one man dropped with rigid limbs swollen and almost paralyzed, and died in a few days from the effects. This instrument of torture consisted of a narrow upright box, about seven feet high, and wide enough to fit an ordinary sized man. It stood in a perpendicular position with its victim without ventilation, and the poor victim and left to sweat to death.

Another instrument of torture used at Elmira was the dreaded barrel shirt. What was known by that name was a very heavy barrel with one head out, and the other containing a hole large enough to admit the head of a man through it. All offenders, twice a day, for two hours, had to wear it. They were drawn up to form a circle, the barrel adjusted over the head the inside of the barrel resting upon the shoulders and the parade commenced. This death dealing instrument would have been a burning shame amongst savages.

This afforded the Negro guard amusement everyday, and also seemed to gratify their beastly officers. Upon the back of every barrel, on a board twenty-four by six inches, was written in large letters the supposed offense, such as, "Liar;" "Liar No. 2;" Liar No. 3;" "Dogeater;" "Dogeater No 1;" and so on. Multitudinous outrages no less revolting were of continued occurrence under the eyes of men high in rank under the Government.

As an explanation of the term "dog-eater" mentioned above I will state on one occasion an officer came into the stockade accompanied by his favorite dog. No sooner was the dog discovered by several hungry prisoners than he was seized and converted into food. A search of the camp soon revealed the dog quartered and dressed and hid away in the rafters. The parties to the wrong were quickly discovered, and were for a long time clothed in barrel shirts.

Rats, dogs, cats nor any other animal would long exist amongst that hungry throng of prisoners. Catching rats and selling them for food became quite a business, and the pursued the avocation with quite a profit, the demand being steady. Would men eat dogs and rats unless suffering from extreme hunger? Many died from insufficient and improper food. I have seen men, almost starved fish scraps from barrels containing hospital refuse and devouring it ravenously, although be so doing were poisoning themselves with the putrid filth they were swallowing. Can it be imagined that human beings imagined that human beings—officers could witness such sights and then return to their sumptuous meals without a thought of the terrible suffering of there starving Confederates.

The customary prison diet consisted of three or four crackers and a small slice of fat pork in the morning. In the afternoon a half pint of water in which the pork was boiled, and a piece of bread— nothing else. There were entirely insufficient to properly preserve health. The diet in the hospital was better, and answered fairly well. No vegetables, tea nor coffee were ever seen. It was repeatedly said, in my presence, that the reason we were denied vegetables, was in retaliation for the refusal of tobacco to their prisoners in the South. On many occasions vegetables sent by friends outside were denied to the prisoners. This occurred oftener at Point Lookout than at Elmira. At the later prison clothes sent to me they refused to deliver, also boots and shoes. In case they did deliver a coat it was not until the tail had been cut off and the tops of boots were similarly curtailed. At Elmira I was one day notified that there was a box at headquarters for me. Upon reporting there for it was opened in my presence by the order of Major Colt who was in command. The articles of clothing therein were of a valuable character. They were refused me. After pleading some time for the new coat, Major Colt consented to having it exchanged in town for another, he said of more suitable color, and detailed. Sent Major Rudd to attend to it. The overcoat was a very handsome and costly one; in return, after charging me five (5) dollars for his trouble he delivered to me a miserable shoddy one almost worthless.

I could relate dozens of other outrages equally disgraceful, but enough is said to illustrate what was the condition of thousands of our Confederates confined in the Northern prison-pens. I hope that many of those who had similar experiences will, some day, make known to the world, the disgraceful scenes they there witnesses.

Walter D. Addison, San Francisco, Sept. 30, 1889

VIEW IN FRONT OF FORT FISHER—SCENE OF THE CHARGE BY THE U. S. MARINES, JAN. 15, SHOWING THE TORPEDOES DUG UP BY REBEL PRISONERS.

Picture from *Frank Leslie's Illustrated Newspaper*, March 4, 1865.

On 4/15/1863 Dr. Albert Marion Baldwin traveled to Fort Fisher and volunteered for duty in the 40th North Carolina Artillery. He was stationed at Fort Holmes, on Bald Head Island. In December, 1864, his company was sent to help defend Fort Fisher.

Wilmington Morning Star News, 12/4/1927

Dr. Albert Marion Baldwin, Confederate veteran, was born in Columbus County, February 9, 1845. He enlisted from Wilmington, Company K., 40th North Carolina heavy artillery, at the age of 18. "I was sent to Fort Fisher where I served one year and was then sent to Bald Head Island, where ten companies were stationed. Here I witnessed the first bombardment of Fort Fisher. I remained one year at Bald Head and was sent back with four other companies to the second bombardment. The coast from Carolina Beach was lined with gunboats about 50. The ironclads came near in shore. We could make no impression on them with our small guns. In front of Fort Fisher there was a channel called the New Channel. It has since filled in by building the wall from the lower end of Fort Fisher to Zeke's Island. This channel was valuable to the blockade runners. I saw the wreck Modern Greece. She was attacked by the Yankees and ran in near shore and was wrecked. She can still be seen off the seas beach at low tide—24 sister blockade runners shared her fate along our coast.

The fort faced the ocean a mile. About every 200 yards a 64-pound gun was mounted and manned by eight to ten men. The largest gun we had was the Armstrong gun. We only had it at the last. I was instructed to stand on tiptoe when the gun went off; I did, and was alright. The bombardment was too terrible to describe. It was a rain of fire, shot and shell over us three days and two nights. Our barracks were all burned. The bombproofs saved some of us, when we could crawl in at night. When the firing ceased and we were captured, we were exhausted, but the Yankees marched us up the beach a mile. Here we camped, with a strong guard around us. They were kind. A soldier gave me something to eat from his haversack. We had no time to eat during the bombardment. We spent two nights on the beach. I had two blankets and the sand was soft. We were marched back and through the fort and put on two transports where the prisoners were taken through the New Channel into the ocean. There were 800 prisoners on the transport I was on.

Our captors were kind and kept the companies together. We put to sea, steaming due north. We entered the Delaware River, cutting through the ice. It was about the 20th of January, and the ice being so heavy our transport was ordered back and we put into New York harbor where we awaited orders from Washington, which was to proceed to Elmira. Our friends on the other transports were taken to Point Lookout. We were to have been sent to Fort Delaware, but our transport could not get through the ice we encountered. From New York we went by train to Elmira. Everything was covered in snow. Crowds came to look at us but no one said anything. We got off in the snow and marched a mile and a half to prison, but it seemed like 10 to me, leaving our southern climate, where I had been put to sleep with the rustling of the palm trees and the warm ocean winds from the Gulf Stream, it was a bitter exchange for this ice and snow—but so I entered my prison January 31, 1865. The officers and guards had icicles hanging from their moustaches. They paid no attention to it, but it was new to me, being from the South, where gentlemen wore no such ornaments.

My bed was a board—we slept in tiers of three along the wall, two to each tier. I occupied a center with a friend, James Lesesne, a member of my company and a comrade at Fort Fisher. I had held on to my two army blankets, and he had two, so we encountered the zero weather. We had two meals a day. We were marched by barracks, 100 to be fed at a time. We ate with our fingers, no plate, knife, fork or spoon. A thin slice of bread—with a thinner slice of meat—pork or corned beef—on it served as a plate. This was breakfast. The next meal and the last of the day was a cup of bean soup and a slice of bread, I was always glad to get the end slice, because it was a little thicker. I was so hungry I felt worse after eating than before. It was just a teaser what they gave me. One day James Lesesne received five dollars from a friend in Vermont, and then we felt as if we had come into a fortune, and so we had. We used it little by little, never more than 75 cents at the time for something to eat, cheese and crackers, which were bought from the sutler, the prison merchant. When money came it was posted on the bulletin board, and what glad news it was; some friend would tell us if we did not see it. I was so thin and weak and hungry that I felt like I was starving to death, and I was. I knew with the fall of Fort Fisher the South could not hold out much longer, and now the question was, would I hold out.

When a prisoner broke a rule he was marched around, up and down through the barracks with a barrel shirt on. The barrel shirt was a barrel with the heads knocked out and a place for the prisoner to put his arms through. The weather was getting better, snow and ice were melting and I could walk outside some days.

The news came, "Lee had surrendered!" Mr. C.C. Covington's uncle was the means of my getting released as soon as I did; he sent my name to Washington. At last the day came when we were ordered to the dining room under strong guard and on the way Lesesne saw on the bulletin board another five was waiting for him. We were so happy release was near. Lesesne was eager to hurry on, but I knew what the money had done for us and would do now, so I had consent to try and get it. I asked permission to see the treasurer, and a guard was given me, and I got the money and again laid in a supply of cheese and crackers. We had to take the oath, then we were marched through a large gate and on to the station.

I was in prison in Elmira four and a half months. I was released June 13, 1865. When I entered I was weighed and measured and a description taken of me. I was six feet and two inches tall and light in weight, 120 pounds, and far less now. From Elmira we went to Baltimore and took a boat to Old Point, changed to a smaller boat and went up the James River to Richmond, from there to Danville, in boxcars to Greensboro, Raleigh, Goldsboro and Wilmington, where I boarded the steamer A.P. Hurt, to Fayetteville, which was my home. My parents were not living, but my sister was there to welcome me—she did not recognize me when I appeared—I was so emaciated and had grown a long black beard. I spent my 20th birthday in prison."

A Tarheel Soldier's Story

Sergeant Thaddeus C. Davis, 3rd Company G, 40th North Carolina

Thaddeus C. Davis enlisted as a private in the 36th Regiment, 2nd Artillery Division, North Carolina troops in Beaufort, NC. Davis was sent to Fort Fisher and was promoted to 3rd sergeant in 3rd Company G on November 14, 1862. He transferred to the 40th Regiment NC, 3rd Artillery division on November 4, 1863 and was stationed at Fort Holmes. During this period he maintained a home at Smithville, NC. On November 22, 1864 five companies of the 40th NC were ordered to Georgia to reinforce Lt. General William J. Hardee, who was contesting Sherman's advance on Savannah. In December the 40th NC along with the 60th NC infantry served as a rear guard as Hardee's army retired through Savannah, Hardeeville, and into Charleston, SC. On December 30th, 1864, the 40th Regiment received orders to return to Wilmington, NC, and reinforce Fort Fisher. Sergeant Davis was captured at Fort Fisher on January 15th, 1865, and sent north to Elmira Prison. After the war he wrote an article about the second battle of Fort Fisher and his imprisonment in Elmira Prison Camp that was published in the *Confederate Veteran* Magazine in the February 1899 issue. Here is a reprint of that article:

T. C. Davis (Fortieth Regiment, North Carolina Troops), of Morehead City, N. C.:

In January, 1865, after the evacuation of Atlanta, five companies of the North Carolina Regiment of Hardee's command were ordered to reinforce the command at Fort Fisher, N. C., which, at that time, was the "key to the Confederacy."

We arrived on the 13th of January, 1865, at the beginning of the second attack on that fort, which was garrisoned with about twelve hundred soldiers. The Federals had a navy of eighty-four vessels, carrying six hundred heavy guns. After bombarding the fort for three days and nights, and disabling all of our guns except two or three, they landed about eleven thousand infantry, under the guns of their navy, and assaulted the fort. They succeeded in making lodgment in the fort about three o'clock Sunday evening, January 15, and the contest kept up until ten o'clock at night. The fort, with its garrison, was captured.

The Federal loss, as stated by Gen. Terry in his official report, was 1,445. The Confederate loss is not known, though it is estimated at 500, including Gen. W. H. C. Whiting and Col. William Lamb.

On January 16 we were put on board a ship and sent to Fortress Monroe, Va., from whence we were to be sent to Fort Delaware; but we got stuck in the ice at the breakwater, and the ship backed out and took us to New York City. We were sent by rail for that den of misery known as Elmira Prison, about one mile from Elmira, N. Y.

We arrived about eight o'clock in the evening, in four feet of snow, and many prisoners had neither blankets nor coats. We were kept standing in ranks in the street for half an hour before starting for the prison. We were halted in an old warehouse and robbed of all valuables by Lieut.

Groves and an unknown Sergeant Major; then we were sent to the barracks-board shanties about fifty yards long, containing one stove. Our beds were planks without blankets.

There were about seven thousand prisoners confined there, and those who had preceded us were in much want. They were dirty, pale, emaciated, and scantily clothed. Our rations consisted of loaves of stale bread an inch thick, tough pieces of steak, and occasionally broth. When prisoners died, their bodies were put in a box and stacked up in a "deadhouse" as high as they could stack them before taking them out for burial.

The Federal Sergeants who had charge of the prison "wards" (as they were called) were the meanest men I ever saw-demons in human flesh. There was a young soldier about eighteen years old, without blanket or coat, who had become deaf from exposure. When he was found near the stove, he was beaten and kicked about unmercifully. Gen. Weyler's treatment of the Cuban prisoners is nothing, compared to the treatment the Confederate' soldiers received at Elmira, N. Y. After the war, we were turned out in squads of two hundred, by taking the oath. I was truly glad to get out of prison, but sorry to be deprived of my watch and ring, which were stolen by Lieut. Groves and the sergeant major. I arrived at home on June 1, 1865, and while memory lasts I shall not forget the Great War and the cruel prison.

UNION SOLDIERS DIGGING UP COTTON FROM THE EARTHWORKS AT FORT FISHER.

Picture showing soldiers removing cotton from Fort Fisher's earthworks. Drawing is from *Frank Leslie's Illustrated Newspaper, March 4, 1865.*

Wilbur W. Gramling Diary

The following excerpts are from a diary kept by Wilbur Wightman Gramling after he was wounded and captured as a Confederate soldier in the Wilderness campaign and while in prison in Washington and in Elmira. A copy of the Macon, Ga., *Southern Christian Advocate* in Mr. Gramling's possession carries an obituary of W.W. Gramling. The newspaper, dated Jan. 25, 1871, said W.W. Gramling was born March 30, 1843, in Spartanburg District, S.C., son of Andrew P. and Elizabeth Gramling. After being captured in the Battle of the Wilderness, he spent 15 months in a federal prison camp and while there contracted pneumonia. He died in Leon County on Dec. 3, 1870, apparently from the effects of this disease, the newspaper said.

The daily diary was kept in ink (some of the entries being badly faded). In the front of the diary is this entry, "W.W. Gramling, May 25th. 1864. Colonial Hospital, Washington, D.C." Inside the back cover are some arithmetic calculations and the entry, 'I-want-to-go-home-so—bad."

Please Note: All spelling and grammatical errors are as they were written by the author of the diary.

Friday, May 6, 1864. Went into battle 2 o'clock. Wounded in the right arm and taken prisoner. Sent to rear in great pain. Had ball out and wound dressed. About 600 prisoners with me.

Saturday, May 7, 1864. Went to Hospital 1st Div. 9th Army Corps. Wound dressed and doing well. Started to rear but cut off by Moseby. Camped on Rappadan River. Considerable uneasyness afraid Mosby will make a dash on them.

Sunday, May 8, 1864. Came back by Chancellorsville and camped near Fredericksburg. All fair weather and wound doing finely. Got on the road to Moseby again today and had to turn back . I have been wishing he would recapture me. Did retake one from my regiment.

Monday, May 9, 1864. Arrived at Fredericksburg only this morning. Established hospital in a Presbyterian Church. Nothing to eat but hard bread, coffee, beef, and tea and every two or three days 2 oz. boiled beef.

Tuesday, May 17, 1864. All quiet. Weather fair. Three butter crackers for supper. Wound still improving. A great many vague rumors among the Yankees in regard to their successes. They have had it read to them on dress parade that Richmond was theirs.

Wednesday, May 18, 1864. A great many wounded came in last night from the front. I asked Dr. to let me walk out for recreation but would not allow me even with a guard. Reports from the front say the forces attacked with bayonets. They repulsed or captured a force including our battery of artillery, their report.

Saturday, May 21, 1864. Arrived at Washington this morning at daybreak. Now in hospital on the north side of town, is called Columbian Hospital. Saw Abe Lincoln's house. Very comfortably situated. Baked bread, coffee, meat, apples, some corn meal and syrup. Another cot to lie on.

Sunday, May 22, 1864. A beautiful morning. Shower rain at noon. Health good and wound doing well. I see negroes riding out in fine carriages with their driver sometimes a negro. Man & a white woman riding together in a carriage with a negro driver. Frequently see them walking together.

Thursday, May 26, 1864. Rainy all day. 200 more wounded came in. Papers are full of vain rumors. Lee is still retreating and nearly cut off from Richmond, Jeff Davis is captured by Grant and paroled. Don't know whether he will be summarily hanged or not. Some believe it, therefore are all very jubilant.

Tuesday, May 31, 1864. Every thing quiet today. The weather fair & pleasant. My health good, wound doing well. Some ladies in today to see Col. Manning. Brought him some grub. Still at Lincoln Hospital. Now what composes it is a building 100 feet long & 25 feet wide forming a triangle and a large number to tents. In all I suppose there is over 3000 wounded here and perhaps 200 rebs. I think this is nearly the last place in creation. It is right out in the open field. It is so very hot. I understand that 18,000 men are to leave here tomorrow for the front. Yanks still in good spirits & are looking up to Grant expecting him to crush out the rebellion this summer. If he does it by the 5th of June will be nominated as candidate for President. He won't do it.

Friday, June 24, 1864. Very fair and warm this morning. Sold $10.00 in gold for $18.00 in greenbacks & bought 1 plug tobacco, 2 boxes of matches & pr suspenders this p.m. Suffering good deal with backache again. The boys all keep in pretty good spirits so far.

Wednesday, July 6, 1864. Weather fair and pleasant. No change in things generally as I know. The wounded are most all doing very well. Some cases of gangrene which I think will be fatal.

Thursday, July 7, 1864. Very fair and pretty day though quite warm. No change in things generally, good deal of excitement about Frederick and Hagerstown, Md. Our forces making pretty good headway. Last dispatches state all the rebs have recrossed the Potomac. Men here sick.

Friday, July 8, 1864. The 8th day of July has passed & nothing has transpired worth note nor to make the day memorable. It has been a rather fair day and quite warm & sultry. The Yankees can't ascertain what force we have invading them with nor their whereabouts.

Sunday, July 10, 1864. The day has passed off very quiet. Nothing of note occurred. It is reported that our boys drove the Yankees 18 miles, killed Gen. Wallace and captured one other general— forget his name—and are now within nine miles of Baltimore. I think Washington is threatened pretty strongly this morning.

Monday, July 11, A.M. Great deal of excitement. Won't allow any one to go out of the ward. Ward master got his repeater on caused from the invaders say they have just about got Baltimore and are coming now to take Washington. Foiled in my plan to escape. Sent part of my party off. Wrote to

142

Irvin. P.M. Things have got a little more quiet. Reports say that they are fighting within six miles of here at Fort Manassas.

Tuesday, July 12, 1864. Fair~& pleasant this morning. Left today at noon & arrived at the old capital prison. They are very strict here. Won't let you get close to the window. Eat twice a day. Quite a dirty place, just alive with chinches one or two out at a time. Think I will get along.

Saturday, July 16, 1864. Every thing quiet today. Nothing occurred worthy note. My principal amusement is looking at the women pass. Some very pretty ones in the city of Washington. Quite a lot of cavalry are passing just now. Weather moderate.

Sunday, July 17, 1864. Today seems a great deal like Sunday & I can't help thinking of home and wishing I was at Old Pisgah. Everything remains about the same. A funeral procession passed. It was a member of the fire company. Five very pretty young ladies passed by in a carriage and one of them waved to me which is frequently the case.

Tuesday, July 19, 1864. Weather quite fair & not very warm. Our room is about 25 or 30 ft. square and has 42 men in it. Pretty well crowded about 600 or 700 prisoners. Prospects are good to be sent away soon but can't judge to what place. Rations are very short, 2 meals per day & is rumored that we will only get one hereafter.

Saturday, July 23, 1864. Left Washington 1 o'clock for Elmira. Arrival at Baltimore at 7. A great many spectators on the street. Got off the cars at Mountain House on Howard St & turned down Franklin. At Franklin house drew rations and left at 8 o'clock.

Sunday, July 24, 1864. Traveled all night and find we 170 miles from Elmira. Corn crops are very sorry. Wheat is gathered. Oats is pretty good. Traveled through the Catskill Mountains up the Susquehanna River. Crossed it 20 times. Got here 6 o'clock.

Monday, July 25, 1864. Raining all day. Very sloppy. Elmira is noted for pretty women and a good many of them. The prison is about 10 acres square with Barracks inside large enough to hold 112 men each. This is Barracks No. 3 commanded by Maj. Colt.

Wednesday July 27, 1864. It is fair & quite warm today. Though the nights are quite cool. We eat twice a day, morning at 7 o'clock & evening at 3 o'clock. Our camp or Barracks are surrounded by mountains, not very high ones though.

Friday, Aug. 5 , 1864. No news today. Every thing perfectly quiet & dull as is natural in prison. Weather remains fair and quite warm. Everything seems to speak in favor of the South. The prisoners are expecting an early exchange or parole.

Thursday, Aug. 11, 1864. Everything very quiet & have rumors of exchange pretty soon but it don't amount to anything, only a falsehood. My health is still improving. Am taking salts in broken doses. My blood seems to be very thin.

Friday, Aug. 12, 1864. This is a beautiful day. The sweet little birds are chirping from branch to branch. There are a great many rumors but I don't pay any attention to these, Dear Friend, when what you do remember is the Guns.

Friday, Aug, 19, 1864. Fair and pleasant today. Suffering very much with jaw-ache. Tried to have an old root extracted & instead of getting it broke a good one off at the gums. Recd. a letter from Irvin today. He was well, also one from Washington. Have some clothes on the road.

Saturday, Aug. 20, 1864. The exchange question is still being agitated very much. Report says (said to be reliable) commencing 10th Sept. all over plus to be paroled & all to have 60 days furlough on our return. Still suffering good deal with neuralgia. Morgan of Co. D died today of Chronic diarrhea.

Friday, Aug. 26, 1864. No change in things generally. It has been a very pleasant day. Little rain this evening. Neuralgia is about well. Received the clothing today that I have been expecting from Washington. Very well pleased. No fine clothing nor provisions are allowed to be brought in—all that come are confiscated.

Saturday, Aug. 27, 1864. Wrote Miss Thomson today. Report says that Lee made a flank movement on Grant & fully demoralized his army. The news generally is very cheering. More rain this evening, I am feeling very well now.

Wednesday, Aug. 31 1864. Last night & this morning was cold, the coldest weather I ever experienced in August. It is quite pleasant this evening. August has been tolerably pleasant and pretty rainy & cloudy most all the time The news generally has been quite cheering. Most all the prisoners are looking forward for an early exchange, also are expecting peace soon. The last report (which are many in regard to exchange) is that Jeff has agreed to exchange the Negroes for the men that have enrolled their names to take the oath of allegiance to the U.S. Thomson is sick with pneumonia. Also Wilford with fever, both in the hospital. My health has been good except neuralgia. The rest of the company are well & doing as well as could be expected. So ended August.

Thursday, Sept, 1, 1864. Good deal of excitement in town last night caused by the nomination of McClellan for President. Quite a number of guns were fired. Weather remained the same as everything else does. No change in anything.

Saturday, Sept. 3, 1864. Weather still remains cool and cloudy, but no rain. Seems be more like November than September. Rumor says Atlanta has fallen with 20,000 prisoners, also that Lee has lost 15,000.

Sunday, Sept. 4, 1864. It is reported that Lee has whipped Grant again & driven him 6 miles. He calls for reinforcements, will have to retreat if not received. Papers advocate a retreat. I think more about home Sundays than any other day, not only home but old Pisgah house. Long to see the dear spot again.

Saturday, Sept. 10, 1864. Rumor says that the exchange is to take place between the 15th & 25th of this month. I can't put much faith in it though I hope it is true. Still fair & very pleasant. We have pretty strict orders. Have to be very careful what we do or how we act.

Friday, Sept. 16, 1864. This has been the most pleasant day we have had in some time. Fair & not cold. There is no news today. Wrote a letter to John T. Desellum for Blanket, draws, pants socks and money. Some rumor about the wounded & sick being sent off.

Wednesday, Sept. 21, 1864. Reported that Gen. Rhodes & Gordon are killed & 15,000 prisoners captured. Am little better today but feel quite bad yet. Men are dying up very fast, average 16 or 18 per day.

Thursday, Sept. 22, 1864. Have got about well again though my breast is very sore yet. The exchange & parole question is being agitated again. Great many are taking the oath. Weather same. Read a letter from Irvin. Is dated the 15th.

Friday, Sept, 23, 1864. There is no news about today. Weather fair & pleasant. Am feeling some better. Wrote to Irvin today. Men are dying very fast, from 15 to 25 per day.

Saturday, Sept. 24, 1864. Surgeons have been round today examining the sick and wounded, they say to parole them. Weather very pleasant though a little cooler this evening. Health improving. I long to get back in Dixie.

Saturday, Oct. 1, 1864. No news of interest stirring today. Weather is cloudy & very cold and unpleasant. Don't expect to sleep much tonight as I only have one blanket to cover with and it is quite thin. Don't see how I am to live this winter without more cover.

Wednesday, Oct. 5, 1864. Weather remains the same. No news at all. Received a letter from & wrote to Mr. Desellum today. Taking names for clothing this evening. Health remains very good.

Friday, Oct.7, 1864. A.M. fair and pleasant. 25 army men made their escape last night by tunneling. They got 25 horses. Commenced 19th of Aug. They dug 64 ft. No news today. Report says the sick leaves in the morning. P.M. cloudy but no rain. Still hauling wood.

Tuesday, Oct. 11, 1864. Elmira Gazette states that all prisoners captured up to June are to be exchanged except those captured by Butler in front of Petersburg. The sick and wounded have got off at—last near 2000. They seemed to be very cheerful.

Thursday, Oct. 14, 1864. No news stirring today. Fair and quite cold. Received a letter from Mattie today of Sept. 17th. All well as usual. Rave not caught any of the men yet that made their escape.

Tuesday, Oct 18, 1864. Still fair & pleasant. Papers says that Sherman's army is completely annihilated. Jeff Davis speaks very cheeringly to the soldiers. I had a mess of cabbage & Irish potatoes todav.

Wednesday, Oct. 19, 1864. No change in the weather & no news of any kind. The general health of the prisoners are a great deal better. Instead of 15 to 20 it is only 5 to 10 per day & it seems to be the general impression that we will winter here.

Thursday, Oct. 20, 1864. Weather somewhat unsettled but no rain. Frost every morning though the weather remains quite moderate. Prisoners are generally pretty well supplied with clothing, shoes especially.

Friday, Oct, 21, 1864. Papers state that England & France have recognized the independence of the Confederacy. Nothing else new.. Weather remains the same. My health is still very good.

Sunday, Oct. 23, 1864. Cloudy but no rain today. My health has generally been good ever since I have been captured. Read my Testament almost every day. They have a Library here now & I have a book reading. The title is the Story of a Pocket Bible. Very good.

Monday, Oct. 24, 1864. More tunneling been going on but were reported by some galvanized demons. Would soon have been through. Weather cloudy but little rain. Wrote to Miss Ida Duncanson today.

Tuesday, Oct. 25, 1864. Reported in camps that Grant has given up Petersburg and is falling back to Washington. My health remains very good. Weather very mild, fair & pleasant. The people of Elmira has kept the old cannon pretty busy today.

Monday, Oct. 31, 1864. Weather warm & wet. We have a very good market here. The principal articles of trade is apples, cooked cabbage, Tobacco, clothing, potatoes, knives &c. Officers have tried several times to break it up but have not succeeded & are not likely to. Received a letter from Mrs. Sawyer yesterday. Boxes of clothing &c, and money are being sent in daily to the men from their relatives & friends but I am somewhat among the unfortunate. The way I spend my time. 1st. Set the table & then clean up afterwards, then 2nd read & knock about until 3 O'clock & 3rd it is dinner, which I have to take an active part in, working after the rest.

Monday, Nov. 7, 1864. Weather fair & pleasant. It is very changeable, one day freezing, the next almost boiling. Comparatively no new dispatches today. Tomorrow is looked upon as the great day. General impression is that it will be a close run between Abe & Mc.

Tuesday, Nov. 8. 1864. Nothing has occurred today more than usual. Far as I know it is quite still for election day. Generally thought that it will be a close run between Abe & Mc. rather in the latter's favor.

Wednesday, Nov. 9, 1864. It is reported that Lincoln is a head as far as known. Little hopes of an exchange. Health good, weather fair & quite pleasant.

Friday, Nov. 11, 1864. Great speculation about the election. Some say that Lincoln is elected & some say Mac. Very fair but some colder though pleasant. Great many boxes packages of clothing come in daily for the rebs.

Monday, Nov. 14, 1864. Have not heard who is elected yet for president—it is a very close run. I believe it inclines to be in Lincoln's favor. Weather unsettled. Little snow & very cold. Health generally very good.

Friday, Nov. 18, 1864. Weather cloudy & warm. Fresh report about exchange. Officers are getting tighter on us every day. Keep trying to break up our market but cant quite outwit. Rebels are too smart at every point.

Saturday, Nov. 19, 1864. Unusually pleasant today & fair. seems to be no doubt but Abe is reelected. Health improving. Everything very quiet in camp. Bought a blanket today for 75 cents.

Wednesday, Nov. 23, 1864. Weather broken & a little snow. Very cold. I am well except a severe cold. N.Y. Papers say Gen. Lee is kill. Beauregard has taken the oath & Jeff is not to be found. Wrote to Mrs. Sawyer and Mr. Wagener.

Thursday, Nov. 24, 1864. No news stirring today. Very strict with the men now. Don't allow the men to bring their rations out of the messroom. Two men were caught tunneling last night.

Friday, Nov. 25, 1864. All quiet along the line today. Fair & pretty warm. Good deal of snow on the ground. Wrote to pa today There is between 7000 & 8000 men in here and about 4000 have applied to take the oath. I am some better this evening.

Saturday, Nov. 26, 1864. Cloudy & a little snow. N.Y. Herald say that Mullord has gone to prepare terms of exchange to Jeff which not doubt he will accept, also that Lee has whipped Grant again, capturing 20,000 prisoners. It predicted that all of us will doubtless eat our Christmas dinner at home.

Thursday, Dec. 1, 1864. No news again today. Weather fair & pleasant. Health very good. Up roar in the cook house. I will try & give a minute description of our camp quarters & surroundings vicinity as well as possible.

Saturday, Dec. 3, 1864. Weather remains the same, No news. On the South Side is the old river bed holding water. Along on the north bank is the cookhouse and mess room & apothecaries &c, then a street 30 ft wide, then a row of Barracks 30 in another street same width.

Sunday, Dec. 4, 1864. Everything remains the same. Next is two more rows of barracks. Along the north side in the west half is the officers quarters, gate in the center along the west side are the Hospital Barracks & kitchen, seven in number.

Monday, Dec. 5, 1864. Everything the same. Major very strict. On the north side of the camp is part of the city, two observatories, 1 regt. in camp & mountains dotted with country farms. On the east side is the principal part of town, depot & another regiment in camp & one 4 gun battery.

Tuesday, Dec. 6, 1864. Our new Maj. is very tyrannical. Had a fight in the ward. Mountains also on the east. On the south side is battery River, broad plain & mountains, slaughter house & farm house &c.

Monday, Dec. 19, 1864. Cloudy but quite pleasant. More prisoners came in today from Washington. Good many cases small pox. Three have died. Prisoners are very sickly as a general thing. My bed fellow Cay is sick with pneumonia.

Tuesday, Dec. 20, 1864. Fair and very cold. Everything is frozen hard. No news again today. Am in very good health. Cay is not any better. The rebs are enjoying themselves daily skating on the pond in the south side of the camp.

Saturday, Dec. 24, 1864. Weather fair & has moderated a great deal. Jeff Davis has poisoned himself, Bob had whipped Grant. There is 40 cases of smallpox, 4 have died. Prospects are bad for Christmas.

Sunday, Dec. 25, 1864. Fair and very pleasant. Christmas but it seems no more than any other day. ground is melting which makes it very slippery. Today is The snow on

Monday, Dec. 26, 1864. Cloudy, warm but no rain. It is reported that Savannah has fallen with 20,000 prisoners. Quite sickly in camp again, from 15 to 25 die a day. Small pox is growing worse every day. Wrote to Mrs. Sawyer.

Thursday, Dec. 29, 1864. Heavy snow last night. Colder today & a little snow. Started to school today. Am taking French lessons. No news. My health remains good. Getting Sunday school lesson, 1st Chapter Acts of the Apostles to 16th verse. Nearly know it.

Tuesday, Jan. 3, 1865. Weather has moderated. A great deal from reports. Confirmed my vaccination has taken finely. Very sickly in camp now. Progressing pretty well in French.

Wednesday, Jan. 4, 1865. Cloudy & a little snow and very cold. Health very good. Arm is pretty soar & is still inflamed. Had quite a fight in my ward this morning between Dunn & Harper about insulting language.

Sunday, Jan. 22, 1865. Had considerable snow again last night. Not very cold. Reported that the authorities have agreed to parole all prisoners. Am not feeling very well this evening. My feet are frost bit again. Lady in camp today.

Tuesday, Jan. 24, 1865. Cloudy but not very cold. Recd. a letter from Matt yesterday. All well but for several deaths. No school today nor no news of interest. All dull.

Thursday, Jan. 26, 1865. Cloudy, no snow nor rain and not very cold. Reported that Buffalo was burnt last night. Supposed to be done by the raiders from Canada. Everything is quiet. 2000 prisoners sent from Point Lookout. Worked on bunk today. (These prisoners were from Fort Fisher. Author)

Thursday, Feb. 2, 1865. Fair and quiet pleasant and beautiful scenery. Mountains all around & perfectly white with snow. Received box & contents today from Mrs. Sawyer & a pair of girls drawers (astonishing).

Sunday, Feb 5, 1865. Very blustery and unpleasant. Thank God the exchange is about to commence at last—have been taking names today. Texas, Louisiana, Tennessee, Kentucky, Arkansas & Missouri are to go first with the sick.

Tuesday, Feb. 7, 1865. A.M. cloudy & moderate. No person allowed to go to Dixie who has applied to take the oath, I entertain very good hopes of getting back soon. Col. Moore says is a general exchange. France seems to be meddling with affairs. P.M. snowing very fast.

Monday, Feb. 13, 1865. Weather fair and pleasant. At noon 300 sick & 200 well men leaves this evening in an hour or more. Are now calling the roll. Reported that they will continue to send fast as possible.

Thursday, Feb, 16, 1865. Reports say there is 1000 to go next load, 600 sick & 400 well also Va. and N.C. will be the last exchanged. Am anxious for my time to come. Am afraid they will only exchange three thousand & stop & leave me here.

Friday, Feb. 17, 1865. Weather very moderate & fair. I have pretty reliable information that the commanding officer has recd orders to clear the camp as quick as possible. Trust to God it is true. Great deal of sickness.

Tuesday, Feb 28, 1865. Another load of 500 signed the paroles today. Don't know when they will get off. Have a load of sick made up also. Hope I will get out soon. Trust to Providence. An unfair way of sending them off. Just whoever has money to buy his way out can go. Some sent an application to the Col. and got off in that way. Great deal of sickness in camp now and the smallpox is more fatal. Great many deaths, from 20 to 30 every day out of about 7000 man. More now than there was last summer and fall when there was some 10,000 here.

Monday, March 13, 1865. Weather quiet moderate. Reported that 13,000 of Earley's men are captured, also that 17,000 of Sherman's surprised old Jube. I don't believe either report. As the saying is those tales have not got any hair in them.

Friday, March 17, 1865. Weather remained the same. River is still rising. Is all over camp 4 or 5 ft deep, in cook house & some of the wards. Moved out all the sick and commissary stores to higher place. Commence fall in it at 6 o'clock.

Saturday, March 18. River has fallen nearly to its old water mark. Mess house 7 & cook houses 4 in deep in mud. Had a bad time cleaning them out. Some houses washed away.

Wednesday, March 22, 1865. Little sleet and rain today, reported that the load on which my name was is broken up. I think it true. They have made up another load of the first on the rolls as we came here. I am knocked out.

Monday, March 27, 1865. Very fair & pleasant. Boys are catching fish today out of the creek. Catches some quite nice perch. Tried my hand but met with no success. Nothing new. All quiet.

Tuesday, March 28, 1865. Weather remains the same. Everything quiet. Papers say Lee attacked Grant thinking his strength was weakened to reinforce Sherman & was repulsed with a loss of 5000 or 6000 men while Grant only lost 500 or 600 men.

Wednesday, March 29, 1865. Very pleasant weather. Every thing very quiet. Discharged from the mess because they were dissatisfied with me but simply good union men. Bob Lee whiped. room today, not to put in some

Thursday, March 30, 1865. My birthday, 22 years old. A very wet morning. More of the waiters discharged. No news about when and more men will leave for Dixie. I think not before next week. Have made one more effort to get off.

Friday, March 31, 1865. Still cool & raining. No news of importance. I hope the Yankees are satisfied now they have discharged all the rebs who were waiters in the mess room and put in oath takers or good union men as they call them. The winter is about over now and it has not been so very hard. I have toughed it out very well. Can't say that I suffered any either from cold or hunger for which I am very thankful. Have been blessed so far. Tried to get off on the next load but I think my chances are very slim. Lt. Smith said the rolls were full. Wards are all consolidated into 30. Mine is still lE.

Monday, April 3, 1865. Weather same. Reports say that Richmond is evacuated & that it will be a month yet before the Baltimore road is repaired. Commenced work today.

Monday, April 4, 1865. A.M. fair and pleasant. Richmond gone up. 12,000 prisoners, 50 pieces artillery. P.M. cloudy and little rain. Nothing new.

Monday, April 10, 1865. Tolerably pleasant today. Reports say, it is published on bulletin board that Lee has surrendered his army also that we are to be paroled immediately.

Tuesday, April 11, 1865. No change in things generally. Still rumors & seems to be confirmation of the surrender of Lee & army. Some seem to be glad, some sorry.

Wednesday, April 12, 1865. Cloudy & rainy. Papers give a list of officers captured, Gen. Finegan one of the number. Great many are confident we will all soon be paroled.

Thursday, April 13, 1865. Seems to be settled that Gen. Lee & Army has surrendered of Grant. Some seem to rejoice while others lament the capture of so noble an army.

Friday, April 14, 1865. Great rejoicing throughout the U.S. Great exultation & blowing in the papers. fairly growing picture. Richmond is entirely destitute of provisions. Recd. Federals with great joy.

Saturday, April 15, 1865. Excitement has only begun. Abe & Seward was murdered last night, first rumors that a Virginian, lastly S.s. clerk Rumored that all Rebel officers at Washington were killed.

Sunday, April 16, 1865. Cloudy and Quite cold. Lincoln's murderer is supposed to be one Booth. Johnson to his seat yesterday at 2 o'clock. Seward considered dangerous. The assassin not apprehended yet.

Monday, April 24, 1865. Weather fair & cold. Great excitement. Took the names of all citizen oath takers, all who willing to take the oath & those who won't take the oath. I am still a R E Reb.

Tuesday, April 25, 1865. Fair and very pleasant. Nothing new. Johnson has not surrendered yet. He & Sherman has been negotiating terms of peace. Lines extend from the Potomac to the Rio Grande. Washington authorities dissatisfied. All armies to be turned over to state authorities just as before the war.

Wednesday, April 26, 1865. Fair & pleasant. Still great excitement. Most all have applied to take the oath & I was weak enough to do so also. Sorry for it since try and & live in the hopes that it will prove for the best.

Thursday, April 27, 1865. Warm & broken. A thunder & shower reminded me of old times very much. Am feeling troubled today, afraid I have done wrong.

Friday, April 28, 1865. Weather broken. No rain & tolerably cool. Latest dispatch is that they commence paroling Monday, Virginians first. Don't place any confidence in the rumor. Health good, smallpox departed

Saturday, April 29, 1865. Another thunder shower. Otherwise fair and pleasant. No news today. All very quiet. Bought some leaf tobacco. These are very dull and all have on hand.

Sunday, April 30, 1865. All quiet. Reported a load leaves tomorrow for Baltimore. There has been a great deal of excitement this month, the whole confederacy has gone. Sad to think of but might be hope.

Friday, May 5, 1865. Fair & warm. No news of importance. Everything quiet. Wrote to Pa of the great improvements going on in camp, and fixing up quite a garden.

Nineteen year-old William R. Greer enlisted in the Confederate Army on January 4, 1863 and was assigned to Hagood's Brigade, 25th South Carolina Regiment. He fought at both battles of Fort Fisher, was captured and sent to Elmira Prisoner of War Camp. This is a small portion of a larger story he had written about his experiences during the War Between the States. His story begins in the trenches of Petersburg, Va., just before the first attack on Fort Fisher. William R. Greer's story is courtesy of the Manuscript Department, William R. Perkins Library, Duke University, North Carolina.

Recollections of a Private Soldier of the Army of the Confederate States by William R. Greer

At 3:30 A. M. December first 1864 there rang out through the bitterly cold air, it was sleeting heavily, the bugle call of "To the Colors" and our brigade started in heavy marching order, southward, destination not divulged. After toiling wearily through heavy mud for ten miles that night we reached Richmond early in the morning. We received no welcome there and no coffee or anything else, although we were bitterly cold and suffering greatly. We were then packed, like cattle, into box cars with no seats therein and so closely packed that we could not move, the redeeming quality of this arrangement being the warmth of such intimacy saved us from freezing to death. We traveled in this fashion all night, reaching Danville, Virginia, the next morning. Upon disembarking one comrade was discovered dead from cold and exposure, a dozen more were hustled to the hospital.

Later on we continued our journey South but with improved Transportation facilities, but owing to the condition of the roads, the rolling stock, and careless or treacherous human assistance, everything pertaining to the transportation department was beginning to disintegrate, we did not reach Wilmington, North Carolina, until December 25th. Rations were not, at that period, superabundant as I recollect while enroute Christmas day, I enjoyed for dinner a large uncooked sweet potato.

On reaching Wilmington we embarked for the neighborhood of Fort Fischer (sic) situated at the mouth of the Cape Fear River. Before our arrival at this destination, an expedition for the reduction of the fort, the land forces under B. F. Butler and a large naval force commanded by Admiral Porter had appeared, but although Porter inaugurated a determined attack, Butler failed in his support and the expedition sailed away December 31st. We were ordered back to Wilmington and there held in reserve.

January 13th a second attack on the fort was imminent. The expedition this time being under command of General Terry supplanting old Butler. Terry's land force of 8,000 men was auxiliary to Porter's fleet officially numbering 58 vessels of various grades.

The garrison of the fort being deemed insufficient our regiment and one other was ordered to proceed with all haste to the point of attack. This journey, my last under Confederate rule, was noteworthy as to the unwillingness or treachery of the Captains of the river steamers to risk their precious lives in close proximity to the bombardment now in progress. My recollection is that the application of a loaded weapon near the head of the recalcitrant sailors proved a persuasive argument, and on to our fatal destination we sailed.

It was a clear, cold morning, Sunday January 15th, when our forces disembarked at the extreme inner end of the landing under cover of a high battery, although we were witnesses of the progress of this continuous and terrific bombardment (up to this time there had been no demonstration from Terry), Porter evidently wished to reduce the fort first; we were soon in a position to realize the magnitude of this unceasing torrent of iron missiles which were being hurled at us. Finding a barrel of "hardtack" flavored with worms, our last ration from Dixie, and thus being prepared for the adventure, we were ordered to proceed singly, keeping a reasonable distance apart, into the main fort, under this enfilade of fire, and ordered to protect ourselves "as well as possible", this was somewhat possible, from gun projectiles as we hugged the intervening batteries and bomb-proofs closely on our hazardous journey to the ramparts of our 1,700 yards but mortar shells are deadly missiles which are difficult to elude. The result of this maneuver which was absolutely correct insofar as necessity demanded, was not quite successful, inas (sic) much as many men perished or were disabled, and many more in consequence partly of the disorganization of the different companies, officers and men being widely apart, and furthermore, many tired out and utterly disheartened men took shelter in the bombproofs on the route and refused to budge, so that only a portion of our force joined the organized garrison on the front who themselves had been of necessity in the bombproofs nearby.

A determined attack by sailors from the fleet who marched up the beach with drawn cutlasses was quickly defeated by our force who manned the breastworks very rapidly. The loss to the attacking party was reported very heavy. Shortly after this incident, a squad of Union soldiers appeared in the fort at the extreme left, the sallyport not only unprotected but left wide open. A larger force appearing there ensued a struggle between the contestants fighting from each bastion when it became useless to resist any further, and Fort Fischer (sic) surrendered.

It was recalled to the memory of the writer that one of the members of our command had in his rapid movement while dodging shells witnessed my complete entombment in the sand from the explosion of a nearby shell and as stated "only one foot sticking out."

As the prison camp (Elmira) was a very large enclosure we did not happen to meet, and it was thirty years after the close of the war, that after much persuasion, he was convinced that the fact of my having one foot out encouraged my extrication.

After a time squads of Federal soldiers marched through the fort gathering up the prisoners saying "fall in" and "Johnny got any tobacco?" We were marched out of the fort in a body and placed on the beach, cold, wet, and hungry, sentinels closely guarding us. The only diversion being the pyrotechnic display from the fleet celebrating the victory. One regret connected with this situation was that before I was ordered to "Fall in" I had unwisely destroyed the diary of my services in the Virginia Campaign, for this proved to have been unnecessary. The possession of this record, written under fire, would have been very valuable in assisting memory at this juncture.

The following morning there occurred a heavy explosion in the magazine of the fort in which it was reported the Confederate who fired the fuse perished as did a number unknown to us of the Union force. As I have no memory of any food being given us I presume we were still hungry, living on the memory of the last Confederate ration mentioned above.

The weather was clear but quite cold, but we were ordered to wade knee deep in the surf and were then hauled in launches, and after boarding a tug, were loaded into a "Greyhound" named General Lyon, said craft being noted as having only one live boiler, its companion having perished as a result of the high rate of speed characterizing the ship, this was confirmed by the fact of its taking ten days to speed from Cape Fear, North Carolina, to Jersey City. The memory of this sea voyage lingers like a sinister dream. I re-visualize the situation in the whole as comparable only to an enlarged box of sardines, the temperature ranging in the 90's and when it is remembered that on deck the yard arms

153

as well as the deck were coated with ice, there could have been only one result, which was speedily achieved by the mortality list shortly after our incarceration in the prison camp, Elmira, N. Y.

Rations for the prisoners appeared to be of the least consequence to our guardians. One day we had, I distinctly recollect, four soda biscuits and some rice gruel. I desire here to emphasize the thought, that what is written about my captivity, that may appear censorious, is related and has lain in memory without sectional prejudice, the term "War" covering the situation and further, if any statement of hardship or suffering is emphasized it is with the view of picturing the horrors of war to some extent with the hope, that even this slight contribution, may assist in producing a situation as outlined by Tennyson "Till the war drums throbbed no longer and the battle flags were furl'd."

On landing at Jersey City we were at once transferred to a train of cars in waiting and then, under guard, commenced our journey to a prison camp on the outskirts of the city of Elmire (sic) in New York State. The journey was long and uncomfortable and on landing at the depot we were marched through the streets, almost waist deep in snow, and being gazed at from the dwellings as if we were wild animals. As the sinister walls of the camp, which proved to be my home for six months, or might, as it was the case of thousands whose graves lie nearby, in mute evidence of their suffering and endurance, have resulted in my relief from earthly existence, the familiar quotation from Dante which I had memorized in my early youth, "All hope abandon ye who enter here." On entering this miniature city, for such it was in a sense, having its own hospitals, guard house, post office, express office, etc. We were at once assigned to barracks, being wooden houses with triple rows of bunks on each wall and two large coal stoves in the center. Being imbued at the time with ideas pertaining to my personal welfare such as warmth and sustenance, I did not interest myself as to the extent of the grounds, number of prisoners, etc., but I did observe that this large area was surrounded by high wooden walls and that sentinels were stationed on platforms on the outside overlooking the camp, and that there existed an area, a prescribed distance from the walls, aptly termed the "Dead Line". This I believe exists in all institutions. There was as far as topography is concerned a river, the name of which is forgotten, flowing past one side of the camp but closely guarded. Still I do not imagine that at that time it was flowing very freely as the whole landscape appeared to be composed of ice and snow; the icicles from the barracks of great lengths and apparently never melting. As an instance of the severity of the climate which so hardly tested our Southern blood and was the cause of great mortality, it was officially stated that on a certain morning in February the relief guard found three sentinels dead from exposure.

On our arrival and assignment, we were ordered to partly unclothe and perform some ablution; as this was effected outside of the building it was performed with great celerity. Our hair being trimmed and very proper instructions given as to keeping away from the stoves we began to settle down and await further orders. I was informed that the number of prisoners at that time was eight thousand.

The most important regulation of the camp was the roll call, outdoors, early morning and again in the evening.

On arrival the prisoners were offered the choice of either remaining loyal to the Confederate cause, or of swearing allegiance to the United States Government, including our oath of never bearing arms during the continuance of the war. Those who availed themselves of this latter opportunity were placed as hospital stewards or assigned other light duties, and furthermore abundantly fed. All of my comrades of the W. L. I. (Washington Light Infantry) decided to remain loyal to the Southern cause. Our duties were in addition to the care and cleanliness of the wards, and our own personal portion thereof, the policing of the streets and other sanitary work. Our rations were poor both in quality and quantity and altogether insufficient for sustenance in such a rigorous climate. In spite of all hygienic precautions, including an enforced vaccination, illness and mortality steadily increased. Pneumonia, typhoid, and small pox simply raged even in the wards. The hospitals, being inadequate to meet the situation, the daily death rate of small-pox alone was registered as forty cases. Finally, I became ill, partly from exposure to the intense cold and from insufficient and improper food. I lay in my bunk without medical attention and was gradually sinking from sheer weakness and exhaustion, when a messenger sent by a friendly hand, appeared at my bedside and silently left a package containing a flask of brandy and some soda crackers. This timely and welcome sustenance restored my strength to an extent that I was again on my feet.

The following narrative may prove of momentary interest, among my messmates in the company there was a gentleman who, for a short period before the secession of South Carolina, had left his native state, Massachusetts, and had come to Charleston with the intention of residing here. In addition to having engaged in mercantile business, he at once evinced a decided interest in the upbuilding (sic) of our Y. M. C. A. His sterling qualities expressed in his various activities very soon resulted, in spite of sectional prejudices, in his acquiring a large circle of friends. This popularity became much greater on his enlisting as a private soldier in the ranks of the W. L. I. (Washington Light Infantry) giving as his reason, his belief in the justice of the Southern cause. Brave soldier as he proved to be in every engagement, he was intensely interested in religious work and whenever occasion offered would assist our chaplain in conducting prayer meetings. He was captured at Fort Fischer (sic) and as, in my case, imprisoned at Elmira. The following information was given me after the close of the war—George S. Baker, such was his name, was the son of the Rev. A. R. Baker of Medford, Massachusetts, this latter being also an author of works more particularly of Sunday School literature. Soon after reaching our prison camp my comrade became desperately ill of pneumonia. Word having been conveyed to his father of the critical situation, he hurried to Washington D. C. and after much difficulty was granted an interview with President Lincoln. After narrating the serious condition of his son he besought the president to grant a pardon and to give an order for his release which might result in saving his life. This plea was at first denied, but as the grief stricken father was on the point of leaving his presence, Mr. Lincoln, for some reason unknown, recalled him, and after some inquiry ascertained that the petitioner was the author of a publication that he (Mr. Lincoln) had used as a textbook while teaching a Sunday school class in former times in Springfield, Illinois. He now signed the order of release and pardon. The patient having, as soon as practicable, been carried to his old homestead, was carefully nursed back to health. It was, as I definitely ascertained, this good hearted messmate, who had directed the conveyance of life saving material by a trusted messenger to my bunk in the prison.

One more rather disagreeable climatic experience in prison is recollected. In the early spring as a consequence of the thaw, the adjacent river overflowing its bank invaded our territory, and for several days the water surged through out barracks to the depth of six feet necessitating an adjournment of the upper banks. After this occurrence things began to grow brighter. The war was over and the gradual release of the prisoners, beginning with the earlier ones, was in inaugurated.

As stated above the earlier prisoners were being released thereby leaving certain positions, clerical and otherwise, to be filled. My vigorous home training being properly brought up supplemented by camp discipline had inculcated a habit of order and neatness not only personally bit in my intimate surroundings. It was, therefore, from habit that my bunk when put in order for the day, was not only proper but was duly decorated with a fringed shawl. So accordingly the established order of little events and their resultant growth, it happened one day, being temporarily on the parade ground and an officer passing through our barracks stopped immediately at my bunk and after obtaining my name left instructions for an immediate appearance at headquarters. Thither I sped with some trepidation, but upon reporting to the said officer and satisfactorily answering certain queries, I was directed to report at Major Beale's tent, the Commandant of the camp, to act as clerk and perform certain duties. I found the Major quite affable and reasonable. He was the ideal expression of an elderly army officer, florid of complexion and in his genial make up gave evidence, from his ample girth, of never permitting any of the comforts of life escaping his vigilance.

After a time the Major, who off duty was really a charming genial personality began to evince a kindly interest in the Confederate boy. I was only twenty years old, and granted the privilege of going into the city during the day. Finally as time wore on and the date of my release from captivity drew near the kind hearted Major expressed a wish that I should remain with him as an adopted son. But, the home urge to a Southern boy, in whose memory of his home in Charleston, South Carolina, with its care, comfort and family affection, dwelt so vividly, and made such an appeal, that I, with grateful thanks and warm appreciation, declined this most unusual tender. I have often thought of the dear old Major who I presume has long since responded to "Taps" of the English—the "Last Post"—"Peace be to his ashes."

On a certain day in August 1865, exact date forgotten, three months after peace was declared and after the administration of the oath of allegiance and other formalities and after twenty-four hours stay in Elmira at the home of a kindly, gracious and elderly Southern gentlewoman, I embarked on a train from New York City enroute for my uncle's residence at Yonkers on the Hudson. There I was graciously received and cared for. After a time, (illegible) and elder brother, (this officer escaped capture with me, being on a furlough at the time, but returned to Virginia and remained with the remnant of the brigade until the surrender of Lee's Army), arrived at Yonkers by invitation and the information that certain business arrangements could be effected for the resumption of the disrupted mercantile business that had existed prior to the war. It can be imagined how this reaction from the hardships and miseries for so long a period was enjoyed, but after a brief period it was determined, that, as our family, then residents of Graniteville, South Carolina, were sorely in need of funds, I was entrusted with a sufficiency of "greenbacks" for first aid. So I took passage on the initial voyage of the steamer "Quaker City" from New York to Charleston. My memory is, that as the good ship entered our ever grand and beautiful harbor and neared her dock, I became deeply despondent at the spectacle of such dilapidation and ruin as our once beautiful city presented at that time. I immediately took passage on the old South Carolina Railroad, and after a varied itinerary of railroads, and crossing streams in lighters and other adventures, arrived safely at Graniteville where I was accorded a joyous welcome.

A pleasant sojourn in the country soon came to a close, as arrangements had been effected for the resumption of the book business in Charleston. The family returned to the old homestead, which fortunately had been out of range of shell fire and was in fair condition for habitation.

I, in company with my father and brothers began the arduous task of rehabilitation of the old business.

William Robert Greer
25th Regiment South Carolina Volunteers

Private William H. Haigh's Letter to his wife Kate, May 24, 1865

Courtesy of the Manuscripts Department, Wilson Library, The University of North Carolina at Chapel Hill

Although William H. Haigh went to Point Lookout Prisoner of War Camp instead of going to Elmira, I felt his statement about his treatment as a captive and his journey north on the steamer *North Point* would be of interest to the reader. Author

24th May 1865
Prisoners Camp: Point Lookout,
Maryland

My dear Kate,

Since the 13th of January last, on the morning of which day at 7:30; the bombardment of Fort Fisher commenced-up to the present time, I have never seen a moment that I could write with ease or satisfaction to you. The system of espionage necessary to be observed in regard to all letters written by prisoners of War, precludes all freedom of thought or expression, and blunts the pen of both husband and lover.

By the terms of the rules prescribed by both Governments, (and I believe the same system prevails in all civilized warfare) every letter written by or to a prisoner is limited in length, and subjected to the scrutiny of an examining clerk. Letters to and from prisoners pass unsealed, their contents being nearly always commonplace, and open to inspection.

How cramped and stiff, and sometimes how little expressive of true feeling these letters are, every days experience and observation testifies. A lover can never tell his sweetheart in the burning eloquence of true love how dear she is to him, how he longs for her presence, to feel the soft and gentle touch of her hand, or in the warm embrace kiss her rosy, pouting lips.

A prisoner fears to tell of hardships here endured; of rations stingingly doled out, of unjust and cruel Corporals lording it over the helpless disarmed soldiers, whose vary looks are enough to excite contempt in the bosoms of those over whom they bear such tyrannical rule.

Then too we seldom receive letters from our real home friends, and when received they prove a source of dissatisfaction, giving us only the dim outlines of home scenes.

So much for the system of letter writing. And yet we all rush to the Post Office daily (Sundays excepted) in quest of letters-because if they bring no good tidings, they (the letters I mean) have been outside prison bounds, have seen people who are free, and are only cramped themselves because they are coming in to a place where everything is bound limited and restrained.

You know that the prisoners from Fort Fisher arrived here on Sunday the 22nd of January, 1865, but you do not know, for no pen could describe, or tongue tell the awful horrors of that terrible sea voyage from Fort Fisher to this place. It was about 1/2 past 10 P. M. Sunday when our little band surrendered to the overpowering force of General Terry. Soon thereafter we were marched up the beach about four miles-sentinels were posted, and we felt ourselves prisoners. It is a sad thought-that first conscious knowledge of being a prisoner.

We slept on the cold beach, the screaming winter blast blowing unobstructed fresh from the Ocean, and the damp ground, (always colder and damper near salt water) chilling us through our blankets. During the night we were waked by a loud explosion of one of our magazines at the fort, but for that, the night passed off in silent slumber, so tired and weary were we with the work, the unceasing, tiresome and perilous work of the past three days.

The morning found us strongly guarded. A line of sentinels surrounded us, and gunboats & frigates lay off in front. Glad enough were we to get anything to eat, and thanks to the Masonic order, I found friends among my enemies. I shall ever remember with grateful heart Captain Wm. S. Marble, 7th Conn. Vols, and Rev Mr. Eaton, Chaplain of the same regt., who not only ministered to my present necessities, but gave me money to aid me as a prisoner.

That was the first time I felt the absolute worthlessness of Confederate money. Since then, even long before the fall of Richmond, I have seen it hawked about camp beginning at 2 1/2 cents & finally dropping down to the fraction of a fourth part of a cent on the dollar. Until now it is only kept in memoriam of a dead treasury and a fast dying nation.

We did not leave the fort until Wednesday. Before leaving we were under guard of Negro soldiers-the first I had ever seen. The Negro makes a good soldier & a good sentinel-but he is somewhat dangerous to white folks.

From Wednesday the 18th, until Sunday the 22nd, late in the evening, six hundred of us were in the hold of the ship "North Point". I will not attempt to describe the scene. Memory sometimes sickens me with a retrospective view of that motley medley of men, almost stifled and crushed to death. There poor McNeill, son of Sh'f McNeill, fell a victim to "Black Hole in Calcutta" cruelty; and others had sown the fatal seed of these terrible maladies that made them inmates of Point Lookout Grave Yard. Cooped up in that "cattle transport" (for such it literally was) midst the darkness of night, the hatches down, men writhing in agony, many blaspheming, cursing and quarreling, it made one feel that he was next door neighbor to the damned spirits of the infernal regions.

Morning after morning came, but still the endless waste of waters, tossed and heaving with a winter's storm. With Elenore of the Signal Corps, I was one of those whose duty it was to give out the rations and this enabled me to move about a little on deck, and thus get a little fresh air, though bitter cold with drifting snow.

Here too on board the North Point in the person of the Mate & Steward of the ship I found a Masonic friend, and while others were huddled below eating their raw pork and wormy crackers, I was under his guidance enjoying a beefsteak and hot cup of coffee. Blessed be his memory.

We came in sight of Point Lookout about daylight Sunday; and lay off until afternoon. That was one of the most cheerless days of my life.

158

John R. King's Account of His Stay at Elmira Prison

United Daughters of the Confederacy, 1917

The prison at Elmira consisted of thirty-six acres enclosed by a wall constructed in the same way as Point Lookout Prison. It was located a short distance from the Chemung River in Chemung County, New York. The river made a bend in front of the prison, but everything indicated that perhaps a hundred or more years before the prison was there the river had run straight and later a beaver dam had changed its course. In our pen there was a body of water within banks very much like a river which occasionally became high. The North side of this body of water had a much higher bank than the South side. Next to the river it became stagnated in the warm season and was not healthful. Elmira was located on the west and near the prison; there were hills on the east which kept our minds on the beautiful and majesty of nature. The Elmira prison looked much cleaner and healthier than Point Lookout, and the water was good. It was a pleasant summer prison for the southern soldiers, but an excellent place for them to find their graves in the winter. The plan was different from the prison at Point Lookout. All our quarters were built on the north side of the water, it being higher than the south side which was a blue grass sod and used for small pox hospitals.

We arrived on Aug. 1st, crossing the water by means of bridges. Our camp was situated in the north east quarter of the pen. The regular prison hospital was in the northeast quarter, the big entrance of the big gate, a cross street leading to the cookhouse; all other of the streets ran east and west. They were ditched and thrown up in the center. The hospital grounds contained frame buildings of medium size, tents and smaller buildings for carpenter shops where coffins were made and other houses for the use of the sergeants, and those who were compelled to be in the prison for various purposes. An undesirable building was erected in the middle of the camp for a guard. We lived in low tents for the first three months, there being no houses and we often suffered with cold.

The manager arranged the building of the houses two months after our arrival and they were completed near Christmas. They were 100 feet long by 25 feet wide; material rough lumber, sawed blocks were set on end and on these sills and lower joists were placed, then a double floor of rough planks was made sided up with ten foot siding, they were stripped roughly and a few binders used, the roof was very flat made by sheeting the rafters with plank this was prepared and covered with pitch gravel. There was no ceiling over head, a large door was arranged at each end and two windows in the sides, three rows of bunks, one above the other, were built on the sides of the building, they were 6 by 4 feet with bottom made of rough plank and six inch boards were railed on the outside, to prevent our rolling out, shavings or bedding of any kind was not permitted as the authorities said they produced vermin, but it mattered little to us for we were already well supplied. Two ventilators were placed in each roof which provided for two stoves. At first we had wooden stoves, but they were not satisfactory and were replaced by Burnside Coal stoves.

The management was somewhat like that at Point Lookout. The head man inside was a major called Provost Marshall, two captains, assistant Provost Marshall, Lieutenants and Sergeants, assisted him. Our first Provost Marshall was Major Colt, his assistants were Captain Mungery and

Captain Peck, they were good men and treated us well, but these officers had nothing to do with feeding, clothing and housing us. This was done by contractors, whose ambition was to make money, they were cruel and caused much suffering. In the tent one night three of us, myself and two boys from Alabama, Burd Messer and Jerry Dingler were sitting on our blankets talking, and suddenly some one in front called out sharply, "Halt" two shots followed tearing through our tent just above my head. The three of us threw ourselves on our backs instantly, and the next morning revealed that the man who fired the shots was an over bearing Lieutenant whom we disliked. At another time Jerry Paugh, one of our companions discovered that some of the boys in our ward planned to escape. Our row of tents was the nearest to the wall and these fellows dug a hole in the bottom of the tent extending to the outside of the prison, a distance of 25 or 30 feet, by means of haversacks they emptied the dirt in the water without being detected. When all was in readiness a few whistles served as a signal for those who desired to exit. Five escaped, two of these later were caught. Others would have ventured the following night, had not the officers been informed.

Our rations were better after we arrived at Elmira, but they soon decreased. We entered the cookhouse by wards, being 42 in all. Soup was placed on long tables in mess pans. Bread and meat was served in the morning, bread and soup in the evening. Marching to the tables two ranks deep, the head of one column stopped at the first place, then the column separated half of them going on each side of the table, each man stopping at the next place and so on down the line. By the time the last man reached his place the first one was leaving, each man was obligated to furnish a vessel in which to carry his soup it being hot and we were given no time to let it cool. Those who could not carry it with them did without soup. Many kinds of vessels were used some had canteens with the neck broken off, others had old tin cans, coffee pots, tin buckets or often a very small wooden bucket which a prisoner by the name of Morgan made to sell and frequently some shiftless fellow had nothing so punished himself trying to swallow the hot soup.

In winter on very cold mornings what a sight we were starting to the cook house for our food; Each ward had a head man called a ward sergeant, he went to the cook house morning and evening to learn when to bring his ward, usually about 200 or 240 men. After securing the information he called out, "Fall in 39 and get your rations." We went in a trot, canteens, buckets, tin cans, coffee pots, rattling, old rags and strings and long unkempt hair, dirt and grey backs, cheek bones projecting for there was very little of us except skin and bones. Our legs were spindling and weak. Here we went over the frozen ground and in crossing ditches some poor fellow frequently fell. We were obliged to leave him struggling to gain his position as our time was limited. This is only a few of the facts. It has often been said that the northern people treated and fed their prisoners well. I wish it were true, but during my imprisonment which was more than a year, I never saw any of the good treatment, except from the old veterans, the men who had been to the front and had seen service in the army were kind.

Tainted meat appeared more frequently and our pieces of bread were perceptibly smaller. The size and weight of our rations, as told heretofore is exactly correct, for many times I measured my piece of bread both in width and thickness. It was very uniform in size, exactly as thick as the distance from the end of middle finger to the first joint inside and just as wide both ways as the length of a table knife blade, this being 5 1\2 inches wide and 1 1\2 inches thick. Our meat ration was very little smaller and often we could see through the soup to the bottom of the pan. At times the officers discovered some dirt or misbehavior near one of our wards, then all the ward was given small rations as a punishment for what one or two had done. We called these morsels of bread

160

detailed rations because men, who were put on detail at cleaning streets or something of the kind, were given small pieces of bread and this was all they had to eat while working. While they were being punished we nearly starved. In the later part of the winter crackers were used in place of soft bread, we enjoyed them but for some reason they were not healthful, causing a stubborn diarrhea and many deaths resulted.

I was in the hospital myself a month with the disease. Weakness and starvation had caused me to lose my sight, consequently often times when wandering some distance from our ward spots appeared before my eyes and I was dependent upon some kind comrade to lead me home. The blindness left me as I grew stronger. Others suffered the same way. Many times a poor fellow staggered along until his old shaky legs failed to support him then he staggered until he was on his feet again with a ghastly smile trying to bear it bravely. It was touching to see the poor, ragged gaunt, half famished, much abused, noble fellows trying to be cheerful through it all. Dear old comrades in misery, how often do I remember you and our friendship. Had all been conducted as well as the government of the prisons, we could have had no cause to complain.

The best treatment came from the citizens, those at home and the contractors. In addition to the other officers there were ward sergeants, who were our prisoners. One of their duties was to examine all letters coming to or going from the prison; also every cent of money sent to the prisoners was credited in a big book and should we find by reading our letters that money had been sent we secured a written order for everything we intended to buy. We never saw any money but there was a Sutler store inside the pen where we made our purchases. First, we ascertained how much to our credit by examining the big book, then a clerk filled out an order blank something like this: "This was the Stutler's name." Demorest, Let J. R. King have 15 cts in apples, 10 cts cabbage, 20c onions, 10 cts on flour, and so on. After receiving the articles we balanced the account to see how much was left to our credit. We had but little money and prices were high; flour five cents per pound, meal the same, onions 15 cents a pound, cabbage 10 cents, small apples one cent each, tobacco 15 cents for a small thin plug, and the man charged to suit himself. Money letters were cried in a public place and it was necessary to answer several questions before it was considered safe to deliver the letter. The people at home never knew how we suffered in prison. If we attempted to tell it in our letters, the Censor saw that they were not mailed. The assistant Provost Marshalls Captain Munger and Captain Peck, and several under officers looked after the inside of the prison. They were responsible for the sanitary condition and the management of the hospitals, cookhouse, the wards, the dead house, burrying the dead and other things. The ward sergeant's duties were to conduct his men to their meals, call the roll, give reports to headquarters concerning his ward, make out requisitions for clothing, coal, etc.

There were nearly 10,000 prisoners at Elmira one time; sometimes less and sometimes more. During the winter those who came from the South felt the cold exceedingly and died from pneumonia. Our clothes poor. The pants I had when arriving at Elmira were in such a bad condition that for a long time I wore nothing but my underwear. However, when the cold weather appeared I was glad to welcome old pants again and after much patching they were a great comfort. In the late winter, out-of-date government coats were presented to us for overcoats: for some reason unknown to us the tails had been cut unevenly, one side being a foot long and others extending only a few inches below the waist line. They helped to keep us warm but should we have been out in the world in such costume, one might have mistaken us for scarecrows eloping from the neighboring cornfield. Oilcloth and two blankets was the covering in our bunks, with a big snow outside and the bitter wind raging around the plank building and whistling in at the cracks. We didn't dream of comforts and many of us had very poor shoes. Mine were ready to be cast aside and did not get a new pair until the last day of February. While in the house I wrapped my feet in old rags which kept them warm, but in the late winter we were compelled to stand in the snow every morning for roll call, consequently my feet and shins were badly frozen. In the spring they had the appearance of a gobbler's legs and it was many years after I returned home before they were entirely cured. Many besides myself had frozen feet.

The man who looked after the fires made only two fires in 24 hours. Each ward had two stoves. The first fire was made at 8:00 in the morning, the other at 8 p.m. Near noon and midnight we were comfortable, but during the twelve hours between fires when the temperature of the stoves lowered we often suffered with the cold. A dead line nailed to the floor three feet in circumference surrounded the stoves. Of course we could not cross the dead lines and often a petty officer entering on a cold evening found some of the ragged shivering men standing too near the fast cooling stove, would become enraged and would run cursing, striking right and left through the crowd, little caring who received the blows or what he did. One day a poor fellow was standing near the stove with an old blanket thrown about his shoulders, held at the throat by an enormous safety pin made from a piece of large wire. The long sharp point of a pin extended through the hook which held it in place. The man of authority struck a swinging blow at the poor fellow when his hand came in contact with the point of that big pin which tore his fingers unmercifully. But it cured him of his fighting propensities. Punishment often resulted from trifling offences and of course we dared not defend ourselves. Some of the men in our ward were powerful men. One was a very tall sergeant who lived in Elmira. His duties kept him inside the prison continually and we called him Long Tom. It gives me pleasure to speak of him for he had a kind heart and was a favorite of every one. He was called our coal sergeant, often when the weather was intensely cold and our fires were low upon request our big friend would get us coal if possible.

Much sickness prevailed among the prisoners In the latter part of the winter many came from near Mobile Bay and brought with them small pox. There were more than forty cases in our ward, and many died. When seven years of age I was vaccinated and although surrounded with it I escaped, there were also many cases of pneumonia, measles and thousands of us were afflicted with the stubborn diarrhea. The poor fellows died rapidly, despondent, homesick, hungry and wretched, I have stood day after day watching the wagons carry the dead outside to be buried and each day for several weeks 16 men were taken through the gate. While the prison was occupied by us which was about one year it was estimated that 3,000 men died. The physicians were very good but it was impossible to save all. At one time scurvy was among us. There were not many deaths, but it caused much suffering. I was among the victims. It frequently attacked the mouth and gums, become so spongy and sore that portions could be removed with the fingers. Others were afflicted in their limbs, the flesh became spotted and the pains were almost unbearable. The remedy was raw vegetables and a medicine called chalk mixture.

Our dead were buried outside by a detail of 16 or 17 prisoners. The name of the company and Regiment of the dead were written on a piece of paper and put in a tightly corked bottle and burried with the corpse, all were buried in that way. Their caskets were made in the pen by prisoners detailed for that purpose. During the early spring the 40th, 41st and 42nd wards were converted into hospitals. We all decided beds made of shavings would be a luxury, so every fellow that was able procured a sharp knife and a pine board and I doubt if the world ever saw such a universal whitling

162

in so short a time. All tried to possess a comfortable bed, but in a few days the Provost Marshall inspected our quarters and ordered every shaving burned. They advocating that the shavings would breed vermin, but we had already been made very uncomfortable by their presence. Near the cookhouse there were vessels for heating water, but few of us could get soap and consequently the few clothes we had never were washed.

The prisoners passed the time making trinkets. Capt. Munger and Capt. Peck, secured the material and after the articles were completed they sold them in the city for the best price possible, always remitting the money. In passing through the prison one would see a boisterous lot playing cards or some other game, numbers making rings out of Gutta-percha buttons and riveting sets on to them of real silver which the captains had purchased, others were making pretty trinkets out of bone, such as tooth picks and seals for watch chains, with birds, squirrels and other figures designed on them Some made watch chains out of horsehair with single links, with two links interlocked and others with three links interlocked making a round chain. This was done with horsehairs and two common needles. We took a board 18 inches wide, near one end a small hole was made into which a flat post a foot in length with a little pole near the top was placed, in that hole was a little round tapered stick running almost to a point. The stick was as large around as we desired the links of the chain inside, after taking the coarse hair from the horses' tails, we placed a small board on a chair and sat on it with the post between our knees, the little stick pointing to us, threaded the needles on both ends of the horse hairs, then make the little links around the stick, slide the needles each way under the link across the hair, and worked the bottom hole stitch around the center of the link, and then interlocked as many links as we wanted. With little practice very pretty chains could be made. Others in our pen made fans out of white pine wood, the board was cut in the shape of a paddle with a fancy handle, then the part which formed the paddle was notched and cut into thin slices with a very sharp knife. The wood was softened with warm water and then the slices bended like a fan. Different colored ribbons were worked through the notches and the ends tied in a bow around the handle. They were very pretty, but frail. One man made a small parasol on the same plan. I saw Capt. Peck, carrying it around one day. I suppose he found a purchaser for it. Another man made a rude engine. One day I gave him a cracker to see it run, that was the admittance. Many wore green shades over their eyes on account of the blazing sun on the sand, tents and water, some of the managers sowed patches of oats which was restful to the eyes.

I will tell you something of the many punishments inflicted on the soldiers; one was wearing the barrel shirt, the big pork barrel with wooden hoops was used, one end was out, a round hole was cut in the other end large enough for a man's head to pass through. The barrel was put over the body by two men leaving the head sticking out through the hole in the end. This he would have to wear two hours before noon and two hours afternoon with a guard behind to keep him in action. Then crosses were nailed on the sides of the barrel on which the man's offense was painted in big black letters. Sometimes it was a lie; other times theft, so here promenaded the man, the barrel, the crosses and the guard; one cross said: "I am a liar." Another said: "I am a thief." This continued day after day. Capt. Whiton, the boss of the cookhouse, had a fat dog which was very friendly and one day was missing. So the Captain found upon investigation that two hungry fellows had killed his dog. Enraged with anger he had the two men taken to headquarters, barrel shirt put on them and dog eater painted on the cross. The prisoners ate every rat they could find and it is well for the rat I didn't find any. They smelt very good while frying. Sometimes men were bucked and gagged or tied up by the thumb for punishment, which was the most cruel of all punishments. I would not punish a dog in that way.

163

Some enterprising fellow built a large frame work outside near the big gate and not more than fifty feet from the wall. The building had three floors besides the ground floor and was called the observatory. There was no roof and it was built for the sole purpose of observation. One on the upper floor had a fine view of our prison and prices were regulated according to the floor on which they stood. The building was forty feet in height. When the weather was pleasant a great many went to the top to look at us. On a beautiful late spring day there was a number of nicely dressed ladies and gentlemen on the top floor. Our provost marshall was sitting on the floor below when presently there came a big Negro among the ladies. He shoved them aside and squared himself to get a good look at us. He was finely dressed and apparently thought himself a very important character. We did not like his attitude so a number of the men groaned at him, hissed, hooted making all sorts of expressions about his impudence but he stood reared back and paid little attention to them. Then the Major got up immediately, went upstairs, took the negro by the shoulders, drew his sword, turned him around and marched him down and out. The negro wanted to argue with the Major but it was useless. Of course we gave the Major a big cheer which seemed to please him. I never saw but one negro who stood guard sometimes in our pen. He behaved like a gentleman.

After warm weather came we had many visitors, often ladies. Some of them spoke pleasantly and were well behaved, while others were impudent and insulting. I remember one day Colonel Moore's son came in our pen with a few young girls, (Colonel Moore was commander of the post), his son was a foppish young fellow and one of the girls overdressed and attracted him. While passing through our ward, with her dainty fingers she tipped up her rustling silken skirts and passed along with an effected air and a disdainful look on her countenance, saying, "Oh, the nasty, dirty, ignorant, beastly Rebels, how filthy they are," and on she continued with a peculiar air, while some of the girls gave us kindly words and looks and were embarrassed by her rudeness; but she was punished for being so unlady like. One of our number, Bish Fletcher, a daredevil, took the opportunity as the girl passed by him to present her with some body lice, 'Grey Backs", we called them. Two sisters of charity visited the prison leaving each a religious tract published by the American Tract Society, and as they passed they treated us with a smile and a kind word. They were real ladies.

I do not want to leave the impression that every prisoner was sick, poor, ragged and weak like the majority of us, for there were many who escaped sickness and numbers who were kept at detail work. Those who worked were fed much better, but of course the majority of us had to work. We had a ray of sunshine occasionally; in the latter part of the winter my good sister, Elizabeth, and my kind parents sent me a box containing biscuits, butter, a piece of bacon, dried apples and a cake. It was all very nice, but unfortunately just before the box arrived I was sick and had no appetite. I ate very little of the contents of my box which was a curiosity to the prisoners. When it came they gathered in a great circle about my bunk and Mr. Breen, a rich iron merchant from Georgia, made a speech to the crowd regarding my dear sister's hands which had prepared it and how my dear parents had remembered their boy in the far away prison. Jaco L. Hale, a large robust man, a Virginian, and one of the "Gray Devils", a company belonging to one of the regiments in the Stonewall Brigade, used the bunk under mine. He was kind to me and was always hungry. I said to Mr. Hale: "Don't you want some butter and bread?" "Yes, sirree," the big fellow answered, and it did me good to watch him sit on the edge of my bunk and eat biscuits and butter. He was a big bony man and a biscuit soon disappeared between those massive jaws. I gave him much of my precious box. He was always my powerful protector and was the last man to whom I spoke in the prison before leaving. Dear old fellow, he had a wife and children at home and was ever the protector of the weak.

164

Prisoners whose homes were within the Yankee lines could receive money at different times and I always got credit in the big book at the headquarters. Everything was so high at the Sutler store we could not get much but it helped to keep the wolf from the door. Some of the prisoners bought and made much for sale so for five cents one could be satisfied for a while. A market place was located near one end of the cookhouse where the prisoners congregated on certain days and tried to sell numberless things to one and another. They sold rings, watch charms and many other trinkets made by the prisoners and besides these men would cry their articles on the market. Some tried to sell eatables. We called a piece of the loaf, cut off the crust end, a "Keno-ration", by reason of a game of chance some of the men played called "Keno". In the game when a certain number was called out the lucky one would cry out: "Keno-o-o". So at the cookhouse when one got a heel ration he called in a loud voice: "Keno-o-o". In the market some would cry: "Here is your keno ration with five chew of tobacco on it for five cents." Still another, "Here's your two rations of meat and ten chews of tobacco on it all for ten cents," and so on. It was a strange medley of things in progress that could never have been seen elsewhere, but little buying was done. Many traded rations. Money was too scarce with which to make purchases. Hunger often caused people to do desperate things. I myself often watched for the bones, after the meat had been eaten off. I got up many times in my bunk with a bone and after knawing the soft ends, sucked at the bone for hours at a time. I wasn't the only one. No bones went to waste as long as there was any substance left on them. One morning while we were eating our beef ration, Dan Singleton, who occupied one of the top bunks, cried out while holding a small rib in his hand, "Look here boys, here's a fine piece of mule meat." The ribs we were eating were all alike, being round and smaller than the ribs of cattle; the cow's ribs are flat as every one knows. The meat was good and we could have relished several more mules had the opportunity been presented.

A few of the under officers were quartered in a little house on a steep bank of a creek. They cooked and ate in front of the house, and here the cook emptied his dishwater which sometimes contained a little meat and bread and I often saw two men on either side of the greasy place scrambling for the crumbs as the dishwater rushed down the bank. It was pitiful. Many men, once strong, would cry for something to eat. I know from experience. A few more of us could have worked in the carpenter shop had we agreed to take the oath of allegiance to the United States, but we refused. Our wages would have been 5 and 10 cents per day according to our capabilities; this didn't tempt me. A day or two after the lamentable death of our President, Abraham Lincoln, the inside officers approached us with a paper telling us that all who would say they were sorry for the President's death would be released first. Not many said they were sorry and those who did stayed there as long as anybody else. I did not say I was sorry and when I came out I left thousands in; yet of course the whole nation was grieved over his death, but we did not care to express our sorrow in that way. However, it was sad to hear the bells tolling in the city when the news came that the President was dead. When Gen. McClellan and Abraham Lincoln ran for president, the majority of the prisoners favored McClellan. They cheered for Little Mac, and one fellow drew the picture of Abraham Lincoln mauling rails and McClellan marching to the White House. Little Mac. was very popular in New York.

Then a flood came in the Chemung, or Gioga River as some called it. There had been much snow during the winter and early in March the thaw caused high water. The snow melted rapidly and soon the little Chemung was raging. The water came into our prison higher and higher, and in a short time the small pox hospital across the creek had to be abandoned. The water increased and in a few hours it reached nearly every house in the prison. The lower bunks were submerged and the second row was threatened. We were surrounded by a wilderness of water. A great part of the prison wall was gone and we could see about half of the cookhouse extending above the water. In every direction men could be seen hustling around in boats trying to save things. The hospitals were flooded and all the sick had to be taken into the city. The dead house was on a little higher ground therefore the dead were not washed away. We were confined in the higher bunks for a day or two with nothing to eat or drink but the dirty river water. After the water receded men came into our wards through the doors in row boats, passing near where we were "roosting". They gave us something to eat. My, but it tasted good! In transferring the sick from the hospitals to the boat, often they fell into the cold water. A poor fellow came out of the hospital next to our ward. He tried to walk a short plank which had been placed from the hospital to the boat, carrying his blanket and some old ragged clothes which belonged to him. Trembling and tottering with weakness, as he stepped on the plank, the boat vacillated and the poor fellow staggered, threw up his arms and went headlong into the water. I feared he would drown, but he was rescued and shivering was taken away in the boat. I have no doubt it caused the man's death.

As soon as we could with safety we waded out to the highest pump in the prison, which was near the dead house, to get some water. On my way to the pump I noticed several old blankets near my feet. Looking closer I discovered a number of dead men concealed under them. The high water had prevented the people from taking them to the graveyard. The walls were rebuilt and in a week or so our old prison was in its natural condition. After the overflow I noticed several extremely large ells lying dead in the water. One day while the cleaning was in progress a petty officer of some sort had four or five men under him working at a crossing. Just as the little platform or little crossing had been nearly placed I happened along and this petty officer was bossing, puffing and swearing at the men. He issued a mighty order to the prison that no man should cross the platform until it was completed. Ignoring the order I crossed and as I was landing on the other side this great man caught me by the shoulders, shoved me roughly towards a Yankee guard who happened to be near and said: "Here, take this man to the guard house and put a barrel shirt on him." The guard asked no questions but conducted me to the guard house and in the afternoon I was wearing the barrel shirt. The Yankee guard at headquarters said in a low voice to me "If I were you I would saw wood for the cookhouse and you will not have to wear the barrel longer." Next morning I told them that I wanted to saw wood, so the old measly pork barrel and I parted company forever. I sawed wood a few hours every day for nearly a week. Major Beall came to the guard house to take the place of Major Colts as Provost Marshall. When I was brought before him he said: "What are you here for?" I said: "For nothing at all." He turned to the jailor and said: "What are the charges against this man?" The jailor after looking at his book said: "No charges." Looking at him sternly the Major said: "Let this man out. What is he here for?" I made my departure never to return.

As the spring passed the number in our wards decreased. At roll call there was no answer to nearly a third of the names. Many had died but early in the spring about 300 of the sick had been sent south to be exchanged. I think the government had intended to send the most of us back to Dixie in the spring had the war not closed, but when Gen. Lee surrendered we then knew that those who lived would return to Dixie. There was great rejoicing and ringing bells at Elmira when the news came that Lee had surrendered. After that we received better treatment from the Yankees and were not guarded so closely. Of course we felt badly when we heard that our beloved Gen. Lee had surrendered, for we knew our noble Army of Northern Virginia would hereafter be only a memory. I am proud to say that I once belonged to the Army of Northern Virginia and marched and fought under the illustrious Robert E. Lee, who, when he had to go down, went down bravely. We started out for what we thought was right and stayed with it faithfully to the bitter end.

I want to speak of some of the characters in our prison who were very interesting. One fellow whom we called Shocky, seemed to have a mysterious influence over the Yankees. He was always well dressed and apparently loyal to the South, but it was always a mystery to us how he could go over the wall at a certain place at anytime he desired and always be respected by the guards. We thought it possible that some free masonry was connected with it. Five of the young Virginians also seemed to be more favored than the rest of us. Among them was Bill McGruder, Bill Hale and a Georgian called Nick Carnochan; the latter pronounced his name Conahan. These young fellows enjoyed many privileges denied the others. Then there was "Old Buttons", a man who sewed buttons on promiscuously to show every battle or skirmish in which he had been. I saw the old fellow die while he and I were in the hospital. We had "Old Blue Ridge" too, a man of gigantic size who wore a home-made blue coat trimmed in various places with fringes, who with all his eccentricities was very kind. Old Pickett, the Florida fisherman, watched from morning till night for the chews of tobacco others had thrown away. He threw them into his mouth as though his life depended upon it. There were many remarkable men with us, of whom I would like to speak but time will not permit.

As the summer drew near we all became restless and were longing for home. Parnell from South Carolina had been employed around headquarters as a messenger boy. As I sat in my bunk despondent and hungry one evening early in June, Parnell appeared, saying in a low voice: "King, you are going out on the next load. I heard your name called today at headquarters. Be still and do not tell anybody but get ready." I asked who also was going from our ward. He said only four: myself, Hoy Reger, Andrew Winster Reger, who was one of my own company in Dixie, and himself. Elated over the news I commenced to get ready. My pants were ragged and dirty. I had an old U. S. blanket and ten cents in money. I went to Bill Goans, who was handy with the needle, and asked him if he would make me a pair of pants out of the blanket. He wanted 25 cents for the job, but I told him I had but 10 cents in the world and that I was to start home on the next load. He hesitated, then said: "All right. I will do it, as you are going home." They were better than the ones I wore but I believe Wanamaker would have made a better fit. All our comrades were soon informed that we were going home and we did not try to keep it a secret. As soon as Mr. Hale, a friend of mine, knew we were going he said: "come and sit down. I want to give you a shave before you leave. He fixed me up the best he could. Then in a day or two we were taken out, measured and our complexion taken down on paper.

The next morning 300 of us were taken to the cookhouse and while standing together with our right hands raised, the oath of allegiance to the U. S. was administered. Then we were given two days rations, our paroles handed to us and we were ready for the journey. I will never forget the march from the cookhouse to the big gate. All the prisoners who were left behind congregated near the street as we went out. No battle scarred veterans ever marched to victory prouder than that ragged, poorly fed, miserable 300 which passed through the big gate never to return. Many of the poor fellows left behind waved us farewells, for but few ever met again. The last familiar face I remember as I went out was that of Mr. Hale, my best friend. He waved his hand and said: "Goodbye, King" This was the tenderessed goodbye for me of all. As I write today the memories of that prison, our suffering, many old comrades I knew well, all rush to my memory so vividly that I seem to live it all over again. It brings a sadness to my heart that I can hardly shake off at times.

We waited in the city until afternoon before taking the train for Baltimore and while there I sold an old blanket I had left for 40 cents and that was all the money with which I had to buy anything to eat on the journey. My two days rations I drew before leaving the prison were so small that I ate all before I passed through the gate, so after getting 40 cents for the blanket I spent 20 cents of it for bread and cheese and ate the most of that before taking the train. The U. S. government gave us free transportation home as far as we could travel by rail or water. In the evening we started for Baltimore on the Pennsylvania North Central R. R. We went through Williamsport, Sunburg, Harrisburg and several other towns and passed long trains of Yankee soldiers going to New York to be discharged. They cheered us as they passed and our train stopped outside of Baltimore for a few minutes. Above us were some women in a garden which had fine onions in it and upon asking for some a Negro girl threw us a few. They were what we called clove onions and were fearfully hot. We ate one or two of them and kept the others.

In Baltimore while waiting at the Band (circled in ink) Depot all day before getting through to West Virginia, I was sitting in the Camden Street station eating one of my hot onions when I noticed some ladies looking at me. I thought probably they were admiring the fit of my new pants, but later one said kindly: "Poor fellow, he looks pitiful." Then I discovered that they thought I was crying and were sympathizing with me. I concluded I would eat more onions, as it was comforting for some one to look at me kindly. I ate my supper that evening at the Soldier's home near the station and I can assure you that I did not leave that table hungry. We took the train in the evening for Grafton, W. Va., and reached there the next day. I spent that night with my Uncle, my Father's brother, John M. King. The next day I went to Clarksburg and from Clarksburg home. I walked 36 miles that night, Hoy Reger and myself. Being timid to approach the house, we slept in a pasture field. The next day we went by way of Buckhannon and parted at the mouth of Turkey Run. I crossed the river at Hyer's Mill and arrived home in the evening, finding all alive and well. I will not try to tell about our happy reunion. There will never be another so happy until we shall meet up there where God will never let us part.

Brother Cyrus is sitting in front of me as I write. I have a beautiful home, children and grandchildren who are tall big men. In a few weeks I will be seventy-four and am hale and hearty and I thank our good master for it all.

In conclusion I will say the war is over. We have peace and prosperity. The North and South are united, but the South is our South. I love it. My heart is with the South and nobler women never lived than our women of the South and there never was in any country nobler women banded together than the Daughters of the Confederacy for the work which they have undertaken. Dear Children of the South, U. D. C.'s, may the kind hand that led me through battles and prisons safely lead everyone securely through the battle of life to a happy old age. To you all I send a greeting. This imperfect sketch was written near Roanoke, W. Va., Feb. 23, 1916.

JOHN R. KING

On April 25, 1861, Lewis Leon joined the Charlotte Grays, Company C, 1st North Carolina Regiment. He began his diary when he joined the Confederate Army and continued to make entries throughout his imprisonment at Point Lookout and Elmira prisons. Because his diary is so extensive I have limited its presentation to cover the time he was captured and sent to prison.

Diary of a Tar Heel Confederate Soldier By Lewis Leon

May 5 - Moved this morning, feeling for the enemy, and came up to them at noon, five miles from the Run, in the Wilderness. It certainly is a wilderness; it is almost impossible for a man to walk, as the woods are thick with an underbrush growth and all kinds of shrubbery, old logs, grapevines, and goodness knows what. My corps of sharpshooters was ordered to the front. We formed in line and advanced to the enemy. We fought them very hard for three hours, they falling back all the time. Our sharpshooters' line got mixed up with Gordon's Brigade, and fought with them. In one charge we got to the most elevated place in the Wilderness. We looked back for our brigade, but saw it not. Just then a Yankee officer came up and we took him prisoner. Some of Gordon's men took him to the rear. Six of our regiment, sharpshooters, myself included, went to the right to join our regiment, but were picked up by the Yankees and made prisoners. We were run back in their line on the double quick. When we got to their rear we

L. LEON

found about 300 of our men were already prisoners. The Yankees lost very heavily in this fight, more than we did. Although we lost heavy enough, but, my Heavens! What an army they have got. It seems to me that there is ten of them to one of us. It looks strange that we could deliver such fearful blows when, in fact, if numbers counted, they should have killed us two years ago. In going to their rear we passed through four lines of battle and reinforcements still coming up, while we are satisfied with, or at least have no more than one line of battle.

May 6 - Fighting commenced at daylight, and lasted all day. So did it last with their everlasting reinforcements. If General Lee only had half their men, and those men were rebels, we would go to Washington in two weeks. When he has fought such an army for four years it certainly shows we have the generals and the fighting-stock on our side, and they have the hirelings. Look at our army, and you will see them in rags and barefooted. But among the Yankees I see nothing but an abundance of everything. Still, they haven't whipped the rebels. Several of our boys came in as prisoners to-day, with them Engle of our company. They think I was killed, so does my brother, but as yet the bullet has not done its last work for your humble servant.

May 7 - We are still penned up as prisoners in the rear of the army, close by General Grant's headquarters. A great many prisoners came in to-day. From some of them I heard that my brother was well.

May 8 - We left this place at dark last night, but only got a distance of two miles, and it took us until 9 in the morning of the 9th.

May 9 - Started again this morning, and passed over the Chancellorsville battlefield. Marched twelve miles today. We passed a brigade of Negro troops. They gave us a terrible cursing, and hollered "Fort Pillow" at us. I am only sorry that this brigade of Negroes was not there, then they certainly would not curse us now. We halted at dark on the plank road seven miles from Fredericksburg.

May 10 - Fighting to-day at Spotsylvania Court House. Prisoners still coming in, two more from my company.

May 11 - This morning about 800 more prisoners came in. Most of them were from my brigade, as well as from Dole's Georgians. I was surprised to see my brother with them. He was taken yesterday, but before he surrendered he sent two of the enemy to their long home with his bayonet.

May 12 - Raining hard all day, and fighting all last night. About 2 o'clock this afternoon about 2,000 prisoners came in, with them Major-General Johnson and Brigadier-General Stewart. We have moved four miles nearer to Fredericksburg. I suppose they think we are too close to our own lines, and they are afraid we will be recaptured, as it was a few days ago. We heard our boys', or, as the Yankees call it, the Rebel yell. We prisoners also gave the Rebel yell. A few minutes after that they brought cannon to bear on us, and we were told to stop, or they would open on us. We stopped.

May 13 - Left here this morning and passed through Fredericksburg. Crossed the Rappahannock on pontoon bridges, and got to Belle Plain on the Potomac at 3 o'clock - nineteen miles to-day. It rained all day, and it is very muddy.

May 14 - We are still camped here. Have been prisoners since the 5th of this month, and have drawn three and a half days' rations. On that kind of a diet I am not getting very fat. We certainly would have suffered a great deal, but our Yankee guard gave us quite a lot of their own rations.

May 15 - Still here. They are fighting very hard on the front.

May 16 - Left this morning at 11 in a tugboat, and from here packed into the Steamer S. R. Spaulding. We are now on our way to a regular prison. We got there at 8 o'clock to-night, and found it to be Point Lookout, Md., fifty miles from Belle Plain. It is in St. Mary's County. We were drawn up in line, searched for valuables, and they taken from us, and marched to prison, one mile from the landing. There are sixteen men in each tent.

May 17 - Saw Mack Sample, Will Stone and several of our company to-day that have been prisoners since the battle of Gettysburg. We get two meals a day.

May 18 - We are divided in divisions and companies. There is a thousand in each division and one hundred in each company. A sergeant commands each company. We get light bread one day and crackers the other.

May 19 - Saw Darnell, of my company, to-day. He was just from the front. He brings us very bad news. Our General Daniels was killed, which is certainly a great loss to us, for he was a good and brave man, also our major of the 53rd, Iredell, and my captain, White, all killed. Colonel Owens, my colonel, was mortally wounded, and quite a number of my company were killed and wounded. He says there is only seven of our company left, and that our Lieutenant-Colonel Morehead is commanding Daniels' Brigade.

May 20 - Three years ago to-day the Old North State left the Union, and we went to the front full of hopes to speedily show the Yankee Government that the South had a right to leave the Union; but to-day, how dark it looks!

May 21 - I heard to-day that my brother Morris was a prisoner at Fort Delaware, Pa. I asked for a parole to-day to go and see my parents in New York, but they could not see it.

May 22 - Nothing new from the front.

May 23 - We are guarded by Negro troops, who are as mean as hell. At each meal there is a guard placed over 500 prisoners, who go to their meals in ranks of four. We are not allowed to cross a certain line, called the "Dead Line," but as 500 men go at one time to meals, of course near the door there is always a rush. To-day one of our men accidentally crossed the line. He was pushed over by the crowd, when a black devil shot and killed him, and wounded two others.

May 24 - One of yesterday's wounded died today. This negro company was taken away to-day, as there is no telling what even men without arms will do to such devils, although they have got guns.

May 25 - Engle received a letter from his father today, who told him they had seen my parents, and I would hear from them soon. This is the first time that I have heard about my parents since the commencement of the war. Thank God, my parents, as well as my sisters and brothers, are well.

May 26 - Received two letters to-day, one from home and one from my brother Pincus, who went to Washington on his way to visit Morris and myself, as he has to get a pass from headquarters before he can see us. He was refused and returned home. Our daily labor as prisoners is that at 5 in the morning we have roll call; 6, breakfast, 500 at a time, as one lot gets through another takes its place, until four lots have eaten; we then stroll about the prison until 1 o'clock, when we eat dinner in the same style as breakfast, then loaf about again until sundown. Roll is called again, thus ending the day. We get for breakfast five crackers with worms in them; as a substitute for butter, a small piece of pork, and a tin cup full of coffee; dinner, four of the above crackers, a quarter of a pound mule meat and a cup of bean soup, and every fourth day an eight-ounce loaf of white bread. Nothing more this month.

171

June 8 - There is nothing new up to to-day, when I received a box of eatables, one or two shirts, and one pair of pants from home. The only way we can pass our time off is playing cards and chess. Six hundred prisoners came in to-day, with them a lady, who is an artillery sergeant. Being questioned by the provost marshal, she said she could straddle a horse, jump a fence and kill a Yankee as well as any rebel. As time in prison is very dull and always the same thing as the day preceding, I shall not mention each day, but only those days upon which something happened.

June 11 - Five hundred more prisoners came in to-day.

June 12 - To-day, as the Negro guard was relieved, two of them commenced playing with their guns and bayonets, sticking at one another. Fortunately one of their guns, by accident, went off and made a hole in the other one's body, which killed him instantly. The other one kicked at him several times, telling him to get up as the rebels were laughing at him, but in a very short time he found out that he had killed his comrade and that we were laughing sure enough.

June 27 - Received money to-day from home, but they gave me sutler's checks for it, as we were not allowed any money, for fear we would bribe the sentinels and make our escape.

July 4 - Four hundred prisoners left here for some other prison, as there were too many here.

July 8 - Engle, Riter and myself received boxes from New York to-day, but as Riter has gone to the other prison with the 400 we have made away with his box.

July 23 - Three hundred more were sent from here to the new prison, which is in Elmira, N. Y., myself with them.

July 25 - Left Point Lookout at 8 o'clock this evening in the frigate Victor for New York. There are 700 prisoners on board.

July 26 - To-day on the ocean a great many of our boys were seasick, but not I. I was promised a guard to take me to see my parents in New York for thirty minutes.

July 27 - We see the Jersey shore this morning. Our vessel was racing with another. We had too much steam up; the consequence was a fire on board, but we soon had it out. We landed at Jersey City at 12 M., and were immediately put in cars, and the officer that promised to send me to my parents refused to do so. We left here at 1, got to Elmira at 8 in the evening.

July 28 - We were treated very good on the road, and especially at Goshen, N. Y. The ladies gave us eatables and the men gave us tobacco.

July 29 - There are at present some 3,000 prisoners here. I like this place better than Point Lookout. We are fenced in by a high fence, in, I judge, a 200-acre lot. There is an observatory outside, and some Yankee is making money, as he charges ten cents for every one that wishes to see the rebels.

August - Nothing worth recording this month, except that the fare is the same as at Point Lookout.

September - It is very cold, worse than I have seen it in the South in the dead of winter.

October - We have got the smallpox in prison, and from six to twelve are taken out dead daily. We can buy from prisoner's rats, 25 cents each, killed and dressed. Quite a number of our boys have gone into the rat business. On the 11th of this month there were 800 sick prisoners sent South on parole.

November and December - Nothing, only bitter cold. We dance every night at some of our quarters. Some of the men put a white handkerchief around one of their arms, and these act as the ladies. We have a jolly good time.

THE YEAR 1865

January - Nothing, only that I fear that our cause is lost, as we are losing heavily, and have no more men at home to come to the army. Our resources in everything are at an end, while the enemy are seemingly stronger than ever. All the prisoners in Northern prisons, it seems, will have to stay until the end of the war, as Grant would rather feed than fight us.

February - The smallpox is frightful. There is not a day that at least twenty men are taken out dead. Cold is no name for the weather now. They have given most of us Yankee overcoats, but have cut the skirts off. The reason of this is that the skirts are long and if they left them on we might pass out as Yankee soldiers.

March - Nothing new. It is the same gloomy and discouraging news from the South, and gloomy and discouraging in prison.

April - I suppose the end is near, for there is no more hope for the South to gain her independence. On the 10th of this month we were told by an officer that all those who wished to get out of prison by taking the oath of allegiance to the United States could do so in a very few days. There was quite a consultation among the prisoners. On the morning of the 12th we heard that Lee had surrendered on the 9th, and about 400, myself with them, took the cursed oath and were given transportation to wherever we wanted to go. I took mine to New York City to my parents, whom I have not seen since 1858. Our cause is lost; our comrades who have given their lives for the independence of the South have died in vain; that is, the cause for which they gave their lives is lost, but they positively did not give their lives in vain. They gave it for a most righteous cause, even if the Cause was lost. Those that remain to see the end for which they fought - what have we left? Our sufferings and privations would be nothing had the end been otherwise, for we have suffered hunger, been without sufficient clothing, barefooted, lousy, and have suffered more than anyone can believe, except soldiers of the Southern Confederacy. And the end of all is a desolated home to go to. When I commenced this diary of my life as a Confederate soldier I was full of hope for the speedy termination of the war, and our independence. I was not quite nineteen years old. I am now twenty-three. The four years that I have given to my country I do not regret, nor am I sorry for one day that I have given - my only regret is that we have lost that for which we fought. Nor do I for one moment think that we lost it by any other way than by being outnumbered at least five if not ten to one. The world was open to the enemy, but shut out to us. I shall now close this diary in sorrow, but to the last I will say that, although but a private, I still say our Cause was just, nor do I regret one thing that I have done to cripple the North.

This article is reproduced from the July, 1878 issue of the journal *Annals of the Army of Tennessee.* The comments in italics below were written by Dr. Edwin L. Drake, the editor of the publication, and a former Lt. Colonel in the Confederate Army.

Nine Months in a Northern Prison
By Sergeant George W. D. Porter, 44th Tenn. Regiment

Elmira is one of the oldest cities in the State of New York. It is situated on the Chemung river, in a beautiful valley surrounded by an almost endless range of peaks and mountains, from which most of the timber has been cleared, leaving a landscape dotted with farmhouses, fields of buckwheat and other grain. It was here, in 1776, the Battle of Chemung was fought, between General Sullivan and the celebrated Iroquois Chief, Thayendanega. He was a half-breed, educated in Connecticut, and was commissioned a colonel in 1775, by the English Crown. He was infamously known to the whites as Joseph Brandt. His cruelties were enacted in the heat of battle, and instigated by the wrongs his people had suffered at the hands of the whites.

Cruelty and cowardice often go hand in hand, but Brandt was brave, and his cruelty to his enemy was only a religious duty naturalized in the savage character through the custom of many ages. His motto was, doubtless, that "war is cruelty," and not open to the amenities which humanity would seek to interpose against its horrors. When I think of Elmira in connection with its historical associations, I am tempted to institute a comparison between Joseph Brandt, the savage, and some of the commandants of her prison-house in 1864, with its thousands of ragged, sick and starved tenants. Brandt was an Indian, tutored from his cradle to deeds of cruelty-these, the representatives of a civilization which boasts of having reached its highest type in this, the nineteenth century of the Christian Era. But this might be called the ravings of hate, and the Democratic Congressman from that district might rise and call me a liar, and affirm that there was no lack of food, fuel and clothing among the Confederate prisoners at Elmira. But to our narrative.

The writer, with about five hundred other prisoners of war, arrived at Elmira about the first of August, 1864, after a confinement of forty-five days at Point Lookout. I spent the first day in a thorough examination of my new abode, and its advantages as a home until fortune would release me from its durance. It contained several acres of ground, enclosed by a plank fence about fourteen feet high; some three feet from the top on the outside ran a narrow footway, or parapet, of plank, supported by braces. On this the sentinels walked day and night, being enabled from this height to command a view of the entire prison. On the inside, large globe lamps were ranged at regular intervals, which were lighted shortly after sunset and extinguished after fair day-light, thus rendering it impossible, even in the darkest night, for anyone to approach without being discovered. For the center of the enclosure, and on the north side, was the main entrance, by large folding doors. East of this point, on the outside about fifty yards from the enclosure, was a large observatory, upon which hundreds would crowd daily to get a view of the prisoners-many to gloat, perhaps, on their sufferings; some to gaze in wonder and awe upon the ragged, bob-tailed crew who had on many fields conquered their best armies; and some, no doubt, to sigh for an exchange of these men for fathers, sons and brothers who were suffering kindred miseries at Libby, Salisbury and Andersonville. A single tree, a walnut, stood opposite the observatory, and its shade was particularly grateful during the month of August.

The south, or rear, line of the enclosure stood on the bank of the Chemung. Through the center ran a deep channel, cut by the river at high tide, the upper and lower ends of which were dry part of the year; the middle always contained water to the depth of two feet or more. During the hot months the prisoners suffered greatly from heat at night, owing to their crowding in tents. In October, materials and tools were furnished, and wooden barracks were built. During our tent life, two blankets were furnished to six men; one stick of green pine or hemlock, from four to six feet long and rarely over six inches in diameter, was the daily allowance of fuel for six men; no tools were allowed to cut and split it. J.W. Daniel was woodchopper for our mess, patiently hacking the wood in two with an old case knife, and splitting it with aid of a railroad spike and a rock. The routine of roll-call was most exactly carried out in spite of bad weather, no one being allowed to break ranks under the most urgent circumstances until the signal was given. Owing to the diet, crowding and other unwholesome surroundings, bowel complaints were exceedingly common and severe, and the requirements of the disease often subjected the unfortunates to a brutish befouling of clothing and person while standing in ranks awaiting the leisurely completion of a simple routine task.

Majors Colt and Beale were at times not only unkind, but unjust and oppressive. Beale, on one occasion, aroused all of the inmates of the prison on a bitter cold night, and made them stand in line until he ascertained how many had United States overcoats, and where they got them. He then had the coats carried to his quarters, where the tails were cut off, and the mutilated garments restored to their owners. These officers had men tied up by the thumbs to make them reveal suppositious plots. An instrument of torture called the "sweat box" will bear describing to the uninitiated. They were made of stout planks, of different dimensions, so as to gauge the victim's size. They were secured upright to a post, with a hinged door, and when a culprit could be squeezed in, so much the better for the violated law. An aperture for the nose was the only evidence of charity in their construction. When a prisoner was to be committed, he was marched to successive boxes until one was found to suit; with his back to the entrance and his arms close to his side, he was thrust in and the door closed with a push and fastened.

Ward inspection was held every Sunday morning by a captain or lieutenant. On these occasions none were excused from attendance. The presence if every man had to be verified; and if any were found in the privies, or on the road there from, they were dragged to the guard-house, where a mysterious performance added terror to the situation. The guard-house had two rooms-the rear one for prisoners; as the victim entered the door a blanket was dropped over his head: and he was forced to the floor and robbed of everything he had. He was then left half-suffocated, without an opportunity of knowing who did the deed. Many of the Federal officers were brutes in the human form. One, whose name I have forgotten, was a fiend. He was a tall, humped-back Scotchman, nicknamed by the boys "Old Hogback," but he was a hog all over. On several occasions I have seen him kick sick men off of the walk with his heavy boots, simply because they were too feeble to get out of his way quickly enough, or did not care to get out in the mud and water to let him pass. I hope some reader of the *Annals* may, perchance, remember his name and report it, so as to impale his memory with the infamy of wanton cruelty to helpless and defenseless fellow-creatures.

Lieutenant Groves, the cashier of the prison bank, was, in every respect, a gentleman, and, for his kindness and humanity, his name is gratefully remembered by every inmate of the Elmira Prison who came in contact with him.

Threats of retaliation for the Fort Pillow affair were often circulated to induce men to take the oath. At one time, it was put out that lots were to be drawn for men to be placed on gunboats under fire of Sumter and other forts. To an officer who was threatening me with such terrors, I replied: "Put me down on that list as a volunteer. I would be delighted with the exchange, and think I can stand anything your men can." I was determined to brag a little, just to cut his feathers, and I succeeded.

My gorge, bile, spleen and phlegm will rise somewhat yet at the recollection of the quantity and quality of the food doled out at the model humanitarian at Elmira in the years 1864-5. I have long since gotten over the sense of soreness begotten of the knocks and hurts incident to honorable warfare; but Elmira, somehow, when I happen to think of it, will play the deuce with my patriotism and loyalty to my country in thought, not act, but only at these times. Ah well! I'd live it down and die content if I was only sure that "Old Hog-Back" will not be able to beat the devil out of his own. Prove me this, and I am "truly loyal." But here's the ration: The strong sustained life on four ounces of sour light bread and three ounces of salt beef or pork for breakfast; for dinner, the same amount of bread was allowed, and, in lieu of the meat, a compound called soup, but in reality nothing more than hot salty water, in which bags of peas or beans had been boiled, but which were carefully removed and kept for other uses than to feed cold, starving prisoners of war. This saltwater diet will account for the large number of cases of scurvy and dysentery which carried off so many. A great number of the men were in rags, and but a small quantity of clothing was issued by the United States government. Of that received from home and friends, the amount was restricted, and only obtainable on a permit approved at headquarters. When the mercury got down to 35 degrees below zero in the winter of 1864-5, I saw numbers of my comrades with frost-bitten hands, ears and faces.

For the truth of these by the evidence of hundreds South. Moore, Colt and could tell a tale if they remember an order that was starved wretches of all food beans which had been stolen can recall the fact that only hundred men, and only half hundreds of wagon-loads But the graves of dead tale, before which every dumb in comparison.

statements, I am willing to abide of living witnesses North and Beale, of the prison authorities, would. They surely can to deprive a prison full of half-until they produced a barrel of by their own underlings. They one stove was allowed to each enough fuel for use, while were stacked on the premises. Southern soldiers at Elmira tell a utterance of the lip or pen is

A SOLDIER'S STORY: PRISON LIFE AND OTHER INCIDENTS

By Miles Sherill

I have been requested to write some incidents, experiences and observations of prison life during the war of 1861-65. After thirty-eight or thirty-nine years it is somewhat difficult to recall anything like all that transpired in those dark days. Some people say it is time to stop talking about that war. Now, that would be a hard thing for those who lived in those days to do: stop talking about that war. The men, women and children at home had almost as hard a time as those at the front-not quite so dangerous, yet it required courage and true patriotism to stand in their places. Furthermore, it seems necessary, in order to keep history straight, that those who lived and participated in that part of our history should occasionally be heard from, otherwise those who write so much, who live north of the Mason and Dixon's line, would make our rising generation believe what is false. So I say to all such: "Nothing in the past is dead to the man who would learn how the present came to be what it is." Much has been written and said by our Northern friends as to the suffering of the Union soldiers in Southern prisons-Andersonville, Salisbury and other places-during the war. They draw an awful picture of their poor soldiers suffering and dying in

Miles Sherrill. Source: Unknown.

Southern prisons. In some respects this was true. To be in prison of itself was bad enough, but to be there without proper food or medicine was very bad indeed. The South did not have the means, neither the medicine, but the prisoners in our care were put on the same footing as our own poor soldiers. The question is: Who was to blame for this state of things? The Confederate authorities made proposition after proposition for exchange of prisoners, but the Government at Washington positively declined. It is said that General Grant said: "It was hard, and a great sacrifice, to leave the Union soldiers in Southern prisons, but it must be made; that the Confederates could not afford to leave their men in prison for want of men to take their place, but the United States could; to exchange the prisoners the Confederates would return to the army and go to fighting again." So here is the key to the responsibility for all to suffering and deaths on both sides in the prisons. The Confederate Government offered to let them send medicine South for their sick prisoners, but they

178

declined to do that. It must be remembered the Confederate Government was shut in from the outside world, and could not secure necessary medicine, etc. Now, as to Andersonville, it was under the command of Wirtz, and since men have had time to cool off it has long since been decided that the hanging of that poor man was simply murder. He did the best he could for the poor prisoners there. General Dick Taylor in his book, "Destruction and Reconstruction," gives the following account of meeting with Wirtz, as his troops were passing Andersonville, during the march of Sherman through Georgia, in 1864: "In this journey through Georgia, at Andersonville, we passed in sight of a large stockade inclosing prisoners of war. The train stopped for a few moments and there entered the carriage to speak to me a man who said his name was Wirtz, and that he was in charge of the prisoners nearby. He complained of the inadequacy of his guard and the want of supplies, as the adjacent country was sterile and thinly populated. He also said that the prisoners were suffering from cold, were destitute of blankets, and that he had not wagons to supply fuel. He showed me duplicates of requisitions and appeals for relief that he had made to different authorities, and these I endorsed in the strongest terms possible, hoping to accomplish some good. I know nothing of this (man) Wirtz, whom I then met for the first and only time, but he appeared to be in earnest in his desire to mitigate the condition of his prisoners. There can be but little doubt that his execution was a 'sop' to the passions of the 'many-headed.'" So, then, poor Wirtz was made a scapegoat to cover the sins of those who could have had those poor prisoners released at anytime but would not. The sacrifice was made to quiet the poor prisoners and their friends. Many things will be settled at the great Assize, when the Judge of all shall sit in judgment.

I was shot in the first charge that was made at Spotsylvania Court House, Virginia, early on the morning of the 9th day of May, 1864. The charge was made by our brigade, composed of the Fifth, Twelfth and Twenty-third N.C., Regiments, led by General R.D. Johnston. The charge was a success so far as the enemy in our front were concerned, but our lines were overlapped by Burnside's troops. Our regiment (the Twelfth) and our company (A), being on the extreme right, were exposed to an enfilading fire clear across an open field; so we were exposed to a fire from front and from the right. The enemy had torn down a rail fence and made temporary breastworks in our front, from which our men drove them, but could not hold the position because Burnside's whole army corps was on hand, and could easily have cut off our little brigade; so General Johnston gave the command to fall back. As our troops fell back, Sergeant Silas Smyre (now county commissioner of Catawba) and Corporal E. G. Bost endeavored to carry me from the battlefield. They were so exhausted from marching and fighting that they could not hold me up so as to prevent the crushed leg from dragging on the ground. To prevent their being captured, I begged them to leave me to my fate. (May I never forget this act of kindness by these brave men, who risked so much for me.) I was in the broiling hot sun, without water, my canteen having been shot in the fight, and the water all run out.

I was concealed from the enemy by some shrubbery. Late in the afternoon I realized that I could not live without water. The loss of blood, together with the burning rays of the sun, made me feel that life was about to ebb out; so I called to the enemy and surrendered. Here I commenced the life of a prisoner, which lasted ten months. Besides the suffering from wounds, the humility, the loss of liberty, the absence of all friends and loved ones, no face but that of enemies, was just about as much as I could bear up under in my condition. In that hour home and friends would have been "a haven of rest" sure enough.

The day following, May 10, 1864, when I was laid on the slaughter table, my eyes caught the sight of arms and legs piled on the ground-an indication of what I might expect. Dr. Cox, of Ohio, examined my leg. The only conversation that passed between us was this: I said, "Doctor, can you save my leg?" He replied, "I fear not, Johnny." Chloroform was applied, and when restored to

179

consciousness I was minus one limb. I lay there in what was designated "a field hospital" for two or three days without further attention to the wound, and the result was the flies "blowed" the amputated limb, and when I reached Alexandria City, some days later, the nurse who dressed the wound found that I was being eat up by the vermin. Just here I will state that on the last day spent at the field hospital there was a great rush in gathering us up in ambulances. Under great excitement, I said to the doctor who was supervising the movement: "Doctor, what is the matter?" He replied that "Burnside was falling back to get a better position." I had been in the army long enough to know that was an evasive answer. The fact was that our troops were driving Burnside back, and the Federals were not willing to lose any of their prisoners though maimed for life. The roads from this place were cut to pieces by the artillery and wagon trains of the Union army going to the front. Those of us who were badly wounded cried for mercy. No mercy came until we reached the boat-landing, where we (those living) were transferred from ambulance to the boat. I do not know how many died en route from the battlefield to the boat-landing. I do know that Charles P. Powell, Adjutant of the Twenty-third North Carolina Regiment, who had lost his leg just as I had, died on this trip, and they stopped on the roadside and covered him up. This young man Powell was from Richmond County, N.C. He was a private soldier at Malvern Hill, July, 1862. When in line of battle, in front of the artillery, a shell fell in the ranks. The men could not leave the line of battle. There lay the shell, sputtering, ready to explode. Young Powell sprang up, grappled the shell and "soused" it into a pool of water nearby. What a risk was that! Yet that heroic act may have saved the lives of several men. Later that day he was wounded, and again at the battle of Gettysburg in July, 1863, and died as above stated. On page 189 of Volume II, North Carolina Regimental Histories, it is stated that C.P. Powell, Adjutant, was killed on the 9th of May, 1864, whereas the truth is he was shot on the 9th and his leg was amputated, and about the 11th or 12th of May he was jolted to death between Spotsylvania Court House and Bell Plains. I venture the assertion that he was not buried two and a half feet deep; and the place is unknown to his people, who think he was buried on the battlefield. We were shipped to Alexandria City, where I spent three months in the "Marshall House," where the proprietor, Jackson, shot and killed Colonel Ellsworth, who tore down his Confederate flag in April, 1861, and Jackson was killed by Frank Brownwell, of Colonel Ellsworth's regiment. This hotel was used as a prison hospital for those who were permanently disabled. For awhile the patriotic women of Alexandria were permitted to visit us, and often when they would bid us good-bye a "green-back" bill or something else was left in our hand. However, before we were removed from there the good women were prohibited from coming to see us.

While a prisoner here our troops, under General Early came down near Washington City, and there was great excitement in Washington and Alexandria, for it did seem that the Confederates were going into Washington. We prisoners were expecting to be released and get home, but our expectations were soon blasted by the Confederates having to retreat back to the south side of the Potomac, and did not come via Alexandria. My next move was to the Lincoln Hospital in Washington City. Here I spent about two months. After I could walk with crutches I was transferred to the old Capitol prison. I was honored with a seat in the old Capitol, but had to look through iron bars.

In November, 1864, I (with others) was shipped off to Elmyra, N.Y. We reached Elmyra on Sunday morning. Being in the mountains, the ground was covered with snow. Arriving at the barracks, we were lined up (I was on my crutches, and had to stand there on one foot for what seemed to me a very long time) just inside the gate, Negro soldiers on guard. The commanding officer, Major Beal, greeted us with the most bitter oaths that I ever heard. He swore that he was going to send us out and have us shot; said he had no room for us, and that we (meaning the Confederate soldiers) had no mercy on their colored soldiers or prisoners. He was half drunk, and I was not sure but that we might be dealt with then and there. Then we were searched and robbed of knives, cash, etc., and sent into our various wards. While we were standing in the snow, hearing the abuse of Major Beal, some poor ragged Confederate prisoners were marched by with what was designated as barrel shirts, with the word "thief" written in large letters pasted on the back of each barrel, and a squad of little drummer boys following beating the drums. The mode of wearing the barrel shirts was to take an ordinary flour barrel, cut a hole through the bottom large enough for the head to go through, with arm-holes on the right and left, through which the arms were to be placed. This was put on the poor fellow, resting on his shoulders, his head and arms coming through as indicated above; thus they were made to march around for so many hours and some many days. Now, what do you suppose they had stolen? Why, something to eat. Yes, they had stolen cabbage leaves and other things from slop barrels, which was a violation of the rules of the prison. One large, robust prisoner from Virginia was brought into the surgical ward where I was, having been seriously wounded by one of the guards. On inquiry, I learned that the poor fellow was caught fishing out scraps from a slop barrel and was shot for it. A small, very thin piece of light-bread with a tin pint cup full of what purported to be soup twice a day was the rations for the prisoners. I heard the men say: "My soup has only three eyes on it."meaning there was no grease in it-only hot water. Now, this fare was not enough to sustain life in healthy, able-bodied men. The result was that where they could not make something-make rings, etc.-and thus secure something from the sutlers, many, yes hundreds of the poor fellows would be attacked with dysentery-so common and often so fatal in camp, and especially in prison life. The food they had seemed to be only enough to feed the disease; the result was that scores and hundreds died. Speaking of the light-bread, the Confederates would sometimes hold it up and declare "that it was so thin that they could read *The New York Herald* through it"; then they would grab it and squeeze it up in one hand till it looked about like a small biscuit. Men died there for the want of food. I do not know, it may be that the Government issued enough rations, but it had to pass through too many hands before reaching the soldiers.

The truth is that there was a great deal of speculation and swindling carried on in the prisons; and I am ashamed to say it, yet it is true that sometimes some of our own men were engaged in the conspiracy to cheat and defraud their fellow-prisoners. It was in this way: those in charge of the prison would take Confederates and make ward-masters, etc., of them (like in prisons now a few are made "trusties"); and a little authority, even of that kind, would ruin some men. Some prisoners, like Jeshrun, grew fat, but others starved for want of suitable food and enough of it. Well, to go back a little, while standing there, receiving the profane blessing from Major Beal, I was drawing near as he dared to venture and old fellow-prisoner that I had met in Washington, who had preceded me to this place. I do not remember his name. I had at Washington nicknamed him "softy." He recognized me, and as Beal closed his eloquent abuse, and we were ordered to march into the barracks, "Softy" ventured in a low tone to speak to me. His greeting was: "Sherill, you have come to hell at last. Did you see those four-horse wagons going out? They were full of dead men, who died last night. They are dying by hundreds here with small-pox and other diseases." He was discovered by one of the guards (standing too near us). He hollowed at him: "Get away from there!" He got away immediately, if not sooner. When I reflected on the situation-the cursing major, the colored guards, the robbing us of our little stock of valuables, the barrel shirts, the wagons with the dead, the appearance of some of the living, the earth covered with snow-I thought, "Well, 'Softy' has given a true bill."

When I was located, I found I had kinsfolk there: J.U. Long (now chairman of the board of county commissioners), Nicholas Sherrill and W.P. Sherrill. There may have been others, but I do not recall them now. My haversack had been supplied with rations on leaving Washington. When I was located in the ward, "Nick" Sherrill came to see me. Of course we were glad to see each other, for it had been many moons since we had met. We were not in the same command in the army. "Nick" asked me if I had anything to eat. I replied, "Yes." He said: "I want to trade you a cup, spoon, etc., for some bread; I am about perished." Poor fellow, he looked the picture of despair. I said: "Nick, I do not want you cup and spoons, but you are welcome to what I have." He devoured in short order all that I had, and wanted more. Poor fellow, he soon died, as did W.P. Sherrill; died away from home and loved ones, buried by their enemies.

I had to spend several days in the barracks before I was transferred to the surgical or hospital ward. I was there long enough to know why Cousin Nicholas was so anxious for my bread. After I was placed in the surgical ward of the hospital I fared fairly well-a great improvement over the fare out in the wards of the regular prison. After a few weeks I was taken with small-pox, and of course was transferred over S. Creek to the small-pox camp. I was carried over on a cot, or "stretcher," with a blanket thrown over my face. When I reached the place, and the blanket was removed, I found myself in a large "wall tent," with several cots, or "bunks," about two and a half feet wide, with two Confederates on each "bunk," in reverse order, i.e., A's head at one end and B's at the other-so your bed-fellow's feet were in very close proximity to your face. They were all sandwiched in this way, because the bed was too narrow to admit of the two to lay shoulder to shoulder. On waking up on a morning one of these poor fellows would be dead and the other alive; this, of course, occurred day after day, and night after night. Well might those poor fellows, who had spent at least a part of the night with a corpse for a bed-fellow, have exclaimed with St. Paul, "Who shall deliver me from the body of this death?" When I took in the situation, I told the man who was going to place me on a bunk by the side of a poor fellow bad off with that awful disease (and who finally died) "that he could not put me on there." He replied "that he would show me whether he could or not." I stuck to it that I would not be put there. The fellow went and brought in the ward-master, and when he appeared it was Jack Redman, from Cleveland County, Company E, my regiment. Redman said, "Why, hello, Sherrill, was it you that was raising such a racket?" I told him it was. He wanted to know what was the matter. I explained that with my amputated limb it would never do to put me on a bunk with another fellow, and he finally consented to arrange for me to gave one to myself. I said: "Redman, you must grant me another favor." He wished to know what it was. I replied: "I want you to let me keep my blanket that came over from the surgical ward." "Why so, Sherrill?" I said: "Jack, you see those blankets that you fellows have been using on these men-there are five 'army lice' to every hair on the blanket." Redman took a hearty laugh. He knew there was more truth in it than poetry, so he granted my request. Redman had had small-pox and was an "immune," hence was made a ward-master. He was especially kind and considerate towards me. When I got well and was carried away, I never knew what became of him. Some of our men, who felt that the thing was gone, and that we could not succeed, never came back South. I am inclined to think that Redman did that thing. After the doctor had declared me well, and directed that I should be removed back to the hospital ward from whence I came, this was indeed glorious news; for all of the diseases that flesh is heir to, small-pox is the filthiest. The small-pox such as we had there was "sure enough" small-pox. Such as we have in North Carolina these days, in comparison with that, is only make-believe. I don't think it an exaggeration to say that seven out of ten who had it died. I was carried over into what was called a bath-house, where I was placed in a large bath-tub of water, almost too hot to bear. The Yankee soldier who had charge went out to look after something else or to loiter around, and I waited and waited for his return (the water was beginning to get cold) so I could get out and get clothing to put on. The atmosphere of the room was colder, if anything, than the water. I was in great distress, and it seemed that I could make no one hear me; so I had to wait the return of the villain, who finally came when the water in the bath-tub seemed to me to be nearly to the freezing point. He came, bringing a full Yankee suit, and when I gave him a piece of my mind he apologized and begged me not to speak of it-said he had actually forgotten me. When I reached the hospital ward I was a blue man in feelings and in appearance. I was dressed in a Yankee suit, even to a cap. I felt humiliated, and my skin was blue from cold. But for the kindness of my comrades there, giving me of their allowance of spirits that night, I don't know but what I would have gone hence.

It is indeed wonderful how the prisoners would work to make a little money. One of the most common occupations was to make finger rings; they did some real nice work. Some of the men would secure a few cents, and on that little capital build up quite a business. Some had teachers and attended school. The teachers were, of course, fellow-prisoners with the pupils. As before stated, I was in the surgical ward while in New York, and had no personal experience in the traffic and trading above alluded to, for it was not allowed in the hospital wards. I am reminded that General Lee says in his memoirs that he used every effort and means at his command to effect an exchange of prisoners, but General Grant refused.

Along toward the close of February, 1865, I with others, was marched to the train and shipped to Richmond. I think that was the happiest day that I ever experienced in my life. To get out of that death-hole was enough to make one happy; and to add to it the prospect of getting home to friends and loved ones, from whom I had been so long separated, not having heard from them in ten months, was indeed a treat. Many and great changes had taken place since I had left Dixie. I never did doubt that we would eventually succeed. I presume I was cheered up and was kept optimistic from the many rumors all the time in circulation that France and England would soon recognize our independence; which, of course, never took place. The air was filled with that and other rumors, not only in the Confederate army, but even in prison. Such rumors of great victories for the Confederate arms were all the time circulating among the poor fellows. As I came on from New York it looked to me as if the whole world was being uniformed in blue and moving toward General Grant's army. As we came up the James River, both sides were lined with soldiers dressed in blue. When we came to the Confederate lines, seeing such few ragged men confronting all that blue host, my courage came near failing me. In fact, I could not see how this little thin line of Confederates could hold at bay such a multitude of well-fed, well-equipped men. The patriotic women of Richmond tried to be cheerful, but I could see plainly enough that they were depressed. While they were just as kind in their attention to the returning soldiers as in former days, yet it was evident that the cheerful hope of former days was gone. When I reached home I soon learned that many who were living on the 9th of May, 1864, when we made that charge, had been numbered with the dead.

There never was any trouble between true soldiers, whether they wore the blue of the gray. It was the warlike civilians who did not fight and the soldiers who were mere hangers-on and camp followers that made the trouble. But for the influence of General Grant and other army officers we would have fared much worse in the South after the close of the war than we did; they, as conquerors, became our protectors. The true soldiers could be seen exchanging coffee for tobacco, going in bathing at the same time, in the same river; and when the enemy fell into his hands as a prisoner he would empty his own haversack and the canteen to relieve his prisoner. When there was no fighting going on, the soldiers of the two armies were on the best of terms. The outrages committed on either side during the war were not attributable to the true soldier; neither can the outrages perpetrated on the South after the war be charged up to the United States Army proper, but to the "bummers," who were no good in the army or at home. The storm has long since gone by. The true soldier has no prejudice against the soldier who fought on the other side.

PRISON EXPERIENCE IN ELMIRA, N.Y.

By Dr. G. T. Taylor, Bismarck, Ark.

Reprinted from *The Confederate Veteran Magazine*, July, 1912.

I belonged to Company C, 1st Alabama Battalion of Heavy Artillery, and served on the Gulf Coast most of the war of 1861-65. I was captured August 23, 1864, at Fort Morgan and was taken to New Orleans and placed in Cotton Press No. 3 on September 18, (?). About 300 of us were sent on board a ship for New York City and placed in Castle Williams, on Governor's Island. We were kept there until December 4, when we were sent to Elmira (N.Y.) Prison. While in New Orleans we fared fairly well under the circumstances. While on Governor's Island a corporal (I think his name was Toby) stole our rations, and we suffered hunger until Colonel Bumford, in command of the prison, removed the man, who was making money while we were starving. While there I took smallpox, as did several others, and we carried the disease to Elmira, where a number died of it.

Talk about Camp Chase, Rock Island, or any other prison as you please, but Elmira was nearer Hades than I thought any place could be made by human cruelty. It was in a bend of the small river, surrounded by a high board inclosure, with sentinels walking on a platform near the top outside, with a dead line some fifteen or twenty feet on the inside; and if prisoners went near the line, a wound or death was the invariable result. Snow and ice several feet thick covered the place from December 6 to March 15, 1865. We were in shacks some seventy or eighty feet long, and they were very open, with but one stove to a house. We had bunks three tiers high, with only two men to a bunk, while we were allowed only one blanket to a man. Our quarters were searched every day, and any extra blankets were taken from us. For the least infraction we were sent to the guardhouse and made to wear a "barrel shirt" or were tied up by the thumbs for hours at a time. There was one Major Beal who, I believe, was the meanest man I ever knew. Our rations were very scant. About eight or nine in the morning we were furnished a small piece of loaf bread and a small piece of salt pork or pickled beef each, and in the afternoon a small piece of bread and a tin plate of soup, with sometimes a little rice or Irish potato in the soup where the pork or beef had been boiled. We were not allowed to have any money, but could make rings or pins or buttons and sell them for sutler tickets and buy tobacco or apples; but we were not allowed to buy rations. After the surrender of General Lee, we thought it would be better, but were mistaken.

In May they commenced to liberate prisoners, sending three hundred every other day. I got out on July 7, 1865, and started for my home in Alabama. Upon arrival in New York City I secured my first "square meal" in over ten months.

My experience was that when you met a Western man you met a gentleman and a soldier; but when you met a "down Easterner" or a Southern renegade, you met the other fellow.

If any of the 1st Battalion of Heavy Artillery of Alabama or any of the 1st Tennessee Heavy Artillery or any of Captain Butt's company, 21st Alabama Infantry sees this, please write me.

Statement of John J. Van Allen

Reprinted from the *Southern Historical Society Papers*, Volume I, page 294-295.

Late in the fall of 1864, and when the bitter sleets and biting frosts of winter had commenced, a relief organization was improvised by some of the generous ladies and gentleman of the city of Baltimore for the purpose of alleviating the wants of those confined in the Elmira Prison, where there were then several thousand prisoners.

I had the honor to be appointed by that organization to ascertain the needs of the prisoners, to distribute clothing, money, etc., as they might require. I had formerly lived at Elmira, where I studied my profession, but then (as now) I resided at this place, twenty miles distant from Elmira, where I resided for nearly twenty-five years and was well known at Elmira.

As soon as appointed I journeyed to that delightful paradise for Confederate prisoners (according to Walker, Tracy and Platt), and stated the object of my visit to the commanding officer, and asked to be permitted to go through the prison in order to ascertain the wants of the prisoners, with the request that I might distribute necessary blankets, clothing, money, medicines, etc.

He treated me with consideration and kindness, and informed me that they were very destitute of clothing and blankets; that not one-half of them had even a single blanket; and that many were nearly naked, the most of them having been captured during the hot summer months with no other than thin cotton clothes, which in most instances were in tatters. Yet he stated that he could not allow me to enter the prison gate or administer relief, as an order of the War Department rendered him powerless. I then asked him to telegraph the facts to the War Department and ask a revocation of the order, which he did; and two or three days were thus consumed by me in a fruitless endeavor to procure the poor privilege of carrying out the designs of the good Samaritans at Baltimore who were seeking to alleviate in a measure the wants of the poor sufferers, who were there dying off like rotten sheep from cold and exposure. The officer in command was an army officer, and his heart nearly bled for those poor sufferers; and I know he did all in his power to aid me, but his efforts were fruitless to assist me to put a single coat on the back of a sufferer. The brutal Stanton was inexorable to all my entreaties, and turned a deaf ear to the tale of their sufferings. The only proposition that could be entertained was this: If I could fetch clothing only of a grey color (Confederate uniforms) I could place it in the hands of some under-strappers of the *loyal persuasion*, as well as such moneys as I might wish to leave in the same hands, and they would distribute the same as they liked.

This could not be allowed to be done by the commanding officer, but must be done by any one of the *loyal* (?) gentry, who I became satisfied would absorb it before any poor Confederate soldier would even catch a glimpse at its shadow; and I was actually forced to give the matter up in despair.

The nearest I could get to the poor skeletons confined in that prison, was a tower built by some speculator in an adjoining field across the way from the prison pen, for which privilege a money consideration was exacted and paid. On taking a position upon this tower what a sight of misery and squalor was presented! My heart was sick, and I blushed for my country—more because of the inhumanity there depicted. Nearly all of the many thousands there were in dirty rags. The rain was

185

pouring, and thousands were without shelter, standing in the mud in their bare feet, with clothes in tatters, of the most unsubstantial material, without blankets. I tell the truth, and Mr. Charles C.B. Watkins dare not deny it, when I say these men suffered bitterly for the want of clothing, blankets and other necessaries. I was denied the privilege of covering their nakedness.

Loading cannon with a block and tackle on a monitor. *Harper's Weekly*

GETTING OUT OF PRISON

By F. S. Wade, Elgin, Texas

Getting Out of Prison is a reprint from *The Confederate Veteran Magazine,* 1926, October.

If there ever was a hell on earth, Elmira prison was that hell, but it was not a hot one, for the thermometer was often 40 degrees below zero. There were about six thousand Confederate prisoners, mostly from Georgia and the Carolinas. We were housed in long prison buildings, say one hundred and twenty feet long and forty feet wide, three tiers of bunks against each wall. A big coal stove every thirty feet was always kept red hot; but for these stoves, the most of us would have frozen. Around each stove was a chalk mark, five feet from the stove, marking the distance we should keep, so that all could be warm. We were thinly clad and not half of us had even one blanket. Our rations were ten ounces of bread and two ounces of meat per day. My weight fell from 180 to 160 in a month. We invented all kinds of traps and deadfalls to catch rats. Every day Northern ladies came in the prison, some of them followed by dogs or cats, which the boys would slip aside and choke to death. The ribs of a stewed dog were delicious, and broiled rat was superb.

One day I was at the guardhouse when about thirty-five of our boys had on barreled shirts, guards marching them around. A barreled shirt was made by knocking out the head of a barrel the cutting a hole in the other head and putting it on the body. On these barreled shirts was written in big letters, "Stole dog," "Stole cat," "Stole ration," "Stole a fur," etc. If a ladies fur was not fastened on, the boys would grab it off, and some of them had been caught.

All the Yankee soldiers were not cruel. The chalk marks were drawn around the stoves so that all could get some of the heat. One day a poor sick boy lay down near the chalk line and went to sleep. In his sleep he threw his leg over the chalk line. A big guard caught him by the shoulder and threw him against the wall, making his nose bleed. I popped my big fist against the guard's jaw, knocking him heels over head. He ran out cursing me. Of course I was scared. In a few minutes, a captain came in with a file of soldiers, having the guard I assaulted in the party, and asked, "Where is the man who knocked this soldier down?" I stepped out and said: "I am the man." Then I called up the sick boy and made him lie down, and I told the captain it made me so mad to see this poor boy so brutally treated that I could not help punishing the bully. He said to our men: Has this man told the truth?" A dozen of our men stepped forward and said that they would swear that I had related the scene correctly. The captain slapped me on the shoulder and said to the brute: "I will put you in the guardhouse." I was called before a court-martial, and, being sworn, related the whole matter as it occurred. The Judge Advocate said to the bully: "You will wear a ball and chain for thirty days and forfeit your pay for a month for brutality to a prisoner."

Good luck came to me after I had been in this prison, say, a month. Some Yankee ladies got up a lot of old schoolbooks and established a prison school, and I was appointed one of the teachers, the pay was an extra ration. I soon got back my twenty pounds of flesh. This was the best pay I ever got for a job in my life.

My father and mother lived in Illinois. I wrote them my starving condition, and they sent me a big box of grub, and told me in their letter that my Uncle Jones lived in Utica, N.Y. I at once wrote him. He sent me a splendid suit of clothes and a pair of boots, and said that he would come to see me. He was what was called a "Copperhead," as he was opposed to the war, and could not get a pass. Then he smuggled a letter to me, asking me to be at the corner of a certain ward at sunset that day, and he would climb up on the observatory, a building outside the prison walls. At sundown, I saw a large old man slowly climb to the top of the observatory. On reaching the top, he faced me. We took off our hats and saluted. He slowly climbed down, with his handkerchief to his eyes. That was the only time I ever saw my dear uncle.

My dear comrade, Jimmie Jones, took the smallpox and was sent to the smallpox hospital. I was immune and got permission to help nurse him. A young Chinese physician, by the name of Sin Lu, had just been put in charge of the ward. The doctor had just become a Mason. Jim and I were very proficient in the work. All the doctor's spare time he spent in Jim's room learning the work. We became great friends. One day the doctor went over to Lake Erie, a few miles away. The next day he told me to go to Jim's room. To my great surprise, Jim was sitting in a coffin with a white sheet around him. He handed me a paper of flour and said: "Sprinkle my face and hands with flour, then slightly fasten the coffin lid down, and when the dead wagon comes around, be sure to put my coffin on top of the other dead." Soon the dead wagon, driven by a Negro, came up. I got help and put Jim's coffin on top. It was forty years before I saw Jim again at a reunion of Green's Brigade at Cuero, Texas.; but a day or two after, I got a letter from him telling me about his experiences. He said when the dead wagon got out of the prison walls, he raised up the coffin lid rapped on it, and said in a sepulchral voice: "Come to judgment." The darky looked around, jumped off the wagon, eyes like saucers, yelling: "Ghosties! Ghosties! Ghosties!" As soon as the darky was out of sight, he stripped off his sheet, wiped the flour off his face and hands, took one of the horses out of the wagon, mounted, and galloped to lake Erie, where he found a boat awaiting him, and was soon in Canada.

Soon after, an order was issued for all prisoners from the subjugated States of Missouri, Kentucky, West Virginia, and Louisiana, to report for parole. All that night I rolled over in my bunk and wished that I was from one of those states. Just before daylight, I had another inspiration. I slipped on my clothes, ran to the office where the prison rolls were kept, and asked the officer in charge to turn to the entry of a certain date. I ran my finger down the list till I came to the name, "F.S. Wade, sergeant of McNeill's Texas Scouts." I said to the officer: "I will give you $10 to erase Texas and substitute Louisiana." Said he: "Show me the money." I started to take it out of my vest pocket, but he put his hand over mine and saw the "X." Then he made the change, and I walked out with my parole.

Soon an officer came in my ward and called my name for parole. I stepped out and fell in line. The boys in the prison kept saying: "He always said he was from Texas." But I kept mum.

188

FEDERAL SOLDIER'S STATEMENTS

The fact that this statement was given voluntarily by a Federal officer guarding Elmira Prison makes it unique and worthy of note.

Chapter XIII is reprinted from the book: *Turned Inside Out:*
Recollections of a Private Soldier in the Army of the Potomac

By Frank Wilkeson

Chapter XIII: The Military Prison at Elmira

After General Early had withdrawn his soldiers from the front of Washington, Battery A Fourth United States Artillery joined the artillery reserve then lying in Camp Barry, near Washington. Life in Camp Barry was exceedingly monotonous, and enlisted men and officers alike were impatient to be ordered to active service. There was joy in the camp one afternoon in late fall, when an order came, directing the commanding officer of Battery A to go at once to Elmira, New York, with a section of artillery, and to report for duty to the commanding officer, of that post. The senior lieutenant, Rufus King, was absent on leave. Lieutenant Cushing, eager to get out of Washington, ordered me to get a section in marching order. I did so, and we marched to the railroad station, and loaded guns, caissons, and horses on the cars, and left Washington in less than two hours after receiving the order.

Captain Frank Wilkeson, 4th US Artillery

We had heard that the Confederate soldiers who were confined in the military prison at Elmira were somewhat unruly, and next day, then we reported for duty to a 100-day colonel, we were not surprised to hear that the prisoners were insubordinate, and that an outbreak was imminent. We marched the battery to the military prison. There we found about twelve thousand Confederate prisoners, who were confined in a large stockade, inside of which were many barracks, and through which the Chemung River flowed. The stockade, made of logs set deeply in the ground on end and standing side by side, was about twelve feet high. About four feet below the top of the stockade, on the outside, was a platform, guarded by a handrail, which extended around the prison. This platform was studded by sentry boxes at short intervals. On it sentinels walked to and fro, day and night, and watched the prisoners. During the night they, at half hour intervals, loudly called the number to their post, and announced that all was well. It was almost dark when we arrived at the prison, and we parked the guns in an open space near the stockade. Around us were many camps, which were occupied by disorderly, undrilled 100-day men. We speedily discovered that there was a lack of discipline in the prison. The Confederates were ugly-tempered and rebellious. That night that gathered in mobs, and the Confederate charging-yell rang out clearly. They threw stones at the sentinels. They refused to go into their barracks. Evidently they knew that the men who guarded them were no soldiers. The uproar increased in volume. I was confident that the prisoners intended to break out that night. Our guns were placed in battery, and the ammunition chests opened. We waited, and waited, and waited, and finally I rode over to an infantry camp in

190

search of information, and there found a 100-day colonel, who was playing cribbage with a sergeant. I asked the meaning of the uproar in the prison, and the colonel said, indifferently: "Oh, that is nothing! They generally make twice as much noise," and he continued to move his pegs up and down the cribbage-board. I returned to camp greatly disgusted.

The next day Cushing and I went into the prison, and after carefully examining it concluded that if an attempt to break guard was made it would be directed against the point where the river left the stockade. As we walked slowly around the prison, groups of Confederates looked curiously at us and talked insultingly about us. One crowd of men followed us to the riverbank and jeered us as we inspected the stockade there. Cushing lost his temper and turned savagely to face them, and said, in a low, clear voice: "See here, ---- ---- ----! I am just up from the front, where I have been killing such infernal wretches as you are. I have met you in twenty battles. I never lost a gun to you. You never drove a battery I served with from its position. You are a crowd of insolent, cowardly scoundrels, and if I had command of this prison I would discipline you, or kill you, and I should much prefer to kill you. I have brought a battery of United States artillery to this pen, and if you will give me occasion I will be glad to dam that river," pointing to the Chemung, "with your worthless carcasses, and silence your insolent tongues forever. I fully understand that you are presuming on your position as prisoners of war when you talk to me as you have: but," and here his hand shook warningly in the faces of the group, "you have reached the end of your rope with me. I will kill the first man of you who again speaks insultingly to me while I am in this pen, and I shall be here daily. Now, go to your quarters." And they went. We returned to camp, moved the guns to a position, which commanded the river, and then rearranged the ammunition, putting all the canister in the chests of the gun lumbers. And we waited for the expected outbreak.

A military prison is not a place where life is enjoyed. The prisoners are enemies, and their keepers care but little for their lives and comfort. It is probable that we fed the Confederates better than they fed Union prisoners. Personally I know nothing of life in Confederate military prisons, as I was not captured. I saw many thousands of our soldiers shortly after they were exchanged. By far the larger portion of these men were in good condition and fit for service. It is true than many of them were diseased and almost dead when they were delivered to us, and these soldiers were grouped and photographed, very unfairly I think, and the illustrated papers which reproduced these photographs were widely circulated throughout the Northern States. I met no Union soldier who had been confined in a Confederate military prison, who thought it to be a pleasant retreat; and I know that the military at good taste. The prisoners, it was alleged, were allowed the same rations, excepting coffee and sugar, that their guards received. They did not get it. I repeatedly saw the Confederate prisoners draw their provisions, and they never got more than two thirds rations. Many of them were diseased, many were slightly wounded, many were feeble and worn out with campaigning in Virginia, and many more were home-sick; and these men died as sheep with the rot. Almost daily a wagon piled high with pine coffins entered the stockade, and these coffins were filled with dead Confederates. The sound men, the men of vigorous constitution, and those possessing aggressive minds, endured prison life without suffering greatly; and this I suspect was true of Union soldiers confined in Confederate prisons. The winter of 1864-65 was exceedingly cold. The Confederate prisoners, thinly clad, enfeebled by campaigning, and further weakened by insufficient supplies of food, were unable to endure the cold of a Northern winter. They died by the hundred. They were mentally depressed, and the inevitable result followed. Their wounds became gangrenous and they died; they were home-sick and they died; Fever stalked among them and struck hundreds down. Bowel disorders carried off other hundreds. I have seen groups of battle-worn, home-sick

Confederates, their thin blankets drawn tightly around their shoulders, stand in the lee of a barrack for hours without speaking to one another. They stood motionless and gazed into one another's haggard faces with despairing eyes. There was no need to talk, as all topics of conversation had long since been exhausted.

The majority of the prisoners were exceedingly ignorant. Many of them could not read or write. I often admired the military skill displayed by the Confederate officers in forging these ignorant men into the almost perfect soldiers they were. The discipline in the Confederate armies must have been exceedingly severe to have enabled their officers to control these reckless, savage-tempered men. The prisoners at Elmira were exclusively Americans. I did not see a foreign-born citizen in that prison. These soldiers were penniless. They could not buy clothing or articles of prime necessity. They were eager to work, to earn money to buy tobacco. On pleasant days a few hundred of them were employed outside the stockade in digging ditches and trenches. For this work they were paid about twenty-five cents per day, which sum they promptly invested in tobacco. And they worked faithfully and honestly, and earned their scanty pay. Thinly clad, with blankets wound around them instead of overcoats, poorly fed, hopeless, these unfortunate soldiers swung heavy picks, and bent low over their shovels, as the cold wind swept through their emaciated frames as through a sieve. It was pitiful to see the poverty-stricken Confederates breaking the hard, frost-bound earth, while armed sentinels passed to and fro about them, and a battery of artillery moved swiftly over the frozen plain in menacing drill.

Outside the stockade, and on the other side of the road, two tall wooden towers had been built by some enterprising Yankees. The owners of these buildings made a profitable show of the Confederate prisoners. Daily their tops were thronged with curious spectators, who paid ten cents each to look into the prison pen. A few weeks after these towers were built, I noticed a young and handsome woman visiting one of them daily. It was evident to me that she was communicating with the prisoners, probably to her friends or relatives who were confined in the stockade. One night seven or eight Confederates escaped from the prison by crawling through a tunnel that they had dug, and were seen no more. I was exceedingly glad that these men had escaped. The young woman disappeared also. Then I reported what I had seen, and the towers were closed by military orders.

One night the uproar in the stockade was terrific. A rifle shot rang out clearly. I heard a sentinel on post call for the officer of the guard. The long roll sounded in the infantry camps. The noise of infantry falling into line hummed in the air. The night was intensely dark. I stood in the door of my tent listening to the uproar in the Confederate pen. I judged that the prisoners were divided into two groups; one standing by the river bank, the other near the gate. Both groups were yelling at the top of their voices. Some of the soldiers of the regular brigade, which had been sent from the Army of the Potomac to assist in guarding the prisoners, were on duty that night. And I heard these cool veterans caution the Confederates not to cross the dead-line, and to repeatedly tell them to stand back or they would fire on them. Another shot rang out clearly. My battery bugler, a Jew, names Samuels, came to me, bugle in hand. "Blow Boots and Saddles," I said. Instantly the artillery camp was alive. Half-dressed men sprang to the guns, horses were harnessed and saddled. I called an old sergeant to me and said: "Trane No. 2 gun on the stockade near the river, and if the prisoners break out, dose the head of the column with double canister until they run over your gun. Fire a blank cartridge to summon Lieutenant Cushing and the enlisted men, who are in town, to the battery. I will take No. 1 gun close to the stockade and smash the flank of the column to flinders if it comes out. I will burn a lantern by the gun so as to mark my position." The sergeant moved off in the darkness. I saw the flash of his gun, heard a shot scream close above my head, and then heard the crash of timber as the shot tore through a barrack. I heard the Confederates cry: "Look out, the artillery has opened!" Instantly the uproar ceased. The great prison was as silent as death, and instantly I knew I was in a scrape, and would probably be court-martialed for firing on the prisoners. Out of town came Cushing, his horse in a lather. I explained to him what had happened. He looked soberly at me for an instant, and then said: "You will be court-marshaled, sure. You must get to your own battery at once (I belonged to battery H), and get off before the 100-day officers prefer charges against you." An officer from headquarters rode up and complained bitterly of the outrage of firing on the prisoners. From him we learned that it was a stone instead of a shot that had been fired into the prison. Early the next morning I left Elmira, having been ordered by a speedily procured telegram to join Battery H, Forth United States Artillery, in the department of the Cumberland. I afterwards learned that a few Confederates were wounded by splinters when the stone struck the barrack, and that they never again made the night hideous by their yells and howls.

STATEMENT OF A UNITED STATES EX-MEDICAL OFFICER

Article Reprinted From *The Southern Historical Society Papers,*
Vol. I. Richmond, VA, March, 1876, No. 4 April, Pages 296-298

To the Editor of the World:

Sir-I beg herewith (after having carefully gone through the various documents in my possession pertaining to the matter) to forward you the following statistics and facts of the mortality of the Rebel prisoners in the Northern prisons, more particularly at that of Elmira, New York, where I served as one of the medical officers for many months. I found, on commencement of my duties at Elmira, about 11,000 Rebel prisoners, fully one-third of whom were under medical treatment for diseases principally owing to an improper diet, a want of clothing, necessary shelter and bad surrounding; the diseases were consequently of the following nature: Scurvy, diarrhea, pneumonia, and the various branches of typhoid, all super induced by the causes, more or less, aforementioned.

The winter of 1864-65 was an unusually severe and frigid one, and the prisoners arriving from the Southern States during this season were mostly old men and lads, clothed in attire suitable only to the genial climate of the South. I need not state to you that this alone was ample cause for an unusual mortality amongst them. The surroundings were of the following nature: narrow, confined limits, but a few acres of ground in extent, and through which slowly flowed a turbid stream of water, carrying along with it all the excremental filth and debris of the camp; this stream of water, horrible to relate, was the only source of supply, for an extended period, that the prisoners could possibly use for the purpose of ablution, and to slack their thirst from day to day; the tents and other shelter allotted to the camp at Elmira were insufficient, and crowded to the utmost extent-hence, small pox and other skin diseases raged through the camp.

Here I may note that, owing to a general order from the Government to vaccinate the prisoners, my opportunities were ample to observe the effects of spurious and diseases matter, and there is no doubt in my mind but that syphilis was engrafted in many instances; ugly and horrible ulcers and eruptions of a characteristic nature were, alas, too frequent and obvious to be mistaken. Small pox cases were crowded in such a manner that it was a matter of impossibility for the surgeon to treat his patients individually; they actually laid so adjacent that the simple movement of one of them would cause his neighbor type prevailed to such an extent, and of such a nature, that the body would frequently be found one continuous scab.

The diet and other allowances by the Government for the use of the prisoners were ample, yet the poor unfortunates were allowed to starve; but why, is a query which I will allow your readers to infer, and to draw conclusions there from.

Out of the number of prisoners, as before mentioned, over three thousand of them now lay buried in the cemetery located near the camp for that purpose; a mortality equal, if not greater than that of any prison in the South. At Andersonville, as I am, well informed by brother officers who endured confinement there, as well as by the records at Washington, the mortality was twelve thousand out of say about forty thousand prisoners. Hence it is readily to be seen that range of mortality was no less at Elmira than at Andersonville.

At Andersonville there was actually nothing to feed or clothe the prisoners with, their own soldiers faring but little better than their prisoners; this, together with a torrid sun and an impossibility of exchange, was abundant cause for their mortality. With our prisoners at Elmira, no such necessity should honestly have existed, as our Government had actually, as I have stated, most bountifully made provision for the wants of all detained, both of officers and men. Soldiers who have been prisoners at Andersonville, and have done duty at Elmira, confirm this statement, and which is in nowise in one particular exaggerated; also, the same may be told of other prisons managed in a similarly terrible manner. I allude to Sandusky, Delaware and other. I do not say that all prisoners at the North suffered and endured the terrors and the cupidity of venal sub-officials; on the contrary, at the camps in the harbor of New York, and at Point Lookout, and at other camps where my official duties from time to time have called me, the prisoners in all respects have fared as our Government intended and designated they should. Throughout Texas, where food and the necessaries of life were plentiful, I found our own soldiers faring well, and to a certain extent contended, so far, at least, as prisoners of war could reasonably expect to be.

The sick in hospitals were curtailed in every respect (fresh vegetables and other antiscorbutics were dropped from the list), the food scant, crude and unfit; medicine so badly dispensed that it was a farce for the medical man to prescribe. At large in the camp the prisoner fared still worse; a slice of bread and salt meat was given him for his breakfast, a poor hatch-up, concocted cup of soup, so called, and a slice of miserable bread, was all he could obtain for his coming meal; and hundreds of sick, who could in nowise obtain medical aid died, "unknelled, unconfined and unknown."

I have in nowise drawn on the imagination, and the facts as stated can be attested by the staff of medical officers who labored at the Elmira prison for Rebel soldiers.

Ex-medical officer United States Army

Confederate States of America, Congress, Joint Select Committee to Investigate the Condition and Treatment of Prisoners of War

---

Text reprinted from *The Southern Historical Society Papers*, Vol. I, pages 132-149

HOUSE OF REPRESENTATIVES, MARCH 3, 1865, on table and ordered to be printed. [By Mr. PERKINS.]

Report of the Joint Select Committee appointed to investigate the Condition and Treatment of Prisoners of War.

The duties assigned to the committee under the several resolutions of Congress designating them, "to investigate and report upon the condition and treatment of the prisoners of war respectively held by the Confederate and United States governments; upon the causes of their detention, and the refusal to exchange; and also upon the violations by the enemy of the rules of civilized warfare in the conduct of the war." These subjects are broad in extent and importance; and in order fully to investigate and present them, the committee propose to continue their labors in obtaining evidence, and deducing from it a truthful report of facts illustrative of the spirit in which the war has been conducted.

Northern Publications

But we deem it proper at this time to make a preliminary report, founded upon evidence recently taken, relating to the treatment of prisoners of war by both belligerents. This report is rendered especially important, by reason of persistent efforts lately made by the Government of the United States, and by associations and individuals connected or co-operating with it, to asperse the honor of the Confederate authorities, and to charge them with deliberate and willful cruelty to prisoners of war. Two publications have been issued at the North within the past year, and have been circulated not only in the United States, but in some parts of the South, and in Europe. One of these is the report of the joint select committee of the Northern Congress on the conduct of the war, known as "Report No. 67." The other purports to be a "Narrative of the privations and sufferings of United States officers and soldiers while prisoners of war," and is issued as a report of a commission of enquiry appointed by "The United States sanitary commission."

This body is alleged to consist of Valentine Mott, M. D., Edward Delafield, M. D., Gouverneur Morris Wilkins, Esquire, Ellerslie Wallace, M. D., Hon. J. J. Clarke Hare, and Rev. Treadwell Walden.

Although these persons are not of sufficient public importance and weight to give authority to their publication, yet your committee have deemed it proper to notice it in connection with the "Report No. 67," before mentioned, because the sanitary commission has been understood to have acted to a great extent under the control and by the authority of the United States government, and because their report claims to be founded on evidence taken in solemn form.

Their Spirit and Intent

A candid reader of these publications will not fail to discover that, whether the statements they make be true or not, their spirit is not adapted to promote a better feeling between the hostile powers. They are not intended for the humane purpose of ameliorating the condition of the unhappy prisoners held in captivity. They are designed to inflame the evil passions of the North; to keep up the war spirit among their own people; to represent the South as acting under the dominion of a spirit of cruelty, inhumanity and interested malice, and thus to vilify her people in the eyes of all on whom these publications can work. They are justly characterized by the Hon. James M. Mason as belonging to that class of literature called the "sensational,"—a style of writing prevalent for many years at the North, and which, beginning with the writers of newspaper narratives and cheap fiction, has gradually extended itself, until it is now the favored mode adopted by medical professors, judges of courts and reverend clergymen, and is even chosen as the proper style for a report by a committee of their Congress.

Photographs

Nothing can better illustrate the truth of this view than the "Report No. 67," and its appendages. It is accompanied by eight *pictures*, or *photographs*, alleged to represent United States prisoners of war, returned from Richmond, in a sad state of emaciation and suffering. Concerning these cases, your committee will have other remarks, to be presently submitted. They are only alluded to now to show that this report does really belong to the "sensational" class of literature, and that, "prima facie," it is open to the same criticism to which the yellow covered novels, the "narratives of noted highwaymen," and the "awful beacons" of the Northern book stalls should be subjected.

The intent and spirit of this report may be gathered from the following extract: "The evidence proves, beyond all manner of doubt, a determination on the part of the rebel authorities, deliberately and persistently practiced for a long time past, to subject those of our soldiers who have been so unfortunate as to fall in their hands, to a system of treatment which has resulted in reducing many of those who have survived and been permitted to return to us, to a condition both physically and mentally, which no language we can use can adequately describe." Report, p. 1. And they give also a letter from Edwin M. Stanton, the Northern Secretary of War, from which the following is an extract: "The enormity of the crime committed by the Rebels towards our prisoners for the last several months, is not known or realized by our people, and cannot but fill with horror the civilized world, when the facts are fully revealed. There appears to have been a deliberate system of savage and barbarous treatment and starvation, the result of which will be that few (if any) of the prisoners that have been in their hands during the past winter, will ever again be in a condition to render any service, or even to enjoy life." Report, p. 4. And the sanitary commission, in their pamphlet, after picturing many scenes of privation and suffering, and bringing many charges of cruelty against the Confederate authorities, declare as follows: "The conclusion is unavoidable, therefore, that these privations and sufferings have been designedly inflicted by the military and other authorities of the Rebel government, and could not have been due to causes which such authorities could not control."

Truth to be sought

After examining these publications, your committee approached the subject with an earnest desire to ascertain *the truth*. If their investigation should result in ascertaining that these charges (or any of them) were true, the committee desired, as far as might be in their power, and as far as they could influence the Congress, to remove the evils complained of, and to conform to the most humane spirit of civilization: and if these charges were unfounded and false, they deemed it a sacred duty, without delay, to present to the Confederate Congress and people, and to the public eye of the enlightened world, a vindication of their country, and to relieve her authorities from the injurious slanders brought against her by her enemies. With these views, we have taken a considerable amount of testimony bearing on the subject. We have sought to obtain witnesses whose position or duties made them familiar with the facts testified to, and whose characters entitled them to full credit. We have not hesitated to examine Northern prisoners of war upon points and experience specially within their knowledge. We now present the testimony taken by us, and submit a report of facts and inferences fairly deducible from the evidence, from the admissions of our enemies, and from public records of undoubted authority.

Facts as to Sick and Wounded Prisoners

First in order, your committee will notice the charge contained both in "Report No. 67," and in the "sanitary" publication, founded on the appearance and condition of the sick prisoners sent from Richmond to Annapolis and Baltimore about the last of April 1864. These are the men, some of whom form the subjects of the photographs with which the United States congressional committee have adorned their report. The disingenuous attempt is made in both these publications to produce the impression that these sick and emaciated men were fair representatives of the general state of the prisoners held by the South, and that all their prisoners were being rapidly reduced to the same state, by starvation and cruelty, and by neglect, ill treatment and denial of proper food, stimulants and medicines, in the Confederate hospitals. Your committee takes pleasure in saying that not only is this charge proved to be wholly false, but the evidence ascertains facts as to the Confederate hospitals, in which Northern prisoners of war are treated, highly creditable to the authorities which established them, and to the surgeons and their aides who have so humanely conducted them. The facts are simply these:

The Federal authorities, in violation of the cartel, having for a long time refused exchange of prisoners, finally consented to a partial exchange of the sick and wounded on both sides. Accordingly, a number of such prisoners were sent from the hospitals in Richmond. General directions had been given that none should be sent except those who might be expected to endure the removal and passage with safety to their lives; but in some cases the surgeons were induced to depart from this rule, by the entreaties of some officers and men in the last stages of emaciation, suffering not only with excessive debility, but with "nostalgia," or home sickness, whose cases were regarded as desperate, and who could not live if they remained, and might possibly improve if carried home. Thus it happened that some very sick and emaciated men were carried to Annapolis, but their illness was *not* the result of ill treatment or neglect. Such cases might be found in any large hospital, North or South. They might even be found in private families, where the sufferer would be surrounded by every comfort that love could bestow. Yet these are the cases which, with hideous violation of decency, the Northern committee has paraded in pictures and photographs. They have taken their own sick and enfeebled soldiers; have stripped them naked; have exposed them before a daguerreian apparatus; have pictured every shrunken limb and muscle—and all for the purpose, not of relieving their sufferings, but of bringing a false and slanderous charge against the South.

Confederate Sick and Wounded—their Condition when returned

The evidence is overwhelming that the illness of these prisoners was not the result of ill treatment or neglect. The testimony of Surgeons Semple and Spence; of Assistant Surgeons Tinsley, Marriott and Miller, and of the Federal prisoners, E. P. Dalrymple, Geo. Henry Brown and Freeman B. Teague, ascertains this to the satisfaction of every candid mind. But in refuting this charge, your committee is compelled by the evidence to bring a counter charge against the Northern authorities, which they fear will not be so easily refuted. In exchange, a number of Confederate sick and wounded prisoners have been at various times delivered at Richmond and at Savannah. The mortality among these on the passage and their condition when delivered were so deplorable as to justify the charge that they had been treated with inhuman neglect by the Northern authorities.

Assistant Surgeon Tinsley testifies: "I have seen many of our prisoners returned from the North, who were nothing but skin and bones. They were as emaciated as a man could be to retain life, and the photographs (appended to 'Report No. 67,') would not be exaggerated representations of our returned prisoners to whom I thus allude. I saw 250 of our sick brought in on litters from the steamer at Rocketts. Thirteen dead bodies were brought off the steamer the same night. At least thirty died in one night after they were received."

Surgeon Spence testifies: "I was at Savannah, and saw rather over three thousand prisoners received. The list showed that a large number had died on the passage from Baltimore to Savannah. The number sent from the Federal prisons was 3,500, and out of that number they delivered only 3,028, to the best of my recollection. Capt. Hatch can give you the exact number. Thus, about 472 died on the passage. I was told that 67 dead bodies had been taken from one train of cars between Elmira and Baltimore. After being received at Savannah, they had the best attention possible, yet many died in a few days"—"In carrying out the exchange of disabled, sick and wounded men, we delivered at Savannah and Charleston about 11,000 Federal prisoners, and their physical condition compared most favorably with those we received in exchange, although of course the worst cases among the Confederates had been removed by death during the passage."

Richard H. Dibrell, a merchant of Richmond, and a member of the "ambulance committee," whose labors in mitigating the sufferings of the wounded have been acknowledged both by Confederate and Northern men, thus testifies concerning our sick and wounded soldiers at Savannah, returned from Northern Prisons and hospitals: "I have never seen a set of men in worse condition. They were so enfeebled and emaciated that we lifted them like little children. Many of them were like living skeletons. Indeed, there was one poor boy about 17 years old, who presented the most distressing and deplorable appearance I ever saw. He was nothing but skin and bone, and besides this, he was literally eaten up with vermin. He died in the hospital in a few days after being removed thither, notwithstanding the kindest treatment and the use of the most judicious nourishment. Our men were in so reduced a condition that on more than one trip up on the short passage of ten miles from the transports to the city, as many as five died. The clothing of the privates was in a wretched state of tatters and filth."—The mortality on the passage from Maryland was very great as well as that on the passage from the prisons to the port from which they started. I cannot state the exact number, but I think I heard that 3,500 were started, and we only received about 3,027."—"I have looked at the photographs appended to 'Report No. 67' of the committee of the Federal Congress, and do not hesitate to declare that several of our men were worse cases of emaciation and sickness than any represented in these photographs."

The testimony of Mr. Dibrell is confirmed by that of Andrew Johnston, also a merchant of Richmond, and a member of the "ambulance committee."

Thus it appears that the sick and wounded Federal prisoners at Annapolis, whose condition has been made a subject of outcry and of wide spread complaint by the Northern Congress, were not in a worse state than were the Confederate prisoners returned from Northern hospitals and prisons, of which the humanity and superior management are made subjects of special boasting by the United States sanitary commission!

Confederate Hospitals for Prisoners

In connection with this subject, your committee takes pleasure in reporting the facts ascertained by their investigations concerning the Confederate hospitals for sick and wounded Federal prisoners. They have made personal examination, and have taken evidence specially in relation to "Hospital No. 21," in Richmond, because this has been made the subject of distinct charge in the publication last mentioned. It has been shown not only by the evidence of the surgeons and their assistants, but by that of Federal prisoners, that the treatment of the Northern prisoners in these hospitals has been everything that humanity could dictate; that their wards have been well ventilated and clean; their food the best that could be procured for them—and in fact, that no distinction has been made between their treatment and that of our own sick and wounded men. Moreover, it is proved that it has been the constant practice to supply to the patients, *out of the hospital funds*, such articles as milk, butter, eggs, tea and other delicacies, when they were required by the condition of the patient. This is proved by the testimony of E. P. Dalrymple of New York, George Henry Brown of Pennsylvania, and Freeman B. Teague of New Hampshire, whose depositions accompany this report.

Contrast

This humane and considerate usage was not adopted in the United States hospital on Johnson's Island, where Confederate sick and wounded officers were treated. Col. J. H. Holman thus testifies: "The Federal authorities did not furnish to the sick prisoners the nutriment and other articles which were prescribed by their own surgeons. All they would do was to permit the prisoners to buy the nutriment or stimulants needed; and if they had no money, they could not get them. I know this, for I was in the hospital sick myself, and I had to buy, myself, such articles as eggs, milk, flour, chickens and butter, after their doctors had prescribed them. And I know this was generally the case, for we had to get up a fund among ourselves for this purpose, to aid those who were not well supplied with money." This statement is confirmed by the testimony of acting assistant surgeon John J. Miller, who was at Johnson's Island for more than eight months. When it is remembered that such articles as eggs, milk and butter were very scarce and high priced in Richmond, and plentiful and cheap at the North, the contrast thus presented may well put to shame the "sanitary commission," and dissipate the self-complacency with which they have boasted of the superior humanity in the Northern prisons and hospitals.

Charge of Robbing Prisoners

Your committee now proceeds to notice other charges in these publications. It is said that their prisoners were habitually stripped of blankets and other property, on being captured. What pillage may have been committed on the battle field, after the excitement of combat, your committee cannot know. But they feel well assured that such pillage was never encouraged by the Confederate generals, and bore no comparison to the wholesale robbery and destitution to which the Federal armies have abandoned themselves, in possessing parts of our territory. It is certain that after the prisoners were brought to the Libby, and other prisons in Richmond, no such pillage was permitted. Only articles which came properly under the head of munitions of war, were taken from them.

Shooting Prisoners

The next charge noticed is, that the guards around the Libby prison were in the habit of recklessly and inhumanly shooting at the prisoners, upon the most frivolous pretexts, and that the Confederate officers, so far from forbidding this, rather encouraged it, and made it a subject of sportive remark. This charge is wholly false and baseless. The "Rules and Regulations" appended to the deposition of Maj. Thomas P. Turner, expressly provide, "Nor shall any prisoner be fired upon by a sentinel or other person, except in case of revolt or attempted escape." Five or six cases have occurred, in which prisoners have been fired on and killed or hurt: but every case has been made the subject of careful investigation and report, as will appear by the evidence. As a proper comment on this charge, your committee report that the practice of firing on our prisoners by the guards in the Northern prisons, appears to have been indulged in to a most brutal and atrocious extent. See the depositions of C. C. Herrington, Wm. F. Gordon, Jr., J. B. McCreary, Dr. Thomas P. Holloway, and John P. Fennell. At Fort Delaware, a cruel regulation as to the use of the "sinks," was made the pretext for firing on and murdering several of our men and officers—among them, Lieut. Col. Jones, who was lame, and was shot down by the sentinel while helpless and feeble, and while seeking to explain his condition. Yet this sentinel was not only not punished, but was promoted for his act. At Camp Douglas, as many as eighteen of our men are reported to have been shot in a single month. These facts may well produce a conviction in the candid observer, that it is the North and not the South that is open to the charge of deliberately and willfully destroying the lives of the prisoners held by her.

Means for securing Cleanliness

The next charge is, that the Libby and Belle Isle prisoners were habitually kept in a filthy condition, and that the officers and men confined there were prevented from keeping themselves sufficiently clean to avoid vermin and similar discomforts. The evidence clearly contradicts this charge. It is proved by the depositions of Maj. Turner, Lieut. Bossieux, Rev. Dr. McCabe, and others, that the prisons were kept constantly and systematically policed and cleansed; that in the Libby there was an ample supply of water conducted to each floor by the city pipes, and that the prisoners were not only not restricted in its use, but urged to keep themselves clean. At Belle Isle, for a brief season (about three weeks), in consequence of a sudden increase in the number of prisoners, the police was interrupted, but it was soon restored, and ample means for washing both themselves and their clothes, were at all times furnished to the prisoners. It is doubtless true, that notwithstanding these facilities, many of the prisoners were lousy and filthy; but it was the result of their own habits, and not of neglect in the discipline or arrangements of the prison. Many of the prisoners were captured and brought in while in this condition. The Federal General Neal Dow well expressed their character and habits. When he came to distribute clothing among them, he was met by profane abuse, and he said to the Confederate officer in charge, "You have here the *scrapings and rakings of Europe.*" That such men should be filthy in their habits, might be expected.

Charge of withholding and pillaging Boxes

We next notice the charge that the boxes of provisions and clothing sent to the prisoners from the North, were not delivered to them, and were habitually robbed and plundered, by permission of the Confederate authorities. The evidence satisfies your committee that this charge is, in all substantial points, untrue. For a period of about one month there was a stoppage in the delivery of boxes, caused by a report that the Federal authorities were forbidding the delivery of similar supplies to our prisoners. But the boxes were put in a warehouse, and were afterwards delivered. For some time no search was made of boxes from the "sanitary committee," intended for the prisoners' hospitals. But a letter was intercepted, advising that money should be sent in these boxes, as they were never searched;" which money was to be used in bribing the guards, and thus releasing the prisoners. After this, it was deemed necessary to search every box, which necessarily produced some delay. Your committee is satisfied that if these boxes or their contents were robbed, the prison officials are not responsible therefore. Beyond doubt, robberies were often committed by prisoners themselves, to whom the contents were delivered for distribution to their owners. Notwithstanding all this alleged pillage, the supplies seem to have been sufficient to keep the quarters of the prisoners so well furnished that they frequently presented, in the language of a witness, "the appearance of a large grocery store."

The Federal Colonel Sanderson's Testimony

In connection with this point, your committee refers to the testimony of a Federal officer, Colonel James M. Sanderson, whose letter is annexed to the deposition of Major Turner. He testifies to the full delivery of the clothing and supplies from the North, and to the humanity and kindness of the Confederate officers—especially mentioning Lieut. Bossieux, commanding on Belle Isle. His letter was addressed to the president of the United States Sanitary Commission, and was beyond doubt received by them, having been forwarded by the regular flag of truce. Yet the scrupulous and honest gentlemen composing that commission have not found it convenient for their purposes to

202

insert this letter in their publication! Had they been really searching for the *truth*, this letter would have aided them in finding it.

Mine under the Libby Prison

Your committee proceed next to notice the allegation that the Confederate authorities had prepared a mine under the Libby prison, and placed in it a quantity of gunpowder for the purpose of blowing up the buildings, with their inmates, in case of an attempt to rescue them. After ascertaining all the facts bearing on this subject, your committee believe that what was done under the circumstances, will meet a verdict of approval from all whose prejudices do not blind them to the truth. The state of things was unprecedented in history, and must be judged of according to the motives at work, and the result accomplished. A large body of Northern raiders, under one Col. Dahlgren, was approaching Richmond. It was ascertained, by the reports of prisoners captured from them, and other evidence, that their design was to enter the city, to set fire to the buildings, public and private, for which purpose turpentine balls in great number had been prepared; to murder the President of the Confederate States, and other prominent men; to release the prisoners of war, then numbering five or six thousand; to put arms into their hands, and to turn over the city to indiscriminate pillage, rape and slaughter. At the same time a plot was discovered among the prisoners to co-operate in this scheme, and a large number of knives and slung-shot (made by putting stones into woolen stockings) were detected in places of concealment about their quarters. To defeat a plan so diabolical, assuredly the sternest means were justified. If it would have been right to put to death any one prisoner attempting to escape under such circumstances, it seems logically certain that it would have been equally right to put to death any number making such attempt. But in truth the means adopted were those of humanity and *prevention*, rather than of execution. The Confederate authorities felt able to meet and repulse Dahlgren and his raiders, if they could prevent the escape of the prisoners.

The real object was to save their lives as well as those of our citizens. The guard force at the prisons was small, and all the local troops in and around Richmond were needed to meet the threatened attack. Had the prisoners escaped, the women and children of the city, as well as their homes, would have been at the mercy of five thousand outlaws. Humanity required that the most summary measures should be used to *deter* them from any attempt at escape.

A mine was prepared under the Libby prison; a sufficient quantity of gunpowder was put into it, and pains were taken to *inform the prisoners* that any attempt at escape made by them would be effectually defeated. The plan succeeded perfectly. The prisoners were awed and kept quiet. Dahlgren and his party were defeated and scattered. The danger passed away, and in a few weeks the gunpowder was removed. Such are the facts. Your committee does not hesitate to make them known; feeling assured that the conscience of the enlightened world and the great law of self-preservation will justify all that was done by our country and her officers.

Charge of Intentional Starvation and Cruelty

We now proceed to notice, under one head, the last and gravest charge made in these publications. They assert that the Northern prisoners in the hands of the Confederate authorities have been starved, frozen, inhumanly punished, often confined in foul and loathsome quarters, deprived of fresh air and exercise, and neglected and maltreated in sickness—and that all this was done upon a deliberate, willful and long conceived plan of the Confederate government and officers, for the purpose of destroying the lives of these prisoners, or of rendering them forever incapable of military service. This charge accuses the Southern government of a crime so horrible and unnatural, that it could never have been made except by those ready to blacken with slander men whom they have long injured and hated. Your committee feel bound to reply to it calmly but emphatically. They pronounce it false in fact and in design; false in the basis on which it assumes to rest, and false in its estimate of the motives which have controlled the Southern authorities.

Humane Policy of the Confederate Government

At an early period in the present contest the Confederate government recognized their obligation to treat prisoners of war with humanity and consideration. Before any laws were passed on the subject, the Executive Department provided such prisoners as fell into their hands, with proper quarters and barracks to shelter them, and with rations the same in quantity and quality as those furnished to the Confederate soldiers who guarded these prisoners. They also showed an earnest wish to mitigate the sad condition of prisoners of war, by a system of fair and prompt exchange—and the Confederate Congress co-operated in these humane views. By their act, approved on the 21st day of May 1861, they provided that "all prisoners of war taken, whether on land or at sea, during the pending hostilities with the United States, shall be transferred by the captors from time to time, and as often as convenient to the Department of War; and it shall be the duty of the Secretary of War, with the approval of the President, to issue such instructions to the Quartermaster General and his subordinates, as shall provide for the safe custody and sustenance of prisoners of war; *and the rations furnished prisoners of war shall be the same in quantity and quality as those furnished to enlisted men in the army of the Confederacy.*" Such were the declared purpose and policy of the Confederate government towards prisoners of war—and amid all the privations and losses to which their enemies have subjected them, they have sought to carry them into effect.

Rations and General Treatment

Our investigations for this preliminary report have been confined chiefly to the rations and treatment of the prisoners of war at the Libby and other prisons in Richmond and on Belle Isle. This we have done, because the publications to which we have alluded refer chiefly to them, and because the "Report No. 67" of the Northern Congress plainly intimates the belief that the treatment in and around Richmond was worse than it was farther South. That report says: "It will be observed from the testimony, that all the witnesses who testify upon that point state that the treatment they received while confined at Columbia, South Carolina, Dalton, Georgia, and other places, *was far more*

204

humane than that they received at Richmond, where the authorities of the so-called Confederacy were congregated." Report, p. 3.

The evidence proves that the rations furnished to prisoners of war in Richmond and on Belle Isle, have been *never* less than those furnished to the Confederate soldiers who guarded them, and have at some seasons been larger in quantity and better in quality than those furnished to Confederate troops in the field. This has been because until February 1864 the Quartermaster's Department furnished the prisoners, and often had provisions or funds, when the Commissary Department was not so well provided. Once and only once, for a few weeks, the prisoners were without meat; but a larger quantity of bread and vegetable food was in consequence supplied to them. How often the gallant men composing the Confederate army have been without meat, for even longer intervals, your committee does not deem it necessary to say. Not less than sixteen ounces of bread and four ounces of bacon, or six ounces of beef, together with beans and soup, have been furnished per day to the prisoners. During most of the time the quantity of meat furnished to them has been greater than these amounts; and even in times of the greatest scarcity, they have received as much as the Southern soldiers, who guarded them. The scarcity of meat and of bread stuffs in the South in certain places has been the result of the savage policy of our enemies in burning barns, filled with wheat or corn, destroying agricultural implements, and driving off or wantonly butchering hogs and cattle. Yet amid all these privations, we have given to their prisoners the rations above mentioned. It is well known that this quantity of food is sufficient to keep in health a man who does not labor hard. All the learned disquisitions of Dr. Ellerslie Wallace on the subject of starvation, might have been spared, for they are all founded on a false basis. It will be observed that few (if any) of the witnesses examined by the "sanitary commission" speak with any accuracy of the quantity (in weight) of the food actually furnished to them. Their statements are merely conjectural and comparative, and cannot weigh against the positive testimony of those who superintended the delivery of large quantities of food, cooked and distributed according to a fixed ratio, for the number of men to be fed.

Falsehoods published as to Prisoners Freezing on Belle Isle

The statements of the "sanitary commission" as to prisoners freezing to death on Belle Isle, are absurdly false. According to that statement it was common, during a cold spell in winter, to see several prisoners frozen to death every morning in the places in which they had slept. This picture, if correct, might well excite our horror; but unhappily for its sensational power, it is but a clumsy daub, founded on the fancy of the painter. The facts are, that tents were furnished sufficient to shelter all the prisoners; that the Confederate Commandant and soldiers on the Island were lodged in similar tents; that a fire was furnished in each of them; that the prisoners fared as well as their guards; and that only one of them was ever frozen to death, and he was frozen *by the cruelty of his own fellow-prisoners*, who thrust him out of the tent in a freezing night, because he was infested with vermin. The proof as to the healthiness of the prisoners on Belle Isle, and the small amount of mortality, is remarkable, and presents a fit comment on the lugubrious pictures drawn by the "sanitary commission," either from their own fancies, or from the fictions put forth by their false witnesses. Lieut. Bossieux proves, that from the establishment of the prison camp on Belle Isle in June 1862, to the 10th of February 1865, more than twenty thousand prisoners had been at various times there received, and yet that the whole number of deaths during this time, was only one hundred and sixty-four. And this is confirmed by the Federal Colonel Sanderson, who states that the average number of deaths per month on Belle Isle, was "from two to five; more frequently the lesser number." The sick were promptly removed from the Island to the hospitals in the city.

Character of the Northern Witnesses

Doubtless the "sanitary commission" have been to some extent led astray by their own witnesses, whose character has been portrayed by Gen. Neal Dow, and also by the Editor of the New York Times, who, in his issue of January 6th, 1865, describes the material for recruiting the Federal armies as "wretched vagabonds, of depraved morals, decrepit in body, without courage, self-respect or conscience. They are dirty, disorderly, thievish and incapable."

Cruelty to Confederate Prisoners at the North

In reviewing the charges of cruelty, harshness and starvation to prisoners, made by the North, your committee has taken testimony as to the treatment of our own officers and soldiers in the hands of the enemy. It gives us no pleasure to be compelled to speak of suffering inflicted upon our gallant men; but the self-laudatory style in which the "sanitary commission" have spoken of their prisons, makes it proper that the truth should be presented. Your committee gladly acknowledge that in many cases our prisoners experienced kind and considerate treatment; but we are equally assured that in nearly all the prison stations of the North—at Point Lookout, Fort McHenry, Fort Delaware, Johnson's Island, Elmira, Camp Chase, Camp Douglas, Alton, Camp Morton, the Ohio Penitentiary, and the prisons of St. Louis, Missouri, our men have suffered from insufficient food, and have been subjected to ignominious, cruel and barbarous practices, of which there is no parallel in any thing that has occurred in the South. The witnesses who were at Point Lookout, Fort Delaware, Camp Morton and Camp Douglas, testify that they have often seen our men picking up the scraps and refuse thrown out from the kitchens, with which to appease their hunger. Dr. Herrington proves that at Fort Delaware unwholesome bread and water produced diarrhea in numberless cases among our prisoners, and that "their sufferings were greatly aggravated by the regulation of the camp which forbade more than twenty men at a time at night to go to the sinks. I have seen as many as five hundred men in a row waiting their time. The consequence was that they were obliged to use the places where they were. This produced great want of cleanliness, and aggravated the disease." Our men were compelled to labor in unloading Federal vessels and in putting up buildings for Federal officers, and if they refused, were driven to the work with clubs.

The treatment of Brig. General J. H. Morgan and his officers was brutal and ignominious in the extreme. It will be found stated in the depositions of Capt. M. D. Logan, Lieut. W. P. Crow, Lieut. Col. James B. McCreary and Capt. B. A. Tracy, that they were put in the Ohio Penitentiary, and compelled to submit to the treatment of felons. Their beards were shaved, and their hair was cut close to the head. They were confined in convicts' cells, and forbidden to speak to each other. For attempts to escape, and for other offences of a very light character, they were subjected to the horrible punishment of the dungeon. In midwinter, with the atmosphere many degrees below zero, without blanket or overcoat, they were confined in a cell without fire or light, with a fetid and poisonous air to breathe—and here they were kept until life was nearly extinct. Their condition on coming out was so deplorable as to draw tears from their comrades. The blood was oozing from their hands and faces. The treatment in the St. Louis prison was equally barbarous. Capt. Wm. H. Sebring testifies: "Two of us, A. C. Grimes and myself, were carried out into the open air in the prison yard, on the 25th of December 1863, and handcuffed to a post. Here we were kept all night in sleet, snow and cold. We were relieved in the day time, but again brought to the post and handcuffed to it in the evening" and thus we were kept all night until the 2nd of January 1864. I was badly frost-bitten, and my health was much impaired. This cruel infliction was done by order of Capt. Byrnes, Commandant of Prisons in St. Louis. He was barbarous and insulting to the last degree."

Our Prisoners put into Camps infected with Small-pox

But even a greater inhumanity than any we have mentioned, was perpetrated upon our prisoners at Camp Douglas and Camp Chase. It is proved by the testimony of Thomas P. Holloway, John P. Fennell, H. H. Barlow, H. C. Barton, C. D. Bracken and J. S. Barlow, that our prisoners in large numbers were put into "condemned camps," where small-pox was prevailing, and speedily contracted this loathsome disease, and that as many as 40 new cases often appeared daily among them. Even the Federal officers who guarded them to the camp, protested against this unnatural atrocity; yet it was done. The men who contracted the disease were removed to a hospital about a mile off, but the plague was already introduced, and continued to prevail. For a period of more than twelve months, the disease was constantly in the camp; yet our prisoners during all this time were continually brought to it, and subjected to certain infection. Neither do we find evidences of amendment on the part of our enemies, notwithstanding the boasts of the "sanitary commission." At Nashville, prisoners recently captured from Gen. Hood's army, even when sick and wounded, have been cruelly deprived of all nourishment suited to their condition; and other prisoners from the same army have been carried into the infected Camps Douglas and Chase.

Many of the soldiers of Gen. Hood's army were frost-bitten by being kept day and night in an exposed condition before they were put into Camp Douglas. Their sufferings are truthfully depicted in the evidence. At Alton and Camp Morton the same inhuman practice of putting our prisoners into camps infected by small-pox, prevailed. It was equivalent to murdering many of them by the torture of a contagious disease. The insufficient rations at Camp Morton forced our men to appease their hunger by pounding up and boiling bones, picking up scraps of meat and cabbage from the hospital slop tubs, and even eating rats and dogs. The depositions of William Ayres and J. Chambers Brent prove these privations.

Barbarous Punishments

The punishments often inflicted on our men for slight offences, have been shameful and barbarous. They have been compelled to ride a plank only four inches wide, called "Morgan's horse;" to sit down with their naked bodies in the snow for ten or fifteen minutes, and have been subjected to the ignominy of stripes from the belts of their guards. The pretext has been used, that many of their acts of cruelty have been by way of retaliation. But no evidence has been found to prove such acts on the part of the Confederate authorities. It is remarkable that in the case of Col. Streight and his officers, they were subjected only to the ordinary confinement of prisoners of war. No special punishment was used except for specific offences; and then the greatest infliction was to confine Col. Streight for a few weeks in a basement room of the Libby prison, with a window, a plank floor, a stove, a fire, and plenty of fuel.

We do not deem it necessary to dwell further on these subjects. Enough has been proved to show that great privations and sufferings have been borne by the prisoners on both sides.

Why have not Prisoners of War been Exchanged

But the question forces itself upon us why have these sufferings been so long continued? Why have not the prisoners of war been exchanged, and thus some of the darkest pages of history spared to the world? In the answer to this question must be found the test of responsibility for all the sufferings, sickness and heart-broken sorrow that have visited more than eighty thousand prisoners within the past two years. On this question, your committee can only say that the Confederate authorities have always desired a prompt and fair exchange of prisoners. Even before the establishment of a cartel they urged such exchange, but could never effect it by agreement until the large preponderance of prisoners in our hands made it the interest of the Federal authorities to consent to the cartel of July 22nd, 1863. The 9th article of that agreement expressly provided, that in case any misunderstanding should arise, it *should not interrupt the release of prisoners on parole*, but should be made the subject of friendly explanation. Soon after this cartel was established, the policy of the enemy in seducing Negro slaves from their masters, arming them and putting white officers over them to lead them against us, gave rise to a few cases in which questions of crime under the internal laws of the Southern States appeared. Whether men who encouraged insurrection and murder could be held entitled to the privileges of prisoners of war under the cartel, was a grave question. But these cases were few in number, and ought never to have interrupted the general exchange. We were always ready and anxious to carry out the cartel in its true meaning, and it is certain that the 9th article required that the prisoners on both sides should be released, and that the few cases as to which misunderstanding occurred should be left for final decision. Doubtless if the preponderance of prisoners had continued with us, exchanges would have continued. But the fortunes of war threw the larger number into the hands of our enemies. Then they refused further exchanges—and for twenty-two months this policy has continued. Our Commissioner of Exchange has made constant efforts to renew them. In August 1864 he consented to a proposition which had been repeatedly made, to exchange officer for officer and man for man, leaving the surplus in captivity. Though this was a departure from the cartel, our anxiety for the exchange induced us to consent. Yet, the Federal authorities repudiated their previous offer, and refused even this partial compliance with the cartel. Secretary Stanton, who has unjustly charged the Confederate authorities with inhumanity, is open to the charge of having done all in his power to prevent a fair exchange, and thus to prolong the sufferings of which he speaks: and very recently, in a letter over his signature, Benjamin F. Butler has declared that in April 1864, the Federal Lieut. General Grant forbade him "to deliver to the Rebels a single able-bodied man:" and moreover, Gen. Butler acknowledges that in answer to Col. Ould's letter consenting to the exchange, officer for officer and man for man, he wrote a reply, "not diplomatically but obtrusively and demonstratively, not for the purpose of furthering exchange of prisoners, but for the purpose of preventing and stopping the exchange, and furnishing a ground on which we could fairly stand."

These facts abundantly show that the responsibility of refusing to exchange prisoners of war rests with the Government of the United States, and the people who have sustained that government; and every sigh of captivity, every groan of suffering, every heart broken by hope deferred among these eighty thousand prisoners, will accuse them in the judgment of the just.

With regard to the prison stations at Andersonville, Salisbury and other places south of Richmond, your committee have not made extended examination, for reasons which have already been stated. We are satisfied that privation, suffering and mortality, to an extent much to be regretted, did prevail among the prisoners there, but they were not the result of neglect, still less of design on the part of the Confederate government. Haste in preparation; crowded quarters, prepared only for a smaller number; want of transportation and scarcity of food, have all resulted from the pressure of the war, and the barbarous manner in which it has been conducted by our enemies. Upon these subjects your committee proposes to take further evidence, and to report more fully hereafter.

But even now enough is known to vindicate the South, and to furnish an overwhelming answer to all complaints on the part of the United States government or people, that their prisoners were stinted in food or supplies. Their own savage warfare has wrought all the evil. They have blockaded our ports; have excluded from us food, clothing and medicines; have even declared medicines contraband of war, and have repeatedly destroyed the contents of drug stores and the supplies of private physicians in the country; have ravaged our country; burned our houses and destroyed growing crops and farming implements. One of their officers (General Sheridan) has boasted in his official report, that in the Shenandoah valley alone be burned two thousand barns filled with wheat and corn; that he burned all the mills in the whole tract of country; destroyed all the factories of cloth, and killed or drove off every animal, even to the poultry, that could contribute to human sustenance. These desolations have been repeated again and again in different parts of the South. Thousands of our families have been driven from their homes, as helpless and destitute refugees. Our enemies have destroyed the rail roads and other means of transportation, by which food could be supplied from abundant districts to those without it. While thus desolating our country, in violation of the usages of civilized warfare, they have refused to exchange prisoners; have forced us to keep fifty thousand of their men in captivity—and yet have attempted to attribute to us the sufferings and privations caused by their own acts. We cannot doubt that in the view of civilization we shall stand acquitted, while they must be condemned.

In concluding this preliminary report, we will notice the strange perversity of interpretation which has induced the "sanitary commission" to affix as a motto to their pamphlet, the words of the compassionate Redeemer of mankind:

"For I was a hungered and ye gave me no meat: I was thirsty and ye gave me no drink: I was a stranger and ye took me not in: naked and ye clothed me not: sick and in prison and ye visited me not."

We have yet to learn on what principle the Federal mercenaries, sent with arms in their hands to destroy the lives of our people; to waste our land, burn our houses and barns, and drive us from our homes, can be regarded by us as the followers of the meek and lowly Redeemer, so as to claim the benefit of his words. Yet even these mercenaries, when taken captive by us, have been treated with proper humanity. The cruelties inflicted on our prisoners at the North may well justify us in applying to the "sanitary commission" the stern words of the Divine Teacher: "Thou hypocrite, first cast out the beam out of thine own eye, and then shalt thou see clearly to cast out the mote out of thy brother's eye."

We believe that there are many thousands of just, honorable and humane people in the United States, upon whom this subject, thus presented, will not be lost; that they will do all they can to mitigate the horrors, of war; to complete the exchange of prisoners, now happily in progress, and to prevent the recurrence of such sufferings as have been narrated. And we repeat the words of the Confederate Congress, in their Manifesto of the 14th of June 1864:

"We commit our cause to the enlightened judgment of the world; to the sober reflections of our adversaries themselves, and to the solemn and righteous arbitrament of Heaven."

ELMIRA PRISONER OF WAR CAMP STATISTICS

These statistics were compiled by the author to illustrate the findings he discovered when researching the Fort Fisher soldiers who were sent to Elmira Prison.

1. What was the average age of Fort Fisher soldiers?

   The average age of the Fort Fisher soldier sent to Elmira was nineteen years old.

2. Who was the youngest soldier?

   The honor as the youngest Fort Fisher soldier to be sent to Elmira falls to Private William H. Faulk of the 36th Regiment North Carolina, 2nd North Carolina Artillery. Faulk was fifteen when he enlisted at Fort St. Philip in Brunswick County, NC, on 4/9/1863. This makes him seventeen-years-old when he was sent to Elmira. He was exchanged on the James River 3/2/1865.

3. Who was the oldest soldier?

   The oldest soldier from Fort Fisher to be sent to Elmira was fifty-six-year-old Private Samuel Hales of the 36th Regiment North Carolina, 2nd North Carolina Artillery. Hales was fifty-four when he enlisted at Blockerville in Cumberland County, NC, on 2/26/1862. He was exchanged on the James River 3/2/1865.

4. What were the top three diseases at Elmira?

   The number one killer at Elmira Prison Camp was chronic diarrhea with 224 deaths. Number two was pneumonia with 149 deaths. Number three was small pox with 62 deaths.

5. Are there any factors that affect whether a prisoner will die from disease?

   Yes. Both the length of time a man spends in prison and his age determine whether he is likely to die from disease. I gathered information concerning the death toll for the different age groups. Generally the older soldiers had a higher death rate because they were unable to shake the effects of disease. Surprisingly the second highest group was the youngest soldiers.

Age	15-19	20-24	25-29	30-34	35-39	40-44	45-49	50-55
Percent Died	29%	16%	23%	26%	26%	36%	36%	34%

6. What was the deadliest month for disease?

   By far the deadliest month was March, 1865. Over 200 prisoners from Fort Fisher died at Elmira that month.

7. Was Elmira intended to become a retaliatory prison?

   No printed evidence exists that Elmira was a retaliatory prison. However, looking at the plethora of written evidence would suggest otherwise. The most obvious statistic is Elmira's 24.4 percent death toll. By comparison the average death by disease rate for Northern prisons was only 11.7 percent. If Elmira was not a retaliatory prison, why was its death rate more than twice what the other Northern prisons were?

8. Why are very few of the Elmira prisoners wounded?

The severity of the wound dictated where the prisoner would be sent. If a prisoner was not likely to survive his journey to prison the soldier usually remained at Fort Fisher until he either recovered enough to travel or he died of his wounds. If a prisoner was gravely wounded but could travel a short distance he was sent to United States Army's Mansfield General Hospital in Morehead City, North Carolina. Most of the wounded men from Fort Fisher that required extended hospital stays were sent either to the hospital's at Point Lookout Prison, Maryland, Fort Monroe, Virginia or Fort Delaware, Delaware. Apparently the United States Army did not think much of the hospital at Elmira because only men with the simplest wounds were sent there.

9. How come there are South Carolina soldiers among the prisoners?

There were elements of three South Carolina infantry regiments inside Fort Fisher for the second battle in January, 1865. Hours before the final battle on January 15th the 11th, 21st and 25th South Carolina regiments were sent to the fort by General Braxton Bragg. Only parts of these regiments were landed at Battery Buchan before the steamer was drive away by intense cannon fire from the Union fleet. The author has researched each South Carolina soldier and found that 482 men were killed or captured inside the fort. This is new information as it was previously thought there were only 350 soldiers captured from these regiments. Of the 482 South Carolina soldiers captured 357 were sent to Elmira Prisoner of War Camp.

10. What became of the Confederate Junior Reserves captured during the first battle of Fort Fisher?

The young men were sent to Point Lookout Prison in Maryland and Fort Delaware Prison in Delaware. They endured the same treatment as the other soldiers and many of them died of disease.

The Most Deadly Northern Prisoner Of War Camps

Rank	Prison	State	Maximum Capacity	Most Prisoners Held At One Time	Number Passed Through	Escapes	Deaths	Percent Died
1.	Elmira	NY	5,000	9,441	12,147	17	2,965	24.4 %
2.	Rock Island	IL	10,080	8,607	12,400	41	1,964	15.8 %
3.	Camp Douglas	IL	6,000	12,082	26,060	317	4,069	15.6 %
4.	Alton	IL	800	1,891	11,764	120	1,508	12.8 %
5.	Camp Morton	IN	2,000	5,000	17,000	150	1,763	10.3 %
6.	Camp Chase	OH	4,000	9,423	25,000	203	2,260	9 %
7.	Fort Delaware	DL	?	12,600	33,000	52	2,460	7.5 %
8.	Point Lookout	MD	10,000	22,000	52,264	50	3,584	6.8 %

Researching the Roster of Fort Fisher Prisoners Sent To Elmira Prisoner of War Camp, Elmira, New York

This roster was researched and compiled by Richard H. Triebe

All these Confederate civilians and soldiers were captured at Fort Fisher, North Carolina, January 15, 1865 by Union forces commanded by Major General Alfred H. Terry. The prisoners were sent to a number of Federal prisoner of war camps. The largest group, 1,180 men, was sent to Elmira Prison Camp during the harsh New York winter. Due to disease raging out of control at Elmira 531 of these men, or 46 percent, would be dead in less than five months. This amounts to more than one hundred men dying per month. This list contains only the names of Confederate prisoners who were sent to Elmira Pri-soner of War Camp unless otherwise indicated.

I have used many resources in compiling this roster. It contains information found in the Confederate soldier's records at the National Archives as well as data obtained from the 1860 United States Census. Various references such as *North Carolina Troops, 1861-1865 A Roster* compiled by Louis H. Manarin, *Service Records of Confederate Enlisted Marines* by Ralph W. Donnelly, numerous letters, soldier's accounts and newspaper articles were also consulted.

The author has discovered the original Elmira Prison Camp ledger which contains all the names of the Fort Fisher soldiers that arrived at the prison. This was an invaluable tool in determining all the men that went to Elmira. Much to my surprise I found there were six possibly seven civilians captured inside the fort on January 15th. I also found 45 more soldiers, marines and sailors. The reason I say there may be seven men captured is because Moses Early is also listed as a soldier in the 40th North Carolina Artillery. There is a question whether this is the same man since his last name is spelled is spelled Early where the soldier's name is spelled Earley. Also both men died from disease in February of 1865, but each man died on different days and from unrelated diseases. Rather than leave this man out from the list of civilians I decided to be cautious by leaving him in. Another reason for leaving him is somewhat intriguing since it shows what methods people will go to escape prison. Private Early may have passed himself off as a civilian thinking these men would be released early. In any event this scheme did not work since both men died from disease the following month. With the discovery of these men a new mystery has arisen. Of the thirteen civilians and soldiers from this group who died four of these individuals do not have graves at Woodlawn Cemetery at Elmira. Currently Confederate the graves cannot be removed from the cemetery, but was it permissible at one time to move them? The four men certainly died at Elmira Prison Camp because their military records at the National Archives tell us they did. So what happened? The only other alternative is that these men were buried in four of the six unknown graves at Woodlawn Cemetery.

Fort Fisher Civilian Prisoner Captured January 15, 1865 and Sent to Elmira Prison Camp, Elmira, New York

NAME & RANK	RESIDENCE AGE & TRADE	RESULT OF BATTLE	PRISON RELEASE
Cook, Doctor H. Political Prisoner	North Carolina Citizen, Unknown	Captured	Oath Of Allegiance 6/20/1865
Early, Moses Political Prisoner	North Carolina Citizen, Unknown	Captured	Died of Chronic Diarrhea 2/12/1865, Grave Not at Woodlawn Cemetery
Herrell, J. G. Political Prisoner	North Carolina Citizen, Unknown	Captured	Died of Variola (Smallpox) 4/18/1865, Grave Not at Woodlawn Cemetery
Hollis, James Political Prisoner	North Carolina Citizen, Unknown	Captured	Died of Rubeola (Measles) 2/16/1865, Grave 2178
Newell, G. S. Political Prisoner	North Carolina Citizen, Unknown	Captured	Died of Variola (Smallpox) 4/18/1865, Grave Not at Woodlawn Cemetery
Randolph, Charles Political Prisoner	North Carolina Citizen, Unknown	Captured	Exchanged On the James River, VA, 3/10/1865
Williams, J. M. Political Prisoner	North Carolina Citizen, Unknown	Captured	Exchanged On the James River, VA, 3/10/1865

Confederate Marines, Sailors and Soldier Captured January 15, 1865 at Fort Fisher, North Carolina

NAME and RANK	PLACE & TYPE OF ENLISTMENT	AGE	RESIDENCE & OCCUPATION	REGIMENT OR BATTALION	RESULT OF BATTLE	REMARKS
Adams, A. Private	Charleston, SC, 5/14/1862	Unk	Unknown	Co H, 25th Regiment South Carolina Volunteers	Captured	Died of Chronic Diarrhea, 2/17/1865 Buried Woodlawn Cemetery, Elmira, NY, Grave No. 2219
Adkins, Robert J. Private	Enfield, NC, Edgecombe County, NC, 10/9/1861, Volunteer	21	Enfield, NC	Co. F, 36th Regiment North Carolina, 2nd Artillery	Captured	Oath of Allegiance 7/7/1865
Allen, Daniel J. Private	Fort Holmes, Brunswick County, 2/24/1864, Volunteer	18	Bladen County, NC, Farmer	2nd Co. K, 40th Regiment North Carolina, 3rd Artillery	Captured	Oath of Allegiance 8/7/1865
Allen, Drewry A. Private	Battery Island, SC, 4/12/1862	37	Gage Station, SC	Co E, 25th Regiment South Carolina Volunteers	Captured	Died of Pneumonia, 2/20/1865 Buried Woodlawn Cemetery, Elmira, NY, Grave No. 2308
Allen, George Frank Private	Elizabethtown, Bladen County, NC, 5/6/1862, Volunteer	20	Bladen County, NC, Farmer	2nd Co. K, 40th Regiment, 3rd North Carolina Artillery	Captured	Exchanged On the James River, VA, 3/2/1865

NAME and RANK	PLACE & TYPE OF ENLISTMENT	AGE	RESIDENCE & OCCUPATION	REGIMENT OR BATTALION	RESULT OF BATTLE	REMARKS
Allen, Joseph B. Private	Elizabethtown, Bladen County, NC 5/6/1862, Mustered in Ft St Philip, Volunteer	27	Bladenboro, NC, Farmer, Detailed as Nurse in Hospital	2nd Co. K, 40th Regiment, 3rd North Carolina Artillery	Captured	Oath of Allegiance 6/12/1865
Allen, Miles, Private	Fort Caswell, Brunswick County, NC, 7/3/1863, Volunteer	18	Eastern Division, Randolph County, NC	2nd Co. D, 36th Regiment North Carolina, 2nd Artillery	Wounded & Captured	Exchanged 3/14/1865, Recaptured at Richmond Hospital, Oath of Allegiance 5/25/1865
Allen, Thomas F. Private	New Berne, Craven County, NC, 1/29/1862, Volunteer	27	New Berne, Craven County, NC Civil Engineer	Co. F, 36th Regiment North Carolina, 2nd Artillery	Captured	Died of Pneumonia, 2/19/1865 Buried Woodlawn Cemetery, Elmira, NY, Grave No. 2327
Allen, William Rufus Private	Elizabethtown, NC, 5/6/1862, Mustered In At Fort St. Philip, Volunteer	20	Prospect Hall, Bladen County, NC, Farmer	2nd Co. K, 40th Regiment, 3rd North Carolina Artillery	Captured	Exchanged On the James River, VA, 2/20/1865
Altman, John J. Private	Marion, SC, 3/15/1864	23	Marion, SC	Co. F, 21st South Carolina	Captured	Exchanged On The James River, VA, 3/10/1865
Altman, Nathan T. Private	Wilmington, NC, New Hanover County, NC, 7/23/1863, Volunteer	18	New Hanover County, NC, Extra Duty as Boatman	3rd Co. G, 40th Regiment, 3rd North Carolina Artillery	Captured	Died of Chronic Diarrhea, 4/18/1865 Buried Woodlawn Cemetery, Elmira, NY, Grave No. 1361
Altman, Owen N. Private	Bay Point, SC, Whippy Swamp, 7/15/1861	21	Edgefield County, SC	Co. F, 11th South Carolina	Captured	Exchanged On The James River, VA, 3/14/1865

NAME and RANK	PLACE & TYPE OF ENLISTMENT	AGE	RESIDENCE & OCCUPATION	REGIMENT OR BATTALION	RESULT OF BATTLE	REMARKS
Anderson, George H. Private	Fort Caswell, Brunswick County, NC, 10/5/1863, Volunteer	45	Sampson County, NC, Laborer	2nd Co. D, 36th Regiment North Carolina, 2nd Artillery	Captured	Died of Chronic Diarrhea, 4/10/1865 Buried Woodlawn Cemetery, Elmira, NY, Grave No. 2674
Anderson, Henry Private	Wayne County, NC, 5/10/1864	49	Goldsboro, Wayne County, NC	Co. D, 40th Regiment, 3rd North Carolina Artillery	Captured	Oath of Allegiance 7/19/1865
Anderson, William J. Private	Duplin County, NC, 10/16/1861, Volunteer	24	Wayne County, NC	3rd Co. G, 40th Regiment, 3rd North Carolina Artillery	Captured	Exchanged On The James River, VA, 2/20/1865
Andrews, Robert A. Private	Chatham County, NC, 3/16/1863, Volunteer	36	Salisbury, NC, Extra Duty as Fisherman	3rd Co. G, 40th Regiment, 3rd North Carolina Artillery	Captured	Oath of Allegiance 6/12/1865
Antley, Furman M. Private	Coles Island, SC, 4/11/1862	Unk	Orangeburg, SC, Overseer of Negro labor	Co. G, 25th South Carolina Volunteers	Captured	Oath of Allegiance 6/27/1865
Ard, Benjamin Private	Williamsburg, SC, 1/27/1861	Unk	Unknown	Co H, 25th Regiment South Carolina Volunteers	Captured	Died of Pneumonia, 6/1/1865 Buried Woodlawn Cemetery, Elmira, NY, Grave No. 2904
Ard, E. G. Private	Battery Island, SC, 4/12/1864	23	Kingstree, SC	Co B, 25th Regiment South Carolina Volunteers	Captured	Oath of Allegiance 7/13/1865
Ard, S. R. Private	Battery Island, SC, 4/12/1862	21	Kingstree, SC	Co C, 25th Regiment South Carolina Volunteers	Captured	Oath of Allegiance 7/26/1865
Arrington, James Lewis Private	New Berne, NC, Craven County, NC, 2/4/1862, Volunteer	25	Heathsville, Halifax County, NC	Co. F, 36th Regiment North Carolina, 2nd Artillery	Captured	Exchanged On the James River, VA, 3/2/1865

NAME and RANK	PLACE & TYPE OF ENLISTMENT	AGE	RESIDENCE & OCCUPATION	REGIMENT OR BATTALION	RESULT OF BATTLE	REMARKS
Arrowood, David Private	Moore County, NC, 3/23/1863	28	Moore County, NC, Farmer	Co. D, 13th Batt. North Carolina Light Artillery	Captured	Died of Chronic Diarrhea, 3/14/1865 Buried Woodlawn Cemetery, Elmira, NY, Grave No. 1815
Atkinson, J.W. Private	Wake County, NC, Date Unknown	30	Raleigh, Wake County, NC, Farmer	Co. D, 1st Battalion, North Carolina Heavy Artillery	Captured	Oath of Allegiance 6/30/1865
Atkinson, Thomas W. Private	Sumter, SC, 3/1/1863	Unk	Unknown	Co G, 21st Regiment South Carolina Volunteers	Captured	Died of Chronic Diarrhea, 4/6/1865 Buried Woodlawn Cemetery, Elmira, NY, Grave No. 2631
Austin, Richard Private	St. Johns, Hertford County, NC, 7/20/1864	Unk	Hertford County, NC	Co. C, 40th Regiment, 3rd North Carolina Artillery	Captured	Died of Chronic Diarrhea, 6/11/1865 Buried Woodlawn Cemetery, Elmira, NY, Grave No. 2886
Autry, Micajah also spelled Autery, Micajah, Private	Clinton, Sampson County, NC, 2/9/1863, Volunteer	33	Owensville, Sampson County, NC, Timber Cutter	2nd Co. C, 36th Regiment North Carolina, 2nd Artillery	Captured	Died of Chronic Diarrhea, 4/9/1865 Buried Woodlawn Cemetery, Elmira, NY, Grave No. 2621
Avant, James H. Private	Coles Island, SC, 4/11/1862	Unk	McCantsville, SC	Co. G, 25th South Carolina Volunteers	Captured	Exchanged 3/2/1865 On The James River, VA
Avant, O.R. Private	Camp Harllee, SC, 12/20/1861	Unk	Kingstree, SC	Co. I, 21st South Carolina Vols.	Captured	Oath of Allegiance 7/11/1865

NAME and RANK	PLACE & TYPE OF ENLISTMENT	AGE	RESIDENCE & OCCUPATION	REGIMENT OR BATTALION	RESULT OF BATTLE	REMARKS
Avinger, Alexander P. Sergeant	Coles Island, SC, 4/11/1862	24	Vans Ferry, South Carolina	Co. F, 25th South Carolina Volunteers	Captured	Oath of Allegiance 7/7/1865

NAME and RANK	PLACE & TYPE OF ENLISTMENT	AGE	RESIDENCE & OCCUPATION	REGIMENT OR BATTALION	RESULT OF BATTLE	REMARKS
Bagnal, Isaac J.M. Sergeant	Georgetown, SC, 1/1/1862	18	Sumter, SC	Co. I, 25th South Carolina Volunteers	Captured	Oath of Allegiance 6/27/1865
Bailey, Charles M. Private	Coles Island, SC, 4/11/1862	22	Farm Laborer	Co. G, 25th South Carolina Volunteers	Captured	Died of Typhoid Fever, 4/19/1865 Buried Woodlawn Cemetery, Elmira, NY, Grave No. 1377
Bailey, Henry L. Private	Orangeburg, SC, 4/14/1862	25	Edisto Island, SC, Merchant	Co. G, 25th South Carolina Volunteers	Captured	Died of Chronic Diarrhea, 3/13/1865 Buried Woodlawn Cemetery, Elmira, NY, Grave No. 2426
Baker, George S. Corporal	Coles Island, SC, 3/28/1862	27	Unknown	Co. B, 25th South Carolina Volunteers	Captured	Exchanged On the James River, VA, 2/11/1865
Baker, Ira D. Private	Chalk Level, NC, Cumberland County, NC, 3/1/62, Volunteer	34	Cumberland County, NC	2nd Co. C, 36th Regiment North Carolina, 2nd Artillery	Captured	Exchanged 3/18/1865 Boulware's Wharf, James River, VA

NAME and RANK	PLACE & TYPE OF ENLISTMENT	AGE	RESIDENCE & OCCUPATION	REGIMENT OR BATTALION	RESULT OF BATTLE	REMARKS
Baker, James Anderson Private	Chalk Level, Cumberland County, NC, 3/1/62, Volunteer	34	Cumberland County, NC	2nd Co. C, 36th Regiment North Carolina, 2nd Artillery	Captured	Died of Variola (smallpox), 3/14/1865, Buried Woodlawn Cemetery, Elmira, NY, Grave No. 1666
Baker, M.R.D. Corporal	Battery Island, SC, 4/12/1862	17	Unknown	2nd Co. C, 25th Regiment, South Carolina Volunteers	Captured	Died of Disease, Chronic Diarrhea, 3/31/1865 Buried Woodlawn Cemetery, Elmira, NY, Grave No. 2601
Baldwin, Albert Marion Private	Fort Fisher, New Hanover County, NC, 4/15/1863, Volunteer	18	Fayetteville, NC, Cumberland County, NC	2nd Co. K, 40th Regiment, 3rd North Carolina Artillery	Captured	Oath of Allegiance 6/12/1865
Baldwin, William Turrentine Corporal	New Hanover County, NC, 2/18/1862, Volunteer	20	Brinkley's Depot, Pender County, NC	2nd Co. D, 36th Regiment North Carolina, 2nd Artillery	Wounded & Captured	Oath of Allegiance 7/11/1865
Ballantine, Brobstone C. Sergeant	Wilmington, New Hanover County, NC 9/27/1861, Volunteer	28	Bladen County, NC	3rd Co. B, 36th Regiment North Carolina, 2nd Artillery	Wounded & Captured	Wounded 12/25/1864, Concussion From Shell, Captured 1/15/1865, Exchanged 3/20/1865
Barber, George D. Private	Coles Island, SC, 4/11/1862	22	Orangeburg, SC	Co. F, 25th South Carolina Volunteers	Captured	Died of Chronic Diarrhea, 6/26/1865, Buried Woodlawn Cemetery, Elmira, NY, Grave No. 2823

NAME and RANK	PLACE & TYPE OF ENLISTMENT	AGE	RESIDENCE & OCCUPATION	REGIMENT OR BATTALION	RESULT OF BATTLE	REMARKS
Barham, Samuel P. Private	Goldsboro, Wayne County, NC, 3/20/1864	19	Goldsboro, Wayne County, NC	Co. F, 10th Reg. 1st North Carolina Artillery	Captured	Died of Chronic Diarrhea, 2/24/1865 Buried Woodlawn Cemetery, Elmira, NY, Grave No. 2258
Barnes, F.H. Private	Manning, SC, 2/23/1863	Unk	Unknown	Co. I, 25th South Carolina Volunteers	Captured	Died of Chronic Diarrhea, 4/1/1865, Buried Woodlawn Cemetery, Elmira, NY, Grave No. 2587
Barnhill, Duncan R. Private	Bladen County, NC 3/9/1862, Mustered in at Wilmington, Volunteer	25	Bladen County, NC, Farmer	Co. H, 36th Regiment North Carolina, 2nd Artillery	Captured	Died of Chronic Diarrhea, 3/9/1865 Buried Woodlawn Cemetery, Elmira, NY, Grave No. 1878
Barrentine, Evander Private	Fort Caswell, NC, 2/25/1863, Substitute for Thomas Barintine,	17	Brunswick County, NC, Extra Duty Cutting Timber	Co. E, 40th Regiment, 3rd North Carolina Artillery	Captured	Died of Chronic Diarrhea, 3/24/1865 Buried Woodlawn Cemetery, Elmira, NY, Grave No. 2453
Barrett, Benjamin J. Private	Mt. Tabor, NC, Forsyth County, NC, 5/1/1862	Unk	Forsyth County, NC,	Co. C, 3rd Battalion, North Carolina Light Artillery	Captured	Exchanged 3/14/1865 Boulware's Wharf, James River, VA
Barrett, James B. Private	Roxobel, NC, 7/1/1864	18	Person County, NC,	Co. C, 3rd Battalion, North Carolina Light Artillery	Captured	Exchanged 3/14/1865 on James River, VA
Barrineau, R.H. Private	Battery Island, SC, 4/12/1862	30	Overseer/Farmer at Castle Pinckney, SC	Co. C, 25th South Carolina Volunteers	Captured	Exchanged 3/2/1865 on James River, VA

NAME and RANK	PLACE & TYPE OF ENLISTMENT	AGE	RESIDENCE & OCCUPATION	REGIMENT OR BATTALION	RESULT OF BATTLE	REMARKS
Barrineau, Ebenezer M. Private	Battery Island, SC, 4/12/1862	16	Kingstree, SC	Co. B, 25th South Carolina Volunteers	Captured	Oath of Allegiance 7/11/1865
Barrington, William T. Private	Craven County, NC, 3/4/1863, Substitute for his father, Rich Barrington	17	Craven County, NC	Co. D, 40th Regiment, 3rd North Carolina Artillery	Captured	Exchanged On the James River, VA, 2/20/1865
Barrow, James Private	Wilson County, NC, 8/18/1863, Volunteer	43	Wilson County, NC	Co. D, 40th Regiment, 3rd North Carolina Artillery	Captured	Died of Chronic Diarrhea, 5/2/1865 Buried Woodlawn Cemetery, Elmira, NY, Grave No. 2746
Barrow, Joseph W. Private	Fort Johnson, Brunswick County, NC, 4/1/1863. Volunteer	16	Lenoir County, NC	3rd Co. G, 40th Regiment, 3rd North Carolina Artillery	Captured	Exchanged 3/18/1865, Boulware's Wharf, James River, VA
Barwick, George W. Private	Charleston, SC, 5/18/1862	18	Georgia	Co. I, 25th South Carolina Volunteers	Captured	Exchanged 2/20/1865 On James River, VA, Died 3/10/1865 from Debility & Frostbite at Howard's Grove General Hospital, Richmond, VA
Barwick, Richard M. Musician	Lenoir County, NC, 11/7/1861, Volunteer	18	Mosely Hall, Lenoir County, NC,	3rd Co. G, 40th Regiment, 3rd North Carolina Artillery	Captured	Exchanged On the James River, VA, 2/20/1865, Drummer
Barwick, William Private	Fort Branch, Brunswick County, NC, 7/17/1863, Volunteer	43	Mosely Hall, Lenoir County, NC, Extra Duty as Assistant at Wagon Yard	3rd Co. G, 40th Regiment, 3rd North Carolina Artillery	Captured	Exchanged 3/14/1865, Boulware's Wharf, James River, VA

NAME and RANK	PLACE & TYPE OF ENLISTMENT	AGE	RESIDENCE & OCCUPATION	REGIMENT OR BATTALION	RESULT OF BATTLE	REMARKS
Bass, Cornelius Private	Union County, NC, 10/14/1861, Volunteer	21	Red Banks, NC, Extra Duty at Fort Campbell and Smithville, NC, as Raftsman, and cutting Timber for Garrison	Co. E, 40th Regiment, 3rd North Carolina Artillery	Captured	Died of Chronic Diarrhea, 5/24/1865 Buried Woodlawn Cemetery, Elmira, NY, Grave No. 2924
Bass, William M. Private	Whippy Swamp, SC, 7/15/1861	21	Unknown	Co. D, 11th South Carolina	Captured	Exchanged On The James River, VA, 3/2/1865
Baugh, Pleasant Private	Edgefield, SC, 9/24/1864	17	Edgefield, SC	Co. H, 25th South Carolina Volunteers	Captured	Oath of Allegiance 7/11/1865
Bell, Manning A. Private	Georgtown, SC, 1/1/1862	16	Sumter, SC	Co. I, 25th South Carolina Volunteers	Captured	Oath of Allegiance 7/3/1865
Bennett, Asa B. Private	Fort St. Philip, NC, 5/5/1862, Volunteer	32	Shallotte, Brunswick County, NC, Extra Duty at Quarter Master Dept.	3rd Co. G, 36th Regiment North Carolina, 2nd Artillery	Wounded & Captured	Died of Chronic Diarrhea, 3/9/1865 Buried Woodlawn Cemetery, Elmira, NY, Grave No. 2371
Benson, Daniel J. Private	Fort St. Philip, Brunswick County, NC, 7/23/1862, Volunteer	27	Wilmington, New Hanover County, NC	3rd Co. G, 36th Regiment North Carolina, 2nd Artillery	Captured	Admitted to Jarvis USA Hospital, Baltimore, MD, with Chronic Diarrhea, 6/25/1865, Released from Hospital 7/7/1865

NAME and RANK	PLACE & TYPE OF ENLISTMENT	AGE	RESIDENCE & OCCUPATION	REGIMENT OR BATTALION	RESULT OF BATTLE	REMARKS
Benson, John M. First Sergeant	Wilmington, New Hanover County, NC, 11/13/1861, Volunteer	22	White Hall, Bladen County NC, Day Laborer	3rd Co. B, 36th Regiment North Carolina, 2nd Artillery	Wounded & Captured	Oath of Allegiance 7/7/1865, Wounded, Concussion of Brain and Contusion Of Right Thigh 12/24/1864,
Beofford, Wesley also spelled Brafford, Wesley, Private	Goldsboro, Wayne County, NC, 9/20/1862, Conscripted at Wilmington, New Hanover County, NC, 9/24/1864	15	Deserted at Goldsboro, October 1862,	Co H, 10th Regiment North Carolina, 1st North Carolina Artillery	Captured	Died of Variola, (smallpox) 4/10/1865, Buried Woodlawn Cemetery, Elmira, NY, Grave No. 2671
Best, Matthew J. Private	Whiteville, Columbus County, NC, 2/6/1863 Conscript	36	Whiteville, NC, Farmer, Detailed as Nurse in the Hospital	Co. E, 36th Regiment North Carolina, 2nd Artillery	Captured	Oath of Allegiance 7/7/1865
Beverly, John Private	Unknown	16	Marion, SC Farm Laborer	Co. D, 25th South Carolina Volunteers	Captured	Died of Chronic Diarrhea, 2/27/1865, Buried Woodlawn Cemetery, Elmira, NY, Grave No. 2123
Biggs, Jefferson Private	Fort St. Philip, NC. 5/15/1862, Volunteer	18	Town Creek, Brunswick County, NC, Extra Duty at Fort Campbell and Smithville as a Raftsman	3rd Co. G, 36th Regiment North Carolina, 2nd Artillery	Captured	Died of "Hospital Gangrene", 3/30/1865 Buried Woodlawn Cemetery, Elmira, NY, Grave No. 2590
Biggs, Moses Private	New Hanover County, NC, 8/5/1861	36	Town Creek, Brunswick County, NC, Extra Duty as Blacksmith	3rd Co. G, 36th Regiment North Carolina, 2nd Artillery	Captured	Oath of Allegiance 6/23/1865
Bilton, Jacob J. Private	Charleston, SC, 2/22/1862, Conscript	31	Charleston, SC, Detailed as Carpenter	Co. E, 25th South Carolina Volunteers	Captured	Oath of Allegiance 5/17/1865

NAME and RANK	PLACE & TYPE OF ENLISTMENT	AGE	RESIDENCE & OCCUPATION	REGIMENT OR BATTALION	RESULT OF BATTLE	REMARKS
Bilton, William H. Private	Charleston, SC, 2/22/1862	31	Charleston, SC, Detailed as Carpenter	Co. E, 25th South Carolina Volunteers	Captured	Exchanged 2/20/1865, Died of Chronic Diarrhea 3/3/1865 at Howard's Grove Hospital, Richmond, VA
Black, John M. Private	Fort Fisher, NC, 8/26/1862, Volunteer	23	New Hanover County, NC, Extra Duty as Teamster at Fort Fisher, NC	Co. E, 36th Regiment North Carolina, 2nd Artillery	Captured	Exchanged On the James River, VA, 3/2/1865
Blackburn, Kinnon Private	Fort Fisher, New Hanover County, NC, 4/6/1862, Volunteer	34	New Hanover County, NC	2nd Co. I, 36th Regiment North Carolina, 2nd Artillery	Captured	Died of Variola (smallpox), 2/28/1865 Buried Woodlawn Cemetery, Elmira, NY, Grave No. 2116
Blackmore, Buckner Lanier Private	Duplin County, NC, 9/15/1861, Volunteer, Mustered In At Fort Caswell	15	Duplin County, NC	2nd Co. A, 36th Regiment North Carolina, 2nd Artillery	Captured	Exchanged On The James River, VA, 2/20/1865 Musician
Blackmore, Harold E. Private	Fort Caswell, Brunswick County, NC, 9/15/1861, Volunteer	21	Warsaw Depot, NC, Laborer at Fort Caswell in Assistant Ordinance Dept.	2nd Co. A, 36th Regiment North Carolina, 2nd Artillery	Captured	Oath of Allegiance 7/7/1865
Blackmore, Romulus A. Private	Duplin County, NC, 5/13/1862, Volunteer	24	Sampson County, NC, Farmer, Detailed in Signal Service at Cape Fear River, NC	Co. A, 36th NC Regiment North Carolina, 2nd Artillery	Captured	Died of Chronic Diarrhea, 6/3/1865, Buried Woodlawn Cemetery, Elmira, NY, Grave No. 2899
Blackwood, G.G. Corporal	Charleston, SC, 1/8/1863	30	Charleston, SC	Co. A, 25th South Carolina Volunteers	Captured	Oath of Allegiance 7/26/1865
Blake, Richard M. Private	Brunswick County, NC, 5/17/1863, Substitute	16	Whitesville, NC	Co. E, 36th Regiment North Carolina, 2nd Artillery	Captured	Oath of Allegiance 7/3/1865

NAME and RANK	PLACE & TYPE OF ENLISTMENT	AGE	RESIDENCE & OCCUPATION	REGIMENT OR BATTALION	RESULT OF BATTLE	REMARKS
Blake, Robert Private	Fort Branch, Brunswick County, NC, 8/6/1863, Volunteer	18	Montgomery County, NC	3rd Co. G, 40th Regiment, 3rd North Carolina Artillery	Captured	Died of Pneumonia, 2/27/1865 Buried Woodlawn Cemetery, Elmira, NY, Grave No. 2129
Blanton, Blaney Private	Wilmington, New Hanover County, NC, 3/25/1862, Volunteer	19	Teachers Depot, Duplin County, NC,	Co. D, 1st Battalion, North Carolina Heavy Artillery	Captured	Oath of Allegiance 7/11/1865
Boggan, James N. Private	Fort Branch, Brunswick County, NC, 8/20/1863, Volunteer	18	Wadesboro, Anson County, NC, Detatched Service as Acting Hospital Steward at Fort Anderson, NC, 1863-64	3rd Co. G, 40th Regiment, 3rd North Carolina Artillery	Captured	Exchanged On The James River, VA, 2/20/1865
Bomar, George W. First Sergeant	Charleston, SC, 2/24/1862	17	Spartinburg, SC	Co. B, 25th South Carolina Volunteers	Captured	Oath of Allegiance 6/16/1865
Bond, Ballas H. Private	Enfield, Halifax County, NC, 10/9/1861, Volunteer	31	Birtee Cay, NC, Extra Duty Laborer at Fort Campbell and Smithville	Co. F, 36th Regiment North Carolina, 2nd Artillery	Captured	Exchanged 3/18/1865, Boulware's Wharf, James River, VA, Recaptured, Oath of Allegiance 6/26/1865
Bond, John F. Private	Fort Ocrecoke, Hyde County, NC, 4/22/1861	21	Washington, Beaufort County, NC	Co. K, 10th Reg. 1st North Carolina Artillery	Captured	Died of Chronic Diarrhea, 2/18/1865 Buried Woodlawn Cemetery, Elmira, NY, Grave No. 2349

NAME and RANK	PLACE & TYPE OF ENLISTMENT	AGE	RESIDENCE & OCCUPATION	REGIMENT OR BATTALION	RESULT OF BATTLE	REMARKS
Bonnett, D.D. Private	Columbia, Richland County, SC, 3/1/1864	44	Orangeburg County, SC, Farmer	Co. D, 25th South Carolina Volunteers	Captured	Exchanged 2/20/1865, Died 3/7/1865 of Chronic Diarrhea at Wayside Hospital No. 9, Richmond, VA
Bordeaux, Enoch Private	Brunswick County, NC, 9/2/1863	18	Brunswick County, NC	Co. H, 36th Regiment North Carolina, 2nd Artillery	Captured	Died of Variola (smallpox), 4/10/1865 Buried Woodlawn Cemetery, Elmira, NY
Boswell, John C. Sergeant	Elizabethtown, Bladen County, NC, 10/19/1861, Volunteer	35	Bladen County, NC, Cooper	2nd Co. I, 36th Regiment North Carolina, 2nd Artillery	Captured	Exchanged 3/14/1865 Boulware's Wharf, James River, VA
Bowden, Joseph N. Private	Wilmington, New Hanover County, NC, 1/17/1863, Volunteer	17	Wilmington, New Hanover County, NC, Clerk	Co. D, 1st Battalion North Carolina Heavy Artillery Battery	Captured	Exchanged On The James River, VA, 2/20/1865,
Boyce, John H. Private	Charleston, SC, 2/22/1862	19	Charleston, SC	Co. E, 25th South Carolina Volunteers	Captured	Oath of Allegiance 5/15/1865
Bozard, David T. Private	Orangeburg, SC, 4/21/1862	28	Orangeburg, SC Lane, SC, Overseer	Co. G, 25th South Carolina Volunteers	Captured	Oath of Allegiance 7/7/1865
Braddock, Ralph Private	Camp Harllee, SC, 1/1/1862	27	Carpenter	Co. D, 21st South Carolina Volunteers	Captured	Exchanged On The James River, VA, 2/20/1865
Braddock, Thomas Private	Chesterfield, SC, 1/1/1862	17	Chesterfield, SC	Co. D, 21st South Carolina Volunteers	Captured	Oath of Allegiance 7/7/1865

NAME and RANK	PLACE & TYPE OF ENLISTMENT	AGE	RESIDENCE & OCCUPATION	REGIMENT OR BATTALION	RESULT OF BATTLE	REMARKS
Bradly, John H. Private	Fort Fisher, New Hanover County, NC, 3/15/1864	18	Enfield, Halifax County, NC	Co. F, 36th Regiment North Carolina, 2nd Artillery	Captured	Died of Variola (smallpox), 2/21/1865 Buried Woodlawn Cemetery, Elmira, NY, Grave No. 2313
Brafford, Joshua Private	Wilmington, New Hanover County, NC, 4/9/1864, Conscript	51	Wayne County, NC, Detailed as Cook at Fort Fisher, NC	Co. F, 10th Regiment, 1st North Carolina Artillery	Captured	Died of Variola (smallpox), 4/21/1865 Buried Woodlawn Cemetery, Elmira, NY, Grave No. 1392
Brafford, Wesley Private	Goldsboro, Wayne County, NC, 9/20/1862, Conscript, 5/15/61864	17	Wilmington, New Hanover County, NC, Deserted October 1862 at Goldsboro, NC	Co. F, 10th Regiment, 1st North Carolina Artillery	Captured	Died of Variola (smallpox), 4/10/1865 Buried Woodlawn Cemetery, Elmira, NY, Grave No. 2671
Brake, Jesse Private	Enfield, Halifax County, NC, 10/9/1861 Volunteer	19	Tarboro, Edgecombe County, NC,	Co. F, 36th Regiment North Carolina, 2nd Artillery	Captured	Oath of Allegiance 6/12/1865
Bray, David C. Private	Wilmington, New Hanover County, NC, 3/5/1862	28	Surry County, NC	Co. D, 1st Battalion North Carolina Heavy Artillery Battery	Captured	Exchanged 2/20/1865, Admitted To Hospital Richmond, VA, Died of Chronic Diarrhea 3/6/1865 Buried Hollywood Cemetery, Richmond, VA

NAME and RANK	PLACE & TYPE OF ENLISTMENT	AGE	RESIDENCE & OCCUPATION	REGIMENT OR BATTALION	RESULT OF BATTLE	REMARKS
Brickett, Joseph H. Also spelled Prickett, Joseph H. Sergeant	Coles Island, SC, 4/11/1862	Unk	St. Matthew, SC	Co. H, 25th South Carolina Volunteers	Captured	Died of Chronic Diarrhea, 6/15/1865, Buried Woodlawn Cemetery, Elmira, NY, Grave No. 2880
Bridgeman, Lewis J. Private	Wilmington, New Hanover County, NC, 8/20/1864	25	Wilmington, New Hanover County, NC	2nd Co. D, 36th Regiment North Carolina, 2nd Artillery	Captured	Oath of Allegiance 7/7/1865
Bridgers, John C. Private	Fort Holmes, Brunswick County, NC, 2/7/1864, Volunteer	18	Brunswick County, NC,	2nd Co. K, 40th Regiment, 3rd North Carolina Artillery	Captured	Exchanged 3/14/1865 Boulware's Wharf, James River, VA
Bright, Samuel S. Private	Wilmington, New Hanover County, NC, 12/26/1861, Volunteer	25	Bladen County, NC, Turpentine	Co. E, 36th Regiment North Carolina, 2nd Artillery	Captured	Died of Chronic Diarrhea, 3/2/1865, Buried Woodlawn Cemetery, Elmira, NY, Grave No. 2008
Brinson, William G. Sergeant	Wilmington, New Hanover County, NC, 7/8/1862	30	New Berne, Craven County, NC, Fisherman	Co. F, 10th Regiment, 1st North Carolina Artillery	Captured	Exchanged on the James River, Va, 2/25/1865
Bristow, Daniel M. Private	Bennettsville, Marlboro District, SC, 4/6/1863	22	Bennettsville, Marlboro District, SC,	Co. F, 21st South Carolina Volunteers	Captured	Died of Pnuemonia, 3/3/1865, Buried Woodlawn Cemetery, Elmira, NY, Grave No. 1998

NAME and RANK	PLACE & TYPE OF ENLISTMENT	AGE	RESIDENCE & OCCUPATION	REGIMENT OR BATTALION	RESULT OF BATTLE	REMARKS
Bristow, Robert N. Private	Bennettsville, Marlboro District, SC, 4/6/1862	29	Bennettsville, Marlboro District, SC,	Co. F, 21st South Carolina Volunteers	Captured	Died of Typhoid Fever, 3/18/1865, Buried Woodlawn Cemetery, Elmira, NY, Grave No. 1719
Britt, George W. Corporal	New Berne, Craven County, NC, 1/13/1862, Volunteer	35	Buncombe County, NC, Farmer	Co. F, 36th Regiment North Carolina, 2nd Artillery	Wounded & Captured	Oath of Allegiance 6/12/1865, Wounded In Arm, 12/25/1864, Captured 1/15/1865
Britt, Lemuel H. Private	Goldsboro, Wayne County, NC, 11/29/1863	28	Lumberton, Robeson County, NC, Farmer	Co. F, 10th Regiment, 1st North Carolina Artillery	Captured	Oath of Allegiance 6/23/1865
Brooks, Thomas D. Private	Chatham County, NC, 8/18/1863, Volunteer	42	Gulf, Chatham County, NC,	3rd Co. G, 40th Regiment, 3rd North Carolina Artillery	Captured	Died of Chronic Diarrhea 3/8/1865, Buried Woodlawn Cemetery, Elmira, NY, Grave No. 2409
Browder, Benjamin R. Private	Williamsburg, SC, 12/29/1861	16	Kingstree, SC	Co. K, 25th South Carolina Volunteers	Captured	Oath of Allegiance 7/11/1865
Browder, Gadsden W. Private	Gourdings Dept, SC, 12/29/1861	36	Kingstree, SC Teamster	Co. I, 25th South Carolina Volunteers	Captured	Oath of Allegiance 6/23/1865
Browder, John J. Private	Charleston, SC, 3/6/1862	16	Kingstree, Williamsburg, District, SC	Co. G, 21st South Carolina Volunteers	Captured	Oath of Allegiance 7/7/1865

NAME and RANK	PLACE & TYPE OF ENLISTMENT	AGE	RESIDENCE & OCCUPATION	REGIMENT OR BATTALION	RESULT OF BATTLE	REMARKS
Browder, William T. Private	Williamsburg, SC, 12/29/1862	39	Kingstree, Williamsburg, District, SC, Farmer	Co. K, 25th South Carolina Volunteers	Captured	Oath of Allegiance 7/19/1865
Brown, Bryant Private	Wilmington, New Hanover County, NC, 4/22/1862, Volunteer	22	Duplin County, NC, Farmer, Detatched to Work on Gunboat CSS Raleigh, February, 1863	Co. D, 1st Battalion North Carolina Heavy Artillery Battery	Captured	Died of Chronic Diarrhea, 4/16/1865, Buried Woodlawn Cemetery, Elmira, NY, Grave No. 2718
Brown, H.J. Private	Battery Island, SC, 4/12/1862	20	Kingstree, SC	Co. C, 25th South Carolina Volunteers	Captured	Oath of Allegiance 6/23/1865
Brown, Henry M. Private	Fort Branch, Brunswick County, NC, 8/19/1862, Volunteer	18	Whiteville, Fair Bluff, Columbus County, NC	Co. E, 36th Regiment North Carolina, 2nd Artillery	Captured	Oath of Allegiance 7/11/1865
Brown, Jesse Private	Duplin County, NC, 3/17/1864, Volunteer	17	Cypress Creek, Duplin County, NC, Farmer	Co. D, 1st Battalion North Carolina Heavy Artillery Battery	Captured	Exchanged On the James River, VA, 3/2/1865 Drummer
Brown, William Private	Unknown	Unk	Unknown	Co. C, Confederate States Marines	Captured	Died of Chronic Diarrhea, 4/4/1865, Buried Woodlawn Cemetery, Elmira, NY, Grave No. 2562
Brown, William W. Sergeant	Cerogordo, NC, 3/1/1862, Mustered in Wilmington, NC, Volunteer	20	Whiteville, Columbus County, NC, Farmer	Co. E, 36th Regiment North Carolina, 2nd Artillery	Captured	Exchanged on the James River, VA, 3/2/1865
Browning, Thomas Jefferson Corporal	Fort Fisher, New Hanover County NC, 12/20/1862, Volunteer	21	Elizabethtown, NC, Bladen County, NC, Turpentine Distiller	2nd Co. I, 36th Regiment North Carolina, 2nd Artillery	Captured	Oath of Allegiance 6/12/1865

NAME and RANK	PLACE & TYPE OF ENLISTMENT	AGE	RESIDENCE & OCCUPATION	REGIMENT OR BATTALION	RESULT OF BATTLE	REMARKS
Bruton, Atlas J. Private	Fort Branch, Brunswick County, NC, 7/22/1863, Volunteer	36	Zion District, Montgomery County, NC	3rd Co. G, 40th Regiment, 3rd North Carolina Light Artillery	Captured	Exchanged On the James River, VA, 2/20/1865
Bruton, Richard N. Private	Fort Branch, Brunswick County, NC, 7/25/1863, Volunteer	42	Mt. Gilead, Montgomery County, NC	3rd Co. G, 40th Regiment, 3rd North Carolina Light Artillery	Captured	Died of Intermittent Fever, 3/20/1865, Buried Woodlawn Cemetery, Elmira, NY, Grave No. 1573
Bryan, Carney J.	Kinston, Lenoir County, NC, 6/28/1862	18	Washington, Beaufort County, NC	Co. D, 13th Battalion North Carolina Light Artillery	Wounded & Captured	Exchanged On the James River, VA, 3/2/1865
Bryan, William T. Private	Fort Caswell, Brunswick County, NC, 9/5/1863, Volunteer	41	Ashboro, Randolph County, NC	3rd Co. G, 36th Regiment North Carolina, 2nd Artillery	Captured	Exchanged On the James River, VA, 3/2/1865
Bryant, George T. Private	Fort Branch, Brunswick County, NC, 8/20/1863, Volunteer	18	Diamond Hill District, Anson County, NC	3rd Co. G, 40th Regiment, 3rd North Carolina Light Artillery	Captured	Oath of Allegiance 6/12/1865
Buckner, John J. Private	Northhampton County, NC, 3/10/1862, Mustered in at Camp Mangum, NC, Volunteer	18	Brunswick County, NC, Farmer, Detailed in Quarter Master's Dept.	Co. C, 3rd Battalion, North Carolina Light Artillery	Captured	Died of Chronic Diarrhea, 4/14/1865, Buried Woodlawn Cemetery, Elmira, NY, Grave No. 2708
Buie, William N. Sergeant	Wilmington, New Hanover County NC, 11/5/1861, Volunteer	18	White Creek, Bladen County, NC	3rd Co. B, 36th Regiment North Carolina, 2nd Artillery	Wounded & Captured	Exchanged on the James River, VA, 2/20/1865, Died of Variola (smallpox), 4/27/1865, Marine USA Hospital, Baltimore, MD

NAME and RANK	PLACE & TYPE OF ENLISTMENT	AGE	RESIDENCE & OCCUPATION	REGIMENT OR BATTALION	RESULT OF BATTLE	REMARKS
Bullard, Jesse F. Private	Gerogordo, NC, 3/1/1862, Mustered in at Wilmington, NC, Volunteer	45	Columbus County, NC	Co. E, 36th Regiment North Carolina, 2nd Artillery	Captured	Died of Pneumonia, 2/15/1865, Buried Woodlawn Cemetery, Elmira, NY, Grave No. 2182
Bullard, John Isom Private	Columbus County, NC, 3/7/1862, Volunteer	17	Columbus County, NC	Co. E, 36th Regiment North Carolina, 3rd Artillery	Captured	Died of Pneumonia, 2/27/1865, Buried Woodlawn Cemetery, Elmira, NY, Grave No. 2206
Bullard, William J. Private	Fort St. Philip, Brunswick County, NC, 8/16/1862, Volunteer	18	White Oak, Bladen County, NC,	2nd Co. K, 40th Regiment, 3rd North Carolina Light Artillery	Captured	Died of Pneumonia, 2/16/1865, Buried Woodlawn Cemetery, Elmira, NY, Grave No. 2154
Bundy, G.W. Private	Bennettsville, Marlboro District, SC, 10/11/1864	Unk	Unknown	Co. F, 21st Regiment South Carolina Volunteers	Captured	Died of Chronic Diarrhea, 3/5/1865, Buried Woodlawn Cemetery, Elmira, NY, Grave No. 2377
Burgess, Joseph C. Corporal	James Island, SC, 5/28/1863	43	Clarendon County, SC, Farmer	Co. I, 25th Regiment South Carolina Volunteers	Captured	Died of Chronic Diarrhea, 7/10/1865, Buried Woodlawn Cemetery, Elmira, NY, Grave No. 2844
Burgess, Shelton H. Private	Camp Harlee, Georgetown, SC, 1/1/1862	19	Lightwood Creek, Lexington, SC	Co. I, 25th Regiment South Carolina Volunteers	Captured	Exchanged 3/2/1865 On James River, VA

NAME and RANK	PLACE & TYPE OF ENLISTMENT	AGE	RESIDENCE & OCCUPATION	REGIMENT OR BATTALION	RESULT OF BATTLE	REMARKS
Burkett, John W. Private	Wilmington, New Hanover County, NC, 4/19/1863, Volunteer	40	Robeson County, NC, Extra Duty for Quarter Master as Teamster at Smithville, NC,	Co. D, 1st Battalion, North Carolina Heavy Artillery	Captured	Died of Chronic Diarrhea, 2/25/1865, Buried Woodlawn Cemetery, Elmira, NY, Grave No. 2289
Burney, John C. Private	Fort Holmes, NC 10/26/1864	16	White Creek, Bladen County, NC	Co. K, 40th Regiment, 3rd North Carolina Light Artillery	Captured	Died of Chronic Diarrhea, 4/23/1865, Buried Woodlawn Cemetery, Elmira, NY,
Burney, William James Private	Elizabethtown, Bladen County, NC, 3/5/1862, Volunteer	23	Elizabethtown, Bladen County, NC, Farmer	3rd Co. B, 36th Regiment North Carolina, 2nd Artillery	Wounded & Captured	Exchanged on the James River, VA, 3/2/1865, Died Of Debility, 4/3/1865, Charlotte, NC
Butler, Edward Private	Wilmington, New Hanover County, NC, 3/10/1863, Volunteer	20	Sampson County, NC, Detailed Quarter Master, Woodcutter at Smithville, NC	Co. D, 1st Battalion, North Carolina Heavy Artillery	Reported Captured	Listed in the National Archives as having died at Elmira, No date is Given,
Butterton, James H. Corporal	Bertie County, NC, 1/23/1862, Mustered in at Camp Mangum, Volunteer	18	Plymouth, NC Farmer, Extra Duty as Laborer at Fort Caswell and Fort Campbell, NC	Co. C, 3rd Battalion, North Carolina Light Artillery	Captured	Oath of Allegiance 6/12/1865
Byrd, John Owen Private	Elizabethtown, Bladen County, NC, 5/12/1862, Mustered in at Ft. St. Philip, Volunteer	25	Lumberton, NC Farmer, Absent for 12 days from June 27, 1863 to attend crops, by order of General Whiting	2nd Co. K, 40th Regiment, 3rd North Carolina Light Artillery	Captured	Oath of Allegiance 7/11/1865
Byrd, Mathew Private	Darlington, SC, 1/13/1862	18	Darlington District, SC,	Co. G, 21st Regiment South Carolina Volunteers	Captured	Died of Pneumonia, 3/28/1865, Buried Woodlawn Cemetery, Elmira, NY, Grave No. 2508

NAME and RANK	PLACE & TYPE OF ENLISTMENT	AGE	RESIDENCE & OCCUPATION	REGIMENT OR BATTALION	RESULT OF BATTLE	REMARKS
Byrd, Robert Private	Fort Fisher, New Hanover County, NC, 7/4/1863, Volunteer	39	Duplin County, NC, Sick at Camp Wyatt, NC, with Rheumatism, December 1863	2nd Co. K, 40th Regiment, 3rd North Carolina Light Artillery	Captured	Died of Chronic Diarrhea, 3/21/1865, Buried Woodlawn Cemetery, Elmira, NY, Grave No. 1534
Byrd, Wiley Private	Darlington, SC, 1/13/1862	20	Darlington District, SC,	Co. G, 21st Regiment South Carolina Volunteers	Captured	Oath of Allegiance 6/23/1865
Byrd, W.C. Private	Charleston, SC, 3/22/1863	24	Charleston, SC	Co. A, 25th South Carolina Volunteers	Captured	Oath of Allegiance 7/7/1865

NAME and RANK	PLACE & TYPE OF ENLISTMENT	AGE	RESIDENCE & OCCUPATION	REGIMENT OR BATTALION	RESULT OF BATTLE	REMARKS
Cade, John L. Sergeant	Georgetown, SC, 12/28/1861	25	Florence, SC	Co. K, 21st Regiment South Carolina Volunteers	Captured	Oath of Allegiance 7/11/1865
Cain, John S. Corporal	Bladen County, NC, 5/6/1862, Mustered in at Wilmington, Volunteer	22	Prospect Hall, SC Farmer	Co. H, 36th Regiment North Carolina, 2nd Artillery	Captured	Oath Of Allegiance 7/7/1865
Cain, Joshua Private	Fort Fisher, New Hanover County, NC, 3/8/1862, Volunteer	20	White Oak, Bladen County, NC, Farmer	2nd Co. I, 36th Regiment North Carolina, 2nd Artillery	Captured	Died of Variola (smallpox), 4/20/1865, Buried Woodlawn Cemetery, Elmira, NY, Grave No. 1384

NAME and RANK	PLACE & TYPE OF ENLISTMENT	AGE	RESIDENCE & OCCUPATION	REGIMENT OR BATTALION	RESULT OF BATTLE	REMARKS
Cain, Travis H. Private	Elizabethtown, Bladen County, NC, 5/6/1862, Mustered in Fort St. Philip, NC, Volunteer	34	Bladen County, NC, Farmer, Absent for 12 days from June 27, 1863 to attend crops, by order of General Whiting	2nd Co. K, 40th Regiment, 3rd North Carolina Light Artillery	Captured	Exchanged On the James River, VA, 2/20/1865
Cain, Wiley Private	Cumberland County, NC, 10/24/1863, Volunteer	38	Fayetteville, NC, Hospital Nurse at Camp Wyatt, NC, July, 1864	Co. E, 36th Regiment North Carolina, 2nd Artillery	Captured	Oath Of Allegiance 6/30/1865
Calder, Edwin Private	Charleston, SC, 2/20/1862	27	Charleston, SC,	Co. A, 25th Regiment South Carolina Volunteers	Captured	Oath Of Allegiance 5/17/1865
Caler, J.E. Private	Battery Island, SC, 4/12/1862	Unk	Unknown	Co. B, 25th Regiment South Carolina Volunteers	Captured	Exchanged 2/20/1865, Died On Route
Callihan, Thomas Private	Charleston, SC, 5/10/1862	34	Nashville, Tenn	Co. E, 25th Regiment South Carolina Volunteers	Captured	Oath Of Allegiance 8/7/1865
Callihan, William J. Private Also Spelled: Callahan	Wilmington, New Hanover County, NC, 11/5/1861, Mustered in at Wilmington, Volunteer	18	White Creek, Bladen County, NC Farmer	3rd Co. B, 36th Regiment North Carolina, 2nd Artillery	Captured	Died of Gangrene of Feet, 3/14/1865, Buried Woodlawn Cemetery, Elmira, NY, Grave No. 1661
Campbell, Archibald Private	Elizabethtown, Bladen County, NC, 10/19/1861, Volunteer	30	Elizabethtown, Bladen County, NC, Turpentine	2nd Co. I, 36th Regiment North Carolina, 2nd Artillery	Captured	Exchanged on the James River, VA, 2/20/1865
Campbell, Charles J. Private	Moore County, NC, 3/11/1863, Volunteer	18	Graham's District, Iredell County, NC,	3rd Co. B, 36th Regiment North Carolina, 2nd Artillery	Captured	Died of Chronic Diarrhea, 2/19/1865, Buried Woodlawn Cemetery, Elmira, NY, Grave No. 2316

NAME and RANK	PLACE & TYPE OF ENLISTMENT	AGE	RESIDENCE & OCCUPATION	REGIMENT OR BATTALION	RESULT OF BATTLE	REMARKS
Campbell, Colen Private	Fort Branch, Brunswick County, NC, 8/15/1863, Volunteer	41	Chesterfield District, SC	3rd Co. G, 40th Regiment, 3rd North Carolina Light Artillery	Captured	Died of Chronic Diarrhea, 3/2/1865, Buried Woodlawn Cemetery, Elmira, NY, Grave No. 1999
Campbell, Duncan D. Private	Bladen County, NC, 9/25/1862, Volunteer	18	Robeson County, NC, Farmer	3rd Co. B, 36th Regiment North Carolina, 2nd Artillery	Captured	Died of Chronic Diarrhea, 3/9/1865, Buried Woodlawn Cemetery, Elmira, NY, Grave No. 1885
Campbell, H.B. Corporal	Chesterfield, SC, 10/10/1863	20	Cheraw, Chesterfield, SC	Co. D, 21st Regiment South Carolina Volunteers	Captured	Oath of Allegiance 7/11/1865
Campbell, John C. Sergeant	Camp Harllee, SC, 1/1/1862	17	Cheraw, Chesterfield, SC	Co. D, 21st Regiment South Carolina Volunteers	Captured	Oath of Allegiance 7/11/1865
Campbell, William A. Private	Wilmington, New Hanover County, NC, 11/5/1861, Mustered in at Wilmington, Volunteer	24	White Creek, Bladen County, NC, Cooper	3rd Co. B, 36th Regiment North Carolina, 2nd Artillery	Captured	Exchanged on the James River, VA, 3/2/1865, Admitted Hospital, Richmond, VA, Died 3/9/1865 Cause Unknown
Campion, Benjamin Franklin Corporal	Chesterfield, SC, 1/1/1862	18	Cheraw, Chesterfield, SC	Co. D, 21st Regiment South Carolina Volunteers	Captured	Oath of Allegiance 5/29/1865
Canaday, William J. Private	Fort Fisher, New Hanover County, NC, 3/15/1863, Volunteer	39	Fayetteville, Cumberland County, NC	2nd Co. C, 36th Regiment, North Carolina, 2nd Artillery	Captured	Oath of Allegiance 6/12/1865

NAME and RANK	PLACE & TYPE OF ENLISTMENT	AGE	RESIDENCE & OCCUPATION	REGIMENT OR BATTALION	RESULT OF BATTLE	REMARKS
Cannon, Archibald Private	New Hanover County, NC, 2/27/1862, Volunteer	26	Pitt County, NC, Detailed as Signal Guard at Battery Gatlin, NC, Extra Duty as Laborer at Fort Caswell, NC	2nd Co. D, 36th Regiment North Carolina, 2nd Artillery	Captured	Exchanged on the James River, VA, 2/20/1865, Admitted Howard Grove Hospital, Richmond, VA, 3/2/1865, Died of Pneumonia, 3/11/1865
Cannon, James Private	Duplin County, NC, 7/21/1863, Volunteer	41	Mount Olive, Duplin County, NC Farmer	3rd Co. G, 40th Regiment, 3rd North Carolina Light Artillery	Captured	Died of Pneumonia, 4/10/1865, Buried Woodlawn Cemetery, Elmira, NY, Grave No. 2667
Cannon, R.J. Private	Gourdin's Dept., SC, 5/11/1862	26	Clarendon, SC	Co. I, 25th Regiment South Carolina Volunteers	Captured	Died of Chronic Diarrhea, 3/9/1865, Buried Woodlawn Cemetery, Elmira, NY, Grave No. 1872
Canoy, John H. Private	Randolph County, NC, 3/23/1863	Unk	Randolph County, NC, Post Office: New Market, NC	Co. K, 10th Reg. 1st North Carolina Artillery	Captured	Oath Of Allegiance 8/7/1865
Capel, Jesse A. Private	Fort Fisher, New Hanover County, 5/20/1864	18	Fayetteville, Cumberland County, NC	Co. H, 36th Regiment North Carolina, 2nd Artillery	Captured	Oath Of Allegiance 7/11/1865
Carmichael, John D. Private	Marion, SC, 3/28/1862	21	Little Rock, Marion, SC	Co. L, 21st South Carolina Volunteers	Captured	Died of Pneumonia, 3/30/1865, Buried Woodlawn Cemetery, Elmira, NY, Grave No. 2592

NAME and RANK	PLACE & TYPE OF ENLISTMENT	AGE	RESIDENCE & OCCUPATION	REGIMENT OR BATTALION	RESULT OF BATTLE	REMARKS
Carroll, Haywood Private	Old Brunswick Town, NC, 4/16/1862, Mustered in at Fort St. Philip	42	Robeson, North West District, Brunswick County, NC, Planter	3rd Co. G, 36th Regiment North Carolina, 2nd Artillery	Captured	Died of Variola (smallpox), 3/25/1865, Buried Woodlawn Cemetery, Elmira, NY, Grave No. 2467
Carroll, James A. Private	Old Brunswick Town, NC, 4/16/1862, Mustered in at Fort St. Philip	44	Brunswick County, NC	3rd Co. G, 36th Regiment North Carolina, 2nd Artillery	Captured	Died of Chronic Diarrhea, 5/16/1865, Buried Woodlawn Cemetery, Elmira, NY, Grave No. 1874
Carroll, Joel G. Private	Old Brunswick Town, Fort St. Philip, NC, 4/16/1862	35	Brunswick County, NC, Extra Duty as Hospital Attendent, July, 1864	3rd Co. G, 36th Regiment North Carolina, 2nd Artillery	Captured	Died of Pneumonia, 3/10/1865, Buried Woodlawn Cemetery, Elmira, NY, Grave No. 1879
Carroll, Joseph Corporal	Elizabethtown, Bladen County, NC, 5/6/1862, Mustered in at Fort St. Philip	21	Prospect Hall, Bladen County, NC, Farmer Brother of Nathaniel	2nd Co. K, 40th Regiment, 3rd North Carolina Light Artillery	Captured	Died of Gangrene Of Feet, 3/9/1865, Buried Woodlawn Cemetery, Elmira, NY, Grave No. 2962
Carroll, Nathaniel Private	Fort Fisher, New Hanover County, NC, 6/1/1863	38	Prospect Hall, Bladen County, NC, Turpentine	2nd Co. K, 40th Regiment, 3rd North Carolina Light Artillery	Wounded & Captured	Exchanged On the James River, VA, 2/20/1865
Carter, Henry C. Private	Fort Fisher, New Hanover County, NC, 3/15/1863	18	Fayetteville, Cumberland County, NC Farm Laborer	2nd Co. C, 36th Regiment North Carolina, 2nd Artillery	Captured	Oath Of Allegiance 6/12/1865,

239

NAME and RANK	PLACE & TYPE OF ENLISTMENT	AGE	RESIDENCE & OCCUPATION	REGIMENT OR BATTALION	RESULT OF BATTLE	REMARKS
Carver, James B. Private	Cumberland County, NC, 6/21/1861	45	Fayetteville, Cumberland County, NC, Farmer	Co. E, 36th Regiment North Carolina, 2nd Artillery	Captured	Oath Of Allegiance 7/11/1865
Casey, Benjamin Private	Wayne County, NC, 4/14/1863	18	Indian Springs District, Wayne County, NC	3rd Co. G, 40th Regiment, 3rd North Carolina Light Artillery	Captured	Oath Of Allegiance 6/12/1865
Casey, Benjamin D. Private	Wayne County, NC, 7/24/1863	17	Goldsboro, Wayne County, NC	3rd Co. G, 40th Regiment, 3rd North Carolina Light Artillery	Captured	Died of Chronic Diarrhea, 2/28/1865, Buried Woodlawn Cemetery, Elmira, NY, Grave No. 2139
Casey, Benjamin F. Private	Wayne County, NC, 7/4/1863	17	Dudley Depot, Wayne County, NC	3rd Co. G, 40th Regiment, 3rd North Carolina Light Artillery	Captured	Oath Of Allegiance 6/12/1865
Casey, Wright Private	Wayne County, NC, 4/14/1863	21	Goldsboro, Wayne County, NC	3rd Co. G, 40th Regiment, 3rd North Carolina Light Artillery	Captured	Exchanged On the James River, VA, 2/20/1865
Cashwell, Marshall Corporal	Fayetteville, Cumberland County, NC, 2/20/1862	20	Fayetteville, Cumberland County, NC	2nd Co. C, 36th Regiment North Carolina, 2nd Artillery	Captured	Oath Of Allegiance 6/12/1865
Center, John A. Also Spelled Senter, Private	Camp Holmes, NC, 10/13/1863	49	South Eastern District, Ashe County, NC	2nd Co. D, 36th Regiment North Carolina, 2nd Artillery	Captured	Oath Of Allegiance 7/3/1865

NAME and RANK	PLACE & TYPE OF ENLISTMENT	AGE	RESIDENCE & OCCUPATION	REGIMENT OR BATTALION	RESULT OF BATTLE	REMARKS
Chambers, James G. Private	Wilmington, New Hanover County, NC, 10/4/1864	Unk	New Hanover County, NC,	Co. K, 10th Reg. 1st North Carolina Artillery	Captured	Died of Chronic Diarrhea, 2/20/1865, Buried Woodlawn Cemetery, Elmira, NY, Died On Route To Be Exchanged
Cheek, John D. Private	Chatham County, NC, 3/26/1863	37	Graham, Alamance County, NC	3rd Co. G, 40th Regiment, 3rd North Carolina Light Artillery	Captured	Oath Of Allegiance 6/12/1865
Cherry, George T. Private	Duplin County, NC, 11/4/1863	23	Mount Olive, Duplin County, NC, Farmer	3rd Co. G, 40th Regiment, 3rd North Carolina Light Artillery	Captured	Oath Of Allegiance 6/12/1865
Clamps, W.C. Private	Unknown	Unk	Unknown	Co. E, 10th Reg. 1st North Carolina Artillery	Captured	Died of Chronic Diarrhea, 3/20/1865, Buried Woodlawn Cemetery, Elmira, NY, Grave No. 1566
Clark, Baty C. Private	Fort Fisher, New Hanover County, NC, 3/11/1863	17	New Hanover County, NC	2nd Co. I, 36th Regiment North Carolina, 2nd Artillery	Captured	Died of Chronic Diarrhea, 3/8/1865, Buried Woodlawn Cemetery, Elmira, NY, Grave No. 2372
Clark, Henry S. Private	Wilmington, New Hanover County, NC, 1/1/1863	40	New Hanover County, NC	Co. K, 10th Reg. 1st North Carolina Artillery	Captured	Exchanged On the James River, VA, 2/9/1865
Clark, James C. Corporal	Wilmington, New Hanover County, NC, 3/11/1862	45	White Hall, Bladen County NC, Farmer	Co. H, 36th Regiment North Carolina, 2nd Artillery	Wounded In Knee & Captured	Oath Of Allegiance 7/11/1865

NAME and RANK	PLACE & TYPE OF ENLISTMENT	AGE	RESIDENCE & OCCUPATION	REGIMENT OR BATTALION	RESULT OF BATTLE	REMARKS
Clark, James D. Private	St Johns, NC, 5/7/1862	Unk	Weldon, NC, Detailed On Garrison Boat, Fort Caswell, NC, March 1864	Co. C, 3rd Battalion, North Carolina Light Artillery	Captured	Oath Of Allegiance 7/11/1865
Clark, John D. Private	Red Springs, Robison County, NC, 9/19/1861	19	Lumberton, NC, Extra Duty As Blacksmith In Quartermaster Dept.,	Co. E, 40th Regiment, 3rd North Carolina Light Artillery	Captured	Oath Of Allegiance 7/11/1865
Clark, John W. Sergeant	Elizabethtown, NC, 5/6/1862, Mustered in at Fort St. Philip	22	Elizabethtown, Bladen County, NC, Student,	2nd Co. K, 40th Regiment, 3rd North Carolina Light Artillery	Captured	Oath Of Allegiance 6/12/1865
Clark, William Savage Private	Fort Holmes, Brunswick County, NC, 10/26/1864	17	White Hall, NC, Bladen County	2nd Co. K, 40th Regiment, 3rd North Carolina Light Artillery	Captured	Oath Of Allegiance 6/12/1865
Clayton, David J. Private	Coles Island, SC, 4/11/1862	23	Poplar, Orangeburg District, SC	Co. F, 25th South Carolina Volunteers	Captured	Exchanged 3/2/1865, Recaptured in Richmond, 5/12/65, Oath 7/19/1865
Clayton, F.R. Private	James Island, SC, 3/7/1863	Unk	Unknown	Co. F, 25th South Carolina Volunteers	Captured	Died of Chronic Diarrhea 3/23/1865, Buried Woodlawn Cemetery, Elmira, NY, Grave No. 2439
Clayton, William W. Private	Coles Island, SC, 4/11/1862	23	Pickens County, SC	Co. F, 25th South Carolina Volunteers	Captured	Exchanged 2/20/1865, Died Chronic Diarrhea 3/26/1865, USA General Hospital, Baltimore, MD
Clemmons, Edward M. Private	Fort Caswell, Brunswick County, NC, 2/6/1863	37	Brunswick County, NC, Extra Duty In Ordinance Dept., November 1863	3rd Co. G, 36th Regiment North Carolina, 2nd Artillery	Captured	Exchanged On the James River, VA, 3/2/1865

NAME and RANK	PLACE & TYPE OF ENLISTMENT	AGE	RESIDENCE & OCCUPATION	REGIMENT OR BATTALION	RESULT OF BATTLE	REMARKS
Clemmons, George M. Private	Fort Caswell, Brunswick County, NC, 2/6/1863	35	Lockwood Folly District, Brunswick County, NC, Quarter Master Dept, July 1864	3rd Co. G, 36th Regiment North Carolina, 2nd Artillery	Captured	Died Of Pneumonia 4/24/1865, Buried Woodlawn Cemetery, Elmira, NY
Clemmons, Thomas Private	Fort St. Philip, NC, 2/6/1863, Mustered in at Wilmington	21	Wilmington, New Hanover County, NC	3rd Co. G, 36th Regiment North Carolina, 2nd Artillery	Captured	Oath Of Allegiance 7/11/1865
Cobb, Calvin A. Private	Robison County, NC, 12/16/1862	18	Lumberton, Robeson County, NC	Co. D, 1st Battalion, North Carolina Heavy Artillery	Captured	Died of Chronic Diarrhea, 3/26/1865, Buried Woodlawn Cemetery, Elmira, NY, Grave No. 2474
Cochran, Allen W. Private	Manning, SC, 8/22/1863	18	Manning, Clarenden District, SC	Co. I, 25th South Carolina Volunteers	Captured	Died of Chronic Diarrhea 3/8/1865, Buried Woodlawn Cemetery, Elmira, NY, Grave No. 2373
Cochran, Elijah P. Private	Enfield, Halifax County, NC, 10/9/1861	20	Enfield, Halifax County, NC	Co. F, 36th Regiment North Carolina, 2nd Artillery	Captured	Died of Chronic Diarrhea, 3/1/1865, Buried Woodlawn Cemetery, Elmira, NY, Grave No. 2025
Cochran, Robert J. Private	Enfield, Halifax County, NC, 10/9/1861	34	Enfield, Halifax County, NC, Extra Duty As Hospital Attendant, April 4, 1864	Co. F, 36th Regiment North Carolina, 2nd Artillery	Captured	Died of Pneumonia, 3/1/1865, Buried Woodlawn Cemetery, Elmira, NY, Grave No. 2099
Coker, John L. Private	Kinston, Lenoir County, NC, 4/4/1863	18	Kinston, Lenoir County, NC	Co. K, 10th Reg. 1st North Carolina Artillery	Captured	Oath Of Allegiance 5/15/1865

NAME and RANK	PLACE & TYPE OF ENLISTMENT	AGE	RESIDENCE & OCCUPATION	REGIMENT OR BATTALION	RESULT OF BATTLE	REMARKS
Coker, Thomas L. Private	Georgetown, SC, 12/20/1861	16	Cheraw, Chesterfield County, SC	Co. D, 21st South Carolina Volunteers	Captured	Exchanged On The James River, VA, 2/20/1865
Cole, William Bright Sergeant	Goldsboro, Wayne County, NC, 7/14/1861	20	Bentonville, Johnston County, NC, Turpentine Maker, On Guard Duty At Plank Road Bridge, 1864	Co. F, 10th Reg. 1st North Carolina Artillery	Wounded In Right Hip & Captured	Oath Of Allegiance 5/19/1865,
Coleman, Daniel J. Private	Fair Bluff, NC, 2/22/1862, Mustered in at Wilmington	19	Fair Bluff, Columbus County, NC	Co. E, 36th Regiment North Carolina, 2nd Artillery	Captured	Oath Of Allegiance 7/3/1865
Coleman, John Q. Private	Brunswick County, NC, 5/3/1862	22	Brunswick County, NC	Co. E, 36th Regiment North Carolina, 2nd Artillery	Wounded by shell in face, nasal bone & Captured	Died of Chronic Diarrhea, 4/21/1865, Buried Woodlawn Cemetery, Elmira, NY, Grave No. 1385
Collins, Richard H. Private	Marion, SC, 2/3/62	Unk	Marion County, SC	Co. L, 21st South Carolina Volunteers	Captured	Died of Typhoid Fever, 2/9/1865, Buried Woodlawn Cemetery, Elmira, NY, Grave No. 1948
Congleton, Owen Private	New Hanover County, NC, 5/8/1864	17	Long Acre, Washington, Beaufort County, NC, Farmer	Co. K, 10th Reg. 1st North Carolina Artillery	Captured	Died of Typhoid Fever, 2/24/1865, Buried Woodlawn Cemetery, Elmira, NY, Grave No. 2271
Conner, Doctor R. Private	Whiteville, Columbus County, NC, 2/9/1863	23	Columbus County, NC	Co. E, 36th Regiment North Carolina, 2nd Artillery	Captured	Exchanged On the James River, VA, 2/20/1865

NAME and RANK	PLACE & TYPE OF ENLISTMENT	AGE	RESIDENCE & OCCUPATION	REGIMENT OR BATTALION	RESULT OF BATTLE	REMARKS
Conner, Pinkney C. Private	Whiteville, Columbus County, NC, 2/9/1863	22	Fair Bluff, Columbus County, NC	Co. E, 36th Regiment North Carolina, 2nd Artillery	Captured	Oath Of Allegiance 7/11/1865
Cook, Alexander Private	Myersville, SC, 5/3/1862	15	Beaufort District, Kingstree, NC	Co. H, 25th South Carolina Volunteers	Captured	Oath Of Allegiance 6/23/1865
Cook, Thomas J. Private	Battery Island, SC, 4/12/1862	24	Kingston Parrish, Horry County, SC	Co. C, 25th South Carolina Volunteers	Captured	Exchanged On the James River, VA, 3/2/1865
Cook, William D. Private	Battery Island, SC, 4/12/1862	27	Camden, Kershaw County, SC	Co. B, 25th South Carolina Volunteers	Captured	Died of Chronic Diarrhea 4/12/1865, Buried Woodlawn Cemetery, Elmira, NY, Grave No. 2541
Cooper, Charles H. Private	Fort Fisher, NC, 10/31/1862, Volunteer	29	Owensville, Sampson County, NC, Farmer	2nd Co. C, 36th Regiment North Carolina, 2nd Artillery	Captured	Died of Variola (smallpox), 3/19/1865, Buried Woodlawn Cemetery, Elmira, NY, Grave No. 1730
Cooper, Hiram B. Private	Fort Fisher, New Hanover County, NC, 10/31/1862	34	Owensville, Sampson County, NC, Farmer	2nd Co. D, 36th Regiment North Carolina, 2nd Artillery	Captured	Died of Disease, Causes Unknown 8/11/1865, Buried Woodlawn Cemetery, Elmira, NY, Grave No. 2861
Corban, Charles Private	Whippy Swamp, SC, 7/15/1861	18	Pocotaligo, Beaufort County, SC	Co. D, 11th South Carolina	Captured	Oath of Allegiance 6/23/1865

NAME and RANK	PLACE & TYPE OF ENLISTMENT	AGE	RESIDENCE & OCCUPATION	REGIMENT OR BATTALION	RESULT OF BATTLE	REMARKS
Corbin, Edward Private	Whippy Swamp, SC, 7/15/1861	28	Prince William Parrish, Beaufort County, SC	Co. D, 11th South Carolina	Captured	Died of Variola (smallpox), 3/23/1865, Buried Woodlawn Cemetery, Elmira, NY, Grave No. 2926
Cordon, Sylverter Corporal	Washington, NC, 9/23/1861	16	South Creek, Beaufort County, NC	Co. D, 13th Battalion, North Carolina Light Artillery	Captured	Died of Chronic Diarrhea, 3/8/1865, Buried Woodlawn Cemetery, Elmira, NY, Grave No. 2408
Cordon, William W. First Sergeant	Washington, NC, 4/22/1861, Mustered in at Fort Ockracoke, NC	21	Washington, Beaufort County, NC, Carpenter	Co. K, 10th Reg. 1st North Carolina Artillery	Captured	Oath Of Allegiance 7/11/1865,
Covington, Benjamin C. Private	Fort Fisher, New Hanover County, NC, 7/21/1863, Volunteer	18	Rockingham District, Richmond County, NC, Farmer	2nd Co. I, 36th Regiment North Carolina, 2nd Artillery	Captured	Oath Of Allegiance 6/16/1865,
Covington, Thomas B. Private	Fort Fisher, New Hanover County, NC, 6/26/1863	18	Rockingham District, Richmond County, NC, Farmer	2nd Co. I, 36th Regiment North Carolina, 2nd Artillery	Captured	Oath Of Allegiance 6/16/1865,
Cowperth-wait, W.B. Private	Charleston, SC, 5/9/1862	25	Charleston, SC	Co. A, 25th South Carolina Volunteers	Captured	Oath Of Allegiance 6/19/1865
Cox, Isaac B. Private	Fort Pender, Brunswick County, NC, 11/24/1863, Volunteer	17	Brunswick County, NC	Co. E, 36th Regiment North Carolina, 2nd Artillery	Captured	Died of Pneumonia, 3/21/1865, Buried Woodlawn Cemetery, Elmira, NY, Grave No. 1542

NAME and RANK	PLACE & TYPE OF ENLISTMENT	AGE	RESIDENCE & OCCUPATION	REGIMENT OR BATTALION	RESULT OF BATTLE	REMARKS
Cozzens, Richard W. Also Spelled: Cousins Private	Washington, Beaufort County, NC, 9/23/1861	19	North Creek, Beaufort County, NC Farmer	Co. D, 13th Battalion, North Carolina Light Artillery	Captured	Died of Variola (smallpox), 3/19/1865, Buried Woodlawn Cemetery, Elmira, NY, Grave No. 1565
Cozzans, Thomas F. Private	Washington, Beaufort County, NC, 9/23/1861	28	Beaufort County, NC	Co. D, 13th Battalion, North Carolina Light Artillery	Captured	Died of Remittent Fever, 4/6/1865, Buried Woodlawn Cemetery, Elmira, NY, Grave No. 2639
Crawford, Mathias Private	Goldsboro, Wayne County, NC, 9/25/1862, Conscript	25	Goldsboro, NC, Deserted 9/11/1863 at Smithville, NC, Arrested 12/15/1863, Put in Military Prison in Wilmington, NC,	Co. F, 10th Reg. 1st North Carolina Artillery	Captured	Died of Pneumonia, 3/12/1865, Buried Woodlawn Cemetery, Elmira, NY, Grave No. 1818
Crawford, William E. Private	Coles Island, SC, 4/11/1862	26	Charleston, SC, Laborer	C. G, 25th South Carolina Volunteers	Captured	Died Of Pnuemonia 3/7/1865, Buried Woodlawn Cemetery, Elmira, NY, Grave No. 2406
Crawley, Hider D. Private	Craven County, NC, 2/18/1862,	18	Brinkleyville, Halifax County, NC, Farmer	Co. F, 36th Regiment North Carolina, 2nd Artillery	Captured	Died of Pneumonia, 3/12/1865, On Route to Be Exchanged
Creech, Doctor L. Private	Bennettsville, Marlboro District, SC, 2/7/62	27	Bennettsville, Marlboro District, SC, Laborer, Teamster	Co. F, 21st South Carolina Volunteers	Captured	Died of Chronic Diarrhea, 6/3/1865, Buried Woodlawn Cemetery, Elmira, NY, Grave No. 2900
Cribb, A.J. Private	Georgetown, SC. 3/23/62	21	Georgetown, Prince George Parish, SC	Co. A, 21st South Carolina Volunteers	Captured	Oath Of Allegiance 7/7/1865

NAME and RANK	PLACE & TYPE OF ENLISTMENT	AGE	RESIDENCE & OCCUPATION	REGIMENT OR BATTALION	RESULT OF BATTLE	REMARKS
Crickman, Solomon Private	New Berne, Craven County, NC, 1/27/1862, Volunteer	19	Battleboro, Nash County, NC, Farmer	Co. F, 36th Regiment North Carolina, 2nd Artillery	Captured	Oath Of Allegiance 7/11/1865
Croom, Isaac Private	Wilmington, New Hanover County, NC, 5/25/1863	Unk	Wilmington, New Hanover County, NC	Co. F, 10th Reg. 1st North Carolina Artillery	Captured	Oath Of Allegiance 5/29/1865
Croom, John A. Private	Wilmington, New Hanover County, NC, 4/18/1862, Volunteer	31	Wilmington, New Hanover County, NC, Fisherman for Company	Co. D, 1st Battalion, North Carolina Heavy Artillery	Captured	Exchanged On the James River, VA, 3/2/1865
Crumpler, Micajah H. Private	New Hanover County, NC, 7/23/1863, Volunteer	42	Clinton, Sampson County, NC	3rd Co. G, 40th Regiment, 3rd North Carolina Light Artillery	Captured	Died of Disease, On Route To Be Exchanged At James River, VA, 2/21/1865
Cudworth, Alfred Private	Charleston, SC, 2/24/1864	20	Charleston, SC	C. A, 25th South Carolina Volunteers	Captured	Oath Of Allegiance 6/16/1865
Culbreth, Daniel M. Private	Sampson County, NC, 9/13/1863, Volunteer	44	Owensville, Sampson County, NC, Farmer	3rd Co. B, 36th Regiment North Carolina, 2nd Artillery	Captured	Died of Chronic Diarrhea, 2/21/1865, Buried Woodlawn Cemetery, Elmira, NY, Grave No. 2265
Culbreth, William Private	Sampson County, NC, 4/10/1863, Volunteer	18	Owensville, Sampson County, NC, Farmer	3rd Co. B, 36th Regiment North Carolina, 2nd Artillery	Captured	Oath Of Allegiance 7/26/1865
Cumbee, Benjamin Private	New Hanover County, NC, 2/12/1862	18	New Hanover County, NC	2nd Co. D, 36th Regiment North Carolina, 2nd Artillery	Captured	Died of Chronic Diarrhea, 3/18/1865, Buried Woodlawn Cemetery, Elmira, NY, Grave No. 1557

NAME and RANK	PLACE & TYPE OF ENLISTMENT	AGE	RESIDENCE & OCCUPATION	REGIMENT OR BATTALION	RESULT OF BATTLE	REMARKS
Cumbee, Solomon J. Private	Wilmington, New Hanover County, NC, 2/12/1862, Volunteer	45	New Hanover County, NC	2nd Co. D, 36th Regiment North Carolina, 2nd Artillery	Captured	Died of Variola (smallpox), 4/12/1865, Buried Woodlawn Cemetery, Elmira, NY, Grave No. 2684
Currie, Nicholas D. Private	Bennettsville, SC, 2/2/1863	24	Marion, SC, Overseer	Co. F, 21st South Carolina Volunteers	Captured	Died of Pneumonia 5/14/1865, Buried Woodlawn Cemetery, Elmira, NY, Grave No. 2802
Cutchen, William T. Also spelled Cutheon Private	Unknown	33	Enfield, Halifax County, NC, Farmer	Co. F, 36th Regiment North Carolina, 2nd Artillery	Captured	Died of Pneumonia, 3/11/1865, Buried Woodlawn Cemetery, Elmira, NY, Grave No. 1837

NAME and RANK	PLACE & TYPE OF ENLISTMENT	AGE	RESIDENCE & OCCUPATION	REGIMENT OR BATTALION	RESULT OF BATTLE	REMARKS
Dailey, Benjamin F. Also Spelled: Daily Private	Wayne County, NC, 4/14/1863, Volunteer	18	Newhope District, Wayne County, NC, Farmer	3rd Co. G, 40th Regiment, 3rd North Carolina Light Artillery	Captured	Died Of Chronic Diarrhea 3/4/1865, Buried Woodlawn Cemetery, Elmira, NY, Grave No. 1984
Dale, James C. Private	Wilmington, New Hanover County, NC, 10/21/1861, Volunteer	18	New Hanover County, NC	2nd Co. D, 36th Regiment North Carolina, 2nd Artillery	Captured	Died Of Pneumonia 3/27/1865, Buried Woodlawn Cemetery, Elmira, NY, Grave No. 2528

NAME and RANK	PLACE & TYPE OF ENLISTMENT	AGE	RESIDENCE & OCCUPATION	REGIMENT OR BATTALION	RESULT OF BATTLE	REMARKS
Daniel, Henry Private	Goldsboro, Wayne County, NC, 7/9/1861, Mustered in at Beaufort, Carteret County, NC	22	Goldsboro, Wayne County, NC, Painter	Co. F, 10th Reg. 1st North Carolina Artillery	Captured	Died from Acute Inflammation Of The Liver 4/18/1865, Buried Woodlawn Cemetery, Elmira, NY, Grave No. 1363
Daniel, William E. Private	Fort Campbell, Brunswick County, NC, 1/2/1864, Volunteer	17	West Brook, Bladen County, NC	3rd Co. G, 36th Regiment North Carolina, 2nd Artillery	Captured	Died Of Variola (smallpox), 3/28/1865, Buried Woodlawn Cemetery, Elmira, NY, Grave No. 1670
Danzlar, Allen P. Private	Coles Island, SC, 4/11/1862	17	Orangeburg, SC	C. F, 25th South Carolina Volunteers	Captured	Exchanged 3/2/1865 On The James River, VA,
Danzlar, B.M. Private	Coles Island, SC, 4/11/1862	20	Orangeburg, SC	C. F, 25th South Carolina Volunteers	Captured	Died Of Chronic Diarrhea 2/20/1865, Buried Woodlawn Cemetery, Elmira, NY, Grave No. 2321
Dantzler, David W. Private	Coles Island, SC, 4/11/1862	27	McCantsville, Orangeburg, SC	Co. F, 25th South Carolina Volunteers	Captured	Died of Pneumonia, 4/1/1865 Buried Woodlawn Cemetery, Elmira, NY, Grave No. 2588
Dantzler, F.W. Private	Coles Island, SC, 4/11/1862	16	Orangeburg District, SC	C. F, 25th South Carolina Volunteers	Captured	Oath Of Allegiance 7/26/1865

NAME and RANK	PLACE & TYPE OF ENLISTMENT	AGE	RESIDENCE & OCCUPATION	REGIMENT OR BATTALION	RESULT OF BATTLE	REMARKS
Darden, George T. Private	Murfreesboro, Hertford County, NC, 6/12/1863	24	Hertford County, NC, Detailed To Carry Mail Between Fort Caswell and Smithville, June 1863	Co. C, 3rd Battalion, North Carolina Light Artillery	Captured	Exchanged 3/14/1865 Boulware's Wharf, James River, VA
Dardin, Calvin Private	Wilmington, New Hanover County, NC 2/2/1863	25	Bull Head District, Greene County, NC	Co. F, 10th Reg. 1st North Carolina Artillery	Captured	Oath Of Allegiance 5/29/1865
David, John Private	Gourdins Dept., SC, 3/25/1863	33	Williamsburg District, SC	C. F, 25th South Carolina Volunteers	Captured	Exchanged 3/2/1865 On The James River, VA,
Davidson, Thomas Private	Duplin County, NC, 9/1/1864	28	Duplin County, NC	Co. D, 10th Reg., 1st North Carolina Artillery	Captured	Died Of Variola (smallpox), 5/10/1865, Buried Woodlawn Cemetery, Elmira, NY, Grave No. 2786
Davis, Alexander Smith Private	Elizabethtown, Bladen County, NC, 5/5/1862, Mustered in at Wilmington, Volunteer	33	Cypress Creek, Bladen County, NC Farmer	Co. H, 36th Regiment North Carolina, 2nd Artillery	Captured	Died Of Chronic Diarrhea 2/18/1865, Buried Woodlawn Cemetery, Elmira, NY, Grave No. 2346
Davis, Amos L. Private	Fort Fisher, New Hanover County, NC, 4/16/1862	18	New Hanover County, NC	2nd Co. I, 36th Regiment North Carolina, 2nd Artillery	Wounded & Captured	Died Of Variola (smallpox), 3/28/1865, Buried Woodlawn Cemetery, Elmira, NY, Grave No. 2486
Davis, E.W. Private	Unknown	50	Stanly County, NC, Farmer	2nd Co. I, 36th Regiment North Carolina, 2nd Artillery	Captured	Died Of Debility 5/26/1865, Buried Woodlawn Cemetery, Elmira, NY, Grave No. 2920

NAME and RANK	PLACE & TYPE OF ENLISTMENT	AGE	RESIDENCE & OCCUPATION	REGIMENT OR BATTALION	RESULT OF BATTLE	REMARKS
Davis, Edward W. Private	Fort St. Philip, Brunswick County, NC, 7/7/1862, Volunteer	23	White Oak, Bladen County, NC, Detailed 1/5/1864 to build wharf at Fort Fisher	2nd Co. K, 40th Regiment, 3rd North Carolina Light Artillery	Captured	Exchanged 2/15/1865, Died of Consumption 5/17/1865, Richmond, VA, Hospital, Buried Hollywood Cemetery, VA
Davis, Hiram Private	Elizabethtown, Bladen County, NC, 10/19/1861, Volunteer	14	Bladen County, NC, Farmer	2nd Co. I, 36th Regiment North Carolina, 2nd Artillery	Captured	Died Of Disease 5/21/1865, Cause Unknown, Buried Woodlawn Cemetery, Elmira, NY,
Davis, John Richardson Private	Fort Fisher, New Hanover County, NC, 3/16/1862, Volunteer	18	Elizabethtown, Bladen County, NC	2nd Co. I, 36th Regiment North Carolina, 2nd Artillery	Captured	Oath Of Allegiance 6/12/1865,
Davis, John W. Sergeant	Carteret County, NC, 10/10/1861, Volunteer	24	Beaufort, Carteret County, NC, Farmer	3rd Co. G, 40th Regiment , North Carolina, 3rd North Carolina Artillery	Captured	Oath Of Allegiance 5/19/1865
Davis, Jordan D. Corporal	Fort St. Philip, Brunswick County, NC, 5/14/1862, Volunteer	33	Lockwoods Folly District, Brunswick County, NC, Farmer	3rd Co. G, 36th Regiment North Carolina, 2nd Artillery	Wounded & Captured	Exchanged 3/2/1865 Boulware's Wharf, James River, VA
Davis, Thaddeus C. Sergeant	Carteret County, NC, 10/16/1861, Volunteer	19	Morehead City, NC	3rd Co. G, 40th Regiment, 3rd North Carolina Light Artillery	Captured	Oath Of Allegiance 5/19/1865
Davis, Thomas Sergeant	Wilmington, New Hanover County, NC, 1/1/1861, Volunteer	23	Prospect Hall, Bladen County, NC, Farmer	3rd Co. B, 36th Regiment North Carolina, 2nd Artillery	Captured	Exchanged 3/2/1865 Boulware's Wharf, James River, VA

NAME and RANK	PLACE & TYPE OF ENLISTMENT	AGE	RESIDENCE & OCCUPATION	REGIMENT OR BATTALION	RESULT OF BATTLE	REMARKS
Davis, William A. Private	Elizabethtown, Bladen County, NC, 10/19/1861, Volunteer	20	White Oak, Bladen County, NC, Farmer	2nd Co. I, 36th Regiment North Carolina, 2nd Artillery	Captured	Exchanged 3/2/1865 Boulware's Wharf, James River, VA
Davis, William H. Private	Fort Fisher, New Hanover County, NC, 5/1/1862, Volunteer	18	New Hanover County, NC	2nd Co. C, 36th Regiment North Carolina, 2nd Artillery	Captured	Died Of Pneumonia 4/27/1865, Buried Woodlawn Cemetery, Elmira, NY, Grave No. 1428
Deal, Linton W. Private	Wilmington, New Hanover County, NC, 2/2/1863, Substitute for Jacob J. Edwards	37	Duplin County, NC, Farmer	Co. D, 1st Battalion, North Carolina Heavy Artillery	Captured	Exchanged 3/2/1865 Boulware's Wharf, James River, VA
Dean, Frank A. Private	Unknown	Unk	Unknown	Co. B, Confederate States Marines	Wounded & Captured	Wounded, Concussion Of Brain, Died Of Chronic Diarrhea 7/18/1865
Dees, John A.W. Private	Richmond County, NC, 4/29/1863, Volunteer	19	Pikesville, Wayne County, NC, Farmer	3rd Co. B, 36th Regiment North Carolina, 2nd Artillery	Captured	Died Of Chronic Diarrhea & Variola (smallpox), 2/27/1865, Buried Woodlawn Cemetery, Elmira, NY, Grave No. 2140
Deloache, Nelson Private	Camp Hardee, Georgetown, SC, 1/1/1862	37	Manning, Clarendon District, SC, Brick Mason	Co. I, 25th South Carolina Volunteers	Captured	Died Of Chronic Diarrhea 3/4/1865, Buried Woodlawn Cemetery, Elmira, NY, Grave No. 1980
Derr, John C. Private	Fort Strong, New Hanover County, NC, 2/2/1863, Volunteer	19	Teacher's Depot, Duplin County, NC,	Co. D, 1st Battalion, North Carolina Heavy Artillery	Captured	Oath Of Allegiance 7/11/1865

NAME and RANK	PLACE & TYPE OF ENLISTMENT	AGE	RESIDENCE & OCCUPATION	REGIMENT OR BATTALION	RESULT OF BATTLE	REMARKS
DeVane, Robert Harvey Also spelled Davane Private	Fort Fisher, New Hanover County, NC, 8/5/1863, Volunteer	18	Colvins Creek, New Hanover County, NC	2nd Co. I, 36th Regiment North Carolina, 2nd Artillery	Captured	Oath Of Allegiance 6/12/1865
DeVoe, James H. Corporal	Charleston, SC, 4/16/1862	25	Unknown	Co. B, 25th South Carolina Volunteers	Captured	Exchanged On the James River, VA, 3/22/1865
Dial, Jacob Private	Bennettsville, Marlboro District, SC, 12/25/1861	41	Bennettsville, Marlboro District, SC	Co. F, 21st South Carolina Volunteers	Captured	Died Of Pneumonia 3/10/1865, Buried Woodlawn Cemetery, Elmira, NY, Grave No. 1583
Dibble, M.W. Corporal	Unknown	Unk	Greenville, SC	Co. B, 25th South Carolina Volunteers	Captured	Oath Of Allegiance 6/15/1865
Dicken, Hiram Private	Enfield, Halifax County, NC, 10/9/1861, Volunteer	34	Heathsville, Halifax County, NC. Farmer	Co. F, 36th Regiment North Carolina, 2nd Artillery	Captured	Exchanged On the James River, VA, 3/14/1865
Dickens, Rovan Sergeant	Fort Caswell, Brunswick County, NC, 8/71863, Volunteer	18	Halifax County, NC	Co. F, 36th Regiment North Carolina, 2nd Artillery	Captured	Died Of Variola (smallpox), 3/18/1865, Buried Woodlawn Cemetery, Elmira, NY, Grave No. 1692
Dickinson, James H. Sergeant	Charleston, SC, 2/24/1862	20	Greenville, SC, Farmer	Co. A, 25th South Carolina Volunteers	Captured	Exchanged On the James River, VA, 3/2/1865

254

NAME and RANK	PLACE & TYPE OF ENLISTMENT	AGE	RESIDENCE & OCCUPATION	REGIMENT OR BATTALION	RESULT OF BATTLE	REMARKS
Dickson, George W. Private	Secessionville, SC, 7/25/1863	30	Columbia, Richland County, SC, Clerk	Co. I, 25th South Carolina Volunteers	Captured	Exchanged On the James River, VA, 3/14/1865
Dill, Samuel L. Private	Wilmington, New Hanover County, NC, 7/1/1863	21	Beaufort, Carteret County, NC, Clerk,	Co. K, 10th Reg. 1st North Carolina Artillery	Captured	Exchanged 3/14/1865, Boulware's Wharf, James River, VA
Dillard, S.H. Private	Sampson County, NC, 9/1/1864	Unk	Sampson County, NC, Overseer	Co. D, 1st Battalion, North Carolina Heavy Artillery	Captured	Exchanged 2/20/1865, Died Of Typhoid Fever 3/8/1865, Hospital Richmond, VA, Buried Hollywood Cemetery, VA
Doares, James D. Private	Old Brunswick Town, NC, 4/16/1862, Mustered in Fort St. Philip	16	Northwest District, Brunswick County, NC, Laborer	3rd Co. G, 36th Regiment North Carolina, 2nd Artillery	Captured	Oath Of Allegiance 8/7/1865
Dorden, Paul Private	Hertford County, NC, 9/1/1864	Unk	Hertford County, NC	Co. C, 3rd Battalion, North Carolina Light Artillery	Captured	Died Of Pneumonia 4/2/1865, Buried Woodlawn Cemetery, Elmira, NY, Grave No. 2571
Doughtie, Alpheus P. Private	Hertford County, NC, 4/30/1862	17	Murfreesboro, Hertford County, NC	Co. C, 3rd Battalion, North Carolina Light Artillery	Captured	Died Of Variola (smallpox), 2/24/1865, Buried Woodlawn Cemetery, Elmira, NY, Grave No. 2261
Douglass, Henry Private	Chesterfield, SC, 5/1/1863	Unk	Unknown	Co. D, 21st South Carolina Volunteers	Captured	Died Of Epilepsy 3/19/1865, Buried Woodlawn Cemetery, Elmira, NY, Grave No. 1699

255

NAME and RANK	PLACE & TYPE OF ENLISTMENT	AGE	RESIDENCE & OCCUPATION	REGIMENT OR BATTALION	RESULT OF BATTLE	REMARKS
Downing, Hayes B. Private	Cumberland County, NC, 10/10/1864	16	Fayetteville, Cumberland County, NC	3rd Co. G, 36th Regiment North Carolina, 2nd Artillery	Captured	Oath Of Allegiance 5/15/1865
Downing, John B. Private	Lock's Creek, Cumberland County, NC, 1/24/1863, Volunteer	28	Fayetteville, Cumberland County, NC, Merchant	2nd Co. I, 36th Regiment North Carolina, 2nd Artillery	Captured	Oath Of Allegiance 6/17/1865
Downing, Valentine Private	New Hanover County, NC, 3/31/1864, Volunteer	18	Downingville, Bladen County, NC	Co. H, 36th Regiment North Carolina, 2nd Artillery	Captured	Died Of Chronic Diarrhea 4/5/1865, Buried Woodlawn Cemetery, Elmira, NY, Grave No. 2552
Dozier, J. Fred also spelled Dospel, J. Fred Private	Unknown,	52	Arringtons District, Nash County, NC, Farmer	Co. E, 36th Regiment North Carolina, 2nd Artillery	Captured	Died Of Chronic Diarrhea 3/9/1865, Buried Woodlawn Cemetery, Elmira, NY, Grave No. 1877
Drew, James Private	Unknown	Unk	Unknown	Co. C, Confederate States Marines	Wounded & Captured	Died Of Pneumonia 2/27/1865, Buried Woodlawn Cemetery, Elmira, NY, Grave No. 2121
Dudley, John R. Private	Fort Caswell, Brunswick County, NC, 9/29/1863, Volunteer	18	Warsaw, Duplin County, NC	2nd Co. A, 36th Regiment North Carolina, 2nd Artillery	Captured	Oath Of Allegiance 7/11/1865
Dudley, Sampson Private	Sampson County, NC, 11/12/1861, Volunteer	19	Dismal District, Northern Division, Sampson County, NC	2nd Co. A, 36th Regiment North Carolina, 2nd Artillery	Captured	Died Of Bronchitis 5/26/1865, Buried Woodlawn Cemetery, Elmira, NY, Grave No. 2918

NAME and RANK	PLACE & TYPE OF ENLISTMENT	AGE	RESIDENCE & OCCUPATION	REGIMENT OR BATTALION	RESULT OF BATTLE	REMARKS
Duncan, John J. Private	Brunswick County, NC, 12/15/1863, Volunteer	38	Enfield, Halifax County, NC, Farm Overseer	Co. F, 36th Regiment North Carolina, 2nd Artillery	Captured	Died Of Chronic Diarrhea 3/31/1865, Buried Woodlawn Cemetery, Elmira, NY, Grave No. 2600
Dunn, Franklin Private	Edgecombe County, NC, 4/1/1864, Volunteer	26	Edgecombe County, NC	Co. D, 40th Regiment, 3rd North Carolina Light Artillery	Captured	Died Of Variola (smallpox) 4/9/1865, Buried Woodlawn Cemetery, Elmira, NY, Grave No. 2618

NAME and RANK	PLACE & TYPE OF ENLISTMENT	AGE	RESIDENCE & OCCUPATION	REGIMENT OR BATTALION	RESULT OF BATTLE	REMARKS
Earls, Daniel Also Spelled: Earle Private	Cleveland County, NC, 2/26/1863	33	New House, Cleveland County, NC	Co. K, 10th Reg. 1st North Carolina Artillery	Captured	Died of Ulcer Around Neck, 4/1/1865, Buried Woodlawn Cemetery, Elmira, NY, Grave No. 2594
Easterling, Andrew Jackson Private	Bennettsville, SC, 5/12/1862	33	Bennettsville, District of Marlboro, SC	Co. F, 21st South Carolina Volunteers	Captured	Died Of Intermittent Fever 3/19/1865, Buried Woodlawn Cemetery, Elmira, NY, Grave No. 2917
Easterling, William T. Private	Bennettsville, SC, 1/1/1864	19	Bennettsville, District of Marlboro, SC	Co. F, 21st South Carolina Volunteers	Captured	Oath Of Allegiance 7/11/1865

NAME and RANK	PLACE & TYPE OF ENLISTMENT	AGE	RESIDENCE & OCCUPATION	REGIMENT OR BATTALION	RESULT OF BATTLE	REMARKS
Earley, Moses C. Private	Hertford County, NC, 9/12/1864	17	Bertie County, NC	Co. C, 3rd Battalion, North Carolina Light Artillery	Captured	Died of Pneumonia & Typhoid Fever, 2/10/1865, Buried Woodlawn Cemetery, Elmira, NY, Grave No. 2047
Edge, Hugh P. Private	Fort Fisher, New Hanover County, NC 5/10/1863, Conscript	24	Elizabethtown, Bladen County, NC Turpentine	2nd Co. I, 36th Regiment North Carolina, 2nd Artillery	Captured	Exchanged 3/14/1865 Boulware's Wharf, James River, VA
Edge, Kelly Private	Elizabethtown, Bladen County, NC, 10/19/1861, Volunteer	39	White Oak, Bladen County, NC Day Laborer	2nd Co. I, 36th Regiment North Carolina, 2nd Artillery	Captured	Exchanged 2/20/1865 Boulware's Wharf, James River, VA
Edge, Robert D. Private	New Hanover County, NC 3/16/1862, Volunteer	30	White Oak, Bladen County, NC, Farmer Detailed as Carpenter at Fort Fisher, NC	2nd Co. I, 36th Regiment North Carolina, 2nd Artillery	Captured	Died of Pneumonia, 3/17/1865, Buried Woodlawn Cemetery, Elmira, NY, Grave No. 1718
Edwards, Edward F. Private	Elizabethtown, Bladen County, NC, 4/1/1862, Mustered in at Wilmington, NC, Volunteer	16	Vicinity of Bryant Swamp, Bladen County, NC, Farmer	Co. H, 36th Regiment North Carolina, 2nd Artillery	Captured	Died of Variola (smallpox), 3/11/1865, Buried Woodlawn Cemetery, Elmira, NY, Grave No. 1849
Edwards, Ralsey Private	Elizabethtown, Bladen County, NC, 5/6/1862, Mustered in at Ft. St. Philip, Volunteer	19	Bladenboro, NC Farmer	2nd Co. K, 40th Regiment, 3rd North Carolina Light Artillery	Captured	Oath Of Allegiance 7/19/1865
Edwards, William Private	Bladen County, NC, 3/10/1863, Volunteer	29	White Creek, Bladen County, NC Turpentine	3rd Co. B, 36th Regiment North Carolina, 2nd Artillery	Captured	Oath Of Allegiance 7/11/1865

NAME and RANK	PLACE & TYPE OF ENLISTMENT	AGE	RESIDENCE & OCCUPATION	REGIMENT OR BATTALION	RESULT OF BATTLE	REMARKS
Ellis, Charles T. Private	New Hanover County, NC, 3/17/1864	44	New Hanover County, NC, Day Laborer	Co. K, 10th Reg. 1st North Carolina Artillery	Captured	Died of Chronic Diarrhea, 3/28/1865, Buried Woodlawn Cemetery, Elmira, NY, Grave No. 2502
Ellis, E. S. Private	Battery Island, SC, 4/12/1862	30	Unknown	Co. C, 25th South Carolina Volunteers	Captured	Died Of Chronic Diarrhea 5/17/1865, Buried Woodlawn Cemetery, Elmira, NY, Grave No. 2953
Ellis, William W. Private	Darlington, SC, 2/19/1863	29	Graniteville, Edgefield, SC	Co. B, 21st South Carolina Volunteers	Captured	Died Of Chronic Diarrhea 3/6/1865, Buried Woodlawn Cemetery, Elmira, NY, Grave No. 1961
Englert, John W. Private	Charleston, SC, 3/25/1863	23	Charleston, SC	Co. I, 25th South Carolina Volunteers	Captured	Oath Of Allegiance 5/15/1865
Epps, J.H Sergeant.	James Island, SC, 4/12/1862	20	Kingstree, SC	Co. C, 25th South Carolina Volunteers	Captured	Oath Of Allegiance 7/7/1865
Ervin, Lawrence N. Private	James Island, SC, 10/17/1863	17	Sumter, Clarendon District, SC	Co. I, 25th South Carolina Volunteers	Captured	Oath Of Allegiance 7/11/1865
Etheridge, Ransom Private	Brunswick County, NC, 8/19/1863, Volunteer	42	Sprights District, Greene County, NC, Overseer	Co. F, 36th Regiment North Carolina, 2nd Artillery	Captured	Exchanged 2/20/1865, Died of Chronic Diarrhea, 4/6/1865, Jackson Hospital, Richmond, VA, Buried Hollywood Cemetery, VA

NAME and RANK	PLACE & TYPE OF ENLISTMENT	AGE	RESIDENCE & OCCUPATION	REGIMENT OR BATTALION	RESULT OF BATTLE	REMARKS
Eure, William W. Sergeant	Halifax County, NC, 10/9/1861, Volunteer	21	Enfield, Halifax County, NC, Mechanic	Co. F, 36th Regiment North Carolina, 2nd Artillery	Captured	Died of Chronic Diarrhea, 3/29/1865, Buried Woodlawn Cemetery, Elmira, NY, Grave No. 2525
Evans, Angus J. Private	Fort Holmes, Brunswick County, NC, 2/24/1864, Volunteer	18	Bladen County, NC, Laborer	2nd Co. K, 40th Regiment, 3rd North Carolina Light Artillery	Captured	Exchanged 3/14/1865 Boulware's Wharf, James River, VA
Evans, Daniel Private	Elizabethtown, Bladen County, NC, 10/19/1861	21	Bladen County, NC, Detailed to catch deserters, 1862	2nd Co. I, 36th Regiment, 3rd North Carolina Light Artillery	Captured	Died of Pneumonia, 2/9/1865, Buried Woodlawn Cemetery, Elmira, NY, Grave No. 1942
Evans, J.H Private	Charleston, SC, 5/16/1862	30	Marion, SC, Farmer	Co. C, 25th South Carolina Volunteers	Captured	Scheduled For Exchange But Died Of Unknown Disease 7/21/1865, Grave No. 2866
Evans, James Private	Fort Fisher, New Hanover County, NC, 3/7/1862, Volunteer	24	New Hanover County, NC	2nd Co. I, 36th Regiment North Carolina, 2nd Artillery	Captured	Exchanged 3/2/1865 Boulware's Wharf, James River, VA
Evans, John Private	Robeson County, NC, 5/8/1862, Volunteer	30	Lumberton, Robeson, NC, Farmer	Co. C, 40th Regiment, 3rd North Carolina Light Artillery	Captured	Oath Of Allegiance 6/20/1865
Evans, Nathan J. Private	Marion, SC, 3/20/1864	19	Marion, SC, Farmer	Co. L, 21st South Carolina Volunteers	Captured	Oath Of Allegiance 7/11/1865

NAME and RANK	PLACE & TYPE OF ENLISTMENT	AGE	RESIDENCE & OCCUPATION	REGIMENT OR BATTALION	RESULT OF BATTLE	REMARKS
Evans, R.M. Private	Coles Island, SC, 4/11/1862	27	Orangeburg, SC, Farmer	Co. F, 25th South Carolina Volunteers	Captured	Died of Pneumonia, 6/2/1865, Buried Woodlawn Cemetery, Elmira, NY, Grave No. 2903
Everett, Neil Private	Cumberland County, NC, Date Unknown	Unk	Fayetteville, Cumberland County, NC	2nd Co. C, 36th Regiment North Carolina, 2nd Artillery	Captured	Oath Of Allegiance 6/12/1865
Evers, Dennis Private	Elizabethtown, Bladen County, NC, 10/23/1863, Volunteer	18	Elizabethtown, Bladen County, NC Farmer	2nd Co. K, 40th Regiment, 3rd North Carolina Light Artillery	Captured	Died of Variola (smallpox), 3/29/1865, Buried Woodlawn Cemetery, Elmira, NY, 2512
Evers, Ephraim Private	Fort Fisher, New Hanover County, NC, 5/7/1863, Volunteer	22	Elizabethtown, Bladen County, NC Farmer	2nd Co. K, 40th Regiment, 3rd North Carolina Light Artillery	Captured	Died of Pneumonia, 3/14/1865, Buried Woodlawn Cemetery, Elmira, NY, Grave No. 1675
Evers, William H. Private	New Hanover County, NC, 10/27/1862, Volunteer	23	New Hanover County, NC, Detailed 1/5/1864 to 8/31/1864 to build a wharf at Fort Fisher	2nd Co. K, 40th Regiment, 3rd North Carolina Light Artillery	Captured	Died of Variola (smallpox), 3/27/1865, Buried Woodlawn Cemetery, Elmira, NY, Grave No. 2478
Exum, Benjamin Private	Wayne County, NC, 5/14/1863	18	Pikeville, Wayne County, NC, Laborer	Co. F, 10th Reg. 1st North Carolina Artillery	Captured	Died of Variola (smallpox), 3/10/1865, Buried Woodlawn Cemetery, Elmira, NY, Grave No. 2361

NAME and RANK	PLACE & TYPE OF ENLISTMENT	AGE	RESIDENCE & OCCUPATION	REGIMENT OR BATTALION	RESULT OF BATTLE	REMARKS
Faircloth, T. Private	Unknown	Unk	Unknown	Co. E, 36th Regiment North Carolina, 2nd Artillery	Captured	Died of Rheumatism, 3/17/1865, Buried Woodlawn Cemetery, Elmira, NY, Grave No. 1703
Faircloth, Thomas H. Private	Terribinth, 2/20/1862, Cumberland County, NC,	20	Ellisville, Bladen County, NC, Farmer	2nd Co. C, 36th Regiment North Carolina, 2nd Artillery	Captured	Died of Chronic Diarrhea, 3/14/1865, Buried Woodlawn Cemetery, Elmira, NY, Grave No. 2430
Faulk, William H. Private	Fort St. Philip, Brunswick County, NC, 4/9/1863, Substitute	15	Brunswick County, NC	Co. E, 36th Regiment North Carolina, 2nd Artillery	Captured	Exchanged On the James River, VA, 3/2/1865
Felder, C.E. Private	Coles Island, SC, 4/11/1862	19	White Cain, Orangeburg, SC	Co. F, 25th South Carolina Volunteers	Captured	Oath of Allegiance 7/11/1865
Ferguson, Dennis or Dorris Private	Fort Holmes, Wake County, NC, 5/11/1863	Unk	Unknown, Detailed to haul wood at Fort Caswell, NC, May, 1863,	Co. C, 3rd Battalion, North Carolina Light Artillery	Captured	Died of Convulsions, 3/10/1865, Buried Woodlawn Cemetery, Elmira, NY, Grave No. 1865
Ferrell, A.S. Private	New Hanover County, NC, 11/25/1864	Unk	New Hanover County, NC	Co. D, 13th Battalion North Carolina Light Artillery	Captured	Exchanged 3/14/1865 Boulware's Wharf, James River, VA
Fersner, W.F. Ordinance Sergeant	Coles Island, SC, 4/11/1862	Unk	Orangeburg, SC	Field And Staff, 25th South Carolina Volunteers	Captured	Oath of Allegiance 7/7/1865

NAME and RANK	PLACE & TYPE OF ENLISTMENT	AGE	RESIDENCE & OCCUPATION	REGIMENT OR BATTALION	RESULT OF BATTLE	REMARKS
Fertic, John Private	Coles Island, SC, 4/11/1862	22	Orangeburg District, Louisville, SC	Co. E, 25th South Carolina Volunteers	Captured	Oath of Allegiance 7/7/1865
Fields, Tobias Private	Fort Branch, Brunswick County, NC, 7/24/1863 Volunteer	19	Moore County, NC Farmer	3rd Co. G, 40th Regiment, 3rd North Carolina Artillery	Captured	Died of Pneumonia 3/4/1865, Buried Woodlawn Cemetery, Elmira, NY, Grave No. 2002
Fisher, Marshall T. Private	Fort Fisher, New Hanover County, NC, 3/15/1863 Volunteer	35	New Hanover County, NC	2nd Co. C, 36th Regiment North Carolina, 2nd Artillery	Captured	Died of Chronic Diarrhea, 5/2/1865, Buried Woodlawn Cemetery, Elmira, NY, Grave No. 2747
Fisher, William T. Private	Fort Fisher, New Hanover County, NC, 3/15/1863 Volunteer	39	Fayetteville, Cumberland County, NC	2nd Co. C, 36th Regiment North Carolina, 2nd Artillery	Captured	Oath of Allegiance 6/12/1865
Flanigan, Alfred Private	Fort Caswell, Brunswick County, NC, 8/22/1863 Volunteer	29	Brunswick County, NC	2nd Co. D, 36th Regiment North Carolina, 2nd Artillery	Captured	Exchanged On the James River, VA, 3/14/1865
Flemming, Samuel W. Private Also Spelled Fleming	James Island, SC, 8/20/1863	33	Columbia, Richland, SC	Co I, 25th Regiment South Carolina Volunteers	Captured	Died of Pneumonia, 4/26/1865, Buried Woodlawn Cemetery, Elmira, NY, Grave No. 1423
Flemming, W.D. Private	Georgetown, SC, 1/1/1862	19	Kingstree, SC	Co. I, 25th South Carolina Volunteers	Captured	Oath of Allegiance 7/11/1865
Flottwell, Richard Private	Charleston, SC, 3/19/1862	27	Mobile, Al	Co. E, 25th South Carolina Volunteers	Captured	Oath of Allegiance 5/29/1865

NAME and RANK	PLACE & TYPE OF ENLISTMENT	AGE	RESIDENCE & OCCUPATION	REGIMENT OR BATTALION	RESULT OF BATTLE	REMARKS
Flowers, James Private	Fort St. Philip, Brunswick County, NC, 5/5/1862 Volunteer	23	Brunswick County, NC	3rd Co. G, 36th Regiment North Carolina, 2nd Artillery	Captured	Exchanged On the James River, VA, 2/20/1865
Flowers, Thomas Private	Darlington, SC, 9/10/1862	21	District of Sumter, SC, Printer	Co. G, 21st South Carolina Volunteers	Captured	Oath of Allegiance 7/11/1865
Fogle, W.J. Private	Orangeburg SC, 4/19/1862	42	Orangeburg District, Bull Swamp, SC, Methodist Clergyman	Co. F, 25th South Carolina Volunteers	Captured	Died of Chronic Diarrhea, 3/16/1865 Buried Woodlawn Cemetery, Elmira, NY, Grave No. 1679
Folks, John A. Private	Columbus County, NC, 10/21/1861, Mustered in at Fort Caswell, NC Volunteer	20	Whiteville, Columbus County, NC Farmer	2nd Co. A, 36th Regiment North Carolina, 2nd Artillery	Captured	Died of Gangrene Of Feet, 3/14/1865, Buried Woodlawn Cemetery, Elmira, NY, Grave No. 1672
Force, George H. Private	Charleston, SC, 3/18/1862	20	Greensboro, Ga	Co. B, 25th South Carolina Volunteers	Captured	Oath of Allegiance 8/14/1865
Ford, John H. also spelled Fort Private	Fort Fisher, New Hanover County, NC, 3/15/1864	27	Fayetteville, Cumberland County, SC, Turpentiner	3rd Co. G, 36th Regiment North Carolina, 2nd Artillery	Captured	Exchanged 3/2/1865, Died of Typhoid Fever, Jackson Hospital, Richmond, VA, 5/2/1865, Buried Hollywood Cemetery, Richmond, VA,
Fox, Isaiah Private	Chatham County, NC, 3/26/1863 Volunteer	34	St. Lawrence, Chatham County, NC,	3rd Co. G, 40th Regiment, 3rd North Carolina Artillery	Captured	Died of Rheumatism, 4/4/1865, Buried Woodlawn Cemetery, Elmira, NY, Grave No. 2561

NAME and RANK	PLACE & TYPE OF ENLISTMENT	AGE	RESIDENCE & OCCUPATION	REGIMENT OR BATTALION	RESULT OF BATTLE	REMARKS
Freeman, Chapman Private	Camp Harllee, SC, 1/1/1862	15	Cheraw, Chesterfield County, SC,	Co. D, 21st South Carolina Volunteers	Captured	Oath of Allegiance 7/11/1865
Freeman, George Private	Marion, SC, 4/20/1862	16	Marion, Gum Swamp, SC, Farmer	Co. I, 25th South Carolina Volunteers	Captured	Died of Pneumonia, 2/25/1865, Buried Woodlawn Cemetery, Elmira, NY, Grave No. 2270
Freeman, William Private	Fort Branch, Brunswick County, NC, 8/17/1863 Volunteer	43	Brunswick County, NC	3rd Co. G, 40th Regiment, 3rd North Carolina Artillery	Captured	Died of Pneumonia, 2/9/1865, Buried Woodlawn Cemetery, Elmira, NY, Grave No. 1939
Furr, John B. Private	Wilmington, New Hanover County, NC, 3/24/1864	Unk	Wilmington, New Hanover County, NC	Co. K, 10th Reg. 1st North Carolina Artillery	Captured	Died of Variola (smallpox), 3/3/1865, Buried Woodlawn Cemetery, Elmira, NY
Furr, Martin Private	Camp Holmes, Wake County, NC, 4/8/1863	20	Mount Pleasant, Cabarrus County, NC, Farmer	Co. C, 3rd Battalion, North Carolina Light Artillery	Captured	Died of Typhoid Fever, 2/22/1865, Buried Woodlawn Cemetery, Elmira, NY, Grave No. 2242

NAME and RANK	PLACE & TYPE OF ENLISTMENT	AGE	RESIDENCE & OCCUPATION	REGIMENT OR BATTALION	RESULT OF BATTLE	REMARKS
Gainey, Thomas W. Private	Darlington, SC, 4/4/1863	24	Darlington District, SC, 4/4/1863, Farmer	Co. G, 21st South Carolina Volunteers	Captured	Oath of Allegiance 7/11/1865

NAME and RANK	PLACE & TYPE OF ENLISTMENT	AGE	RESIDENCE & OCCUPATION	REGIMENT OR BATTALION	RESULT OF BATTLE	REMARKS
Gainor, William T. Private	Greenville, Pitt County, NC, 5/14/1862	Unk	Washington, NC	Co. K, 10th Reg. 1st North Carolina Artillery	Captured	Died of Chronic Diarrhea, 3/4/1865 Buried Woodlawn Cemetery, Elmira, NY, Grave No. 2001
Galloway, Abram M. Private	Darlington, SC, 4/15/1861	19	Darlington District, SC, Farmer	Co. H, 21st South Carolina Volunteers	Captured	Oath of Allegiance 8/7/1865
Galloway, L. Chappel Private	Darlington, SC, 5/20/1862	24	Darlington District, SC, Farmer	Co. B, 21st South Carolina Volunteers	Captured	Died of Chronic Diarrhea, 4/25/1865, Buried Woodlawn Cemetery, Elmira, NY, Grave No. 1417
Galloway, Pipkin Private	James Island, SC, 3/1/1864	38	Darlington District, SC, Farmer Father of Abram Galloway	Co. H, 21st South Carolina Volunteers	Captured	Died of Gangrene Of Feet 3/7/1865, Buried Woodlawn Cemetery, Elmira, NY, Grave No. 2397
Gamble, Joseph M. Private	Gourdins Dept., SC, 12/29/1861	37	Sumter, SC	Co. K, 25th South Carolina Volunteers	Captured	Oath of Allegiance 7/3/1865
Gamble, Thomas E. Private	Charleston, SC, 5/16/1862	27	New Zion, Clarendon County, SC, Farmer	Co. I, 25th South Carolina Volunteers	Captured	Died of Chronic Diarrhea, 4/7/1865, Buried Woodlawn Cemetery, Elmira, NY, 2645
Ganns, Wiley Private	Fort Caswell, NC, 10/20/1863 Volunteer	20	Fair Bluff, Columbus County, NC	2nd Co. D, 36th Regiment North Carolina, 2nd Artillery	Captured	Oath of Allegiance 7/7/1865

266

NAME and RANK	PLACE & TYPE OF ENLISTMENT	AGE	RESIDENCE & OCCUPATION	REGIMENT OR BATTALION	RESULT OF BATTLE	REMARKS
Gardner, Benjamin W. Private	Smithville, Brunswick County, NC, 5/15/1864	17	Stony Creek District, Goldsboro, Wayne County, NC, Farmer	Co. F, 10th Reg. 1st North Carolina Artillery	Captured	Died of Intermittent Fever, 3/5/1865 Buried Woodlawn Cemetery, Elmira, NY, Grave No. 2375
Gardner, Robinson Private	Elizabethtown, Bladen County, NC, 10/19/1861 Volunteer	16	Fayetteville, Cumberland County, NC,	Co. E, 36th Regiment North Carolina, 2nd Artillery	Captured	Died of Variola (smallpox), 3/2/1865 Buried Woodlawn Cemetery, Elmira, NY, 2018
Garner, David F. Private	Shepardsville, NC, Carteret County, NC, 7/20/1861, Mustered in at Beaufort, NC Volunteer	21	Shepardsville, Carteret County, NC, Farmer	Co. F, 10th Reg. 1st North Carolina Artillery	Captured	Died of Chronic Diarrhea, 5/8/1865 Buried Woodlawn Cemetery, Elmira, NY, Grave No. 2778
Garner, William J. Private	Seccessionville, SC, 1/25/1864	29	Marion, SC	Co. K, 25th South Carolina Volunteers	Captured	Exchanged 2/20/1865, Died Of Unknown Disease 3/9/1865 In Howard's Grove Hospital, Richmond, VA
Gasque, J.M. Private	Marion Dist., SC, 3/13/1862	18	Marion Dist., SC	Co. L, 21st South Carolina Volunteers	Captured	Oath of Allegiance 7/11/1865
Gasque, Samuel O. Private	Marion, SC, 5/14/1862	21	Marion, SC, Farm Laborer	Co. L, 21st South Carolina Volunteers	Captured	Died of Chronic Diarrhea, 3/28/1865, Buried Woodlawn Cemetery, Elmira, NY, Grave No. 2503
Gause, William Q. Private	Brunswick County, NC, 2/26/1863 Volunteer	18	Whiteville, Columbus County, NC	Co. H, 36th Regiment North Carolina, 2nd Artillery	Captured	Oath of Allegiance 7/7/1865

NAME and RANK	PLACE & TYPE OF ENLISTMENT	AGE	RESIDENCE & OCCUPATION	REGIMENT OR BATTALION	RESULT OF BATTLE	REMARKS
Gay, P.W. Private	Bennettsville, Marlboro District, SC, 1/21/1864	38	Bennettsville, Marlboro District, SC, Farmer	Co. F, 21st South Carolina Volunteers	Captured	Died of Pneumonia 2/13/1865, Buried Woodlawn Cemetery, Elmira, NY, Grave No. 2063
Gerken, E.F. Henry Private	Charleston., SC, 2/22/1862	38	Charleston, SC	Co. D, 25th South Carolina Volunteers	Captured	Oath of Allegiance 5/15/1865
Gibson, Albert Sergeant	Marion, SC, 1/26/1862	23	Marion, SC	Co. L, 21st South Carolina Volunteers	Severe Gunshot Wound Left Hip, Femur Fracture & Captured,	Oath of Allegiance 7/11/1865
Gibson, Ebenezer B. Private	Laurenburg, Richmond County, NC, 8/17/1863 Volunteer	18	Richmond County, NC	Co. E, 40th Regiment, 3rd North Carolina Artillery	Captured	Died of Chronic Diarrhea, 3/10/1865 Buried Woodlawn Cemetery, Elmira, NY, Grave No. 1883
Gibson, Raiford Private	Fort Holmes, Brunswick County, NC, 12/24/1864	16	Williamson District, Richmond County, NC	Co. E, 40th Regiment, 3rd North Carolina Artillery	Captured	Oath of Allegiance 6/12/1865
Gilcott, George H. Private	St. Johns, Hertford County, NC, 7/1/1862	Unk	Plymouth, NC	Co. C, 3rd Battalion, North Carolina Light Artillery	Captured	Oath of Allegiance 6/12/1865
Ginnett, Matthew Private	Goldsboro, Wayne County, NC, 7/22/1861, Mustered in at Beaufort, NC Volunteer	19	Goldsboro, Wayne County, NC, Farmer	Co. F, 10th Reg. 1st North Carolina Artillery	Captured	Oath of Allegiance 7/11/1865

NAME and RANK	PLACE & TYPE OF ENLISTMENT	AGE	RESIDENCE & OCCUPATION	REGIMENT OR BATTALION	RESULT OF BATTLE	REMARKS
Ginnett, Needham Private	Fort Holmes, New Hanover County, NC, 1/10/1864	Unk	New Hanover County, NC	Co. F, 10th Reg. 1st North Carolina Artillery	Captured	Exchanged On the James River, VA, 2/20/1865
Glover, John B. Private	Charleston, SC, 2/24/1862	25	Augusta, Ga	Co. B, 25th South Carolina Volunteers	Gunshot Wound Of Chest & Captured	Oath of Allegiance 7/26/1865
Godwin, Ichabod Private	Wilmington, NC, New Hanover County, 3/1/1862 Volunteer	17	Fair Bluff, Columbus County, NC	Co. E, 36th Regiment North Carolina, 2nd Artillery	Captured	Oath of Allegiance 7/11/1865
Gooden, David James Private	Elizabethtown, NC, Bladen County, NC 2/3/1862 Volunteer	18	Bladen County, NC	2nd Co. I 36th Regiment North Carolina, 2nd Artillery	Captured	Exchanged 3/14/1865 Boulware's Wharf, James River, VA
Gooding, Eldred B. Sergeant	Whippy Swamp, SC, 7/15/1861	18	Prince William Parish, Beaufort District, SC, Farmer	Co. E, 11th South Carolina	Captured	Exchanged On the James River, VA, 3/2/1865
Goodman, Henry E. Private	Lenoir County, NC, 7/18/1863 Volunteer	41	Goldsboro, Wayne County, NC	3rd Co. G, 40th Regiment, 3rd North Carolina Artillery	Captured	Oath of Allegiance 6/12/1865
Goodman, Henry H. Private	Old Brunswick Town, NC, 4/16/1862, Mustered in at Fort St. Philip, NC Volunteer	32	Town Creek District, Brunswick County, NC, Farmer	3rd Co. G, 36th Regiment North Carolina, 2nd Artillery	Captured	Died of Variola (smallpox), 2/21/1865 Buried Woodlawn Cemetery, Elmira, NY, Grave No. 2237
Gowan, Peter Private	Charleston, SC, 2/24/1862	20	Charleston, SC	Co. A, 25th South Carolina Volunteers	Captured	Oath of Allegiance 6/21/1865

NAME and RANK	PLACE & TYPE OF ENLISTMENT	AGE	RESIDENCE & OCCUPATION	REGIMENT OR BATTALION	RESULT OF BATTLE	REMARKS
Gower, Henry S. Private	Camp Holmes, NC, 10/13/1863	Unk	Wake County, NC	2nd Co. D, 36th Regiment North Carolina, 2nd Artillery	Captured	Died of Chronic Diarrhea, 5/14/1865 Buried Woodlawn Cemetery, Elmira, NY, 2800
Grady, Lewis H. Private	Duplin County, NC, 7/13/1863 Volunteer	22	Mount Olive, Duplin County, NC, Farmer	3rd Co. G, 40th Regiment, 3rd North Carolina Artillery	Captured	Exchanged 3/2/1865, Died of Pneumonia, 3/15/1865, Richmond, VA Buried Hollywood Cemetery, VA
Graham, James Private	Marion, SC, 4/20/1862	18	Gum Swamp, Marion, SC,	Co. D, 25th South Carolina Volunteers	Captured	Died of Remittent Fever, 2/4/1865, Buried Woodlawn Cemetery, Elmira, NY, Grave No. 1887
Grambling, Martin L. Private	Coles Island, SC, 4/11/1862	27	Orangeburg, SC Farmer, Teamster	Co. F, 25th South Carolina Volunteers	Captured	Oath of Allegiance 7/7/1865
Grant, Solomon E. Private	Wilmington, New Hanover County, NC, 4/16/1864	15	Wilmington, New Hanover County, NC	Co. K, 10th Reg. 1st North Carolina Artillery	Captured	Died of Chronic Diarrhea, 3/6/1865 Buried Woodlawn Cemetery, Elmira, NY, Grave No. 2411
Grant, William R. Private	Camp Harllee, SC, 1/1/1862	30	Marlboro District, SC	Co. D, 21st South Carolina Volunteers	Captured	Exchanged On the James River, VA, 3/2/1865

NAME and RANK	PLACE & TYPE OF ENLISTMENT	AGE	RESIDENCE & OCCUPATION	REGIMENT OR BATTALION	RESULT OF BATTLE	REMARKS
Grantham, John Q. Private	Fort Holmes, Brunswick County, NC, 12/11/1864	Unk	Brunswick County, NC	Co. E, 40th Regiment, 3rd North Carolina Artillery	Captured	Exchanged 3/18/1865, Died of Typhoid Fever 4/5/1865, Richmond, VA Buried Hollywood Cemetery
Grantham, Josiah L. Private	Fort Caswell, Brunswick County, NC, 8/19/1863 Volunteer	44	Brunswick County, NC	Co. E, 40th Regiment, 3rd North Carolina Artillery	Captured	Died of Chronic Diarrhea, 3/23/1865, Buried Woodlawn Cemetery, Elmira, NY, Grave No. 1514
Grantham, Robert W. Private	Darlington, SC, 1/20/1862	18	Darlington District, SC, Farmer	Co. H, 21st South Carolina Volunteers	Captured	Died of Pneumonia 3/5/1865, Buried Woodlawn Cemetery, Elmira, NY, Grave No. 2398
Gray, James Alexander Private	Fort Fisher, New Hanover County, NC, 7/16/1864	19	Wilmington, New Hanover County, NC	2nd Co. C, 36th Regiment North Carolina, 2nd Artillery	Captured	Exchanged On the James River, VA, 3/2/1865
Green, Samuel Private	Fort Pender, Brunswick County, NC, 12/29/1863 Volunteer	19	Alamance County, NC, Farmer	Co. E, 36th Regiment North Carolina, 2nd Artillery	Captured	Oath of Allegiance 7/3/1865
Greer, William Robert	Charleston, SC, 1/4/1863	19	Charleston, SC,	Co. B, 25th South Carolina Volunteers	Captured	Oath of Allegiance 6/23/1865
Gregg, Alex M. Sergeant	Pee Dee, SC, 1/1/1862	19	Mars Bluff, Marion County, SC	Co. K, 21st South Carolina Volunteers	Captured	Oath of Allegiance 6/23/1865
Gregg, Thomas C. Private	Camp Mannigaulp, SC, 5/2/1862	23	Mars Bluff, Marion County, SC	Co. I, 21st South Carolina Volunteers	Captured	Oath of Allegiance 6/23/1865

NAME and RANK	PLACE & TYPE OF ENLISTMENT	AGE	RESIDENCE & OCCUPATION	REGIMENT OR BATTALION	RESULT OF BATTLE	REMARKS
Gregg, W.W. Private	Marion, SC, 9/1/1863	19	Marion County, SC	Co. I, 21st South Carolina Volunteers	Captured	Died Of Unknown Disease On Boat To Be Exchanged 3/3/1865
Grice, Giles W. Private	Sampson County, NC, 10/23/1861, Mustered in at Fort Caswell, NC Volunteer	32	Sampson County, NC, Hireling	2nd Co. A, 36th Regiment North Carolina, 2nd Artillery	Captured	Died of Chronic Diarrhea, 3/22/1865 Buried Woodlawn Cemetery, Elmira, NY, Grave No. 1517
Grier, Thomas C. Private	Georgetown, SC, 1/1/1862	34	Prince George Parish, Georgetown, SC, Farmer	Co. A, 21st South Carolina Volunteers	Captured	Exchanged On the James River, VA, 3/2/1865
Grier, William S. Private	Charleston, SC, 4/1/1864	17	Prince George Parish, Georgetown, SC, Farmer	Co. A, 21st South Carolina Volunteers	Captured	Died of Chronic Diarrhea, 3/12/1865, Buried Woodlawn Cemetery, Elmira, NY, Grave No. 1852
Griffin, Absalom B. Private	Coles Island, SC, 4/11/1862	Unk	Unknown	Co. F, 25th South Carolina Volunteers	Captured	Died of Chronic Diarrhea, 5/6/1865, Buried Woodlawn Cemetery, Elmira, NY, Grave No. 2765
Griffin, Henry J.F. Private	Coles Island, SC, 4/11/1862	36	Lance's Ferry, Orangeburg District, SC, Overseer	Co. F, 25th South Carolina Volunteers	Captured	Died of Chronic Diarrhea, 5/16/1865, Buried Woodlawn Cemetery, Elmira, NY, Grave No. 2963
Griffin, S.D. Private	Coles Island, SC, 4/11/1862	Unk	Orangeburg, SC	Co. F, 25th South Carolina Volunteers	Captured	Oath of Allegiance 7/11/1865

NAME and RANK	PLACE & TYPE OF ENLISTMENT	AGE	RESIDENCE & OCCUPATION	REGIMENT OR BATTALION	RESULT OF BATTLE	REMARKS
Griggs, Elisha Private	Fort Branch, Brunswick County, NC, 7/25/1863 Volunteer	18	Charlotte, NC	3rd Co. G, 40th Regiment, 3rd North Carolina Artillery	Captured	Oath of Allegiance 6/12/1865
Gurgainus, James R. Private	Wilmington, New Hanover County, NC, 10/20/1864	19	Tarboro, Edgecombe County, NC	Co. K, 10th Regiment, 1st North Carolina Artillery	Captured	Oath of Allegiance 7/7/1865
Guy, William Private	Lillington, Harnett County, NC, 4/30/1862 Volunteer	24	Raleigh, Wake County, NC	2nd Co. C, 36th Regiment North Carolina, 2nd Artillery	Captured	Oath of Allegiance 6/12/1865
Gyles, F.A. Sergeant	Coles Island, SC, 3/22/1862	21	Unknown	Co. B, 25th South Carolina Volunteers	Captured	Exchanged On the James River, VA, 3/14/1865

NAME and RANK	PLACE & TYPE OF ENLISTMENT	AGE	RESIDENCE & OCCUPATION	REGIMENT OR BATTALION	RESULT OF BATTLE	REMARKS
Haggard, John D. Private	St. Johns, Hertford County, NC, 7/18/1864 Conscript	30	Garysburg, NC	Co. C, 3rd Battalion, North Carolina Light Artillery	Captured	Oath Of Allegiance 5/29/1865
Haigler, F.G. Private	Secessionville, SC, 5/22/1862	18	Orangeburg District, SC	Co. F, 25th South Carolina Volunteers	Captured	Oath Of Allegiance 7/26/1865
Hales, Samuel Private	Blockerville, Cumberland County, NC, 3/2/1862 Volunteer	53	Fayetteville, Cumberland County, NC, Farm Hand	2nd Co. D, 36th Regiment North Carolina, 2nd Artillery	Captured	Exchanged On the James River, VA, 3/2/1865
Haley, Harvey V. Corporal	Camp Hardee, Georgetown, SC, 1/1/1862	33	Manning, Clarendon District, SC	Co. I, 25th South Carolina Volunteers	Captured	Died Of Chronic Diarrhea 3/12/1865, Buried Woodlawn Cemetery, Elmira, NY, Grave No. 1821

NAME and RANK	PLACE & TYPE OF ENLISTMENT	AGE	RESIDENCE & OCCUPATION	REGIMENT OR BATTALION	RESULT OF BATTLE	REMARKS
Hall, Alexander A. Private	Hardeeville, SC, 3/6/1863	18	Unknown	Co. D, 11th South Carolina	Captured	Died Of Rubeola 4/2/1865, Buried Woodlawn Cemetery, Elmira, NY, Grave No. 2581
Hall, Amos J. Private	Fort Fisher, New Hanover County, NC, 12/2/1862 Volunteer	31	Owensville, Sampson County, NC	2nd Co. C, 36th Regiment North Carolina, 2nd Artillery	Captured	Exchanged On the James River, VA, 3/2/1865
Hall, Daniel Private	Darlinton, SC, 1/3/1862	25	Unknown	Co. G, 21st South Carolina Volunteers	Captured	Died of Pneumonia 2/25/1865, Buried Woodlawn Cemetery, Elmira, NY, Grave No. 2281
Hall, David T. Private	Ellisville, NC, Bladen County, NC, 3/4/1862 Volunteer	38	Ellisville, Bladen County, NC	2nd Co. C, 36th Regiment North Carolina, 2nd Artillery	Captured	Oath Of Allegiance 7/7/1865
Hall, Gaston W. Private	Fort Fisher, New Hanover County, NC, 3/15/1864 Volunteer	19	Fayetteville, Cumberland County, NC, Detailed as Scout for Lt. Faison	Co. H, 36th Regiment North Carolina, 2nd Artillery	Captured	Died of Chronic Diarrhea, 3/1/1865, Buried Woodlawn Cemetery, Elmira, NY, Grave No. 2109
Hall, James H. Private	Georgetown, SC, 1/1/1862	23	New Prospect, Spartanburg, SC	Co. K, 21st South Carolina Volunteers	Captured	Died of Chronic Diarrhea, 8/26/1865, Buried Woodlawn Cemetery, Elmira, NY, Grave No. 2857
Hall, Jesse Private	Fort Fisher, New Hanover County, NC, 6/1/1863 Volunteer	19	Ellisville, Bladen County, NC	2nd Co. I, 36th Regiment North Carolina, 2nd Artillery	Captured	Died of Rubeola, 2/10/1865, Buried Woodlawn Cemetery, Elmira, NY, Grave No. 2093

NAME and RANK	PLACE & TYPE OF ENLISTMENT	AGE	RESIDENCE & OCCUPATION	REGIMENT OR BATTALION	RESULT OF BATTLE	REMARKS
Hall, Lewis Private	St. Johns, Hertford County, NC, 8/7/1864 Volunteer	17	Yadkinville, Yadkin County, NC	Co. C, 3rd Battalion, North Carolina Light Artillery	Captured	Died of Chronic Diarrhea, 3/7/1865, Buried Woodlawn Cemetery, Elmira, NY
Hall, Lewis D. Private	Fort Fisher, New Hanover County, NC, 9/20/1863	Unk	New Hanover County, NC	2nd Co. A, 36th Regiment North Carolina, 2nd Artillery	Captured	Died of Variola (smallpox), 3/19/1865, Buried Woodlawn Cemetery, Elmira, NY, 1960
Hall, Lorenzo Dow Private	Cumberland County, NC, 9/8/1863 Volunteer	45	Fayetteville, Cumberland County, NC	3rd Co. B, 36th Regiment North Carolina, 2nd Artillery	Captured	Oath Of Allegiance 7/7/1865
Hall, Malcom Private	Fort Fisher, New Hanover County, NC, 3/8/1863 Volunteer	39	Owensville, Sampson County, NC, Farmer	2nd Co. D, 36th Regiment North Carolina, 2nd Artillery	Captured	Oath Of Allegiance 7/11/1865
Hall, Maurice Private	Fort Fisher, New Hanover County, NC, 7/8/1862	Unk	Fayetteville, Cumberland County, NC	2nd Co. C, 36th Regiment North Carolina, 2nd Artillery	Captured	Oath Of Allegiance 6/12/1865
Hall, Stephen W. Private	Harrison Creek, Cumberland County, NC, 3/5/1862 Volunteer	23	Ellisville, Bladen County, NC, Farmer	2nd Co. C, 36th Regiment North Carolina, 2nd Artillery	Captured	Oath Of Allegiance 6/12/1865
Hall, Thomas H. Private	Fort Fisher, New Hanover County, NC, 8/20/1864	Unk	New Hanover County, NC	2nd Co. I, 36th Regiment North Carolina, 2nd Artillery	Captured	Died of Pneumonia, 2/16/1865, Buried Woodlawn Cemetery, Elmira, NY, Grave No. 2204

NAME and RANK	PLACE & TYPE OF ENLISTMENT	AGE	RESIDENCE & OCCUPATION	REGIMENT OR BATTALION	RESULT OF BATTLE	REMARKS
Hall, William D. Private	Clinton, Sampson County, NC, 2/24/1863 Volunteer	24	Red Plains, Yadkin County, NC, Farm Laborer	2nd Co. C, 36th Regiment North Carolina, 2nd Artillery	Captured	Oath Of Allegiance 7/7/1865
Hall, William J. Private	Fort Fisher, New Hanover County, NC, 5/8/1862 Volunteer	34	Ellisville, Bladen County, NC Turpentine	2nd Co. C, 36th Regiment North Carolina, 2nd Artillery	Captured	Oath Of Allegiance 6/12/1865
Hamer, C.H. Private	Bennettsville, SC, 10/20/1863	38	Unknown	Co. F, 21st South Carolina Volunteers	Captured	Died of Pneumonia 2/6/1865, Buried Woodlawn Cemetery, Elmira, NY, Grave No. 1919
Hamer, James C. Private	Bennettsville, Marlboro District, SC, 5/1/1864	36	Bennettsville, Marlboro District, SC, Farmer	Co. F, 21st South Carolina Volunteers	Captured	Died of Chronic Diarrhea, 3/2/1865, Buried Woodlawn Cemetery, Elmira, NY, Grave No. 2022
Hamlet, Nathaniel M. Musician	New Berne, Craven County, NC, 1/1/1862	20	Weldon, Halifax County, NC Farmer	Co. F, 36th Regiment North Carolina, 2nd Artillery	Captured	Exchanged On the James River, VA, 3/2/1865
Hammonds, Moses Private	Fort Caswell, Brunswick County, NC, 5/3/1862 Volunteer	27	Asheboro, Randolph County, NC Carpenter	Co. E, 36th Regiment North Carolina, 2nd Artillery	Captured	Oath Of Allegiance 6/23/1865
Hancock, Zumariah Private	Wilmington, New Hanover County, NC, 7/18/1863	Unk	High Point, Guilford County, NC	Co. K, 10th Reg. 1st North Carolina Artillery	Captured	Oath Of Allegiance 7/11/1865
Harrelson, Isham West Private	Old Brunswick Town, 4/16/1862, Mustered in at Fort St. Philip, NC, Volunteer	30	Lockwood Folly District, Brunswick County, NC, Cooper	3rd Co. G, 36th Regiment North Carolina, 2nd Artillery	Captured	Exchanged On the James River, VA, 3/2/1865

NAME and RANK	PLACE & TYPE OF ENLISTMENT	AGE	RESIDENCE & OCCUPATION	REGIMENT OR BATTALION	RESULT OF BATTLE	REMARKS
Harris, Edward Private	Old Brunswick Town, 4/16/1862, Mustered in at Fort St. Philip, NC Volunteer	40	Town Creek District, Brunswick County, NC Laborer	3rd Co. G, 36th Regiment North Carolina, 2nd Artillery	Wounded & Captured	Died of Pneumonia, 4/2/1865, Buried Woodlawn Cemetery, Elmira, NY, Grave No. 2585
Harris, Franklin H. Private	Darlington, SC, 1/20/1862	18	Charlotte, NC, Farmer	Co. H, 21st South Carolina Volunteers	Captured	Oath Of Allegiance 7/11/1865
Hart, Harris Private	Chatham County, NC, 3/26/1863 Volunteer	39	Chatham County, NC, Wood Cutter	3rd Co. G, 40th Regiment, 3rd Regiment, North Carolina Light Artillery	Captured	Exchanged Boulware's Wharf, James River, VA, 3/14/1865
Harvey, Robert James Sergeant	New Berne, Craven County, NC, 1/23/1862 Volunteer	49	New Berne, Craven County, NC, Turpentine Distillery	Co. F, 36th Regiment North Carolina, 2nd Artillery	Captured	Exchanged On the James River, VA, 3/2/1865
Haskins, William Private	Wayne County, NC, 10/11/1864	Unk	Wayne County, NC	Co. D, 40th Regiment, 3rd Regiment, North Carolina Light Artillery	Captured	Died of Chronic Diarrhea, 3/21/1865, Buried Woodlawn Cemetery, Elmira, NY, Grave No. 1529
Haste, Calvin A. Private	St. Johns, Hertford County, NC, 7/8/1862	30	Hertford County, NC, Farmer	Co. C, 3rd Battalion North Carolina Artillery	Captured	Died of Peritonitis, 2/14/1865, Buried Woodlawn Cemetery, Elmira, NY, Grave No. 2060
Hatcher, William H. Private	Chesterfield, SC, 12/31/1863	14	Bennettsville, Marlboro District, SC	Co. D, 21st South Carolina Volunteers	Captured	Died Of Pneumonia 6/29/1865, Buried Woodlawn Cemetery, Elmira, NY, Grave No. 2826

NAME and RANK	PLACE & TYPE OF ENLISTMENT	AGE	RESIDENCE & OCCUPATION	REGIMENT OR BATTALION	RESULT OF BATTLE	REMARKS
Hawkins, Major B. Private	Enfield, Halifax County, NC, 10/9/1861 Volunteer	19	Halifax County, NC	Co. F, 36th Regiment North Carolina, 2nd Artillery	Captured	Died of Pneumonia, 2/13/1865, Buried Woodlawn Cemetery, Elmira, NY, Grave No. 2046
Hays, Charles F. Private	Marion, SC, 4/20/1862	Unk	Unknown	Co. D, 25th South Carolina Volunteers	Captured	Died of Pneumonia, 3/20/1865, Buried Woodlawn Cemetery, Elmira, NY, Grave No. 1515
Hays, James N. Private	James Island, SC, 6/6/1863	33	Oak Grove, Marion, SC, Farmer	Co. D, 25th South Carolina Volunteers	Captured	Oath Of Allegiance 6/23/1865
Heady, Charles Private	Wilmington, New Hanover County, NC, 10/23/1861 Volunteer	30	Wilmington, New Hanover County, NC	2nd Co. D, 36th Regiment North Carolina, 2nd Artillery	Captured	Died of Rheumatism, 5/27/1865, Buried Woodlawn Cemetery, Elmira, NY, Grave No. 2914
Heckle, Andrew J. Private	James Island, SC 9/1/1862	Unk	Unknown	Co F, 25th Regiment South Carolina Volunteers	Captured	Died of Typhoid Fever, 2/9/1865, Buried Woodlawn Cemetery, Elmira, NY, Grave No. 1951

NAME and RANK	PLACE & TYPE OF ENLISTMENT	AGE	RESIDENCE & OCCUPATION	REGIMENT OR BATTALION	RESULT OF BATTLE	REMARKS
Hedgepath, John S. Private	Unknown	17	Tarboro, Edgecombe County, NC	Co. F, 36th Regiment North Carolina, 2nd Artillery	Captured	Died of Pneumonia, 2/10/1865, Buried Woodlawn Cemetery, Elmira, NY, Grave No. 1945
Herring, Benjamin Private	Fort Holmes, Brunswick, County, NC, 9/25/1864 Volunteer	38	Lumberton, Robeson County, NC, Farmer	3rd Co. G, 40th Regiment, 3rd Regiment, North Carolina Light Artillery	Captured	Died of Chronic Diarrhea, 5/22/1865, Buried Woodlawn Cemetery, Elmira, NY, Grave No. 2932
Herring, Benjamin F. Corporal	Red Banks, Robeson County, NC, 10/14/1861 Volunteer	15	Colvin's Creek, New Hanover County, NC	3rd Co. G, 40th Regiment, 3rd Regiment, North Carolina Light Artillery	Captured	Oath Of Allegiance 5/17/1865
Herring, James Private	Wayne County, NC, 7/14/1863 Volunteer	16	Sleepy Creek, Indian Springs District, Wayne County, NC,	3rd Co. G, 40th Regiment, 3rd Regiment, North Carolina Light Artillery	Captured	Died of Chronic Diarrhea, 4/21/1865, Buried Woodlawn Cemetery, Elmira, NY, Grave No. 1386
Hester, David D. Private	Elizabethtown, Bladen County, NC, 1/1/1864 Volunteer	18	Bladen County, NC	2nd Co. K, 40th Regiment, 3rd Regiment, North Carolina Light Artillery	Captured	Died of Pneumonia/Typhoid, 2/6/1865, Buried Woodlawn Cemetery, Elmira, NY, 1910

NAME and RANK	PLACE & TYPE OF ENLISTMENT	AGE	RESIDENCE & OCCUPATION	REGIMENT OR BATTALION	RESULT OF BATTLE	REMARKS
Hester, Jasper Private	Fort Holmes, Brunswick, County, NC, 6/8/1864	18	Elizabethtown, Bladen County, NC, Detached service at Fort Holmes, November 1864	2nd Co. K, 40th Regiment, 3rd Regiment, North Carolina Light Artillery	Captured	Died of Typhoid Fever, 2/28/1865, Buried Woodlawn Cemetery, Elmira, NY, Grave No. 2133
Hester, William B. Private	Elizabethtown, Bladen County, NC, 1/1/1864 Volunteer	18	Bladen County, NC	2nd Co. K, 40th Regiment, 3rd Regiment, North Carolina Light Artillery	Captured	Exchanged On the James River, VA, 3/2/1865
Hester, William J. Private	Elizabethtown, Bladen County, NC, 5/6/1862, Mustered in Fort St. Philip, Volunteer	19	Bladen County, NC, Farmer Sick at home for 60 days, July, 1864	2nd Co. K, 40th Regiment, 3rd Regiment, North Carolina Light Artillery	Captured	Died of Pneumonia, 3/29/1865, Buried Woodlawn Cemetery, Elmira, NY, Grave No. 2589
Hewitt, Dority W. Last name also spelled Hewett Private	Fort Campbell, Brunswick, County, NC, 10/26/63	17	Brunswick, County, NC, Extra duty at Quarter Master Dept.	3rd Co. G, 36th Regiment North Carolina, 2nd Artillery	Captured	Died of Pneumonia, 3/26/1865, Buried Woodlawn Cemetery, Elmira, NY, Grave No. 1680
Hewitt, Ephram Last name also spelled Hewett Private	Brunswick, County, NC, 5/4/64	19	Lockwood Folly District, Brunswick, County, NC Farmer	3rd Co. G, 36th Regiment North Carolina, 2nd Artillery	Captured	Exchanged On the James River, VA, 3/2/1865

NAME and RANK	PLACE & TYPE OF ENLISTMENT	AGE	RESIDENCE & OCCUPATION	REGIMENT OR BATTALION	RESULT OF BATTLE	REMARKS
Hewitt, Isaiah Last name also spelled Hewett Private	Fort Caswell, Brunswick, County, NC, 9/4/63 Volunteer	26	Piney Greene, Onslow County, NC, Farmer	3rd Co. G, 36th Regiment North Carolina, 2nd Artillery	Captured	Exchanged On the James River, VA, 2/20/1865
Hewitt, J. R. Private	Unknown	Unk	Unknown	3rd Co. B, 36th Regiment North Carolina, 2nd Artillery	Captured	Transferred to USA General Hospital 7/13/1865, Released 7/13/1865
Hickman, Stewart Corporal	Old Brunswick, NC, 4/16/62, Mustered in Fort St. Philip, Volunteer	24	Shallotte, Brunswick, County, NC, Laborer	3rd Co. G, 36th Regiment North Carolina, 2nd Artillery	Captured	Oath Of Allegiance taken at Elmira US Hospital 8/7/1865
Hickman, William B. Private	Unknown	17	Whiteville, Columbus County, NC Farmer	Co. E, 36th Regiment North Carolina, 2nd Artillery	Captured	Died of Chronic Diarrhea, 2/28/1865, Buried Woodlawn Cemetery, Elmira, NY, Grave No. 2117
Hicks, George T. Private	Fort Johnston, Brunswick, County, NC, 6/25/63 Volunteer	18	North Western District, Wake County, NC	3rd Co. G, 40th Regiment North Carolina, 2nd Artillery	Captured	Died of Pneumonia, 3/31/1865, Buried Woodlawn Cemetery, Elmira, NY, Grave No. 2599
Hildreth, Thomas Private	Fort Branch, Brunswick, County, NC, 8/20/1863 Volunteer	43	Anson County, NC	3rd Co. G, 40th Regiment, 3rd Regiment, North Carolina Light Artillery	Captured	Died of Pneumonia, 3/2/1865, Buried Woodlawn Cemetery, Elmira, NY, Grave No. 2007

NAME and RANK	PLACE & TYPE OF ENLISTMENT	AGE	RESIDENCE & OCCUPATION	REGIMENT OR BATTALION	RESULT OF BATTLE	REMARKS
Hill, Elias Private	Darlington, SC, 5/12/1862	43	York County, SC, Teamster	Co. B, 21st South Carolina Volunteers	Captured	Died Of Chronic Diarrhea 5/2/1865, Buried Woodlawn Cemetery, Elmira, NY, Grave No. 2744
Hill, Webb H. Private	Enfield, Wayne County, NC, 10/9/1861, Volunteer	21	Goldsboro, Wayne County, NC, Detailed as blacksmith	Co. F, 36th Regiment North Carolina, 2nd Artillery	Captured	Oath Of Allegiance 5/29/1865,
Hinson, Eli Private	Fort Pender, Brunswick, County, NC, 12/8/1863, Volunteer	17	Fair Bluff, Columbus County, NC	Co. E, 36th Regiment North Carolina, 2nd Artillery	Captured	Oath Of Allegiance 7/19/1865,
Hinson, Elias A. Corporal	Wilmington, New Hanover County, NC, 3/4/1862 Volunteer	21	Wilmington, New Hanover County, NC	Co. E, 36th Regiment North Carolina, 2nd Artillery	Captured	Died of Pneumonia, 3/13/1865, Buried Woodlawn Cemetery, Elmira, NY, Grave No. 2431
Hinson, Jimpsey Private	New Hanover County, NC, 4/28/1864	Unk	New Hanover County, NC	Co. E, 36th Regiment North Carolina, 2nd Artillery	Captured	Died of Chronic Diarrhea, 3/7/1865, Buried Woodlawn Cemetery, Elmira, NY, Grave No. 2401
Hinson, John Private	Camp Harllee, SC, 1/1/1862	19	Bennettsville, Marlboro District, SC, Clerk	Co. A, 21st South Carolina Volunteers	Captured	Died of Pneumonia, 5/18/1865, Buried Woodlawn Cemetery, Elmira, NY, Grave No. 2947

NAME and RANK	PLACE & TYPE OF ENLISTMENT	AGE	RESIDENCE & OCCUPATION	REGIMENT OR BATTALION	RESULT OF BATTLE	REMARKS
Hinson, Joshua P. Private	Fort Anderson, Brunswick, County, NC, 7/29/1863 Volunteer	18	Brunswick, County, NC	Co. E, 36th Regiment North Carolina, 2nd Artillery	Captured	Died of Chronic Diarrhea, 4/7/1865, Buried Woodlawn Cemetery, Elmira, NY, Grave No. 2636
Hinson, Richard D. Private	Goldsboro, Wayne County, NC, 4/28/1864	64	Goldsboro, Wayne County, NC,	Co. F, 10th Reg. 1st North Carolina Artillery	Captured	Oath Of Allegiance 5/29/1865
Hinson, William H. Private	Chatham County, NC, 3/26/1863, Volunteer	36	Graham, Alamance County, NC	3rd Co. G, 40th Regiment North Carolina, 3rd North Carolina Artillery	Captured	Oath Of Allegiance 6/12/1865
Hinton, Bernard A. Private	Elizabethtown, Bladen County, NC, 10/19/1861	21	Bladen County, NC	2nd Co. I, 36th Regiment North Carolina, 2nd Artillery	Captured	Exchanged On the James River, VA, 3/2/1865
Hirschler, Isaac Private	Wilmington, New Hanover County, NC, 7/7/1862, Volunteer	22	Wilmington, New Hanover County, NC	Co. D, 1st Battalion, North Carolina Heavy Artillery	Captured	Oath Of Allegiance 5/13/1865
Hobbs, George A. Corporal	Williamston, Martin County, NC, 3/31/1862	Unk	Hamilton, Martin County, NC	Co. K, 10th Reg. 1st North Carolina Artillery	Captured	Died of Phthisis, 3/21/1865, Buried Woodlawn Cemetery, Elmira, NY, Grave No. 1546
Hockaday, Bennett Private	Fayetteville, Cumberland County, NC, 2/26/1862, Volunteer	26	Rockfish, Hoke County, NC, Detached service at Battery Gatlin	2nd Co. A, 36th Regiment North Carolina, 2nd Artillery	Captured	Died of Variola (smallpox), 3/5/1865, Buried Woodlawn Cemetery, Elmira, NY, Grave No. 1966

NAME and RANK	PLACE & TYPE OF ENLISTMENT	AGE	RESIDENCE & OCCUPATION	REGIMENT OR BATTALION	RESULT OF BATTLE	REMARKS
Hodge, John P. Private	Whippy Swamp, SC, 7/15/1861	18	Gillisonville, St. Peter's Parrish, Beaufort District, SC, Farmer	Co. D, 11th South Carolina	Captured	Oath Of Allegiance 8/7/1865
Hodge, James B. Private	Camp Harlee, Georgetown, SC, 1/1/1862	22	Brewington, Clarendon District, SC, Farmer	Co. I, 25th South Carolina Volunteers	Captured	Died Of Chronic Diarrhea 4/10/1865, Buried Woodlawn Cemetery, Elmira, NY, Grave No. 2606
Hodge, Lewis Private	Whippy Swamp, SC, 7/15/1861	22	St. Peters Parrish Beaufort District, SC,	Co. D, 11th South Carolina	Captured	Oath Of Allegiance 7/13/1865
Hodge, Samuel N. Private	Camp Harlee, Georgetown, SC, 1/1/1862	21	Clarendon District, SC,	Co. I, 25th South Carolina Volunteers	Captured	Died Of Chronic Diarrhea 2/11/1865, Buried Woodlawn Cemetery, Elmira, NY, Grave No. 2175
Hodges, Elihue S. Private	Camp Hardee, Georgetown, SC, 1/1/1862	18	Sumter District, SC, Farmer	Co. I, 25th South Carolina Volunteers	Captured	Exchanged 2/20/1865, Died Of Unknown Disease at Wayside Hospital No. 9, Richmond, VA, 3/4/1865, Buried Hollywood Cemetery, Richmond, VA

NAME and RANK	PLACE & TYPE OF ENLISTMENT	AGE	RESIDENCE & OCCUPATION	REGIMENT OR BATTALION	RESULT OF BATTLE	REMARKS
Hodges, John H. Private	Robeson County, NC, 9/1/1863 Volunteer	44	Pleasant Exchange, NC	3rd Co. B, 36th Regiment North Carolina, 2nd Artillery	Captured	Exchanged Boulware's Wharf, James River, VA, 3/14/1865 Died of Chronic Diarrhea, 3/27/1865, C.S. Way Hospital #2, Greensboro, NC
Hodges, William H. Sergeant	Georgetown, SC, 1/1/1862	21	Manning, Clarendon District, SC, Farmer	Co. K, 21st South Carolina Volunteers	Captured	Died Of Chronic Diarrhea 3/7/1865, Buried Woodlawn Cemetery, Elmira, NY, Grave No. 2392
Holden, Nathan E. Private	Brunswick, County, NC, 9/25/1862	20	Brunswick, County, NC	3rd Co. G, 36th Regiment North Carolina, 2nd Artillery	Captured	Died of Chronic Diarrhea, 2/28/1865, Buried Woodlawn Cemetery, Elmira, NY, Grave No. 2130
Holden, Richard A. Private	Fort Fisher, NC, 2/28/1864, Volunteer	17	Brunswick County, NC	3rd Co. G, 36th Regiment North Carolina, 2nd Artillery	Wounded & Captured	Oath Of Allegiance 7/3/1865
Holden, Richard W., Jr. Private	Fort Campbell, Brunswick, County, NC, 10/9/1863, Volunteer	18	Brunswick, County, NC	3rd Co. G, 36th Regiment North Carolina, 2nd Artillery	Captured	Exchanged 2/20/1865, Died of Variola (smallpox), 3/12/1865, Howard Grove Hospital, Richmond, VA

NAME and RANK	PLACE & TYPE OF ENLISTMENT	AGE	RESIDENCE & OCCUPATION	REGIMENT OR BATTALION	RESULT OF BATTLE	REMARKS
Holland, Matthew Private	Clinton, Sampson County, NC, 10/9/1863, Volunteer	37	Clinton, Sampson County, NC, Farmer	2nd Co. C, 36th Regiment North Carolina, 2nd Artillery	Captured	Died of Chronic Diarrhea, 4/7/1865, Buried Woodlawn Cemetery, Elmira, NY, Grave No. 2657
Holmes, William E. Corporal	Charleston, SC5/9/1862	27	Spartanburg, SC	Co. A, 25th South Carolina Volunteers	Captured	Oath Of Allegiance 6/19/1865
Holstein, Joseph A. Private	James Island, SC, 4/21/1863	17	Ridge, Edgefield District, SC, Farmer	Co. G, 21st South Carolina Volunteers	Captured	Died of Chronic Diarrhea, 3/7/1865, Buried Woodlawn Cemetery, Elmira, NY, Grave No. 2381
Honeycutt, Hillery H. Private	Wilmington, New Hanover County, NC, 7/23/1863, Volunteer	42	Sampson County, NC	3rd Co. G, 40th Regiment, 3rd Regiment, North Carolina Light Artillery	Captured	Exchanged On the James River, VA, 3/2/1865
Hook, Samuel P. Private	Coles Island, SC, 4/11/1862	21	Saluda Town, Columbia, Richland County, SC	Co. D, 25th South Carolina Volunteers	Captured	Died of Pneumonia, 3/8/1865, Buried Woodlawn Cemetery, Elmira, NY, Grave No. 2374
Horn, Little Berry Private	Wilmington, New Hanover County, NC, 3/5/1862, Volunteer	33	Columbus County, NC	Co. E, 36th Regiment North Carolina, 2nd Artillery	Captured	Exchanged On the James River, VA, 2/20/1865
Horn, W.W. Private	Gourdins Dept., SC, 5/11/1862	38	Kingston, SC	Co. K, 25th South Carolina Volunteers	Captured	Oath Of Allegiance 7/11/1865

NAME and RANK	PLACE & TYPE OF ENLISTMENT	AGE	RESIDENCE & OCCUPATION	REGIMENT OR BATTALION	RESULT OF BATTLE	REMARKS
Horne, Daniel W. Private	Fort Fisher, New Hanover County, NC, 5/7/1862, Volunteer	31	New Hanover County, NC	2nd Co. C, 36th Regiment North Carolina, 2nd Artillery	Captured	Died of Variola (smallpox), 3/26/1865, Buried Woodlawn Cemetery, Elmira, NY, Grave No. 2470
Horne, William J. Private	Fort Fisher, New Hanover County, NC, 7/26/1863, Volunteer	18	Downingsville, Bladen County, NC, Farmer	2nd Co. C, 36th Regiment North Carolina, 2nd Artillery	Captured	Died of Chronic Diarrhea, 3/7/1865, Buried Woodlawn Cemetery, Elmira, NY, 2399
Horton, George P. Private	Fort Holmes, NC, 6/29/1864	24	Oak Spring, Flint Hill District, Rutherford County, N C, Farmer	3rd Co. G, 40th Regiment, 3rd Regiment, North Carolina Light Artillery	Captured	Oath Of Allegiance 6/12/1865
House, John H. Private	Brunswick, County, NC, 9/15/1863, Volunteer	18	Halifax County, NC,	Co. F, 36th Regiment North Carolina, 2nd Artillery	Captured	Oath Of Allegiance 7/7/1865
Howard, William Private	Duplin County, NC, 9/1/1864	18	Magnolia, Duplin County, NC, Farmer	Co. D, 1st Battalion, North Carolina Heavy Artillery	Captured	Died of Chronic Diarrhea, 5/1/1865, Buried Woodlawn Cemetery, Elmira, NY, Grave No. 2736
Howell, Curtis D. Private	Goldsboro, Wayne County, NC, 9/20/1862	18	Goldsboro, Wayne County, NC, Farmer	Co. F, 10th Reg. 1st North Carolina Artillery	Captured	Oath Of Allegiance 5/29/1865

NAME and RANK	PLACE & TYPE OF ENLISTMENT	AGE	RESIDENCE & OCCUPATION	REGIMENT OR BATTALION	RESULT OF BATTLE	REMARKS
Howell, Levi D. Private	Goldsboro, Wayne County, NC, 3/8/1864	43	Goldsboro, Fork District, Wayne County, NC	Co. F, 10th Reg. 1st North Carolina Artillery	Captured	Died of Chronic Diarrhea, 5/22/1865, Buried Woodlawn Cemetery, Elmira, NY, Grave No. 2933
Howell, Richard M. Private	Beaufort, Carteret County, 6/28/1861	27	Wayne County, NC, Farmer	Co. F, 10th Reg. 1st North Carolina Artillery	Wounded & Captured	Exchanged On the James River, VA, 2/20/1865
Howell, Ralph Private	Wilmington, New Hanover County, 3/3/1862	22	Fayetteville, Cumberland County, NC	2nd Co. D, 36th Regiment North Carolina, 2nd Artillery	Captured	Oath Of Allegiance 7/7/1865
Hubbard, John B. Private	Unknown	16	Martin's Creek, Pickens District, SC	Co. H, 25th South Carolina Volunteers	Captured	Oath Of Allegiance 7/19/1865
Hudson, Thomas Private	Fort Johnson, SC, 9/8/1863	27	Darlington District, SC, Farmer	Co. K, 21st South Carolina Volunteers	Captured	Oath Of Allegiance 6/30/1865
Huffman, Andrew Private	Coles Island, SC, 4/11/1862	24	St. Matthews, Orangeburg District, SC	Co. F, 25th South Carolina Volunteers	Captured	Died of Chronic Diarrhea, 4/6/1865, Buried Woodlawn Cemetery, Elmira, NY, Grave No. 2641
Huffman, D.J. Private	Coles Island, SC, 4/11/1862	38	Louisville, SC	Co. F, 25th South Carolina Volunteers	Captured	Oath Of Allegiance 7/11/1865

NAME and RANK	PLACE & TYPE OF ENLISTMENT	AGE	RESIDENCE & OCCUPATION	REGIMENT OR BATTALION	RESULT OF BATTLE	REMARKS
Huffman, Milton Last name also spelled Huffham Private	Camp Wyatt, New Hanover County, NC, 4/14/1864	18	New Hanover County, NC	2nd Co. D, 36th Regiment North Carolina, 2nd Artillery	Captured	Exchanged 3/14/1865, Recaptured in Jackson Hospital, Richmond, Va, 4/3/1865, Released 6/28/1865
Huggins, Christopher Private	Marion Dist., SC, 2/21/1862	24	Mullins Depot, SC	Co. K, 21st South Carolina Volunteers	Captured	Oath Of Allegiance 6/23/1865
Hunter, William W. First Sergeant	Lenoir County, NC, 10/16/1861	19	Kinston, Lenoir County, NC	3rd Co. G, 40th Regiment, 3rd Regiment, North Carolina Artillery	Captured	Oath Of Allegiance 6/12/1865
Huntley, Elijah D. Corporal	Fort Branch, Brunswick, County, NC, 7/20/1863	30	Wadesboro, Anson County, NC Farmer	3rd Co. G, 40th Regiment, 3rd Regiment, North Carolina Artillery	Captured	Exchanged Boulware's Wharf, James River, VA, 3/14/1865
Hux, Benjamin G. Private	Fort Caswell, Brunswick, County, NC, 6/18/1863	18	Western District, Halifax County, NC, Farmer	Co. F, 36th Regiment, North Carolina, 2nd Artillery	Captured	Oath Of Allegiance 7/26/1865
Hux, Gardner H. Private	Halifax County, NC, 10/25/1864	15	Western District, Halifax County, NC, Farmer	Co. F, 36th Regiment, North Carolina, 2nd Artillery	Captured	Oath Of Allegiance 6/23/1865

NAME and RANK	PLACE OF ENLISTMENT	AGE	RESIDENCE & OCCUPATION	REGIMENT or BATTALION	RESULT OF BATTLE	REMARKS
Inabet, Andrew J. Private	Coles Island, SC, 4/11/1862	41	St. Matthews, Orangeburg, SC	Co. G, 25th South Carolina Volunteers	Captured	Oath of Allegiance 6/23/1865

NAME and RANK	PLACE OF ENLISTMENT	AGE	RESIDENCE & OCCUPATION	REGIMENT or BATTALION	RESULT OF BATTLE	REMARKS
Inabet, Charles G. Private	Coles Island, SC, 4/11/1862	Unk	Orangeburg, SC	Co. G, 25th South Carolina Volunteers	Captured	Oath of Allegiance 7/7/1865
Irby, William Private	Fort Caswell, Brunswick County, NC, 2/2/1863	18	Enfield, Halifax County, NC	Co. F, 36th Regiment North Carolina, 2nd Artillery	Captured	Oath of Allegiance 6/12/1865, Enlisted As a Substitute
Irick, Elliott H. Private	Secessionville, SC, 5/1/1862	32	St. Matthews, Orangeburg, SC	Co. G, 25th South Carolina Volunteers	Captured	Exchanged On the James River, VA, 2/20/1865
Irick, Laban A. Private	Coles Island, SC, 4/15/1862	Unk	Orangeburg, SC	Co. G, 25th South Carolina Volunteers	Captured	Oath of Allegiance 7/11/1865
Ivey, John A. Private	Fort Fisher, New Hanover County, NC, 12/21/1861	46	New Hanover County, NC	2nd Co. I, 36th Regiment North Carolina, 2nd Artillery	Captured	Exchanged 3/2/1865, Dispatch Bearer in Fort Fisher Telegraph Office
Izlar, Adolphus M. Private	Coles Island, SC, 4/11/1862	Unk	Unknown	Co. G, 25th South Carolina Volunteers	Captured	Exchanged On the James River, VA, 3/14/1865
Izlar, Benjamin P. First Sergeant	Coles Island, SC, 4/11/1862	25	Orangeburg, SC, Teacher	Co. G, 25th South Carolina Volunteers	Captured	Oath of Allegiance 6/14/1865

NAME and RANK	PLACE & TYPE OF ENLISTMENT	AGE	RESIDENCE & OCCUPATION	REGIMENT OR BATTALION	RESULT OF BATTLE	REMARKS
Jackson, Alfred Webb Private	Fort Fisher, New Hanover County, NC, 10/25/1863	37	Fayetteville, Cumberland County, NC, Farmer	Co. E, 36th Regiment North Carolina, 2nd Artillery	Captured	Exchanged 3/2/1865 Died of Chronic Diarrhea 3/24/1865 at Way Hospital #1, Weldon, NC

NAME and RANK	PLACE & TYPE OF ENLISTMENT	AGE	RESIDENCE & OCCUPATION	REGIMENT OR BATTALION	RESULT OF BATTLE	REMARKS
Jackson, Allen M. Private	Fort Fisher, New Hanover County, NC, 5/6/1863	42	Fayetteville, Cumberland County, NC, Farmer	Co. E, 36th Regiment North Carolina, 2nd Artillery	Captured	Oath of Allegiance 7/3/1865
Jackson, Blackman Private	Sampson County, NC, 2/18/1863	37	Dismal District, Sampson County, NC, Farm Laborer	2nd Co. A, 36th Regiment North Carolina, 2nd Artillery	Captured	Exchanged 3/14/1865, Boulware's Wharf, James River, VA
Jackson, Nathan H. Private	Sampson County, NC, 2/18/1863	38	Mingo District, Sampson County, NC,	2nd Co. A, 36th Regiment North Carolina, 2nd Artillery	Captured	Died of Pneumonia, 2/11/1865, Buried Woodlawn Cemetery, Elmira, NY, Grave No. 2094
Jacobs, Snowden Private	Bennettsville, Marlboro District, SC, 12/25/1861	24	Sidehill, SC	Co. F, 21st South Carolina Volunteers	Captured	Oath Of Allegiance 7/7/1865
James, H.V. Private	James Island, SC, 6/23/1863	Unk	Madisonville, Fl	Co. H, 25th South Carolina Volunteers	Captured	Oath of Allegiance 7/19/1865
Jeffords, Joseph B. Private	Pee Dee, SC, 2/20/1862	26	Timmonsville, Darlington District, SC, Carpenter	Co. K, 21st South Carolina Volunteers	Captured	Oath Of Allegiance 7/3/1865
Jenkins, Samuel Private	Fort Branch, Brunswick County, NC, 8/19/1863	41	Ragland District, Granville County, NC, Farmer	3rd Co. G, 40th Regiment North Carolina Artillery	Captured	Oath of Allegiance 6/23/1865
Johnson, Amos Private	Robeson County, NC, 1/25/1862	28	Fayetteville, Cumberland County, NC, Cooper	3rd Co. B, 36th Regiment North Carolina, 2nd Artillery	Captured	Died of Chronic Diarrhea 4/16/1865, Buried Woodlawn Cemetery, Elmira, NY, Grave No. 2721
Johnson, James Private	Fort Fisher, New Hanover County, NC, 5/16/1863	18	New Hanover County, NC	2nd Co. C, 36th Regiment North Carolina, 2nd Artillery	Captured	Exchanged On the James River, VA, 2/20/1865

NAME and RANK	PLACE & TYPE OF ENLISTMENT	AGE	RESIDENCE & OCCUPATION	REGIMENT OR BATTALION	RESULT OF BATTLE	REMARKS
Johnson, James Henry Sergeant	Goldsboro, Wayne County, NC, 7/21/1861, Mustered in at Beaufort, NC	22	Goldsboro, Wayne County, NC,	Co. F, 10th Regiment North Carolina Artillery	Captured	Oath of Allegiance 7/13/1865
Johnson, John Private	Goldsboro, NC, 7/9/1861, Mustered in at Beaufort, NC	45	Goldsboro, Wayne County, NC,	Co. F, 10th Regiment North Carolina Artillery	Captured	Oath of Allegiance 7/11/1865
Johnson, John A. Private	Fort Fisher, NC, 1/6/1863, New Hanover County, NC	18	Summerville, Harnett County, NC, Farmer	2nd Co. C, 36th Regiment North Carolina, 2nd Artillery	Captured	Died from Dysentery, 2/23/1865, Buried Woodlawn Cemetery, Elmira, Grave No. 2257
Johnson, John F. Private	Marion City Hall, SC, 4/20/1862	16	Unknown	Co. D, 25th South Carolina Volunteers	Captured	Exchanged On the James River, VA, 2/20/1865
Johnson, John J. Private	Camp Harlee, Georgetown, SC, 1/1/1862	38	Unknown	Co. D, 25th South Carolina Volunteers	Captured	Died from Remittent Fever, 2/16/1865, Buried Woodlawn Cemetery, Elmira, NY, Grave No. 2210
Johnson, Larry Private	Wayne County, NC, 7/8/1861, Mustered in at Beaufort, NC	23	Goldsboro, Wayne County, NC, Farmer	Co. F, 10th Regiment North Carolina Artillery	Captured	Died from Pneumonia, 2/26/1865, Buried Woodlawn Cemetery, Elmira, NY, Grave No. 2158
Johnson, M.P. Private	James Island, SC, 8/1/1863	Unk	Unknown	Co I, 25th Regiment South Carolina Volunteers	Captured	Died of Variola (smallpox), 3/23/1865, Buried Woodlawn Cemetery, Elmira, NY, Grave No. 2443

NAME and RANK	PLACE & TYPE OF ENLISTMENT	AGE	RESIDENCE & OCCUPATION	REGIMENT OR BATTALION	RESULT OF BATTLE	REMARKS
Johnson, Nathan Thomas Private	Brunswick County, NC, 8/28/1863	Unk	Wayne County, NC	Co. F, 10th Regiment North Carolina Artillery	Captured	Oath of Allegiance 7/11/1865
Johnson, Richard M. Private	Fayetteville, Cumberland County, NC, 5/12/1862	18	Hunting Creek, Wilkes County, NC, Farmer	2nd Co. C, 36th Regiment North Carolina, 2nd Artillery	Captured	Died from Pneumonia, 2/20/1865, Buried Woodlawn Cemetery, Elmira, NY, 2332
Johnson, William F. Private	Wilmington, New Hanover County, NC, 10/28/1861	27	Wilmington, New Hanover County, NC,	Co. E, 36th Regiment North Carolina, 2nd Artillery	Captured	Exchanged 3/2/1865, Died from Chronic Diarrhea Moore Hospital, Richmond VA 3/9/1865
Jones, Bartemus P. Ordinance Sergeant	Beaufort County, NC, 9/30/1861, Mustered in near Washington, NC	33	North Creek, Beaufort County, NC, Laborer	Co. B, 40th Regiment North Carolina, 3rd Artillery Division	Captured	Died of Variola (smallpox), 4/1/1865, Buried Woodlawn Cemetery, Elmira, NY, Grave No. 2583
Jones, D.H. Sergeant	Charleston, SC, 7/2/1862	20	Charleston, SC	Co A, 25th Regiment South Carolina Volunteers	Captured	Oath of Allegiance 6/19/1865
Jones, Daniel S. Private	New Hanover County, NC, 6/17/1863	16	South Division, Guilford County, NC	Co. K, 10th Regiment, North Carolina Artillery	Captured	Oath of Allegiance 6/23/1865
Jones, David Britton Private	Washington County, NC, 8/21/1864	Unk	Rocky Mount, Edgecombe County, NC	Co. D, 40th Regiment North Carolina Artillery	Captured	Oath of Allegiance 7/7/1865
Jones, Franklin Private	Wayne County, Transferred From N.C. Local Defense Troops 8/17/1864	Unk	Goldsboro, Wayne County, NC,	Co. D, 40th Regiment North Carolina Artillery	Captured	Oath of Allegiance 5/29/1865

NAME and RANK	PLACE & TYPE OF ENLISTMENT	AGE	RESIDENCE & OCCUPATION	REGIMENT OR BATTALION	RESULT OF BATTLE	REMARKS
Jones, J.A. Private	Marion, SC, 1/23/1864	46	Floydsville, Marion, SC,	Co. L, 21st South Carolina Volunteers	Captured	Died of Chronic Diarrhea, 2/26/1865, Buried Woodlawn Cemetery, Elmira, NY, Grave No. 2122
Jones, James E. Private	Edgecombe County, NC, 3/23/1864	18	Rocky Mount, Edgecombe County, NC	Co. D, 40th Regiment North Carolina Artillery	Captured	Oath of Allegiance 6/21/1865
Jones, P.D. Private	Unknown	Unk	Unknown	Co. D, 40th Regiment North Carolina Artillery	Captured	Oath of Allegiance 7/7/1865
Jordan, Kenion Private	Beaufort, Carteret County, NC, 7/29/1861	23	Wayne County, NC, Farmer	Co. F, 10th Regiment North Carolina Artillery	Captured	Died of Chronic Diarrhea, 3/10/1865, Buried Woodlawn Cemetery, Elmira, NY, Grave No. 1864
Jordan, Wilson Private	Newland, Avery County, NC, 3/26/1862	58	Morrisville, Wake County, NC, Farmer	Co. C, 3rd Battalion North Carolina Artillery	Captured	Exchanged 3/14/1865, Boulware's Wharf, James River, VA
Joyner, James H. Last name also spelled Joiner Private	Fort St. Philip, NC, Brunswick County, NC, 5/16/1862, Volunteer	34	Unknown	3rd Co. G, 36th Regiment North Carolina, 2nd Artillery	Wounded & Captured	Exchanged 2/20/1865, Died of Unknown Disease at Pettigrew Hospital, Raleigh, NC, 3/20/1865
Joyner, Samuel Sergeant	Whiteville, Columbus County, NC, 3/1/1862, Mustered in at Wilmington, NC	43	Whiteville, Columbus County, NC, Merchant	Co. E, 36th Regiment North Carolina, 2nd Artillery	Captured	Died of Gangrene of Feet, 2/28/1865, Buried Woodlawn Cemetery, Elmira, NY, Grave No. 2148

NAME and RANK	PLACE & TYPE OF ENLISTMENT	AGE	RESIDENCE & OCCUPATION	REGIMENT OR BATTALION	RESULT OF BATTLE	REMARKS
Judge, John J. Sergeant	Enfield, NC, Halifax County, NC, 10/9/1861	20	Halifax County, NC	Co. F, 36th Regiment North Carolina, 2nd Artillery	Captured	Exchanged 3/19/1865, Boulware's Wharf, James River, VA
Junes, S.N. Private	Battery Island, SC, 4/12/1862	17	Gourdine Station, SC	Co C, 25th Regiment South Carolina Volunteers	Captured	Oath of Allegiance 7/13/1865
Justice, Benjamin H. Musician	Conscript 4/4/1863	25	New Hanover County, NC, Sail Maker	3rd Co. G, 36th Regiment North Carolina, 2nd Artillery	Captured	Oath of Allegiance 5/15/1865

NAME and RANK	PLACE & TYPE OF ENLISTMENT	AGE	RESIDENCE & OCCUPATION	REGIMENT OR BATTALION	RESULT OF BATTLE	REMARKS
Keith, Duncan Private	Wilmington, New Hanover County, NC, 4/24/1863	Unk	Fayetteville, Cumberland County, NC	Co. F, 10th Regiment North Carolina, 1st North Carolina Artillery	Captured	Oath of Allegiance 6/12/1865
Kelley, James Private	Unknown	39	Camden, Kershaw County, SC, Overseer	Co. B, 25th South Carolina Volunteers	Captured	Died Of Disease 2/6/1865, Buried Woodlawn Cemetery, Elmira, NY, Grave No. 1912
Kelley, John Private	Anderson, SC, 5/1/1862	37	Greenville County, SC, Farmer	Co. H, 25th South Carolina Volunteers	Captured	Died Of Variola (smallpox) 2/28/1865, Buried Woodlawn Cemetery, Elmira, NY, Grave No. 2112
Kelley, John M. Private	Charleston, SC, 5/28/1862	24	Charleston, SC,	Co. H, 25th South Carolina Volunteers	Captured	Died of Pneumonia, 2/13/1865, Buried Woodlawn Cemetery, Elmira, NY, Grave No. 2067

NAME and RANK	PLACE & TYPE OF ENLISTMENT	AGE	RESIDENCE & OCCUPATION	REGIMENT OR BATTALION	RESULT OF BATTLE	REMARKS
Kelley, Simon Private	Darlington, SC, 3/15/1864	18	Bishopville, Sumter County, SC	Co. G, 21st South Carolina Volunteers	Captured	Died Of Pneumonia 2/16/1865, Buried Woodlawn Cemetery, Elmira, NY, Grave No. 2202
Kelly, Henry Private	Unknown	16	Darlington District, SC	Co. G, 21st South Carolina Volunteers	Captured	Oath Of Allegiance 6/14/1865
Kelly, James A. Private	Darlington, SC, 1/1/1862	18	Darlington District, SC	Co. B, 21st South Carolina Volunteers	Captured	Died Of Pneumonia 2/6/1865, Buried Woodlawn Cemetery, Elmira, NY
Kelly, Thomas Private	Darlington, SC, 5/1/1862	38	Darlington District, SC, Farmer,	Co. G, 21st South Carolina Volunteers	Captured	Oath of Allegiance 7/3/1865
Kennedy, Levi B. Private	Camp Holmes, NC, 4/15/1864	20	Kinston District, Lenoir County, NC, Farmer	Co. K, 10th Regiment North Carolina, 1st Artillery	Captured	Died of Chronic Diarrhea 2/6/1865, Buried Woodlawn Cemetery, Elmira, NY, 1893
Kennedy, William J. Last name also spelled Canaday Private	Fort Fisher, New Hanover County, NC, 3/15/1863	39	Fayetteville, Cumberland County, NC	2nd Co. C, 36th Regiment, North Carolina, 2nd Artillery	Captured	Oath of Allegiance 6/12/1865
King, Barnabus S. Private	Wilmington, New Hanover County, NC, 3/30/1863	46	Johnston County, NC	Co. F, 10th Regiment North Carolina, 1st Artillery	Captured	Died of Chronic Diarrhea 2/24/1865, Buried Woodlawn Cemetery, Elmira, NY, Grave No. 2252

NAME and RANK	PLACE & TYPE OF ENLISTMENT	AGE	RESIDENCE & OCCUPATION	REGIMENT OR BATTALION	RESULT OF BATTLE	REMARKS
King, George B. Private	Elizabethtown, Bladen County, NC, 5/6/1862, Mustered in at Fort St. Philip	18	Bladenboro, Bladen County NC Farmer	2nd Co. K, 40th Regiment North Carolina, 3rd Artillery	Captured	Oath of Allegiance 6/21/1865
King, I.P.Z. Sergeant	Darlington, SC, 3/15/1863	Unk	Charlotte, NC	Co. B, 21st South Carolina Volunteers	Captured	Oath of Allegiance 7/11/1865
King, James Private	Fort St. Philip, NC, 8/2/1862	31	West Brook, Bladen County, NC,,	3rd Co. G, 36th Regiment, North Carolina, 2nd Artillery	Captured	Died of variola (smallpox) 3/2/1865, Buried Woodlawn Cemetery, Elmira, NY, Grave No. 2115
King, T.P. Private	Darlington, SC, 2/20/1862	18	Charlotte, NC	Co. B, 21st South Carolina Volunteers	Captured	Oath of Allegiance 7/11/1865
King, W. Private	Unknown	Unk	Unknown	Co. E, 25th South Carolina Volunteers	Captured	Died Of Disease 6/3/1865, Buried Woodlawn Cemetery, Elmira, NY, Grave No. 2818
King, Wesley Private	James Island, SC, 12/9/1863	35	Darlington District, SC	Co. H, 21st South Carolina Volunteers	Captured	Died Of Chronic Diarrhea 6/23/1865, Buried Woodlawn Cemetery, Elmira, NY
Kingman, John W. Private	Charleston, SC, 2/18/1862	30	Charleston, SC, Clerk	Co A, 25th Regiment South Carolina Volunteers	Captured	Exchanged On the James River, VA, 3/14/1865
Kinlaw, Anderson W. Private	Fort Holmes, Brunswick County, NC, 11/20/1864	Unk	Brunswick County, NC, Farmer	2nd Co. K, 40th Regiment North Carolina, 3rd N.C. Artillery	Captured	Exchanged On the James River, VA, 2/20/1865

NAME and RANK	PLACE & TYPE OF ENLISTMENT	AGE	RESIDENCE & OCCUPATION	REGIMENT OR BATTALION	RESULT OF BATTLE	REMARKS
Kinlaw, Benjamin Corporal	Elizabethtown, Bladen County, NC, Mustered in at Fort St. Philip, Brunswick County, NC, 5/6/1862, Volunteer	27	Farmer & Turpentine Distiller Prospect Hall, Bladen County NC,	2nd Co. K, 40th Regiment North Carolina, 3rd N.C. Artillery	Captured	Transferred For Exchange 2/20/1865. Died of Chronic Diarrhea 4/16/1865, Buried Woodlawn Cemetery, Elmira, NY, Grave No. 2720
Kinlaw, Neill Private	Lumberton, Robeson County, NC, 8/18/1863	38	Farmer, Lumberton, Robeson County, NC	2nd Co. K, 40th Regiment North Carolina, 3rd Artillery	Captured	Died of Chronic Diarrhea 2/20/1865, Buried Woodlawn Cemetery, Elmira, NY, Grave No. 2334
Kirby, Dixon Private	Camp Holmes, NC, 3/29/1864	Unk	Wake County, NC	Co. K, 10th Regiment North Carolina, 1st Artillery	Captured	Died of Variola (smallpox) 4/13/1865, Buried Woodlawn Cemetery, Elmira, NY, Grave No. 2700
Knight, John Private	St. Johns, NC, Hertford County, NC, 8/3/1864	26	Gates County, NC	Co. C, 3rd Battalion North Carolina Light Artillery	Captured	Died of Typhoid Fever 4/15/1865, Buried Woodlawn Cemetery, Elmira, NY, Grave No. 2714
Kornegay, Dixon W. Corporal	Wayne County, NC, 10/16/1861	16	Sleepy Creek, Indian Springs District, Wayne County, NC, Farmer	3rd Co. G, 40th Regiment North Carolina, 3rd Artillery	Captured	Died Chronic Diarrhea 4/27/1865, Buried Woodlawn Cemetery, Elmira, NY, Grave No. 2725

NAME and RANK	PLACE & TYPE OF ENLISTMENT	AGE	RESIDENCE & OCCUPATION	REGIMENT OR BATTALION	RESULT OF BATTLE	REMARKS
Kornegay, Joseph E. Private	Fort Holmes, NC, 4/13/1864	16	Mount Olive, Duplin County, NC, Farmer	3rd Co. G, 40th Regiment North Carolina, 3rd Artillery	Captured	Exchanged On the James River, VA, 3/2/1865
Kornegay, Wesley Corporal	Duplin County, NC, 10/16/1861	17	Duplin County, NC	3rd Co. G, 40th Regiment North Carolina, 3rd Artillery	Captured	Died of Chronic Diarrhea 4/27/1865, Buried Woodlawn Cemetery, Elmira, NY,

NAME and RANK	PLACE & TYPE OF ENLISTMENT	AGE	RESIDENCE & OCCUPATION	REGIMENT OR BATTALION	RESULT OF BATTLE	REMARKS
Lamb, James Private	Fort Holmes, NC, 1/10/1864	44	Colvin Creek, New Hanover County, NC, Farm Laborer	Co. F, 10th Regiment North Carolina, 1st Artillery	Captured	Died of Chronic Diarrhea 2/19/1865, Buried Woodlawn Cemetery, Elmira, NY, Grave No. 2335
Lamberson, Eli Private	Elizabethtown, Bladen County, NC, 3/20/1862, Mustered in at Wilmington, NC	21	White Creek, Bladen County, NC, Turpentine	Co. H, 36th Regiment North Carolina, 2nd Artillery	Captured	Died of Chronic Diarrhea 3/7/1865, Buried Woodlawn Cemetery, Elmira, NY, Grave No. 2382
Lanneau, W.S. Private	Charleston, SC, 5/9/1863	24	Charleston, SC	Co A, 25th Regiment South Carolina Volunteers	Captured	Oath of Allegiance 6/14/1865
Lassiter, James Henry' Private	Winton, Hertford County, NC, 2/13/1862, Mustered in at Camp Mangum, NC, 3/27/1862	24	Murfreesboro, Herford County, NC, Farmer, Detailed in Quarter Master Dept.	Co. C, 3rd Battalion, North Carolina Light Artillery	Captured	Oath of Allegiance 6/12/1865

NAME and RANK	PLACE & TYPE OF ENLISTMENT	AGE	RESIDENCE & OCCUPATION	REGIMENT OR BATTALION	RESULT OF BATTLE	REMARKS
Lassiter, John F. Private	Winton, Hertford County, NC, 1/28/1862, Mustered in at Camp Mangum	19	Murfreesboro, Herford County, NC, Farmer	Co. C, 3rd Battalion North Carolina Light Artillery	Captured	Oath of Allegiance 6/12/1865
Lassiter, Leroy Private	Winton, Hertford County, NC, 1/28/1862, Mustered in at Camp Mangum	33	Murfreesboro, Herford County, NC, Farmer	Co. C, 3rd Battalion North Carolina Light Artillery	Captured	Oath of Allegiance 6/12/1865
Lassiter, Richard Private	St. Johns, Hertford County, NC, 4/15/1862	19	Plymouth, Washington County, NC	Co. C, 3rd Battalion North Carolina Light Artillery	Captured	Oath of Allegiance 5/17/1865
Lawhon, James Private	Duplin County, NC, 11/6/1861 Mustered in at Fort Caswell, NC,	39	Duplin County, NC,	2nd Co. A, 36th Regiment North Carolina, 2nd Artillery	Captured	Died of Chronic Diarrhea 4/10/1865, Buried Woodlawn Cemetery, Elmira, NY, Grave No. 2670
Lawrence, James M. Private	New Berne, NC, Craven County, NC, 1/1/1862	26	Tarboro, Edgecombe County, NC	Co. F, 36th Regiment North Carolina, 2nd Artillery	Captured	Died of Pneumonia 4/23/1865, Buried Woodlawn Cemetery, Elmira, NY, Grave No. 1403
Lawson, William Private	Unknown	Unk	Unknown	Co. K, 10th Regiment North Carolina, 1st Artillery	Captured	Died of Chronic Diarrhea 2/20/1865, Buried Woodlawn Cemetery, Elmira, NY, Grave No. 2320
Lawson, William R.S. Sergeant	Georgetown, SC, 1/25/1862	25	Charlotte, NC	Co. H, 21st South Carolina Volunteers	Captured	Oath of Allegiance 7/11/1865

NAME and RANK	PLACE & TYPE OF ENLISTMENT	AGE	RESIDENCE & OCCUPATION	REGIMENT OR BATTALION	RESULT OF BATTLE	REMARKS
Leach, Hugh Private	Randolph County, NC, 3/16/1863	31	Trinity College, Ashboro, Randolph County, NC	Co. K, 10th Regiment North Carolina, 1st Artillery	Captured	Died of Chronic Diarrhea 3/30/1865, Buried Woodlawn Cemetery, Elmira, NY, Grave No. 2591
Leary, Lemuel Private	Enfield, Halifax County, NC, 10/9/1861	18	Halifax County, NC	Co. F, 36th Regiment North Carolina, 2nd Artillery	Captured	Exchanged on the James River, VA, 3/2/1865
Lee, W.J. Private	Pee Dee, SC, 4/27/1862	Unk	Timmonsville, SC	Co. K, 21st South Carolina Volunteers	Captured	Oath of Allegiance 7/11/1865
Legett, Andrew J. Private	Bennettsville, Marlboro County, SC, 4/4/1862	25	Marion County, SC, Farm Laborer	Co. F, 21st South Carolina Volunteers	Captured	Oath of Allegiance 6/14/1865
Legrand, Hosmar Private	Fort Fisher, New Hanover County, NC, 9/14/1863	17	New Hanover County, NC, Detailed to Mounted Scouts, Fort Fisher, NC	2nd Co. I, 36th Regiment North Carolina, 2nd Artillery	Captured	Died on steamer to be Exchanged at James River of Chronic Diarrhea/ Typhoid Fever 3/8/1865
Legrand, Julius E. Private	Fort Fisher, New Hanover County, NC, 3/8/1864	17	New Hanover County, NC, Detailed as a Hospital Attendant	2nd Co. I, 36th Regiment North Carolina, 2nd Artillery,	Captured	Exchanged 3/2/1865, Died of Chronic Diarrhea/ Typhoid Fever 3/10/1865, Wayside Hospital #9, Richmond, Va
Lehue, Benjamin W. Private	Fort St. Philip, Brunswick County, NC, 5/14/1862	28	Brunswick County, NC	3rd Co. G, 36th Regiment North Carolina, 2nd Artillery	Captured	Exchanged On the James River, VA, 3/2/1865

NAME and RANK	PLACE & TYPE OF ENLISTMENT	AGE	RESIDENCE & OCCUPATION	REGIMENT OR BATTALION	RESULT OF BATTLE	REMARKS
Lemon, Alexander Private	Elizabethtown, Bladen County, NC, 5/7/1862	27	Elizabethtown, Bladen County, NC Farmer	Co. H, 36th Regiment North Carolina, 2nd Artillery	Captured	Oath of Allegiance 6/12/1865
Lemons, John A. Private	Union County, NC, 3/23/1863	Unk	Post Office Corbaus Store, NC	Co. K, 10th Regiment North Carolina, 1st Artillery	Captured	Died of Pneumonia 5/20/1865, Buried Woodlawn Cemetery, Elmira, NY, Grave No. 2939
Leonard, Asa Corporal	Fort St. Philip, Brunswick County, NC, 5/16/1862	34	Wilmington, New Hanover County, NC	3rd Co. G, 36th Regiment North Carolina, 2nd Artillery	Captured	Oath of Allegiance 7/7/1865
Lesesne, James Private	Fort Holmes, Bladen County, NC, 5/25/1864	17	Elizabethtown, Bladen County, NC	2nd Co. K, 40th Regiment North Carolina, 3rd Artillery	Captured	Oath of Allegiance 6/12/1865
Lesesue, Paul Private	Fort Fisher, New Hanover County, NC, 12/4/1862	17	Bladen County, NC, Student	2nd Co. K, 40th Regiment North Carolina, 3rd Artillery	Captured	Exchanged 3/14/1865 Boulware's Wharf, James River, VA
Lewis, Alexander Private	Fort St. Philip, Brunswick County, NC, 4/16/1862	23	Lumberton, Robeson County, NC	3rd Co. G, 36th Regiment North Carolina, 2nd Artillery	Captured	Exchanged 2/20/1865, Died in Hospital in Raleigh of Pneumonia 3/20/1865
Lewis, Gains Private	Fort Branch, Brunswick County, NC, 7/23/1863	28	Wayne County, NC	3rd Co. G, 40th Regiment North Carolina, 3rd Artillery	Captured	Exchanged On the James River, VA, 2/20/1865
Lewis, William E. Private	Goldsboro, Wayne County, NC, 10/6/1863	17	Goldsboro, Wayne County, NC	Co. F, 10th Regiment North Carolina, 1st Artillery	Captured	Oath of Allegiance 5/29/1865

NAME and RANK	PLACE & TYPE OF ENLISTMENT	AGE	RESIDENCE & OCCUPATION	REGIMENT OR BATTALION	RESULT OF BATTLE	REMARKS
Liddon, David S. Private	Fort Ocracoke, Beaufort County, NC, 4/22/1861	21	Washington, NC	Co. K, 10th Regiment North Carolina, 1st Artillery	Captured	Oath of Allegiance 5/14/1865
Lide, Robert T. Private	Chesterfield, SC, 2/24/1863	26	Cheraw, Chesterfield, SC	Co. D, 21st South Carolina Volunteers	Captured	Oath of Allegiance 7/7/1865
Lifrage, Theodore M. Sergeant	Williamsburg, SC, 12/29/1861	29	Murray's Ferry, Williamsburg, SC,	Co K, 25th Regiment South Carolina Volunteers	Captured	Died of Chronic Diarrhea, 4/3/1865 Buried Woodlawn Cemetery, Elmira, NY, Grave No. 2567
Lilly, William B. Private	Beaufort County, NC, 10/5/1861	18	Tarboro, Edgecombe County, NC	Co. K, 10th Regiment North Carolina, 1st Artillery	Captured	Oath of Allegiance 7/19/1865
Lime, William Private	Unknown	Unk	Unknown	2nd Co. I, 36th Regiment North Carolina, 2nd Artillery	Captured	Died of Unknown Disease 3/31/1865, Buried Woodlawn Cemetery, Grave No. 2595
Little, Robert Augustus Private	Tarboro, Edgecombe County, NC, 5/30/1863	31	Beaufort County, NC	Co. D, 13th Battalion North Carolina Light Artillery	Captured	Died of Chronic Diarrhea 3/20/1865, Buried Woodlawn Cemetery, Elmira, NY, Grave No. 1577
Lockemy, Resin Private	Fort Caswell, Brunswick County, NC, 7/6/1863	28	Brunswick County, NC	2nd Co. D, 36th Regiment North Carolina, 2nd Artillery	Captured	Died of Pneumonia 3/13/1865, Buried Woodlawn Cemetery, Elmira, NY, Grave No. 2423

NAME and RANK	PLACE & TYPE OF ENLISTMENT	AGE	RESIDENCE & OCCUPATION	REGIMENT OR BATTALION	RESULT OF BATTLE	REMARKS
Lockrema, Daniel Private Also Spelled: Lockerman	Unknown	30	Northern Division, Sampson County, NC, Cooper	2nd Co. D, 36th Regiment North Carolina, 2nd Artillery	Captured	Died of Typhoid Fever 4/29/1865, Buried Woodlawn Cemetery, Elmira, NY, Grave No. 2729
Lofton, Isaac N. Private	Fort Holmes, Brunswick County, NC, 4/20/1864	18	Jerecho, Indian Springs District, Wayne County, NC,	3rd Co. G, 40th Regiment North Carolina, 3rd Artillery	Captured	Died of Chronic Diarrhea 3/30/1865, Buried Woodlawn Cemetery, Elmira, NY, Grave No. 2534
Long, Alexander Private	Elizabethtown, Bladen County, NC, 10/19/1861	20	Elizabethtown, Bladen County, NC	2nd Co. I, 36th Regiment North Carolina, 2nd Artillery	Captured	Oath of Allegiance 7/11/1865
Long, Lillington D. Private	Elizabethtown, Bladen County, NC, 2/3/1862	35	Downsville, NC	2nd Co. I, 36th Regiment North Carolina, 2nd Artillery	Captured	Exchanged 2/20/1865 Died of Unknown Disease 4/2/1865 at Howard's Grove Hospital, Richmond, Va
Love, Robert A. Private	Red Springs, Robeson County, NC, 9/15/1861	24	Robeson County, NC	Co. E, 40th Regiment North Carolina, 3rd Artillery	Captured	Exchanged On the James River, VA, 3/2/1865
Love, Thomas J. Sergeant	Red Springs, Robeson County, NC, 9/19/1861	24	Robeson County, NC	Co. E, 40th Regiment North Carolina, 3rd Artillery	Captured	Exchanged 3/2/1865 Died in Raleigh General Hospital #8 of Chronic Diarrhea 3/15/1865
Lowder, H.S. Private	Camp Harlee, Georgetown, SC, 5/16/1862	31	Manning, Clarendon District, SC, Farmer	Co. I, 25th South Carolina Vols.	Captured	Exchanged On the James River, VA, 3/14/1865

NAME and RANK	PLACE & TYPE OF ENLISTMENT	AGE	RESIDENCE & OCCUPATION	REGIMENT OR BATTALION	RESULT OF BATTLE	REMARKS
Lowder, James D. Private	Charleston, SC, 5/28/1862	29	Manning, Clarendon District, SC, Farmer	Co. I, 25th South Carolina Vols.	Captured	Oath of Allegiance 7/3/1865
Lucas, Henry Private	Clinton, NC, Sampson County, NC, 2/91863	37	Sampson County, NC, Farmer	2nd Co. D, 36th Regiment North Carolina, 2nd Artillery	Captured	Exchanged 3/14/1865 at Boulware's Wharf, James River, VA
Lucas, John T. Private	Wilmington, New Hanover County, NC, 3/20/1864, Transferred From Provost Guard, Goldsboro, NC	Unk	Goldsboro, Wayne County, NC	Co. F, 10th Regiment North Carolina, 1st Artillery	Captured	Died of Chronic Diarrhea 4/15/1865, Buried Woodlawn Cemetery, Elmira, NY, Grave No. 2711

NAME and RANK	PLACE & TYPE OF ENLISTMENT	AGE	RESIDENCE & OCCUPATION	REGIMENT OR BATTALION	RESULT OF BATTLE	REMARKS
Mallison, David B. Private	Wilmington, New Hanover County, NC, 1/1/1863	17	Washington, NC	Co. K, 10th Regiment North Carolina, 1st Artillery	Captured	Oath of Allegiance 5/19/1865
Malloy, Edward Private	Robeson County, NC, 5/9/1862	29	Robeson County, NC	Co. D, 1st Battalion North Carolina Heavy Artillery	Captured	Died of Chronic Diarrhea 4/19/1865, Buried in Woodlawn Cemetery, Elmira, NY, Grave No. 1369
Marlain, William T. Private	Robeson County, NC, 1/6/1865	17	Wadesboro, Anson County, NC	Co. D, 1st Battalion North Carolina Heavy Artillery	Captured	Oath of Allegiance 5/17/1865

NAME and RANK	PLACE & TYPE OF ENLISTMENT	AGE	RESIDENCE & OCCUPATION	REGIMENT OR BATTALION	RESULT OF BATTLE	REMARKS
Marler, Jesse Private	Goldsboro, NC, Wayne County, NC, 9/20/1863	Unk	Goldsboro, Wayne County, NC	Co. K, 10th Regiment North Carolina, 1st Artillery	Captured	Oath of Allegiance 6/23/1865
Marsh, Neill Private	Cumberland County, NC, 9/20/1863	40	Gray's Creek, Fayetteville, Cumberland County, NC,,	3rd Co. B, 36th Regiment North Carolina, 2nd Artillery	Captured	Exchanged 3/2/1865 Died of Typhoid/Pneumonia in Pettigrew Hospital #13, Raleigh, NC, 3/19/1865
Marshall, Andrew M. Private	Fort Branch, Brunswick County, NC, 8/17/1863	44	Orange County, NC	3rd Co. G, 40th Regiment North Carolina, 3rd Artillery	Captured	Oath of Allegiance 6/12/1865
Martin, John Private	Charleston, SC, 4/15/1862	39	Charleston, SC	Co. E, 25th South Carolina Vols.	Wounded & Captured	Oath of Allegiance 5/17/1865
Mathews, Archibald B. Private	Fort Caswell, NC, Brunswick County, NC, 5/15/1863	18	Brunswick County, NC	Co. E, 40th Regiment North Carolina, 3rd Artillery	Captured	Died of Pneumonia 2/10/1865, Buried in Woodlawn Cemetery, Elmira, NY, Grave No. 2090
Mathews, Charles M. Private	Gourdins Dept., SC, 4/15/1862	16	Kingstree, SC	Co. K, 25th South Carolina Vols.	Captured	Oath of Allegiance 8/7/1865
Mathews, J.M. Private	Battery Island, SC, 4/12/1862	22	Murray's Ferry, Williamsburg District, SC, Farmer	Co. B, 25th South Carolina Vols.	Captured	Oath of Allegiance 7/11/1865

NAME and RANK	PLACE & TYPE OF ENLISTMENT	AGE	RESIDENCE & OCCUPATION	REGIMENT OR BATTALION	RESULT OF BATTLE	REMARKS
Mathews, W.J. Private	Meyersville, SC, 5/3/1862	24	Murray's Ferry, Williamsburg District, SC, Clerk	Co H, 25th Regiment South Carolina Volunteers	Captured	Died of Variola (smallpox) 4/7/1865, Buried in Woodlawn Cemetery, Elmira, NY, Grave No. 2649
Matthews, Edwin J. Private	Fayetteville, Cumberland County, NC, 2/26/1862	18	Cumberland County, NC	2nd Co. C, 36th Regiment North Carolina, 2nd Artillery	Captured	Died of Pneumonia 3/17/1865, Buried in Woodlawn Cemetery, Elmira, NY, Grave No. 1555
Matthews, Jacob M. Private	Fayetteville, Cumberland County, NC, 2/26/1862	22	Barkleysville, NC, Cumberland County, NC	2nd Co. C, 36th Regiment North Carolina, 2nd Artillery	Captured	Died of Variola (smallpox) 4/19/1865, Buried in Woodlawn Cemetery, Elmira, NY, Grave No. 1370
Matthews, John Allen Musician	Lillington, Harnett County, NC, 2/20/1862	28	Raleigh, NC, Blockersville, NC, Sampson, NC, Farmer	2nd Co. C, 36th Regiment North Carolina, 2nd Artillery	Captured	Oath of Allegiance 6/12/1865
Matthews, John R. Private	Fort Caswell, Brunswick County, NC, 3/8/1863	24	Sampson County, NC, Farmer	2nd Co. D, 36th Regiment North Carolina, 2nd Artillery	Wounded & Captured	Exchanged On the James River, VA, 3/2/1865
Matthews, Neill A. Private	Fort Fisher, New Hanover County, NC, 12/12/1862	18	Raleigh, Wake County, NC	2nd Co. C, 36th Regiment North Carolina, 2nd Artillery	Captured	Oath of Allegiance 6/12/1865
Matthews, William H. Private	Lillington, Harnett County, NC, 2/26/1862, Mustered in at Fort Caswell	26	Harnett County, NC	2nd Co. C, 36th Regiment North Carolina, 2nd Artillery	Captured	Died of Variola (smallpox) 3/27/1865, Buried in Woodlawn Cemetery, Elmira, NY, Grave No. 2471

NAME and RANK	PLACE & TYPE OF ENLISTMENT	AGE	RESIDENCE & OCCUPATION	REGIMENT OR BATTALION	RESULT OF BATTLE	REMARKS
Matthis, Neill Private	Harnett County, NC, 11/15/1863	37	Raleigh, Wake County, NC	3rd Co. B, 36th Regiment North Carolina, 2nd Artillery	Captured	Oath of Allegiance 7/7/1865
Maxwell, Whitford Private	Camp Wyatt, New Hanover County, NC, 6/16/1864	35	New Hanover County, NC, Farmer	2nd Co. D, 36th Regiment North Carolina, 2nd Artillery	Captured	Died of Chronic Diarrhea 3/11/1865, Buried in Woodlawn Cemetery, Elmira, NY, Grave No. 1835
Maxwell, William S. Private	Camp Wyatt, New Hanover County, NC, 3/15/1864	35	New Hanover County, NC,	2nd Co. D, 36th Regiment North Carolina, 2nd Artillery	Captured	Exchanged On the James River, VA, 3/14/1865
May, Patrick F. Private	Charleston, SC, 2/22/1862	18	Charleston, SC	Co. E, 25th South Carolina Vols.	Captured	Oath of Allegiance 5/17/1865
McCalister, E. Private	Williamsburg, SC, 5/13/1862	18	Murray's Ferry, Williamsburg District, SC, Farmer	Co. H, 25th South Carolina Vols.	Captured	Died of Variola (smallpox) 4/20/1865, Buried in Woodlawn Cemetery, Elmira, NY, Grave No. 1378
McCall, Barnabus Private	Marion, SC, 5/12/1862	20	Selkirk, Marion, SC, Farm Laborer	Co. K, 21st South Carolina Volunteers	Captured	Oath of Allegiance 7/7/1865
McCaskill, Francis M. Private	Montgomery County, NC, 4/29/1863	18	High Point, Guilford County, NC	3rd Co. B, 36th Regiment North Carolina, 2nd Artillery	Captured	Oath of Allegiance 7/11/1865

NAME and RANK	PLACE & TYPE OF ENLISTMENT	AGE	RESIDENCE & OCCUPATION	REGIMENT OR BATTALION	RESULT OF BATTLE	REMARKS
McCaskill, John C. Private	Fort Branch, NC, Brunswick County, NC, 7/30/1863	40	Montgomery County, NC	3rd Co. G, 40th Regiment North Carolina, 3rd Artillery	Captured	Died of Rheumatism 3/18/1865, Buried in Woodlawn Cemetery, Elmira, NY, Grave No. 1553
McCauley, John	Fort Caswell, Brunswick County, NC, 12/19/1862	Unk	Brunswick County, NC	2nd Co. D, 36th Regiment North Carolina, 2nd Artillery	Captured	Exchanged On the James River, VA, 3/2/1865
McClary, D.S. Private	James Island, SC, 4/5/1864	16	Kingstree, SC, Murray's Ferry, Williamsburg District, SC, Farmer	Co. C, 25th South Carolina Vols.	Captured	Oath of Allegiance 7/11/1865
McClendon, Joel Private	Fort Branch, Brunswick County, NC, 7/24/1863	30	Montgomery County, NC	3rd Co. G, 40th Regiment North Carolina, 3rd Artillery	Captured	Died of Remittent Fever 2/18/1865, Buried in Woodlawn Cemetery, Elmira, NY, Grave No. 2218
McCorkle, J.F. Private	Marion, SC, 4/20/1862	Unk	Marion, SC	Co. D, 25th South Carolina Vols.	Captured	Oath of Allegiance 7/7/1865
McCormick, Duncan Private	Red Springs, Robeson County, NC, 9/17/1861	19	Robeson County, NC, Carpenter	Co. E, 40th Regiment North Carolina, 3rd Artillery	Captured	Died of Unknown Causes 7/21/1865, Buried in Woodlawn Cemetery, Elmira, NY, Grave No. 2867
McDaniel, Joe R. Sergeant	Marion, SC, 1/8/1862	23	Allen's Bridge, Marion, SC, Farmer	Co. I, 21st South Carolina Volunteers	Captured	Died of Pneumonia, 6/11/1865, Buried Woodlawn Cemetery, Elmira, NY, Grave No. 2885

NAME and RANK	PLACE & TYPE OF ENLISTMENT	AGE	RESIDENCE & OCCUPATION	REGIMENT OR BATTALION	RESULT OF BATTLE	REMARKS
McDaniel, William L. Private	Fort Branch, New Hanover County, NC, 8/1/1863	44	New Berne, Craven County, NC	3rd Co. G, 40th Regiment North Carolina, 3rd Artillery	Captured	Oath of Allegiance 6/12/1865
McDuffie, Daniel K. Private	Fort St. Philip, Brunswick County, NC, 7/16/1862	21	Brunswick County, NC	2nd Co. K, 40th Regiment North Carolina, 3rd Artillery	Captured	Exchanged On the James River, VA, 3/2/1865
McDuffie, Henry F. Private	Fort St. Philip, Brunswick County, NC, 7/16/1862	18	Brunswick County, NC	2nd Co. K, 40th Regiment North Carolina, 3rd Artillery	Captured	Died on Boat to be Exchanged From Unknown Disease 2/20/1865
McEwen, Archibald Daniel Corporal	Elizabethtown, Bladen County, NC, 5/6/1862, Mustered in at Fort St. Philip, NC	23	Elizabethtown, Bladen County, NC, Farmer	2nd Co. K, 40th Regiment North Carolina, 3rd Artillery	Captured	Oath of Allegiance 6/12/1865, Died of Chronic Diarrhea June 19th at Manchester, VA
McFeeley, James G. Private	Charleston, SC, 5/5/1862	Unk	Charleston, SC	Co. H, 25th South Carolina Vols.	Captured	Oath of Allegiance 5/7/1865
McGhee, William H. Private	Elizabethtown, Bladen County, NC, 10/19/1861	19	Bladen County, NC	2nd Co. I, 36th Regiment North Carolina, 2nd Artillery	Captured	Exchanged 3/14/1865 at Boulware's Wharf, James River, VA
McGregor, Benjamin F. Private	Fort Caswell, Brunswick County, NC, 1/23/1863	18	Laurinburg, Scotland County, NC	Co. E, 40th Regiment North Carolina, 3rd Artillery	Captured	Oath of Allegiance 6/12/1865
McIntosh, Daniel Private	Camp Holmes, NC, 4/12/1864	18	Wake County, NC	Co. K, 10th Regiment North Carolina, 1st Artillery	Captured	Died of Chronic Diarrhea 4/2/1865, Buried in Woodlawn Cemetery, Elmira, NY, Grave No. 2586

NAME and RANK	PLACE & TYPE OF ENLISTMENT	AGE	RESIDENCE & OCCUPATION	REGIMENT OR BATTALION	RESULT OF BATTLE	REMARKS
McIntyre, Duncan Musician	Wilmington, New Hanover County, NC, 2/6/1863	38	Cumberland County, NC, Farmer	Co. F, 10th Regiment North Carolina, 1st Artillery	Captured	Oath of Allegiance 5/15/1865
McIntyre, John T. Sergeant	Bennettsville, Marlboro District, SC, 5/12/1862	17	Bennettsville, Marlboro District, SC,	Co. F, 21st South Carolina Volunteers	Captured	Died of Chronic Diarrhea, 3/5/1865, Buried Woodlawn Cemetery, Elmira, NY, Grave No. 2413
McIver, David A. Private	Coles Island, SC, 4/11/1862	Unk	Unknown	Co. F, 25th South Carolina Vols.	Captured	Exchanged On the James River, VA, 3/2/1865
McKay, John L. Private	Fort Fisher, New Hanover County, NC, 7/22/1863	18	New Hanover County, NC	2nd Co. K, 40th Regiment North Carolina, 3rd Artillery	Captured	Exchanged 3/14/1865 Boulware's Wharf, James River, VA
McKinnie, Robert Private	Camp Holmes, 9/22/1863	44	Wayne County, NC	3rd Co. G, 40th Regiment North Carolina, 3rd Artillery	Captured	Exchanged On the James River, VA, 2/20/1865
McKnight, William M. Corporal	Battery Island, SC, 4/12/1862	28	Unknown	Co. C, 25th South Carolina Vols.	Captured	Exchanged On the James River, VA, 2/20/1865
Mclain, Joshua B. Private	Fort St. Philip, Brunswick County, NC, 7/2/1863	17	Brunswick County, NC	Co. E, 36th Regiment North Carolina, 2nd Artillery	Wounded In Right Thigh & Captured	Died of Unknown Disease 5/10/1865, Buried in Woodlawn Cemetery, Elmira, NY, Grave No. 2792

NAME and RANK	PLACE & TYPE OF ENLISTMENT	AGE	RESIDENCE & OCCUPATION	REGIMENT OR BATTALION	RESULT OF BATTLE	REMARKS
McLaurin, John Private	Fort Branch, NC, Brunswick County, NC, 8/18/1863	41	Anson County, NC	3rd Co. G, 40th Regiment North Carolina, 3rd Artillery	Captured	Died of Eyrsipelas 2/13/1865, Buried in Woodlawn Cemetery, Elmira, Grave No. 2065
McLeish, John W. Sergeant	Charleston, SC, 2/22/1862	26	Charleston, SC	Co. E, 25th South Carolina Vols.	Captured	Oath of Allegiance 5/29/1865
McLellan, Enos T. Private	Camp Harllee, Marion, SC, 5/1/1862	17	Britton's Neck, Marion District, SC,	Co. I, 21st South Carolina Volunteers	Captured	Died of Chronic Diarrhea 3/2/1865, Buried in Woodlawn Cemetery, Elmira, NY, Grave No. 2020
McLeod, Daniel Private	Harnett County, NC, 4/30/1862	33	Raleigh, Wake County, NC	2nd Co. C, 36th Regiment North Carolina, 2nd Artillery	Captured	Oath of Allegiance 6/12/1865
McLivane, J.H. Private	Darlington, SC, 1/1/1862	22	Florence, SC	Co. B, 21st South Carolina Volunteers	Captured	Oath of Allegiance 7/7/1865

NAME and RANK	PLACE & TYPE OF ENLISTMENT	AGE	RESIDENCE & OCCUPATION	REGIMENT OR BATTALION	RESULT OF BATTLE	REMARKS
McMasters, Wesley W. Private	Asheboro, Randolph County, NC, 3/25/1863	29	Randolph County, NC	3rd Co. G, 40th Regiment North Carolina, 3rd Artillery	Captured	Exchanged 3/2/1865, Died of Remittent Fever 3/18/1865 At Jackson Hospital, Richmond, VA, Buried in Hollywood Cemetery, VA
McMillan, Daniel Private	Fort Caswell, Brunswick County, NC, 8/12/1864	16	Fayetteville, Cumberland County, NC	Co. C, 3rd Battalion North Carolina Light Artillery	Captured	Oath of Allegiance 6/12/1865, Also reported as having "died on the route" to be exchanged 2/20/1865
McNair, Daniel P. Private	Robeson County, NC, 8/8/1863	36	Robeson County, NC	3rd Co. B, 36th Regiment North Carolina, 2nd Artillery	Wounded & Captured, Wounded in Hand 12/24/1864	Died of Chronic Diarrhea 3/10/1865, Buried in Woodlawn Cemetery, Elmira, NY, Grave No. 1881
McNeill, Daniel Private	Cumberland County, NC, 11/21/1863	18	Cumberland County, NC, Detailed as scout under Lt. Faison	3rd Co. B, 36th Regiment North Carolina, 2nd Artillery,	Captured,	Died of Chronic Diarrhea 3/10/1865, Buried in Woodlawn Cemetery, Elmira, NY, Evidence Suggests that McNeill died of suffocation aboard the transport *North Point* while sailing to Point Lookout, MD

NAME and RANK	PLACE & TYPE OF ENLISTMENT	AGE	RESIDENCE & OCCUPATION	REGIMENT OR BATTALION	RESULT OF BATTLE	REMARKS
McNeill, Franklin Purcell Private	Robeson County, NC, 4/22/1863	18	Robeson County, NC	Co. D, 1st Battalion North Carolina Heavy Artillery	Captured	Oath of Allegiance 6/26/1865
McQueen, Daniel M. Private	Unknown	16	Lumberton, Robison County, NC,	Co. E, 40th Regiment North Carolina, 3rd Artillery	Captured	Died of Chronic Diarrhea 2/22/1865, Buried in Woodlawn Cemetery, Elmira, NY, Grave No. 2243
Mears, Elihu Private	Elizabethtown, Bladen County, NC, 10/19/1861	19	Elizabethtown, Bladen County, NC	2nd Co. I, 36th Regiment North Carolina, 2nd Artillery	Captured	Oath of Allegiance 6/12/1865
Meeks, Brantley Private	Wilmington, New Hanover County, NC, 2/27/1863	26	New Hanover County, NC,	Co. D, 1st Battalion North Carolina Heavy Artillery	Captured	Exchanged 3/14/1865, Died of Scorbutus in Jackson Hospital, Richmond, VA. 4/2/1865, Buried Hollywood Cemetery
Mellichampe, James M. Private	Charleston, SC, 2/24/1862	25	Charleston, SC, Clerk	Co A, 25th Regiment South Carolina Volunteers	Captured	Died of Pneumonia 2/12/1865 Buried Woodlawn Cemetery, Elmira, NY, Grave No. 2052
Melvin, Daniel M. Private	Wilmington, New Hanover County, NC, 1/1/1861	18	Wilmington, NC, New Hanover County, NC	2nd Co. I, 36th Regiment North Carolina, 2nd Artillery	Captured	Died of Pneumonia 3/18/1865, Buried in Woodlawn Cemetery, Elmira, NY, Grave No. 1716

NAME and RANK	PLACE & TYPE OF ENLISTMENT	AGE	RESIDENCE & OCCUPATION	REGIMENT OR BATTALION	RESULT OF BATTLE	REMARKS
Melvin, Marshall H. Private	Fort Fisher, New Hanover County, NC, 3/7/1862	17	Harrison's Creek, NC	2nd Co. I, 36th Regiment North Carolina, 2nd Artillery	Captured	Oath of Allegiance 7/11/1865
Melvin, A. W. Private	Fayetteville, Cumberland County, NC, 2/26/1862	26	Fayetteville, Cumberland, NC,	2nd Co. C, 36th Regiment North Carolina, 2nd Artillery	Captured	Died of Variola (smallpox) 3/18/1865, Buried in Woodlawn Cemetery, Elmira, NY, Grave No. 1710
Melvin, William Private	Alamance County, NC, 3/14/1863	Unk	Alamance County, NC	Co. K, 10th Regiment North Carolina, 1st Artillery	Captured	Oath of Allegiance 6/12/1865
Melvin, William Snowden Private	Bladen County, NC, 5/13/1862	51	Bladen County, NC	Co. H, 36th Regiment North Carolina, 2nd Artillery	Captured	Died of Unknown Causes 3/18/1865, Buried in Woodlawn Cemetery, Elmira, NY, Also Reported Being Released 7/11/1865
Mercer, Absalum Private	Fort Caswell, NC, 5/5/1864	18	Mount Olive, Duplin County, NC	2nd Co. A, 36th Regiment North Carolina, 2nd Artillery	Captured	Died On Route to Be Exchanged, 2/20/1865
Mercer, Calvin W. Private	Fort Caswell, NC, 5/14/1862	24	Brunswick County, NC, Laborer	2nd Co. A, 36th Regiment North Carolina, 2nd Artillery	Captured	Exchanged 3/2/1865, Died of Unknown Causes in Richmond Hospital 3/29/1865, Buried Hollywood Cemetery

NAME and RANK	PLACE & TYPE OF ENLISTMENT	AGE	RESIDENCE & OCCUPATION	REGIMENT OR BATTALION	RESULT OF BATTLE	REMARKS
Mercer, Chancy G. Private	Fort Caswell, NC, Brunswick County, NC, 1/9/1864	17	Brunswick County, NC	2nd Co. A, 36th Regiment North Carolina, 2nd Artillery	Captured	Died From "Gangrene of Feet" 3/11/1865, Buried Woodlawn Cemetery, Elmira, NY, Grave No. 1839
Mercer, Lott Private	Duplin County, NC, 11/6/1861, Mustered Fort Caswell, NC	42	Birmington, Wake County, NC	2nd Co. A, 36th Regiment North Carolina, 2nd Artillery	Captured	Exchanged On the James River, VA, 2/20/1865
Mercer, Noah J. Private	Fort Caswell, NC, Brunswick County, NC, 5/14/1862	27	Brunswick County, NC	2nd Co. A, 36th Regiment North Carolina, 2nd Artillery	Captured	Died of Typhoid Fever 3/17/1865, buried in Woodlawn Cemetery, Elmira, NY, Grave No. 1696
Meritt, Richard D. Private	Fort St. Philip, NC, Brunswick County, NC, 4/21/1863	35	Elizabethtown, Bladen County, NC, Turpentine	Co. E, 36th Regiment North Carolina, 2nd Artillery	Captured	Exchanged 3/14/1865 at Boulware's Wharf, James River, VA
Merritt, John A. Private	Enfield, Halifax County, NC, 10/9/1861	20	Enfield, NC	Co. F, 36th Regiment North Carolina, 2nd Artillery	Captured	Oath of Allegiance 6/12/1865
Miller, Alexander Private	Beaufort County, NC, 2/12/1862	Unk	Unknown	2nd Co. A, 36th Regiment North Carolina, 2nd Artillery	Captured	Exchanged On the James River, VA, 2/20/1865
Miller, Chancy W. Private	Fort Caswell, Brunswick County, NC, 2/6/1864	17	Brunswick County, NC	2nd Co. A, 36th Regiment North Carolina, 2nd Artillery	Captured	Exchanged On the James River, VA, 2/20/1865

NAME and RANK	PLACE & TYPE OF ENLISTMENT	AGE	RESIDENCE & OCCUPATION	REGIMENT OR BATTALION	RESULT OF BATTLE	REMARKS
Miller, Clayton Private	Charleston, SC, 12/5/1863	15	Parish of Prince George, George Town, SC,	Co. A, 21st South Carolina Volunteers	Captured	Exchanged On the James River, VA, 2/20/1865
Miller, Daniel Private	Charleston, SC, 12/5/1863	21	Charleston, SC,	Co. A, 21st South Carolina Volunteers	Captured	Exchanged 2/20/1865
Millican, Francis O. Sergeant	Wilmington, New Hanover County, NC, 3/5/1862	26	Whiteville, Columbus County, NC	Co. E, 36th Regiment North Carolina, 2nd Artillery	Captured	Died of Chronic Diarrhea 3/16/1865, Buried in Woodlawn Cemetery, Elmira, NY, Grave No. 1676
Mills, John H. Private	Old Brunswick, NC, 4/16/1862, Mustered in Fort St. Philip	41	Brunswick County, NC	3rd Co. G, 36th Regiment North Carolina, 2nd Artillery	Captured	Exchanged On the James River, VA, 3/2/1865
Mints, Stephen Private	Old Brunswick, NC, 4/16/1862, Mustered in Fort St. Philip	48	Brunswick County, NC	3rd Co. G, 36th Regiment North Carolina, 2nd Artillery	Captured	Exchanged 2/20/1865, Died of Unknown Disease in Howard Grove Hospital, Richmond, Va 3/20/1865
Mints, William Private	Old Brunswick, NC, 4/16/1862, Mustered in Fort St. Philip	21	Brunswick County, NC	3rd Co. G, 36th Regiment North Carolina, 2nd Artillery	Captured	Died of Typhoid Fever 4/10/1865, Buried in Woodlawn Cemetery, Elmira, NY, Grave No. 2605
Mitchum, John S. Private	Battery Island, SC, 4/12/1862	21	Kingston, SC	Co. K, 25th South Carolina Vols.	Captured	Oath of Allegiance 7/11/1865

NAME and RANK	PLACE & TYPE OF ENLISTMENT	AGE	RESIDENCE & OCCUPATION	REGIMENT OR BATTALION	RESULT OF BATTLE	REMARKS
Mitchum, S.S. Sergeant	Battery Island, SC, 4/12/1862	45	Unknown	Co. C, 25th South Carolina Vols.	Captured	Exchanged On James River, VA, 2/20/1865
Mitchum, W.E. Private	Gourdins Dept, SC, 5/1/1864	20	Kingstree, SC	Co. K, 25th South Carolina Vols.	Captured	Oath of Allegiance 7/7/1865
Mixon, A.W. Private	Camp Harllee, Georgetown, SC, 1/1/1862	41	Unknown	Co. I, 25th South Carolina Volunteers	Captured	Died Of Chronic Diarrhea 2/14/1865, Buried Woodlawn Cemetery, Elmira, NY, Grave No. 2185
Mixon, W.P. Sergeant	Darlington, SC, 1/20/1862	20	Darlington District, SC, Farmer	Co. H, 21st South Carolina Volunteers	Captured	Exchanged On James River, VA, 2/20/1865
Molloy, Lawrence E. Private	James Island, SC, 5/4/1862	Unk	Charleston, SC	Co. B, 25th South Carolina Volunteers	Captured	Oath of Allegiance 7/7/1865
Montgomery, Edward P. Private	Battery Island, SC, 4/12/1862	20	Kingstree, SC	Co. C, 25th South Carolina Volunteers	Captured	Oath of Allegiance In USA General Hospital 8/7/1865
Montgomery, Isaac Sergeant	Georgetown, SC, 1/1/1862	25	Kingstree, SC	Co. C, 25th South Carolina Volunteers	Captured	Oath of Allegiance 7/26/1865
Montgomery, J.A. Private	Battery Island, SC, 4/12/1862	22	Kingstree, SC	Co. C, 25th South Carolina Volunteers	Captured	Oath of Allegiance 7/26/1865
Montgomery, S.E. Private	Georgetown, SC, 4/17/1862	29	Overseer Holms House	Co. B, 25th South Carolina Volunteers	Captured	Exchanged On James River, VA, 3/14/1865

NAME and RANK	PLACE & TYPE OF ENLISTMENT	AGE	RESIDENCE & OCCUPATION	REGIMENT OR BATTALION	RESULT OF BATTLE	REMARKS
Moore, Andrew Private	Fort Fisher, New Hanover County, NC, 3/13/1862, Volunteer	22	Fayetteville, Cumberland County, NC	2nd Co. I, 36th Regiment North Carolina, 2nd Artillery	Captured	Oath of Allegiance 6/12/1865
Moore, Benjamin Franklin Private	Darlington, SC, 5/19/1863	16	Bennettsville, Marlboro District, SC	Co. B, 21st South Carolina Volunteers	Captured	Died Of Chronic Diarrhea 4/10/1865, Buried Woodlawn Cemetery, Elmira, NY, Grave No. 2607
Moore, Enoch Private	Fort Caswell, Brunswick County, NC, 12/8/18633, Volunteer	18	Pitt County, NC	Co. F, 36th Regiment North Carolina, 2nd Artillery	Captured	Exchanged On the James River, VA, 2/20/1865
Moore, J.F. Private	Darlington, SC, 1/1/1862	19	Columbia, Richland County, SC, Carpenter	Co. B, 21st South Carolina Volunteers	Captured	Oath of Allegiance 8/7/1865
Moore, James R. First Sergeant	Bennettsville, Marlboro District, SC, 12/25/1861	28	Charleston District, SC, Sailor	Co. F, 21st South Carolina Volunteers	Captured	Died Of Unknown Disease 7/18/1865, Buried Woodlawn Cemetery, Elmira, NY, Grave No. 2872
Moore, James R. Private	Brunswick County, NC, 7/24/1863	40	Anson County, NC	3rd Co. G, 40th Regiment North Carolina, 3rd Artillery	Captured	Exchanged On the James River, VA, 2/21/1865
Moore, William H. Private	Brunswick County, NC, 7/27/1863, Volunteer	18	Anson County, NC, Extra duty as laborer in Quarter Master Dept.	3rd Co. G, 40th Regiment North Carolina, 3rd Artillery	Captured	Died of Remittent Fever 2/28/1865, Buried in Woodlawn Cemetery, Elmira, NY, Grave No. 2151

NAME and RANK	PLACE & TYPE OF ENLISTMENT	AGE	RESIDENCE & OCCUPATION	REGIMENT OR BATTALION	RESULT OF BATTLE	REMARKS
Morton, Hardy Owen Private	Bladen County, NC, 1/28/1862' Volunteer	26	Flemington, NC	3rd Co. B, 36th Regiment North Carolina, 2nd Artillery	Wounded in Left Knee & Captured	Oath of Allegiance 7/3/1865
Munn, John B. Private	Brunswick County, NC, 8/13/1863, Volunteer	18	Montgomery County, NC	3rd Co. G, 40th Regiment North Carolina, 3rd Artillery	Captured	Died of Phthisis Pulmonalis 2/26/1865, Buried in Woodlawn Cemetery, Elmira, NY, Grave No. 2157
Murphy, B.F. Private	Unknown	Unk	Unknown	Co. G, 25th South Carolina Volunteers	Captured	Exchanged 3/2/1865 On James River, VA, Died of Variola (smallpox), 3/24/1865 Howard's Grove Hospital, VA
Murphy, David F. Private	Orangeburg, SC, 4/30/1862	27	Orangeburg District, SC Farm Labore	Co. G, 25th South Carolina Volunteers	Captured	Died of Chronic Diarrhea, 2/28/1865 Buried Woodlawn Cemetery, Elmira, NY
Murphy, James W. Private	Brunswick County, NC, 6/25/1863, Volunteer	26	Brunswick County, NC	3rd Co. G, 40th Regiment North Carolina, 3rd Artillery	Captured	Exchanged 2/20/1865, Died of Unknown Disease At Richmond Hospital 3/16/1865, Buried in Hollywood Cemetery, Richmond, VA

NAME and RANK	PLACE & TYPE OF ENLISTMENT	AGE	RESIDENCE & OCCUPATION	REGIMENT OR BATTALION	RESULT OF BATTLE	REMARKS
Murphy, Miles Private	Wake County, NC, 3/29/1864	unk	Unk	Co. K, 10th Regiment North Carolina, 1st N.C. Artillery	Captured	Exchanged 3/2/1865, Face Burned By Gunpowder 12/25/1864
Murrell, George W. Private	Camp Holmes, Wake County, NC, 9/5/1863	32	Wilmington, New Hanover County, NC	3rd Co. B, 36th Regiment North Carolina, 2nd Artillery	Captured	Oath of Allegiance 7/11/1865
Myers, Fred M. Private	James Island, SC, 10/19/63	43	Branchville, Orangeburg, SC	Co. G, 25th South Carolina Vols.	Captured	Oath of Allegiance 6/23/1865
Myers, Luther Private	Coles Island, SC, 4/11/62	31	Midway, Orangeburg District, SC, Farmer	Co. G, 25th South Carolina Vols.	Captured	Oath of Allegiance 7/7/1865

NAME and RANK	PLACE & TYPE OF ENLISTMENT	AGE	RESIDENCE & OCCUPATION	REGIMENT OR BATTALION	RESULT OF BATTLE	REMARKS
Nance, Everett Private	Cerogordo, Brunswick County, NC, 11/17/1862, Volunteer	28	Fair Bluff, Columbus County, NC	Co. E, 36th Regiment North Carolina, 2nd North Carolina Artillery	Captured	Oath of Allegiance 7/3/1865
Neal, George M. Private	Enfield, NC, Halifax County, NC, 10/9/1861, Volunteer	18	Edgecombe County, NC	Co. F, 36th Regiment North Carolina, 2nd North Carolina Artillery	Captured	Exchanged On the James River, VA, 2/20/1865
Newman, Archibald W. Private	Fort Caswell, Brunswick County, 7/15/1862, Volunteer	31	Sampson County, NC Farmer	2nd Co. A, 36th Regiment North Carolina, 2nd North Carolina Artillery	Captured	Oath of Allegiance 8/7/1865
Newton, D.D. Corporal	Bennettsville, Marlboro District, SC, 11/18/1862	19	Cheraw, Chesterfield County, SC,	Co. F, 21st South Carolina Volunteers	Captured	Oath of Allegiance 7/11/1865

NAME and RANK	PLACE & TYPE OF ENLISTMENT	AGE	RESIDENCE & OCCUPATION	REGIMENT OR BATTALION	RESULT OF BATTLE	REMARKS
Nichols, Hazard Private	Fayetteville, NC, Cumberland County, 2/20/1862, Volunteer	22	Gray's Creek, NC	2nd Co. C, 36th Regiment North Carolina, 2nd North Carolina Artillery	Captured	Died of Chronic Diarrhea 3/20/1865, Buried Woodlawn Cemetery, Elmira, NY, Grave No. 1579
Nichols, William A. Private	Hertford County, 7/15/1862, Mustered in Camp Mangum, NC	25	Weldon, Halifax County, NC Farmer	Co. C, 3rd Battalion North Carolina Light Artillery	Captured	Oath of Allegiance 7/11/1865
Niven, Dougal Private	Brunswick County, 7/27/1863, Volunteer	40	Mecklenburg County, NC	3rd Co. G, 40th Regiment North Carolina, 3rd Regiment Artillery	Captured	Oath of Allegiance 6/12/1865
Nobles, John Private	Cerogordo, NC, 3/3/1862, Mustered in Wilmington, New Hanover County, NC	18	Fair Bluff, Columbus County, NC	Co. E, 36th Regiment North Carolina, 2nd North Carolina Artillery	Captured	Oath of Allegiance 7/7/1865
Noles, Alfred Private	Cerogordo, 3/4/1862, Mustered in at Wilmington, New Hanover County, NC, Volunteer	22	Columbus County, NC	Co. E, 36th Regiment North Carolina, 2nd North Carolina Artillery	Captured	Died of Chronic Diarrhea 5/21/1865, Buried Woodlawn Cemetery, Elmira, NY, Grave No. 2937
Norman, James S. Corporal	Washington, Beaufort County, NC, 4/16/1862	26	Washington, Beaufort County, NC Sail Maker	Co, K, 10th Regiment North Carolina, 1st N.C Artillery	Captured	Oath of Allegiance 7/11/1865
Northcutt, Henry L. Private	Marion, SC, 2/29/1864	Unk	Mullins, SC	Co. I, 21st South Carolina Volunteers	Captured	Oath of Allegiance 7/11/1865

NAME and RANK	PLACE & TYPE OF ENLISTMENT	AGE	RESIDENCE & OCCUPATION	REGIMENT OR BATTALION	RESULT OF BATTLE	REMARKS
Northcutt, John W. Corporal	Darlington, SC, 11/1/1863	42	Darlington District, SC, Farmer	Co. B, 21st South Carolina Volunteers	Captured	Exchanged On the James River, VA, 3/2/1865
Northcutt, S. T. Private	Darlington, SC, 1/25/1862	20	Darlington District District, SC	Co. B, 21st South Carolina Volunteers	Captured	Oath of Allegiance 7/19/1865
Nunn, Benjamin F. Sergeant	Lenoir County, NC, 10/16/1861, Volunteer	18	Lenoir County, NC	3rd Co. G, 40th Regiment North Carolina, 3rd Regiment Artillery	Captured	Exchanged On the James River, VA, 2/20/1865

NAME and RANK	PLACE & TYPE OF ENLISTMENT	AGE	RESIDENCE & OCCUPATION	REGIMENT OR BATTALION	RESULT OF BATTLE	REMARKS
Oats, J.P. Private	Darlington, SC, 1/1/1862	19	Darlington District, SC	Co. B, 21st South Carolina Volunteers	Captured	Oath of Allegiance 7/7/1865
Oats, John C. Private	New Hanover County, NC, Date Unknown	16	Town Creek District, Brunswick County, NC	3rd Co. G, 36th Regiment North Carolina, 2nd Artillery	Wounded Severe & Captured	Oath of Allegiance 6/23/1865
Odom, Arnold Private	Fort Fisher, New Hanover County, NC, 11/28/1862	24	New Hanover County, NC	2nd Co. I, 36th Regiment North Carolina, 2nd Artillery	Captured	Exchanged 3/14/1865 Boulware's Wharf, James River, VA
Odom, William B. Sergeant	Bennettsville, Marlboro District, SC, 12/25/1861	21	Charlotte, NC	Co. I, 21st South Carolina Volunteers	Captured	Oath of Allegiance 7/26/1865

NAME and RANK	PLACE & TYPE OF ENLISTMENT	AGE	RESIDENCE & OCCUPATION	REGIMENT OR BATTALION	RESULT OF BATTLE	REMARKS
Ott, Elmore W. Private	Secessionville, SC, 3/10/1864	13	Poplar, Orangeburg District, SC, Farmer	Co. G, 25th South Carolina Vols.	Captured	Died of Pneumonia, 3/5/1865, Buried Woodlawn Cemetery, Elmira, NY, Grave No. 1981
Ott, Samuel Private	Secessionville, SC, 5/9/62	23	St. Matthews, Orangeburg District, SC, Farmer	Co. E, 25th South Carolina Vols.	Captured	Oath of Allegiance 7/14/1865
Ott, William E. Private	Unknown	18	Unknown	Co C, 25th Regiment South Carolina Volunteers	Captured	Died of Unknown Disease, 3/5/1865, Buried Woodlawn Cemetery, Elmira, NY
Ottaway, Robert M. Private	Fort Fisher, NC, 2/25/1864; Volunteer	17	Brunswick County, NC	3rd Co. G, 36th Regiment North Carolina, 2nd Artillery	Captured	Died of Variola (smallpox), 5/5/1865, Buried Woodlawn Cemetery, Elmira, NY, Grave No. 2762
Outlaw, Jackson K. Private	Brunswick County, NC, 4/26/1864	17	Mount Olive, Duplin County, NC,	3rd Co. G, 40th Regiment North Carolina, 3rd Artillery	Captured	Exchanged On the James River, VA, 2/20/1865
Outlaw, John Lewis Private	Winton, Hertford County, NC, 2/5/1862, Mustered in at Camp Mangum, NC	26	Bertie County, NC, Farmer	Co. C, 3rd Battalion North Carolina Light Artillery	Captured	Died of Pneumonia, 3/28/1865, Buried Woodlawn Cemetery, Elmira, NY, Grave No. 2511
Owen, Michael Private	Elizabethtown, NC, Bladen County, NC, 10/19/1861, Volunteer	19	Bladen County, NC	2nd Co. I, 36th Regiment North Carolina, 2nd Artillery	Captured	Died of Chronic Diarrhea 4/19/1865, Buried Woodlawn Cemetery, Elmira, NY, Grave No. 1367

NAME and RANK	PLACE & TYPE OF ENLISTMENT	AGE	RESIDENCE & OCCUPATION	REGIMENT OR BATTALION	RESULT OF BATTLE	REMARKS
Owen, Thomas S. Private	Fort Fisher, New Hanover County, NC, 3/7/1862, Volunteer	25	Fayetteville, Cumberland County, NC, Detailed Carpenter at Fort Fisher	2nd Co. I, 36th Regiment North Carolina, 2nd Artillery	Captured	Oath of Allegiance 6/21/1865
Owens, Samuel Private	Charleston, SC, Morris Island, 2/20/1863	Unk	Charleston, SC,	Co A, 21st Regiment South Carolina Volunteers	Captured	Died of "Lung Fever", 2/21/1865 Buried Woodlawn Cemetery, Elmira, NY, Grave No. 2301
Owens, William Private	Georgetown, SC, 1/5/1862	18	Prince George Parish, Georgetown, SC,	Co. C, 21st South Carolina Volunteers	Captured	Died of Chronic Diarrhea 4/26/1865, Buried Woodlawn Cemetery, Elmira, NY, Grave No. 1424
Owens, William C. Sergeant	Charleston, SC, Charleston, 2/24/1862	19	Prince George Parish, Georgetown, SC,	Co K, 25th Regiment South Carolina Volunteers	Captured	Died of Catarrh, 3/21/1865 Buried Woodlawn Cemetery, Elmira, NY, Grave No. 1537

NAME and RANK	PLACE & TYPE OF ENLISTMENT	AGE	RESIDENCE & OCCUPATION	REGIMENT OR BATTALION	RESULT OF BATTLE	REMARKS
Page, Bennett Private	Fort Caswell, NC, Brunswick County, NC, 2/24/1863, Volunteer	37	Charlotte, NC	3rd Co. G, 36th Regiment North Carolina, 2nd Artillery	Captured	Died of "Rheumatic Pericarditis" 3/7/1865, Buried Woodlawn Cemetery, Elmira, NY, Grave No. 2400

NAME and RANK	PLACE & TYPE OF ENLISTMENT	AGE	RESIDENCE & OCCUPATION	REGIMENT OR BATTALION	RESULT OF BATTLE	REMARKS
Parker, Abner P. Private	Mount Tabor, Forsyth County, NC, 7/15/1863	Unk	Boykin Station, VA	Co. C, 3rd Battalion North Carolina Light Artillery	Captured	Oath Of Allegiance 6/12/1865
Parker, Badgegood B. Private	Chesterfield, SC, 1/8/1862	32	Unknown	Co. E, 21st South Carolina Vols.	Captured	Died of Chronic Diarrhea 7/12/1865, Buried Woodlawn Cemetery, Elmira, NY, Grave No. 2847
Parker, George F. Private	Kinston, Lenoir County, NC, 9/20/1863	30	Everittsville, Cross Roads District, Wayne County, NC Farmer	Co. F, 10th Regiment North Carolina, 1st Artillery	Captured	Oath Of Allegiance 7/11/1865
Parker, George R. Private	Fort Caswell, NC, Brunswick County, NC, 7/15/1862 Volunteer	36	Brunswick County, NC	2nd Co. A, 36th Regiment North Carolina, 2nd Artillery	Captured	Died of Chronic Diarrhea 6/18/1865, Buried Woodlawn Cemetery, Elmira, NY, Grave No. 2808
Parker, John Private	New Hanover County, NC, 12/15/1864	19	Pitt County, NC, Laborer	Co. D, 13th Battalion North Carolina Light Artillery	Captured	Exchanged On the James River, VA, 2/20/1865
Parnell, Joshua Private	Morris Island, SC, 6/12/1863	18	Darlington District, SC, Farmer	Co. H, 21st South Carolina Volunteers	Captured	Oath Of Allegiance 6/14/1865
Parnell, Thomas N. Private	Darlington, SC, 1/1/1862	22	Darlington District, SC, Farmer	Co. B, 21st South Carolina Volunteers	Captured	Exchanged On the James River, VA, 3/14/1865
Parrott, Joseph M. Sergeant	Darlington, SC, 5/12/1862	39	Darlington District, SC, Farmer	Co. B, 21st South Carolina Vols.	Captured	Died Of Unknown Disease 7/17/1865, Buried Woodlawn Cemetery, Elmira, NY, Grave No. 2873

NAME and RANK	PLACE & TYPE OF ENLISTMENT	AGE	RESIDENCE & OCCUPATION	REGIMENT OR BATTALION	RESULT OF BATTLE	REMARKS
Partin, John Private	Wake County, NC, 8/18/1863, Volunteer	44	Wake County, NC, Detailed as laborer.	3rd Co. B, 36th Regiment North Carolina, 2nd Artillery	Captured	Died of Chronic Diarrhea 3/10/1865, Buried Woodlawn Cemetery, Elmira, NY, Grave No. 1865
Pate, Asa Private	Fort Holmes, NC, Bladen County, NC, 2/5/1864	Unk	Bladen County, NC, Detached service at Smithville, June 1864	Co. F, 10th Regiment North Carolina, 1st Artillery	Captured	Died of Pneumonia 4/2/1865, Buried Woodlawn Cemetery, Elmira, NY, Grave No. 2580
Pate, Daniel Private	Bladen County, NC, 5/6/1862	24	Wayne County, NC, Farmer, Detached service at Smithville, June 1864	2nd Co. K, 40th Regiment North Carolina, 3rd Artillery	Captured	Died of Chronic Diarrhea 5/9/1865, Buried Woodlawn Cemetery, Elmira, NY, Grave No. 2782
Pate, Daniel Private	Goldsboro, Wayne County, NC, 12/8/1862	19	Goldsboro, Stony Creek District, Wayne County, NC	Co. F, 10th Regiment North Carolina, 1st Artillery	Captured	Oath Of Allegiance 7/3/1865
Pate, Edwin A. Private	Columbus County, NC, 5/15/1862	54	Whiteville, Columbus County, NC,	1st Battalion, North Carolina Heavy Artillery	Captured	Oath Of Allegiance 7/3/1865
Pate, Jackson Private	Beaufort, Carteret County, NC, 7/6/1861	24	Goldsboro, Wayne County, NC, Farmer, Detached service at Smithville, June 1864	Co. F, 10th Regiment North Carolina, 1st Artillery	Captured	Oath Of Allegiance 5/29/1865
Pate, John C. Private	Brunswick County, NC, 3/20/1864	18	Brunswick County, NC	2nd Co. K, 40th Regiment North Carolina, 3rd Artillery	Captured	Died of Remittent Fever 3/26/1865, Buried Woodlawn Cemetery, Elmira, NY, Grave No. 2466
Pate, John Lewis Private	Beaufort, Carteret County, NC, 3/20/1864	19	Goldsboro, Wayne County, NC Farmer	Co. F, 10th Regiment North Carolina, 1st Artillery	Captured	Oath Of Allegiance 7/26/1865

327

NAME and RANK	PLACE & TYPE OF ENLISTMENT	AGE	RESIDENCE & OCCUPATION	REGIMENT OR BATTALION	RESULT OF BATTLE	REMARKS
Pate, Richard W. Private	Beaufort, Carteret County, NC, 7/2/1861	20	Goldsboro, Wayne County, NC Farmer	Co. F, 10th Regiment North Carolina, 1st Artillery	Captured	Oath Of Allegiance 7/7/1865
Pate, Stephen Private	Brunswick County, NC, 9/23/1863, Volunteer	27	Bladen County, NC, Farmer	2nd Co. K, 40th Regiment North Carolina, 3rd Artillery	Captured	Exchanged On the James River, VA, 3/2/1865
Paul, Peter Private	Brunswick County, NC, 12/28/1863	18	Lumberton, Robeson County, NC,	2nd Co. K, 40th Regiment North Carolina, 3rd Artillery	Captured	Oath Of Allegiance 6/4/1865
Pearson, J.W. Private	Orangeburg, SC, 12/20/1862	Unk	Orangeburg, SC	Co H, 25th Regiment South Carolina Volunteers	Captured	Oath Of Allegiance 7/11/1865
Peel, James Private	Brunswick County, NC, 10/31/1864	Unk	Brunswick County, NC	3rd Co. G, 40th Regiment North Carolina, 3rd Artillery	Captured	Died of "Dropsy From Hepatic Disease" 4/4/1865, Buried Woodlawn Cemetery, Elmira, NY, Grave No. 2554
Peltier, L.L. Private	Chesterfield, SC, 2/1/1863	34	Cheraw, Chesterfield, NC, Cooper	Co. D, 21st South Carolina Vols.	Captured	Oath Of Allegiance 7/7/1865
Perdue, Charles Private	Lenoir County, NC, 10/16/1861, Volunteer	30	Lenoir County, NC, Detailed as teamster in wagon yard.	3rd Co. G, 40th Regiment North Carolina, 3rd Artillery	Captured	Died of "Continued Fever" 3/22/1865, Buried Woodlawn Cemetery, Elmira, NY, Grave No. 1539
Perdue, Charles Private	Chesterfield, SC, 5/1/1862	17	Unknown	Co. E, 21st South Carolina Vols.	Captured	Died of Pneumonia 6/21/1865, Buried Woodlawn Cemetery, Elmira, NY, Grave No. 2812

NAME and RANK	PLACE & TYPE OF ENLISTMENT	AGE	RESIDENCE & OCCUPATION	REGIMENT OR BATTALION	RESULT OF BATTLE	REMARKS
Perdue, William Private	Brunswick County, NC, 4/22/1863, Substitute	49	Lenoir County, NC, Detailed as teamster in wagon yard.	3rd Co. G, 40th Regiment North Carolina, 3rd Artillery	Captured	Exchanged 3/2/1865, Died of "Chronic Diarrhea and Febris Typhoides" 3/21/1865 at Raleigh Hospital
Perry, John C. Private	Brunswick County, NC, 3/20/1864	18	Bladen County, NC, Farmer	3rd Co. B, 36th Regiment North Carolina, 2nd Artillery	Captured	Died of Variola (smallpox) 3/20/1865, Buried Woodlawn Cemetery, Elmira, NY, Grave No. 1562
Perry, Lewis H. Last name also spelled Perrey Private	Wilmington, New Hanover County, NC, 10/20/1864	Unk	Tarboro, Edgecombe County, NC	Co. K, 10th Regiment North Carolina, 1st Artillery	Captured	Oath Of Allegiance 7/19/1865
Perry, Orren Private	Chatham County, NC, 10/20/1863 Volunteer	37	Chatham County, NC	3rd Co. G, 40th Regiment North Carolina, 3rd Artillery	Captured	Died of Chronic Diarrhea 4/2/1865, Buried Woodlawn Cemetery, Elmira, NY, Grave No. 2578
Perry, Wiley N. Private	Bladen County, NC, 1/28/1862, Volunteer	19	Bladen County, NC	3rd Co. B, 36th Regiment North Carolina, 2nd Artillery	Captured	Exchanged 3/2/1865, Died in Moore Hospital, Richmond, Va, of Typhoid Fever 3/15/1865, Buried in Hollywood Cemetery, Richmond, VA

NAME and RANK	PLACE & TYPE OF ENLISTMENT	AGE	RESIDENCE & OCCUPATION	REGIMENT OR BATTALION	RESULT OF BATTLE	REMARKS
Phelps, William Thomas Private	Windsor, Bertie County, NC, 1/23/1862, Mustered in at Camp Mangum, NC	21	Plymouth, NC Farmer	Co. C, 3rd Battalion North Carolina Light Artillery	Wounded In Leg & Captured	Oath Of Allegiance 6/12/1865
Phillips, Bryant Private	Chatham County, NC, 3/26/1863, Volunteer	18	Chatham County, NC	3rd Co. G, 40th Regiment North Carolina, 3rd Artillery	Captured	Died of Chronic Diarrhea 4/8/1865, Buried Woodlawn Cemetery, Elmira, NY, Grave No. 2633
Phillips, Eli Private	Georgetown, SC, 1/1/1864	34	Marion District, SC, Farmer	Co. A, 21st South Carolina Vols.	Captured	Died of Chronic Diarrhea 2/20/1865, Buried Woodlawn Cemetery, Elmira, NY, Grave No. 2328
Phillips, John Private	Camp Harllee, Georgetown, SC, 1/1/1862	32	Prince George Parish, Georgetown, SC	Co. A, 21st South Carolina Vols	Captured	Died of Chronic Diarrhea 2/6/1865, Buried Woodlawn Cemetery, Elmira, NY, Grave No. 1916
Phipps, Richard Private	Columbus County, NC, 10/25/1861, Volunteer	22	Columbus County, NC, Teamster at Fort Caswell, NC	2nd Co. A, 36th Regiment North Carolina, 2nd Artillery	Captured	Oath Of Allegiance 7/13/1865
Plowden, John Covert Private	Georgetown, SC, 3/18/1862	36	Manning, Clarendon District, SC, Sub. Overseer	25th South Carolina Vols	Captured	Died of Chronic Diarrhea 5/2/1865, Buried Woodlawn Cemetery, Elmira, NY, Grave No. 2754
Polk, Joel C. Private	Petersburg, VA, 5/20/1864	19	Darlington District, SC, Farmer	Co. D, 21st South Carolina Vols.	Captured	Oath Of Allegiance 7/7/1865

NAME and RANK	PLACE & TYPE OF ENLISTMENT	AGE	RESIDENCE & OCCUPATION	REGIMENT OR BATTALION	RESULT OF BATTLE	REMARKS
Pope, Stephen Private	Brunswick County, NC, 9/23/1863	41	Duplin County, NC	3rd, Co. G, 40th Regiment North Carolina, 2nd Artillery	Captured	Oath Of Allegiance 6/12/1865
Pope, William Streety Corporal	Elizabethtown, Bladen County, NC, 10/19/1861, Volunteer	28	Fayetteville, Cumberland County, NC, Detailed as assistant in Ordinance Dept.	2nd Co. I, 36th Regiment North Carolina, 2nd Artillery	Captured	Oath Of Allegiance 6/12/1865
Potter, Rufus H. Private	Bladen County, NC, 12/4/1861, Volunteer	17	Bladen County, NC	3rd Co. B, 36th Regiment North Carolina, 2nd Artillery	Captured	Died of Chronic Diarrhea 4/9/1865, Buried Woodlawn Cemetery, Elmira, NY, Grave No. 2613
Pouns, Jacob A. Sergeant	Old Brunswick, NC, 4/23/1862, Mustered in at Fort St. Philip, NC, Volunteer	22	Brunswick County, NC, Promoted to sergeant 12/15/1862	3rd Co. G, 36th Regiment North Carolina, 2nd Artillery	Captured	Died of Pneumonia 2/13/1865, Buried Woodlawn Cemetery, Elmira, NY, Grave No. 2051
Pouns, Samuel J. Private	Fort Fisher, New Hanover County, NC, 4/19/1864	17	New Hanover County, NC	3rd Co. G, 36th Regiment North Carolina, 2nd Artillery	Captured	Died on Route to be Exchanged, Cause Unknown 2/20/1865
Powe, Ellerbe Private	Camp Harllee, SC, 1/1/1862	40	Cheraw, Chesterfield, SC, Farmer	Co. D, 21st South Carolina Vols.	Captured	Oath Of Allegiance 7/7/1865
Powe, James F. Private	Camp Marrigault, Chesterfield, SC, 4/3/1862	36	Cheraw, Chesterfield, SC, Farmer	Co. D, 21st South Carolina Vols.	Captured	Died of Pneumonia 5/5/1865, Buried Woodlawn Cemetery, Elmira, NY, Grave No. 2764
Powe, Joseph Corporal	Chesterfield, SC, 4/30/1862	48	Cheraw, Chesterfield, SC, Overseer	Co. D, 21st South Carolina Vols.	Captured	Died of Pneumonia 3/8/1865, Buried Woodlawn Cemetery, Elmira, NY, Grave No. 2364

NAME and RANK	PLACE & TYPE OF ENLISTMENT	AGE	RESIDENCE & OCCUPATION	REGIMENT OR BATTALION	RESULT OF BATTLE	REMARKS
Powell, Charles Private	Myersville, SC, 5/13/1862	15	Cheraw, Chesterfield, SC,	Co. H, 25th South Carolina Vols.	Captured	Exchanged 3/2/1865, Admitted To Charlotte Hospital with Variola (smallpox) 3/15/1865
Powell, David Private	Myersville, SC, 5/13/1862	Unk	Unknown	Co. H, 25th South Carolina Vols.	Captured	Exchanged On the James River, VA, 2/20/1865
Powell, E. Private	Myersville, SC, 5/7/1862	Unk	Unknown	Co. H, 25th South Carolina Vols.	Captured	Died of Inflammation of the Liver, 6/23/1865, Buried Woodlawn Cemetery, Elmira, NY, Grave No. 2815
Powell, Warren T. Private	Robeson County, NC, 9/24/1861, Volunteer	20	Red Springs, Robeson County, NC, Detailed as teamster	Co. E, 40th Regiment North Carolina, 3rd Artillery	Captured	Exchanged 3/2/1865, Died of Chronic Diarrhea in Jackson Hospital, Richmond 4/24/1865, Buried Hollywood Cemetery, VA
Pressley, H.M. Private	James Island, SC, 4/9/1863	17	Murray's Ferry, Williamsburg District, SC, Farmer	Co. C, 25th South Carolina Vols.	Captured	Exchanged On the James River, VA, 3/2/1865
Price, Robert T. Private	Wayne County, NC, 8/19/1863, Volunteer	18	Wayne County, NC	3rd Co. G, 40th Regiment North Carolina, 3rd Artillery	Captured	Died of Pneumonia 2/13/1865, Buried Woodlawn Cemetery, Elmira, NY, Grave No. 2066

NAME and RANK	PLACE & TYPE OF ENLISTMENT	AGE	RESIDENCE & OCCUPATION	REGIMENT OR BATTALION	RESULT OF BATTLE	REMARKS
Prickett, Joseph H. Private	Coles Island, SC, 4/12/1862	Unk	Unknown	Co. H, 25th South Carolina Vols.	Captured	Died of Chronic Diarrhea 6/15/1865, Buried Woodlawn Cemetery, Elmira, NY, Grave No. 2880
Pridgen, Edwin S. Private	Brunswick County, NC, 7/23/1863	17	Lenoir County, NC, Student	3rd Co. G, 40th Regiment North Carolina, 3rd Artillery	Captured	Oath Of Allegiance 6/12/1865
Pridgen, Melvin Private	Wilmington, NC, New Hanover County, NC, 3/3/1862, Volunteer	22	Wilmington, NC, New Hanover County, NC	2nd Co. D, 36th Regiment North Carolina, 2nd Artillery	Captured	Died of Chronic Diarrhea 4/15/1865, Buried Woodlawn Cemetery, Elmira, NY, Grave No. 2713
Pridgen, Thomas J. Sergeant	Fort Caswell, NC, 2/16/1863	28	Canetuck, Pender County, NC	2nd Co. D, 36th Regiment North Carolina, 2nd Artillery	Captured	Oath Of Allegiance 6/16/1865
Pridgen, William Lafayette Private	Wilmington, New Hanover County, NC, 5/15/1862, Volunteer	20	Canetuck, Pender County, NC	2nd Co. D, 36th Regiment North Carolina, 2nd Artillery	Captured	Oath Of Allegiance 6/16/1865
Priest, John A. Private	Wilmington, New Hanover County, NC, 11/12/1861	18	White Hall, Bladen County NC	3rd Co. B, 36th Regiment North Carolina, 2nd Artillery	Captured	Oath Of Allegiance 7/7/1865
Provost, Clarence Private	Charleston, SC, 2/24/1862	28	Anderson, SC Merchant	Co. A, 25th South Carolina Vols.	Captured	Oath Of Allegiance 6/19/1865
Pugh, William Washington Private	Wilmington, New Hanover County, NC, 4/22/1861, Mustered in at Fort Branch	19	Beaufort County, NC	Co. F, 10th Regiment North Carolina, 1st Artillery	Captured	Exchanged on the James River, VA, 2/20/1865

NAME and RANK	PLACE & TYPE OF ENLISTMENT	AGE	RESIDENCE & OCCUPATION	REGIMENT OR BATTALION	RESULT OF BATTLE	REMARKS
Purcell, Duncan Private	Fort Fisher, NC, New Hanover County, NC, 3/12/1862, Volunteer	35	New Hanover County, NC	2nd Co. C, 36th Regiment North Carolina, 2nd Artillery	Captured	Died of Chronic Diarrhea 4/10/1865, Buried Woodlawn Cemetery, Elmira, NY, Grave No. 2668
Purnell, Calvin Private	Red Springs, Robeson County, NC, 9/24/1861, Volunteer	30	Robeson County, NC, Detailed cutting timber	Co. E, 40th Regiment North Carolina, 3rd Artillery	Captured	Died of Chronic Diarrhea 3/15/1865, Buried Woodlawn Cemetery, Elmira, NY, Grave No. 1664
Purvis, Henry Also Spelled: Pervis Private	Georgetown, SC, 1/1/1862	25	Darlington District, SC, Farmer	Co. K, 21st South Carolina Vols.	Captured	Died of Chronic Diarrhea 2/12/1865, Buried Woodlawn Cemetery, Elmira, NY, Grave No. 2057

NAME and RANK	PLACE & TYPE OF ENLISTMENT	AGE	RESIDENCE & OCCUPATION	REGIMENT OR BATTALION	RESULT OF BATTLE	REMARKS
Quick, Angus P. Private	Bennettsville, Marlboro District, SC, 12/25/1861	32	Unknown	Co. F, 21st South Carolina Vols.	Captured	Exchanged On the James River, VA, 3/2/1865
Quinn, John T. Private	Wilmington, New Hanover County, NC, 4/26/1862	23	Magnolia, Duplin County, NC	Co. D, 1st Battalion North Carolina Heavy Artillery	Captured	Exchanged 3/2/1865, Admitted To Hospital in Richmond 3/8/1865 with Debility
Quinn, Sylonus Private	Unknown	47	Duplin County, NC, Cooper	Co. D, 40th Regiment North Carolina, 3rd Artillery	Captured	Exchanged On the James River, VA, 3/2/1865

NAME and RANK	PLACE & TYPE OF ENLISTMENT	AGE	RESIDENCE & OCCUPATION	REGIMENT OR BATTALION	RESULT OF BATTLE	REMARKS
Rabon, George W. Private	Old Brunswick Town, NC, 4/16/1862, Mustered in at Fort St. Philip, NC	33	Wilmington, New Hanover County, NC	3rd Co. G, 36th Regiment North Carolina, 2nd Artillery	Captured	Oath Of Allegiance 7/19/1865
Rabon, William P. Private	Fort Caswell, NC, 9/11/1863	18	Wilmington, New Hanover County, NC	3rd Co. G, 36th Regiment North Carolina, 2nd Artillery	Captured	Oath Of Allegiance 7/3/1865
Rascoe, Alexander H. Private	Bennettsville, Marlboro District, SC, 12/25/1861	23	Bennettsville, Marlboro District, SC, Farmer	Co. F, 21st South Carolina Vols.	Captured	Exchanged On the James River, VA, 3/14/1865
Ratley, Hinant Private	Fort Fisher, NC, New Hanover County, NC, 3/19/1863, Subtitute for John F. Bryne of Cumberland County, NC	50	New Hanover County, NC	2nd Co. K, 40th Regiment North Carolina, 3rd Artillery	Captured	Died of Chronic Diarrhea 2/10/1865, Buried Woodlawn Cemetery, Elmira, NY, Grave No. 2087
Rawls, Hosey Private	St. Johns, NC, Hertford County, NC, 7/27/1864	26	Murfreesboro, Hertford County, NC	Co. C, 3rd Battalion North Carolina Artillery	Captured	Died of Debility 5/27/1865, Buried Woodlawn Cemetery, Elmira, NY, Grave No. 2915
Rawles, J. Private	Unknown	17	Vicinity of Rocky Well, Lexington, SC,	Co. K, 21st South Carolina Vols.	Captured	Exchanged On the James River, VA, 3/14/1865
Rawles, James Last name also spelled Rauls Private	Georgetown, SC, 12/20/1861	30	Georgetown, Prince George Parish, SC, Farmer	Co. A, 21st South Carolina Vols.	Captured	Died of Chronic Diarrhea 4/5/1865, Buried Woodlawn Cemetery, Elmira, NY, Grave No. 2548

NAME and RANK	PLACE & TYPE OF ENLISTMENT	AGE	RESIDENCE & OCCUPATION	REGIMENT OR BATTALION	RESULT OF BATTLE	REMARKS
Rawls, Joseph A. Private	St. Johns, NC, Hertford County, NC, 8/3/1864	Unk	Plymouth, NC	Co. C, 3rd Battalion North Carolina Artillery	Captured	Exchanged 3/21/1865 At Boulware's Wharf, James River, VA, Died of Debility In Jackson Hospital 3/23/1865, Richmond, VA, Buried Hollywood Cemetery, VA
Rawls, Joseph J. Private	Greenville, NC, Pitt County, NC, 5/14/1862	Unk	Tarboro, Edgecombe County, NC	Co. K, 10th Regiment North Carolina, 1st Artillery	Shot In Arm & Breast 12/25/1864 Captured 1/15/1865	Oath Of Allegiance 7/26/1865
Rawls, William R. Private	St. Johns, NC, Hertford County, NC, 7/28/1864	32	Murfreesboro, Hertford County, NC,	Co. C, 3rd Battalion North Carolina Artillery	Captured	Exchanged 3/14/1865 At Boulware's Wharf, James River, VA
Reaves, Jerry P. Private	Fort Fisher, New Hanover County, NC, 5/10/1863	40	New Hanover County, NC, Detailed in Gatlin Battery, NC	2nd Co. I, 36th Regiment North Carolina, 2nd Artillery	Captured	Exchanged On the James River, VA, 2/20/1865
Reaves, John W. Private	Fort Caswell, NC, Brunswick County, NC, 10/7/1863, Volunteer	33	Brunswick County, NC	2nd Co. D, 36th Regiment North Carolina, 2nd Artillery	Captured	Died of Bronchitis 3/26/1865, Buried in Woodlawn Cemetery, Elmira, NY, Grave No. 2477
Reaves, Samuel F. Private	Old Brunswick, Brunswick County, NC, 4/16/1862, Mustered in Fort St. Philip, Volunteer	35	Whiteville, Columbus County, NC	3rd Co. G, 36th Regiment North Carolina, 2nd Artillery	Captured	Died of Variola (smallpox) 4/13/1865, Buried in Woodlawn Cemetery, Elmira, NY, Grave No. 2701

NAME and RANK	PLACE & TYPE OF ENLISTMENT	AGE	RESIDENCE & OCCUPATION	REGIMENT OR BATTALION	RESULT OF BATTLE	REMARKS
Reaves, Samuel W. Private	Fort Anderson, NC, 4/27/1863 Conscript	18	Columbus County, NC	Co. E, 36th Regiment North Carolina, 2nd Artillery	Captured	Exchanged On the James River, VA, 3/2/1865
Reed, James Private	Charleston, SC, 4/2/1862	35	Orangeburg District, SC, Farmer	Co. H, 25th South Carolina Vols.	Captured	Died of Variola (smallpox) 3/13/1865, Buried Woodlawn Cemetery, Elmira, NY, Grave No. 2192
Regan, Addison Private	Fort Fisher, New Hanover County, NC, 6/28/1863, Volunteer	17	Robeson County, NC	2nd Co. I, 36th Regiment North Carolina, 2nd Artillery	Captured	Exchanged 3/14/1865 At Boulware's Wharf, James River, VA
Regan, Neill Private	Fort Fisher, NC, New Hanover County, NC, 3/4/1864, Volunteer	17	New Hanover County, NC, Detailed as mounted scout, Fort Fisher, NC	2nd Co. I, 36th Regiment North Carolina, 2nd Artillery	Captured	Died of Pneumonia 5/23/1865, Buried in Woodlawn Cemetery, Elmira, NY, Grave No. 2929
Reid, Louis H. Sergeant Major	Washington, NC, 9/23/1861	21	Wilson, Wilson County, NC	Co. D, 13th Battalion North Carolina Light Artillery	Captured	Oath Of Allegiance 6/14/1865
Renneker, John H. Private	James Island, SC, 3/21/1863	Unk	Charleston, SC	Co. B, 25th South Carolina Vols.	Captured	Oath Of Allegiance 6/23/1865
Renneker, F.W. Private	Charleston, SC, 2/24/1862	21	Unknown	Co. B, 25th South Carolina Vols.	Captured	Exchanged On the James River, VA, 3/14/1865

NAME and RANK	PLACE & TYPE OF ENLISTMENT	AGE	RESIDENCE & OCCUPATION	REGIMENT OR BATTALION	RESULT OF BATTLE	REMARKS
Rentfrow, James Private	Smithville, NC, Brunswick County, NC, 7/11/1863	Unk	Brunswick County, NC, Detached service at Smithville, NC	Co. F, 10th Regiment North Carolina, 1st Artillery	Captured	Died of Pneumonia 3/4/1865, Buried in Woodlawn Cemetery, Elmira, NY, Grave No. 1988
Reynolds, James M. Private	Fort Caswell, Brunswick County, NC, 5/4/1863, Volunteer	37	Brunswick County, NC	3rd Co. G, 36th Regiment North Carolina, 2nd Artillery	Captured	Exchanged On the James River, VA, 2/20/1865
Reynolds, James W. Private	Sampson County, NC, May 4, 1863 Volunteer	33	Sampson County, NC, Farm Laborer	3rd Co. G, 36th Regiment North Carolina, 2nd Artillery	Captured	Died of Pneumonia 4/9/1865, Buried in Woodlawn Cemetery, Elmira, NY, Grave No. 2619
Reynolds, William Private	Sampson County, NC, 2/19/1862, Volunteer	37	Sampson County, NC, Detailed as raftsman at Fort Campbell & Smithville, NC	2nd Co. A, 36th Regiment North Carolina, 2nd Artillery	Captured	Died of Pneumonia 3/5/1865, Buried in Woodlawn Cemetery, Elmira, NY, Grave No. 1971
Reynolds, William H. Private	Smithville, NC, 2/19/1862, Mustered in at Fort Johnson, NC, Volunteer	39	Town Creek, Brunswick County, NC, Detailed as raftsman at Fort Campbell & Smithville, NC	Co. K, 36th Regiment North Carolina, 2nd Artillery	Captured	Exchanged 2/20/1865, Died 4/9/1865 of Pneumonia, Buried Woodlawn Cemetery, Elmira, NY

NAME and RANK	PLACE & TYPE OF ENLISTMENT	AGE	RESIDENCE & OCCUPATION	REGIMENT OR BATTALION	RESULT OF BATTLE	REMARKS
Rhames, Nathaniel E. Private	Charleston, SC, 4/17/1864	Unk	Unknown	Co. A, 21st South Carolina Vols.	Captured	Died of Chronic Diarrhea 6/10/1865, Buried Woodlawn Cemetery, Elmira, NY, Grave No. 2887
Rhodes, A.J. Private	Darlington, SC, 10/23/1863	Unk	Darlington District, SC	Co. B, 21st South Carolina Vols.	Captured	Oath Of Allegiance 7/7/1865
Rhodes, John D. Private	Fort Caswell, NC, 3/26/1862	18	Fair Bluff, Columbus County, NC	Co. E, 36th Regiment North Carolina, 2nd Artillery	Captured	Oath Of Allegiance 7/7/1865
Richards, Miah Sergeant	Marrion, SC, 4/20/1862	24	Marrion, SC, Merchant	Co. D, 25th South Carolina Vols.	Captured	Oath Of Allegiance 5/13/1865
Richardson, P.G. Private	Camp Harllee, SC, 2/14/1862	Unk	Kingstree, SC	Co. I, 21st South Carolina Vols.	Captured	Oath Of Allegiance 7/11/1865
Richburg, Benjamin D. Private	James Island, SC, 2/23/1863	29	Bradford Springs, Sumter District, SC, Overseer	Co. I, 25th South Carolina Vols.	Captured	Died of Pneumonia 4/24/1865, Buried Woodlawn Cemetery, Elmira, NY, Grave No. 1409
Richburgh, J.E. Private	Camp Harllee, Georgetown SC, 1/1/1862	18	Kingstree, SC	Co. I, 25th South Carolina Vols.	Captured	Oath Of Allegiance 6/23/1865

NAME and RANK	PLACE & TYPE OF ENLISTMENT	AGE	RESIDENCE & OCCUPATION	REGIMENT OR BATTALION	RESULT OF BATTLE	REMARKS
Ridgeway, Joseph M. Private	James Island, SC, 11/15/1861	Unk	Unknown	Co. I, 25th South Carolina Vols.	Captured	Died of Pneumonia 4/6/1865, Buried Woodlawn Cemetery, Elmira, NY, Grave No. 2549
Ridgeway, Joseph N. Also Spelled: Ridgway Private	Camp Harllee, Georgetown, SC, 2/23/1863	33	Manning, Clarendon District, SC, Miller	Co. I, 25th South Carolina Vols.	Captured	Died of Unknown Disease 4/24/1865, Buried Woodlawn Cemetery, Elmira, NY, Grave No. 1409
Ridgeway, Reuben F. Sergeant	James Island, SC, 10/24/1862	30	Manning, Clarendon District, SC, Farmer	Co. I, 25th South Carolina Vols.	Captured	Exchanged On the James River, VA, 2/20/1865
Riley, Daniel Private	Fort Fisher, NC, New Hanover County, NC, 3/15/1863, Volunteer	32	Fayetteville, Cumberland County, NC, Farmer	2nd Co. D, 36th Regiment North Carolina, 2nd Artillery	Captured	Died of Pneumonia 2/16/1865, Buried in Woodlawn Cemetery, Elmira, NY, Grave No. 2203
Rinaldi, Eugene W. Private	Fort Holmes, NC, Brunswick County, NC, 8/21/1864	17	Elizabethtown, Bladen County, NC	2nd Co. K, 40th Regiment North Carolina, 3rd Artillery	Captured	Died of Chronic Diarrhea 4/26/1865, Buried Woodlawn Cemetery, Elmira, NY, Grave No. 1426
Rivers, Jacob M. Private	Whippy Swamp, SC, 7/15/1861	25	Prince William Parish, Beaufort District, SC, Farmer	Co. D, 11th South Carolina	Captured	Exchanged On The James River, VA, 3/2/1865

NAME and RANK	PLACE & TYPE OF ENLISTMENT	AGE	RESIDENCE & OCCUPATION	REGIMENT OR BATTALION	RESULT OF BATTLE	REMARKS
Rives, William C. Private	Secessionville, SC, 5/11/1862	20	Orangeburg, SC	Co. G, 25th South Carolina Vols.	Captured	Oath Of Allegiance 6/16/1865
Robbins, William W. Private	Fort Caswell, NC, Brunswick County, NC, 8/29/1863, Volunteer	36	Brunswick County, NC	3rd Co. G, 36th Regiment North Carolina, 2nd Artillery	Wounded & Captured	Died of Variola (smallpox) 3/22/1865, Buried Woodlawn Cemetery, Elmira, NY, Grave No. 1538
Roberson, Harrison Also Spelled: Robason Private	Transferred From F Co., 17th Regiment 4/27/1864, North Carolina Troops	21	Martin County, NC	Co. K, 10th Regiment North Carolina, 1st Artillery	Captured	Died of Pneumonia 3/7/1865, Buried in Woodlawn Cemetery, Elmira, NY, Grave No. 2405
Roberts, John Troy Private	Fort Fisher, New Hanover County, NC, 6/21/1864	17	Spout Spring Depot, NC, Student	Co. H, 36th Regiment North Carolina, 2nd Artillery	Captured	Oath Of Allegiance 7/11/1865
Robeson, Matthew P. Private	Elizabethtown, Bladen County, NC, 3/15/1862, Mustered in at Wilmington, NC, Volunteer	42	Duplin County, NC, Farmer	Co. H, 36th Regiment North Carolina, 2nd Artillery	Captured	Died of Variola (smallpox) 2/22/1865, Buried in Woodlawn Cemetery, Elmira, NY, Grave No. 2247
Robinson, Jesse Private	Goldsboro, Wayne County, NC, 7/3/1863, Mustered in at Beaufort, NC,	36	Greene County, NC, Farmer	Co. F, 10th Regiment North Carolina, 1st Artillery	Captured	Died of Rubeola (measles) 2/19/1865, Buried in Woodlawn Cemetery, Elmira, NY, Grave No. 2337

NAME and RANK	PLACE & TYPE OF ENLISTMENT	AGE	RESIDENCE & OCCUPATION	REGIMENT OR BATTALION	RESULT OF BATTLE	REMARKS
Robinson, John P. Private	Fort St. Philip, Brunswick County, NC, 5/14/1862, Volunteer	28	Brunswick County, NC	3rd Co. G, 36th Regiment North Carolina, 2nd Artillery	Captured	Oath Of Allegiance 7/3/1865
Robinson, Julius C. Private	Fort Fisher, NC, New Hanover County, NC, 3/1/1864, Volunteer	18	New Hanover County, NC	2nd Co. I, 36th Regiment North Carolina, 2nd Artillery	Captured	Died of Chronic Diarrhea 2/15/1865, Buried Woodlawn Cemetery, Elmira, NY, Grave No. 2170
Robinson, Napoleon A. Private	Fort Branch, Brunswick County, NC, 7/9/1863	17	Charlotte, NC	3rd Co. G, 40th Regiment North Carolina, 3rd Artillery	Captured	Oath Of Allegiance 6/12/1865
Robison, A. Private, may be same person as Robeson, Albert	Fort Pender, NC, 12/2/1863, Volunteer	18	White Hall, Bladen County NC	Co. H, 36th Regiment North Carolina, 2nd Artillery	Captured	Exchanged 3/14/1865 At Boulware's Wharf, James River, VA
Robinson, William Private	Goldsboro, NC, Wayne County, NC, 8/23/1862	20	Goldsboro, Wayne County, NC	Co. F, 10th Regiment North Carolina, 1st Artillery	Captured	Died of Pneumonia 3/7/1865, Buried in Woodlawn Cemetery, Elmira, NY, Grave No. 2407
Rogers, Thomas G. Private	Camp Harllee, Georgetown, SC, 1/8/1862	27	Marion District, SC, Silver Smith	Co. I, 21st South Carolina Volunteers	Captured	Died of Chronic Diarrhea, 2/16/1865, Buried Woodlawn Cemetery, Elmira, NY, Grave No. 2188
Rodgers, William J.J. Private	Enfield, NC, Halifax County, NC, 10/9/1861, Volunteer	23	Wayne County, NC	Co. F, 36th Regiment North Carolina, 2nd Artillery	Captured	Died of Typhoid Fever 2/27/1865, Buried in Woodlawn Cemetery, Elmira, NY, Grave No. 2120

NAME and RANK	PLACE & TYPE OF ENLISTMENT	AGE	RESIDENCE & OCCUPATION	REGIMENT OR BATTALION	RESULT OF BATTLE	REMARKS
Rook, E.C. Private	Coles Island, SC, 4/11/1862	Unk	Unknown	Co. F, 25th South Carolina Vols.	Captured	Exchanged On the James River, VA, 3/2/1865
Rouse, Noah Private	Fort Fisher, New Hanover County, NC, 2/9/1863, Volunteer	21	Whiteville, Columbus County, NC	2nd Co. K, 40th Regiment North Carolina, 3rd Artillery	Captured	Oath Of Allegiance 6/12/1865
Rowland, Benjamin W. Private	Fort Caswell, Brunswick County, NC, 8/2/1863, Volunteer	18	Henderson, Vance County, NC	Co. F, 36th Regiment North Carolina, 2nd Artillery	Captured	Oath Of Allegiance 6/12/1865
Royal, Molton Private	Fort Fisher, New Hanover County, NC, 10/31/1862, Volunteer	22	Unknown	2nd Co. C, 36th Regiment North Carolina, 2nd Artillery	Captured	Exchanged On the James River, VA, 3/2/1865
Royal, Ollin Private	Sampson County, NC, 2/18/1863	35	Warsaw, Duplin County, NC	2nd Co. A, 36th Regiment North Carolina, 2nd Artillery	Captured	Oath Of Allegiance 6/12/1865
Rozier, Reuben Private	Fort Fisher, New Hanover County, NC, 8/1/1863, Volunteer	43	Lumberton, Robeson County, NC	2nd Co. K, 40th Regiment North Carolina, 3rd Artillery	Captured	Oath Of Allegiance 6/12/1865
Rush, Robert T. Private	Fort Branch, Brunswick County, NC, 7/20/1863, Volunteer	18	Montgomery County, NC	3rd Co. G, 40th Regiment North Carolina, 3rd Artillery	Captured	Exchanged On the James River, VA, 3/2/1865
Rushing, James B. Private	Marion, SC, 4/20/1862	17	Marion County, SC,	Co. D, 25th South Carolina Vols.	Captured	Exchanged On the James River, VA, 2/20/1865

NAME and RANK	PLACE & TYPE OF ENLISTMENT	AGE	RESIDENCE & OCCUPATION	REGIMENT OR BATTALION	RESULT OF BATTLE	REMARKS
Russ, William H. Private	Fort Campbell, Brunswick County, NC, 1/16/1864 Volunteer	17	Wilmington, New Hanover County, NC	3rd Co G, 36th Regiment North Carolina, 2nd Artillery	Captured	Oath Of Allegiance 7/7/1865
Russell, John Private	Fort Branch, NC, Brunswick County, NC, 7/28/1863, Volunteer	42	Anson County, NC	3rd Co. G, 40th Regiment North Carolina, 3rd Artillery	Captured	Died of Pneumonia 3/4/1865, Buried in Woodlawn Cemetery, Elmira, NY, Grave No. 1975
Ryan, James T. Private	Fort Caswell, Brunswick County, NC, 7/1/1863	18	Enfield, NC	Co. F, 36th Regiment North Carolina, 2nd Artillery	Captured	Oath Of Allegiance 7/7/1865

NAME and RANK	PLACE & TYPE OF ENLISTMENT	AGE	RESIDENCE & OCCUPATION	REGIMENT OR BATTALION	RESULT OF BATTLE	REMARKS
Salmon, Sidney Private	Chatham County, NC, 3/26/1863, Volunteer	18	Goldston, Chatham County, NC, Farmer, Wood Cutter	3rd Co. G, 40th Regiment North Carolina, 3rd Artillery	Captured	Exchanged 3/2/1865 at James River, VA, Died of unknown Disease 3/2/1865
Sanders, Benjamin H. Private	Coles Island, SC, 4/11/1862	14	Midway, Barnwell County, SC,	Co. G, 25th South Carolina Vols.	Captured	Oath Of Allegiance 7/7/1865
Sanders, Joseph T. Sergeant	Charleston, SC, 4/1/1862	19	Charleston, SC, Clerk	Co. E, 25th South Carolina Vols.	Captured	Exchanged On the James River, VA, 2/20/1865

NAME and RANK	PLACE & TYPE OF ENLISTMENT	AGE	RESIDENCE & OCCUPATION	REGIMENT OR BATTALION	RESULT OF BATTLE	REMARKS
Sanford, Jesse Private	Columbia, Richland County, SC, 8/13/1864	34	Blackville, Orangeburg District, SC, Mechanic	Co. G, 25th South Carolina Vols.	Captured	Died of Chronic Diarrhea 3/20/1865, Buried Woodlawn Cemetery, Elmira, NY, Grave No. 1549
Saunders, James R. Private	Fort Caswell, Brunswick County, NC, 7/15/1863, Volunteer	18	Halifax County, NC	Co. F, 36th Regiment North Carolina, 2nd Artillery	Captured	Exchanged 3/14/1865 at Boulware's Wharf, James River, VA
Schirer, John	James Island, SC, 7/20/1862, Volunteer	Unk	Providence, RI	Co. B, 25th South Carolina Vols.	Captured	Oath Of Allegiance 6/16/1865
Schuler, George L.V.S. Also Spelled: Shuler Private	Cole's Island, SC, 4/11/1862	25	McCantsville, Orangeburg, SC, Carpente	Co. F, 25th South Carolina Vols.	Captured	Exchanged On the James River, VA, 3/2/1865
Schuler, Fred P.H. Private Also Spelled: Shuler	Cole's Island, SC, 4/11/1862	15	Orangeburg District, SC,	Co. F, 25th South Carolina Vols.	Captured	Exchanged 3/2/1865, Died at Jackson Hospital Of Chronic Diarrhea 4/3/1865, Buried Hollywood Cemetery, Richmond, VA
Schulte, J.H. Private	Charleston, SC, 4/4/1862	29	Charleston, SC, Lumber Dealer	Co. B, 25th South Carolina Vols.	Captured	Oath Of Allegiance 7/7/1865
Scott, J.E. Private	James Island, SC, 5/16/1863	18	Murray's Ferry, Williamsburg District, SC,	Co. C, 25th South Carolina Vols.	Captured	Oath Of Allegiance 6/30/1865

NAME and RANK	PLACE & TYPE OF ENLISTMENT	AGE	RESIDENCE & OCCUPATION	REGIMENT OR BATTALION	RESULT OF BATTLE	REMARKS
Scott, John L. Private	James Island, SC, 8/29/1863	34	Lynchburg, Sumter District, SC, Contractor	Co. G, 25th South Carolina Vols.	Captured	Oath Of Allegiance 7/11/1865
Seagraves, James M. Private	Camp Hill, NC, 8/8/1862, Transferred From Co. D, Camp Holmes Guard 3/1863	Unk	Detailed as Brick Mason at Fort Campbell & Fort Caswell, NC	Co. C, 3rd Battalion North Carolina Light Artillery	Captured	Exchanged 3/14/1865 at Boulware's Wharf, James River, VA
Secrest, Lafayette A. Private	Wilmington, NC, New Hanover County, NC, 5/11/1864	18	Monroe, Union County, NC	Co K, 10th Regiment North Carolina, 1st Artillery	Captured	Died of "Spasm Of Glottis" 4/13/1865, Buried Woodlawn Cemetery, Elmira, NY, Grave No. 2717
Sellars, David Private	Fort Caswell, NC, 10/20/1863, Volunteer	35	New Hanover County, NC	2nd Co. D, 36th Regiment North Carolina, 2nd Artillery, Detailed to Signal Corp.	Captured	Died of Variola (smallpox) 3/20/1865, Buried Woodlawn Cemetery, Elmira, NY, Grave No. 1544
Sellars, Duncan C. Private	Bladen County, NC, 1/28/1862	26	Rosendale, NC	3rd Co. B, 36th Regiment North Carolina, 2nd Artillery	Captured	Oath Of Allegiance 7/3/1865
Sellars, George Private	Wilmington, New Hanover County, NC, 10/28/1861, Volunteer	19	Wilmington, New Hanover County, NC	2nd Co. D, 36th Regiment North Carolina, 2nd Artillery	Captured	Oath Of Allegiance 5/27/1865, Died of Chronic Diarrhea 5/27/1865, Buried Woodlawn Cemetery, Elmira, NY, Grave No. 2916

NAME and RANK	PLACE & TYPE OF ENLISTMENT	AGE	RESIDENCE & OCCUPATION	REGIMENT OR BATTALION	RESULT OF BATTLE	REMARKS
Sellars, John Private	Wilmington, NC, New Hanover County, NC, 3/3/1862, Volunteer	38	New Hanover County, NC	2nd Co. D, 36th Regiment North Carolina, 2nd Artillery	Wounded & Captured	Died of Variola (smallpox) 3/1/1865, Buried Woodlawn Cemetery, Elmira, NY, Grave No. 2023
Sellars, William Private	Wilmington, New Hanover County, NC, 3/3/1862, Volunteer	28	New Hanover County, NC	2nd Co. D, 36th Regiment North Carolina, 2nd Artillery	Captured	Died of "Congestion Of Lungs" 2/10/1865, Buried Woodlawn Cemetery, Elmira, NY, Grave No. 1944
Sellers, James B. Private	Fort Fisher, New Hanover County, NC, 5/23/1864	17	Town Creek District, Brunswick County, NC	3rd Co. G, 36th Regiment North Carolina, 2nd Artillery	Captured	Oath Of Allegiance 7/7/1865
Sellers, John First Sergeant	Fort St. Philip, NC, Brunswick County, NC, 5/14/1862, Volunteer	34	Brunswick County, NC, Detailed to string Telegraph lines to Fort Caswell, NC	3rd Co. G, 36th Regiment North Carolina, 2nd Artillery	Captured	Died of Chronic Diarrhea 3/29/1865, Buried Woodlawn Cemetery, Elmira, NY, Grave No. 2537
Sellers, John M. Private	Old Brunswick Town, NC, 4/16/1862, Mustered in at Fort St. Philip, NC, Volunteer	41	Brunswick County, NC	3rd Co. G, 36th Regiment North Carolina, 2nd Artillery	Captured	Died of Variola (smallpox) 3/20/1865, Buried Woodlawn Cemetery, Elmira, NY, Grave No. 1560
Sellers, John W. Musician	Fort Caswell, NC, Brunswick County, NC, 2/24/1863, Volunteer	37	Brunswick County, NC	3rd Co. G, 36th Regiment North Carolina, 2nd Artillery	Captured	Died of Variola (smallpox) 5/14/1865, Buried Woodlawn Cemetery, Elmira, NY, Grave No. 2804

NAME and RANK	PLACE & TYPE OF ENLISTMENT	AGE	RESIDENCE & OCCUPATION	REGIMENT OR BATTALION	RESULT OF BATTLE	REMARKS
Sellers, Lorenzo Private	Fort Caswell, NC, Brunswick County, NC, 9/25/1862, Volunteer	21	Lockwood Folly, NC, Worked Extra Duty as a Nurse in the Hospital	3rd Co. G, 36th Regiment North Carolina, 2nd Artillery	Captured	Exchanged 3/21/1865 at Boulware's Wharf, James River, VA
Sellers, Robert A. Private	Fort Johnson, Brunswick County, NC, 3/16/1863, Volunteer	17	Smithville, Brunswick County, NC	3rd Co. G, 40th Regiment North Carolina, 3rd Artillery	Captured	Oath Of Allegiance 6/12/1865
Sellers, Thomas A. Private	Fort Caswell, Brunswick County, NC, 2/8/1863, Volunteer	38	Brunswick County, NC	3rd Co. G, 36th Regiment North Carolina, 2nd Artillery	Captured	Exchanged 2/20/1865 at Boulware's Wharf, James River, VA
Sellers, William H. Private	Cerro Gordo, NC, 3/5/1862, Mustered in at Wilmington, NC, Volunteer	25	Whiteville, Columbus County, NC	Co. E, 36th Regiment North Carolina, 2nd Artillery	Wounded & Captured	Oath Of Allegiance 7/3/1865
Sellers, William R. Private	Brunswick County, NC, 8/24/1863, Volunteer	30	Brunswick County, NC,	3rd Co. G, 36th Regiment North Carolina, 2nd N.C. Artillery	Wounded & Captured	Died of Congestion Of Lungs, 2/10/1865
Senter, John A. Private	Camp Holmes, NC, 10/13/1863	Unk	Raleigh, Wake County, NC	2nd Co. D, 36th Regiment North Carolina, 2nd Artillery	Captured	Oath Of Allegiance 7/3/1865
Sessoms, Neill Private	Blockersville, NC, 2/26/1862, Volunteer	26	Fayetteville, Cumberland County, NC	2nd Co. C, 36th Regiment North Carolina, 2nd Artillery	Captured	Oath Of Allegiance 6/12/1865

NAME and RANK	PLACE & TYPE OF ENLISTMENT	AGE	RESIDENCE & OCCUPATION	REGIMENT OR BATTALION	RESULT OF BATTLE	REMARKS
Sessoms, Thomas S. Last name also spelled Sessons Private	Wilmington, New Hanover County, NC, 11/4/1861, Volunteer	21	Harrison's Creek Landing, NC	2nd Co. I, 36th Regiment North Carolina, 2nd Artillery	Captured	Oath Of Allegiance 6/12/1865
Shadding, Henry J. Private	Fort Pender, NC, Brunswick County, NC, 12/7/1863, Volunteer	18	Brunswick County, NC, Detached Service as Mounted Scout	Co. H, 36th Regiment North Carolina, 2nd Artillery	Captured	Died of Chronic Diarrhea 3/31/1865, Buried Woodlawn Cemetery, Elmira, NY, Grave No. 2598
Shaffer, R.R. Private	Charleston, SC, 2/24/1862	33	Charleston, SC	Co. B, 25th South Carolina Vols.	Captured	Oath Of Allegiance 7/11/1865
Shaw, Bennett Private	Elizabethtown, Bladen County, NC, 5/6/1862, Mustered in at Fort St. Philip, NC, Volunteer	22	Brown Marsh, Bladen County, NC Farmer	2nd Co. K, 40th Regiment North Carolina, 3rd Artillery	Captured	Oath Of Allegiance 6/12/1865
Shaw, Daniel F. Private	Elizabethtown, Bladen County, NC, 5/6/1862, Mustered in at Fort St. Philip, NC, Volunteer	33	Brown Marsh, Bladen County, NC Farmer	2nd Co. K, 40th Regiment North Carolina, 3rd Artillery	Captured	Oath Of Allegiance 6/12/1865
Shaw, Daniel M. Private	Fort Caswell, Brunswick County, NC, 9/19/1863, Volunteer	41	Brunswick County, NC	Co. E, 40th Regiment North Carolina, 3rd Artillery	Captured	Exchanged On the James River, VA, 3/2/1865
Shaw, Duncan Private	Elizabethtown, Bladen County, NC, 5/6/1862, Mustered in at Fort St. Philip, NC, Volunteer	18	Brown Marsh, Bladen County, NC Farmer	2nd Co. K, 40th Regiment North Carolina, 3rd Artillery	Captured	Oath Of Allegiance 6/12/1865

NAME and RANK	PLACE & TYPE OF ENLISTMENT	AGE	RESIDENCE & OCCUPATION	REGIMENT OR BATTALION	RESULT OF BATTLE	REMARKS
Shaw, H.D. Private	Battery Island, SC, 4/12/1862	17	Kingstree, Murray's Ferry, Williamsburg District, SC	Co. C, 25th South Carolina Vols.	Captured	Oath Of Allegiance 7/11/1865
Shaw, John Private	Wilmington, New Hanover County, NC, 12/28/1861, Volunteer	40	Fayetteville, Cumberland County, NC	Co. E, 36th Regiment North Carolina, 2nd Artillery	Captured	Oath Of Allegiance 7/3/1865
Shaw, John W. Private	Elizabethtown, Bladen County, NC, 5/6/1862, Mustered in at Fort St. Philip, NC, Volunteer	18	Elizabethtown, Bladen County, NC	2nd Co. K, 40th Regiment North Carolina, 3rd Artillery	Captured	Oath Of Allegiance 6/12/1865
Shaw, Malcom Private	Unknown	16	Whiteville, Columbus County, NC	Co. K, 36th Regiment North Carolina, 2nd Artillery	Captured	Oath Of Allegiance 7/7/1865
Shaw, Mitchell Private	Fort Holmes, Brunswick County, NC, 10/26/1864	41	Brunswick County, NC	2nd Co. K, 40th Regiment North Carolina, 3rd Artillery	Captured	Exchanged On the James River, VA, 3/2/1865
Shaw, Solomon Musician	Fort St. Philip, Brunswick County, NC, 2/7/1863, Volunteer	36	Whiteville, Columbus County, NC,	Co. E, 36th Regiment North Carolina, 2nd Artillery	Captured	Exchanged 3/14/1865 at Boulware's Wharf, James River, VA
Sheahan, William S. Private	St John, Hertford County, NC, 5/2/1862	Unk	Hertford County, NC	Co. C, 3rd Battalion North Carolina Light Artillery	Captured	Oath Of Allegiance 8/7/1865
Shephard, John J. Private	Wilmington, New Hanover County, NC, 2/13/1862 Volunteer	17	Wilmington, New Hanover County, NC	2nd Co. D, 36th Regiment North Carolina, 2nd Artillery	Captured	Exchanged 3/14/1865 at Boulware's Wharf, James River, VA

NAME and RANK	PLACE & TYPE OF ENLISTMENT	AGE	RESIDENCE & OCCUPATION	REGIMENT OR BATTALION	RESULT OF BATTLE	REMARKS
Shepherd, Ethemore Private	Cerogordo, NC, 3/1/1862, Mustered in at Wilmington, NC	18	Fair Bluff, Columbus County, NC	Co. E, 36th Regiment North Carolina, 2nd Artillery	Captured	Oath Of Allegiance 7/26/1865
Shipman, William Private	Bladen County, NC, 7/8/1862, Volunteer	24	Elizabethtown, Bladen County, NC	3rd Co. B, 36th Regiment North Carolina, 2nd Artillery	Captured	Oath Of Allegiance 7/7/1865
Shirer, Henry W. Private	Cole's Island, SC, 4/11/1862	23	Charleston, SC	Co. F, 25th South Carolina Vols.	Captured	Died of Variola (smallpox) 6/30/1865, Buried Woodlawn Cemetery, Elmira, NY, Grave No. 2830
Shirley, John Private	Fort Ellis, Craven County, NC, 12/25/1861, Volunteer	25	Gibbs Woods District, Carrituck County, NC	Co. F, 36th Regiment North Carolina, 2nd Artillery	Captured	Exchanged On the James River, VA, 2/20/1865
Shoemaker, Ira Thomas Sergeant	Coles Island, SC, 4/11/62	Unk	Grahams P.O., SC	Co. G, 25th South Carolina Vols.	Captured	Oath Of Allegiance 6/14/1865
Sikes, Amos Private	Fort Fisher, NC, New Hanover County, NC, 9/28/1863, Conscript	42	New Hanover County, NC	2nd Co. I, 36th Regiment North Carolina, 2nd Artillery	Captured	Died of Typhoid Fever 5/6/1865, Buried Woodlawn Cemetery, Elmira, NY, Grave No. 2766

NAME and RANK	PLACE & TYPE OF ENLISTMENT	AGE	RESIDENCE & OCCUPATION	REGIMENT OR BATTALION	RESULT OF BATTLE	REMARKS
Sikes, Lucian Private	Fort Fisher, NC, New Hanover County, NC, 5/12/1862, Conscript	28	New Hanover County, NC	2nd Co. I, 36th Regiment North Carolina, 2nd Artillery	Captured	Exchanged at James River, VA, 3/14/1865, Died of Debility In Jackson Hospital, Richmond , Va, 4/7/1865, Buried Hollywood Cemetery, VA
Sillivent, Hardy Private	Goldsboro, NC, Wayne County, NC, 8/27/1862	Unk	Goldsboro, NC, Wayne County, NC	Co F, 10th Regiment North Carolina, 1st Artillery	Captured	Died of Typhoid Fever 4/20/1865, Buried Woodlawn Cemetery, Elmira, NY, Grave No. 1383
Simmons, Asberry Private	Fort St. Philip, Brunswick County, NC, 5/13/1862, Volunteer	33	Smithville, NC	3rd Co. G, 36th Regiment North Carolina, 2nd Artillery	Captured	Oath Of Allegiance 6/23/1865
Simmons, John W. Private	Fort Fisher, New Hanover County, NC, 6/11/1864, Conscript	36	Sampson County, NC, Farmer	2nd Co. I, 36th Regiment North Carolina, 2nd Artillery	Captured	Exchanged 3/14/1865 at Boulware's Wharf, James River, VA
Simmons, Samuel Private	Fort Fisher, New Hanover County, NC, 7/13/1864	34	Sampson County, NC, Farmer	3rd Co. G, 36th Regiment North Carolina, 2nd Artillery	Captured	Exchanged on the James River, VA, 3/2/1865
Simms, John H. Private	Fort Fisher, NC, New Hanover County, NC, 3/15/1863, Volunteer	18	New Hanover County, NC	2nd Co. C, 36th Regiment North Carolina, 2nd Artillery	Captured	Died of Chronic Diarrhea/Pneumonia 2/24/1865, Buried Woodlawn Cemetery, Elmira, NY, Grave No. 2269
Simons, W. Lucas Private	Charleston, SC, 5/1/1862	19	Unknown	Co. B, 25th South Carolina Vols.	Captured	Exchanged On The James River, VA, 3/10/1865

NAME and RANK	PLACE & TYPE OF ENLISTMENT	AGE	RESIDENCE & OCCUPATION	REGIMENT OR BATTALION	RESULT OF BATTLE	REMARKS
Sinclair, James J. Private	Fort Holmes, NC, Brunswick County, NC, 3/24/1864, Volunteer	18	Brunswick County, NC	2nd Co. K, 40th Regiment North Carolina, 3rd Artillery	Captured	Exchanged on the James River, VA, 3/2/1865
Singletary, Calvin Private	Elizabethtown, NC, Bladen County, NC, 5/6/1862, Mustered in at Fort St. Philip, NC, Volunteer	33	Bladen County, NC, Farmer	2nd Co. K, 40th Regiment North Carolina, 3rd Artillery	Captured	Died of Pneumonia 2/24/1865, Buried Woodlawn Cemetery, Elmira, NY, Grave No. 2287
Singletary, Dennis Lennon Private	Elizabethtown, NC, 5/6/1862, Mustered in at Fort St. Philip, NC, Volunteer	34	Bladen County, NC, Farmer, Detailed to build a wharf at Fort Fisher, 1-5-1864	2nd Co. K, 40th Regiment North Carolina, 3rd Artillery	Captured	Exchanged on the James River, VA, 3/2/1865
Singletary, George S. Private	Elizabethtown, NC, 5/6/1862, Mustered in at Fort St. Philip, NC, Volunteer	23	Lumberton, Robeson County, NC Farmer	2nd Co. K, 40th Regiment North Carolina, 3rd Artillery	Captured	Oath Of Allegiance 6/12/1865
Singletary, Jonathan L. Private	Elizabethtown, Bladen County, NC, 5/6/1862, Mustered in at Fort St. Philip, NC, Volunteer	20	Elizabethtown, Bladen County, NC Farmer	2nd Co. K, 40th Regiment North Carolina, 3rd Artillery	Captured	Oath Of Allegiance 6/12/1865
Singletary, Joshua K. Private	Bladen County, NC, 8/28/1862, Volunteer	20	Elizabethtown, Bladen County, NC, Farmer	3rd Co. B, 36th Regiment North Carolina, 2nd Artillery	Captured	Exchanged on the James River, VA, 3/2/1865
Singletary, Matthew Young Private	Bladen County, NC, 12/20/1861, Mustered in at Wilmington, NC, Volunteer	25	Pleasant Exchange, NC, Extra Duty as Hospital Nurse at post	3rd Co. B, 36th Regiment North Carolina, 2nd Artillery	Captured	Exchanged on the James River, VA, 2/20/1865,

NAME and RANK	PLACE & TYPE OF ENLISTMENT	AGE	RESIDENCE & OCCUPATION	REGIMENT OR BATTALION	RESULT OF BATTLE	REMARKS
Singletary, Wright Private	Wilmington, NC, New Hanover County, NC, 1/1/1862, Volunteer	30	Elizabethtown, Bladen County, NC	3rd Co. B, 36th Regiment North Carolina, 2nd Artillery	Captured	Oath Of Allegiance 7/7/1865
Sizemore, Wiiliam J. Private	Chatham County, NC, 3/26/1863, Volunteer	37	Halifax County, NC	3rd Co. G, 40th Regiment North Carolina, 3rd Artillery	Captured	Died of Pneumonia 3/21/1865, Buried Woodlawn Cemetery, Elmira, NY, Grave No. 1528
Skinner, Franklin Private	James Island, SC, 9/1/1863	Unk	Carpenter	Co. H, 21st South Carolina Vols.	Captured	Died of Chronic Diarrhea 4/9/1865, Buried Woodlawn Cemetery, Elmira, NY, Grave No. 2612
Skipper, William M. Private	Old Brunswick Town, NC, 4/23/1862, Mustered in at Fort St. Philip, NC, Volunteer	15	Brunswick County, NC	3rd Co. G, 36th Regiment North Carolina, 2nd Artillery	Wounded & Captured	Exchanged on the James River, VA, 3/2/1865
Smith, Archibald Private	Fort Fisher, New Hanover County, NC, 10/16/1863, Conscript	45	Elizabethtown, Bladen County, NC	2nd Co. I, 36th Regiment North Carolina, 2nd Artillery	Captured	Oath Of Allegiance 6/12/1865, Detailed to Cut Timber in Bladen County, NC, July 1864
Smith, Bunyon M. Private	Elizabethtown, Bladen County, NC, 10/19/1861, Volunteer	18	Fayetteville, Cumberland County, NC	2nd Co. I, 36th Regiment North Carolina, 2nd Artillery	Captured	Oath Of Allegiance 6/12/1865
Smith, Chesley Private	Sampson County, NC, 10/18/1861, Volunteer	38	Bladen County, NC	2nd Co. A, 36th Regiment North Carolina, 2nd Artillery	Captured	Died of Chronic Diarrhea 6/23/1865, Buried Woodlawn Cemetery, Elmira, NY, Grave No. 2817

354

NAME and RANK	PLACE & TYPE OF ENLISTMENT	AGE	RESIDENCE & OCCUPATION	REGIMENT OR BATTALION	RESULT OF BATTLE	REMARKS
Smith, Daniel Private	Elizabethtown, Bladen County, NC, 7/8/1862, Volunteer	27	Bladen County, NC, Detailed as a Carpenter Building Batteries, Oct. 1862	2nd Co. I, 36th Regiment North Carolina, 2nd Artillery,	Captured	Died of Variola (smallpox) 3/29/1865, Buried Woodlawn Cemetery, Elmira, NY, Grave No. 2517
Smith, E.B. Private	Marion, SC, 4/26/1864	26	Marion, SC,	Co. D, 21st South Carolina Volunteers	Captured	Died On Route To Be Exchanged 3/2/1865, Buried Woodlawn Cemetery, Elmira, NY
Smith, Edom Private	Fort Fisher, NC, New Hanover County, NC, 6/11/1863, Volunteer	20	New Hanover County, NC, Detailed as a Carpenter	2nd Co. I, 36th Regiment North Carolina, 2nd Artillery	Captured	Died of Pneumonia 2/18/1865, Buried Woodlawn Cemetery, Elmira, NY, Grave No. 2352
Smith, F.C. Private	Unknown	Unk	Warsaw, Duplin County, NC,	2nd Co. A, 36th Regiment North Carolina, 2nd Artillery	Captured	Oath Of Allegiance 7/11/1865
Smith, Henry Clay Private	Pitt County, NC, 8/17/1864	21	Maysville, Greene County, NC,	Co. D, 40th Regiment North Carolina, 3rd Artillery	Captured	Exchanged 3/14/1865 at Boulware's Wharf, James River, VA
Smith, John B. Private	Chatham County, NC, 3/26/1863, Volunteer	37	Chatham County, NC, Detailed as Wood Cutter, Smithville, NC, November 1863	3rd Co. G, 40th Regiment North Carolina, 3rd Artillery	Captured	Died of Pneumonia 2/8/1865, Buried Woodlawn Cemetery, Elmira, NY, Grave No. 1936

NAME and RANK	PLACE & TYPE OF ENLISTMENT	AGE	RESIDENCE & OCCUPATION	REGIMENT OR BATTALION	RESULT OF BATTLE	REMARKS
Smith, John B. Private	Fort Fisher, NC, New Hanover County, NC, 10/26/1863, Conscript	45	New Hanover County, NC, Detailed as a Carpenter, August, 1864	2nd Co. I, 36th Regiment North Carolina, 2nd Artillery	Captured	Died of Pneumonia 4/10/1865, Buried Woodlawn Cemetery, Elmira, NY, Grave No. 2609
Smith, John O.D. Private	Wilmington, NC, New Hanover County, NC, 10/19/1861, Volunteer	19	Bladen County, NC	2nd Co. I, 36th Regiment North Carolina, 2nd Artillery	Captured	Exchanged 3/2/1865, Died of Chronic Diarrhea At Richmond Hospital 3/16/1865, Buried Hollywood Cemetery, VA,
Smith, John W. Private	Orangeburg, SC, 3/30/1862	29	Vance's Ferry, Orangeburg District, SC	Co. F, 25th South Carolina Vols.	Captured	Oath Of Allegiance 7/11/1865
Smith, Josephus C. Private	Fort Fisher, NC, New Hanover County, NC, 6/11/1863, Volunteer	18	New Hanover County, NC	2nd Co. I, 36th Regiment North Carolina, 2nd Artillery	Captured	Died of Chronic Diarrhea 3/22/1865, Buried Woodlawn Cemetery, Elmira, NY, Grave No. 1523
Smith, Nathan Private	Fort Fisher, NC, New Hanover County, NC, 5/5/1864	26	New Hanover County, NC	2nd Co. A, 36th Regiment North Carolina, 2nd Artillery	Captured	Died of Pneumonia 2/24/1865, Buried Woodlawn Cemetery, Elmira, NY, Grave No. 2267
Smith, Philip D. Private	Darlington, SC, 1/20/1862	23	Darlington District, SC, Farmer	Co. H, 21st South Carolina Volunteers	Captured	Oath Of Allegiance 7/11/1865

NAME and RANK	PLACE & TYPE OF ENLISTMENT	AGE	RESIDENCE & OCCUPATION	REGIMENT OR BATTALION	RESULT OF BATTLE	REMARKS
Smith, Peter W. Private	Fort Fisher, NC, 4/5/1864, Volunteer	17	New Hanover County, NC	Co. H, 36th Regiment North Carolina, 2nd Artillery	Captured	Died of Chronic Diarrhea 3/13/1865, Buried Woodlawn Cemetery, Elmira, NY, Grave No. 2432
Smith, Randal H. Private	Lillington, NC, Harnett County, NC, 4/30/1862, Volunteer	26	Harnett County, NC	2nd Co. C, 36th Regiment North Carolina, 2nd Artillery	Captured	Exchanged on the James River, VA, 3/14/1865
Smith, Robert Private	Elizabethtown, Bladen County, NC, 4/5/1862, Volunteer	31	Cypress Creek, NC, Bladen County, NC, Farmer	Co. H, 36th Regiment North Carolina, 2nd Artillery	Captured	Died On Route To Be Exchanged, 2/20/1865
Smith, Robert J. Private	James Island, SC, 3/24/1864	17	Bradford Springs, Sumter District, SC, Farmer	Co. F, 25th South Carolina Vols.	Captured	Died of Chronic Diarrhea 2/24/1865, Buried Woodlawn Cemetery, Elmira, NY, Grave No. 2159
Smith, Simeon Private	Fort Caswell, Brunswick County, NC, 3/6/1863, Volunteer	25	Laurenburg, NC	Co. E, 40th Regiment North Carolina, 3rd Artillery	Captured	Oath Of Allegiance 6/12/1865
Smith, Stephen Allen Private	Wilmington, NC, New Hanover County, NC, 3/3/1862, Volunteer	19	New Hanover County, NC	2nd Co. D, 36th Regiment North Carolina, 2nd Artillery	Wounded & Captured	Died of Variola (smallpox) 3/1/1865, Buried Woodlawn Cemetery, Elmira, NY, Grave No. 2098

NAME and RANK	PLACE & TYPE OF ENLISTMENT	AGE	RESIDENCE & OCCUPATION	REGIMENT OR BATTALION	RESULT OF BATTLE	REMARKS
Smith, Thomas Gibson Private	Fort Caswell, Brunswick County, NC, 3/6/1863, Volunteer	20	Laurenburg, NC	Co. E, 40th Regiment North Carolina, 3rd Artillery	Captured	Oath Of Allegiance 6/12/1865
Smith, Thomas M. Private	Fort Fisher, NC, 10/26/1863, Conscript	45	Elizabethtown, Bladen County, NC	Co. K, 36th Regiment North Carolina, 2nd Artillery	Captured	Oath Of Allegiance 6/30/1865
Smith, William E. Private	Fort Fisher, New Hanover County, NC, 2/12/1864, Volunteer	18	Halifax County, NC	2nd Co. C, 36th Regiment North Carolina, 2nd Artillery	Captured	Oath Of Allegiance 7/7/1865
Smith, William H. Private	Brunswick County, NC, 12/4/1862	18	Halifax County, NC	Co. F, 36th Regiment North Carolina, 2nd Artillery	Captured	Oath Of Allegiance 7/7/1865
Smithwick, William Hyman Sergeant	Windsor, Bertie County, NC, 1/23/1862, Mustered in at Camp Mangum, NC	21	Plymouth, NC Farmer	Co. C, 3rd Battalion North Carolina Light Artillery	Captured	Oath Of Allegiance 6/12/1865
Smoke, Andrew E. Private	Orangeburg, SC, 4/24/1864	23	Bull Swamp, Orangeburg District, SC, Farmer	Co. H, 25th South Carolina Vols.	Captured	Died of Chronic Diarrhea 2/21/1865, Buried Woodlawn Cemetery, Elmira, NY, Grave No. 2264
Smothers, Simeon Private	Chesterfield, SC, 12/26/1861	24	Unknown	Co. G, 21st South Carolina Vols.	Captured	Exchanged On The James River, VA, 2/20/1865

NAME and RANK	PLACE & TYPE OF ENLISTMENT	AGE	RESIDENCE & OCCUPATION	REGIMENT OR BATTALION	RESULT OF BATTLE	REMARKS
Snead, Jonathan Bonaparte Private	Old Brunswick Town, NC, 4/30/1862, Mustered in at Fort St. Philip, Volunteer	30	Wilmington, New Hanover County, NC, Detailed Sept. 1863 as guard for the Wilmington & Manchester Rail Road	3rd Co. G, 36th Regiment North Carolina, 2nd Artillery	Captured	Oath Of Allegiance 5/29/1865
Snipes, John Private	Goldsboro, NC, Wayne County, NC, 7/6/1861, Mustered in at Beaufort, NC	24	Goldsboro, Wayne County, NC, Mason, Detailed as Overseer at Fort Holmes, June, 1864	Co F, 10th Regiment North Carolina, 1st Artillery	Captured	Died of Pneumonia 2/20/1865, Buried Woodlawn Cemetery, Elmira, NY, Grave No. 2326
Snipes, Sion Private	Elizabethtown, NC, 2/3/1862, Volunteer	25	Bladen County, NC	Co. E, 36th Regiment North Carolina, 2nd Artillery	Captured	Oath Of Allegiance 8/7/1865
Soots, Adam Private	Camp Holmes, NC, 5/9/1863	Unk	Wake County, NC	Co. C, 3rd Battalion North Carolina Light Artillery	Captured	Died of Chronic Diarrhea 3/1/1865, Buried Woodlawn Cemetery, Elmira, NY, Grave No. 2097
Spell, David Private	Fort Fisher, NC, New Hanover County, NC, 4/10/1863, Volunteer	18	New Hanover County, NC	2nd Co. C, 36th Regiment North Carolina, 2nd Artillery	Captured	Died of Chronic Diarrhea 3/24/1865, Buried Woodlawn Cemetery, Elmira, NY, Grave No. 2456

NAME and RANK	PLACE & TYPE OF ENLISTMENT	AGE	RESIDENCE & OCCUPATION	REGIMENT OR BATTALION	RESULT OF BATTLE	REMARKS
Spell, Hardy Private	Fort Fisher, NC, New Hanover County, NC, 10/18/1862, Volunteer	18	New Hanover County, NC	2nd Co. C, 36th Regiment North Carolina, 2nd Artillery	Captured	Died of Chronic Diarrhea 2/13/1865, Buried Woodlawn Cemetery, Elmira, NY, Grave No. 2044
Spence, John A. Private	Fort Fisher, NC, New Hanover County, NC, 3/15/1863, Volunteer	18	New Hanover County, NC, Laborer	2nd Co. D, 36th Regiment North Carolina, 2nd Artillery	Captured	Died of "Congestion Of Lungs" 2/10/1865, Buried Woodlawn Cemetery, Elmira, NY, Grave No. 2086
Spigner, Edward Private	Cole's Island, SC, 5/19/1864	29	Orangeburg District, SC, Overseer	Co. F, 25th South Carolina Vols.	Captured	Oath Of Allegiance 7/7/1865
Spivey, William J. Private	Fort Fisher, New Hanover County, NC, 4/28/1864	17	Whiteville, Columbus County, NC Laborer	Co. E, 36th Regiment North Carolina, 2nd Artillery	Captured	Oath Of Allegiance 7/7/1865
Springs, William Vincent Private	Charleston, SC, 4/7/1864	18	Mars Bluff, Marion County, SC, Laborer	Co. A, 21st South Carolina Vols.	Captured	Died of Chronic Diarrhea 2/19/1865, Buried Woodlawn Cemetery, Elmira, NY, Grave No. 2340
Squires, John H. Musician	Bladen County, NC, 3/7/1862, Volunteer	23	Bladen County, NC	3rd Co. B, 36th Regiment North Carolina, 2nd Artillery	Captured	Exchanged on the James River, VA, 3/2/1865

NAME and RANK	PLACE & TYPE OF ENLISTMENT	AGE	RESIDENCE & OCCUPATION	REGIMENT OR BATTALION	RESULT OF BATTLE	REMARKS
Stallings, Slade R. Private	Washington, NC, Beaufort County, NC, 4/22/1861, Mustered in at Ocracoke, NC	26	Greeneville, NC	Co K, 10th Regiment North Carolina, 1st Artillery	Captured	Died of Pneumonia 3/10/1865, Buried Woodlawn Cemetery, Elmira, NY, Grave No. 1884
Stanaland, Stephen B. Private	Fort Caswell, Brunswick County, NC, 6/21/1863, Volunteer	17	Columbus County, NC	Co. E, 40th Regiment North Carolina, 3rd Artillery	Captured	Oath Of Allegiance 7/26/1865
Standin, William H. Private	New Hanover County, NC, 8/7/1863	50	Edenton, Chowan County, NC	Co. D, 13th Battalion North Carolina Light Artillery	Captured	Oath Of Allegiance 6/27/1865
Starling, Thomas E. Last name also spelled Sterling Private	Fort Fisher, New Hanover County, NC, 5/1/1863, Volunteer	38	Fayetteville, Cumberland County, NC	2nd Co. D, 36th Regiment North Carolina, 2nd Artillery	Captured	Oath Of Allegiance 7/19/1865
Stean, Allen Private	Bennettsville, SC, 9/13/1864	18	Bennettsville, Marlboro District, SC, Farm Laborer	Co. F, 21st South Carolina Vols.	Captured	Died of Pneumonia 2/17/1865, Buried Woodlawn Cemetery, Elmira, NY, Grave No. 2221
Stephens, James Private	Chesterfield, SC, 12/25/1861	27	Cheraw, Chesterfield County, SC, Laborer	Co. F, 21st South Carolina Vols.	Captured	Died of Pneumonia 2/23/1865, Buried Woodlawn Cemetery, Elmira, NY, Grave No. 2254

NAME and RANK	PLACE & TYPE OF ENLISTMENT	AGE	RESIDENCE & OCCUPATION	REGIMENT OR BATTALION	RESULT OF BATTLE	REMARKS
Stevenson, William M. Private	Ashboro, Randolph County, NC, 3/25/1863, Volunteer	31	Greensboro, Guilford County, NC,	3rd Co. G, 40th Regiment North Carolina, 3rd Artillery	Captured	Oath Of Allegiance 5/29/1865
Stewart, Auguis Private	Camp Wyatt, New Hanover County, NC, 4/1/1864, Volunteer	40	New Hanover County, NC	2nd Co. D, 36th Regiment North Carolina, 2nd Artillery	Captured	Died of Pneumonia 3/14/1865, Buried Woodlawn Cemetery, Elmira, NY, Grave No. 1668
Stewart, Charles A. Musician	Sampson County, NC, 11/4/1861, Mustered in at Fort Caswell, NC, Volunteer	26	Sampson County, NC	2nd Co. A, 36th Regiment North Carolina, 2nd Artillery	Captured	Died of Variola (smallpox) 3/14/1865, Buried Woodlawn Cemetery, Elmira, NY, Grave No. 1669
Stewart, Duncan J. Musician	Fort Caswell, Brunswick County, NC, 10/20/1863	25	Fayetteville, Cumberland County, NC	2nd Co. D, 36th Regiment North Carolina, 2nd Artillery	Captured	Oath Of Allegiance 7/7/1865
Stewart, John Private	Brunswick County, NC, 10/20/1863, Volunteer	35	Brunswick County, NC	2nd Co. D, 36th Regiment North Carolina, 2nd Artillery	Captured	Died of Chronic Diarrhea 4/9/1865, Buried Woodlawn Cemetery, Elmira, NY, Grave No. 2610
Stewart, Samuel C. Private	Darlinton, SC, 1/1/1862	17	Darlington District, SC,	Co. B, 21st South Carolina Vols.	Captured	Died of Chronic Diarrhea 4/9/1865, Buried Woodlawn Cemetery, Elmira, NY, Grave No. 2555

NAME and RANK	PLACE & TYPE OF ENLISTMENT	AGE	RESIDENCE & OCCUPATION	REGIMENT OR BATTALION	RESULT OF BATTLE	REMARKS
Stinson, Henry M. Private	Chatham County, NC, 7/21/1862, Volunteer	18	Chatham County, NC, Employed in Signal Corp. at Fort Holmes and Wilmington, New Hanover County, NC, 1863	2nd Co. I, 36th Regiment North Carolina, 2nd Artillery	Captured	Died of "Jaundice" 5/17/1865, Buried Woodlawn Cemetery, Elmira, NY, Grave No. 2956
Stoy, Walter P. Private	Charleston, SC, 3/14/1862	19	Augusta, Ga	Co. E, 25th South Carolina Vols.	Captured	Oath Of Allegiance 8/7/1865
Strickland, Alexander Last name also spelled Stricklin Private	Cerro Gordo, NC, Columbus County, NC, 3/12/1862, Volunteer	18	Columbus County, NC	Co. E, 36th Regiment North Carolina, 2nd Artillery	Captured	Died of Typhoid/Pneumonia 2/18/1865, Buried Woodlawn Cemetery, Elmira, NY, Grave No. 2216
Strickland, Alva Private	Wilmington, NC, New Hanover County, NC, 5/1/1862, Volunteer	18	New Hanover County, NC	2nd Co. D, 36th Regiment North Carolina, 2nd Artillery	Captured	Died of Typhoid Fever 4/23/1865, Buried Woodlawn Cemetery, Elmira, NY, Grave No. 1402
Strickland, David Last name also spelled Stricklin Private	Cerro Gordo, Columbus County, NC, 3/1/1862, Mustered in at Wilmington, New Hanover County, NC	20	Fair Bluff, Columbus County, NC	Co. E, 36th Regiment North Carolina, 2nd Artillery	Captured	Oath Of Allegiance 7/7/1865

NAME and RANK	PLACE & TYPE OF ENLISTMENT	AGE	RESIDENCE & OCCUPATION	REGIMENT OR BATTALION	RESULT OF BATTLE	REMARKS
Strickland, Jacob Last name also spelled Stricklin Private	Cero Gordo, NC, Columbus County, NC, 3/11/1862, Mustered in at Wilmington, NC, Volunteer	18	Columbus County, NC, Detailed at Fort Pender as a Teamster, 1863	Co. E, 36th Regiment North Carolina, 2nd Artillery	Captured	Died of Chronic Diarrhea 5/16/1865, Buried Woodlawn Cemetery, Elmira, NY, Grave No. 2959
Strickland, Martin Last name also spelled Stricklin Private	Sampson County, NC, 2/18/1863, Volunteer	36	Sampson County, NC	2nd Co. A, 36th Regiment North Carolina, 2nd Artillery	Captured	Died of Chronic Diarrhea 4/8/1865, Buried Woodlawn Cemetery, Elmira, NY, Grave No. 2602
Strickland, Nathaniel Last name also spelled Stricklin Private	Wilmington, New Hanover County, NC, 3/1/1864, Transferred From CS Navy, Conscript	45	Wilmington, New Hanover County, NC	Co. E, 36th Regiment North Carolina, 2nd Artillery	Captured	Died of Pneumonia 3/12/1865, Buried Woodlawn Cemetery, Elmira, NY, Grave No. 1848
Strickland, William H. Last name also spelled Stricklin Private	Whiteville, Columbus County, NC, 2/9/1863, Conscript	36	Whiteville, Columbus County, NC	Co. E, 36th Regiment North Carolina, 2nd Artillery	Captured	Exchanged 3/14/1865 at Boulware's Wharf, James River, VA, Died From Unknown Disease At Richmond Hospital, 3/31/1865, Buried In Hollywood Cemetery, VA
Strock, Emery B. Private	Coles Island, SC, 4/13/1864	17	Vicinity of Vance's Ferry, Orangeburg District, SC, Farmer	Co. E, 25th South Carolina Vols.	Captured	Exchanged 2/20/1865, Died 3/16/1865 of Rubeola, Jackson Hospital, Richmond, VA

NAME and RANK	PLACE & TYPE OF ENLISTMENT	AGE	RESIDENCE & OCCUPATION	REGIMENT OR BATTALION	RESULT OF BATTLE	REMARKS
Stroman, Charles Private	Cole's Island, SC, 4/11/1862	24	St. Matthews, Orangeburg District, SC, Farmer	Co. F, 25th South Carolina Vols.	Captured	Died of Variola (smallpox) 5/10/1865, Buried Woodlawn Cemetery, Elmira, NY, Grave No. 2788
Stubbs, D.D. Private	Bennettsville, Marlboro District, SC, 12/25/1861	18	Charlotte, NC	Co. F, 21st South Carolina Vols.	Captured	Oath Of Allegiance 7/11/1865
Stubbs, Samuel F. Private	Bennettsville, Marlboro District, SC, 4/16/1863	22	Bennettsville, Marlboro District, SC, Student	Co. F, 21st South Carolina Vols.	Captured	Died of Typhoid Fever/Pneumonia 2/11/1865, Buried Woodlawn Cemetery, Elmira, NY, Grave No. 2059
Suggs, James McKay Private	Fort Anderson, NC, Brunswick County, NC, 12/18/1862, Volunteer	38	Brunswick County, NC	Co. H, 36th Regiment North Carolina, 2nd Artillery	Captured	Died of Variola (smallpox) 4/19/1865, Buried Woodlawn Cemetery, Elmira, NY, Grave No. 1371
Suit, William J. Private	Fort Branch Brunswick County, NC, 8/17/1863, Volunteer	40	Durham, NC, Detailed as Nurse in Hospital	3rd Co. G, 40th Regiment North Carolina, 3rd Artillery	Captured	Exchanged on the James River, VA, 2/20/1865
Sullivan, Richard T. Private	Fort Fisher, NC, New Hanover County, NC, 7/14/1863, Volunteer	18	New Hanover County, NC	2nd Co. I, 36th Regiment North Carolina, 2nd Artillery	Captured	Died of Pneumonia 2/28/1865, Buried Woodlawn Cemetery, Elmira, NY, Grave No. 2144

NAME and RANK	PLACE & TYPE OF ENLISTMENT	AGE	RESIDENCE & OCCUPATION	REGIMENT OR BATTALION	RESULT OF BATTLE	REMARKS
Sumerlin, Wiley N. Private	Wilmington, New Hanover County, NC, Transferred from Provost Guard, Goldsboro, N.C. Troops, 3/20/1864	40	Goldsboro, Wayne County, NC Carpenter	Co F, 10th Regiment North Carolina, 1st Artillery, Appointed Artificer in Smithville, 6/1/1864	Captured	Died of Chronic Diarrhea 3/20/1865, Buried Woodlawn Cemetery, Elmira, NY, Grave No. 1545
Sutton, Bryan Private	Wilmington, New Hanover County, NC, 1/3/1863	29	Sampson, NC, Farmer	Co F, 10th Regiment North Carolina, 1st Artillery	Captured	Died of Pneumonia 3/6/1865, Buried Woodlawn Cemetery, Elmira, NY, Grave No. 2414
Sutton, John C. Private	Camp Holmes, NC, Conscript, Transferred From CS Navy 6/10/1863	18	Unknown	3rd Co. G, 36th Regiment North Carolina, 2nd Artillery	Captured	Died of Pneumonia 4/16/1865, Buried Woodlawn Cemetery, Elmira, NY, Grave No. 2716
Sykes, Edmund Private	Fort Fisher, NC, 5/1/1862	28	New Hanover County, NC	2nd Co. C, 36th Regiment North Carolina, 2nd Artillery	Captured	Died of Chronic Diarrhea 3/3/1865, Buried Woodlawn Cemetery, Elmira, NY, Grave No. 1991
Syphret, Obedia J. Private	Orangeburg, SC, 4/15/1862	Unk	Orangeburg, SC	Co. G, 25th South Carolina Vols.	Captured	Oath Of Allegiance 6/23/1865

NAME and RANK	PLACE & TYPE OF ENLISTMENT	AGE	RESIDENCE & OCCUPATION	REGIMENT OR BATTALION	RESULT OF BATTLE	REMARKS
Tallivast, Alex Private	Darlington, SC, 9/1/1863	Unk	Unknown	Co. B, 21st South Carolina Vols.	Captured	Died of Chronic Diarrhea 4/4/1865, Buried Woodlawn Cemetery, Elmira, NY, Grave No. 2556
Talton, A.J. Private	Chesterfield, SC, 1/8/1862	20	Cheraw, Chesterfield County, SC,	Co. E, 21st South Carolina Vols.	Captured	Oath Of Allegiance 7/7/1865
Tatom, Alexander J. Private	Fort Anderson, NC, 12/12/1862, Volunteer	30	Brunswick, County, NC	Co. H, 36th Regiment North Carolina, 2nd .C. Artillery	Captured	Died of Variola (smallpox), 3/13/1865, Buried in Woodlawn Cemetery, Elmira, NY, Grave No. 1832
Taylor, A.J. Private	Unknown	30	Richardson's District, Craven County, NC,	2nd Co. K, 40th Regiment North Carolina, 3rd Artillery	Captured	Died of Chronic Diarrhea 2/16/1865, Buried in Woodlawn Cemetery, Elmira, NY, Grave No. 2208
Taylor, Isaac J. Private	Fort Caswell, NC,, 2/20/1862, Volunteer	28	Kenansville, Duplin County, NC,	2nd Co. A, 36th Regiment North Carolina, 2nd Artillery	Captured	Died of Chronic Diarrhea 3/11/1865, Buried in Woodlawn Cemetery, Elmira, NY, Grave No. 1861
Taylor, Middleton E. Private	Coles Island, SC, 4/11/1862	27	Orangeburg District, SC, Overseer, Ambulence Driver	Co. F, 25th South Carolina Vols.	Captured	Exchanged On the James River, VA, 2/20/1865
Taylor, P.H. Private	Coles Island, SC, 4/11/1862	26	Georgia Station, Orangeburg District, SC, Farmer	Co. F, 25th South Carolina Vols.	Captured	Oath Of Allegiance 7/7/1865

NAME and RANK	PLACE & TYPE OF ENLISTMENT	AGE	RESIDENCE & OCCUPATION	REGIMENT OR BATTALION	RESULT OF BATTLE	REMARKS
Teal, G.W. Private	Chesterfield, SC, 1/25/1864	Unk	Unknown	Co. D, 21st South Carolina Vols.	Captured	Died of Pneumonia 4/8/1865, Buried in Woodlawn Cemetery, Elmira, NY, Grave No. 2646
Terry, George W. Corporal	Williamsburg, SC, 2/6/1862	21	Kingstree, SC	Co. F, 25th South Carolina Vols.	Captured	Oath of Allegiance 7/11/1865
Thaggard, Amos Jerome Private	Elizabethtown, Bladen County, NC, 5/6/1862, Mustered in at Fort St. Philip, Volunteer	30	Bladen County, NC, Farmer	2nd Co. K, 40th Regiment North Carolina, 3rd Artillery	Captured	Exchanged On the James River, VA, 3/2/1865
Thaggard, James B. Private	Fort Fisher, New Hanover County, NC, 3/15/1863, Volunteer	35	Fayetteville, Cumberland County, NC	2nd Co. C, 36th Regiment North Carolina, 2nd .C. Artillery	Captured	Oath of Allegiance 6/12/1865, Died of Chronic Diarrhea in Hospital At City Point, VA, 6/27/1865
Thally, David J. Private	Old Brunswick, NC, 4/16/1862, Mustered in at Fort St. Philip, Volunteer	21	Duplin County, NC	3rd Co. G, 36th Regiment North Carolina, 2nd .C. Artillery	Captured	Exchanged 2/20/1865, Died of Bronchitis 4/9/1865 at CSA General Hospital, Charlotte, NC
Thomas, J.H. Private	Chesterfield, SC, 1/24/1864	17	Cheraw, Chesterfield County, SC, Farmer	Co. D, 21st South Carolina Vols.	Captured	Oath Of Allegiance 7/7/1865

NAME and RANK	PLACE & TYPE OF ENLISTMENT	AGE	RESIDENCE & OCCUPATION	REGIMENT OR BATTALION	RESULT OF BATTLE	REMARKS
Thompson, Willis Andrew Private	Fort Fisher, New Hanover County, NC, 6/4/1863	Unk	Warsaw, Duplin County, NC	2nd Co. C, 36th Regiment North Carolina, 2nd .C. Artillery	Captured	Oath of Allegiance 6/12/1865
Thompson, David V. Private	Coles Island, SC, 4/11/1862	16	Orangeburg District, SC, Farm Laborer	Co. F, 25th South Carolina Vols.	Captured	Oath Of Allegiance 7/11/1865
Thompson, Edward D. Private	Resided In Robeson County, NC,	Unk	Lumberton, Robeson County, NC	Co. F, 40th Regiment North Carolina, 3rd Artillery	Captured	Oath of Allegiance 7/11/1865
Thompson, James D. Private	Union County, NC, 8/30/1861, Volunteer	23	Lumberton, Robeson County, NC	Co. F, 40th Regiment North Carolina, 3rd Artillery	Captured	Oath of Allegiance 7/11/1865
Thompson, Wesley Private	Laurenburg, Richmond County, NC, 8/17/1863, Volunteer	18	Lumberton, Robeson County, NC	Co. F, 40th Regiment North Carolina, 3rd Artillery	Captured	Oath of Allegiance 7/11/1865
Thompson, William F. Private	Unknown	34	Georgetown, Prince George Parish, SC, Farmer	Co. B, 21st South Carolina Vols.	Captured	Died of Chronic Diarrhea 2/17/1865, Buried Woodlawn Cemetery, Elmira, NY, Grave No. 2230
Thorp, James Last name also spelled Tharp Corporal	Old Brunswick Town, NC, 4/16/1862, Mustered in at Ft. St. Philip, NC, Volunteer	21	Brunswick County, NC	3rd Co. G, 36th Regiment North Carolina, 2nd .C. Artillery	Wounded & Captured	Oath of Allegiance 7/7/1865

NAME and RANK	PLACE & TYPE OF ENLISTMENT	AGE	RESIDENCE & OCCUPATION	REGIMENT OR BATTALION	RESULT OF BATTLE	REMARKS
Tillman, John R. Private	Fort Fisher, New Hanover County, NC, 10/28/1863, Conscript	25	Charlotte, NC	2nd Co. I, 36th Regiment North Carolina, 2nd .C. Artillery	Captured	Oath of Allegiance 6/12/1865
Tindall, Calvin Private	Fort Fisher, NC, 10/31/1862, Volunteer	19	New Hanover County, NC	2nd Co. C, 36th Regiment North Carolina, 2nd .C. Artillery	Captured	Died of Chronic Diarrhea 3/4/1865, Buried in Woodlawn Cemetery, Elmira, NY, Grave No. 1992
Tisdale, W.W. Private	Battery Island, SC, 4/12/1862	19	Kingston, SC	Co. B, 25th South Carolina Vols.	Captured	Oath Of Allegiance 6/30/1865
Tobias, John S. Private	Charleston, SC, 2/1/1864	18	Brewington, Clarendon District, SC, Farmer	Co. I, 25th South Carolina Vols.	Captured	Died of Pneumonia 2/23/1865, Buried in Woodlawn Cemetery, Elmira, NY, Grave No. 2244
Tolar, Robert M. Private	Bladen County, NC 11/6/1864, Volunteer	34	Fayetteville, Cumberland County, NC, Extra Duty Setting Range Lights	3rd Co. B, 36th Regiment North Carolina, 2nd .C. Artillery	Captured	Oath of Allegiance 7/7/1865
Tumage, Luke Private	Unknown	26	Cheraw, Chesterfield County, SC, Laborer	Co. F, 21st South Carolina Vols.	Captured	Oath Of Allegiance 7/3/1865

NAME and RANK	PLACE & TYPE OF ENLISTMENT	AGE	RESIDENCE & OCCUPATION	REGIMENT OR BATTALION	RESULT OF BATTLE	REMARKS
Tune, Thomas Private	Enfield, NC, 10/9/1861, Volunteer	28	Halifax County, NC,	Co. F, 36th Regiment North Carolina, 2nd .C. Artillery	Captured	Died of Pneumonia 4/1/1865, Buried in Woodlawn Cemetery, Elmira, NY, Grave No. 2574
Tune, William Private	New Berne, Craven County, NC, 1/30/1862, Volunteer	27	Halifax County, NC	Co. F, 36th Regiment North Carolina, 2nd .C. Artillery	Captured	Died of Variola (smallpox) 3/31/1865, Buried in Woodlawn Cemetery, Elmira, NY, Grave No. 2574
Turner, John Private	Wilmington, New Hanover County, NC, 5/8/1862, Volunteer	32	Bladen County, NC, Farmer, Deserted August 1862, Captured and Court Marshalled 3/5/1863	Co. H, 36th Regiment North Carolina, 2nd .C. Artillery	Captured	Died of Pneumonia 3/8/1865, Buried in Woodlawn Cemetery, Elmira, NY, Grave No. 2385
Tyler, James Private	Fort Caswell, Brunswick County, NC, 1/25/1862, Volunteer	31	Fair Bluff, Columbus County, NC	2nd Co. A, 36th Regiment North Carolina, 2nd .C. Artillery	Captured	Oath of Allegiance 7/11/1865
Tyler, Lucius A. Private	St. John's, Hertford County, NC, 4/1/1862	Unk	Hertford County, NC	Co. D, 3rd Battalion North Carolina Light Artillery	Captured	Oath of Allegiance 6/21/1865
Tyson, Gideon A. Private	Wilmington, New Hanover County, NC, 4/30/1862, Volunteer	22	Greenville, NC Cooper, Extra Duty at Fort Holmes as Overseer, January 1864	Co. H, 36th Regiment North Carolina, 2nd .C. Artillery	Captured	Oath of Allegiance 7/7/1865

NAME and RANK	PLACE & TYPE OF ENLISTMENT	AGE	RESIDENCE & OCCUPATION	REGIMENT OR BATTALION	RESULT OF BATTLE	REMARKS
Ulmer, George L. Private	Coles Island, SC, 4/11/1862	20	Poplar, Orangeburg District, SC, Farm Laborer	Co. F, 25th South Carolina Vols.	Captured	Oath Of Allegiance 7/11/1865
Utley, Jasper T. Musician	Orange County, NC, 6/23/1864	34	Hillsboro, Orange County, NC	Co D, 1st Battalion North Carolina Heavy Artillery	Captured	Oath Of Allegiance 6/23/1865, Appointed Drummer 7/1864

NAME and RANK	PLACE & TYPE OF ENLISTMENT	AGE	RESIDENCE & OCCUPATION	REGIMENT OR BATTALION	RESULT OF BATTLE	REMARKS
Veal, Joseph T. Private	Enlisted In November Of 1864	17	Windsor, Bertie County, NC,	Co. D, 3rd Battalion North Carolina, 3rd Light Artillery	Captured	Exchanged 2/20/1865, No Record of Exchanged taking Place
Vines, Henry Private	Old Brunswick Town, NC, 4/30/1862 Mustered in at Fort St. Philip, NC, Volunteer	18	Wilmington, New Hanover County, NC, Extra Duty in Engineering Dept. October 1863	3rd Co. G, 36th North Carolina, 2nd Artillery,	Captured	Oath Of Allegiance 7/26/1865, Oath Of Allegiance 7/26/1865, Had both legs amputated to the knees because of Frostbite.
Vinson, Daniel J. Private Name Also Spelled: Vincent	Goldsboro, Wayne County, NC, 6/8/1863	18	Goldsboro, Stoney Creek District, Wayne County, NC Farm Laborer	Co. F, 10th Regiment North Carolina, 1st Artillery	Wounded In Face & Captured	Died Of Chronic Diarrhea 3/16/1865, Buried In Woodlawn Cemetery, Elmira, NY, Grave No. 1701

NAME and RANK	PLACE & TYPE OF ENLISTMENT	AGE	RESIDENCE & OCCUPATION	REGIMENT OR BATTALION	RESULT OF BATTLE	REMARKS
Vinson, Uriah T. Private Name Also Spelled: Vincent	Goldsboro, Wayne County, NC, 9/12/1862	19	Goldsboro, Stoney Creek District, Wayne County, NC, Detailed to Fort Anderson	Co. F, 10th Regiment North Carolina, 1st Artillery	Wounded In Face & Captured	Died Of Pneumonia 3/19/1865, Buried In Woodlawn Cemetery, Elmira, NY, Grave No. 1581
Vocelle, Augustus Private	Charleston, SC, 2/22/1862	37	Charleston, SC,	Co. F, 25th South Carolina Vols.	Captured	Died Of Pnuemonia 3/21/1865, Buried In Woodlawn Cemetery, Elmira, NY, Grave No. 1527

NAME and RANK	PLACE & TYPE OF ENLISTMENT	AGE	RESIDENCE & OCCUPATION	REGIMENT OR BATTALION	RESULT OF BATTLE	REMARKS
Walker, David J. Private	Brunswick County, NC, 9/7/1863, Volunteer	18	Brunswick County, NC	3rd Co. G, 36th Regiment North Carolina, 2nd Artillery	Captured	Died Of Chronic Diarrhea 3/21/1865, Buried In Woodlawn Cemetery, Elmira, NY, Grave No. 1533
Wall, Mial Private	Fort Branch, Brunswick County, NC, 8/17/1863, Volunteer	41	Charlotte, NC, Extra Duty as Keeper of the Lights	3rd Co. G, 40th Regiment North Carolina, 3rd Artillery	Captured	Oath Of Allegiance 6/12/1865
Wallace, Henry W. Private	Fort St. Philip, NC, 5/15/1862, Volunteer	48	Brunswick County, NC	3rd Co. G, 36th Regiment North Carolina, 2nd Artillery	Captured	Died Of Pneumonia 2/18/1865, Buried In Woodlawn Cemetery, Elmira, NY, Grave No. 2359
Walling, J.A. Private	Coles Island, SC, 4/11/1862	Unk	Columbia, Richland County, SC	Co. F, 25th South Carolina Vols.	Captured	Oath Of Allegiance 7/7/1865

NAME and RANK	PLACE & TYPE OF ENLISTMENT	AGE	RESIDENCE & OCCUPATION	REGIMENT OR BATTALION	RESULT OF BATTLE	REMARKS
Ward, James M. Private	Fort St. Philip, NC, 5/16/1862, Substitute	17	Brunswick County, NC	3rd Co. G, 36th Regiment North Carolina, 2nd Artillery	Captured	Died Of Chronic Diarrhea 3/17/1865, Buried In Woodlawn Cemetery, Elmira, NY, Grave No. 1556
Ward, Joel Reaves Sergeant	Old Brunswick, NC, 4/16/1862, Mustered in at Fort St. Philip, Volunteer	18	Brunswick County, NC, Extra Duty Engineering Dept. July 1864	3rd Co. G, 36th Regiment North Carolina, 2nd Artillery	Captured	Exchanged 3/14/1865 Boulware's Wharf, James River, VA
Ward, Joseph W. Private	Fort Ellis, NC, 11/1/1861, Volunteer	39	Halifax County, NC	Co. F, 36th Regiment North Carolina, 2nd Artillery	Captured	Exchanged 2/20/1865 Boulware's Wharf, James River, VA
Ward, Solomon R. Private	Old Brunswick Town, NC, 4/16/1862, Mustered in at Fort St. Philip, NC, Volunteer	19	Brunswick County, NC, Extra Duty at Fort Caswell & Smithville for Engineering Dept. working on Revetment Turf	3rd Co. G, 36th Regiment North Carolina, 2nd Artillery	Captured	Exchanged on the James River, VA, 3/14/1865, Admitted to USA Hospital Bermuda Hundred 3/21/1865 with Small Pox
Ware, John H. Private	New Hanover County, NC, 6/1/1864	20	Yancyville, Caswell County, NC, Extra Duty for Engineering Dept. as Foreman of Carpenters	Co. D, 13th Battalion North Carolina Light Artillery	Captured	Exchanged On the James River, VA, 3/2/1865
Warren, William H. Private	Beaufort County, NC, 9/30/1861, Volunteer	41	Beaufort County, NC, Detailed to Engineering Dept as Carpenter	Co. C, 40th Regiment North Carolina, 3rd Artillery	Captured	Exchanged On the James River, VA, 3/2/1865
Warrick, William Private	Goldsboro, Wayne County, NC, 10/28/1862	29	Falling Creek, Cross Roads District, Wayne County, NC	Co. F, 10th Regiment North Carolina, 1st Artillery	Captured	Died Of Variola (smallpox) 2/26/1865, Buried In Woodlawn Cemetery, Elmira, NY, Grave No. 2147

NAME and RANK	PLACE & TYPE OF ENLISTMENT	AGE	RESIDENCE & OCCUPATION	REGIMENT OR BATTALION	RESULT OF BATTLE	REMARKS
Waters, James C. Private	Washington, NC, 4/24/1861, Mustered in at Fort Ocracoke, Hyde County, NC	28	Unknown, Taken Prisoner at Fort Hatteras, NC, 8/29/1861 taken to Fort Monroe, Va, Released 2/3/1862	Co. K, 10th Regiment North Carolina, 1st Artillery	Captured	Exchanged on James River, VA, 2/20/1865
Watson, John Private	New Berne, Craven County, NC, 1/27/1862, Volunteer	38	Edgecombe County, NC, Extra Duty as Laborer and Boatman at Fort Caswell, NC	Co. F, 36th Regiment North Carolina, 2nd Artillery	Captured	Oath Of Allegiance 7/26/1865
Watson, John H. Private	Elizabethtown, Bladen County, NC, 10/19/1861, Volunteer	19	Elizabethtown, Bladen County, NC	Co. E, 36th Regiment North Carolina, 2nd Artillery	Captured	Oath Of Allegiance 8/7/1865
Watson, Nathaniel S. Private	Red Springs, Robeson, NC, 9/5/1861, Volunteer	18	Robeson County, NC	Co. F, 40th Regiment North Carolina, 3rd Artillery	Captured	Died Of Pneumonia 3/18/1865, Buried In Woodlawn Cemetery, Elmira, NY, Grave No. 1722
Way, W.B. Private	Coles Island, SC, 4/11/1862	20	McCantsville, Orangeburg District, SC	Co. F, 25th South Carolina Vols.	Captured	Oath Of Allegiance 7/26/1865
Welch, John Private	Chatham County, NC, 3/26/1863, Volunteer	19	Chatham County, NC, Extra Duty in Smithville, NC as Woodcutter for Garrison	3rd Co. G, 40th Regiment North Carolina, 3rd Artillery	Captured	Died Of Pneumonia 3/22/1865, Buried In Woodlawn Cemetery, Elmira, NY, Grave No. 1524
Wells, Alfred M. Private	Unknown	Unk	Unknown	3rd Co. G, 36th Regiment North Carolina, 2nd Artillery	Captured	Exchanged on James River, 2/20/1865, Died Of Smallpox 3/5/1865, US Army Hospital, Bermuda Hundred, VA

NAME and RANK	PLACE & TYPE OF ENLISTMENT	AGE	RESIDENCE & OCCUPATION	REGIMENT OR BATTALION	RESULT OF BATTLE	REMARKS
Wells, David Private	Wilson, Wilson County, NC, 8/18/1863, Volunteer	41	Edgecombe County, NC	Co. D, 40th Regiment North Carolina, 3rd Artillery	Captured	Exchanged 3/14/1865 Boulware's Wharf, James River, VA,
Wells, Jacob Private	Fort Caswell, NC, 8/23/1863	Unk	Brunswick County, NC	2nd Co. D, 36th Regiment North Carolina, 2nd Artillery	Captured	Died Of Pneumonia 2/15/1865, Buried In Woodlawn Cemetery, Elmira, NY, Grave No. 2171
Wescoat, George W. Private	Fort Holmes, NC, 9/5/1863, Conscript	40	Wake County, NC	3rd Co. G, 36th Regiment North Carolina, 2nd Artillery	Captured	Exchanged On the James River, VA, 3/2/1865
Wescoat, St. Julian D. Private	Charleston, SC, 5/13/1862	18	Edisto Island, St John's Coleton, SC, Planter	Co. F, 25th South Carolina Vols.	Captured	Exchanged On the James River, VA, 2/20/1865
West, Arthur M. Private	Elizabethtown, Bladen County, NC, 10/19/1861, Volunteer	18	Fayetteville, NC, Assistant in Ordinance Department at Fort Fisher, NC	2nd Co. I, 36th Regiment North Carolina, 2nd Artillery	Captured	Oath Of Allegiance 6/12/1865
West, George W. Private	Fort Fisher, New Hanover County, NC, 8/1/1864	16	Fayetteville, Cumberland County, NC	Co. H, 36th Regiment North Carolina, 2nd Artillery	Captured	Oath Of Allegiance 6/12/1865
West, William J. Private	Elizabethtown, Bladen County, NC, 10/19/1861, Volunteer	21	Bladen County, NC	2nd Co. I, 36th Regiment North Carolina, 2nd Artillery	Captured	Died Of Acute Dysentery 4/9/1865, Buried In Woodlawn Cemetery, Elmira, NY, Grave No. 2614

NAME and RANK	PLACE & TYPE OF ENLISTMENT	AGE	RESIDENCE & OCCUPATION	REGIMENT OR BATTALION	RESULT OF BATTLE	REMARKS
Wheeler, Owen Private	Fayetteville, Cumberland County, NC, 2/26/1862, Volunteer	40	Cumberland County, NC	2nd Co. D, 36th Regiment North Carolina, 2nd Artillery	Captured	Died Of Pneumonia 5/3/1865, Buried In Woodlawn Cemetery, Elmira, NY, Grave No. 2748
White, Eli M. Private	Unknown	23	Waccamaw District, Brunswick County, NC, Farm Laborer	2nd Co. K, 40th Regiment North Carolina, 3rd Artillery	Captured	Died Of Pneumonia 4/23/1865, Buried In Woodlawn Cemetery, Elmira, NY, Grave No. 1401
White, Hardy Private	Unknown	17	Scotland's Neck, Halifax County, NC,	3rd Co. G, 36th Regiment North Carolina, 2nd Artillery	Captured	Exchanged 3/14/1865 Boulware's Wharf, James River, VA
White, John B. Private	Chesterfield, SC, 1/1/1862	18	Cheraw, Chesterfield, SC,	Co. D, 21st South Carolina Vols.	Captured	Exchanged On The James River, VA, 3/2/1865
White, J.B. Private	Camp Harllee, Georgetown, SC, 1/1/1862	42	Sumter, SC	Co. I, 25th South Carolina Vols.	Captured	Oath Of Allegiance 6/23/1865
White, Jerry M. Private	Georgetown, SC, 1/1/1862	18	Darlington District, SC,	Co. K, 21st South Carolina Vols.	Captured	Exchanged On the James River, VA, 3/2/1865
White, William R. Private	Camp Harllee, Georgetown, SC, 1/1/1862	42	Darlington District, SC,	Co. I, 25th South Carolina Vols.	Captured	Oath Of Allegiance 6/27/1865

NAME and RANK	PLACE & TYPE OF ENLISTMENT	AGE	RESIDENCE & OCCUPATION	REGIMENT OR BATTALION	RESULT OF BATTLE	REMARKS
Whitehead, Eli M. Private	New Berne, Craven County, NC, 1/1/1862, Volunteer	22	Craven County, NC	Co. F, 36th Regiment North Carolina, 2nd Artillery	Captured	Died Of Chronic Diarrhea 4/10/1865, Buried In Woodlawn Cemetery, Elmira, NY, Grave No. 2665
Wiggs, Henry L. Private	Goldsboro, Wayne County, NC, 7/24/1861, Mustered in at Beaufort, NC	18	Goldsboro, Wayne County, NC, Farmer	Co. F, 10th Regiment North Carolina, 1st Artillery	Captured	Oath Of Allegiance 7/11/1865
Wilder, Benjamin K. Private	Gourdin's Dept., SC, 5/1/1862	39	Vicinity of Murray's Ferry, Williamsburg District, SC,	Co. K, 25th South Carolina Vols.	Captured	Died Of Pneumonia 3/16/1865, Buried In Woodlawn Cemetery, Elmira, NY, Grave No. 1693
Wilder, L. E. Private	James Island, SC, 3/10/1863	32	Vicinity of Murray's Ferry, Williamsburg District, SC, Farm Laborer	Co. K, 25th South Carolina Vols.	Captured	Died Of Intermittent Fever 4/2/1865, Buried In Woodlawn Cemetery, Elmira, NY, Grave No. 2575
Wiles, William Private	Coles Island, SC, 4/11/1862	26	Poplar, Orangeburg District, SC, Overseer	Co. F, 25th South Carolina Vols.	Captured	Died Of Acute Diarrhea 5/11/1865, Buried In Woodlawn Cemetery, Elmira, NY, Grave No. 2795
Wilkinson, James Private	Marion, SC, 4/20/1862	42	Fair Bluff, Columbus County, NC, Company Cook	Co. D, 25th South Carolina Vols.	Captured	Oath Of Allegiance 7/7/1865,

NAME and RANK	PLACE & TYPE OF ENLISTMENT	AGE	RESIDENCE & OCCUPATION	REGIMENT OR BATTALION	RESULT OF BATTLE	REMARKS
Willets, Benjamin B. Private	Fort St. Philip, Brunswick County, NC, 7/20/1862, Volunteer	18	Wilmington, New Hanover County, NC	3rd Co. G, 36th Regiment North Carolina, 2nd Artillery	Captured	Oath Of Allegiance 7/11/1865
Willets, Jacob L. Private	Old Brunswick Town, NC, 4/16/1862, Mustered in at Fort St. Philip, NC, Volunteer	22	Brunswick County, NC	3rd Co. G, 36th Regiment North Carolina, 2nd Artillery	Wounded & Captured	Died Of Chronic Diarrhea 4/14/1865, Buried In Woodlawn Cemetery, Elmira, NY, Grave No. 2707
Willets, John J. Private	Old Brunswick Town, NC, 4/16/1862, Mustered in at Fort St. Philip, NC, Volunteer	21	Brunswick County, NC, Extra Duty Engineer Work, Smithville and Fort Caswell, NC	3rd Co. G, 36th Regiment North Carolina, 2nd Artillery	Wounded & Captured	Died Of Pneumonia 5/7/1865, Buried In Woodlawn Cemetery, Elmira, NY, Grave No. 2770
Willets, William J. Private	Old Brunswick Town, NC, 4/16/1862, Mustered in at Fort St. Philip, NC, Volunteer	26	Brunswick County, NC	3rd Co. G, 36th Regiment North Carolina, 2nd Artillery	Wounded & Captured	Died Of Pneumonia 3/4/1865, Buried In Woodlawn Cemetery, Elmira, NY, Grave No. 1977
Williams, Alexander Private	Chesterfield, SC, 1/25/1862	37	Cheraw, Chesterfield, SC, Farmer	Co. D, 21th South Carolina Vols.	Captured	Died Of Acute Diarrhea 4/20/1865, Buried In Woodlawn Cemetery, Elmira, NY, Grave No. 1379
Williams, Amos Private	Wilmington, New Hanover County, NC, 3/7/1862, Volunteer	38	Whiteville, Columbus County, NC, Detailed as Mounted Scout	Co. E, 36th Regiment North Carolina, 2nd Artillery	Captured	Died On Route To Be Exchanged On the James River, VA, 2/20/1865

NAME and RANK	PLACE & TYPE OF ENLISTMENT	AGE	RESIDENCE & OCCUPATION	REGIMENT OR BATTALION	RESULT OF BATTLE	REMARKS
Williams, Andrew T. Private	Bladen County, NC, 2/16/1863, Volunteer	22	Bladenboro, Bladen County, NC,	3rd Co. B, 36th Regiment North Carolina, 2nd Artillery	Captured	Oath Of Allegiance 7/11/1865
Williams, Charles O. Private	Union County, NC, 8/27/1861, Volunteer	30	Robeson County, NC	Co. E, 40th Regiment North Carolina, 3rd Artillery	Captured	Exchanged On the James River, VA, 3/2/1865
Williams, Isaac W. Private	Fort Caswell, Brunswick County, NC, 3/5/1863, Volunteer	22	Brunswick County, NC, Detailed as Cart Driver Engineer Dept.	Co. E, 40th Regiment North Carolina, 3rd Artillery	Captured	Exchanged 2/20/1865, Died Of Chronic Diarrhea 3/12/1865 Richmond Hospital, VA, Buried Hollywood Cemetery, VA
Williams, J.H. Private	Unknown	20	Bladen County, NC, Detailed as a Carpenter on Smith Island, NC	Co. F, 40th Regiment North Carolina, 3rd Artillery	Captured	Died Of Chronic Diarrhea 4/3/1865, Buried In Woodlawn Cemetery, Elmira, NY, Grave No. 2550
Williams, Joel Private	Clinton, Sampson County, NC, 2/9/1863, Volunteer	34	Sampson County, NC Farmer	2nd Co. D, 36th Regiment North Carolina, 2nd Artillery	Captured	Died Of Pneumonia 3/4/1865, Buried In Woodlawn Cemetery, Elmira, NY, Grave No. 1972
Williams, John Private	Bennettsville, Marlboro District, SC, 4/4/1862	32	Cheraw, Chesterfield County, SC, Farmer	Co. I, 21st South Carolina Vols.	Captured	Oath Of Allegiance 7/11/1865
Williams, John W. Private	Fort Holmes, NC, 5/18/1864	Unk	Brunswick County, NC	2nd Co. K, 40th Regiment North Carolina, 3rd Artillery	Captured	Died Of Typhoid Fever 3/24/1865, Buried In Woodlawn Cemetery, Elmira, NY, Grave No. 2458

NAME and RANK	PLACE & TYPE OF ENLISTMENT	AGE	RESIDENCE & OCCUPATION	REGIMENT OR BATTALION	RESULT OF BATTLE	REMARKS
Williams, Richard Private	Clinton, Sampson County, NC, 2/9/1863, Volunteer	36	Sampson County, NC	2nd Co. C, 36th Regiment North Carolina, 2nd Artillery	Captured	Exchanged On the James River, VA, 3/2/1865
Williams, William D. Private	Robeson County, NC, 6/10/1862, Volunteer	18	Lumberton, Robeson County, NC	Co. E, 40th Regiment North Carolina, 3rd Artillery	Captured	Oath Of Allegiance 7/11/1865
Williamson, Dallas M. Private	Wilmington, New Hanover County, NC, 3/3/1862, Volunteer	18	Fair Bluff, Columbus County, NC	Co. E, 36th Regiment North Carolina, 2nd Artillery	Captured	Oath Of Allegiance 7/11/1865
Williamson, Daniel S. Private	Fort Caswell, NC, Brunswick County, NC, 5/8/1862, Volunteer	30	Brunswick County, NC	Co. E, 36th Regiment North Carolina, 2nd Artillery	Captured	Died Of Chronic Diarrhea 3/14/1865, Buried In Woodlawn Cemetery, Elmira, NY, Grave No. 1674
Williamson, Hosea W. Private	Wilmington, New Hanover County, NC, 3/1/1862, Volunteer	20	Fair Bluff, Columbus County, NC	Co. E, 36th Regiment North Carolina, 2nd Artillery	Captured	Oath Of Allegiance 7/11/1865
Williamson, James Private	Whiteville, NC, Columbus County, NC, 8/20/1863, Volunteer	42	Columbus County, NC	Co. E, 36th Regiment North Carolina, 2nd Artillery	Captured	Died Of Pneumonia 4/11/1865, Buried In Woodlawn Cemetery, Elmira, NY, Grave No. 2692

NAME and RANK	PLACE & TYPE OF ENLISTMENT	AGE	RESIDENCE & OCCUPATION	REGIMENT OR BATTALION	RESULT OF BATTLE	REMARKS
Williamson, James Wilds Sergeant	Darlington, SC, 3/18/1862	27	Darlington District, SC, Farmer	Co. B, 21th South Carolina Vols.	Captured	Died Of Pneumonia 3/15/1865, Buried In Woodlawn Cemetery, Elmira, NY, Grave No. 1690
Williamson, Joseph W. Private	Fort Caswell, NC, 7/16/1862, Volunteer	34	Columbus County, NC	Co. E, 36th Regiment North Carolina, 2nd Artillery	Captured	Died Of Chronic Diarrhea 6/21/1865, Buried In Woodlawn Cemetery, Elmira, NY, Grave No. 2813
Williamson, Joshua Robert Private	Cerro Gordo, Columbus County, NC, 3/1/1862, Volunteer	19	Columbus County, NC	Co. E, 36th Regiment North Carolina, 2nd Artillery	Captured	Died Of "Congestion Of Lungs" 2/15/1865, Buried In Woodlawn Cemetery, Elmira, NY, Grave No. 2183
Willis, Cass Private	Fort Fisher, New Hanover County, NC, 4/24/1863, Substitute	16	Fayetteville, Cumberland County, NC	2nd Co. I, 36th Regiment North Carolina, 2nd Artillery	Wounded & Captured	Oath Of Allegiance 6/12/1865
Willis, Charles T. Private	Fort Fisher, New Hanover County, NC, 7/1/1862	16	Washington, Beaufort County NC, Detailed in Engineering Dept. Wilmington, NC	Co. K, 10th Regiment North Carolina, 1st Artillery	Captured	Oath Of Allegiance 6/16/1865
Willis, John S. Sergeant	Elizabethtown, Bladen County, NC, 1/6/1861, Volunteer	38	Fayetteville, Cumberland County, NC	2nd Co. I, 36th Regiment North Carolina, 2nd Artillery	Captured	Oath Of Allegiance 6/12/1865
Willis, William N. Private	Fort Fisher, New Hanover County, NC, 8/29/1863, Volunteer	17	Fayetteville, Cumberland County, NC, Detailed to Tend Range Lights	2nd Co. I, 36th Regiment North Carolina, 2nd Artillery	Wounded & Captured	Oath Of Allegiance 6/12/1865

NAME and RANK	PLACE & TYPE OF ENLISTMENT	AGE	RESIDENCE & OCCUPATION	REGIMENT OR BATTALION	RESULT OF BATTLE	REMARKS
Wilson, Burrell Private	Unknown	16	Vicinity of Hawley's Store, Sampson County, NC, Farmer	2nd Co. A, 36th Regiment North Carolina, 2nd Artillery	Wounded & Captured	Exchanged Exchanged On the James River, VA, 3/2/1865
Wilson, John H.	Sampson County, NC, 2/18/1863, Volunteer	20	Sampson County, NC	2nd Co. A, 36th Regiment North Carolina, 2nd Artillery	Captured	Exchanged On the James River, VA, 3/2/1865
Wilson, Lucian W. Private	Fort Caswell, Brunswick County, NC, 1/6/1864, Volunteer	18	Brunswick County, NC	2nd Co. D, 36th Regiment North Carolina, 2nd Artillery	Captured	Died Of Chronic Diarrhea 4/3/1865, Buried In Woodlawn Cemetery, Elmira, NY, Grave No. 2565
Windham, John Private	Williamsburg, Gourdin's Dept., SC, 4/20/1862	18	Vicinity of Murray's Ferry, Williamsburg District, Farm Laborer	Co. K, 25th South Carolina Vols.	Captured	Exchanged On the James River, VA, 2/20/1865
Wise, V.F. Private	James Island, SC, 3/5/1863	Unk	Unknown	Co. F, 25th South Carolina Vols.	Captured	Exchanged On the James River, VA, 2/20/1865
Wolfe, D.W. Private	Unknown	Unk	Unknown	Co. G, 25th South Carolina Vols.	Captured	Died Of Chronic Diarrhea 3/1/1865, Buried In Woodlawn Cemetery, Elmira, NY, Grave No. 2100
Wolfe, Jacob A. Corporal	Orangeburg, SC, 4/24/1864	46	Orangeburg District, SC, Farmer	Co. H, 25th South Carolina Vols.	Captured	Oath Of Allegiance 7/7/1865

NAME and RANK	PLACE & TYPE OF ENLISTMENT	AGE	RESIDENCE & OCCUPATION	REGIMENT OR BATTALION	RESULT OF BATTLE	REMARKS
Woodard, John A. Private	Fort Fisher, New Hanover County, NC, 4/5/1864, Volunteer	19	New Hanover County, NC	Co. H, 36th Regiment North Carolina, 2nd Artillery	Captured	Died Of Pneumonia 2/7/1865, Buried In Woodlawn Cemetery, Elmira, NY, Grave No. 1927
Worrell, Ervin Private	Wilmington, New Hanover County, NC, 2/15/1863	41	Goldsboro, Wayne County, NC, Barrel Maker	Co. F, 10th Regiment North Carolina, 1st Artillery	Captured	Died Of Pneumonia 2/9/1865, Buried In Woodlawn Cemetery, Elmira, NY, Grave No. 1947
Worrell, John Private	Goldsboro, Wayne County, NC, 10/15/1862	28	Nahunta District, Wayne County, NC Farmer	Co. F, 10th Regiment North Carolina, 1st Artillery	Captured	Died Of Pneumonia 3/11/1865, Buried In Woodlawn Cemetery, Elmira, NY, Grave No. 1843
Worsham, Joseph R. Private	Camp Glover, Ridgeville, SC, 6/10/1861	21	Brewington, Clarendon County, SC,	Co. I, 25th South Carolina Vols.	Captured	Died Of Pneumonia 2/24/1865, Buried In Woodlawn Cemetery, Elmira, NY, Grave No. 2241
Wright, James D. Private	Brunswick County, NC, 1/18/1864, Volunteer	18	Halifax County, NC	Co. F, 36th Regiment North Carolina, 2nd Artillery	Captured	Exchanged 2/20/1865, Died Of Smallpox, Jackson Hospital, Richmond, VA, 5/28/1865
Wright, James L. Private	Camp Holmes, NC, 4/10/1864	34	Montgomery County, NC,	Co. K, 10th Regiment North Carolina, 1st Artillery	Captured	Died Of Variola (smallpox) 4/18/1865, Buried In Woodlawn Cemetery, Elmira, NY, Grave No. 1365

NAME and RANK	PLACE & TYPE OF ENLISTMENT	AGE	RESIDENCE & OCCUPATION	REGIMENT OR BATTALION	RESULT OF BATTLE	REMARKS
Wyndham, P.M. Private	Louisa City Hall, VA, 4/8/1862	Unk	Sumter, SC	Co. I, 25th South Carolina Vols.	Captured	Oath Of Allegiance 7/11/1865

NAME and RANK	PLACE & TYPE OF ENLISTMENT	AGE	RESIDENCE & OCCUPATION	REGIMENT OR BATTALION	RESULT OF BATTLE	REMARKS
Yarboro, Moses Private	Georgetown, SC, 1/25/1862	23	Society Hill, SC	Co. D, 21st South Carolina Vols.	Captured	Oath Of Allegiance 7/26/1865
Yarborough, Thomas L. Private	Darlington, SC, 5/19/1862	30	Darlington District, SC, Farmer	Co. B, 21st South Carolina Vols.	Captured	Died Of Pneumonia 4/28/1865, Buried At Woodlawn Cemetery, Elmira, NY, Grave No. 2728
Young, James H. Private	Battery Island, SC, 4/12/1862	18	Unknown	Co. C, 25th South Carolina Vols.	Captured	Exchanged On the James River, VA, 3/2/1865

Orders of Battle

Second Battle of Fort Fisher, January 13-15, 1865

Confederate States Army, Department of North Carolina, Third Military District, Major General Braxton Bragg, commander

FORT FISHER

Major General William Henry Chase Whiting,
observer and adviser

Colonel William Lamb,
36th Regiment North Carolina Troops, 2nd North Carolina Artillery, commander

1st Battalion North Carolina Heavy Artillery, Company D,
Captain James L. McCormic

3rd Battalion North Carolina Heavy Artillery, Company C, (Sutton's Battery)
Captain John M. Sutton

10th North Carolina Troops, 1st North Carolina Artillery,
Major James Reilly, commander
Company F, Captain Edward D. Walsh
Company K, (Shaw's Battery), Captain William Shaw, Jr.

13th Battalion North Carolina Artillery, Company D,
Captain Zachariah T. Adams

36th Regiment North Carolina Troops, 2nd North Carolina Artillery,
Colonel William Lamb, commander
2nd Company A, (Murphy's Battery) Captain Robert Murphy
2nd Company C, (Braddy's Battery), Captain Kinchen Braddy
2nd Company D, (Anderson's Artillery), Captain Edward Dudley
Company E, (Powell's Artillery), Captain Oliver Powell
Company F, (Hunter's Company), Captain Exum Lewis Hunter
3rd Company G, (Russell's Battery), Lieutenant William Swain
Company H, (Clarendon Guards), Captain Daniel Patterson
2nd Company I, (Bladen Artillery), Captain John T. Melvin
Company K, (Brunswick Artillery), Captain William Brooks

40th Regiment North Carolina Troops, 3rd North Carolina Artillery,
Company D, (Bay River Artillery), Captain James Lane
Company E, (Scotch Greys), Captain Malcomb H. McBrydie
3rd Company G, Captain George Buchan
2nd Company K, (Bladen Artillery Guards), Captain Daniel James Clark

Detachment of Confederate States Navy
Lieutenant Robert T. Chapman

Detachment of Confederate States Marines
Captain Alfred C. Benthuysen

Johnson Hagood's Brigade
11th South Carolina Infantry (detachment),
21st South Carolina Infantry (detachment), Captain D. G. DuBose
25th South Carolina Infantry (detachment), Captain James Carson

SUGAR LOAF

Hoke's Division, Major General Robert F. Hoke

Clingman's Brigade, Colonel Hector McKethan
8th North Carolina Infantry, Lt. Colonel Rufus A. Barrier
31st North Carolina Infantry, Lt. Colonel Charles Knight
51st North Carolina Infantry, Captain James W. Lippitt
61st North Carolina Infantry, Colonel William S. Devane

Colquitt's Brigade, Brig. General Alfred H. Colquitt
6th Georgia Infantry, Colonel John T. Lofton
19th Georgia Infantry, Colonel James H. Neal
23rd Georgia Infantry, Colonel Marcus R. Ballenger
27th Georgia Infantry, Captain Elisha D. Graham
28th Georgia Infantry, Captain John A. Johnson

Hagood's Brigade, Colonel Robert F. Graham
7th Battalion South Carolina Infantry, Lt. Colonel James H. Rion
11th South Carolina Infantry, Colonel F Hay Gantt
21st South Carolina Infantry,
25th South Carolina Infantry,
27th South Carolina Infantry,

Kirkland's Brigade, Brig. General William W. Kirkland
17th North Carolina Infantry, Lt. Colonel Thomas H. Sharp
42nd North Carolina Infantry, Colonel John E. Brown
66th North Carolina Infantry, Colonel John H. Nethercutt
2nd South Carolina Cavalry, Colonel Thomas J. Lipscomb

3rd Battalion North Carolina Light Artillery
Company A, (Northampton Artillery), Captain Andrew J. Ellis

10th Regiment North Carolina Troops, 1st North Carolina Artillery
2nd Company I, (Southerland's Battery), Captain Thomas Southerland

Staunton Hill Artillery (Paris' Battery) Captain Andrew B. Paris

FEDERAL FORCES

United States Army, Department of Virginia and North Carolina, Terry's Provisional Corps, Bvt. Major General Alfred H. Terry, commander

XXIV Army Corps

First Division

Second Brigade

Colonel Joseph C. Abbott,Commander
6th Connecticut Infantry, Colonel Alfred P. Rockwell
7th Connecticut Infantry, Captain John Thompson
Captain William S. Marble
3rd New Hampshire Infantry, Captain William H. Trickey
7th New Hampshire Infantry, Lt. Colonel Augustus W. Rollins

16th New York Heavy Artillery (detachment)
Companies A, B, C, F, G, K, Major Frederick W. Prince

Second Division

Brig. General Adelbert Ames, commander

First Brigade

Colonel N. Martin Curtis, commander
Major Ezra L. Walrath

3rd New York Infantry, Captain James H. Reeve
Lt. Edwin A. Behan
112th New York Infantry, Colonel John F. Smith
117th New York Infantry, Lt. Colonel Francis X. Meyer
142nd New York Infantry, Lt. Colonel Albert M. Barney

Second Brigade

Colonel Galusha Pennypacker, commander
Major Oliver P. Harding

47th New York Infantry, Captain Joseph M. McDonald
48th New York Infantry, Lt. Colonel William B. Coan,
Major Nere A. Elfwing

76th Pennsylvania Infantry, Colonel John S. Littell,
Major Charles Knerr
97th Pennsylvania Infantry, Lt. John Wainwright
203rd Pennsylvania Infantry, Colonel John W. Moore
Lt. Colonel Jonas W. Lyman
Major Oliver P. Harding
Captain Heber B. Essington

Third Brigade

Colonel Louis Bell, commander
Colonel Alonzo Alden

13th Indiana Infantry, Lt. Colonel Samuel M. Zent
4th New Hampshire Infantry, Captain John H. Roberts
115th New York Infantry, Lt. Colonel Nathan J. Johnson
169th New York Infantry, Colonel Alonzo Alden
Lt. Colonel James A. Colvin

Artillery Brigade, Captain Richard H. Lee
16th New York Independent Battery Light Artillery (detachment)

XXV Army Corps

Third Division

Brig. General Charles J. Paine, commander

Second Brigade

Colonel John W. Ames, commander

4th U.S. Colored Troops, Lt. Colonel George Rogers
6th U.S. Colored Troops, Major Augustus S. Boernstein
30th U.S. Colored Troops, Lt. Colonel Hiram A. Oakman
39th U.S. Colored Troops, Colonel Ozora P. Stearns

Third Brigade

Colonel Elias Wright, commander

1st U.S. Colored Troops, Lt. Colonel Giles H. Rich
5th U.S. Colored Troops, Major William R. Brazie
10th U.S. Colored Troops, Lt. Colonel Edward H. Powell
27th U.S. Colored Troops, Bvt Brig. General Albert M. Blackman
37th U.S. Colored Troops, Colonel Nathan Goff, Jr.

Artillery Brigade

1st Connecticut Heavy Artillery
Companies B, G, L, Captain William G. Pride
3rd U.S. Regular Army, Battery E, Lt. John Myrick
Artillery Bvt. Brig. General Henry L. Abbot
New York Light, 16th Battery, Captain Richard H. Lee

Engineers
15th New York
Companies A, I, Lt. K. Samuel O'Keefe

United States Navy, North Atlantic Blockading Squadron, Cape Fear Task Force,
Rear Admiral David D. Porter, commanding fleet

Line No. 1

VESSEL	GUNS	COMMANDING OFFICER
Brooklyn	26	Captain James Alden
Canonicus (monitor)	2	Lt. Cmdr. George Belknap
Huron	5	Lt. Cmdr. Thomas O. Selfridge
Kansas	8	Lt. Cmdr. Pendleton Watmough
Mahopac (monitor)	2	Lt. Cmdr. A.W. Weaver
Maumee	8	Lt. Cmdr. Ralph Chandler
Mohican	9	Cmdr. Daniel Ammen
Monadnock (monitor)	4	Cmdr. Enoch G. Parrott
New Ironsides (ironclad)	20	Cmdr. William Radford
Nyack	4	Lt. Cmdr. L.H. Newman
Pawtuxet	10	Cmdr. James H. Spotts
Pequot	8	Lt. Cmdr. Daniel Braine
Pontoosuc	12	Lt. Cmdr. William G. Temple
Saugus (monitor)	2	Cmdr. Edmund R. Colhoun
Seneca	5	Lt. Cmdr. Montgomery Sicard
Tacony	12	Lt. Cmdr. William T. Truxtun
Unadilla	6	Lt. Cmdr. Frank M. Ramsey
Yantic	5	Lt. Cmdr. Thomas C. Harris

Line No. 2

VESSEL	GUNS	COMMANDING OFFICER
Colorado	50	Commodore Henry K. Thatcher
Juanita	14	Captain William R. Taylor
Mackinaw	10	Cmdr. John C. Beaumont

Minnesota	46	Commodore Joseph Lanman
Powhatan	24	Commodore James F. Schenck
Shenandoah	6	Captain Daniel B. Ridgely
Susquehanna	18	Commodore Sylvanus W. Godon
Ticonderoga	14	Captain Charles Steedman
Tuscarora	10	Cmdr. James M. Frailey
Vanderbilt	16	Captain Charles W. Pickering
Vicksburg	7	Lt. Cmdr. Baker
Wabash	44	Captain Melancton Smith

Line No. 3

VESSEL	GUNS	COMMANDING OFFICER
Alabama	10	Acting Vol. Lt. Amos Langthorne
Chippewa	6	Lt. Cmdr. E.E. Potter
Fort Jackson	11	Captain Benjamin F. Sands
Iosco	10	Cmdr. John Guest
Keystone State	16	Cmdr. H. Rolando
Maratanza	6	Lt. Cmdr. George Young
Montgomery	6	Acting Vol. Lt. Thomas C. Dunn
Monticello	6	Lt. Cmdr. William B. Cushing
Osceola	10	Cmdr. J.M.B. Clitz
Quaker City	7	Cmdr. William F. Spicer
R.R. Cuyler	12	Cmdr. Charles H.B. Caldwell
Rhode Island	12	Cmdr. Stephen D. Trenchard
Santiago de Cuba	11	Captain Oliver S. Glisson
Sassacus	12	Lt. Cmdr. John L. Davis

Reserves

VESSEL	GUNS	COMMANDING OFFICER
A.D. Vance	5	Lt. Cmdr. John H. Upshur
Aries	7	Acting Vol. Lt. Francis S. Wells
Britannia	6	Acting Vol. Lt. William Sheldon
Cherokee	6	Acting Vol. Lt. William Dennison
Emma	8	Acting Vol. Lt. James Williams
Eolus	4	Acting Mstr. Edward S. Keyser
Fort Donelson	1	Acting Mstr. George W. Frost
Gettysburg	7	Lt. R. H. Lamson
Gov Buckingham	6	Acting Vol. Lt. J. MacDiarmid
Howquah	9	Acting Vol. Lt. Balch
Launch No. 6	1	Gunner Hubert Peters
Lillian	2	Acting Vol. Lt. T.A. Harris
Little Ada	2	Acting Mstr. Samuel P. Crafts

Malvern	12	Lt. Cmdr. Benjamin H. Porter
Moccasin	3	Acting Ensign Brown
Nansemond	3	Acting Mstr. James H. Porter
Nereus	11	Cmdr. J.C. Howell
Republic	1	Acting Mstr. John W. Bennett
Tristram Shandy	4	Acting Vol. Lt. Edward F. Green
Wilderness	4	Acting Mstr. Henry Arey

U.S. Army Transports

Atlantic, Blackstone, California, Champion, Charles Leary, Commodore DuPont, DeMolay, Euterpe, General Lyon, Governor Chase, Idaho, L.C. Livingston, McCellan, Montauk, North Point, Prometheus, Russia, Thames, Thomas, R. Scott, Tonawanda, Varuna, Weybosett

Notes

Chapter 1 Lincoln Takes Office

1. Lincoln, President Abraham, *First Inaugural Address*, March 4, 1861
2. Fonvielle Jr., Dr. Chris E., *The Wilmington Campaign: Last Rays of Departing Hope*, pages. 6-7; Gragg, Rod, *Confederate Goliath: The Battle of Fort Fisher*, page 8
3. Lamb, William, *Colonel Lamb's Story of Fort Fisher*, pages 2-5; *Histories of Several Regiments and Battalions from North Carolina in the Great War 1861-65*, by Walter Clark, Volume V, pages 218-220
4. *The Atlas to Accompany the Official Records of the Union and Confederate Armies*, Plate 75, numbers 1-3, Plate 76, numbers 2, 4, Washington, D.C.: U.S. Government Printing Office, 1891;
5. Dr. Chris E., *The Wilmington Campaign: Last Rays of Departing Hope*, page 44; Robinson III, Charles M., *Hurricane of Fire*, Page 66; Ripley, Warren, *Artillery and Ammunition of the Civil War*, pages 140-141
6. Wilkinson, John, *Narrative of a Blockade-Runner*, page 152
7. Lamb, William, *Colonel Lamb's Story of Fort Fisher*, pages 4-5; Fonvielle Jr., Dr. Chris E., *The Wilmington Campaign: Last Rays of Departing Hope*, Page 45; Rod Gragg, *Confederate Goliath: The Battle of Fort Fisher*, page 19

Chapter 2 Wilmington Takes On New Importance

1. Mark A. Moore, *The Wilmington Campaign and the Battles for Fort Fisher*, page 14
2. Rod Gragg, *Confederate Goliath: The Battle of Fort Fisher*, page 39; Shelby Foote, *The Civil War: A Narrative, vol. I*, pp. 370, 533
3. Butler, Major General Benjamin, *Butler's Book*, pages 775-776, Rod Gragg, *Confederate Goliath: The Battle of Fort Fisher*, pages 39-40; Holzman Robert S., *Stormy Ben Butler*, pages 103-105, 147
4. Richard B. McCaslin, *The Last Stronghold: The Campaign for Fort Fisher*, page 52-53
5. Porter to Butler, December 13, 1864, *O.R.N,. Series I, Vol 11*, page 191; Richard B. McCaslin, *The Last Stronghold: The Campaign for Fort Fisher*, page 42; Fonvielle Jr., Dr. Chris E., *The Wilmington Campaign: Last Rays of Departing Hope* Page 79;
6. Gragg, Rod *Confederate Goliath: The Battle of Fort Fisher*, page 49

Chapter 3 The First Attack

1. Fonvielle Jr., Dr. Chris E., *The Wilmington Campaign: Last Rays of Departing Hope*, Page 124; Report of A.C. Rhind, December 26, 1864, *ORN 11*, pages 226-227; Gragg, Rod, *Confederate Goliath*, p. 52
2. Fonvielle Jr., Dr. Chris E., *The Wilmington Campaign: Last Rays of Departing Hope*, Page 125; Lamb, William, *Lamb Diary*, December 24, 1864
3. Lamb, Colonel William, *Colonel Lamb's Story of Fort Fisher* page 14
4. Lamb, William, *Colonel Lamb's Story of Fort Fisher*, pages 15-16; Gragg, Rod, *Confederate Goliath*, page 63; Trotter, William R., *Ironclads and Columbiads*, page 358; Fonvielle Jr., Dr. Chris E., *The Wilmington Campaign: Last Rays of Departing Hope*, Page 119

5. Blair, B.F., letter *To Mother*, December 27, 1864, B.F. Blair Papers, Archives Division, U.S. Army Military History Institute

6. Gragg, Rod, *Confederate* Goliath, page 65, Robinson III, Charles M., *Hurricane of Fire*, P 123

7. Selfridge, Thomas, *Battles and Leaders of the Civil War*, Vol. 4, page 657

8. Simms, Joseph, *Personal Experience in the Volunteer Navy During the Civil War*, page 12

9. Lamb, William, *Colonel Lamb's Story of Fort Fisher*, page 15

10. Robinson III, Charles M., *Hurricane of Fire*, pages 124-125; Trotter, William R., *Ironclads and Columbiads*, page 360

11. *O.R.N,. Series I*, Vol. XI, pages 298-299

12. Fonvielle Jr., Dr. Chris E., *The Wilmington Campaign: Last Rays of Departing Hope*, Pages 137-138

13. Gragg, Rod, *Confederate Goliath*, page 69

14. Lamb, William, *Colonel Lamb's Story of Fort Fisher*, pages 16-17

15. *O.R.N,. Series I, Vol. 11*, page 253

16. Fonvielle Jr., Dr. Chris E., *The Wilmington Campaign: Last Rays of Departing Hope*, Page 141

17. Gragg, Rod, *Confederate Goliath: The Battle of Fort Fisher, page 77*; Turner, Henry M. *Civil War Times Illustrated*, 31 (October/November, 1980)

18. Longacre, Edward G., *Antietam to Fort Fisher*, page 223-224; Trotter, William R., *Ironclads and Columbiads*, page 369

19. Fonvielle Jr., Dr. Chris E., *The Wilmington Campaign: Last Rays of Departing Hope*, Page 143; Mark A. Moore, *The Wilmington Campaign and the Battles for Fort Fisher*, page 23

20. *O.R. Series I, Vol. XLII, part 1*, pages 985-986,

21. Robinson III, Charles M., *Hurricane of Fire*, Pages 133-134

22. *O.R. Series I, Vol. XLII, part 1*, pages 1020-1022

23. *O.R., Series I, Vol. XLII, part III*, page 1307; Gragg, Rod, *Confederate Goliath: The Battle of Fort Fisher*, pages 85-86;

24. Gragg, Rod, *Confederate Goliath: The Battle of Fort Fisher*, pages 83-84; Fonvielle Jr., Dr. Chris E., *The Wilmington Campaign: Last Rays of Departing Hope*, Pages 151-152; Walker, James L., *Rebel Gibraltar*, page 285

25.   Fonvielle Jr., Dr. Chris E., *The Wilmington Campaign: Last Rays of Departing Hope*, Page 152; Gragg, Rod, *Confederate Goliath: The Battle of Fort Fisher*, page 85

26. Gragg, Rod, *Confederate Goliath: The Battle of Fort Fisher*, page 85; Fonvielle Jr., Dr. Chris E., *The Wilmington Campaign: Last Rays of Departing Hope*, Page 152

27. *O.R.N,. Series I, Vol. XI*, page 295

28. *O.R.N., Series I, Vol. XI*, pages 296-297

29. *O.R.N. Vol. XI*, pages 298-299

30. *O.R. Series I, Vol. XLII, part 1*, page 986

31. Edited by W. F. Beyer and O. F. Keydel, *Deeds of Valor: How America's Heroes Won the Medal of Honor, Volume I*, page 471

32. Fonvielle Jr., Dr. Chris E., *The Wilmington Campaign: Last Rays of Departing Hope*, Page 157; Lamb, William, *Colonel Lamb's Story of Fort Fisher*, page 18

33. Fonvielle Jr., Dr. Chris E., *The Wilmington Campaign: Last Rays of Departing Hope*, Pages 159-160; Gragg, Rod, *Confederate Goliath: The Battle of Fort Fisher*, page 87-90

34. Fonvielle Jr., Dr. Chris E., *The Wilmington Campaign: Last Rays of Departing Hope*, pages. 169-170; Gragg, Rod, *Confederate Goliath: The Battle of Fort Fisher*, page 95; Walker, James L., *Rebel Gibraltar*, pages 290-191; Mowris, Regimental Surgeon James A., *A History of the 117th Regiment, New York Volunteers,(Fourth Oneida)* page 157;

35. *O.R. Series I, Vol. XLII, part 1*, page 981; *O.R. Series I, XLII, part 1*, page 986; Gragg, Rod, *Confederate Goliath: The Battle of Fort Fisher*, pages 88-89;
36. Simpson, George, *Capture of Fort Fisher*, page 8, Curtis Collection, Chicago Historical Society
37. *O.R. Series I, Vol. XLII, part 1*, Pages 979 to 980; Lamb, William, *Colonel Lamb's Story of Fort Fisher*, page 21
38. *O.R.N., Series I, Vol. 11*, pages 261-262, 264; Whiting's reply to questions submitted by General Butler, *O.R. Series I, Vol. XLII, part 1*, page 981; Lamb, William, *Colonel Lamb's Story of Fort Fisher*, page 21; *O.R. Series I, Vol. XLII, part 1*, page 66
39. *O.R. Series I, Vol. XLII, part 3*, page 1087; Walker, James L., *Rebel Gibraltar*, page 298
40. Gragg, Rod, *Confederate Goliath: The Battle of Fort Fisher*, pages 105-107
41. Lamb, William, *Colonel Lamb's Story of Fort Fisher*, page 20
42. *Daily Journal*, January 6, 1865; Walker, James L., *Rebel Gibraltar*, pages 295-296
43. Gragg, Rod, *Confederate Goliath: The Battle of Fort Fisher*, pages 99-100
44. Fonvielle Jr., Dr. Chris E., *The Wilmington Campaign: Last Rays of Departing Hope*, page 178

Chapter 4 The Second Attack

1. *O.R.N., Series I, Vol. 11*, page 391; Fonvielle Jr., Dr. Chris E., *The Wilmington Campaign: Last Rays of Departing Hope*, page 191; Mark A. Moore, *The Wilmington Campaign and the Battles for Fort Fisher*, page 35
2. Jones, Reverend J. William, *Personal Reminiscences, Anecdotes, and Letters of Gen. Robert E. Lee*, page 40
3. Lamb, William, *Colonel Lamb's Story of Fort Fisher*, page 35; *O.R Series I, Vol. XVIII*, Pages 818-819; Lee to Smith, January 4, 1863
4. *O.R. Series I, Vol. XLVI, part 2*, page 1023
5. Fonvielle Jr., Dr. Chris E., *The Wilmington Campaign: Last Rays of Departing Hope*, pages 204-205; Gragg, Rod, *Confederate Goliath: The Battle of Fort Fisher*, page 111; Lamb, William, *Colonel Lamb's Story of Fort Fisher*, page 22-23; Robinson III, Charles M., *Hurricane of Fire*, Page 152
6. Lamb, William, *Colonel Lamb's Story of Fort Fisher*, page 23; Fonvielle Jr., Dr. Chris E., *The Wilmington Campaign: Last Rays of Departing Hope*, page 218; Gragg, Rod, *Confederate Goliath: The Battle of Fort Fisher*, page 121,
7. *O.R. Series I, Vol. XLVI, part 2*, page 1048, 1056,
8. *O.R. Series I, Vol. XLVI, part 2*, pages 1056-1057, 1061-1062
9. Gragg, Rod, *Confederate Goliath: The Battle of Fort Fisher*, pages 112-113
10. Buell, Augustus, *The Cannoneer: Recollections Of Service In The Army of the Potomac*, Page 329
11. Deeds of Valor Volume 2, pages 85-86,
12. Longacre, Edward G., *Civil War Times Illustrated*, volume XXI, No. 10, February, 1983, *The Task Before Them*, page 38,
13. Fonvielle Jr., Dr. Chris E., *The Wilmington Campaign: Last Rays of Departing Hope*, page 210,
14. Little, Lieutenant Henry F., *The Seventh Regiment New Hampshire Volunteers in the War Of the Rebellion*, pages 358-359,
15. Fonvielle Jr., Dr. Chris E., *The Wilmington Campaign: Last Rays of Departing Hope*, page 210; *New York Tribune*, January 18, 1865; *National Tribune*, "Fort Fisher: The Part Taken by the 27th US Colored Troops*, July 17, 1865; *The Cannoneer: Recollections Of Service In The Army of the Potomac* Page 327; Gragg, Rod, *Confederate Goliath: The Battle of Fort Fisher*,

pages 116-117; Little, Lieutenant Henry F., *The Seventh Regiment New Hampshire Volunteers in the War of the Rebellion*, pages 358-359;

16. Little, Lieutenant Henry F., *The Seventh Regiment New Hampshire Volunteers in the War Of the Rebellion*, pages 358-359,

17. *O.R. Series I, Vol. XLVI, part I,* page 397, Gragg, Rod, *Confederate Goliath: The Battle of Fort Fisher*, pages 123-124, Fonvielle Jr., Dr. Chris E., *The Wilmington Campaign: Last Rays of Departing Hope,* pages 219-220

18. Fonvielle Jr., Dr. Chris E., *The Wilmington Campaign: Last Rays of Departing Hope,* page 228

19. Fonvielle Jr., Dr. Chris E., *The Wilmington Campaign: Last Rays of Departing Hope,* page 214; Asa King Memoir, *Confederate Veterans' Talks,* Lower Cape Fear Historical Society, Wilmington, North Carolina; Gragg, Rod, *Confederate Goliath: The Battle of Fort Fisher,* page 117

20. *O.R. Series I, Vol. XLVI, part 2,* page 1047, Colonel William Lamb to Major Hill

Chapter 5 The Final Day of Battle

1. Lamb, William, *Colonel Lamb's Story of Fort Fisher,* page 25

2. McNeill, Sergeant Thomas A., *Histories of Several Regiments and Battalions from North Carolina in the Great War 1861-65,* by Walter Clark, volume IV, page 308-309

3. Curtis, Colonel Newton Martin, *The Capture of Fort Fisher, Personal Recollections of the War of the Rebellion, Addresses Delivered Before the Commandery of the State of New York, Military Order of the Loyal Legion of the United States,* pages 47-48

4. Sand, Benjamin, *From Reefer to Rear Admiral,* page 263

5. Fonvielle Jr., Dr. Chris E., *The Wilmington Campaign: Last Rays of Departing Hope,* page 217; Gragg, Rod, *Confederate Goliath: The Battle of Fort Fisher,* pages 121-122; James Montgomery papers, Confederate Veterans' Talks, Lower Cape Fear Historical Society Archives; R.P.C. to "My Dearest Cousin," January 24, 1865, Lybrook Collection, N.C. Department of Archives and History; *North Carolina State Troops,* volume I page 214; Still, William N., Jr., ed., *The Yankees Are Landing Below Us: The Journal of Robert Watson, C.S.N., Civil War Times Illustrated,* Volume XV, No. 1, April 1976, page 15,

6. *O.R.N.,* Series I, *Vol. XI,* page 438, 477,

7. Longacre, Edward G., *The Task Before Them,* Letter from Captain Adrian Terry to his wife, page 41, *Civil War Times Illustrated,* February 1983, Volume XXI, Number 10,

8. McNeill, Sergeant Thomas A., *Histories of Several Regiments and Battalions from North Carolina in the Great War 1861-65,* by Walter Clark, volume IV, page 309,

9. *O.R. Series I, Vol. XLVI, part 2,* page 1053; Fonvielle Jr., Dr. Chris E., *The Wilmington Campaign: Last Rays of Departing Hope,* pages 234-235,

10. Terry, Major General Alfred H, *O.R.,* Series I, XLVI, part I, page 398; Fonvielle Jr., Dr. Chris E., *The Wilmington Campaign: Last Rays of Departing Hope,* page 242; Gragg, Rod, *Confederate Goliath: The Battle of Fort Fisher,* page 169;

11. Curtis, Colonel Newton Martin, *The Capture of Fort Fisher,* page 49, *Personal Recollections of the War of the Rebellion, Addresses Delivered Before the Commandery of the State of New York, Military Order of the Loyal Legion of the United States*; Little, Lieutenant Henry F.W., *New Hampshire Volunteers in the War of the Rebellion,* pages 391-392; Mark A. Moore, *The Wilmington Campaign and the Battles for Fort Fisher,* pages 49, 50,

12. Mowris, Regimental Surgeon James A., *A History of the 117th Regiment, New York Volunteers, (Fourth Oneida)* page 167-168; Walrath, Colonel E. L., *The Syracuse Daily Courier and Union,*

February 3, 1865;

13. *O.R.N., Vol.* XI, page 427, Merrill, James M., ed. *The Fort Fisher and Wilmington Campaign: Letters From Rear Admiral David D. Porter, North Carolina Historical Review,* XXXV (October, 1958) page 467, Fonvielle Jr., Dr. Chris E., *The Wilmington Campaign: Last Rays of Departing Hope,* page 231; Gragg, Rod, *Confederate Goliath: The Battle of Fort Fisher,* page 134,

14. Letter from Admiral David D. Porter to Secretary of the Navy Gideon Wells, *O.R.N.,* Series I, *Vol. XI,* page 439; *O.R., Series I, Vol. XLVI,* part I, page 397,

15. Dawson, Captain Lucien L., *O.R.N., Series I, Vol. XI,* page 576

16. Dawson, Captain Lucien L., *O.R.N.,* Dawson, Lucien L. Captain, *ORN, Series I, Vol. XI,* page 576,

17. Simms, Lieutenant Commander Joseph, *Personal Experiences in the Volunteer Navy During the Civil War: War Papers Read Before the Military Order of the Loyal Legion, Commandery of the District of Columbia,* page 365, Parker, Lieutenant Commander James, *Personal Recollections of the War of the Rebellion: Addresses Delivered Before the Commandery of the State of New York, Military Order of the Loyal Legion of the United States,* page 112, Harris, Ensign Ira, Military Essays and Recollections, Papers Read Before the Commandery of the State of Illinois: Military Order of the Loyal Legion of the United States, Volume II, page 173,

18. Breese, Lieutenant Commander Randolph Kidder, *O.R.N., Series I, Vol. XI,* page 446, Report of Captain Lucien L. Dawson, U.S. Marine Corps, answering criticisms of Rear-Admiral Porter, *O.R.N., Series I, Vol. XI,* page 578; Little, Lieutenant Henry F.W., *New Hampshire Volunteers in the War of the Rebellion,* page 388,

19. Evans, Ensign Robley, *A Sailor's Log,* page 87,

20. Simms, Ensign Joseph, *Personal Experiences in the Volunteer Navy During the Civil War, War Papers Read Before the Military Order of the Loyal Legion, Commandery of the District of Columbia,* page 365, Gragg, Rod, *Confederate Goliath: The Battle of Fort Fisher,* page 154,

21. Breese, K. Randolph, *O.R.N., Series I, Volume XI,* page 446, Fonvielle Jr., Dr. Chris E., *The Wilmington Campaign: Last Rays of Departing Hope,* page 254-255; Gragg, Rod, *Confederate Goliath: The Battle of Fort Fisher,* page 164, Grattan, John W., *Under the Blue Pennant,* pages 183-188, Mark A. Moore, *The Wilmington Campaign and the Battles for Fort Fisher,* page 45,

22. *O.R.N., Series I, Vol. XI,* p 446-447, Sands, Francis, p. 20, Buel, Augustus, *Cannoneer,* p. 332, Grattan, "Under the Blue Pennant, page 168,

23. Lamb, Colonel William, *Colonel Lamb's Story of Fort Fisher,* page 26,

24. Evans, Robley, *A Sailor's Log,* pages 88-89,

25. Evans, Robley, *A Sailor's Log,* pages 86-87, Fonvielle Jr., Dr. Chris E., *The Wilmington Campaign: Last Rays of Departing Hope,* page 252, Gragg, Rod, *Confederate Goliath: The Battle of Fort Fisher,* page 156, Robinson III, Charles M., *Hurricane of Fire,* Page 156,

26. *O.R.N., Series I, Vol. XI,* page 578, Letter of Lieutenant John Bartlett, U. S. Navy, to his sisters,

27. Lanman, Commodore Joseph, *O.R.N., Series I, Vol. XI,* page 498,

28. Lamson, Lieutenant Roswell H., *O.R.N., Series I, Vol. XI,* page 450,

29. Evans, Ensign Robley D., *A Sailor's Log,* page 95-96, Porter, Rear-Admiral David D., *O.R.N.,* Series I, Volume XI, page 448,

30. Lieutenant Commander William T. Truxton, *O.R.N., Series I, Vol. XI,* page 471, Breese, Lieutenant Commander Randolph Kidder, *O.R.N., Series I, V Vol. XI,* page 446,

31. Lamb, Colonel William, Colonel Lamb's Story of Fort Fisher, page 27,

32. Harris, Ensign Ira, Military Essays and Recollections, Papers Read Before the Commandery of the State of Illinois: Military Order of the Loyal Legion of the United States, Volume II, page 172-173,

33. Cobb, Seaman William T. Papers, *Dear Father*, Fort Fisher State Historic Site

34. Fonvielle Jr., Dr. Chris E., *The Wilmington Campaign: Last Rays of Departing Hope*, page 256; Gragg, Rod, *Confederate Goliath: The Battle of Fort Fisher*, pages 166-167,

35. Lanman, Commodore Joseph, *ORN*, Series I, Volume XI, pages 498-499; Breese, Lieutenant Commander Randolph Kidder, *ORN*, Series I, Volume XI, pages 446-447; Selfridge, Lieutenant Commander Thomas O., Battles and Leaders, Volume IV, page 660; Robinson III, Charles M., *Hurricane of Fire*, Page 172; Walker, James L., *Rebel Gibraltar*, page 338; Letter of Lieutenant John Bartlett to his sisters, ORN, Series I, Volume XI, page 528,

36. Lanman, Commodore Joseph, *O,R.N.*, *Series I, Vol. XI*, page 499

37. Lanman, Commodore Joseph, *O,R.N.*, *Series I, Vol. XI*, page 499

38. Letter of Lieutenant John Barlett, U.S. Navy, to his sisters, *ORN*, Series I, Volume XI, page 528

39. Curtis, Colonel Newton Martin, *The Capture of Fort Fisher*, page 47, *Personal Recollections of the War of the Rebellion, Addresses Delivered Before the Commandery of the State of New York, Military Order of the Loyal Legion of the United States*; Dawson, Captain Lucien L., *ORN, Series I, Vol. XI*, pages 581-582; Fonvielle Jr., Dr. Chris E., *The Wilmington Campaign: Last Rays of Departing Hope*, page 258; Gragg, Rod, *Confederate Goliath: The Battle of Fort Fisher*, page 167,

40. Lamb, William, *Colonel Lamb's Story of Fort Fisher*, page 27; Fonvielle Jr., Dr. Chris E., *The Wilmington Campaign: Last Rays of Departing Hope*, pages 260-261; Gragg, Rod, *Confederate Goliath: The Battle of Fort Fisher*, page 168

41. Curtis, Colonel Newton Martin, *The Capture of Fort Fisher*, page 40, *Personal Recollections of the War of the Rebellion, Addresses Delivered Before the Commandery of the State of New York, Military Order of the Loyal Legion of the United States*; Lamb, William, *Colonel Lamb's Story of Fort Fisher*, pages 27-28; Fonvielle Jr., Dr. Chris E., *The Wilmington Campaign: Last Rays of Departing Hope*, pages 260-261; Gragg, Rod, *Confederate Goliath: The Battle of Fort Fisher*, page 168, 191; Robinson III, Charles M., *Hurricane of Fire*, Page 172,

42. Fonvielle Jr., Dr. Chris E., *The Wilmington Campaign: Last Rays of Departing Hope*, page 243; Gragg, Rod, *Confederate Goliath: The Battle of Fort Fisher*, pages 176-177,

43. Terry, Major General Alfred H, *O.R.*, Series I, XLVI, Part I, Page 398, 407; Fonvielle Jr., Dr. Chris E., *The Wilmington Campaign: Last Rays of Departing Hope*, pages 243-244; Gragg, Rod, *Confederate Goliath: The Battle of Fort Fisher*, page 171; Robinson III, Charles M., *Hurricane of Fire*, Page 173,

44. Fonvielle Jr., Dr. Chris E., *The Wilmington Campaign: Last Rays of Departing Hope*, pages. 244-245; Gragg, Rod, *Confederate Goliath: The Battle of Fort Fisher*, page 172,

45. Towle, Captain George F., *Terry's Fort Fisher Expedition*, page 297, *Old and New*, Volume XI,

46. Terry, Major General Alfred H, *O.R.*, Series I, Vol. XLVI, part I, page 398; Ames, Colonel Adelbert, *The Capture of Fort Fisher, January 15, 1865, Personal Recollections of the Rebellion*, pages 11-12; Fonvielle Jr., Dr. Chris E., *The Wilmington Campaign: Last Rays of Departing Hope*, pages. 244, 261; Gragg, Rod, *Confederate Goliath: The Battle of Fort Fisher*, page 172-173; Curtis, Colonel Newton Martin, *The Capture of Fort Fisher, Personal Recollections of the Rebellion*, pages 38-39; Lockwood, Colonel Henry C., *The Maine Bugle, A True History of the Army At Fort Fisher*, page 45,

47. Curtis, Colonel Newton Martin, *The Capture of Fort Fisher, Personal Recollections of the Rebellion*, pages 38-39,

48. Longacre, Edward G., *The Task Before Them,* Letter from Captain Adrian Terry to his wife, page 42, *Civil War Times Illustrated,* February 1983, Volume XXI, Number 10,

49. Thomas, Leonard R., *Story of Fort Fisher, January 15, 1865,* page 19; Hyde, William L., *History of the 112th New York Volunteers*, pages 122-123; Mowris, Regimental Surgeon James A., *A History of the 117th Regiment, New York Volunteers,(Fourth Oneida)* page 175,

50. Ames, Colonel Adelbert, O.R., *Series I, Vol. XLVI,* page 417; Fonvielle Jr., Dr. Chris E., *The Wilmington Campaign: Last Rays of Departing Hope,* page 265; Gragg, Rod, *Confederate Goliath: The Battle of Fort Fisher*, page 177,

51. Towle, Captain George F., *Terry's Fort Fisher Expedition,* page 298, *Old and New,* Vol. XI; N. M. Robinson in a letter dated February 27, 1865, Private collection of Dr. Chris E. Fonvielle, Jr.

52. Lamb, Colonel William, *The Battles of Fort Fisher, Southern Historical Society Papers*, Volume XXI, page 283,

53. Hyde, William L., *History of the 112th New York Volunteers*, pages 120, 123; Walker, James L., *Rebel Gibraltar,* page 339,

54. McNeill, Sergeant Thomas A., *Histories of Several Regiments and Battalions from North Carolina in the Great War 1861-65,* by Walter Clark, volume IV, page 310; Lockwood, Colonel Henry C., *The Maine Bugle, A True History of the Army At Fort Fisher,* page 48,

55. Fulmore, Judge Zachary F., in a letter to Colonel William Lamb, *Southern Historical Society Papers,* Volume XXI, page 283,

56. Simpson, 2nd Lieutenant George, *Capture of Fort Fisher,* page 12,

57. Curtis, Colonel Newton Martin, *The Capture of Fort Fisher, Personal Recollections of the Rebellion,* page 48; Fonvielle Jr., Dr. Chris E., *The Wilmington Campaign: Last Rays of Departing Hope,* page 265; Gragg, Rod, *Confederate Goliath: The Battle of Fort Fisher,* page 178; Walker, James L., *Rebel Gibraltar,* page 340,

58. Lamb, Colonel William, *The Battles of Fort Fisher, The Southern Historical Society Papers,* Volume XXI, page 284; Lamb, Colonel William, *Colonel Lamb's Story of Fort Fisher,* page 32, The Blockade Runner Museum, 1966

59. McQueen, Corporal Henry Clay, Henry Clay McQueen papers, *Confederate Veterans' Talks,* Lower Cape Fear Historical Society Archives; Fonvielle Jr., Dr. Chris E., *The Wilmington Campaign: Last Rays of Departing Hope,* pages 265, 281; Gragg, Rod, *Confederate Goliath: The Battle of Fort Fisher,* page 186; Moore, Mark A., *The Wilmington Campaign and the Battles for Fort Fisher,* page 50,

60. Mowris, Regimental Surgeon James A., *History of the 117th Regiment New York Volunteers,* page 169,

61. Curtis, N. Martin, *Capture of Fort Fisher,* pages 39-40; Fonvielle Jr., Dr. Chris E., *The Wilmington Campaign: Last Rays of Departing Hope,* page 266; Gragg, Rod, *Confederate Goliath: The Battle of Fort Fisher,* page 186,

62. Ames, General Adelbert, O.R., *Series I, Vol. LVIII,* page 417; Lockwood, Colonel Henry C., *The Maine Bugle, A True History of the Army At Fort Fisher,* page 46; Gragg, Rod, *Confederate Goliath: The Battle of Fort Fisher,* page 184

63. Lockwood, Colonel Henry C., *The Maine Bugle, A True History of the Army At Fort Fisher,* page 49; O.R., *Series I, Vol. XLVI* page 420; Fonvielle Jr., Dr. Chris E., *The Wilmington Campaign: Last Rays of Departing Hope,* page 268; Gragg, Rod, *Confederate Goliath: The Battle of Fort Fisher,* page 184,

64. Lockwood, Colonel Henry C., *The Maine Bugle, A True History of the Army At Fort Fisher,* page 49; O.R., *Series I, Vol. XLVI,* page 420; Fonvielle Jr., Dr. Chris E., *The Wilmington Campaign:*

Last Rays of Departing Hope, page 268; Gragg, Rod, *Confederate Goliath: The Battle of Fort Fisher*, page 184; Fox, Lt Colonel William F., *Regimental Losses in the American Civil War 1861-1865*, pages 19, 459,

65. Price, Major Isaiah, *History of the Ninety-seventh Regiment, Pennsylvania Volunteer Infantry During the War of the Rebellion*, pages 355-356; Harding, Major Oliver P., *O.R. Series I, Vol. LVIII, part 1*, page 420; Gragg, Rod, *Confederate Goliath: The Battle of Fort Fisher*, page 186,

66. Fulmore, Zachariah T., *Wilmington Messenger*, June 27, 1897,

67. Braddy, Captain Kinchen, Kitchen Braddy letter to Z.T. Fulmore, March 25, 1901, misc. Civil War papers, Division of Archives and History, Raleigh, North Carolina; Fonvielle Jr., Dr. Chris E., *The Wilmington Campaign: Last Rays of Departing Hope*, page 273;

68. Pennypacker, General Galusha, to journalist Philip R. Dillon, *The Pittsburg Press*, November 16, 1911,

69. Colonel Curtis, *The Capture of Fort Fisher*, page 41, *Personal Recollections of the War of the Rebellion*, Fonvielle Jr., Dr. Chris E., *The Wilmington Campaign: Last Rays of Departing Hope*, page 281;

70. Bouton, John Bell, *A Memoir of General Louis Bell*, page 26-28; Gragg, Rod, *Confederate Goliath: The Battle of Fort Fisher*, pages 195-197;

71. Terry, Adrian's letter to his wife, *The Task Before Them*, page 43, Longacre, Edward G., *Civil War Times Illustrated*, volume XXI, No. 10, February, 1983;

72. Bouton, John Bell, *A Memoir of General Louis Bell*, pages 28-29; Fonvielle Jr., Dr. Chris E., *The Wilmington Campaign: Last Rays of Departing Hope*, pages 274-275; Gragg, Rod, *Confederate Goliath: The Battle of Fort Fisher*, page 197;

73. Bouton, John Bell, *A Memoir of General Louis Bell*, page 29; Gragg, Rod, *Confederate Goliath: The Battle of Fort Fisher*, page 198;

74. Lamb, William, *Colonel Lamb's Story of Fort Fisher*, page 34; Harkness, Edson J, *The Expeditions Against Fort Fisher and Wilmington*, page 174, *Military Essays and Recollections; Papers Read Before the Commandery of the State of Illinois, Military Order of the Loyal Legion of the United States*, Vol II; Gragg, Rod, *Confederate Goliath: The Battle of Fort Fisher*, pages 191-193;

75. Lamb, William, *Colonel Lamb's Story of Fort Fisher*, page 32-33; Towle, Captain George F., *Terry's Fort Fisher Expedition*, page 297, *Old and New*, Vol. XI;

76. *O.R. Series I, Vol. XLVI, part 2*, page 1062; Barefoot, Daniel W., *General Robert F. Hoke: Lee's Modest Warrior*, pages 258-259; Fonvielle Jr., Dr. Chris E., *The Wilmington Campaign: Last Rays of Departing Hope*, pages 278-279; Gragg, Rod, *Confederate Goliath: The Battle of Fort Fisher*, page 187-188;

77. Harkness, Edson J, *The Expeditions Against Fort Fisher and Wilmington*, pages 177-178, *Military Essays and Recollections; Papers Read Before the Commandery of the State of Illinois, Military Order of the Loyal Legion of the United States*, Vol. II,

78. Lamb, Colonel William, *The Defense of Fort Fisher*, page 229, Histories of Several Regiments and Battalions from North Carolina, Vol. 5, by Walter Clark;

79. Lamb, William, *Colonel Lamb's Story of Fort Fisher*, page 33-34;

80. Lamb, William, *Colonel Lamb's Story of Fort Fisher*, page 34; Fonvielle Jr., Dr. Chris E., *The Wilmington Campaign: Last Rays of Departing Hope*, page 284; Gragg, Rod, *Confederate Goliath: The Battle of Fort Fisher*, pages 201-202;

81. *O.R., Series I, Vol. XLVI, Part 2*, pages 1064-1065;

82. James Reilly's Account of Fort Fisher, W. L. DeRossett papers, North Carolina Department of

Archives and History; Fonvielle Jr., Dr. Chris E., *The Wilmington Campaign: Last Rays of Departing Hope,* page 285; Gragg, Rod, *Confederate Goliath: The Battle of Fort Fisher,* page 203;

83. O.R., Series I, Vol. LVIII, Part 2, page 426;

84. Curtis, Colonel N. Martin, *The Capture of Fort Fisher, Personal Recollections of the War of the Rebellion, Addresses Delivered Before the Commandery of the State of New York, Military Order of the Loyal Legion of the United States,* page 41;

85. Curtis, N. Martin, *The Capture of Fort Fisher, Personal Recollections of the War of the Rebellion, Addresses Delivered Before the Commandery of the State of New York, Military Order of the Loyal Legion of the United States,* page 43; Fonvielle Jr., Dr. Chris E., *The Wilmington Campaign: Last Rays of Departing Hope,* page 287;

86. Curtis, N. Martin, *The Capture of Fort Fisher, Personal Recollections of the War of the Rebellion, Addresses Delivered Before the Commandery of the State of New York, Military Order of the Loyal Legion of the United States,* page 44;

87. Comstock, Lt Colonel Cyrus B., *The Diary of Cyrus B. Comstock,* pages 303-304, Gragg, Rod, *Confederate Goliath: The Battle of Fort Fisher,* page 212;

88. Gragg, Rod, *Confederate Goliath: The Battle of Fort Fisher,* pages 213-214; Fonvielle Jr., Dr. Chris E., *The Wilmington Campaign: Last Rays of Departing Hope,* pages 289-290

89. Ames, General Adelbert, *The Capture of Fort Fisher,* page 15, *Personal Recollections of the War of the Rebellion, Addresses Delivered Before the Commandery of the State of New York, Military Order of the Loyal Legion of the United States;*

90. Gragg, Rod, *Confederate Goliath: The Battle of Fort Fisher,* pages 214-215; Fonvielle Jr., Dr. Chris E., *The Wilmington Campaign: Last Rays of Departing Hope,* pages 289-290;

91. Lamb, Colonel William, *Colonel Lamb's Story of Fort Fisher,* pages 34-35; Gragg, Rod, *Confederate Goliath: The Battle of Fort Fisher,* pages 216-217; Fonvielle Jr., Dr. Chris E., *The Wilmington Campaign: Last Rays of Departing Hope,* pages 292-294;

92. Lamb, Colonel William, *Colonel Lamb's Story of Fort Fisher,* pages 34-35;

93. Lamb, Colonel William, *Colonel Lamb's Story of Fort Fisher,* pages 36-37; Fonvielle Jr., Dr. Chris E., *The Wilmington Campaign: Last Rays of Departing Hope,* page 293; Yearns and Barrett, *North Carolina Civil War Documentary,* pages 88-89;

94. Lamb, Colonel William, *Colonel Lamb's Story of Fort Fisher,* pages 4-5; Fonvielle Jr., Dr. Chris E., *The Wilmington Campaign: Last Rays of Departing Hope,* page 45;

95. Fonvielle Jr., Dr. Chris E., *The Wilmington Campaign: Last Rays of Departing Hope,* page 293-294; Gragg, Rod, *Confederate Goliath: The Battle of Fort Fisher,* page 218;

96. Reilly, Major James, *James Reilly's Account of the Battle of Fort Fisher,* W.L. DeRossett Papers, North Carolina Department of Archives and History;

97. Reilly, Major James, *James Reilly's Account of the Battle of Fort Fisher,* W.L. DeRossett Papers, North Carolina Department of Archives and History;

98. Watson, Seaman Robert, *Robert Watson's Diary, Yankees were landing below us,* page 16;

99. Yearns and Barrett, *North Carolina Civil War Documentary,* page 89;

100. Reilly, Major James, *James Reilly's Account of the Battle of Fort Fisher,* W.L. DeRossett Papers, North Carolina Department of Archives and History; Fonvielle Jr., Dr. Chris E., *The Wilmington Campaign: Last Rays of Departing Hope,* page 295;

101. *O.R. Series I, Vol. XLVI, part 2,* pages 442-447; Lamb, Colonel William, *Colonel Lamb's Story of Fort Fisher,* page 37; Fonvielle Jr., Dr. Chris E., *The Wilmington Campaign: Last Rays of Departing Hope,* page 295; Gragg, Rod, *Confederate Goliath: The Battle of Fort Fisher,* pages 224-225

102. Terry, Adrian's letter to his wife, *The Task Before Them,* page 43, Longacre, Edward G., *Civil War Times Illustrated,* volume XXI, No. 10, February, 1983; Fonvielle Jr., Dr. Chris E., *The Wilmington Campaign: Last Rays of Departing Hope,* page 296; Gragg, Rod, *Confederate Goliath: The Battle of Fort Fisher*, page 228;

103. Rockwell, Colonel Alfred P., *OR* LVIII, Series I, page 411;

104. Eldridge, Captain Daniel, *The Third New Hampshire and All About It, 1861-1865,* page 616;

105. Grattan, John W., *Under the Blue Pennant,* page 182;

106. Gragg, Rod, *Confederate Goliath: The Battle of Fort Fisher*, page 220;

107. *New York Herald-Tribune,* January 26, 1865;

108. Manarin, Louis H. and Weymouth T. Jordan, eds., *North Carolina Troops 1861-1865: A Roster,* volume I, Artillery, page 263;

Chapter 6, The Aftermath

1. *New York Tribune,* January 17, 1865; Canning, Joseph, Joseph Canning's journal, McEachern and Williams Collection, UNCW; Fonvielle Jr., Dr. Chris E., *The Wilmington Campaign: Last Rays of Departing Hope,* pages 302-303;

2. Cleer, Seaman James J., James Cleer in a letter to his mother and father, January 17, 1865, James J. Cleer papers, Manuscript Department, William R. Perkins Library, Duke University; Gragg, Rod, *Confederate Goliath: The Battle of Fort Fisher*, pages 231-232;

3. Perrien, Joseph, *Historic Incidents From the fall of Fort Fisher,* page 473-474, *Deeds of Valor: How America's Heroes Won the Medal of Honor;*

4. Grattan, Acting Ensign John W., *Under the Blue Pennant or Notes of a Naval Officer 1863-1865*, page 176;

5. Rogers, Henry Munroe, *Memories of Ninety Years,* page 109-110;

6. Jones, Regimental Chaplain T.D., *Welshman in the Union Armies, Civil War History,* page 172, Published Quarterly by the State University of Iowa, Vol. 4, 1958

7. Turner, Reverend Henry M., *Rocked in the Cradle of Consternation,* page 79, *American Heritage Magazine,* October/November 1980;

8. *O.R., Series I, Vol. XLVI,* page 430; Turner, Reverend Henry M., *Rocked in the Cradle of Consternation,* page 78, *American Heritage Magazine,* October/November 1980; Walker Jr., James L., *Rebel Gibralter,* page 363; Fonvielle Jr., Dr. Chris E., *The Wilmington Campaign: Last Rays of Departing Hope,* page 306; Gragg, Rod, *Confederate Goliath: The Battle of Fort Fisher,* pages 232-233;

9. Lamb, Colonel William, *Colonel Lamb's Story of Fort Fisher,* page 37-38; Clark, Lt James, *The Iron Hearted Regiment,* page 165;

10. Mowris, Regimental Surgeon James A., *A History of the 117th Regiment, New York Volunteers,(Fourth Oneida)* pages 179-180; Fonvielle Jr., Dr. Chris E., *The Wilmington Campaign: Last Rays of Departing Hope,* pages 304-305; Gragg, Rod, *Confederate Goliath: The Battle of Fort Fisher,* pages 233-234;

11. Mowris, Regimental Surgeon James A., *A History of the 117th Regiment, New York Volunteers,(Fourth Oneida)* page 182;

12. Clark, Lt James, *The Iron Hearted Regiment,* page 166;

13. *O.R. Series I, Vol. XLVI, part 1,* page 427; Fonvielle Jr., Dr. Chris E., *The Wilmington Campaign: Last Rays of Departing Hope,* page 305; Gragg, Rod, *Confederate Goliath: The Battle of Fort Fisher,* page 234; Johnston, John M, *Personal Recollections,* pages 2-3, Collection

of Bob Cook;

14. Turner, Reverend Henry M., *Rocked in the Cradle of Consternation,* page 79, *American Heritage Magazine,* October/November 1980;

15. *O.R. Series I, Vol. XLVI, part 1*, page 427; Fonvielle Jr., Dr. Chris E., *The Wilmington Campaign: Last Rays of Departing Hope,* page 305;

16. Quimby, First Lt. George, *OR,* XLVI, Series I, part I, page 430; Gragg, Rod, *Confederate Goliath: The Battle of Fort Fisher*, page 233;

17. *O.R. Vol. LVIII, Series I,* pages 399-401; Battles and Leaders, Volume IV, page 401; Fonvielle Jr., Dr. Chris E., *The Wilmington Campaign: Last Rays of Departing Hope,* page 393; Gragg, Rod, *Confederate Goliath: The Battle of Fort Fisher*, page 235; Mark A. Moore, *The Wilmington Campaign and the Battles for Fort Fisher*, page 80; Walker, James L., *Rebel Gibraltar,* page 362;

18. Lamb, William, *Colonel Lamb's Story of Fort Fisher,* pages 26-27; Triebe, Richard H., *South Carolina Troops Killed or Captured At Fort Fisher, January 15, 1865*;

19. Gragg, Rod, *Confederate Goliath: The Battle of Fort Fisher*, page 236;

20. Haigh, William H., *William H. Haigh Papers*, pages 2-3, Manuscripts Department, Wilson Library, University of North Carolina at Chapel Hill;

21. Haigh, William H., *William H. Haigh Papers*, pages 2-3, Manuscripts Department, Wilson Library, University of North Carolina at Chapel Hill;

22. Thomas, Leonard R., *The Story of Fort Fisher*, page 16, *The United Service: A Monthly Review of Military and Naval Affairs,* vol. X; Gragg, Rod, *Confederate Goliath: The Battle of Fort Fisher*, page 237;

23. Haigh, William H., *William H. Haigh Papers*, pages 2-3, Manuscripts Department, Wilson Library, University of North Carolina at Chapel Hill;

24. Haigh, William H., *William H. Haigh Papers*, pages 3-4, Manuscripts Department, Wilson Library, University of North Carolina at Chapel Hill;

25. Johnston, John M, *Personal Recollections,* pages 2-3, Collection of Bob Cook;

26. Gragg, Rod, *Confederate Goliath: The Battle of Fort Fisher*, pages 242-243;

27. *O.R., Series I, part II, Vol.* XLVI, page 1078;

28. *O.R., Series II, Vol. LVIII,* page 434;

29. *Wilmington Messenger* June 27, 1897;

30. *O.R., Series II, Vol. LVIII,* pages 440, 442;

31. Lamb, William, *Histories of the Several Regiments and Battalions From North Carolina In the Great War 1861-65,* volume I, edited by Walter Clark, pages 530-531;

Chapter 7   Elmira Prisoner of War Camp

1. F.S. Wade, *Getting Out of Prison,* page 1

2. Thaddeus C. Davis, *Confederate Veteran* Magazine, February, 1899, page 65

3. James Huffman, *Ups and Downs of a Confederate Soldier,* page 96; Clarence Poe, *True Tales of the South At War, How Soldiers Fought and Families Lived, 1861-1865,* page 147

4. *O.R., Series II, Vol. VI,* page 226, 8/25/1863 General S. A. Meredith to Major General E. A. Hitchcock, Report of refusal to exchange Negro troops. Meredith's report also advises Hitchcock the South will not exchange white officer who captured commanding Negro troops; Major General Robert E. Lee to General-in-Chief U. S. Grant, 10/3/1864, the South will exchange Negro troops, if they are free blacks, but not if they are escaped slaves. General Grant refuses

Lee's offer.

5. Michael Horigan, *Elmira: Death Camp of the North*, page 65, General-in-Chief U. S. Grant to Butler explaining reason for halting the prisoner exchange.

6. *O.R., Series II, Vol. VI*, page 606-607, General-in-Chief U. S. Grant to Butler explaining real reason for halting the prisoner exchange.

6. Michael Horigan, *Elmira: Death Camp of the North*, page 59; Michael P. Gray, *The Business of Captivity: Elmira and Its Civil War Prison*, page 23

6. Michael P. Gray, *The Business of Captivity: Elmira and Its Civil War Prison*, page 23

7. *Rochester Daily Union and Advertiser*, New York, reprinted in *Elmira Daily Advertiser*, August 13, 1864

8. Keiley, Anthony M., *In Vinculis; or, The Prisoner of War*, pages 157-158; Michael P. Gray, *The Business of Captivity: Elmira and Its Civil War Prison*, page 24

9. Michael Horigan, *Elmira: Death Camp of the North*, page 60

10. Michael Horigan, *Elmira: Death Camp of the North*, page 60

11. *Rochester Daily Union and Advertiser*, September 13, 1864; Michael P. Gray, *The Business of Captivity: Elmira and Its Civil War Prison*, page 23

12. G.W. D. Porter, "Nine Months in a Northern Prison," *Annuals of the Army of Tennessee and Early Western History* 1.4 (July 1878): page 159

12. James Huffman, *Ups and Downs of a Confederate Soldier*, page 105

13. Ausburn Towner, *A History of the Valley and County of Chemung from the Closing Years of the Eighteenth Century*, Syracuse, N.Y.: D. Mason, 1892, page *270*

14. Michael P. Gray, *The Business of Captivity: Elmira and Its Civil War Prison*, page 23-26

15. Michael Horigan, *Elmira: Death Camp of the North*, page 62

16. Anthony M. Keiley, *In Vinculis Or, The Prisoner of War: Being The Experience Of A Rebel In Two Federal Pens*, page 158

17. *O.R., Series II, Vol. VII*, page 80-81

18. *O.R., Series II, Vol. VII*, page 113-114

19. *O.R., Series II, Vol. VII*, page 114

20. T. Harry Williams, *Lincoln and the Radicals*, page 344-45

21. Senate Resolution 97, Library of Congress, web page: http://memory.loc.gov/cgi-bin/ampage?collId=llsr&fileName=038/llsr038.db&recNum=105

22. *New York Times*, October 2, 1864, Michael Horigan, *Elmira: Death Camp of the North*, 94.

23. Richard N. Current, *The Lincoln Nobody Knows*, page 176

24. Michael Horigan, *Elmira: Death Camp of the North*, page 86

25. *O.R.*, Series II, Vol. VII, page 72-75, Lonnie Speers, *War of Vengeance, Acts of Retaliation Against Civil War POWs*, page 117

26. *O.R., Series II, Vol. VI*, page 504;

27. *O.R., Series II, Vol. VI*, page 489

28. James F. Crocker, *Prison Reminiscences*, page 43-44

29. John Allan Wyeth, *Cold Cheer at Camp Morton, Century Magazine* 41 no. 6 (April 1891) 848

30. R.B. Ewan, *Prison Life*, page 14

31. Michael Horigan, *Elmira: Death Camp of the North*, page 98

32. Berry Benson, *Civil War Book*, page 134

33. Berry Benson, *Civil War Book*, page 134

34. John R. King, *My Experience in the Confederate Army and in Northern Prisons*, page 42

35. Marcus B. Toney, *Privations of a Private*

36. Walter D. Addison, *Recollections of a Confederate Soldier*

37. R.B. Ewan, *Prison Life*, page 14

37. Michael P. Gray, *The Business of Captivity: Elmira and Its Civil War Prison*, page 75, Berry Benson, *Civil War Book*, page 133, James Huffman, *Up and Downs*, 97

38. Michael P. Gray, *The Business of Captivity: Elmira and Its Civil War Prison*, page 75, Benson, *Civil War Book*, page 133-34, John R. King, *My Experience*, 45, Marcus B. Toney, *Privations*, 101

39. John R. King, *My Experience in the Confederate Army and in Northern Prisons*, page 42

40. *O.R., Series II, Vol. VIII*, 52-53

41. *O.R., Series II, Vol. VII*, 604-605, 1092-10984

42. Horigan, Michael, *Elmira: Death Camp of the North*, page 67;

43. Frank Wilkeson, *Turned Inside Out: Recollections of a Private Soldier in the Army of the Potomac*, page 4-5

44. *Elmira Daily Advertiser*, January 19, 1865

45. John N. Opie, *A Rebel Cavalryman With Lee, Stuart, and Jackson*, page 318

46. John R. King, *My Experiences in the Confederate Army and in Northern Prisons*, page 38

47. James Huffman, *Prisoner of War*, page 548

49. 50. Michael P. Gray, *The Business of Captivity: Elmira and Its Civil War Prison*, page 63

50. *O.R.*, Series II, Vol. VII, 878; Horigan, Michael, *Elmira: Death Camp of the North*, page 90; Gray, Michael, *The business of Captivity: Elmira and Its Civil War Prison*, page 30;

51. John R. King, *My Experiences in the Confederate Army and in Northern Prisons*

52. Ibid., *O. R., Series II, Vol. VII*, 573-74; Horigan, Michael, *Elmira: Death Camp of the North*, page 150;

53. Sergeant George W.D. Porter, *Nine Months In A Northern Prison*; Horigan, Michael, *Elmira: Death Camp of the North*, pages 151-152;

54. *The Treatment of Prisoners during the War, Southern Historical Society Paper 1*, no. 4 (April 1876): 294, Michael Horigan, *Elmira: Death Camp of the North*, page 151-52

55. *Southern Historical Society Paper vol. 1, no. 4 (April 1876): 295, Elmira: Death Camp of the North by Michael Horigan 151-52;*

56. *The Southern Historical Society Papers*, vol. 1, No. 4, April 1876, page 295; *The Confederate Veteran*, April 1907, page 163; Pratt, Fletcher, *Stanton: Lincoln's Secretary of War*, page 357;

57. Horigan, Michael, *Elmira: Death Camp of the North*, page 155

58. *O. R.*, Series II, *Vol. VIII*, Series II, page 23-24; Horigan, Michael, *Elmira: Death Camp of the North*, page 157

59. Horigan, Michael, *Elmira: Death Camp of the North*, page 157

60. *O.R., series II, Vol. VII*, page 891-892

61. Anthony Keiley, *In Vinculis*, 181-182

62. *O.R., Series II, Vol. VII*, page 892-93

63. *O.R., Series II, Vol. VII*, page 894; Horigan, Michael, *Elmira: Death Camp of the North*, page 116

64. *O.R., Series II, Vol. VII*, page 894

65. *O.R., Series II, Vol. VII*, page 894

66. Dibrell, Richard H., *Confederate States of America, Congress, Joint Select Committee to Investigate the Condition and Treatment of Prisoners of War, The Southern Historical Society Papers*, Vol. I, pages 136-137

67. W.W. Gramling Diary, *Fort Fisher To Elmira*, page 147

68. Keiley, Anthony M., *In Vinculis; or, The Prisoner of War,* page 185
69. Keiley, Anthony M., *In Vinculis; or, The Prisoner of War,* page 174-75, 185
70. Keiley, Anthony M., *In Vinculis; or, The Prisoner of War,* page 138
71. Holmes, Clay, *Elmira Prison Camp*, page 117-18
72. Michael P. Gray, *The Business of Captivity: Elmira and Its Civil War Prison,* page 51; Holmes, Clay, *Elmira Prison Camp*, page 328
73. Eugene F. Sanger Papers, Records of the Office of the Adjutant General, Regimental Correspondence, 1861-1865, Maine State Archives. Michael Horigan, *Elmira: Death Camp of the North,* page 129
74. Horigan, Michael, *Elmira: Death Camp of the North,* page 131
75. Butler, Benjamin F., *Butler's Book: Autobiography and Personal Reminiscences of Major-General Benjamin F. Butler*, page 610-611,
76. Michael Horigan, *Elmira: Death Camp of the North,* page 193
77. *O.R., Series II, Vol. VI*, pages 647-649

Bibliography

Articles and Periodicals:

Bouton, John Bell, *A Memoir of General Louis Bell, Massachusetts Historical Society,* December 14, 1866;

Conway, Alan, *Welshmen In The Union Armies, Published Quarterly By the State University of Iowa,* pages 143-174, *Civil War History,* Vol. 4, 1958, Berkeley Square House, London,

Davis, Thaddeus C., *Confederate Veteran* Magazine, February, 1899, page 65

Dillon, Philip R., *Great Moments In War, Told by Living Generals,* November 16, 1911, *The Pittsburg Press*

Ewan, R.B., *Reminiscences of Prison Life at Elmira, N.Y.,* January 1908

Harkness, Edson J, *The Expeditions Against Fort Fisher and Wilmington,* page 174, *Military Essays and Recollections; Papers Read Before the Commandery of the State of Illinois, Military Order of the Loyal Legion of the United States,* Vol II;

Huffman, James, *Prisoner of War, Atlantic Magazine* 163, no. 4, April 1939

Jones, James P., *A Rebel's Diary of Elmira Prison Camp, Chemung Historical Journal* 20, no. 3, March 1975

Leon, Lewis, *Diary of a Tar Heel Confederate Soldier,* Stone Publishing, Charlotte, NC

Lamb, Colonel William, *Colonel Lamb's Story of Fort Fisher*, The Blockade Runner Museum, 1966

Lamb, Colonel William, *The Battles of Fort Fisher, The Southern Historical Society Papers*, Volume XXI, page 284;

Longacre, Edward G., *The Task Before Them,* page 36-43, *Civil War Times Illustrated,* February, 1983

Sherrill, Miles, *A Soldier's Story: Prison Life and Other Incidents,* University of North Carolina at Chapel Hill, 1998,

Taylor, G.T., *Prison Experience in Elmira, N.Y., Confederate Veteran* Magazine 20, no. 7, July 1912

Terry, Adrian's letter to his wife, *The Task Before Them,* page 43, Longacre, Edward G., *Civil War Times Illustrated,* volume XXI, No. 10, February, 1983;

The Treatment of Prisoners during the War between the states, Southern Historical Society Papers 1, no. 3, March 1876

The Treatment of Prisoners during the War, Southern Historical Society Papers 1, no. 4, April 1876

Towle, Captain George F., *Terry's Fort Fisher Expedition, Old and New,* Vol. XI, edited by Edward E. Hale, pages 290-304;

Turner, Henry M. *Civil War Times Illustrated,* 31 (October/November, 1980)

Wade, F.S., *Getting Out of Prison, Confederate Veteran* magazine 34, no. 10, October 1926

Ward, John Shirley, *Responsibility for the Death of Prisoners, Confederate Veteran* magazine 4, no. 1. January 1896

Watson, Robert, *The Yankees Were Landing Below Us: The Journal of Robert Watson, C.S.N., Civil War Times Illustrated,* April, 1976, Edited by William N. Still, Jr.

Wyeth, John Allan, *Cold Cheer at Camp Morton, Century Magazine* 41 no. 6 (April 1891) 848

Books:

Badeau, Adam, *Military History of Ulysses S. Grant, From April, 1861, To April, 1865.,* Vol. III, New York: D. Appleton and Company, 1885

Barefoot, Daniel W., *General Robert F. Hoke: Lee's Modest Warrior*, John F. Blair Publisher, 1996

Benson, Susan W., ed. *Berry Benson's Civil War Book: Memoirs of a Confederate Scout and Shapshooter,* Athens, Ga.: University of Georgia Press, 1962

Butler, Benjamin F., *Butler's Book: Autobiography and Personal Reminiscences of Major-General Benjamin F. Butler,* A. M. Thayer & Co. Publishers, 1892

Canney, Donald L., *The Old Steam Navy,Frigaates, Sloops, and Gunboats, 1815-1885,* Vol. 1, Naval Institute Press, Annapolis, Maryland, 1990

Current, Richard N., *The Lincoln Nobody Knows,* Hill and Wang, 1958

Fonvielle, Chris E., *The Wilmington Campaign: Last Rays of Departing Hope,* Savas Publishing, 1997

Fox, Lt. Colonel William F., *Regimental Losses In the American Civil War, 1861-1865, Albany Publishing Company, 1889*

Gragg, Rod, *Confederate Goliath: The Battle of Fort Fisher,* Harper Collins, 1991

Grattan, John W., *Under the Blue Pennant: Or Notes of a Naval Officer, 1863-1865, John Wiley and Sons, Inc.,* pages 162-173, New York, 1999

Gray, Michael P., *The Business of Captivity: Elmira and It's Civil War Prison,* The Kent State University Press, 2001

Hallock, Judith Lee, *Braxton Bragg and Confederate Defeat*, vol II, University of Alabama Press, 1991

Hampson, Helen (Wyeth), My Great-Great Grandfather Was a Prisoner of War . . . Libby Prison, 2002

Horigan, Michael, *Elmira: Death Camp of the North,* Stackpole Books, 2002

Holmes, Clay W., *The Elmira Prison Camp: A History of the Military Prison at Elmira, N.Y. July 6, 1864, to July 10, 1865.* New York: Knickerbocker Press, 1912

Huffman, James, *Ups and Downs of a Confederate Soldier,* New York: William E. Rudge's Sons, 1940

Keiley, Anthony M., *In Vinculis; or, The Prisoner of War: Being The Experience Of A Rebel In Two Federal Pens,* Petersburg, Va.: Vindex, 1866

King, John R., *My Experiences in the Confederate Army and in Northern Prisons,* Clarksburg, W.Wa.: United Daughters of the Confederacy, 1917

Leon, Louis, *Diary of a Tarheel Confederate Prisoner,* Charlotte, N.C.: Stone, 1913

Levy, George, *To Die In Chicago, Confederate Prisoners at Camp Douglas 1862-65,* Pelican, 1999

Manarin, Louis H. and Weymouth T. Jordan, eds., *North Carolina Troops1861-1865: A Roster,* 13 volumes, Raleigh, North Carolina: Division of Archives and History, 1966-1993

Mast, Greg, *State Troops and Volunteers*, A Photographic Record Of North Carolina Civil War Soldiers, North Carolina Department of Cultural Resources, Volume I, 1995

McCaslin, Richard B., *The Last Stronghold: The Campaign For Fort Fisher,* McWhiney Foundation Press, 2003

Moore, Mark A., *The Wilmington Campaign and the Battles For Fort Fisher,* Savas, 1999

Opie, John N., *A Rebel Cavalryman with Lee, Stuart, and Jackson,* Chicago: W.B. Conkey, 1899

Pickenpaugh, Roger, *Captives In Gray,* The University of Alabama Press, 2009

Poe, Clarence, *True Tales of the South At War, How Soldiers Fought and Families Lived, 1861-1865,*

Pratt, Fletcher, *Stanton: Lincoln's Secretary of War,* W. W. Norton & Company Inc., 1953

Rogers, Henry Munroe, *Memories of Ninety Years,* Cambridge, Massachusetts: Houghton, Miflin, 1928

Speer, Lonnie R., *Portals To Hell: Military Prisons of the Civil War,* Stackpole Books, 1997

Speer, Lonnie R., *War of Vengeance: Acts of Retaliation Against Civil War POWs,* Stackpole Books, 2002

Stephens, Alexander H., *A Constitutional View of the Late War Between the States,* vol. II, Chicago: National Publishing Co. 1868

Styple, William B. & Fitzpatrick, John J., *The Andersonville Diary & Memoirs of Charles Hopkins,* Belle Grove Publishing, 1988

Thomas, Leonard R., *The Story of Fort Fisher,* page 16, *The United Service: A Monthly Review of Military and Naval Affairs,* vol. X, Philadelphia: L.R. Hamersly & Co., 1893

Toney, Marcus B., *The Privations of a Private,* Nashville and Dallas: M.E. Church, South, Smith and Lamar, 1907

Wilkeson, Frank, *Turned Inside Out: Recollections of a Private Soldier in the Army of the Potomac,* New York and London: G.P. Putnam's Sons, 1887

Internet:

American Civil War Research Database, Historical Data Systems
Chemung Valley History Museum
Footnotes.com

Manuscripts:

Blair, B.F., letter *To Mother*, December 27, 1864, B.F. Blair Papers, Archives Division, U.S.,

Braddy, Captain Kinchen, Kitchen Braddy letter to Z.T. Fulmore, March 25, 1901, misc. Civil War papers, Division of Archives and History, Raleigh, North Carolina;

Cleer, Seaman James J., James Cleer in a letter to his mother and father, January 17, 1865, James J. Cleer papers, Manuscript Department, William R. Perkins Library, Duke University;

Cobb, Seaman William T. Papers, *Dear Father*, Fort Fisher State Historic Site

Confederate Veterans' Talks, Lower Cape Fear Historical Society, Wilmington, North Carolina, McQueen, Corporal Henry Clay, Henry Clay McQueen papers, *Confederate Veterans' Talks*, Lower Cape Fear Historical Society Archives;

Greer, William R. Papers, *Recollections of a Private Soldier of the Army of the Confederate States,* Manuscript Department, William R. Perkins Library, Duke University, North Carolina

Montgomery, James, James Montgomery papers, *Confederate Veterans' Talks*, Lower Cape Fear Historical Society Archives;

Reilly, James, James Reilly's Account of Fort Fisher, W. L. DeRossett papers, North Carolina Department of Archives and History;

Sanger, Eugene F., Eugene F. Sanger Papers, Records of the Office of the Adjutant General, Regimental Correspondence, 1861-1865, Maine State Archives.

College of William and Mary

William Lamb Collection

William M. Reaves Collection

Newspapers:

Elmira Daily Advertiser
Elmira Daily Gazette

New York Times
New York Tribune
New York World
The Pittsburg Press
The Syracuse Daily Courier and Union
Wilmington Daily Journal
Wilmington Messenger

Official Publications:

Confederate States of America, Congress, *Joint Select Committee to Investigate the Condition and Treatment of Prisoners of War,* March, 1865

United States War Department, ed. *The War of the Rebellion: A Compilation of the Official Records of the Union and Confederate Armies,* 128 vols. Washington, D.C.: Government Printing Office

Official Records of the Union and Confederate Navies In the War of the Rebellion 1861-65, Published Under the Direction Of the Honorable H.A. Herbert, Secretary of the Navy, by Lt. Commander Richard Rush, U.S. Navy

Pubished Primary Sources:

"A Yankee Account of the Battle of Fort Fisher." *Our Living and Our Dead,* Vol. 1, No. 4, December, 1874.

Ames, Adelbert, "The Capture of Fort Fisher, North Carolina, January 15, 1865." Commandery of the Loyal Legion of the State of New York, 1897.

INDEX

418

428

430

About the Author:

Richard H. Triebe is a freelance writer and historian publish-ed in multiple periodicals. He is the author of several historical novels and has done extensive research work regarding the Fort Fisher prisoners. Two of his books, *Fort Fisher to Elmira* and *Point Lookout Prison Camp and Hospital,* were awarded the coveted Jefferson Davis Historical Gold Medal Award for outstanding achievement of a literary work. His ground breaking research resulted in hundreds of names being added to the rolls of Confederate prisoners who died at both prisons. This list contains the names of the Confederate dead which include civilians, marines, sailors and soldiers.

Richard has an Associate's Degree in Marine Technology. He is a former Chicago police officer and was a Provost Marshal investigator in the United States Army. Richard is a member of the Coastal Carolina Writers Guild, a Brunswick Writers Forum panelist, and has appeared as a guest on several television shows, including *The Artist's Craft* hosted by Stacy Cochran and WWAY TV's *Book Corner* with Marcy Cuevas. He is a member of the Cape Fear Civil War Round Table, and has presented historical overviews of the battles of Fort Fisher to many local organizations. Richard is also presenting a PowerPoint talks about the northern prisons at Elmira, New York, and Point Lookout, Maryland. He and his wife, Barbara, live in Wilmington, North Carolina.

432